A SINGLE
SQUARE
PICTURE

*A Korean Adoptee's
Search for Her Roots*

Katy Robinson

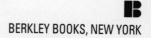

BERKLEY BOOKS, NEW YORK

B

A Berkley Book
Published by The Berkley Publishing Group
A division of Penguin Putnam Inc.
375 Hudson Street
New York, New York 10014

PRINTING HISTORY
Berkley trade paperback edition / August 2002

Visit our website at
www.penguinputnam.com

Library of Congress Cataloging-in-Publication Data

Robinson, Katy.
A single square picture / Katy Robinson.
p. cm.
ISBN 0-425-18496-X
1. Robinson, Katy. 2. Korean American women—Biography. 3. Korean Americans—Biography. 4. Adopted children—United States—Biography. 5. Seoul (Korea)—Biography. I. Title.

E184.K6 R63 2002
973'.04957'0092—dc21
2001052922

Dedicated to my two mothers

Acknowledgments

Love and gratitude to my family—on both sides of the Pacific; to the Jefferson Fellowship at the East-West Center and the Bang Il–Young Fellowship for making my two trips to Korea possible; to the many mentors at the Asian American Journalists Association; to my most influential teachers at SCU, Tennant C. Wright, S. J.; to Brian Boyd, whose advice, editing, and encouragement went above and beyond the call of duty; to my agent, Jandy Nelson, for her unwavering enthusiasm; to my editor at Berkley, Natalee Rosenstein, for her guidance and belief; to the many friends and family members who cheered me on each step of the way; and finally, to John—my greatest gift and partner in all things.

Prologue

When I was seven years old, my mother and grand-mother took me to the airport and watched as I boarded a plane for America.

At first, I clung to the scent of roasted seaweed and peppery *kimchee,* the feel of my grandmother's body next to mine, and the last look on my mother's face. But with time, I became convinced my life simply began the moment I stepped off the airplane on the other side of the world. One day I was Kim Ji-yun growing up in Seoul, Korea; the next day I was Catherine Jeanne Robinson living in Salt Lake City, Utah.

When I first learned English, I told people my new name and announced, "I 'pose to be Korean!" like I didn't believe it my-self. In my new home, there was no face that mirrored my own, no one to describe how I got that dime-sized scar imprinted on my left knee. To tell me, perhaps, that I have my mother's eyes, my father's wit.

Left as I was to my own devices, memories of Korea became little more than blurred visions that flash and skip like a broken movie projector. In times of confusion, I return to the photographs—the undeniable evidence. A baby in a traditional Korean birthday costume. A five-year-old skipping down a brick path in a pink ruffled dress. A solemn face that disguises the scabby red remnants of chicken pox. Pasted to the top right-hand corner of the last photograph is a white label with my adoption number—3833—the one that gave me passage to this new life. Finally, I come to the Polaroid taken at the airport that day. The once shiny finish has dulled with time and the smudge of fingerprints. A hairline crack shoots down the left side of the photo, temporarily resting on my mother's shoulder bone. But the center of the photograph remains undisturbed. I am the little girl standing between two Korean women. I know this for a fact and yet I do not recognize myself.

But as I study the still faces, I hear the voices of ghosts. At first formal: *Kim Ji-yun* . . . then more familiar: *Ji-yun-ah!* They call me by a distant childhood name and beg me to remember.

And for a short time, I do.

That day, *Halmoni,* my grandmother, spotted a man walking across the airport with a large camera hanging from his neck. She waved him over and asked him to take a picture of us. Posing for the man's camera, I stood between my mother and *Halmoni* with my right hand lifted to curl loosely over my mother's index finger. I smiled a sheepish, close-lipped grin and scrunched my eyes into half-open slits as I tilted my chin toward the lens. My hair was parted down the center and brushed until it hung straight and shining over my shoulders. Red wool tights sagged at the knees under my short brown jumper and a red plaid school pack was strapped to my back.

I was the only one smiling. My mother and grandmother's pale faces shared a similar expression: lips drawn tight and long across their wide faces; dark eyes staring blankly into the camera. Together we stood as three generations of the same blood; our eyes, nose, and mouth only slightly varied from one another to mark the progression of years.

Halmoni wore a familiar brown-patterned dress and a thin gray sweater that seemed too small for her broad shoulders. The pointed toes of her worn rubber slippers peered out from her gown like the ends of two white canoes, barely revealing her pink socks. The blue scarf I had given her as a present a few weeks earlier was tied around her head so that no hair was visible around her face. Dark circles set around her eyes and the lines of her face sank downward in a way that formed a knot in the pit of my stomach.

As I stood framed by my mother and grandmother, it seemed as though we were the only three people in the world. Soon after the man handed my grandmother a single square picture, the sound of sharp heels echoing against the floor drew closer like the ticking of a clock.

When so many memories fail me, this one stands out as a capsule of my childhood—the precise moment when the direction of my life suddenly and irreversibly changed.

Above the click-click of high heels is a slim, iron-backed woman dressed in a navy-blue suit and matching cap. She taps my mother on the shoulder with two short motions of her extended finger, cups her white-gloved hand to my mother's ear, and whispers something I cannot hear. As the woman draws away, my mother tightens her grip on my fingers and I look up to see her painted lips quiver slightly and her hair sway back and forth as she shakes her head. Her hand releases my fingers, shoots up my arm, and grips my shoulder. As she does this, I feel a shot of panic travel up my chest.

The time has come.

But another eternity passes before my mother releases her clawlike grip on my shoulder bone and moves her hand to cover her eyes. My grandmother has been watching her daughter with eyes sinking deeper into the lines of her face, her lips pursed into a tight ball before she breaks the spell and comes alive behind me. She unfastens the flap of my backpack and shoves something into an inside pocket.

"Ji-yun-ah, listen to me." She grabs me by the shoulders and turns me toward her. "Carefully guard your pack on the airplane. Don't let anyone take it away from you. Understand?"

"Ne, Halmoni." Yes, Grandmother.

Something about her voice frightens me and I can feel the tears starting to well up. But she spins me around and pulls the straps of my pack onto my shoulders so tightly that I nearly topple over. She then hands me a roll of my favorite crackers and the folder of paper dolls my mother bought me after our last trip to the bathhouse.

She gives me a slight push forward.

Before I can form a response, I do as instructed and follow the blue cap and clicking heels away from my mother and grandmother, toward the giant revolving glass doors. I want to go, and yet I don't—both reactions are expected of me. I don't know which to choose, so I obey.

Just before I reach the doors, I glance back.

Words once again catch in my throat. I see my mother and grandmother standing in the same spot on the black-and-gray-checkered floor of Kimpo Airport. Their expressions are frozen like two statues. The urge to turn around and sprint back toward them runs down my legs like a slow tickle. But I turn away and continue through the glass doors, knowing they are still standing in the spot where we took the photograph minutes before.

1

)

The first time I witnessed the expanse of city lights come to life from the back balcony of my new home, I thought I could see the whole world from my perch high above the ground. The lights formed colorful specks like thousands of stars that stretched on forever and ever, until they dropped off into the blackness of night. If I stood on tiptoe, stretched my neck, and scouted the last flicker of light on the horizon—that's where I thought Korea was.

Growing up, I secretly searched for Korea out there in the darkness and sometimes imagined myself returning into the arms of my grandmother, who would be there waiting for me in the same spot at Kimpo Airport as if she had never left. Now, twenty years later, I was on a plane headed toward Seoul. I was going in search of my mother, grandmother, and all of the other lost figures of my childhood. It was time to make sense of the disjointed snapshots and blurred visions of the life that had ended so abruptly. I wanted, once and for all, to piece together the two halves of myself and create one continuous story that was my life—something that I assumed came naturally to everyone else not adopted.

I awoke to the ding of the "Fasten Seat Belt" sign surrounded by rapid, deep-throated sounds that I should have recognized as my native language, but didn't. As the buzz of voices increased, so did my awareness of the foreign faces around me. Then it hit me—these people looked like me. I scanned the crowd and stared into different reflections. No one could mistake the similarity of our dark narrow eyes, rounded faces, and small flat noses. I was no longer the lone Asian in the crowd. Yet the feeling that I was an outsider intensified as the plane made its bumpy descent. I gripped the seat back in front of me and prepared to touch down in the place where I had last seen my mother and grandmother.

The strength of my earlier conviction gave way to the ripples in my stomach. As passengers shook their companions awake and gathered their belongings, I studied different faces, once again trying to match their reflections to my own. Did I look like that woman? Or that girl? Surely other Koreans could sense my difference. But maybe I would set foot on the soil of my homeland and transform into a Korean. As I filed out of the plane with rows of other black-haired heads, perhaps my American-ness would drop away like loose skin. With a secret smile, I pictured myself stepping off the plane and saying "I am home" with glistening eyes as a violin score lifted into crescendo in the background.

As I walked down the narrow hallway to baggage claim, I noticed a mother up ahead leading a girl by the hand. The girl's fine brown hair was pulled into high pigtails that bounced up and down beneath red satin ribbons that matched the trim of her velvet dress. The girl's size and the way she held her mother's hand made me want to run after her as if I were chasing a scene from my past. I was certain she was seven years old. Because of the vast hole in my childhood that was simply the "pre-America period," I often thought of myself as an unaware and uncomprehending infant when I left my family in Korea.

How would that girl react if I pulled her away from her mother and told her to board a plane for America? Would she obey without protest, as I had?

The bouncing pigtails had long disappeared into a sea of moving legs and I stood in the middle of the airport hit by the full reality of what I was about to do. I had expected a feeling of déjà vu. I was returning through the same glass doors. As an American. As a Korean-American. I imagined myself awaking from amnesia to remember everything about my native country, including the long-forgotten language. In the dream, I watched a stream of words flow out of my mouth that suddenly remembered the twists, shapes, and sounds of my native tongue. I spoke without knowing what I was saying, only other Koreans understood perfectly. "Aiee-yah! We told you," they exclaimed excitedly. "We knew the Korean was still in you! After all, this is your country. You are Korean. Welcome back to your country. Welcome home!"

But as I looked around at the sea of Korean faces, I knew that I was just another foreigner visiting Korea—a *kyopo,* overseas Korean, here for a short visit before returning home to a land that was not Korea. This was confirmed at the customs counter when a grandfatherly man spoke to me in rapid Korean without looking up. I shook my head in shame, "No. I'm sorry, I don't speak Korean."

He lifted his head in surprise (was that a look of disapproval in his eyes?) and waved me through, only saying, "Okay." I picked up my luggage and loaded it onto a cart, repeating to myself like a soothing mantra, "I am back in Korea . . ." I wheeled the cart through the thick crowd, not bothering to look up at the anxious faces and bobbing heads awaiting passengers from the other side of the glass doors. I knew that no one would be here to greet me.

I looked around for a sign pointing to a shuttle bus to take me to my hotel. Then I saw a cardboard sign with my name printed in black marker. Above the sign was a young woman dressed in a pale yellow suit staring at me with a questioning look.

"Miss Robinson?" She approached, handing me a silk rose tied with a glittery pink ribbon.

"Yes . . ."

"I have been waiting for your arrival for a long time!"

"You have?"

"Yes, my name is Miss Yoo. I am General Chang's secretary, and he sent me to meet you."

"I am so happy to see you!" I squeezed her hand and pumped it up and down.

I had met the general two months earlier in Boise while working on a story for the newspaper. He was a retired general of the South Korean Army and an important businessman who now served as a trade representative to Idaho. When a mutual acquaintance discovered that I was going to Seoul, he suggested that I contact the general when he came to town. But I was given this subtle warning: "He can be kind of stern and well, you know, he's a traditional Korean man so . . ."

When I gathered the nerve to approach the general at the conference, he dismissed me with a nod and moved to shake hands with an American businessman next to me. After the brush-off, I arranged to interview a less intimidating representative from Taiwan named Eddie Yen. I arrived at the hotel lobby and was confused to find the general, not Eddie, waiting for me.

"I understand that you want to talk to me," he said, and led me to a table inside the hotel coffee shop. "Well?"

"I am traveling to Asia next month with a group of journalists and will stop in Seoul," I began. "You see, I was adopted from Korea and this will be my first trip back. I hope to search for some records of my Korean family, but I don't know anyone in Seoul and . . ."

His face was unmoved. I lowered my eyes, feeling that I had made a mistake by appealing, so personally, to this stranger. I could feel the heat of embarrassment spread across my chest. But when I looked up, I saw no trace of his earlier sternness. Instead, an unexpected look of familiarity settled on his distinguished face. His dark eyes looked at me with a hint of fond sadness from beneath a thick fold of skin. The lines of his face lifted as a small smile crept across his lips.

"Don't worry," he said. "When you come to Korea, I will treat you just like my own granddaughter."

Now I discovered that the general had been true to his word. He sent Miss Yoo to serve as my guide during the length of my stay in Korea. Together we boarded a shuttle bus to the hotel. Her first question was how old I was.

"Twenty-seven."

"Then I must address you as *Unnee,* older sister, since you are a year older than me," she exclaimed. "*Unnee,* are you married?"

I nodded.

"Oh, you are very lucky! I want to be married by the end of this year. I do not have much time left to find a husband." When I laughed, she explained earnestly, "In Korea, we believe finding a husband at twenty-four is the best luck; twenty-five is okay. But if you are not married by age twenty-six, then perhaps it will be too late. So you see, I am running out of time."

"Really? But you are so young. I'm sure you'll meet someone

soon." My attempt to console her sounded lame considering her apparent distress.

"Thank you. I hope so." She laughed then changed to a more confident tone as she pulled out a typed itinerary of "Miss Katy Robinson's Visit to Korea" from her purse.

"The general says you want to search for your parents. Please tell me your Korean name, age, and the year you were adopted so I can prepare an advertisement for the newspaper."

"An advertisement?"

"Yes. There is a section in the newspaper where children who have been adopted overseas can post their information. Usually their Korean names and dates of adoption, or anything else they can remember. If their parents or relatives see it, they can call a number to arrange for a reunion. Many adopted children have found their families this way."

"Really?" I was surprised and a little disappointed that my search was something as common as a classified advertisement in a daily newspaper.

"There is also a television show that tries to unite adopted children with their parents. Maybe we could try to get you on."

"Oh no. I don't want to go on TV!" I pictured myself holding up a name card in front of my chest like someone on *America's Most Wanted*. I offered a more practical solution. "Could you take me to a place called Korea Social Services, maybe tomorrow?"

"Korea Social Services? What is that?"

"I'm not sure, but I think they are an agency that may have information about my adoption records. When I wrote to the adoption agency in America asking for help, they told me to contact Korea Social Services in Seoul."

"Okay." Miss Yoo scribbled herself a note on the back of her copy of the itinerary. "I'll look them up tomorrow and try to call them for you. I hope you will enjoy your time in our beau-

Miss Yoo met me at the hotel the next morning dressed in pumps, a short tan skirt, and matching jacket. "I looked in the phone book and found three listings for Korea Social Services," she reported. "I called each of them and I think this is the right one."

We jumped into a taxi and passed by towering downtown skyscrapers and billboards the size of movie screens, then moved to what appeared to be the outskirts of the city. We drove through winding neighborhood streets with iron gates and cement walls encircling sloping tile-roofed homes. Shiny earth-colored ceramic *kimchee* pots and dried red peppers decorated balconies and courtyards.

I remembered playing with groups of children in streets just like this one, except they weren't paved back then. We ran around in large packs, kicking balls, cans, or whatever else we could get our feet on until our clothes were covered with dirt. I was tall for my age and could run fast enough to keep up with the neighborhood boys. As dusk faded into night, I was often the last one remaining by the dim light of street lamps. I would sit quietly by the side of the road and enjoy the feeling of grubbiness, dirt, and pure exhaustion before I went inside to where the adults were. Once in America, surrounded by a bedroom full of toys and freshly cut grass, I never experienced that same feeling of joyful grunge again.

We passed through more narrow paved streets lined with old women sitting on the sidewalk. In between gossiping and fanning themselves, they hawked garlic and onions that were gathered into tall bundles with fresh dirt still clinging to the bulbs. Our taxi screeched and halted behind a motorcycle carrying large bundles of fabric strapped to the back bumper. While the two male drivers debated who had cut off whom, I seized the opportunity to take a closer look at the surrounding scene. Across the street was a neighborhood market with a mishmash of items stacked floor to ceiling in unsteady columns. Outside the store, female shoppers sniffed and squeezed an assortment of tangerines, purple grapes, and large round Asian pears that were lined up in wooden crates and cardboard boxes. Through the clear glass doors of restaurants, I could see rows of low tables with built-in gas burners in the center for grilling marinated meats. In the corner, a hunchbacked grandmother leaned over an enormous rice cooker and shoveled heaping scoops into metal bowls. I rolled down the window and breathed in the air, which hung heavy with the combined scent of car exhaust, ripe produce, grilled meats, and rotting garbage.

The smells triggered sudden flashes.

Once, when I was about five, I got lost in a narrow hilly neighborhood just like this one. Every winding street looked the same and I couldn't remember where I had been or where I had come from. Up one steep street and down another, I walked for what seemed like hours, searching for the way home.

I had the same sensation as we passed through an alley and pulled up in front of a redbrick building with a green iron gate. My heart beat faster as I craned my head out the window. There was a distant sense of recognition as though I had been here once before, but I could not put my finger on it. I followed Miss Yoo in silence and we entered a long hallway that echoed with our footsteps.

"Whatever happens is meant to be," I said to myself. And for once, I truly believed it.

A woman with shoulder-length hair and a kind oval face met us at the end of the hall. "Hello, my name is Miss Kim. I am a social worker here," she said in hesitant English.

"This is Miss Katy Robinson." Miss Yoo introduced me in Korean. "She was adopted in 1977 and wishes to find her parents."

I smiled from behind Miss Yoo.

"Do you know the exact date of your adoption?"

"Yes, November seventh, 1977. Also my Korean name is Kim Ji-yun, if that helps." I hoped that I was pronouncing my own name correctly.

"Okay, please wait here."

My reply hung in the air as Miss Kim turned her back and started digging in a metal file cabinet.

A few minutes later, she pulled out a worn brown file folder with my Korean name printed across the top. Resting her hand on the small of my back, she led us to a table in the corner of the room. As we sat down, I noticed a Korean grandmother sitting alone opposite us. Her black-and-gray hair was pulled back into a tight old-fashioned bun and deep wrinkles creased her leathery brown face. Her lips looked like a prune shriveled into the gaps in her mouth where her teeth had once been. Her milky-gray eyes followed everything that was being said. When I caught her staring at me, she shifted with embarrassment, only to steal another look a second later.

My attention shifted to Miss Kim, who took a seat across from me and placed the file in front of her. I took a deep breath and deliberately folded my hands in front of me in an attempt to appear calm. A single nugget of information contained in the file held the power to change the course of my life—for better or for worse, I didn't know. There was a big difference between searching and finding.

A numb anticipation settled through my body as I waited for the first words to be spoken.

As Miss Kim opened the worn file folder, my eyes locked on a wallet-size black-and-white photograph stapled to the inside corner. It was a picture of a little girl posing next to a rosebush with a half smile on her face. There was a white label stuck on the top right-hand corner with the number 3833.

The photograph was taken when I was still recovering from chicken pox. On that day, my grandmother took me to a strange place dressed in a hand-me-down sleeveless dress hitting high on my thighs. It was a thin polyester dress with purple and pink flowers shaped like daisies. A man with a camera arranged me next to some rosebushes and told me to smile like a model. I squatted between a cluster of thorny bushes and squinted into the camera as my grandmother looked on disapprovingly from a distance.

"Open your eyes and try to look happier," she instructed.

This photograph was the duplicate of a picture my American parents had at home. I knew from my mother's stories that this was the picture the adoption agency had sent to my parents asking if they would be willing to take this girl (me!) instead of the younger one they had anticipated. That girl, expected to arrive in America within a few weeks, had suddenly developed an ear infection and was unable to fly. But another little girl— a few years older than they had requested—was available to take her place immediately if they were willing to make the switch.

Later, my mother told me the story of the girl whose place I had taken and I filed away every detail as if she had been talking about me.

After a year of waiting, Welcome House sent us a picture of a little girl, three years old. Of course, she was darling and I fell in love with her immediately. The ladies at church and my work had a shower for her. We set up the quilting frame and the ladies took part in sewing the rosebud quilt you used as a bedspread. Probably forty or fifty people came. Others sent gifts even if they couldn't come. Remember the little blue suit you had? There were picture frames, necklaces, medals, dresses, and toys.

Suddenly we received a letter saying the little girl—Mei-lee, I think—was no longer available for adoption. We were heartbroken. I remember sitting at church with the tears running down my face and trying to hide them. But a few months later, they sent your picture.

You looked much older, a little sad I think. Standing there very formally. You weren't smiling and had just had chicken pox, we were told. Once again, our hearts lifted. We started planning again.

I grew up a little envious of Mei-lee, who had first occupied a place in my mother's heart. I secretly taunted her, wherever she was, and relished the good luck that made her sick and found me adoptive parents even at an undesirable older age. I felt even more important when I heard the next part, about how my parents had to conquer political forces in order to get me.

Suddenly the political climate changed. President Carter threatened to pull the troops out of Korea. South Korea was frightened they would be overrun by the North, so in retaliation the government said there would be no more children adopted out of Korea. Well, it was a good strategy because everyone who was waiting for a child began writing to their congressmen. Once again, our friends came forward and we spent days of writing letters asking for help to get you here. I also wrote to people in Korea. One of them was a nun working in a home for unwed mothers. She promised to help you if she could.

We finally got notice that you would be able to be adopted if we went to Korea to get you. So we dashed about getting a passport and visa to travel to Korea. To save money, I was planning on going alone. But several weeks before I was going to go, the nun in Korea wrote saying not to get tickets to Korea, that you would be sent here. And so you were!

The story always ended with a mutual declaration of our good luck and how it must have been fate that gave Mei-lee an earache and brought my mother and me together.

It had been a long time since I thought about Mei-lee. As I sat studying the photograph, I was still grateful for the twist of fate that had sent me into the Robinson family, but also a little sad and frightened. What if it had been *me* who got an ear infection instead of Mei-lee? Then my mother would have told another Korean girl how lucky they were to be together.

The thought made me feel disposable and rootless. A drifter, passed randomly from one set of hands to another.

Miss Kim turned the first page and slid the folder toward me until I gazed down at a brownish document with Korean writing on it.

"This was the document your Korean mother signed relinquishing all rights to you."

The finality of those words struck me as I reached for the document and studied the faded signature and imprint of a red stamp above the black line. I ran my fingers over the ink even though I could not make out my mother's name. Just seeing the document made it somehow more official—my mother gave me up, "relinquished all rights." I pictured my mother sitting at this same table twenty years earlier and signing the papers that would hand me over to strangers. Had her hand trembled that day as she signed her name? Had she been sad? Ashamed? Or maybe relieved and hopeful for a new beginning? There were a thousand different guesses and I longed to hear the answer directly from my mother's lips. I never knew the intensity of that longing—to hear every detail of my mother's life and mine— until I sat before a folder containing the brief synopsis of my childhood.

My fingers shaking now, I touched the full length of each document in the folder and began turning the pages faster and faster. I ran across a paper with my American mother's handwriting. The familiar right slant and long curve of her writing stopped me cold. It was a recent letter she had written to the agency telling them of my planned visit to Seoul.

"This is an important journey for Katy. Please help her in any way you can," she had written.

I turned the page to find typed documents and forms written in Korean. The angular writing appeared like a secret code.

"What does this paper say?" I asked Miss Yoo.

Instead of answering, the two women spoke back and forth in Korean for what seemed like ages. Each minute they spoke in the language I once knew, but could no longer understand, I grew more agitated. "What is Miss Kim saying now? What were you two just talking about? What do these papers say about me and my mother?" I prodded Miss Yoo like an impatient child. She listened to my questions with a frustrated expression on her face.

Still there was no reply.

Miss Kim closed the folder and took it out of my hands. As if to mitigate the brusqueness of this act, she smiled and finally spoke. And Miss Yoo translated: "I can try to answer your questions about the information in your file, but I can't let you look at it yourself or give you much personal information about your mother because of privacy issues. We have to protect your Korean mother, you see? But I'll try to answer as many questions as I can."

She opened the folder once again and flipped through its pages until she found a report typed in English. She turned the paper toward me and waited for me to read. It was a summary written by the caseworker who had observed me at the orphanage.

Ji-yun is a very beautiful, sweet, and charming-looking little girl, who appears to be in good health and to be quite mature physically for her age. She has a pretty oval face with medium-fair complexion, dark long hair, dark smiling eyes, and typical Korean features. Her recent pictures and medical certificate are herewith attached. She gives the impression of being a very cheerful, lively, bright, sociable, friendly, and good-natured girl who can make friends easily even with strangers and gets along well with other children. She can express her feelings and thoughts well. She talks clearly in a polite manner and is responsive to what is told or asked of her. She looks alert, intelligent, and sensitive enough for her age. Her housemother reports that she is cooperative and faithful to adults and that no particular care, medical problem, or habit has been observed in her yet.

She is very clever and can read easy storybooks almost perfectly and deal with her own things very well by herself. She sings very well and enjoys drawing. She is anxious about her future and looking forward to the foster parents. She is considered to be quite grown up for her age and to be capable of making a proper adjustment to any adoptive home without presenting much difficulty if it would be arranged for her properly.

Ji-yun is in need of any proper adoptive placement to provide her with better opportunity for normal growth and development in the future and is recommended for consideration in an overseas adoptive placement.

I blinked several times in silence, then laughed as I finished reading the report. I devoured this information that was about me, and yet not about me. It was like reading about a stranger who was being put up for sale. I imagined parents-to-be anxiously reading about their future children, relieved that they were getting a good one. The report told them exactly what they wanted to hear. Or, perhaps, I really was the model adoptive child.

Miss Kim reached across to cup my hand. "Your mother was in a very bad situation. Understand, women in Korea had very little choice at that time. Your mother had to make a very difficult decision, but she would be happy to know that you turned out so well and that you are a grown woman now. You have grown up so tall and beautiful and intelligent. I am so proud of you."

As she patted my hand and stroked my hair, I resisted the urge to lay my head on her breast.

It was then that I noticed the old grandmother once again and realized that she had been sitting across from us, watching and listening the entire time. As our eyes met, she began to wail, tears streaming down her face as she rocked back and forth in her chair. She reached out and grabbed my hands with both of her wrinkled brown ones. She sobbed and stroked my hands over and over again while shaking her head. Between sobs, she spoke to me in loud passionate words.

"What is she saying?" I glanced around the room in confusion. A woman ran across the room.

"I'm sorry," she said as she scooped up the grandmother and led her out of the room. "She is here searching for information about her daughter who she gave up for adoption many years ago."

I turned around and tried to smile at the old woman through my own wet eyes. My heart ached for this *halmoni,* who could have been my own grandmother wondering where I was. I wondered if my grandmother still thought about me or had plans to search for me one day.

I watched the grandmother disappear down the hall and turned around to face the file once again. Miss Kim visibly relaxed her posture and looked at me through the eyes of a mother rather than a complete stranger.

"Your mother was young and unmarried when she had you. Do you have many memories of her?"

"Not a lot . . . some, I guess." How could I tell her, or anyone else, about memories I could not explain, even to myself?

"You lived with your mother and grandmother as a child. I

think your grandmother raised you and spent the most time with you?"

"Yes, that I remember."

"After you were born, your mother separated from your father and didn't have money to take care of you. We understand that your grandmother was ill and could no longer care for you."

"Yes, she had a bad cough. She was trying to quit smoking. She wasn't supposed to, but she bought cartons of cigarettes anyway." I remembered how just before I left, I bought a carton of cigarettes for my grandmother as a present. I wrapped the box in brown paper and across the top of the package I wrote, "*Halmoni, don't smoke these!*" as a reminder.

"I think your mother planned to get married after you left for America. You understand that in Korean culture, your mother could not get married if her future husband discovered that she already had a child by another man. That would have been impossible."

"Yes, I understand." Even as I said the words, I wondered, had my mother wanted to get rid of me just so she could get married?

Miss Kim studied my face and spoke slowly. "I am sure it was a very difficult decision for her. She only wanted what was best for you. I don't think you would have had as many opportunities in Korea."

Tears flooded my eyes and I no longer tried to hold them back. I wept openly without knowing for whom—the child who had boarded the airplane so obediently, my young unwed mother, or my stoic grandmother? I couldn't grasp the enormity of the decision my mother had made—for both of us. Now I wanted more than anything to find my mother and tell her that I was okay, that all of her hopes and dreams for me had come true, and that I still loved her—the same way I had as a child.

"Do you have any information about where my mother is now? Do you think I can find her?"

"I don't know. We have no information about where your mother is now."

"What about my *halmoni*? Do you think she is still alive?"

"I don't know that either." She hesitated before continuing. "But our records show that your father visited our office about ten years ago. He was here looking for you. We still have his old address and a telephone number. Here, write down your address in the United States so we can contact you if we find out anything. Also write down the name of your hotel so I can call if I find out anything sooner."

Even though I had known about my Korean father's attempt to find me years before, I now envisioned him sitting at the table and waiting patiently just as the old grandmother had done while Miss Kim searched through my case file. That my father had come in search of me was remarkable, all the more so since he had not made the effort when I was within his grasp.

I could picture an abstract figure of a man, but not a face or a voice. My father was like a ghost that floated in and out of my childhood at his own will.

One day my father came to visit me at my grandmother's house—the last day I ever saw him. He brought with him an offering—three new dresses. I gasped with joy as I opened the boxes to discover the dresses lying carefully folded in pink tissue paper. One was a lime-green-and-white sleeveless sundress decorated with tiny apples. The second dress was trimmed with cherry-red ruffles above princess sleeves and a high waist. The third and fanciest dress sported colored feathers fanning out from puffed sleeves and a white chiffon skirt that formed a bell at my waist when I spun.

My grandmother had dismissed them with a grimace and a flip of her hand. "They look so cheap and gaudy. I bet they won't even fit you."

"Go try them on for Daddy," my father countered with a pleading smile, avoiding my grandmother's piercing eyes. I obliged my father by shedding my old clothes on the floor and slipping into the cool fabric of each new dress.

I skipped down the brick walkway in faded leather sandals, wearing each dress in turn and twirling in front of the adults. Despite what my grandmother said, each dress fit perfectly, hitting high above my knobby knees. My father positioned me by a cluster of blooming rosebushes in the backyard and took my picture. He snapped the camera over and over again as I modeled in various corners of the yard.

I basked in my father's attention until I remembered my grandmother's earlier warning. "Your father is a bad man. I'm sorry you have to spend the day with him. But it's your duty."

When it was time to leave for our scheduled outing, I thought about my grandmother's words once again and began to cry and protest that I didn't want to go. I cried not because I was really scared of my father, but because I thought it was what my grandmother expected of me.

Later, when I sat at the back of the bus holding my father's hand, he asked me, "Why did you cry like that? Don't you love me?"

I loved him but couldn't make myself say the words out loud. Instead I looked down at my swinging feet without responding. I sensed his hurt, and a feeling of guilt mixed with confusion washed over me. I felt pulled in two opposite directions, wanting to please my grandmother, and then my father.

•   •   •

Miss Kim searched my face for an answer and repeated her question.
"If we can find him, would you like to meet your father while you are here?" There was a hint of doubt in her voice.

"Yes, of course I want to meet him!"

She took down the number of my hotel in Seoul. "I'll try my best to locate your father, but please don't get your hopes up too much. This phone number for him is ten years old and he has probably moved since then."

After we exchanged information, I went to a bathroom around the corner from the office and splashed my face with cold water. Both Miss Kim and Miss Yoo seemed relieved when I came out smiling. The three of us walked outside into a spring day painted with pink cherry blossoms. As we passed tall shady trees and the deep red of Japanese maples, the sense of recognition grew stronger.

Miss Kim studied my face as if reading my thoughts. Finally she asked, "Did you know that you lived here?"

"I did?"

"Yes, this is the orphanage where you stayed before you went to America. I don't think it was called Korea Social Services then. But according to our records, this is where you lived before you were adopted. Do you remember living here?"

I shook my head even as I began to remember. I seldom thought about my brief stay at the orphanage, but Miss Kim's question unleashed flashbacks of group showers with other naked children and cold meals devoured at long tables, heads of short-cropped hair, ill-fitting clothes, and rows of bodies at night.

I couldn't remember what my grandmother told me the day she dropped me off. But soon after she left, they took away the clothes, books, and paper dolls. (I made a mental note to report this to my grandmother the next time I saw her.) The next morning, a woman told me to select a shirt and a pair of pants from a mound of ratty clothes piled in the middle of a room. I asked for my own school clothes back, but the woman refused, saying I had to save those for my trip.

"You were one of many children living in the orphanage during the 1970s waiting to be adopted by families overseas," Miss Kim said. "These days, we only have twenty-four infants, most of them with developmental problems. The oldest baby we have here is three." She pointed to a little girl playing in the grass.

She had beautiful almond-shaped eyes and brown hair. When she heard Miss Kim's voice, the little girl looked up and smiled impishly with her hands twisting behind her back.

"Her father was killed in a car accident. She is going to a family in Minnesota next Wednesday."

I dropped to my knees so we were at eye level and smiled at the child, suppressing a desire to scoop her up into my arms. I wanted to explain what was about to happen to her, to whisper in her ear not to be afraid on the airplane. But as soon as she heard my English "hello," she ran behind a tree.

As I smiled at the girl peeking out from behind the tree trunk, all I could think about was how she was about to begin the journey that I was now completing.

"Can I see the other babies?"

The little girl walked alongside Miss Kim as we headed toward another building. I expected to see a brightly colored nursery filled with musical mobiles and gurgling babies with slobber running down their faces. Instead I was hit by the sight of a sterile room, more like a hospital intensive care unit than a nursery. The room was clean and lined with incubators, rectangular glass bins, and connecting wooden cribs holding tiny, barely moving bodies. Miss Kim held out her arm, blocking my entrance. From the doorway, I could make out fuzzy black heads and tiny tan legs. Two baby boys lay still and silent on a Mickey

Mouse quilt on the floor. One was on his stomach, his face buried in the quilt. The other baby was on his back, one bony leg deformed and twisted to the side beside his normal chubby leg.

Miss Kim quickly led me out of the room and back outside. "Our records show that you lived here about six months."

I looked at her blankly, trying to comprehend my time in this place. She continued, "Your rooms would have been over there. And this was the old bathroom."

All that remained was a pile of broken bricks.

Then I saw the gate up ahead, the same one I had noticed coming in. As I approached the iron gate, the pieces suddenly clicked. Of course, the gate! As a child, it had towered above my head. For all of these years I had pictured thick iron poles shooting into the sky with the sole purpose of keeping my grandmother and me apart.

Halmoni had come to see me at the orphanage.

A man met her at the gate, but refused to let her in. From across the lawn, I overheard them argue, softly at first then louder. When he disappeared inside the building, I ran over to my grandma.

"Halmoni, anyonghaseyo."

"Ji-yun-ah, here. I brought you a surprise." She shoved a thick package wrapped in brown paper through the slats of the gate.

I grabbed the package from my *halmoni* and tore it open to discover my first *hanbok*. I unfolded the pink silk skirt that wrapped around the middle of my chest and cascaded to the ground. The short brocaded vest with a starched white V-neck trim tied together with a pair of long rainbow-colored ribbons that looped in a half bow over my left breast. The round sleeves of the vest curved below my elbows in colorful stripes like the wings of a bird.

This *hanbok* was just like the one I had seen in a window display while walking downtown with my grandmother.

"There's more," she said.

The full outfit included yellow pantaloons to be worn underneath my skirt, padded white socks with upturned toes that fit inside the rainbow-striped rubber *komusin* slippers. There was also a matching coin purse that tied with miniature Korean drums dangling from lime-green tassels.

I buried my hands in mountains of soft cool silk. I had seen other children dress up in *hanboks* on New Year's Day and *Chusok* harvest-moon celebration. I knew from pictures that I had worn a baby version of the elaborate costume during *ddol*, my first birthday celebration. But never a real grown-up *hanbok*.

"*Halmoni*, where did you get this?"

"I had it made especially for you."

Her words made me grin. I was not like these other unwanted children without families to visit them, their hair cropped in random zigzags around their faces and ragged pants that hit above their ankles. They did not even dream of owning *hanboks*.

This was proof that I did not belong here.

After admiring the dress some more, I looked up to see a funny expression cross my grandmother's face. I noticed too how she wore the same brown-patterned dress as the week before, with a scarf tied sloppily over her hair.

Her voice changed as she spoke.

"Change your clothes and put this on before you meet your new American parents. Be sure to smile and say, 'Hel-lo. I love you.' " Her wide mouth twisted into funny shapes as she pronounced the only words of English she knew. I could tell she had been practicing the phrases.

I nodded my head and twisted my mouth into the same shapes as I repeated the English words. "Hel-lo! I love you!"

"Good. Oh, and one more thing, Ji-yun-ah. In America, they

don't count their ages like we do in Korea. So if anyone asks you how old you are, don't say your real age, okay? Tell them that you are six."

"You want me to lie about my age?"

"It's not lying. It's just a different way of counting." Her voice dropped as she saw the man step out of the building. "I have to go now. But your mother and I will meet you at the airport."

I watched her tall, bulky figure disappear down the hill. *"Halmoni!"* I yelled, just to see if she would turn around.

The next morning, the house *ajuma* shook me awake and led me into the dining room. Normally, the room was filled with children pushing and shoving their way toward little white bowls of rice lined up at the long wooden table. But this morning I sat alone on the bench. It felt strange to sit in silence without the clicks of metal chopsticks and spoons scraping the insides of bowls or the chorus of slurps, chomps, and belches rising from the table. Only the sound of my own slurping echoed in the empty room as I ate a bowl of cold rice soup and *kimchee*.

I set a piece of long cabbage onto my spoon, dipped it into the bowl, and watched the water turn a peppery red. I was about to do it again when I heard her voice hit the back of my neck.

"Pali-pali! Mogo, mogo! Hurry! Eat, eat!" The *ajuma* moved to my side and flapped the back of her hand toward my face as she spoke. "You need to fill up for your long journey." She paused to look me over with squinty eyes, then smiled and added, "Aren't you the lucky one to find a family in America?"

As soon as I scooped the last bit of rice into my mouth, she rushed me into another room to change my clothes. She yanked the stained shirt above my head and set my old school clothes in front of me, saying, "Ah, you recognize these? Put them on. Quickly!"

I peeled off my torn pants and slipped into a pair of red wool tights. I pulled the brown wool jumper over my head and buckled my leather shoes. I couldn't wait to see my mother and grandmother.

I could hardly believe that the monstrous gate of my childhood now hit barely above my chest. I looked around the yard to see what else I could remember. "There used to be a swing set over there with grapevines growing over the top of it."

"Yes, that's right," Miss Kim answered.

I remembered sitting on the swing set with another girl close to my age and the two of us trying to make each other cry—a not so difficult task. She began by saying she was tired of being locked behind a gate and living in an orphanage. I said that I wanted to return to my old school and live with my family again like a normal child. We then harvested our successful crop of tears and folded them into a leaf from the vine creeping above our heads. Although no blood had been exchanged, I still felt the bond of that moment.

Where is she now? I wondered. Did she find a good home?

Miss Kim squeezed my hand one last time before I got into a taxi and pulled away from the orphanage.

2

I stared at the ringing phone, frozen by the realization that this could be the call. How did one prepare to hear such news—that they did or did not find your father, and that he did or did not want to see you? On the fourth ring, I gathered enough courage to answer. "Hel-lo?"

"Miss Robinson?"

"Yes . . ."

"This is Miss Kim. We found your *aboji*! Your father. He come to your hotel tomorrow—okay with you?"

Her short breath hung suspended on the other end, waiting for my response. Her words washed over me in slow ripples until the full weight of them dropped me back to the sound of her voice.

"Hello? You still there? You still want to meet your father? You want me to call him and tell him okay, come to hotel?"

"Yes! I'm here. And yes, I still want to meet my father."

I was laughing now as tears ran down my cheeks.

"Okay, good. He come to hotel tomorrow four o'clock. I think your daddy is happy to meet his daughter at long last!"

"Miss Kim? What about my mother? Were you able to find her?"

"No, not your *omma*. I don't know. But don't worry, I still try for you, okay?"

"Yes, okay. Thank you! Thank you for finding my father."

I stared at the phone, trying to convince myself that what had just happened wasn't a dream. When the reality sank in, I laughed and sobbed, feeling disbelief, fear, and excitement all tangled together in one giant swell of emotion.

I was about to meet my Korean father!

I let out a squeal, danced around the room, then collapsed onto the bed. Still out of breath, I called my husband, John, to tell him the news, then made a collect call to Salt Lake City.

I smiled as I heard my mother's familiar voice echo through a tunnel. "Yes, I'll accept the call . . . Katy?"

"Mom, they found my dad and I'm meeting him tomorrow!" My words tumbled out in one long breath.

"Katy!" my mother exclaimed, and I pictured her face as she thought of what to say next. There was silence, then I heard her blow her nose into the phone and sniffle.

"Today, I went to that place, Korea Social Services, and guess what? It was the actual orphanage where I stayed. Miss Kim, the social worker, said I stayed there six months—"

"That's not true," she interrupted. "I know you were only at that orphanage for about two weeks. That's why you still had long hair while the other children coming off the plane had short-cropped hair."

Neither my mother nor I had expected it to happen so suddenly. Meeting my Korean family had always been a remote possibility that we would deal with when, and if, we came to it. Now that it was suddenly upon us, we each clung to our end of the phone and searched in silence for the proper words.

Finally my mom spoke. "I hope your meeting with your father will be everything you want it to be."

Even after we hung up, I could still hear my mom tweaking her nose back and forth with a Kleenex. On the eve of meeting my Korean father, my thoughts remained preoccupied with my American mother and the letter I sent her before leaving for Korea. The thoughts and emotions had been overwhelming when I scribbled them. I still meant them, although gentler emotions had settled in since that day I spat pages of angry words at her.

I knew many mothers and daughters whose relationships tee-tered on spoken and unspoken accusations and past hurts that festered like an open wound. But that was not true of my mom and me. From the beginning, we treasured the relationship made possible by a remarkable twist of fate. I had never felt anything but the deepest gratitude and affection for my adoptive mother. Whenever I thought about her, I pictured myself with my head resting on her cushioned chest, breathing in the tingly scent of Mentholatum on her thin lips and feeling the greasy night cream caked on her freckled cheek. She would be wrapped in an old pink quilted robe, propped up on her bed doing a *New York Times* crossword puzzle with oversized plastic drugstore glasses (held together by safety pins) hanging off the edge of her long pointy nose.

My mother had a habit of rubbing the bottoms of her scaly chapped feet together, making scraping sounds like a cricket. She traveled with a Ziploc bag containing packets of Sweet'N Low and fat-free Jenny Craig bars. I could always rely on her to have extra Kleenex stuffed up her sleeve and loose breath mints at the bottom of her bulging black purse. For weeks after her

visits to our house in Boise, I would discover pink plastic fingernails and her wax earplugs, still shaped into the mold of her
ear, nestled in our carpet.

From early on, ours was a different kind of relationship, with
me as much my mother's protector as she attempted to be mine.
Just after I finished high school, she finally left my father after
twenty-seven years of turbulent marriage and got a small apartment across town for the two of us. Many children view divorce
as a tragedy. But I was grateful to escape the turmoil that had
come to define our family as my parents' fights escalated and
two of my brothers battled raging drug addictions, which resulted in the arrest and imprisonment of one of them for multiple
armed robberies at local pharmacies—an event played out on
the evening news.

After the divorce, my mother and I forged a partnership and
found a kind of freedom other people took for granted. We'd
go shopping and Mom would whip out her credit card with
obvious glee. "I can buy whatever I want!" she'd exclaim to the
amused salesclerk. We'd go out to dinner and she would declare
to the waiter, "I like my steak medium, not rare," as if in direct
defiance to Dad, who liked his meat bloodred. After any little
mishap—running out of gas or taking the wrong exit—we'd
brace ourselves until we realized no one was screaming or be-
rating us and we would end up giggling in relief like two schoolgirls.

The bond between us did not go through the natural breaks
that come with adolescence or even adulthood. It wasn't until
after I got married and the reality of becoming a mother myself
one day neared that our relationship took on a strange new
shape. For the first time, I saw my mother not as the model of
a perfect, infallible mother, as I had believed her to be, but as
an aging woman who had made mistakes. I don't know if this
realization comes as a shock to all children, but it had a profound

effect on me. It allowed me, finally, to bring up the question of my other mother—the one who gave me birth—and to ask the questions I had previously dismissed as a betrayal.

One of the curses of being adopted is wanting to know the whys—why our birth parents gave us up and why our adoptive parents wanted us. In my case, my adoptive mother (after growing up with four brothers and giving birth to three sons) desperately wanted a daughter, and my father, foremost, wanted to make her happy. Later, I learned that my mother had had a miscarriage and she got the idea to adopt after meeting a couple through their church who had adopted a little girl from Korea. Other children, I imagined, chalked their birth up to fate or circumstance, whereas my mother always made me feel chosen. "I am the luckiest mother," she would tell me, usually when I was bemoaning my looks. "Most parents have no say about their children. They get who they get. But I got to choose exactly who I wanted for a daughter. Out of all the little girls in the world, I chose you."

When I was little, that answer had been enough. But now my questions dug deeper. I wanted to know about what came after the choosing.

Why didn't you teach me about my Korean heritage? Why didn't you help me keep my name or language? Why didn't you have any Korean friends or move someplace that was more ethnically diverse?

I had never bothered to ask such questions when they might have done some good. Still, I couldn't get over the feeling that my parents should have known better (a curse of *all* children). The families I met as an adult who adopted children from China and Korea did things so much differently than my parents had. First, they traveled to the countries where their children were born to experience and gather information about their children's

cultures. They met regularly with other families and their
adopted children and surrounded their children with books
about adoption, their native cuisine, information, and artwork
from their countries. Adoptive parents increasingly recognize
the importance of interweaving their children's birth culture
into the fabric of their family's daily lives. By contrast, my parents had never been to Korea and knew little about the country.
There were no tangible signs of Korean culture in our household. Most important, there was nothing said or done to make
me feel proud of being Korean (at least nothing that worked).
As I wrote to my mother, every hurt that I had ever suffered
came spilling out in a way that surprised even myself.

*How could you pluck me from a country halfway around the world
and drop me in a place like Salt Lake City?*

*Why did you make me feel like I would hurt your feelings by
searching for my birth parents? Why didn't you tell me immediately
about my Korean father trying to contact me? Why didn't you ever
take me on a trip to Korea like you promised?*

*Do you know what it feels like to have an Asian shell while long-
ing to be white just like you?*

*Well, I am not one of you. I am not a Connole. I am not Irish. I
am Korean and I want to find out what that means. I no longer want
to be the little girl in braided pigtails, marching under the Connole
banner in the St. Patrick's Day parade wearing an "Honorary Irish-
man" badge. I do not resemble anyone in our family, no matter how
many times you joke that we have the same cheekbones. The truth is,
nothing about us is similar.*

*I do not know if addiction runs in my blood like the rest of our
family. I do not know who I take after in looks or personality—my
Korean mother, father, or grandmother?*

*How can I pass down my heritage to my children if it is one giant
question mark?*

I wasn't sure what kind of response I expected, except perhaps, some kind of acknowledgment. But my mother never replied to the letter. She has saved every card, picture, and letter I have given her since kindergarten—except this one. When I asked her about it, she said she only vaguely remembered receiving it and would look for it.

She never found it, although my guess was that it was lying in a place too close to her heart to search.

3

I *jumped out of bed as the realization that this was*
the day I would meet my father pierced through
my sleep. My initial joy soon gave way to fits of
panic. How would we greet each other and what
would we say? Would we feel like two strangers
or like long-lost family? Fortunately, I could not spend the next
six hours fretting over the possibilities. General Chang had
scheduled a hike at "0700 hours," as directed on my itinerary,
and I was glad for the distraction.

Like many older Koreans, the general and a group of his male
friends hiked every Saturday throughout the year, regardless of
the weather. He picked Miss Yoo and me up at the hotel and
drove us to a national park located in the middle of the city,
although it was a world far removed from the surrounding skyscrapers, noise of traffic, and hurried feet scampering across the
pavement. The cool morning air greeted us as we stepped out
of the car, and I welcomed the sight of lush trees and the pink
and purple blossoms splashed across the mountainside.

As we started the climb up the mountain, my nervous anticipation about the reunion with my father slowly gave way to the serenity of the scenery. It seemed like the perfect start to the momentous day ahead.

Although the general and his friends were in their mid-seventies, they bounded up the steep mountain without effort, climbing over boulders and cliffs like mountain goats. I scrambled to keep up with the men, and at one point raced ahead of them feeling proud of my athletic abilities. Delicate Korean woman—ha! I would show them, I thought to myself, setting an even faster pace. A few minutes later, I felt a tap on my shoulder from a red-faced and out-of-breath Miss Yoo.

"Katy, please slow down and wait for the general," she said, giving a backward glance to the general with a look of alarm on her face.

I quickly realized my mistake. To everyone's relief, I fell back and allowed the general to once again assume the lead. For the rest of the hike, Miss Yoo and I walked a few paces behind the men. When we took a break to drink ladles of water from a mountain spring, the general's friend complimented me.

"You are very strong for a woman."

"Oh, thank you," I replied as my face turned hot. "Actually, the general is in such good shape, he is wearing me out. This is more like rock climbing than hiking."

"Yes, the general is in very good health." He shot his friend an admiring glance. "Every week, he hikes—even in the rain or snow."

The general took my hand and pointed to the trees, to the top of the steep mountain, and to each bright cluster of color. "This is Korea! That is Korea! You remember this beauty as Korea—your country. When you leave here, you remember this as the true Korea."

At that moment, his unbridled enthusiasm did not seem all

that exaggerated. The scene was indeed breathtaking and magical. The jagged mountains of Korea had an air of tranquillity and grace unlike anything I had ever experienced. As we climbed higher up the peak, the sloping black-tile roof of a Buddhist temple peered out from the pine trees and a low melodic chanting drifted up from below. But we did not need to be inside the temple to participate in the ceremony. It was as if the trees and cliffs themselves formed the walls of a living temple of worship, and each step we took was a silent prayer.

We walked quietly until we reached the top of the world, where everyone squeezed onto a single boulder and sat with their feet dangling off the edge. The men cupped their hands around their mouths and yelled into the wind.

"Yaaa-hoo!"

We waited for the echo of our voices to travel the peaks and bounce back to us and repeated several more hikers' yells.

The general then pulled out a tiny book from his back pocket and recited a poem with all the theatrics of a Shakespearean actor. When he finished, he looked down at his pocket watch and suddenly exclaimed, "Katy, the meeting with your father! We have to get you back to the hotel."

We scrambled down the mountain. Along the way, we passed groups of older men and women dressed in typical Korean hiking fashion: red vests worn over long-sleeve shirts, visors or hats, loose pants tucked into colorful argyle socks, and knitted white gloves with rubber grips. Luckily, we had gone early enough to avoid the rush of people to the mountains, which on weekends could get as crowded as city streets.

As I raced down the hill, my body pulsed with anticipation. Now that the reality of meeting my father drew closer, new fears rose inside. How was I supposed to act—like a Korean daughter or like myself?

It didn't help that the men began a lengthy discussion about how I should greet my *appa,* "daddy," and what kind of gift I should present to him on our first meeting.

"It should be something that will remind him of you every day when he sees it," the general's friend said.

"Yes, and something that shows how much you love him," another friend added. Finally, it was decided that I should buy him a set of expensive silver chopsticks and a matching spoon— the only eating utensils Koreans used.

"That way, every time he eats, your daddy will think of his daughter."

With less than an hour to go before my father arrived at the hotel, we piled back in the car and drove to Lotte, the most popular department store in downtown Seoul, to buy my father's gift.

"We don't have time to park," the general said. "Miss Yoo, run up with Katy and help her find the perfect gift. Hurry!"

Miss Yoo grabbed my hand and together we raced down the street and into a shining twelve-story building. We squeezed into an elevator packed like sardines and fell out on the top floor of the department store, where Miss Yoo led me to a glass counter lined with rows of chopsticks as far as the eye could see.

"Which one?" she asked while tapping her finger on the glass.

I had no idea one could spend hundreds of dollars on a single set of chopsticks. They came in every kind of metal, weight, and design. Pairs of elaborate chopsticks stretched out in a dizzying number of choices and I debated which price range would properly honor my father.

"I don't know." I finally sighed.

"Okay, how about these?" She pointed to a pair with the long necks of Korean white cranes carved along the tops.

I nodded and Miss Yoo directed the salesclerk to wrap the gift as quickly as possible.

We arrived back at the hotel with just twenty minutes to spare.

"You can't meet your father like this. Hurry, you must curl your hair and put on makeup," Miss Yoo directed me, suddenly sounding like a Korean mother.

I tore off my dirty socks and sweats and rummaged through my suitcase, throwing out possibilities. "What should I wear?"

Miss Yoo shook her head disapprovingly. One skirt was wrinkled, another too short. The room suddenly filled with tension as I threw Miss Yoo an annoyed look. I finally selected a gray silk blouse, scarf, and knee-length skirt and rushed to the bathroom to apply a healthy dose of makeup and curl my hair. I hadn't even met my father yet, and already I felt a need to comply with the standards of a proper *Korean* daughter.

Miss Yoo instructed me how to bow to my father when he entered the room, bending deeply from the waist to show proper respect. Next I should hand him the wrapped gift with both hands while looking down. The nervousness took hold in my stomach and I ran to the bathroom.

I heard Miss Yoo's persistent voice outside the door. "How will we know if he is truly your father? What if they made a mistake?"

A new wave of panic washed over me. Oh God! What if this was someone else's father? That kind of mix-up was not unheard of. In fact, there was a well-known story of a Korean adoptee who reunited with her birth parents on national television, only to discover later that they were not really her parents!

I did not possess a single photograph of my father. How would I know if he really *was* my father? It wasn't like I could order a blood test on the spot.

Emerging from the bathroom, I sat on the edge of the bed and mentally rehearsed the bow I would give this man. My heart jumped with each ding of the elevator out in the hallway. Finally, I heard the elevator doors slide open on the eighth floor. I heard a man clear his throat in the hallway and pause outside the door.

My father had arrived.

Two soft knocks came at the door and I slowly released my breath. Miss Yoo pushed me off the bed toward the door.

I opened the door slowly.

"Ji-yun-ah!" He stumbled forward and called out my name. In one arm he carried a dozen red roses and several small wrapped packages. The other arm was in a cast up to his elbow and supported by a sling. My father stepped toward me and hugged me to his chest as his eyes reddened with tears. I forgot all about my proper Korean greeting and bow as we held each other, then pushed apart far enough to stare unbelievingly at each other's face.

I took the flowers and gifts from him and led him to a table. We sat in silence, studying each other as tears streamed down my face. Without speaking, we seemed to be asking each other, "Is that really you?"

Miss Yoo broke our silence with an air of business, offering my father a can of juice from the hotel refrigerator. She gave a painfully long introduction of herself, as if bringing a meeting to order. She explained how I had come to know the general.

"The general is a very kind and good man," she told my father. "He helped to arrange this meeting between you and Katy today."

My father nodded his appreciation. "Please thank your boss, the general, for me. I am indebted to him for making the meeting with my daughter possible."

Miss Yoo looked pleased, and after a short pause began translating my father's first words.

"Ji-yun-ah, I'm so sorry I could not do my duties to you as a father." He looked at me with a shy smile that lingered somewhere between joy and sorrow. His voice was low and soothing as he spoke and he studied my face as if probing for a reaction to his apology.

I smiled at him and searched his face for a sign, a hint of resemblance between us. His smooth shiny skin was pulled tightly around his cheekbones, except for the folds of loose skin that hooded his small, dark eyes. His eyelids were red and puffy from crying, but he released no tears. His straight black hair was parted on the side and cut squarely around his face; a thinning spot created a circle in the back of his head. He was tall and so skinny that his shoulder bones stuck out as he slouched forward. The white cast on his right arm accentuated his rough brown hands and the dirt under his fingernails.

I could not see myself in him, and yet there was an undeniable bond.

"After I received the phone call from Miss Kim, I could not sleep," he continued. "I lay awake, my heart pounding with excitement for the meeting with my daughter."

"Me too!"

After another moment of silence, he reached into his jacket pocket with his left hand and pulled out a white envelope. Turning to Miss Yoo, my father spoke for a long time as I anxiously awaited her translation.

"Your father's house burned down in a fire several months ago. It started a few houses down and spread to his house. It was a very bad fire. He lost everything, including most of his clothes, and he broke his arm while escaping. That is why your father apologizes for not wearing more formal clothes for his meeting with you today. He wishes he could look better for you."

"I'm so sorry to hear about the fire. Is he all right now?"

"Your father says you shouldn't worry about his arm. It is healing fine and he is getting the cast taken off next month. Other than the arm, your father is very healthy and strong. He thinks that after meeting you, his bad luck will change. In the fire, he lost most of his things, but he rescued these photographs of you. Your father says he has treasured and carried these pictures of you for all of these years that you have been gone."

He handed me the envelope.

The first photograph was a black-and-white snapshot of a tiny baby with a round face, chubby cheeks, and fuzzy black hair. This was the first picture I had ever seen of myself as an infant, but sitting there next to my Korean father, I recognized myself as the baby in the photograph. It was an indescribable feeling to see a picture of myself at this age, like discovering a lost period of my life. I was seated in an ornate wooden chair with a gold-plated back, my head tilted slightly, with a bored, lofty look on my face. I wore a gold ring on a finger of my right hand.

The next pictures were a series of me posing in different party dresses. A big smile spread across my face and I turned to my father. "I remember the day you brought me those dresses!"

My father's eyes disappeared under the folds of his eyelids as he laughed with joy at my recollection. All of my previous doubts dissipated as we made our first reconnection to a shared past.

In one of the pictures, an old school sweater was draped over my shoulders (a sign of my grandmother's invisible hand on that day). Next was a photograph of my father as a strikingly handsome twenty-year-old in the Korean Army. All of the lines were erased from his face to reveal much fuller cheeks with buttery skin and eyes that had an air of quiet confidence. That this stately man was my father filled my heart with pride. To me, he looked like a movie star.

The last picture was of my father and mother together. My father was dressed in a suit and tie and looked like a professor with thick black-framed glasses. He was seated on a brick wall in front of some trees on what looked like a university campus.

He was much older than in the previous picture. He could have passed for my mother's father instead of her lover. My mother looked like a young schoolgirl, much younger than I was now. She stood by my father's side with her hand resting affectionately on his thigh. Her hair was pulled back into a loose ponytail and she wore a short pleated skirt, jacket, and scarf. She had just a hint of a smirk on her face that made me guess they were on a secret outing on that autumn day.

I was entranced by this photograph as a voice in my head screamed, "These two people are my parents." I was the combination of these two people in flesh and blood . . . They made me . . . I looked like my mother! We shared a similar face, eyes and nose, and the same long legs. I stared at the photograph, not wanting to release my eyes from the image. Now that I discovered them, I desperately wanted to know their story—how they met and fell in love, what happened after I was born, why they separated, why they put me up for adoption.

"Your mother, Miss Korea." My father pointed to her face, using the expression that was synonymous in Korea with "beautiful woman." "You take after her, but I think I gave you your brains."

We both laughed.

Then the tears began to stream down my face and I was afraid that once they started, they would never stop. Suddenly my father spoke to me in near-perfect English. "Get my hankie from my pocket."

"What?"

"Get my hankie from my pocket," he repeated. I reached into his pocket, pulled out a worn, white handkerchief, and blew my nose through laughter and tears.

"You can speak English!"

"No, no. Not very good."

I reluctantly slid the photographs back into the envelope and handed it to my father. "No, for you." He pushed my hand back.

Then it was my turn to share photographs. I had packed an envelope of them—just in case. I pulled out pictures from my wedding the year before and pointed. "This is my husband, John, on our wedding day."

My father took the photograph from me and held it close to his eyes, slanting it right then left toward the light. "Your husband—he is American?" His eyebrows wrinkled in puzzlement and he returned to speaking Korean.

"Yes," I said, laughing at my father's surprise. "Where I grew up in Salt Lake City, there were not many other Koreans. In fact, I was the only Asian at my school."

"I see," he said slowly, still looking a little shocked. "If you lived in New York City or Los Angeles, there are lots of Koreans."

"Yes, but not in Utah or Idaho."

After a pause, my father spoke again with a look of concern. "Did you suffer racism while growing up?"

I laughed at the enormity of his question and opted for the simplest response. "No, I had a very good life and a very loving family. I have three older brothers."

"Are they Korean too?"

"No, they are American. I was the only one in the family who was adopted."

"Your American parents—"

"My parents divorced when I was in high school."

"Oh, I see. Did they treat you nice?"

"Yes, I had a very loving family." I wanted him to know everything about my life and understand the person I had become, but it was impossible to describe twenty years in one meeting, in one sentence. "My American father and I didn't get along so well. But my mother and I are very close."

"If your parents divorced, what about the money? Were they able to support you and pay for school?"

"Yes. I went away to a private university in California—Santa Clara University—and that's where I met John. We met in a meditation class."

My father was amused. "Does your husband practice Buddhism?"

"No, but we are both interested in it. I studied English and I am now working as a journalist at a newspaper in Idaho."

"I thought you studied to become a doctor! That's what I was told by the adoption agency—that you were a doctor living in New York City. They told me many lies, I think."

"No, I'm not a doctor! I was never good at math or science. I always wanted to be a writer—ever since I was little."

"Of course! At your first birthday, you picked up a pen, so it makes perfect sense that you are a writer."

I suspected he was lying, but his effort made me smile.

"Your husband, does he have a good job?"

"Yes, he is an electrical engineer."

"Good, good." My father nodded his approval.

Another long silence followed before my father cleared his throat as if preparing to give a rehearsed speech. He paused after each sentence so that Miss Yoo could echo back the translation.

"For twenty-one years, not a single day went by that I did not think of you, my lovely daughter. Now that I see how you have turned out, all grown up as an adult, my mind can finally be at peace. I can die knowing all of my wishes have come true. You have grown into a beautiful, intelligent woman. Please thank your American mother for me for raising you so well. I'm very grateful to her that she could provide for you when I could not."

I felt my insides soften with each word.

"My mother told me to tell you that she also is grateful to you."

"But I did nothing. She is the one who raised you for the past twenty years," he said with a smile.

"I have missed you so much and tried many times to find you. About ten years ago, I went to the orphanage to try and find out where you lived in America. They told me you lived in New York City. Before I died, I was going to go to America and search for you in New York City. But you came to me first."

"My mom told me that you tried to contact me when I was still in high school. She said she wrote you a letter telling you about me. Did you get it?"

"No. I never got such a letter."

He stole shy glances at my face as we sat in silence. Then, suddenly, a series of questions flew out of my mouth before I could think about what I was saying. "How did you meet my mother? What happened between you? Why did you give me up for adoption?"

With each question, tears rolled down my cheeks. These were the questions I had longed to ask for all of these years, and with their utterance, I found myself sobbing like a child.

A look of pain flashed across my father's face, but he nodded as if he had been expecting these questions. "Your mother and I worked together. We were business associates. I had been divorced for fifteen years when I met her. You have a half brother and sister from my previous marriage. Do you remember them?"

I strained to remember a brother and a sister, but my mind remained blank. "No. Do they live in Seoul?"

"Yes."

"But you don't live together?"

"No. I live alone. Do you remember your grandmother—my mother—and your uncle?"

I shook my head.

"Oh, you don't? That's right, maybe she died when you were very young. Well, we all lived together after you were born— you, your mother, and me. I owned a clothing export business then, but it went bankrupt shortly after you were born and your mother and I separated because of economic reasons.

"We talked about sending you to America to go to school. We thought you were very smart and that would be the best thing for you. If you had not been so smart, we would not have sent you to America. We asked you if you wanted to go and you said yes."

He paused and looked at me as if to jog my memory before continuing.

"But then I changed my mind. I wanted another chance to provide for you myself. But your mother and grandmother decided to go ahead with the plan without me. They secretly arranged the adoption and took you to the airport without telling me. I didn't know until afterward that you were gone. That is why I was not there to say good-bye to you at the airport.

"After you left, your mother and I tried to get back together. We were together for a short time after you left, but it didn't work out between us. I have never forgotten about her. I never remarried. I live alone now. Have you tried to find your mother?"

"Yes, I asked the adoption agency to help me find her. They are looking. Do you know where she might be living now?"

"No, I don't know anything. But if you find her, I want to see her too. I want you to tell me if you find her so we can both meet her together."

"Okay." I nodded. "Do you know anything about my *halmoni* and whether she is still alive?"

He shook his head slowly. "Do you have memories of me?

Did you have a picture of me while growing up?" His look was a mixture of sadness and faint hope.

Rather than tell him the truth, I remained silent.

"We spent a lot of time together, you and I. We went to the park together and I took you out on many outings. I brought you presents all the time and paid for you to go to school."

"Yes, I know. I remember. I still have the red plaid backpack you bought me for school. I took it to America with me, filled with my Korean schoolbooks."

He grinned. "You were my favorite out of all the children."

We met again the next afternoon to have lunch and tour the city. At the restaurant, my father watched closely to see what I ate. When he saw me enjoying everything with a ravenous appetite using expert chopstick skills—including the *kimchee*—he smiled. "Ah, you like *kimchee*. You are truly Korean!" He threw back his head and laughed.

I walked with my arm linked through my father's on a spring day through a city park. It was Korea's wedding season. Brides adorned in elaborate white Western wedding gowns posed with grooms in black tuxedos by a tall water fountain. The brides looked like fashion models with their hair curled and piled high on their heads and their faces painted in rich makeup. I was told that Korean families often go into lifetime debt for their daughters' weddings, spending more than $30,000. In addition to the generous gifts for the groom, elaborate makeovers for the bride, rental of a Western gown, as well as a traditional Korean wedding *hanbok* and full-day outdoor photo sessions took up a large chunk of that sum. By contrast, my simple handmade gown and backyard wedding must have looked subdued to my father. I wondered what went through his mind when he saw the photos of my wedding.

My father squeezed my hand tightly whenever we rested on a bench, examining my face in silence. We walked to Insadong, a historic art district near downtown Seoul composed of a main street and alleyways lined with displays of calligraphy brushes, scrolls, pottery, masks, and traditional Korean dresses. The festive streets were packed with people and vendors. Men dressed in casual loose-fitting *hanboks* demonstrated pottery techniques, sold Korean flags, and pounded blocks of glutinous rice with a huge wooden hammer to create *ddok*—a rice cake made into a popular chewy snack dusted with red bean powder.

"Do you want Daddy to buy that for you?" My father pointed to some candy.

I shook my head.

"How about this?" He picked out a small drum ornament with lime-green tassels.

"Okay." I smiled, feeling as though time had rolled back twenty years. He gave the vendor a few coins and handed me the gift with a pat on my shoulder.

Our day together ended with a night parade in celebration of Buddha's birthday, although to me it felt more like a parade in honor of my return to Korea. We joined the crowds lining downtown streets. My father took my hand and elbowed his way toward the front of the crowd, where parents stood with their pint-size toddlers. As dusk fell over the cool night air, the parade began with a grand procession of gray-robed monks holding round paper lanterns lit from the inside with candles. Groups of male drummers dressed in loose white pants and colorful jackets followed behind them. Older boys banged on the huge drums hanging off their chests while smaller boys clanged brass cymbals. Rows of women dressed in *hanboks* of bright pinks, deep reds and greens danced and twirled gracefully while displaying elaborate paper lanterns in the shapes of fish, animals, and flowers. Hundreds of uniformed schoolchildren and university students marched with waving Korean flags and banners. Finally, an enormous statue of a golden praying Buddha sitting atop a glowing pink lotus flower floated down the street.

I prepared to leave Seoul and the father I had just met feeling, strangely, like a child leaving home for the first time. I reluctantly repacked my huge suitcase and carry-on, loading it down with Korean souvenirs and gifts, including the ten packages of *kim*—toasted dried seaweed—my father had brought me.

"You are traveling all by yourself." My father shook his head and scanned the luggage. "Will there be someone to meet you?"

"Yes, don't worry, *Aboji*."

"Do you think you will ever return to Korea?"

"Yes! I want to come again and bring John to meet you. Maybe you could come visit me in Boise?"

My father smiled. "We'll see."

Together we took a shuttle bus back to Kimpo Airport. He squeezed my hand all during the long ride through the city. As I looked out the window at the spring rain washing over the city, I bid good-bye to Seoul as if it was an old friend. I did not consider myself a religious person, but I felt that a higher power had guided me during this journey and made everything fall into place exactly as it should. The short time in Seoul had been like floating through time, riding a sweeping wave, and unlocking a mystery after so many years.

I thought about my father's words—he had thought about me every day since I left. So this is what it feels like, I thought, to be adored by a father.

We arrived at the airport early and waited in the boarding area. My father alternated between checking his pocket watch and studying my face, as I nervously chewed my nails. Finally, it was time for me to board.

"I better get in line now," I told my father.

He looked at his watch one more time and checked it against a clock on the wall. "Okay," he said reluctantly.

He walked me to the line of passengers snaking around the corner. As the line got shorter and shorter, I hugged his bony shoulders and kissed him on the cheek. My father wiped his puffy eyes with the same handkerchief I had used to blow my nose. I laughed as I remembered how he had told me to get his hankie from his pocket. I handed my boarding pass to the agent and looked back one last time at my father, who was now standing on his tiptoes and leaning over the railing.

He waved his hankie in the air as I reluctantly stepped around the corner.

I had arrived in America.

I was on a moving staircase riding slowly down. From what my *halmoni* had told me, I knew that waiting for me at the bottom would be my new parents. I saw them in the distance—two foreigners who looked as strange as monsters. The woman had a long pointy nose, white skin splashed with tiny brown spots, orange hair, and pale green eyes. The man had only a few strands of long silvery hair brushed across his shiny head, while large bushy clumps of hair hung from his chin like a lion. So this is what Americans looked like! I didn't know what I had expected them to look like exactly, except that I was surprised by how different they looked from Koreans and my own family.

As I rode closer to the foreigners, I understood that these people were vital to my future. My grandmother had told me many times that I had to impress them, but I wanted to run back up the stairs as fast as my legs could carry me. The strangers talked to each other and to me in strange sounds that I could not understand. I saw a tear run down the woman's face and I became even more frightened. I wondered if she was crying because she was disappointed.

I gulped down my own tears and stepped off the escalator dressed in my *hanbok*. As soon as the plane landed, a woman had helped me change into my *hanbok* just as my grandmother instructed.

I stood before my new parents as the rest of my grandmother's instructions echoed through my head: *Be sure to smile and say, "Hel-lo. I love you."* I wanted to make my grandmother proud of me and show these strangers how smart I was. But a lump formed in my throat as I stared at my new parents. Before, "parents" had seemed like just another word, similar to the ones Korean children were taught to use in addressing near strangers—"our aunt" or "uncle," and sometimes even "our mother"—as a show of respect. But as I stood before these two foreigners, everything that my grandmother told me about going to America became a jumble in my head. I tried to hold back the tears by keeping my lips pressed together.

My breath froze midway as a slap whipped across my face. It took a second for me to realize that the slap had come from the Korean escort standing next to me.

"Why are you behaving in this shameful way?" she lashed out. "You are embarrassing me. Do you know how lucky you are to have an American mommy and daddy? Stop crying this instant and show proper respect."

The woman shoved me toward the strangers and ordered me to bow.

I blinked back the tears in shock. My mind continued to reel: *Be sure to smile...lucky...American mommy and daddy...proper respect...I love you.*

I did not smile, bow, or say the instructed words. Instead, I cried even harder. At that moment, I wanted more than anything to be back at the airport in Korea.

4

The day you arrived in America actually began the day before, when we flew to Sea-Tac Airport. We stayed at the motel by the airport. I couldn't sleep, but was afraid to make any noise because I didn't want to wake your father. We weren't sure you would be on the plane. They said that if you were sick or something, you might not be put on the plane and we wouldn't know until the plane took off. We could then check and see if your name was on the list. At about 2 A.M., I could tell your dad was restless and tossing and turning too. So we woke up and called to see if you were on the plane.

You were!

We were then too excited to sleep. We got to the airport early and visited with the people at Travelers Aid. They were very excited to see some parents. Usually the children landed then went directly to other destinations and the people in Seattle never saw the elated parents when their children or babies arrived. We met a young Korean girl who would translate for us and talk to you. She was thin, dressed in her white school blouse and blue skirt. She had an intense, studious face.

We were so nervous waiting, pacing and rehearsing what we would say and do. We were told we shouldn't cry, as you would interpret that as being disappointed and unhappy. So we were determined not to cry, or be loud and scare you, or talk too much.

Since it was an international airport, there was a big wall between the arriving overseas passengers and the terminal. If we stayed on the upper floor we could look over the wall into a glassed portion and see you coming down the escalator. All the children started coming off the plane and down the escalator. Some with shaved heads, some with hair cut in various lengths, cut quickly without any thought to style. Then a little girl dressed in a beautiful Korean dress, with a little purse and shoes to match. Her straight, black hair hung below her shoulders. Her brown eyes, not crying but with tears rimming. She was frightened and timidly walking very straight.

"That's her," I told your dad.

"Do you think it really is?" he replied. She was the most beautiful of all the children.

The girl took your hand and led you to us. I was trying so hard not to cry, but I was overwhelmed with emotion. We had waited so long, and here you were. When you came over to us, the tears welled in your eyes. The girl said something to you in Korean, then she slapped your face. You were startled, but so was I. I picked you up and told you that I was sorry she slapped you and hugged you. The girl said it wasn't good to spoil you and it was wrong to cry.

The ladies that brought you took us into the office of Travelers Aid and got the papers in order. You and I went to the rest room and washed away our tears. Your father and I gave you a little rag doll to carry. The ladies said you had been very sick on the plane and had thrown up several times. They said they had been told to dress you in the hanbok *before you met your new parents. It was a gift from your grandmother.*

It didn't dawn on us that this was the first of many clues that the story they had given us from Korea wasn't really true.

• • •

When I hear mothers talk about the birth of their children, I have a hard time envisioning my own birth. Instead of emerging out of my mother's womb naked, I picture my arrival at age seven fully dressed, traveling down the escalator and being delivered to my adoptive parents. Upon delivery, I cried, received a slap from the Korean escort, and was thus awakened to the reality of my new life.

The foreign woman (whom I understood to be my new mother) made soft cooing sounds that I could not understand, wiped my face, and helped me change out of my *hanbok*. After that, there was another plane ride, then a car ride with other members of my new family—three big boys whom I later understood were my *oppa,* elder brothers, named Dave, Mike, and Kelly. Mike had a head of curly dark hair; the other two had long brown hair that hung straight over their eyes and to their shoulders in the fashionable style of the seventies. Their faces looked like my new mother's, with the same pale eyes, pointy nose, and splash of brown freckles.

As we headed down a highway with me sandwiched between the boys in the backseat, the car filled with noise. Everyone talked in loud, excited voices all at once and laughed whenever they looked at me.

During the ride home, Mike introduced me to PEZ candy. He had purchased a Goofy dispenser for his new little sister and showed me how to press the dog's head to release the little colored candies. Unable to communicate anything else, he resorted to animal sounds, not realizing even those were different in our respective languages.

"Woof, woof." He made Goofy bark at me.

"Mong, mong." I barked back the sound of a Korean dog.

After a nauseating car ride (I wasn't used to riding in automobiles and got sick several times during the trip), we finally pulled up in front of an enormous redbrick house with a large open yard in front covered with a smooth green blanket of grass. All down the street, the houses looked the same. Everything appeared so vast and open, clean, and void of the noises and smells that had surrounded me in Korea. There were no walls or gates around the houses, clothes hanging from a line, *kimchee* pots lined up on the balcony, or children running in the street.

Even the air was sterile and still.

My new home was located at the top of a long steep hill, at the foot of the majestic Wasatch Mountains that stood guard over the Salt Lake Valley. Directly across the street was the bishop of our neighborhood Mormon ward, who was always nice to us even though we were the only Catholic family for miles around. (He even remained cordial after making the unfortunate mistake of backing into my grandmother's white Cordova. Grandma Ruth didn't give a damn if he was a Mormon bishop or the Catholic pope. She ignored his apologies while yelling for my brother at the top of her lungs. "This bastard just hit my car. Michael, come out here and beat him up!") Just down the street and around the corner from us lived a polygamist family that always had a dozen bicycles parked in their front yard. Sometimes we would see a group of young women leave the house in homemade ankle-length dresses and matching braids in their hair. Years later, when it occurred to them, my family would joke that I was hit with the double whammy of being an ethnic and a religious minority in Utah, as if just being Catholic wasn't bad enough.

That first day, I stopped on the front porch to unbuckle my shoes and place them toes facing outward. I looked up to see the rest of the family stare down at me in surprise and amusement. Kelly tried to suppress a giggle. But I was equally surprised to see that no one else removed their dirty shoes before walking directly into the house. We entered a room covered with fuzzy brown stuff (the first time I had seen carpet) and I was shocked to see that these people allowed a big, hairy dog to roam free inside the house.

The inside of the home was a maze, with stairs, numerous doors leading outside, long hallways, and so many separate rooms filled with furniture. My grandmother was right—Americans must be very wealthy, I thought as I explored the rooms.

My father led me to a bathroom and undressed me. He lifted me into a huge pink bathtub of warm water and continued the same growling noises he had made on the plane as he washed my hair and scrubbed my body. I was embarrassed to have a man touch me and see me naked for the first time, so I laughed nervously and tried to hide the lower parts of my body. Not only was I unaccustomed to having a man participate in my life, I found my new father a little scary. He had thick hair everywhere except the top of his head. It grew on his face, down his neck, along his arms, and to the middle of his fingers. He made loud noises and seemed gruff even when he played. The more I giggled in discomfort, the more my father growled and laughed loudly.

After the bath, I remember that first night as a grand party. My brothers took turns tickling me, giving me bucking piggyback rides, and making strange, playful sounds. We spoke to one another through gestures and by shaking or nodding our heads. My parents attempted to read Korean phrases they had practiced from a sheet of paper. But when I could not distinguish their Korean from their English, they gave up and resorted to motioning with their hands. "Do you want to eat?" They scooped up an invisible spoon and moved it up and down to their mouths. "Do you want a drink? Are you sleepy?"

After a strange-tasting meal of fish sticks and rice, my mother led me by the hand to a room that I understood was mine—at least it was the only room in the house decorated for a girl. It was a huge room with thick red carpet and sheer white curtains over two square windows. A four-poster brass bed stood at the center of the room. A comforter decorated with red roses tied in strips of red yarn covered the bed. A doll with dark brown eyes and straight black hair sat on a desk next to the bed. The doll looked a bit like me—not like the yellow-hair American doll my mother had kept in a glass display case in Korea.

As evening turned dark, everyone went to separate parts of the house and I lay alone in my room, aware of the open space, huge elevated bed, and the quiet solitude. This was the first time I had ever slept by myself. In Korea, I had always taken comfort in being on an *ondol* heated floor next to my grandmother or other relatives in one cozy room. I took the blanket off my bed, tiptoed down the hall, and entered the room where my parents slept. I lay down on the floor next to their tall bed while Murphy, our brown furry dog, snored underneath it.

I didn't cry that first night.

The next morning, I watched as my mother searched through my school pack and emptied the contents onto my bed. She found my schoolbooks, pieces of leftover silk fabric from my *hanbok,* and a piece of folded brown paper where my grandmother had written my Korean name above my American father's misspelled name in clunky English letters. Buried deep in one of the pockets, my mother found the bundle of photographs that my grandmother had secretly placed inside my pack.

As she flipped through the pictures more and more slowly, her face became still as she realized that everything the orphanage had told her about me was a lie. I had not been abandoned at birth and left at the doorsteps of a Pusan police station with a note pinned to my sweater. And I had not grown up in an orphanage, as the adoption records indicated.

Her eyes rested on a picture of me at my first birthday party and she let out a mixture of a gasp and a laugh. In the photo, I was dressed in a baby *hanbok* and my head poked up from behind an elaborate banquet table piled with platters of fruit, carefully arranged towers of candy, rice cakes, round sugar cookies, presents, and a fan of crisp new bills. According to Korean tradition, symbolic items such as a pen, thread, money, and books are placed before a child on his first birthday. Whichever he selects first symbolizes his future—writer, long life, wealth, or scholar. As for my destiny, I held a round pink sugar cookie in one hand and a spoon in the other.

In the bundle there were also pictures of me at age two, looking like a chubby boy with short black hair. Me with longer hair under a sunbonnet, the crotch of my white tights hanging below my blue dress as I clung to my mother's leg. Me with my grandmother several years later with hair chopped every which way around my sulky face—the result of sleeping with gum in my mouth the night before. And last, the Polaroid taken at the airport just a few days before.

My mother's eyes froze on that picture.

She focused for a long time on the picture of me standing between my mother and grandmother until tears filled her eyes. She looked at me, then back to the little girl in the picture. Then, as if shaking off a sleepy dream, she yelled for my father.

They both stared at me as if I had the answers to their silent question.

I reached for the Polaroid and pointed to my mother and grandmother. "This is my mother and this is my grandmother," I told them in Korean. "They must miss me, so I want to go home now, okay? I—go—home—now." I tried speaking more slowly.

They continued to stare at me in silence.

• • •

People often ask me what those first weeks were like in a strange country with a new family and a language I could not understand. Was I scared? More than I can express all of these years later. Feeling abandoned by those closest to you is a hard thing for a seven-year-old mind to grasp. Seven is a precarious age— too young to understand the big picture, but old enough to feel the kind of grief that leaves imprints. Minus the very first night, I cried for two weeks straight as my new mother rocked me in her lap like a baby. The nights were most frightening as the isolation and darkness settled over my new surroundings. For weeks I didn't unpack anything so that I would be ready for my trip back to Korea at a moment's notice.

Each day I waited to go home brought a lesson in strange new customs and ways. I wasn't used to the huge bathtub for one; American toilet paper gave me a rash and most of the food tasted bland and mushy compared with Korean cuisine. (I had never before eaten a meal that did not include *kimchee*.) There were no chopsticks at the table and I was scolded for chewing with my mouth open—something that came naturally to Koreans. The hardest part, besides not being able to communicate with anyone, was sleeping in a bed, all alone in a large room. Each night, my parents tucked me in and turned out the light. But each morning, my parents or one of my brothers would find me wrapped in a blanket on the floor next to their beds. At first, they were surprised to find me beneath their feet when they got up. But with time, they learned to step over the lump on the floor.

Soon after my arrival, I was introduced to Thanksgiving. I wore my *hanbok* for the occasion and drew a turkey by tracing the outline of my open hand with a crayon. My mother pasted my turkeys all over the front window and made the family pose in front of them for a picture. That night, both sets of grand-parents, aunts, uncles, and cousins came to our house for dinner. I gripped an enormous drumstick with both hands and tore into the skin and flesh unaware that I was the center of attention. At the end of the meal all that remained on my china plate was one clean bone sucked dry with the ends chewed off.

I also embraced the idea of Santa Claus, even if I didn't un-derstand all of the rituals at first. The first time my mother showed me the sequin snowman stocking she was sewing, I held it up to my right foot and gestured that it was way too big. I slipped my bare foot inside the green felt stocking to prove my point, but my family laughed. I didn't see what was so funny since the green stocking was shaped just like a traditional Korean padded sock worn with *hanboks*. How strange, I thought, to hang a sock on the wall.

One day my mom and grandma took me shopping at the downtown mall. The fancy stores, bright lights, and Christmas decorations were an amazing sight. I had never seen anything like it. All day long, we bought gifts for my brothers—boxes and bags full of them, making several trips to the car to unload it all. I secretly wondered if only my brothers got presents and if my mother and grandmother thought me undeserving. My feelings grew more hurt as the day wore on. When I saw an enormous wood-shingled dollhouse on display at ZCMI de-partment store, I ran to my mother and pulled her by the sleeve to the display. I pointed out the miniature furniture, wooden staircase, rugs, and lights that turned on and off. I stood there mesmerized by the dollhouse and wondered if it was my turn yet to get a gift.

When my mother shook her head and pulled me away, I began to wail and speak in Korean. "Why nothing for Katy? Just the boys!"

My mother and grandmother exchanged puzzled looks and tried to console me.

Come Christmas morning, I woke up to find piles of presents—the most I had ever seen or imagined in my wildest dreams. Each of my brothers had piles of wrapped gifts stacked high in separate parts of the living room. And in the corner, there was a pile for me. I was overjoyed to think they had not forgotten about me after all. It was just the opposite—lavishing me with a whole toy store full of goodies. My favorite gift was a plastic baby doll with deep blue marble eyes that opened and shut.

During the day, my parents' friends stopped by to meet me with their arms loaded with presents. I gathered the stuffed animals, books, and toys and carefully laid them in the center of a sheer blue-and-green scarf I had brought with me from Korea. The scarf had been my Korean mother's favorite and she often wore it around her neck tied into a loose knot. After I arrived in America, I was surprised to find her scarf tucked in among the photographs and books in my school pack. When I lifted the scarf to my face, I could still smell my mother's perfume. After tying the corners of the scarf into a tight knot, I slid the bundle under the bed. I couldn't wait to show my mother and grandmother all of my new American things. The toys and books they had spoken to me about. And all of my new clothes—a whole closet full of them. I would tell my grandmother that everything she had told me about America was true.

I kept waiting for someone to tell me that it was time to go home. I struggled in frustration to talk to my parents in Korean, but they could not understand me no matter how slowly or loudly I spoke; and I could not understand them.

One day an American missionary who spoke Korean came to our house.

"You are a very lucky girl. How do you like your new home and your new mommy and daddy?" he asked.

"My new American family is very nice, but they don't understand anything I say and I miss my grandmother and mother. Can I go back home to Korea now?" I asked excitedly.

"No, Korea is no longer your home. This is your home now."

"What do you mean?"

"Well, you are now an American and you are going to live and grow up in this fine country with your new family. You are very lucky to have American parents who will love and take care of you as their own daughter and send you to school. This is what your Korean mommy wished and wanted for you."

"No, wait." I tried, patiently at first, to explain to this man how there had been some kind of mix-up. My grandmother had never said anything about me becoming an American. That was stupid since I was Korean—not like these people. "She said I could return home anytime," I explained. "Besides, she's sick and she needs me to take care of her. If only I could call her, she will straighten everything out."

The man stared at me for a long time with a half smile painted on his face. Finally, he said, "I'm sorry to tell you this. But you cannot return to Korea or see your mother and grandmother ever again. This is your new home."

I took several deep breaths and tried to think of a way to reason with this ignorant man.

"Could I at least call my grandmother on the phone?" I asked, running to the dining room and lifting up the receiver of a heavy, yellow dial phone.

"No." His voice was firm and the sad smile was now a stern look.

"Okay, could I go home to Korea just for a short visit if I promise to return to America later?"

"No."

"Could my grandmother and mother come live with us in America? Look, this house is plenty big and they won't eat much food."

"No."

It took a minute for all of his "noes" to sink in. When I finally realized I had just exhausted all of my options, I flopped to the floor and threw the biggest fit of my life. I had either been kidnapped by Americans or betrayed by my own family—I wasn't sure which. I didn't care anymore about acting polite or impressing anyone. Or about stupid American dolls or presents. I just wanted to go home. I pounded my fists into the brown carpet and banged my head as hard as I could. Never before had I been as out of control as I was that moment.

I ran into my bedroom, pulled out the packet of photographs from my backpack, and tried to tear them up. I wanted to rip those faces into shreds and banish them from my memory.

I felt my American mother pry the photographs from my hands and I turned my anger toward her.

"I don't care," I spat in Korean. "I would rather kill myself than leave my family in Korea!"

Trying to console me, the befuddled missionary made a promise. "Okay, look. You may write letters to your mother and grandmother in Korea. Your American mommy has promised to mail them for you. That would make you feel better, wouldn't it?"

That night, after my anger turned to sorrow, then a glimmer of hope, I sat at the dining-room table and composed a letter. Despite my earlier outburst, I addressed my grandmother in polite form as Korean children are taught to do.

Dear Halmoni,
This is Kim Ji-yun.
I am here in America. My American mother has orange hair and green eyes like a monster. My American father has no hair on his head.
Halmoni, when can I come home? Don't you want to see me? I want to come home now. Are you coming to get me soon? I miss you and want to come home to Korea. Please write to me soon.
I am waiting.

Each letter became a little more subdued with time as my memories of Korea began to dim. Years later I found one of my letters that never got mailed. I discovered the childish handwriting in large block Korean letters stuck between pages of English homework.

Halmoni, hello.
Grandmother, Mother too, I want to see you.
Grandma, did you smoke all of the cigarettes I bought you? I still have my school pack.
Grandma, don't you want to see me?
Mother, don't you want to see me?
I am doing fine, so don't worry too much. Grandma, I promise to become a medical doctor and come back to you. Good-bye.
*   —Kim Ji-yun*

Weeks, then months, went by without a reply. Then one day my mother called me in from the backyard. In her hand she held a square envelope with short red and blue stripes around the edges.

"Did I get a letter from Korea?" I asked.

My mother's eyes shifted to the envelope in her hand, which she then set down on the counter. "No, honey, I'm sorry. Your letters to Korea got returned. We mailed them to the orphanage in Korea, but your mother and grandmother didn't leave a forwarding address. The orphanage had nowhere to send the letters, so they just shipped them back. I know you're disappointed, but I think that maybe it would have been too difficult for your mother and grandmother to hear from you. It would just remind them of how much they love and miss you."

My last hope for contact with my Korean grandmother and mother vanished. My mother stared at me with a worried look on her face. I nodded my head and tried to force a smile even though a feeling of betrayal spread deep inside. If I acted too sad, I would hurt my American mother's feelings. She would think that I was ungrateful and that I didn't want to live with her, and then I would have no place to go.

A few days later, I pulled out the bundle from under the bed. I untied the ends of my Korean mother's scarf and released the stuffed animals and toys into my bedroom. I took the empty scarf and found my mother in her bedroom.

She accepted the gift with tears in her eyes.

tiful country, which is your country too. I will do everything I can to help you."

We exchanged hopeful smiles.

I had less than five days in Korea. I knew better than to expect too much in that amount of time. Many adoptees, after all, never find their birth families even after a lifetime of searching. The best I hoped for was to find some records that would give me the names of my parents. (Wasn't it funny that I had lived with my birth mother for seven years and couldn't even remember her name? I wondered if this was normal or if that information, along with other memories, was waiting to be unlocked from some corner of my brain.) If I could at least discover my mother's name, I could continue the search when I returned home.

Before dropping me off at the hotel, Miss Yoo walked me down a side street to a small nondescript restaurant. The only menu was some foreign words written in vertical columns on a board on the wall. "Do you want soup or noodles?" Miss Yoo asked.

"Soup."

Miss Yoo spoke a few words to the old woman behind the counter, who immediately began delivering small white bowls of vegetables and *kimchee*. We sat next to each other at the high counter enjoying our spicy fish soup and nibbling at the pickled vegetables with our silver chopsticks. I thought about trying to make conversation until I noticed how my companion bent her head into her steaming bowl, absorbed in the act of slurping her spicy soup with heaping spoonfuls of rice. I kept quiet and enjoyed my first meal in Korea by imitating her actions. It tasted perfect, the familiar spices dancing on my tongue.

• • •

5

After I had been in America less than three months, my parents made a tape recording of me talking in English and Korean—the only time I have been able to flow in and out of both with relative ease. We sat on the living-room floor one evening and my parents plugged in a big microphone to a tape recorder. My mom encouraged me to sing and read from my Korean schoolbooks. I was eager to perform, boldly declaring to the world, "My Korean book, I can 'member forty-thlee pages!"

That high-pitched Korean voice still amazes me each time I hear it. I find myself wondering, Where did it go? But it was already beginning to slip away just after three months. The long pause and halting words as I struggle to remember the lyrics to the songs I learned at school and the words to beloved Korean folktales I once read with ease. Slowly I try to sound out the words. Finally, I give up and switch to halting English with this simple explanation: "I can't 'member, so I'm gonna talk now."

The rest of the tape is in English, where I already seem to find myself more comfortable than in my native tongue.

Of all the mementos from my American childhood, I treasure this recording, which is perhaps the best evidence of my moment of transformation. A freeze-frame of my brief time as a true "Korean–American." As I listen, I can almost see myself shedding my Korean language and identity and stepping into a new American skin. Half in, half out. Adopting new English words as the once familiar Korean words slip away into the ocean that is memory.

My name is Catherine Jeanne Robinson, Ka-ty. I 'posed to be Korean! So here first came I cry and sad, and then I happy. My mom and daddy so nice. Thlee brothers little bit tease just to me. Big brothers David, Michael, and Kelly, thlee brothers all day tease me!

I got a thlee school. One is a ski school. One is a writing and reading school. One is just an easy, play, and just a easy.

Today is party, Korean food. Mom so so a good job, I'm happy.

I got a two doggies, one dog is dumb. One dog is girl, dumb. Bathroom, couch. One dog is so smart, boy, a name of dog is Murphy. Murphy is so smart. Girl dog is Tabby. Murphy is so smart, and kitty cat does all day long meow, meow, meow.

And a boy likes kitty cat and Daddy likes TV. Mommy likes me!

I got a two grandma, two grandpas, one grandma is Grandma Ruth. Another grandma is Grandma Jeanne. Grandma Ruth is Mommy's grandma, I mean Mommy's mommy. Grandpa Harold is Daddy's daddy and Grandpa Art is Mommy's daddy. Daddy's dog go boo, boo, boo all day long.

My family every day is ha-ha-ha like that.

You did that Korean names? Kimchee, you know? Hot, you know? I got a thlee window book now, whoa! Birthday is eighty days. Daddy says my birthday, big whole bunch, big book reading to Daddy.

My boys, just a minute I'm going to count, one, two, thlee, floor, my daddy too, tease me all day long. Two girls gonna be . . . scared!

I got happy Christmas. My Christmas, a Korean girl come to here, writing, paper in mailbox. I see I so happy now. No more crying, sometimes I not even cry and Daddy spanky me.

I got a room, pretty. My room 'posed to be my brother Michael's. Michael gave it to me, nice present. I make a Valentine cards; I make a birthday cards, everybody happy. And I got a thlee dollies—almost one hundred, whoa! I got a lots and lots of dollies for Christmas.

I first came I Christmas present for my mom and dad.

I got a nice room and a baby bed, high chair, work deskee. I got a big bed, whoa pretty. That's new one, yeah I got a lots and lots dolly, bye.

I'm sorry, I gotta more talk, whoa, lots, lots singing and talk. Umm, I got a hanbok, *you know* hanbok? *Mom, say yes. Hanbok,* Korean *dress, pretty.*

Okay, I teach you Korean words. Pihanghi *is "airplane."* Migook— *"America."* Cha dong cha— *"automobile."* Almoni— *"mother."*

6

My entrance into first grade was marked by both a sense of pride at having escaped kindergarten (which I deemed too easy after attending two years of school in Korea) and a sense of shame after the first open ridicule of my foreign features. That kind of teasing was to be expected, I suppose, at a private Catholic school that spanned from kindergarten to eighth grade where I was the only Asian student. For most of the students, I am sure I was the only Asian they had ever encountered, with the exception, perhaps, of a kung-fu character on a television show. I must have seemed as foreign to them as my American family had appeared to me at first. But I was still shocked when a group of older boys (probably third grade or so) stopped in their tracks and stared at me wide-eyed.

"She's a chink!" one of them finally blurted out. As if following a script, his friend pulled at the ends of his eyes and asked, "Hey, do you speakee Chinese?"

No, I didn't speak Chinese. I had problems enough with English at that point. But I knew enough to cringe at the word "chink," and later "gook." It sounded like they were eating dirt, the way they scrunched their faces and spat those names at me. I have often wondered why my parents didn't raise me in Los Angeles or San Francisco, where my ethnicity might not have been such a source of shock to those around me. But both my parents were born and raised in Salt Lake City, and that was their home. Besides, in those days, my mom likes to remind me, the popular opinion was to make me forget about Korea and assimilate me into the white culture as fast as they could. And for that, there was no better place than Salt Lake City, Utah. Over the years, I progressed along the apple-pie trail leading to student council, cheerleading, and drill team (where I spent half my time globbing on eye makeup and trying to get my hair to the required fluff).

On that first day of school, I swallowed hard and tried to ignore the boys' ridicule. I walked down the hallway of Cosgriff Elementary dressed in a uniform just like the older students. Beginning in the first grade, girls at our school wore the typical Catholic uniform: round-collared white blouses under green-checked polyester jumpers, white knee-high socks, and saddle shoes.

My first-grade teacher was Sister Muriel. She was tall and thin with wire-rimmed glasses and white hair poking out from beneath her navy-blue habit and matching dress. She wore a grave expression as she greeted me at the doorway and showed me to a desk at the back of the classroom. Back at the front of the room, she said something to the class, and students immediately responded by lifting the lids of their desks and fishing out thick blue-covered books and pieces of lined paper. Soon I was lost in a jumble of rapid English and the shuffle of papers. I felt like crawling under my desk and crying. Everyone around me wrote rows of words on their papers while I sat there like an idiot and chewed my nails until my fingers began to bleed. (A nervous habit which often forced my mother to send me to school with the ends of all ten fingers bandaged.)

In Korea, I had been a good student who was always eager to answer the teacher's questions. On the first day of school in Korea, I was assigned a seat at the back of a long classroom where it was hard to see the chalkboard. I shared a wooden seat and wide desk with a boy. The next week, my mom gave me an envelope filled with money to give to my teacher. Soon after, my teacher moved me to a seat at the front of the class. Maybe I should tell my American mother to give my new teacher some money too, I thought.

By the time the bell rang for afternoon recess, I desperately had to use the bathroom. I filed out of the classroom and into a chaotic hallway filled with the stampede of running feet and chatter of excited voices. I had no idea where the girls' bathroom was located and was too scared to ask anyone. While I pondered my dilemma I felt a warm trickle snake around my thighs and down the back of my legs. Before I could stop myself, a small flood gushed out from beneath my uniform.

If I had been quiet and neat in Korea, I quickly adapted to the ways of my new family. Upon walking through the front door, I threw my books and school bag on the living-room floor and stripped off my polyester plaid uniform while standing on the couch. Sometimes I performed a few leg-splitting bounces before grabbing a snack and preparing for my daily battle with Kelly for the remote control.

From the moment the novelty of a new sister wore off, Kelly (who had been the baby of the family before I came along) and I became rivals and often divided our parents—Dad on his side, Mom on mine. When he wasn't locking me in my room, reading out loud from my Judy Blume diary (a passage each day for maximum torment), or farting in my face, Kelly had his head stuck in a fantasy novel or an Atari game. He also liked old kung-fu movies and loved that one TV show—the one where an ugly white guy plays a kung-fu master named Grasshopper—which was on at the same time as Wonder Woman. Of course he didn't understand that Lynda Carter was my first great American Superhero. From the moment I saw her blue eyes, I thought she was the most beautiful creature on earth. I lived to see her spin into her skimpy Wonder Woman outfit each afternoon and lasso the bad guys.

"Won-der Wo-man . . ." I sang along with the theme song while jumping off the couch, which I imagined to be the tallest skyscraper on earth. I spun around as fast as I could and pictured myself transforming into Lynda Carter's curvy body poured into those star-spangled satin blue bottoms and glittery red-and-white top. I wanted the crown that doubled as a boomerang in my loosely curled hair and eyes as ocean blue as hers. I wanted to lasso up Kelly and throw him in a dungeon.

Invariably, I would get home from school first and be fully engrossed in the latest battle against evil when Kelly would come down and switch the channel, thus declaring war.

Grasshopper vs. Wonder Woman.

Sometimes Wonder Woman won out if I fought back hard enough. But most of the time I screamed from under the weight of Kelly's body while Grasshopper's sedated-sounding voice (meant to sound more "Eastern"?) boomed from the television.

"Shut up, Kate, I can't hear the TV," he'd say before turning the volume up another notch.

Sometimes Dad came down to ask what in the hell all the racket was about and sent us both to our rooms until dinner.

· · ·

I grew up with a large extended family—both sets of grandparents;
numerous aunts; uncles; first, second, and third cousins—who
converged on our house during the holidays or any special occasion. Each Saturday, but especially before a family gathering,
was deemed cleaning day at our house. We had assigned rooms
or sometimes drew chores from a hat (it took a while for me to
catch on that my brothers rigged the drawing to give me both
the bathrooms and the kitty litter). During those times of rush
cleaning, the hallway closet was an especially convenient place
to hide things that had no place else to go, and my brothers and
I took secret joy in booby-trapping it for the next person who
opened it.

"Goddammit," we heard Dad screech one time, "who in the
hell put this here?" I can't remember what fell on his balding
head. Perhaps he had gone to look for a pair of gloves and ended
up being clobbered by a fishnet.

"I swear to God," he would mutter at such times, "no one
in this family has the brains God gave a soda cracker." (Our
family's mental capacity alternated between that of a soda cracker
and a dead bush.)

I can't remember ever using a bottle opener in our house.
Instead, we positioned the grooved cap of our soda bottles under
a kitchen drawer handle and yanked upward, carving a deep
groove in the wood. Deep cleaning was done out of necessity
rather than a set schedule. The freezer (before the days of frost-
free) only got cleaned when opening it meant dodging flying
chicken legs and frost-covered ice-cream cartons. The garage
was cleaned out when dozens of empty Pepsi bottles, bags of
outgrown clothes, and miscellaneous parts from one of our
broken-down cars blocked all paths out. Clearing it out for, say,
a car was a major two-day family feat, involving numerous trips
to the city dump.

Similarly, the shower only got cleaned when the flowering algae and green mold and gunk made the inside tile unrecognizable. Only then would Dad enter with a potent cleaning solution while still wearing his glasses and thongs on his feet. The laundry got done when the mountain of clothes thrown in the hallway grew knee-deep. Then someone would throw a load or two in the wash. But how quickly the clothes made it out of the dryer and into our dressers was another story. Most of the time, the clean clothes sat crumpled on top of a card table until the mound grew large enough to call for Mom's attention one Sunday afternoon. She would then spend the better half of an afternoon transporting baskets of laundry out to the couch and folding them into dozens of piles for people to put away. Until then, it was up to individuals to fish from the mound of clothes for two matching socks or a school jumper.

My brothers seemed to navigate around this chaos with ease, probably because they were the cause of most of it. They were not even bothered by the disasterlike state of their own bedrooms and only cleaned when my mother made an ultimatum. I, on the other hand, developed a habit of staying up half the night to organize my room. The clothes in the closet had to hang just so, each hanger spaced exactly half an inch apart and each pair of shoes lined up perfectly against the back wall before I could crawl into bed. Then I would spot a crooked book or a slightly off-center stuffed animal and hop back up. Sometimes I would make my bed in the middle of the night, pulling the sheets tightly under the mattress then sliding under them to create the least amount of wrinkles. In the morning, if I slipped out just right, it would look as though no one had slept there. All of this strikes me as crazy now, but perhaps that was the only way to regain control of a world that had flipped upside down and catapulted me onto the other side of the Pacific Ocean.

The state of our household was not due to my mother's neglect, for she spent most Saturdays dressed in her oversized orange-pumpkin sweatshirt and gray sweatpants with a scarf tied around her frizzy hair. She deemed Saturdays "cobweb days," a day filled with cleaning, grocery shopping, running errands, and cooking. In the middle of this, she always mustered the energy to rescue each of us from our brewing crisis. While my woes remained mostly fixable, my brothers' problems grew more complex. Most of the details were fuzzy to me then, other than the closed-door whispers, my mother's swollen eyes, trips to our house by the police, and calls ending with my father telling the other person never to call our house again before slamming down the phone.

There was a lot of yelling by my father—the red-faced, chicken casserole–chucking kind. Sometimes he exploded over the biggies (lies, thefts, drug paraphernalia in the bedroom). But more often it was the little, unpredictable thing that set him off like a firecracker (an empty ice tray, a wrong look, using two of his stamps to join a Howard Jones fan club). This added an element of surprise to his outbursts and increased the fear factor.

One recurring battle had to do with rousing my sleepy brothers—usually Kelly, since he lived at home the longest—for church on Sunday mornings. (We were the family who arrived ten minutes early and sat in the front pew.)

"Goddammit." My dad's voice boomed from the basement as my mother twirled my hair into ringlets in the upstairs bathroom. "Get your lazy ass out of bed and get ready for church. This is the last time I'm telling you."

One Sunday battle resulted in a fistfight. I think my dad gave up on his sons' religious education after that. Through the years, my two older brothers moved in and out of the house on the crests and falls of their addiction and troubles with the law. During that time, I was busy trying to fit in and become a Robinson.

I never understood kids who pretended to be, or wished they

were, adopted. As a child, all I ever wanted was to *not* be adopted. I grew up convincing myself that I was just like the rest of my family—copying their personality traits, mannerisms, and idiosyncrasies as my own. It wasn't until much later that I realized I was different with a capital *D,* and not just in looks. It hit me on a Christmas morning not that long ago as I looked around the room at my family and felt utterly alone.

The irony, of course, was that I had tried so hard to deny my true identity.

The first time my parents took me to an annual gathering of Asian people, I had been happy to see other faces like mine. It reminded me of home and I enjoyed eating spicy foods and running around with other black-haired children. There was even a man at the party who spoke to me in Korean and I bowed to him and called him *ajashi,* uncle.

The second year I began to feel uncomfortable and shy, and could barely understand the Korean man when he spoke to me. By the third year I flat-out refused to go.

"I am not going to the stupid Asian festival," I told my parents, stomping my foot on the ground for emphasis.

"But, Katy, why don't you want to go?" My mom looked genuinely surprised.

"Because I am not like any of those people. And it makes me feel stupid to be there!"

My mother was silent, my protest a success. After that, my parents never asked again if I wanted to attend an Asian cultural event.

All I could think about then was that I was an American. I could speak perfect English and had completely forgotten Korean. It made me feel ashamed to be with a group of black-headed, slant-eyed people who spoke in rough up-and-down sounds that I couldn't understand but was somehow expected to. Their foreign sounds made me cringe. Their language sounded like the same singsongy babble children used to make fun of me at school. Their foreign faces were ugly, especially their small eyes that became slits when they smiled.

I hated the way some people made me feel like something I wasn't or how our neighbor slowed her speech and raised her voice a notch whenever she spoke to me—long after English had become my best subject at school. There were no other Asians in my neighborhood, church, or school. My parents didn't have any Asian friends. I figured my parents didn't like them much either, even when they used to take me to those gatherings. My dad tried too hard, his loud chuckle strained as he said, "Katy, this man is from Korea, just like you!" Sometimes it felt as if I had "Made in Korea" stamped on my forehead, just like a sticker found on the bottom of my leather sandals.

One evening, I made an announcement to my family. "I know you think I'm Korean. But I'm not. I'm Hawaiian!"

"What are you babbling on about now, Kate?" my brother Kelly asked as the rest of the family looked up, trying to swallow their laughter.

I hummed a tropical tune and demonstrated a hula dance by rolling my hips in slow wide circles just like the girls I'd seen on television. I made believe I had waist-length hair by draping a white bath towel over my head. The idea first popped into my head after I saw a television advertisement for C&H pure cane sugar. "C&H—pure cane sugar. From Ha-wai-ii," the jingle went. In the commercials, dark-skinned women walked barefoot on a sandy beach against an orange-lit sky. They wore red flowers in their flowing hair and grass skirts hanging low off their bony hips. They too had long black hair and dark eyes like me. But you could tell those Hawaiian girls were considered exotic and beautiful.

• • •

My friends shared their beauty tips with me.

"Maybe if you sleep with a clothespin on your nose," Jenny suggested one night during a sleep-over. She pinched my nose into a wooden clothespin and told me to sleep with it on there all night. But about ten minutes of pain was all I could handle before I freed my nose. I tried other things, like stretching my eyelids with my fingers and trying to open my eyes wider.

But nothing worked.

One day while reading a magazine, I discovered a more permanent fix. There were doctors who could give you pointed noses and larger eyes with folds above them just like Jenny's. The article said this cosmetic surgery was becoming popular with Asian people living in California and it seemed like the perfect solution to my problems.

"Look, Mom, I want to have this done to my eyes." I showed her the article.

"Oh Katy! Why on earth would you want to do that?"

"Because they look so much prettier. I hate my small eyes. I want to have it done."

"Over my dead body." She shut the magazine with a grimace. "Your eyes are beautiful just the way they are. If you had this done, you would regret it for the rest of your life and there would be no way to undo it."

"I don't care what you say. As soon as I turn eighteen—I'm saving my money and going to San Francisco to have it done."

"Oh no, you're not."

"Oh yes, I am!"

I couldn't wait for that day. Besides, how could my mom understand how I felt? Sitting on the bathroom counter with my feet in the sink, I watched my mother put on her makeup before she went out. First she covered her brown freckles with a beige foundation then brushed her cheeks with a rosy blush. She drew in long eyebrows with a brown pencil before applying dark mascara and green liner around her hazel eyes. By the time she smacked her lips and dabbed them on a folded tissue, she looked like a movie star.

"I wish I looked like you," I sighed as I stared at her reflection in the mirror.

"Oh Katy, you should be thankful you don't look like me," my mother said, rolling her eyes. "When I was your age, I hated the way I looked. This pointy nose, all of my freckles, and skin that burned so quickly in the sun."

"Really? But I would give anything to look like you. I'm so ugly. I hate my eyes."

"No, you are beautiful." Then she would tell me the part about choosing me out of all the children in the world.

7

I decided on a career as a journalist when I was eigh-teen.

A few months before, I broke the news to my parents that I wanted to quit ballet lessons. My father had introduced me to the idea of becoming a ballerina during my first week in America. For a short time, he took care of me during the days when my mom went back to her teaching job. He took me on outings to the playground down the street or to McDonald's, where I got some of my first English lessons.

"French fry." My dad held up a golden potato, pleading for me to repeat after him.

"Plench fly," I repeated. (My pronunciation would provide family amusement for years to come, much to my chagrin.)

One day after our trip to McDonald's, my dad took me into the Grand Central store next door, where I fell in love with a ballerina doll in an aisle display. She had reddish-pink hair that curled up at the ends and blue eyes, with a painted-in sparkle, that took up half her face. She was dressed in a pink outfit with a silver star emblazoned on her chest, and if you stuck her plastic toe shoe into a hole in the star-shaped stage and cranked the handle, she twirled. The doll was a worthwhile investment on my father's part because my fascination with ballet lasted eleven years, all the way through the pain of mangled feet crammed inside the torture chamber called toe shoes.

My father took the news that I wanted to stop my lessons the hardest. "I didn't know I was raising a quitter," he spat as the disappointment shone in his clear blue eyes. "All of these years I paid for those expensive lessons, all for nothing. First you quit this, and next you'll be quitting everything you ever start."

His prediction was a crushing blow and his anger a surprise that added to my own sense of failure. I remember thinking, did he really believe I was going to become rich and famous as a ballerina? But perhaps it was the end of a dream for him as well, one that started during my first weeks in America. That time with my dad, before I could speak English, was the closest we have ever been.

While I never truly believed in my prospects as a ballerina, I secretly fantasized about becoming a writer. I had spent my life trapped between two identities and figured that journalism would offer me the chance to write about life's complexities. The summer before my senior year of high school, I won a scholarship to a journalism camp at Northern Arizona University and my mom and I made the long drive across the desert alone. She was contemplating leaving my father at that time and used the trip as an excuse to think things through.

We had been driving for half a day when my mom turned off the radio and cleared her throat in a way that immediately sounded alarms in my head. What came next marked a turning point in our relationship, although I did not realize it at the time.

"I have something to tell you," she said.

"What?"

She blew her nose before continuing. The words tumbled out clumsily, as if she couldn't wait to shed their burden. "Last year, your Korean father tried to find you. He wrote to the adoption agency we used asking if he could get in touch with you. The agency—Welcome House—called me out of the blue."

Your Korean father. Those were the last three words I ever expected to hear. Just the word "father" and the way it sounded when she said the words together—"your Korean father"—sounded so strange, yet held so much promise. My hand tightened around the steering wheel and I looked straight ahead even though I could feel my mother's eyes probing the side of my face. I waited in silence for her to continue.

"Oh Katy, I didn't want to tell you before because I thought he would want to take you back now that you have nearly finished high school." Her voice shook and she blew her nose again. "I'm so sorry. Things have been so bad at home with Dad and me fighting all the time. I was afraid you might want to go back to Korea. I was afraid of losing you."

She broke out into a full sob now, and I was both moved and annoyed that I had to comfort her. This was supposed to be about my Korean father and me and about something even larger than that—the unspoken possibility that had loomed over us ever since the day she discovered the photographs of my Korean family. We had both ignored the possibility that I might want to find them someday, hoping that unspoken desire might fade away quietly until it vanished altogether. It was as if we were both secretly hoping that by remaining silent, the desire would never return inside me.

But now, even though the subject had been broached, it still felt forbidden. Felt like a betrayal somehow. And the impulse to protect my mother took over.

"Oh Mom, I would never want to return to Korea! Why would I want to do that? That's crazy. This is my home and my country now. I can't even speak Korean anymore. What would I do there?"

It didn't occur to me to be angry with my mother for withholding this information about my father for more than a year. Instead I felt sorry for the anguish my Korean father had caused her. I also wondered if my father really could take me back to Korea against my will. I pictured myself being taken from my American family and sent back to a foreign country where I couldn't speak the language, to live with strangers whom I didn't know even though they were my biological family.

I couldn't do it all over again. I never wanted to go back to Korea.

But in the middle of this nightmarish scenario, I went back to my mother's earlier words. *Last year, your Korean father tried to find you. He wrote to the adoption agency asking if he could get in touch with you.*

The second time around, the words caused my insides to pulse with a mixture of incredible joy and anguish. I had a father in Korea who was looking for me—someone who remembered me and loved me enough to search for me! I imagined his torment and all of the years of wondering about me. But in the next second, I struggled to control a wave of emotions hurling me back into a past I had tried so hard to forget.

"I panicked when I received the phone call from the agency," my mother continued, calmer now. "All I could think was, he thinks it's time for you to come home. You've grown up, almost finished high school, and now he wants you back."

"So what did you tell him?"

"I never talked to him directly. I asked the agency not to tell your father where you lived or to give him our address or phone number."

"Oh."

"But I did write your father a letter telling him all about you—that you had grown up to be a beautiful young lady. That you took ballet lessons, you were a good student, and had applied and been accepted into good universities. I sent the letter to the agency, to pass on to your father."

"Do you think he got it?"

"I don't know."

We drove on silently, neither of us knowing what else to say.

My hand trembled as I wrote to the adoption agency and asked them how I could get in touch with my Korean father. Three years after my mother first told me about my father, I took the first timid step that gave weight to his existence and finally lifted his shadow from my back. I argued with myself all the way to the mailbox and closed my eyes as I dropped the envelope down the chute.

Several weeks later, I received a reply:

Dear Ms. Robinson,

I would be happy to forward a letter from you to Korea Social Services to give to your Korean father. All you need to do is write a letter telling about yourself and perhaps include a picture, send it here, and I'll forward it to Korea. If you would like to correspond directly, include your address in the letter.

Your parents told us a little about you in 1987 and we sent the information to Korea at that time.

I'm sure your Korean father will be very happy to hear from you.

I came so close and yet never responded.

In the years following, I never forgot about my Korean father or lost the image of a faceless man searching for his lost daughter. I simply tried to bury those thoughts along with other memories of my childhood. I concentrated once again on being "an American" and nothing else as if pouring myself into someone else's mold.

But that all changed the day I discovered two letters.

I saw the thin sheets of Korean writing buried among old class pictures and ribbons I'd won in the third grade. I vaguely remembered the letters written on white sheets as thin as tissue paper. They were in response to the letters I'd written home to Korea soon after my arrival in America. I wrote that I wanted to go home and begged my grandmother to come and get me. My pleas never reached my mother or grandmother, but they somehow made it into the hands of a Korean nun working with unwed mothers in Seoul. Although I wrote many letters home, the only response I ever received from Korea was from this stranger. At the time, I had not liked this woman—who was not my grandmother—or what she had to say to me. But my mother made me save her letters anyway, for the neat Korean writing, she said.

"Someday you'll go back and read these and be glad you saved them," she said.

But for twenty years the letters sat neglected. I had long forgotten their significance, and by the time I rediscovered them, I could no longer make out the Korean words. The angular Korean writing was full of connecting circles, dashes, and lines—backward and upside-down Ls and squares. The only characters I still recognized were the ones forming my Korean name at the top of the page—Kim Ji-yun.

As I held the letters in my hands, I sensed that my life was about to change. From those translucent sheets of paper, the voices of the past—of this stranger, my father, of my mother and grandmother—rose up in one chorus, beckoning me to come home.

And I knew in an instant that I could no longer ignore them.

To Kim Ji-yun:

I am someone working with the sisters here. I heard about you and am writing to you.

I know some children who went to America from here. They too missed home and friends, and were sad at first, but they are all doing well, I understand. Make friends, and study hard. Because of the different customs America and Korea have, they went through some difficulty at first, but now they have adjusted and are very happy, I understand.

Ji-yun too—listen to your adoptive parents, and study hard. Think about it. Why did your parents bring you over to America? To help you: to teach and to love you. So, always be thankful and try to follow them. And always be honest. Don't feel ashamed of being poor. If you had rich parents in Korea, your parents would not have brought you over. If you have anything to ask me, write to me. I heard that you write and read well.

Write to me.

To Miss Kim Ji-yun,

Did you have a happy New Year? Got a year older? But they don't count the ages like that in America. At your birthday, you get a year older. So, Ji-yun too, since you live in America, count the American way. Don't think you are a year older at the New Year. Don't think it strange. Since it's America, do everything their way. Follow and obey.

Why did your American mommy bring you over? To think about you and love you just as she would her own birth daughter. However, if you don't get along with your mom, her heart would be sad. Many children search for adoptive parents, but because of the lack of their availability they can't go over to the USA.

I received a letter from your American mom. You are getting better all the time and listen to her well, she says. As a Korean, I am happy too. If I hear that you are disobedient and rude, I would feel sad.

I will answer what you asked me in your last letter. Could you come to Korea in the future? Certainly you can come to Korea again. Study hard. Grow big, get a job, make money—then you can come anytime.

Dear Appa,

I've been back home for two weeks now and have thought about you every day. My trip to Korea seems like a dream and you seem so far away. I look at the pictures you gave me and replay the scene when we met. I have so much that I want to tell you and wish that I could pick up the phone and call you. But I am working on my Korean.

I'm sorry that I didn't find you sooner. I can't tell you the feeling it brought me to be hugged by you. I have been missing you for so long and it felt so right to be with you. You are the father that I have always dreamed of finding one day.

I always knew that I was very loved while growing up in Korea. Because of that, I grew up secure and was able to succeed in my new life here. I feel so lucky to have been loved by families on both sides of the globe.

—Katy

Dearest Daughter:

I am now thinking about our meeting, which I can never forget, as I write this letter. I look at the pictures you sent me and think of you all the time. You have become such a beautiful and intelligent person. I can't believe you're the little girl I said good-bye to twenty years ago! For twenty years I always thought of you as a seven-year-old girl. But the moment I met you, those thoughts changed so fast.

I think you made a big step in life by coming back to Korea. It was a brave step. I was very happy to know you tried so hard to learn about your Korean roots. You should be proud of yourself. You are a citizen of the great United States of America and have a loving and caring mother. You have found your lost Korean life, so now you have an even better life spread out before you.

I am very happy to hear that you are learning Korean and even planning to live in Seoul for a year. But let's take things one step at a time. As I told you, my going to Boise should be thought over with care. So I think we should discuss this matter with time.

I have written a letter to your mom. I don't know how to thank her. I hope your friendship with your mother lasts a lifetime. The years people spend with each other are precious.

I love you.

—Appa

8

After returning from Korea, I resumed my life with a feeling of detachment, like I was carrying around a secret others could not fathom. By finally meeting my Korean father, my world opened up to endless new possibilities, questions, and discoveries.

I gazed for hours at the pictures my father gave me and imprinted every detail of those faces in my mind. A framed photograph—the one of my Korean mother and father posed together—sat on our mantel next to a picture of my American mom. Just as my father had tried to do for me, I tried to fill in the gaps for him with photographs of me in ballet class, a Girl Scout uniform, high-school graduation, posing with John in front of our apartment, and later, our first home.

Each week I ran to our mailbox on the street corner hoping to find the familiar red-and-blue striped airmail envelope from Korea with my father's neatly slanted writing on the front. When I'd discover one of his letters nestled in among the bills and catalogs, I'd rip open the envelope and hold the pages like a treasure. Just the mere act of holding my father's writing in my hands often made my eyes well up. Sometimes his graceful and restrained words made me sob uncontrollably.

In my dreams, my Korean childhood and family intermingled with scenes of America. In and out, I drifted between the two worlds with ease until the lines of reality became blurred. Sometimes I awoke with a crystal-clear image of my old life in Korea, only to have it fade seconds later. But I made up for the failures of memory with more recent thoughts of Korea. The country glowed in my imagination as a place of beauty, warm people, blooming mountainsides, and pulsing energy. Korea had wrapped itself around me like a warm, comforting blanket.

John and I enrolled in Korean lessons at a small Korean Presbyterian church in town. We entered the building late one Friday afternoon and ran into a room full of preschool kids playing tag. A few volunteer female teachers rounded them up into a room and began teaching Korean songs and games.

"Excuse me," I asked one of the Korean women, "my husband and I are interested in learning Korean."

"Do you already know how to read or write?"

"Um, no. We need to start at the very beginning."

"Our beginning class is for children. They are in there." She pointed then paused. "Wait a minute, please." She went and whispered to another woman. She returned a few minutes later. "Okay, we will make a special beginning class just for you."

We sat at a card table with our notebooks open and began learning the Korean alphabet. As we repeated the letters after our teacher, I struggled with the pronunciation. "Your husband can speak Korean better than you." Our teacher laughed. "Show her again how to pronounce the sound."

I could hardly believe that I once spoke, read, and wrote Korean. This could have been any foreign language I was learning for the first time. We repeated the sounds and copied the linear letters in our notebooks with arrows to show the order in which to draw the lines. Our first words were *pah* ("green onion"), *cha* ("car" or "tea") and *koe* ("nose").

Before, I had hardly noticed other Koreans living in town, but now I began to note members of the Korean community living in Boise as if each one were a personal friend. Whenever I recognized a teacher from the language school I would point that person out to John. "See, she is Korean. Can you tell?"

When people mistook me for Japanese or Chinese, I replied proudly, "No, I am Korean!"

I couldn't wait to return to Korea.

Dear Mr. Kim,

When Katy arrived from Korea, she was very frightened. The adoption agency told us that she had been abandoned as an infant, but then we discovered the pictures of her mother and grandmother. We called the agency here in the United States and talked to them about what had happened. They stood by their false story, so we did not know what to do. It took a long time for her to finally give up on her quest to return to her family.

As you know, Katy loved school and thought that American schools were too easy when she first started. She was also very sociable and made many friends even though she was the only Korean child in the school.

I got a divorce just before she went to college. Although a divorce is sometimes a tragic thing, in this case it was a happy time for both of us. My husband was not a warm man and had a difficult time controlling his temper. Luckily, I had a good education and could provide for Katy and myself. Katy and I were more than just mother and daughter. We were best friends, and I have always felt blessed that she came into my life. And because of that special relationship, I would like to thank you for giving me the opportunity to have Katy as a daughter and a friend.

There are many stories I want you to know about her. But I know this letter will be just the start of a communication between us that will give us all an increased appreciation of what a wonderful experience this life has been, for us to know and connect with each other.

The pictures you gave Katy were so beautiful. You gave her a good start and the strong emotional security she needed to adjust to a new life and to make the very best of whatever life gave her. Thank you.

—Sue Robinson

Dear Sue,

I feel very lucky, getting a chance to meet again with my daughter. For the past twenty years I had tried so hard to reach my daughter. But the managing agency who took care of the adoption gave me no information about her life in America.

I could tell by your letter that you are a respectable person and a loving mother. In Korea, we believe that the daughter takes after her mother—especially the mother's personality. So you can get a slight idea what kind of person the mother is by meeting the daughter. The moment I met Katy I knew that you should be someone intelligent and a person with a lot of love. I feel you accomplished a better life for Katy. In many ways, you have given her a life I was unable to give her. She is truly your loving daughter. I'm just someone who gave her a start in life.

When Katy was five, I was bankrupt. Because of economic reasons, Katy's birth mother and I decided to separate and I agreed to take care of our daughter. I was able to send her to elementary school. When she turned seven, after thinking it over and over again, we thought it would be best for Katy's future to put her up for adoption.

I am very grateful for your honesty. Telling me about the hard times and good times you had. In your letter, you told me you were very lucky to have met a daughter like Katy. The togetherness that has developed between you and Katy now has made you and me a family beyond the Pacific.

I know you and Katy have worked hard to find Katy's birth mother. I believe everyone has questions about their unknown past. Because of those questions, one goes through a lot of pain and doubt. Thinking about the situation Katy is in, I find myself wanting to help her.

Dear Appa:

I have read about Korea's economic crisis and wonder how you are doing. I am sorry that times are so difficult. I am sending this letter and package through General Chang's office. I find myself thinking about you every day and wanting to make up for all of the lost time between us.

I wanted to ask you if you have heard any more information about my Korean mother and grandmother. As I told you, the adoption agency tried to find them when I was in Korea. I haven't heard anything more from them.

I hope you are doing well. I love you.

Dear Daughter:

Making up for all of the lost years is exactly the same for you and me. Since I met you so far away, we're bodies apart, but your mind and heart are always sitting next to mine. Before, I could only picture you as a grown woman in my imagination. Now I can imagine you as you are.

I am healthy—maybe because of the vitamins I received among the many gifts you sent me. Right after your last phone call, I received the money into my bank account. I bought myself a new suit and many other things. I truly thank you. But don't worry too much about Daddy. When I hear news that you are healthy and happy, I am also happy and relieved. Spend many happy and steadfast years with your husband and in-laws.

As you know, the Korean economy is not doing very well right now. The international news is not very popular because of IMF. Ko-

reans living overseas may be embarrassed about their country. When I think about that, it hurts my feelings. However, if we Koreans stick it out and persevere, then we will recover.

It is good to know that John has started a new job. I am happy to know that our daughter truly loves John. Tell him I am very thankful.

I am very proud of my daughter for her participation in the Chosun Ilbo Fellowship. In Korea, Seoul National University, Korea University, and Yonsei University are the most prestigious. The entrance exams are very difficult. If I may, I would recommend your father's alma mater, Korea University.

Appa,

We are very excited to come to Korea to live for a year!

I wanted to tell you a little bit more about my fellowship. The Bang Il-Young Foundation, which publishes the Chosun Ilbo newspaper, awards scholarships to foreign journalists who want to learn more about Korea. I will be a full-time student studying the Korean language. John will try to transfer or get a job teaching English. He is very excited to meet you and live in Korea.

We will be arriving at the beginning of September. I can't wait to see you and get to know you better. Please write to me soon and let me know what you think.

Dear Daughter:

You are coming in September to attend Daddy's alma mater on a scholarship. That is very good! In a few months, I will see my dear daughter often. I am so proud of my daughter and brag often to my friends. Daddy would like to study English. But I am too old, so it is difficult for me to learn. So you must study Korean very quickly. How good it would be if we could talk to each other without an interpreter!

I am continually asking about news of your birth mother and grandmother. Please wait a little longer.

9

This time sitting on the plane among other Koreans, I felt a strange sense of belonging. I basked in my newfound identity and felt bound to the people and country that were foreign yet so familiar. It felt as though my entire life had been a preparation for this journey.

As I drifted into half sleep, memories of Korea floated in and out of my mind beginning with the trip to America and traveling backward in time. I grabbed at the floating pieces: the sensation of boarding my first plane with a name tag strapped around my wrist. Landing in America and waving good-bye to the little boy next to me, hoping that he would find the candy and toys I had promised him. The day my Korean mother bought me a book of paper dolls. A song I learned at school about mountain rabbits that went *san toki, toki-yo.* My mind rushed to chase down the memories and hold on to them a little longer. But when the images disappeared, I recalled the reunion with my father a year earlier. Every detail was still fresh: the high-pitched ding of the elevator bell. The sweet smell of red roses in his arms. The sound of my Korean name rolling off his tongue and our first embrace. This time I was not heading into the unknown. I was going to meet my father and continue the search for my mother.

When the voice of a Korean stewardess came over the loudspeaker, John and I took a deep breath and smiled at each other. We were in Korea. In many ways, this felt like a natural phase in our life together. From the time we first met in college, we had shared a desire to see the world. But unlike our friends who zoomed in and out of as many countries as possible on their Eurailpasses, we preferred a slower-paced method—that of actually living in other cultures for as long as possible. After graduating a year ahead of me, John went to the Basque region of Spain for a year to study Spanish, art history, and Basque dancing and cooking (a welcome break from electrical engineering). Then, after I graduated and finished a newspaper internship, we moved to Durango, Mexico, for a year to teach English. After the school year, we traveled until our pesos ran out. We ended up in Boise because that was where we had free lodging with John's parents until we found "real" jobs. When John and I announced our move to Korea, it didn't come as much of a shock to our families.

Still, I wondered if John knew what he was in for. Like an overnight expert, I drilled him on Korean customs and ways. "Just make sure to bow to everyone—the deeper the better. And don't do anything with one hand. Use both hands like this. Seoul is very crowded and Korean people are always in a hurry, so make sure you're assertive in a crowd." As I said this, I had visions of John—who avoided confrontations, however minor, like the plague—getting trampled in the market by a group of Korean grandmothers.

"Don't worry." He laughed. "I'll just follow you."

Usually I traveled to other countries without expectations. But this was Korea—*my* country—and I felt like John's tour guide. In preparation for our trip, we had read about Seoul and knew that it was a crowded metropolitan city with nearly thirteen million people—a quarter of South Korea's population. We had heard about nightmarish traffic jams, pollution, and the high price of housing. But, of course, I had been too enthralled to notice any of those things during my first trip.

As we stepped off the plane, my worries turned into excitement at the thought of seeing my father again. I wanted to impress him at our reunion and had planned to change into a dress, fix my hair, and put on some makeup in an attempt to erase the damage done by seventeen hours on an airplane. But when I saw the crowded airport bathroom, I decided to forgo any visions of glamour and proceed in my stretch pants, sweatshirt, and ponytail. (Besides, my father would have to see the true me sooner or later.)

After we picked up our luggage and exchanged some money, we went through the doors to the arrival area. I scanned the crowd waiting for their loved ones to step through the doors. Finally, I saw my father's face peering above the sea of heads. As our eyes locked on each other, a smile spread across both of our faces at the same time.

"There he is!" I pulled John's arm. "Come on."

My father ran toward us, tripping over someone's luggage in his excitement. He was dressed in what looked like a new dark blue suit that still held sharp creases down the center of his pants. He wore a wide red tie over a sheer white shirt that revealed the outline of a cotton tank top underneath. His jacket was unbuttoned to reveal a pager clasped prominently on his leather belt.

"Ji-yun-ah!" He hugged me quickly then shook John's hand.

"John, nice to meet you," he said in English.

"I'm happy to finally meet you." John gave a faint bow and his cheeks turned red.

"Please, wait here." My father scanned the airport and ran outside. I couldn't help but laugh when I saw him dashing up and down among the rows of cars waiting at the curb, excited as a groom preparing to whisk away his bride. We waited for my father to return as the crowds swarmed around us. People greeted and hugged family members in rapid, excited voices. Others whisked by carting luggage and huge cardboard boxes wrapped with white string. We were like two children landed on a foreign planet—at the mercy of my father for guidance. He returned a few minutes later accompanied by a young Korean man.

"Please call me Lee. I am here to translate for your father," the man said in English.

The four of us stood together smiling awkwardly and waiting for my father's next instructions. A few minutes later, a pretty woman walked up to us. My father said something to me in Korean and gestured to her.

"Your father wants you to meet your older sister," Lee echoed back.

I extended my hand when the words sank in. During times of particular torment at the hands of my brother Kelly, I had prayed to God to banish him and send me a sister in his place. A kind and loving sister—at least another girl in the family— had seemed like the solution to the rampant teasing in our family. Now that the real thing stood before me, I wasn't so sure anymore. I knew that my father had other children from his earlier marriage, but I had not connected them to myself until this moment. The last thing I expected was to meet a half sister upon my arrival in Korea.

I tried to get used to the idea that this pretty, slender woman standing before me was my *unnee*—my older sister!

I finished my handshake and forced a greeting. "Hello. Nice to meet you."

The woman stepped closer and searched my face. It might have been different if we resembled each other in some way, but we looked nothing alike. She was shorter than I was, with a slender frame, pale skin, and large dark eyes. She was dressed in a black jumpsuit with a rhinestone belt, white jacket, and high heels.

"Katy?" she said questioningly. She stepped within inches of my face and tucked a loose strand of hair behind my ear.

My father laughed at our cautious reaction to each other. "She is your older sister," he repeated to me as if expecting us to embrace each other with joy.

My sister continued to observe me in silence for a full minute before saying, *"Kapshida"*—let's go—with a smile. She grabbed my hand and led me out of the airport.

Hard, gritty rain tapped against the rooftop of our car as we crept through traffic heading into downtown Seoul. Drivers honked impatiently and jammed their dark Hyundai, Daewoo, and Kia cars into disarrayed formations on the wide road. In the distance, rows of apartment buildings punched through the sky for as far as the eye could see. Up ahead, I saw a familiar sign for Burger King among the rows of foreign letters written across colorful billboards and storefronts.

"Did you see that?" I whispered to John, amused to see that we were not that far from home after all.

"Ka-ty." My sister said my name slowly in an accent that made it sound like a command. "Are you hungry?" She had caught me eyeing Burger King.

"No, we're fine."

"Katy, how old are you?"

"Twenty-eight."

"And John?"

"Twenty-nine," I answered for him. "How old are you?" The question slipped out naturally, but I realized my mistake as soon as I saw her expression. She laughed politely and remained silent.

"Your sister thirty-eight!" my father yelled from the backseat. "Your sister—not married!"

Through the rearview mirror, my sister and I looked at each other with horrified expressions. She quickly changed the subject. "Katy, how long have you and John been married?"

"We dated a long time. But we've only been married three years."

"Three years already? When do you plan to have a baby?"

"I want to see your baby!" my father stated with a big smile.

With this topic, the whole car livened up. I knew even before I had spoken that my Korean family would be disappointed by my answer. If I had been smart, I would have invented the correct answer—something like "as soon as humanly possible!" or "next year, for sure," or better yet, "I'm already pregnant!" But stupidly, I thought out loud. "Um, we don't know . . . probably not for a while—at least a couple more years."

My sister and father both turned to look at me with surprise.

"First we want to travel and do some other things," I explained. "But we want to have a baby someday."

Everyone laughed politely once more. But I could tell my Korean family thought I was crazy.

"What are you going to do in Korea?" my sister asked.

"I have a scholarship to study Korean at Korea University—"

"*Chosun Ilbo* newspaper gives her money each month," my father interrupted.

"You must be very intelligent," my sister replied. "And what about John?"

"I'm going to teach English at ELS," he answered. "It is a large language institute. I think I will be teaching adults and college students."

"John, how much money you make?" my father wanted to know.

"Not very much."

My father laughed at John's evasive response as if it had been a joke.

"Katy, are there Koreans where you live in America?" my sister asked.

"No, not very many."

"I think you and your husband are brave to come back to Korea. Katy, do you have memories of me?"

I shook my head. "Do you remember me?"

"Of course. I used to give you piggyback rides when you were little." She looked at me with a smile that seemed a little sad.

After colliding in the doorway where all of us stopped to take off our shoes, we stepped inside a two-hundred-square-foot studio apartment like four giants entering a dollhouse. The walls were covered with pastel-colored wallpaper, and in one corner, turquoise metal cupboards hung above two gas burners. Our Western-style bed was decorated with a peach flowered bedspread and two pillows as big as sofa cushions. We stood around the perimeter of the room with our luggage stacked in the middle.

"What did you bring?" My father stared at our two backpacks, a suitcase, and duffel bag. "This apartment is too small. Closet too small. Sorry it's so small!"

"No, no this is perfect. It's everything we need."

"No. Not good enough," my father insisted. After we assured him again that the apartment was fine, he pointed to the bedspread. "Your sister bought for you."

"Kam-sa-ham-nida." I bowed and thanked her in Korean. She mimicked my Korean and giggled.

"Katy, your Korean is cute. You speak like a baby."

My father had selected the apartment for us and helped prepare it for our arrival. It was obvious he had gone to great trouble. He opened the refrigerator and held up each of the items—ketchup, American-style hamburger patties, Coke, and instant coffee. He opened the cupboards and showed us the dishes, glasses, teacups, and silverware, making a special point to show John the forks purchased especially for him. My father had even brought over a used television set with a built-in VCR.

"It's okay?" my father asked with a worried look.

"Yes, it's perfect. Thank you, *Appa,*" I answered.

"Rest now. I come six o'clock."

After my father and sister left, we unpacked and explored our new home. We discovered that my father had chosen a new, modern building with an elevator, surveillance cameras, and an upstairs landlord with a daughter who spoke English. I smiled as I pictured him shopping for our perceived American tastes. He had thought of every detail to make us comfortable. Two pairs of red flowered slippers were laid out for us by the front door to wear inside the house. Inside the bathroom was another pair of slippers, plastic ones for the wet floor. Our blue-tiled bathroom had a drain in the middle of the floor and a showerhead that splashed over the toilet and everything else in the room. Two towels that were slightly bigger than washcloths hung on a bar. In our giddy state, we laughed at how anyone could dry their hair and body with them. But we later discovered, after searching shops in our neighborhood, that large bath towels were hard to come by. My father and most other Koreans did not take showers at home. Instead they washed from a collection of buckets on the bathroom floor and went to public bathhouses for a full-body wash.

Our apartment opened up to an enclosed balcony, which housed a plastic washing machine that looked like it belonged to a play set. From our balcony, we could see our neighbor's flat rooftop, which was lined with several *kimchee* pots, clothes hanging from a line, and hot red peppers drying in the sun. In the distance, we overlooked a hazy skyline dotted with construction cranes and rows of high-rise apartment buildings.

My father returned that evening with a video of L.A. Confidential. "Come, I show you *bee-dio-bang*," he said, motioning for us to follow him outside.

Our neighborhood was set back from a busy five-lane road and was like a self-enclosed city, with everything we needed within walking distance. The narrow curving streets held a mixture of small apartment buildings, homes, restaurants, an elementary school, shops, and outdoor grocers. We noticed that people often sectioned off a portion of their homes to run a business—either a restaurant, sewing shop, or clothing store.

My father held my hand as we walked and pointed out the video store where he had set up an account for us under his name, the butcher store, a hair salon, Laundromat, and grocery store. In the absence of a translator, he strained to think of words in English and I struggled to use my limited Korean vocabulary. We looked at each other with puzzled expressions and tried to guess what the other person wanted. His face became solemn and I could tell he was wondering how John and I would ever get along in Seoul without knowing Korean. I could see his mind churning with a list of things he needed to teach us.

"Money—no in house. Go to bank. Okay?"

"*Ne, Appa.* Okay. We're going to open an account at the bank tomorrow."

"That store, no. Here store, everything ten percent discount. You buy." He pushed us into a cramped grocery store and watched us wander the aisles.

When we walked out, he continued checking off his list. "No open door. First you say, *Noo-goo-sayo?* Understand?"

"*Ne, Appa.* I know." I smiled, wondering how long it had been since I was told not to open the door before asking "Who is it?" I wanted to tell him that John and I had traveled to many other countries, that we were capable adults and could handle it. But when I saw his furrowed brows, I squeezed his hand and said, "*Cwen-cha-nayo.* It's okay. Don't worry, *Appa.*" This soon became my favorite expression when speaking to my father.

He looked at me with surprise as I spoke in a mixture of Korean and English, then relaxed his face. We walked out of our neighborhood to the busy main street, where we dodged speeding motorbikes weaving in and out of traffic and on and off the sidewalk, taking little notice of pedestrians. After a while we turned down an alley and found ourselves in an open-air market that stretched ahead for blocks. Women sat on cardboard boxes next to their neatly arranged piles of fresh vegetables, fried foods, and assorted *kimchee.* Styrofoam containers of water held live eels and rays next to rows of old rubber shoes and shower caps for sale. We saw wrinkled grandmothers toasting chestnuts with darkened hands and peeling mountains of garlic. Men passed by pulling makeshift wooden wheelbarrows loaded with tomatoes, cherries, and other freshly picked produce.

My father continued to point and advise us which stores were the cheapest and best. We walked around the labyrinth of goods and produce until the scent of toasted sesame oil, spicy *kimchee,* and fresh fruit made my stomach growl. My father heard the rumble and remembered my comment from the year before that *bi-bim-bap* was my favorite Korean food. He began inquiring at restaurants to see if they served traditionally prepared *bi-bim-bap*.

"It's okay, *Appa*. I like *all* Korean food," I said after my father struck out at several restaurants.

He ignored me and continued to search up and down side streets for *bi-bim-bap*. He finally led us to a small restaurant located on the second floor of an old building. We sat cross-legged on flat square pads on the warm floor and wiped our hands on rolled damp washcloths as my father ordered for all of us. Our *bi-bim-bap* arrived in heated cast-iron bowls filled with a bed of rice and topped with spinach, roots, radishes, and other vegetables. The dish came with a fried egg on top and a dollop of hot pepper paste and sesame oil on the bottom. We mixed together the ingredients until the rice and egg crackled against the side of the bowl and turned light red from the pepper paste. While we stirred our *bi-bim-bap,* soup and an assortment of side dishes arrived at our table. Hot steam from the dish mixed with the hot peppery paste in our mouths produced beads of sweat on our foreheads.

My father smacked his lips loudly with each bite and emitted deep burps as he ate. He ordered a small green bottle of *soju,* a potent Korean liquor made from potatoes and similar to vodka. We held up our shot glasses and toasted each other with a *"kum-bae!"* After throwing back his shot of *soju* in one gulp, my father turned to John. His face was relaxed and reddened from our steamy meal and the strong liquor. He spoke in perfect English; as if he had rehearsed this line beforehand.

"John, how much do you love my daughter?"

John's face flushed a deep red before he came up with an answer. "I love Katy very much. I feel very lucky to have found Katy and have this opportunity to return to Korea with her and meet her Korean family."

My father's normally stoic face transformed into a wide grin. "Very good, thank you. Thank you for loving my daughter and taking care of her. My daughter is lucky to have a good husband. Please take good care of her," he said in a mixture of English and Korean.

"What do you mean? I take care of him," I said.

"I think my daughter is very lucky to have a good husband like you," he repeated.

After dinner, my father walked us back to the apartment. "Tomorrow I come at one o'clock," he told us before running to catch a bus that would take him to his house across town.

We went to bed our first night in Seoul surrounded by foreign sounds and smells. Our Samsung refrigerator hummed like a piece of loud machinery, and each time our upstairs neighbors flushed their toilet, the sound of water rushed over our heads and roared down the pipes in our thin walls. There was something exhilarating about not knowing what to expect the next morning and having no routine, schedules, or deadlines. In just twenty-four hours, we had left behind all of our old worries and possessions. Our minds were clean slates ready to be imprinted with our new environment.

We awoke the next morning to the full realization that we were in a foreign country. Our neighbor's alarm echoed down the hallway and the Korean national anthem blared from the speakers at a nearby elementary school. Soon the streets came alive and vendors yelled through their bullhorns in Korean, "Onions, cabbage, shoes, televisions for sale." Around nine o'clock, the smell of fried fish and *dwang-jong,* fermented soybean paste, wafted in from the neighbor's apartment, introducing us to Korean-style breakfast.

· · ·

I recognized my father's soft knock on our door. He wore the same suit and tie as the day before and cleared his throat in the hallway just as he had done outside my hotel room the first time we had met.

I opened the door and bowed.

"No open door." He wagged his finger in my face. "First say, 'Who is it?' "

I was busted. "Oh *Appa!*"

He repeated his instructions, this time in Korean. "Okay?" he asked.

"*Ne,* I understand."

I could tell by the smell of liquor on his breath that he had come from drinking *soju* with his friends. I had seen groups of old men sitting under a tent on the sidewalk sharing bottles of liquor and engaging in lively conversations.

"*Appa,* have you eaten? Do you want me to fix you something?"

He shook his head. "I ate with my friends."

He handed me a sack filled with tangerines, a bottle of orange juice, and a bundle of government-issue garbage sacks. After examining the inside of our refrigerator to see what we had eaten of his purchases, he took a seat at the table. We looked at each other in silence and through smiles as I tried to conjure up enough Korean to start a conversation. I reached for my pocket Korean phrase book and tried not to massacre the language.

"Do you want some tea?"

"Huh?" My father couldn't tell which language I was speaking—English or Korean.

"Here." I pointed to the line in the book.

He took the book and squinted at the tiny words. "Okay. I go now." To my puzzlement, he patted my hand and abruptly ended his visit.

The next day, he continued the tour of our neighborhood, the bank, and anywhere else he thought we needed to go. Through mostly silent gestures, my father showed us how to catch the bus and made us practice with him. He pointed out John's school and walked me to the Chosun Ilbo offices, where I would have to pick up my stipend each month.

"Okay?" he asked, to make sure I knew my way around. I nodded, thinking once again of being lost as a child on a Seoul street.

My father led me by the hand to the university like a parent guiding a child to her first day of school. Together we stepped onto the campus of Korea University, where he had studied economics fifty years earlier. A Gothic-style stone building stood at the center of the large campus and was surrounded by rows of potted yellow flowers, trees, and a manicured lawn where families picnicked. The rest of the campus was composed of nondescript cement buildings decorated with student-made flyers and banners announcing upcoming events and protesting America's role in the International Monetary Fund (IMF), which had recently lent South Korea a large sum of money. We passed students dressed formally in varying shades of black and gray and wearing similar hairstyles—short crew cuts for the men and long hair with bangs pinned off the forehead for the women. This was the first college campus I had seen where hardly anyone wore T-shirts or shorts or displayed any marks of individuality such as a pierced tongue or purple hair.

We made our way to the office for foreign students, where I registered for language classes.

"Let's see, fall quarter begins September twentieth." My father pulled out his university schedule. "Your scholarship is for four quarters, so you will go summer quarter too."

"Actually, as I told you, I'm not going to school during the summer. John and I would like to spend some time traveling around Korea before we have to return home."

"But they will pay for four quarters." Instead of raising his voice, my father smiled wider to make his point.

"I know, *Appa,* but I think we want to spend some time traveling and exploring Korea before returning to our jobs."

"You're not going to school in the summer?"

"No."

"Okay, you can think about it and tell me your answer later." He carefully folded the schedule and returned it to his suit pocket.

I swallowed a sigh and tried to fight back a growing sense of impatience and a feeling that I was losing control. It was hard not to notice how my father smiled proudly as he walked holding my hand and introduced me to people as his daughter. I didn't want to rob him of that happiness, but I felt my independence and American identity dissolve with each passing second I spent with him. It was obvious that he thought of me as a helpless child and not a grown woman. But I suppose it was just as difficult for me to rewind the years as it was for my father to fast-forward through my missed childhood. I wasn't sure which role to play—that of a "dutiful Korean daughter" or myself. In him, I wanted the father of my childhood dreams, but also an adult friend who would accept me for who I was. We struggled to find the middle ground where we could start our relationship anew. As we continued our tour of the city, I wondered if we would ever make up for the lost years.

10

Dear my sister Cady,

It's becoming Autumn now. Your country, Korea's fall is very smart and beautiful, sky is blue and high, air is fresh and many kinds of trees are proud its variety of colorful leaves. When I got the news which you would come to Korea for studying Korean from father, I was very surprised of it. Expecting and waiting the day to meet you had made my mind shaking. No sleeping some day nights. I had missed you for a long time. I have kept a sorrow and heart breaking memory of your childhood in my mind about twenty years.

Sometimes it had made me feeling deep sadness.

With the dream memory of your childhood I had met you at the airport. But I had found that you had become a good lady and housewife of a good gentleman. Your husband must be good, smart, and diligent. I am proud you as a career woman.

I never got a sorrow mind of you in the future. I must thank to God for your growing up with health in a strange foreign country. It is sure that you have studied and worked very hard until today.

Even though we could not conversate with a language each other, I

*could tell you with my eyes, and I felt your warm heart by my one. I
will try to learn English conversation to talk with you and your husband. You also should study Korean to talk with me.*

*During your staying in Korea, please make good memories in our
country, Korea. Korea is your country and the place which you were
born.*

Please take care of your health and study hard Korean.

I will often contact with you.

—Your elder sister

"Katy? This is your elder sister." My sister spoke timidly then giggled
at her use of English.

"Oh *Unnee! Anyonghaseyo*. Hello."

She laughed at my Korean pronunciation, then switched to
Korean herself. "If you have time, can you meet me? I want to
buy you and John some delicious Korean food."

"Yes, we have time."

"Katy, do you know how to take the subway?"

"Yes."

"Take the green line and get off at Hangik University. I'll
meet you in front of Popeye's restaurant."

Remarkably, between her poor English and my poor Korean,
we managed to arrange a meeting place and time. I was only
halfway sure that I had understood her instructions correctly, so
I was happy to see her waving to us from a car as we emerged
from the subway station. To my relief, I saw that she brought
Lee to translate for us once again, along with another male
friend. As we stepped inside the car, she said something and
gestured to the male driver.

"Hello, nice to meet you." I greeted the stranger, removing
my sunglasses and bowing my head. The man turned around to
look at me more closely.

My sister and the two Korean men laughed. "Did you understand what your sister said to you?" Lee asked in English.

I shook my head.

"She said to you, 'Katy, meet *Oppa*—your older brother!' "

I looked at the man in the driver's seat more closely and was struck by his resemblance to my father. His face was the exact image of my father forty years earlier! They had the same narrow eyes, long nose, and full lips that turned slightly downward at the ends. His black silk shirt hung off his bony shoulders and emphasized his thin frame.

"Hello!" I repeated, and continued to stare at his face. He was a complete stranger, just as my sister had been. But here he was—my older brother—appearing before me like a magic trick.

He laughed and nodded. "You are so tall—just like your mother. But we have the same hair—brown, not black, see?" He pulled at a strand of his hair. "And the same eyes."

I stared into the eyes that were supposed to be a reflection of my own. As much as I wanted to, I did not see a resemblance or sense a connection with my new siblings. I struggled to place a brother or sister in my memory. I remembered walking to school with several older children. Perhaps it had been them.

My sister moved to the backseat next to me. She patted my thigh and squeezed my wrists with concern.

"Are you getting enough to eat these days?"

I laughed and nodded. If she only knew how much I ate, she'd be encouraging me to diet along with half the female population in Korea.

"Are you staying warm enough?"

I nodded, wondering why she was asking me about staying warm when the weather was hot and muggy.

"What about John?"

"*Unnee,* we are both doing fine."

"Well, don't worry. We will feed you and John a Korean feast today."

We arrived at Sam Won Gardens, a garden restaurant popular among foreigners for its expensive Korean barbecued meats and extensive menu complete with pictures.

I sat across from my brother and he continued to watch me with shy amusement. He bounced his leg up and down and drummed the table with his fingers before speaking. "Do you remember me? When you were little, you liked me a lot! I was your favorite. Do you have many memories of Korea?"

As he spoke, a scene popped into my mind. Drop by drop, memories of my past began to trickle in. When I was about five or six, I was sent away to live with some relatives in the countryside, where I attended school for a short time. There were many other children in this village. Families lived together in connecting rooms built above the ground around a dirt courtyard and a well.

One day, an older boy, who was perhaps a cousin, snatched the book I was reading and ran along the wooden planks into a dark attic.

"Give that back," I yelled, and chased after him.

"If you want it that bad, come and get it," he said, stuffing my book down his pants. I chased him into the attic and followed his instructions, reaching deep into his pants to feel a mound of warm, pulsing flesh.

"Where is my book?"

"Squeeze it," he demanded, pressing my hand against the mass of hard flesh. He released a long groan and lay back with a smile. My face flushed hot, but I obeyed his order and squeezed the hard long mass that felt like a warm hot dog.

"Harder," he said, short of breath now.

I rescued my book and ran away.

At this village, there were no indoor toilets. We used an old wooden outhouse with a rectangular hole cut into the floor. It was difficult to straddle the wide hole while squatting down to do your business. One day, my foot slipped and sent me splashing to the bottom of the pit. I was buried shoulder-deep in thick brown muck and screaming my head off from the dark hole while gagging on the stench. Since there was no way I could climb out by myself, I prayed that someone would hear my cries for help. A few minutes later, a group of adults fished me out and carried me by the shoulders to the middle of the courtyard. There was a lot of screaming and running around as I stood there with one missing brown sandal. Women splashed me with buckets of water while shaking their heads in dismay and plugging their noses. At first, the other children were fearful of the sight of me looking and smelling like the swamp monster. But as soon as they heard what had happened, they broke out into hysterical laughter and taunting chants of "She fell in! She fell in!"

During this time of living with relatives, I waited for my grandmother to send for me. Then I would travel alone by bus back to my mother and grandmother's modern apartment building in the city. It was a concrete skyscraper, and each time I visited, I was impressed by the clean streets, sidewalks, and people riding by on bicycles—and an indoor flushing toilet! After a short visit, I returned to relatives and cousins at the village. But before taking me to the bus station, my grandmother stopped at a street vendor—usually an old woman stirring a large stainless-steel vat under a tent—and treated me to a bowl of steaming pig-intestine soup. The sliced liver and wormlike strands popping out of the sausage casing were a delicacy. My grandmother watched me eat with a smile on her face.

Old women still sold intestine soup under tents. Although liver and intestines no longer sounded appetizing to me, the smell brought back my grandmother. That vivid memory suddenly triggered other scenes of Korea. They were random and scattered pieces: sitting on a warm vinyl floor and crawling over to a red ant, which bit me with a painful pinch. *Halmoni* making me bean-sprout porridge, then carrying me outside on her back after I had been sick with the chicken pox. Emerging with my mother from the sauna house with hot red skin and sipping a cool drink. Skipping through the archways of school with a new backpack and pencil case.

I longed to stretch out each image until they all blended into one seamless story.

When my thoughts drifted back, my brother was waiting for an answer to his question: Did I have many memories of Korea?

"Yes, some. I remember going away to school in the countryside. I think I lived with some relatives."

"Yes! That's right." A smile broke out on his face. "We were sent away to live with an uncle for a while. Do you remember him? He was our father's older brother. I was there with you. You remember a lot."

"What would John like to eat?" My sister interrupted our conversation with a look of unease.

"Oh, anything. We both like all Korean food," I answered.

After discussing back and forth, my brother and sister ordered practically one of everything on the menu. First came a colorful procession of *ban chun,* an assortment of side dishes, and three or four different kinds of *kimchee* that we soon learned were typical of every Korean meal. A dozen small dishes containing lettuce, soybean sprouts, spinach, sauces, and unknown roots arrived at our table. Next, a man from the kitchen carried out a metal basket of red-hot coals and set it inside a pit built into the center of our table. A beautiful, young waitress dressed in a simple *hanbok* followed behind with platters of raw meat for our grilled *kalbi* ribs and marinated beef *bulgogi*. My brother and sister unrolled strips of ribs with metal tongs and arranged them on the grill. Just when I thought the table couldn't possibly hold any more food, another waitress brought a bowl of bubbling soup and placed it in the center of the group. This was followed by a steaming dish of rice baked with pine nuts and dates, and a huge bowl of cold buckwheat noodles in ice water flavored with sliced Asian pears, slivered cucumber, and boiled eggs.

The sizzle and delicious aroma of grilled meat made our mouths water with anticipation as my brother and sister took turns flipping the ribs.

"Like this." My sister demonstrated the art of eating Korean barbecue. First she selected a large red leaf lettuce with her left hand and dropped a dollop of hot pepper paste into the center. She then picked up a piece of beef with her metal chopstick and dipped it in a mixture of sesame oil and salt before placing it inside the lettuce. She topped it off with a piece of raw garlic and a string of sweet pickled radish and folded the lettuce around the meat like an envelope.

"Here, John, eat," she commanded.

John stuffed the whole thing in his mouth and nodded his approval while he chewed with his cheeks bulging. My sister laughed and directed everyone else to dig in. It was the most delicious meal I had ever eaten.

As our feeding frenzy waned, we laughed nervously and tried to make conversation like people on a blind date.

"John, you use chopsticks very well," my sister said as she placed the biggest piece of meat into his dipping sauce. "Katy, eat, eat." She patted my ballooning stomach.

"John, how do you like Korea?" Lee asked. "Do you like Korean food? And what do you think about the city of Seoul?"

As apparently the sole representative American (I didn't count), John had the weight of public opinion on his shoulders—something he never got used to during his time in Korea, although he did much to dispel the stereotype of the loud, cocky American male. The group hung on his every word. After John carefully phrased his praises of Korea, the food, the people, and the city, my brother beamed.

"John, I think you are a good diplomat," he said, patting him on the back.

The laughter was followed by an uncomfortable silence. We looked at one another, unsure of how to broach the subject of the past that was on everyone's minds. Finally, I set down my chopsticks, wiped my mouth, and took the plunge.

"When I first went to America, I was very sad and wanted to return to Korea. I spent many days crying because I missed my family."

I wanted to tell them too about how I had threatened to kill myself rather than leave my family in Korea. "I wrote many letters home. But they all got returned and I never heard from anyone."

My sister dabbed her eyes with a napkin.

"We didn't know that you had gone to America," my brother said. "You were just gone one day and no one told us children anything. We thought you had gone to live with your mother and grandmother. When Father told us about meeting you last year, we couldn't believe it. I wanted to go to Idaho to see you. If you had not come back to Korea, I would have gone to Idaho to find you.

"When you were little, we all lived together in the same house for a short time. You also had another brother; he was my twin. Do you remember him?"

I shook my head.

"You two would always fight and I was in the middle trying to keep the peace. He died in a car accident when we were eighteen. That was the saddest day of my life.

"I also knew your mother . . ."

His last words hung in the air as my heart beat with excitement. If he had known my mother, then maybe he could help me find her, or perhaps he already knew where she was! Those were going to be his next words.

"Katy, your mommy—have you tried to look for her?" my sister asked.

"Yes. I went to the orphanage and tried to get information about her last year when I met our father. They promised to look for her, but I haven't been able to find out anything so far. I want to try again to find her while I'm here."

My sister was setting the stage for the good news, I thought as my heart pounded. My brother looked across at his older sister before he spoke.

"I'm not sure, but I heard your mother is dead."

I sat back, dazed, as if someone had just punched me in the stomach. I didn't know how many seconds passed before I recovered enough to speak. "Dead? What do you mean? How do you know?"

"That's just what we heard—that she died a while ago. I don't know any more."

"But exactly when did she die? And how?"

He shrugged his shoulders in silence and lit a cigarette to signal the end of the conversation.

11

I had never known how much I wanted to find my birth mother until that possibility was taken away. For weeks, I mourned her death as if losing her all over again, this time as an adult. The feeling of loss was greater than anything I could have imagined, given her long absence from my life. I could not explain it even to John, who watched helplessly as I sobbed into the wall for hours at a time. Perhaps it was overdue grief or the sense that I had made the journey too late.

When people discovered the age at which I had been adopted, the conversation inevitably ended in this question: "Do you plan to search for your parents? Um, your real ones, I mean at least your mother? Do you know why she gave you up?"

A hint of sympathy lingered on their faces, along with embarrassment in their voices for prying. Yet they couldn't help but entertain the question and, of course, neither could I even as I gave my stock answer: "You know, sometimes I'm curious, but it doesn't really matter to me if I find my biological parents or not. I've never been one of those adoptees with a lifelong mission to find their birth parents. I'm grateful to my mom for her sacrifice, but Korea was another life and I'm here now."

At this, a smile of approval and look of relief would cross their faces.

Looking back, I suppose that was the easiest answer and one that made everyone feel good. I had said it so many times that I almost believed it. But as I pondered my mother's death and the reality of never seeing her again, I knew I had lied all those times. She was the reason I had returned to Korea.

There is something about the bond with the woman who gave you birth that is like no other in the world.

What I never told anyone else, and was afraid to admit to myself, was a secret fantasy I harbored about meeting my birth mother again. It was as real to me as Santa Claus is to an impressionable child. I often replayed every detail in my mind and believed in my heart that it would happen in just this way.

We would meet in a plush hotel suite.

My mother is waiting for me, sitting on a deep velvet couch, her long slender body dressed in an elegant white pantsuit. Her dark hair falls to her shoulders and is slightly curled, as it was the last time that I saw her at Kimpo Airport. Her face too is nearly unchanged—the creamy complexion, arched eyebrows, and painted lips—just as she looks in the Polaroid picture. She is only slightly aged from that day with a few fine lines around her crescent-shaped eyes.

I see in her the same air of restraint as the last time I saw her. Her face does not contort into a sob at the first sight of me. Rather, she stares calmly into my face without rushing to explanation or defense. By contrast, all of my emotion bubbles to the surface like a boiling pot at the sight of a face that is a mirror of my own. After a few silent moments, she approaches me with open arms and folds me to her chest. As her voice hits the air,

I caught a hint of surprise and amusement cross my brother's face whenever I did something "un-Korean"—laugh without covering my mouth, speak a Korean phrase with a mangled accent, or extend my right hand instead of bowing from my waist. It was from these subtle looks that I became aware of how much I had to learn about the culture that was supposed to be mine.

When we emerged from the subway station, my brother was waiting for us in his car. He drove us to Insadong, the same arts-and-antiques district where my father had taken me the year before. The area was located just a few blocks from the clusters of movie theaters, English language institutes, and American fast-food chains that lined Chong-no Street. John's school was on this street, and we noticed that regardless of what day or hour we came, the sidewalks hummed with activity that enveloped the senses. Each block displayed a mind-boggling assortment of items for sale, ranging from toy-sized sewing machines and animal-shaped alarm clocks to toasted squid and boiled silk-worms. The sheer number of people packed into the streets was overwhelming to someone who was used to living in Idaho, where trees outnumbered people and one took wide-open spaces for granted. While mostly older men and women set up shop along the sidewalks, crowds of twenty-somethings—styl-ishly dressed in black jackets and leather shoes—flowed grace-fully between cars and motorcycles, oblivious to whose shoulder or elbow bumped and ground against theirs. I, on the other hand, felt crushed in the crowd like a misplaced fan at a rock concert each time I stepped onto the streets.

My brother crept along in traffic for a while before letting us out to walk the rest of the way to the restaurant up ahead. On these outings, my brother always brought along friends, at least one who could speak English and help translate. That job usually fell to one of my brother's employees named Jin-ho, or Kurt, as he was known to us. Kurt had studied and lived in the States for ten years and could slip easily between Korean and English with all of the mannerisms to go with it. One minute he bowed humbly to my brother and addressed him in the honorific title befitting a boss: "Mr. President." The next second he shook our hands loosely and greeted us with a "What's up?" His appearance too was a seamless blend of East and West. He dressed conservatively in dark suits and ties typical of Korean men, but wore his hair long and gelled.

Kurt led us down an alley and around the corner into a restaurant decorated with a small pond, bonsai trees, and potted flowers out front. Inside, an L-shaped raised floor held low lacquered tables and embroidered square mats arranged around a stage located at the center of the room.

"Tonight your *oppa* wants you and John to taste a Korean royal banquet," Kurt told us. "And introduce you to traditional Korean dancing and music."

Our six-course royal banquet included prawns wrapped in lettuce, steamed fish in a sweet-and-sour sauce, pickled cow-knee cartilage, and braised beef ribs along with the usual assortment of *kimchee* and side dishes. As per Korean custom, shots of liquor accompanied our delicious meal.

Kurt filled *Oppa*'s shot glass first, since my brother was the eldest at the table. "John, watch carefully. This is how you should fill Mr. Kim's glass," he said, supporting his right elbow with his left hand as he poured. "In the old days, royal servants did this so the sleeves of their robes wouldn't get in the way. We continue to do it today as a sign of respect. When we toast, we should hold our glasses lower than Mr. Kim's. And when we drink, we should cover our mouths and turn to the side because

Koreans believe it's improper for young people to drink in front of an elder."

We noticed other customs as well. As the eldest, my brother decided where to go and what to order for the group. He always paid for every activity, regardless of the number of people involved or the size of the bill. We learned that my brother spent most evenings going out for dinner and drinks with his co-workers. He ran a small concert promotion company that brought Western performers to Korea. The year before, his company helped bring Michael Jackson and Celine Dion to Seoul. But because of the current economic crisis, the Korean government had put a cap on what promoters could pay foreign entertainers and that limited my brother's choices mainly to heavy-metal bands. Most of the employees at his company were male, but evening outings often included several attractive young women—never the wives, I noticed. Entertainment centered on alcohol, and guests—especially males—never declined a drink the host offered them and were often expected to match shot for shot until everyone was happily drunk and boisterous.

Kurt emphasized this last point to John. "In Korea, you must always finish what is poured for you. So bottoms up!"

We clanked our glasses and I watched the men swallow their *soju* with a grimace while I reluctantly sipped mine. Out of necessity, John learned to raise his alcohol tolerance during the year, since drinking was an act of male bonding. But to my brother's surprise, John's understated demeanor never altered, no matter how many shots of *soju* he downed.

After a few shots, my brother relaxed and cleared his throat. "Katy," he began with a serious look, "you and I had different paths while growing up. But we shared the same difficult childhood, I think. Growing up I had difficult times after my parents separated and Father left us. We didn't have any money and we children really struggled a lot. But no matter our hardships, we turned out to be good, straight people. Even when times were hard, I never veered from the right path. I had to grow up without a father and make difficult choices. But I never chose the easy road even though the temptation was there. Your *oppa* is a good, honest person. Everyone in our family is an honest, good person. Even though we grew up apart, I think we share the same mind and the same blood.

"Kurt, don't you think Katy looks like me?" My brother smiled and reached for my hand.

"Don't insult her, Mr. Kim."

My brother ignored Kurt and became serious again. "You are my *yul dong-seang,* younger sister. John, from now on you call me *Hyong,* older brother. Say it."

"Hyong?" John obeyed and filled my brother's shot glass the way Kurt had taught him to do earlier.

"Your brother loves you very much," Kurt said to me. "In Korea, we believe that relationship by blood is the most important thing. So you know, since you and your brother share the same blood, he feels very close to you. When he first heard about you, he called me up and said, 'Kurt, we have to meet and drink—just you and me.' And that's when he told me that he had a sister in the United States."

I was both touched and embarrassed by the heartfelt declarations and struggled to find the proper words to respond. "Tell my brother thank you for welcoming me back and for treating us so nicely."

"Your brother said to never thank him again. He is your brother!"

An awkward silence settled over the table as I thought about all my brother and I didn't know about each other's life. I wondered how we would ever overcome the language barrier and cultural differences. When would he stop talking about the importance of sharing the same blood?

"Kurt, is my brother married?" I asked, realizing that I didn't even know this.

"Of course! He has a son who is seven, American age."

"*Oppa*"—I addressed my brother—"how did you and your wife meet?"

My brother became animated and spoke rapidly while Kurt struggled to keep up his translation. "Your *oppa* met his wife while they were in college. He didn't really study during that time like you did in college. Instead your brother joined Korea's student movement for democracy—that was in the 1980s. His wife was also a protester."

"Yankee, go home!" my brother broke into English and pumped his fist in the air to supplement Kurt's translation.

"Yeah, during that time a lot of Korean people wanted the American soldiers to leave Korea," Kurt said. "The Korean government was also very corrupt and the students wanted reform. Your brother was arrested and went to jail for demonstrating. During those days, many young people were taken to jail without a trial. After they were released, those students were blacklisted and banned from attending national universities, so your brother never went back to school."

This wasn't the first time I had heard about Korea's student protest movement. It was impossible to spend any amount of time in Seoul without running into groups of chanting protesters or hearing about the famous student movement for democracy. It sounded similar to the student activism of the sixties and seventies in the United States, but with more deaths and greater results. At one point, South Korea's government declared martial law and brutally broke up the protests. Hundreds of civilians were killed and thousands more were injured and arrested in what became known as the Kwangju Massacre—a favorite topic among university students. One of the leading government protesters and opposition politicians who was jailed and tried for treason during that time was Kim Dae-jung, who, of course, was the current president of South Korea.

After the Kwangju Massacre, protests against the government grew across the country and finally, after international outrage and pressure, the Korean dictatorship crumbled. The students were credited with leading the country to its first democratic presidential elections. Since then, student protests had taken on a life of their own, becoming a kind of rite of passage. Throughout the year, but especially in the spring, chanting students clashed with equally young military police garbed in full riot gear. The first time John and I saw hundreds of blue-uniformed riot police file out of their special buses and line downtown streets, we were frightened by the unusual show of force. We peeked out our bus window and braced ourselves for mayhem. But what we observed was mostly macho posturing and light shoving back and forth as our bus made a U-turn on the blocked street. Older people hardly took notice of the ruckus outside. And after a few months in Seoul, neither did we. Protesters were as common a sight as congregating *harabojis,* grandfathers, dressed in traditional loose white pants and Panama hats.

"After your brother and his wife got married," Kurt continued, "they moved to Taejon and tried to organize a labor union at a textile factory. In those days, labor unions were illegal and factories were notorious for their horrible working conditions and abuse of laborers, many of them female. For three years, your brother and his wife worked twelve-hour shifts in the factory. Your brother says they treated workers worse than animals."

As I listened, my brother's life and personality started to take shape and I understood what he had meant by his earlier comments about his difficult life and not veering from the right path.

"Wow. Tell my brother that I admire his courage in all that he has done."

Kurt translated his response: "I don't tell you these stories to brag, but so that you may understand me. You are lucky to have grown up in America and to have American citizenship. Because you are an American citizen, you have many more freedoms. It's very hard for Koreans to get a visa to visit America, but it's very easy for Americans to visit Korea. But don't worry because *Oppa* already has a visa, so I can visit you in America."

"Yes, we hope you will visit us. When you come, you can stay with us. You should bring your wife and son too. We would like to meet your family."

My brother tugged at his shirt collar and smiled with discomfort. "Someday I want you to come to my house and meet my wife and son and see how we live. But our mother also lives with us and she does not know that you are in Seoul. Sister and I are afraid of how our mother might react if she finds out. We haven't told her about you yet because our mother has hard feelings for our father. She is still very hurt by him. But don't worry. I want to tell her about you soon. I wanted to tell her right away, but Sister does not agree with me."

My brother and sister's mother was my father's first wife, whom he left in order to have an affair with my much younger mother. I guessed that my father had contacted my siblings in secret and asked them to help him prepare for my arrival. Perhaps this explained the discomfort I had sensed in my sister during our first meeting. Understandably, my sister felt the need to protect her mother from memories and ghosts that might rekindle old shame. I would do the same in her shoes. But I wondered when I might see my sister again and when, or if, my siblings would tell their mother about me.

• • •

As the lights were turned off and the candles lit, we pushed back from our table to watch the performance. My brother signaled for me to move closer to him. He held my hand and smoothed the skin back and forth as he spoke without translation. "Katy, I love you."

I knew he was waiting for a reply, but I could not bring myself to say the words back. Instead I smiled and squeezed his hand. We turned our attention to the stage, where young Korean women dressed in elaborate costumes appeared holding open fans in front of their faces. "Katy, do you know the traditional fan dance?" my brother asked.

I shook my head and watched the women, mesmerized by their beauty and grace. Their black hair was slicked back into tight buns at the base of their necks, their faces lightened with powder and painted with thick makeup around their eyes, cheeks, and lips. Each one's mouth was frozen in a soft smile. The petite dancers were dressed in bright pink *hanboks* and their feet glided over the floor in tiny, smooth steps.

These dancers symbolized the Korean ideal of feminine beauty, and at first I was entranced. But as the performance continued, I was struck by how all of the women wore the exact unchanging expression in every dance—a studied look that mingled demure humility and frail beauty with subtle flirtation. As their frozen smiles blurred together, it was impossible to differentiate one woman from another. Their faces seemed to me like the masks of painted dolls more than real individuals.

After the performance, my brother patted my leg and said, "I understand how you must have suffered growing up without knowing your culture, away from your family and country. While you are in Korea, I will teach you everything I can about your culture."

13

The day before, my father had ended his visit to our apartment with an order: "Tomorrow, you cook me dinner."

I reluctantly agreed. His choppy English sounded brusque and the request felt a little bit like I was going to be tested on my skills as a Korean woman and daughter. But I reminded myself that having one's father over for dinner was not such an unusual thing. Since I had not had a relationship with my American father in some years, I was walking in unfamiliar territory. But I was eager to gain my father's approval and surprise him with my Korean cooking skills (I had taken lessons from a Korean friend in Boise). I walked to the farthermost market, the one my father said had the best produce, and searched for the vegetables, meat, and spices I needed. In preparation for the solo venture, I had looked up words such as "sesame seeds," "ginger," "sugar," and "rice" in my English-Korean dictionary and wrote the Korean spellings on a slip of paper. I managed to get by at the market by pointing to various vegetables and other items and nodding yes to any questions. I was studying Korean four hours a day at school, but I was beginning to wonder if the language had been wiped from my brain forever.

On the first day of language class, I couldn't understand anything as the teacher addressed the group of students who had come from all over the world to study Korean. She passed out sheets of blank paper and continued in her rapid Korean. People around me began writing as I raised my hand in confusion.

"Excuse me, I didn't understand anything you just said."

The teacher smiled and answered me in Korean. I turned for help to the male student with an earring and spiky blond hair sitting next to me. "She wants you to write a self-introduction," he said in a thick Australian accent. I glanced at his paper and was amazed to see that he had already filled half the page with Korean writing. It looked as impressive as a physics formula.

"What if I can't write anything?" I whispered.

The teacher came by, picked up my blank sheet of paper, and pointed to a small group in the corner. "Level one, over there," she said.

I felt like I was back in the first grade.

I was desperate to reclaim the Korean language. Outside of class, I was afraid to open my mouth for fear Koreans would recognize me as a stranger among them. I wanted more than anything to belong and blend into the crowded streets of Seoul. But if I was going to learn Korean, I knew I had to practice speaking. I decided to try out a phrase I had learned in class the week before. In what I thought was clear Korean pronunciation, I asked the male store clerk for some water.

"Mu-o?" he asked with a puzzled expression. "What?"

"Moo-ul," I repeated. Water.

"Mu-o?"

"Moo-ul." I pointed to the bottled water on the shelf behind him.

"Oh, wah-ta!" he said with a laugh. "Are you Korean?"

I nodded.

He gazed at me with a curious expression until I began to feel like an alien. Not only could I not speak Korean, but I was suddenly aware of how I looked and dressed. I was in jeans and hiking boots—not the formfitting blouses, short skirts or slacks, and high heels women my age wore outside the house. My hair was not colored or curled, and bangs covered my forehead—a sign of disrespect toward my husband, I was later told. While Korean women walked with umbrellas to protect their skin from the sun, I soaked up the rays until my face and arms turned a dark brown. My great tan was a source of envy at home, but here, it turned into a source of shame.

"Were you adopted?" the clerk asked in Korean. I recognized the question because I had recently looked up the word for "adopted" in the dictionary.

"*Ne,*" I answered.

"America?"

When I answered yes again, he nodded with understanding and continued to examine me with his mouth open, as if he had something more to say. I didn't understand his next question and apologized in English as I walked away.

"I'm sorry. My Korean is not very good."

"Okay. Bye-bye," he said in English, and waved as I ducked into the crowd.

Back at the apartment, I went to work on my father's dinner. Soon, sacks of vegetables and spices were strewn all over our bed, table, and desk as I turned every corner of our apartment into a kitchen. My father came early and walked into the middle of the mess.

"I see my daughter is a good cook," he said, and laughed. (I was beginning to understand that Koreans laughed most when a potentially embarrassing situation needed defusing.)

Under his watchful eye, I struggled to re-create the Korean dishes I had cooked at home. I marinated strips of beef in a sauce made of minced garlic and ginger, sesame oil, soy sauce, and sugar. I prepared rice in a medium saucepan, wishing for the rice cooker I always used at home. Soon the water in the pan boiled over and bits of rice spluttered on the flames of the gas burner. I doused the pan with cold water and felt my pride dissipate with each tiny explosion on the stove. The list of failures grew in my head: I couldn't speak Korean. I didn't look right. And I didn't know how to cook rice!

"This is my fault." My father made it worse by apologizing. "I should have bought you a rice cooker. I will get you one."

"No, no, that's okay," I answered.

We sat down for a meal with store-bought *kimchee* and rice that had the consistency of wallpaper paste. I wanted to tell my dad that I really was a good cook at home. But instead, I apologized in Korean fashion.

"*Appa,* you don't have to eat this. This food is terrible. I'm sorry." Usually when a Korean woman apologized for her cooking, it meant that she had prepared an extra-special meal to impress a guest and the food, of course, was delicious. My father pretended this was the case now.

"It's very delicious," he said. "I am happy to know that my daughter learned how to cook Korean food."

The disastrous meal typified the new direction of our relationship. I tried hard to be the person I guessed my father wanted me to be. Back and forth, we tried to please each other with growing unease as our expectations kept getting in the way. We were two strangers, pretending to be a father and daughter and not wanting to admit the wide gulf that separated us. Our letters to each other the year before had been filled with the disbelief and joy of our reunion and an outpouring of instant love and affection. But now that my father and I were face-to-face, it was much harder to cross the barrier created by language, culture, and lost time.

Before I came, I had heard about the important role of Confucian values in Korea's culture. Confucianism set the rules for social conduct and outlined the Five Relationships (between ruler and subject, father and son, husband and wife, old and young, and between friends). Regardless of what I read about this belief system, I could not have fathomed how much it was to color the relationship with my father. While I sought an adult friend and companion, he naturally assumed his role as patriarch, with all the powers that afforded him. I was surprised when he barked out orders, kept a set of keys to our apartment, and dropped in unannounced at will.

I interpreted his short Korean words as brusqueness reminiscent of my American father and found myself retracting on impulse. Even as my Korean father searched my face, the booming voice of my American father flooded my mind until I was suddenly angry at the man before me.

Then my father smiled at me.

And I remembered that I was in Korea, where no two people were ever equal in a relationship—least of all a parent and child. My father held the highest position in the Korean social hierarchy, and I held the lowest as a daughter and wife. A person's age and social position dictated everything, down to the manner of speaking and eating. I struggled to balance a respect for Korean culture and the pressure to obey and serve with my own feeling of loss of control.

We both hid our disappointments with uncomfortable smiles and tried to bend to each other's will.

"Miss Yoo, you call her now," my father said, referring to the general's secretary, who had translated for us during our first meeting.

"I already left a message for her last week. I think she is very busy at work," I replied. Seeing my father's disappointment, I thought of another person who could translate for us. The week before, I met a Korean male student at school who wanted a language exchange partner to practice his English. His English already seemed good enough for him to act as a translator and I told my father about him.

"What are you doing meeting with a boy?" he asked.

"Oh *Appa,* he's just a student who wants to practice speaking English. He's going to help me with my Korean. Lots of students at school arrange a language exchange."

"But you must be very careful of his intentions."

"What do you mean? He knows I'm married. It's not like that. Don't worry."

"Still, you must be careful." My father was persistent. "Don't meet with him ever again. He may misunderstand you."

"Okay," I said with a forced smile. "I won't ask him to translate. I'll call Miss Yoo."

"Your father has something very important to tell you—something that he did not tell you before," Miss Yoo began.

My father, dressed in a three-piece suit, studied my face in the same shy, apologetic manner that he had shown during our first meeting. He suddenly looked vulnerable as he sat across from me with his shoulders hunched over and his mouth stretched into a long line. I noticed a red *kimchee* stain on the front of his tie and wondered who washed his clothes or cooked and cleaned for him. He cleared his throat and continued speaking without pause as Miss Yoo took notes to help her translate when my father was finished.

I caught a familiar word here and there. He said something about my mother!

After what seemed like forever, the translation came.

"After your father divorced your mother, he remarried—"

"What do you mean divorced?" I asked Miss Yoo, and looked at my father. "My father and mother never *married* . . . did they?"

Miss Yoo laughed and blushed with embarrassment. "Do you want me to ask your father that?"

I nodded, even though I already knew the answer. When she told him what I had asked, he smiled at me sadly, so that I was instantly sorry.

"No, we were never married," he said.

Miss Yoo went back to her notes and continued. "After your mother and father divorced—um, broke up—he married another woman. They had two children. This is what your father has been wanting to tell you. His wife died of cancer about five years ago. And now your father lives with his two children. He is taking care of them."

I should not have been surprised to hear that my father had married another woman after his affair with my mother. But I sat stunned by his confession and the realization that he had lied to me at our first meeting.

"How old are his other children?" I asked.

"He has a son and daughter. His son is eighteen and his daughter is fifteen. They are in high school."

"I don't understand. My father told me he never remarried, that he lived alone. Why?"

Miss Yoo looked at me silently, knowing that she did not need to translate my reaction for my father.

My father suddenly laughed and said something before rising from the table.

"Your father said that he has not had much luck with women."

"Your younger brother and sister, do you want to meet them?" my father asked before he left. "I can bring them over tomorrow."

I couldn't believe that he expected me to be excited, to accept kinship with my younger siblings just because half of our blood was the same. I stared him in the eye with an anger that I did not attempt to mask.

"Think about it," he said, shifting his eyes. "I can bring them over anytime."

Suddenly I was crying. I no longer knew how to feel, what was expected, or how I should react. "I need some time," I told him. "This is all very confusing."

"Okay. I understand. Before you leave Korea, you meet your younger brother and sister."

He turned the doorknob to leave, then added, "Your brother told me the news about your mother. I'm sorry. I would have been happy if she was alive and you could have met her."

Long after my father left the apartment, his words echoed in the air. Was he really sorry about my mother? What did he mean about his not having much luck with women? It seemed to me that it was women who did not seem to have much luck with my father. Everything—our joyous meeting and the year of letters— seemed like a sham. He had led me to believe that he still cared about my mother. Said he wanted to meet her if I found her and that he thought about me every day. But he was too busy marrying other women and having children. If he lied about this, what else was he keeping from me?

What kind of man was my father?

He was seventy-two years old and had fathered children, the youngest of whom was still in her teens, by three different women. He left his first wife and abandoned their three children. He got my young mother pregnant and had not married her. Had failed to raise me in a proper family—had failed in his duties to me as a father by his own admission.

I wondered why my mother hadn't given me up for adoption right after I was born, as was customary for single Korean mothers. Why had she waited those seven years? Had she clung to the false hope that my father would marry her? She had waited as long as possible, until she herself hit twenty-seven—almost beyond the marriageable age for Korean women.

I knew that my father could not undo his past or change who he was any more than I could change into a traditional Korean daughter. But why had he lied to me for the past year? And if my brother knew, how long had my father known about my mother's death? How long had my father also known and not told me? If only he had told me the truth from the beginning, I wouldn't have built up this fantasy or felt so betrayed. But now I had no idea how to behave or what startling news to expect next.

It was dawning on me that I would never truly understand my father or the life he led. I despised my father and loved him with equal strength, as I did Korea itself, for the strong hold it had on me, while at the same time rejecting me as one of its own.

I thought about my father's shy, apologetic look and wanted to forgive him everything. But when he laughed and referred to his lack of luck with women, I had begun to resent all of the choices he made during his life. Still, regardless of how I felt about him, I could no longer dream of meeting another father to replace the ones I had. My American father, I was bound to by life's circumstances. This one, by blood.

My father. The smooth shiny skin of his face hardly looked like that of a seventy-year-old man. The expression etched into his face whenever he gazed at me was three parts male pride and one part sadness mixed with shame. His long face naturally sank downward, but lifted like sunshine during one of his rare smiles. His eyelids were thick overhangs above narrow eyes, but his nose was long and stately. My father's suit pants hung off his bony hips and made him appear more fragile than he was. I had seen him break into an agile sprint to chase down a bus or cross a street before the light changed. He was a factory of noises— loud burps and deep-throated hacking followed by a thick wad of spit landing wherever it pleased like a mark of territory. Eating for him was a noisy experience as well, whether it was smacking his lips with each bite or slurping small mountains of noodles with his face buried in the bowl.

Each time he left our apartment, he mistook our wooden incense holder for a shoehorn.

After the first day of rain, he bought John a used trench coat like the kind worn by old men who hung out in a park. He bought me a suede one like what young schoolgirls wore. As I lifted the coat from the gift box, I felt him waiting for me to try it on and twirl in front of him like the little girl I once was.

I saw the vision of my perfect father slip away and take with it a piece of my childhood. In its place, I saw a sudden stranger— perhaps the bad man my grandmother had warned me about.

The Polaroid of me with my mother and grandmother
at Kimpo Airport in Korea, 1977.

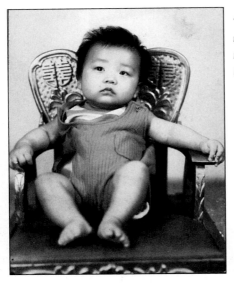

The only photo I have of myself as an infant, given to me by my Korean father during out first reunion.

안길 기념
1971. 4. 21

A studio shot taken on my first or second birthday.

My first birthday celebration. According to Korean tradition,
symbolic items are placed before the child to determine his or her calling in life.
My father swears I chose a pen (not the cookie I am holding in my hand).

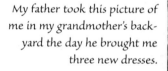

Sitting on the heated floor of my grandmother's house, I am about a second away from sticking my tongue out at the person holding the camera— who I imagine is my mother.

My father took this picture of me in my grandmother's back-yard the day he brought me three new dresses.

Modeling another new dress on that same day, but not before my grandmother threw an old sweater over my shoul-ders to keep me warm.

My grandmother and me,
when I was about five years old.

The referral picture the adoption agency sent
to my American parents, asking if they
would take me instead of the younger child they
had been expecting.

The only photo I have showing my parents together, given to me by my Korean father during our first reunion.

A recent photo of my Korean father, who is now in his seventies.

My American family (from left to right):
older brothers Dave, Kelly and Mike; my mom, Sue; and me.

14

"Have you found your Korean mommy yet?"

The unexpected question made me feel like a lost child. Mr. Sim, who gave me my fellowship stipend each month, waited for my answer with a look of concern on his round face. He, of course, knew that I was adopted and wanted to find my birth mother, but I was surprised by his sudden interest in my search. Mr. Sim worked in a crowded office with rows of connecting desks, so when surrounding colleagues overheard his question, they lifted their heads and waited for my response.

"No," I replied. "My brother told me that my mother was dead. But he doesn't have much information about when or how she died. Maybe you would know—would it be possible for me to find a death certificate for her?"

"You can't find your mommy?" The woman who sat across from Mr. Sim clucked her tongue and frowned as if she didn't believe that my mother was dead. "Maybe we can help you. Don't you think we could help her?" she asked some colleagues.

"Yes," Mr. Sim answered. "I think we can help you. It is

very easy to find information about your mother. You see, in Korea, every family has a registration number and detailed family documents. Your father would know. If you can get that number from your father, we can find your mother's records."

He noticed the look of hesitation on my face.

"If you want, I can call your father and ask him for the registration number. Once we have that, we can run it through the police records for you."

I breathed a grateful sigh and nodded.

"Good luck! I hope you find out about your mommy," several people in the office said as I left.

My father came to the apartment the next day visibly upset. Instead of the usual greeting, his mouth was twisted into a scowl. Without speaking, he sat down at the table and slipped on a pair of plastic reading glasses that had the price sticker still on the lens. He reached into his suit pocket and pulled out a bundle of folded papers.

"I received a call from Mr. Sim yesterday." He looked at me like a parent called in by a school principal. "He said you were searching for information about your mother. Look here, these are your mother's family registration papers."

He unfolded the papers and pointed to a box. "This is your mother. This is your mother's mother—your grandmother. Do you understand what these papers are? They are"—he paused to look up the English translation—"family documents."

I learned that in Korea, the family register was a sacred record of a family's lineage, traced through the male line. Many family registers contained the names of paternal ancestors going back for over five hundred years. Because of its importance, I heard that written evidence of mistresses and illegitimate children was most often deleted from the records. I doubted whether a record of my birth would appear on my father's family register—or anywhere, for that matter.

While these thoughts drifted through my mind, I answered my father's questioning look. "Yes, I understand what this is. Mr. Sim said I needed our family registration number to—"

"It took me a very long time to get these papers. These documents show that your mother is alive and not married."

My heart stopped at that one word—*alive*.

"See here," my father continued in a raised voice, "her name would be crossed out in black if she were dead. But it's not, so that means she is alive! Also look here, this line shows that she is not married."

My father sat back and examined my face to see if I comprehended what he had just said. My mind raced in excitement as I sifted through his Korean words and finally returned to that one incredible phrase: *These documents show that your mother is alive.*

My mother was alive!

I struggled to stave off shifting waves of joy and shock as a cautioning voice in my head took over. I wanted proof. I reached for the papers and searched through long columns of Chinese characters and Korean writing. I had no idea what I was reading.

"*Odi?* Where?" I asked my father. "Which person is my mother and where does it say she is alive?"

"Here. She is alive," my father repeated in a firm voice, and pointed to the box containing my mother's name.

I didn't know whether to weep for joy, scream, or laugh at the sudden reversal of my mother's fate. I gazed down at her name typed out in Korean letters. Should I believe it, and if so, why did my brother tell me she was dead? And why had my father confirmed that information when he had these papers saying she was alive?

I grabbed a piece of paper and a pencil and copied the information—my mother's name and birth date. For the first time,

I had solid bits of fact to put with the face in my dreams. My mother was Lee Kyung-woo. Born December 10, 1949. Just having this information in my possession made her more real and alive to me.

Lee Kyung-woo. Her name danced in my mind.

I once again planned our reunion. Perhaps she would come to our apartment or we would meet at a coffee shop.

I pieced together the bits of information. My mother had been the same age I was now when she gave me up for adoption. She was only forty-nine now. I found my father's insistence that she was not married strange and hard to believe. Wasn't that the reason she had given me up—to get married? Regardless of what my father said, I pictured her married with other children by now—perhaps even another daughter.

Did she know I was looking for her? And the biggest question of all: did she want to see me?

As I studied the documents, I convinced myself of this truth: this was my mother, her name and birth date. She was alive! Perhaps she was walking around Seoul at this very moment. We could have ridden on the same subway or walked along the same street. If we saw each other in a crowd, would we recognize the other person? I turned the pages of the document and found the box for my grandmother and the names of my mother's siblings. This meant I had an aunt and uncle who could tell me what happened to my mother and help me to find her. I wondered if there was a chance that my grandmother was still alive. Sudden new possibilities spread before me and I wanted to run in every direction at once.

All this time I felt my father's eyes locked on my face.

I returned his look while unspoken questions lingered on my lips. How long had he had these documents and why had he kept them from me until now? Did he really want me to find my mother or were there more family secrets yet to be unveiled?

"Look, I talked to Mr. Sim and I know you want to find your mother," he said. "I will help you. You can't find her without my help, understand? If you meet her, I want to be there."

What if I didn't want him there? He, after all, was the one who abandoned her with a child. Why would my mother want to see him again? Suddenly I distrusted my father and his intentions. The only thing he was interested in was saving face. He did not want me to meet my mother alone for fear of what she might tell me. All of my suspicions hardened into one giant ball of anger that I wanted to hurl at my father.

"On my own," I said with my limited Korean vocabulary. My voice shook and I tried not to cry. "Please just give me a copy of the documents so I can search on my own."

"You can't do it without my help," he repeated firmly. He quickly gathered the papers and put them back inside his coat pocket.

I felt like a defeated child and hated my father for making me choose sides.

"My mother and grandmother hate you!" I spat through the tears that were now rolling down my cheeks. That wasn't what I had meant to say, but before I could stop myself, the next words came flying out in broken Korean words sloppily strung together. "They don't want to see you. It would be strange. This is strange. I want to meet my mother by myself—without you!"

I felt myself shrink smaller and smaller. My father gazed at me with that familiar look of hurt. "Don't you love me?" I heard him ask through his silence.

"Don't worry," he finally said, patting my hand across the table. "We'll find your mother."

•   •   •

Left alone in the room, I wept with confusion, confusion about the renewed hope of meeting my mother and about the decaying relationship with my father. I longed to share this new information about my mother with John and get his perspective, which always tended to be more objective and measured than mine. But I looked at the clock and saw that he would be at work for another three hours. I couldn't stand to be alone in my anguish and decided to call my brother's employee, Kurt, on his cell phone.

"Kurt, hi. My dad was just here and he told me that my mother is alive. But my brother told me she was dead. Everyone is lying to me and I don't know what to believe."

I hadn't meant to lose it like this on the phone.

"Katy, take it easy." I heard Kurt translate my words back to my brother then come back on the line. "Hold on and wait for your brother. We're coming to your apartment right now."

I had time to compose myself before my brother arrived. I retold my story in a calmer voice. "Our father showed me the family document, but wouldn't give me a copy of it. He said the documents show that my mother is alive and not married, but that I can't find her without his help. I don't think he's going to help me. He doesn't want me to meet my mother alone. I just want to find out the truth. Why did you tell me she was dead?"

"That's what I was told," my brother said, shrugging his shoulders. "I honestly didn't know for sure. But don't worry, I'll help you find her. I'll get the documents from our father."

As my brother dialed our father's number, I felt tangled in a quiet but widening battle for the truth. I heard the echo of my father's loud, excited voice on the other end of the line as he recounted his version of our earlier meeting to my brother.

"Can you meet with Katy again tomorrow?" my brother

asked my father. "I'll arrange for one of my employees to translate for you.

"Don't worry," he told me as he hung up the phone. "Kurt
will meet with you and father tomorrow and he'll make sure to
get a copy of the papers for you." He turned to Kurt and spoke
in Korean. "Don't come back to the office without those papers."

I began to relax and realized this was the first time my brother
had been to our apartment or met with me outside of a fancy
restaurant. For once we could carry on a conversation without
the aid of alcohol or formal speeches and forced declarations of
love. I fixed everyone a cup of green tea and the three of us sat
on the bed and talked. What I wished most from my new Korean family was a sense of comfort and trust, to be able to let
down our guards and speak openly—something I had always
taken for granted with my American family.

"*Oppa.*" I turned to face my brother. "You don't have to
protect me from anything. I just want to know the truth about
my past and my mother—whatever that may be."

"Of course," he answered quickly. "*Oppa* believes in telling
the truth."

After a pause, he began speaking again with Kurt as our translator. "After Father left our mother, she was very ashamed and
embarrassed. Back then, she did not want to see us children very
much. I, especially, reminded her of our father because our faces
are exactly the same. All of us kids lived together with you for
a while at our uncle's house. Then I don't know where you
went. I think maybe with your mother and grandmother. After
that, our sister moved in with my mother and I lived with my
twin brother in our own place. After my brother died, I felt
alone. Because I lost my brother, I feel very lucky to have met
you again."

"What kind of relationship do you have with our father?"

"No relationship." My brother laughed without joy. "I didn't see our father for fifteen years. He didn't come to my twin brother's funeral or to my wedding. He has never met my son. Two years ago, our older sister located our father through a friend of hers at the police department. She arranged for us to meet with him. She felt like it was time for us to make peace with him. And then right before you came to Korea, Father called us and told us you were coming to live here for a year."

After a long pause, my brother said, "I think you were always our father's favorite."

His comment made me sad somehow. Perhaps I was the one who had caused my father the most guilt. As I listened to my brother, I was struck by the parallels in our lives, even as we grew up oceans apart. I hadn't spoken to my adoptive father for six years. He also had not come to my wedding, graduation, or any of the other events that have marked my life. In many ways, my brother and I both grew up fatherless, and that was the strongest link between us.

"And what about our father's other children?" I asked him. "Have you ever met his son and daughter?"

"No, not really. I saw his son from a distance on one occasion. I've never met the girl."

"Do you know how they are doing? Is Father able to take care of them?"

"Fine. I don't know. His daughter is in high school and I think his son will probably do his military service before college, in order to save money."

"He wants me to meet them. But I don't know how I feel about that yet. I mean, I feel like they are complete strangers with no real relation to me."

"It's the same for me. I feel that you are my sister because I knew you growing up. But them . . . I don't know. You don't have to meet them if you don't want to. I don't have a choice. I know the time will come one day when I will have to meet them, but until then . . ." My brother paused while Kurt explained Korean custom.

"You see, your brother is the oldest son in the family. And as the oldest son, he is expected to take care of the rest of his family. Your father is pretty old, so if anything happens to him, your brother will be responsible for your father's children—even though he isn't close to them."

"I think it would be best if you didn't meet our father's children right now," my brother said. "You and John don't want to be put under any obligations until you are ready."

His advice was another subtle reminder of our cultural differences. As a Korean, my brother felt a sense of obligation to family members, no matter how distant, and knew his role without having to be told. But before my brother's last statement, I hadn't really considered what it would mean to meet my younger siblings, that this might open the doors to some form of obligation to fulfill later, as my brother implied. Developing a relationship with these new siblings and helping them out financially or otherwise was fine—as long as it was a personal choice and not something thrust upon us. Perhaps this was the main difference between the Korean and American: my brother accepted his role without question while I boiled everything down to a matter of personal choice.

I didn't know whether I was being selfish for not wanting to meet these other half siblings. If I were to gauge my reactions and emotions by degrees of Korean-ness, I knew I would fail. I wondered how my older brother and sister had initially reacted to the news of my coming to live in Korea. Was it their Korean sense of duty and obligation that bound them to me or was there a deeper connection? Perhaps they were one and the same.

My brother and I were both deep in our own thoughts in

the quietness of the room. Finally, he laughed and said, "Our father," while shaking his head. "You and I feel the same way about him."

What, exactly, was that feeling toward our father? Certainly we loved him, but we also felt betrayed by him in our own way.

"Our father is seventy-two years old and has high blood pressure," my brother said with a sudden change of expression. "I want to prepare for his eventual death in my mind instead of being taken by surprise. No matter what our father did in the past, I want to give him a proper burial as my last act as his son. I want to fulfill my duties so that I have no regrets later. I will take care of him and his children, so don't worry about that."

I wondered if I also was prepared. I was just beginning to know my father, and already our relationship was strained. If he were to die tomorrow, I knew that I would be filled with regret for the missed opportunities and for the forgiveness that would come too late.

My father and I avoided each other's eyes like two friends after a quarrel. While we waited for Kurt to arrive, John served us tea and tried to soothe the waves of tension in the air by showing my father pictures we had taken around Seoul. "John, you make me copies," my father said, pointing to pictures of me standing in front of Korea University.

"Sure. I can get you copies of all of these," he answered.

Watching the two of them carry on a conversation, I envied John's ability to remain detached while my emotions bent and twisted with the wind. When I recounted the visit with my father and brother to him the night before, John had reacted cautiously.

"I don't know that you're ever going to get the truth from

your Korean family," he said after a long pause. The way he said it, this was neither an accusation nor insult, but a simple fact.

"What do you mean? You don't believe that my mother is alive?"

"Well, she may be. But I don't know that they really know, or would tell you if they did. I didn't believe your brother when he told you that she was dead."

"You didn't?" I was incredulous to think that the whole time I had been mourning my mother's death, my husband had kept these suspicions to himself. But I also knew him well enough to know how his mind worked. My feelings were my own and I was entitled to them. It was not his place to interfere with someone else's pent-up grief, least of all mine.

"Think about it. All that your brother said was that he *heard* from someone that your mother was dead. No other details, like when or how. He couldn't even say who told him. And now your father says she is alive, again with no details. I don't think you can take any of this as absolute fact."

"But why would my brother tell me something like that on our very first meeting if it wasn't true? Why would he want to hurt me like that?"

"I don't think he wanted to hurt you. He probably wants to protect you, or your family is more like it."

"So you think he lied?"

"I don't think he would look at it like that. It's just a cultural difference we can't understand."

"I don't care which culture you're in. A lie is a lie." Perhaps I was being overly sensitive, but it seemed dangerous to chalk everything up to cultural differences.

"I don't think you should look at it that way. Your family is going to protect you whether you want them to or not."

As I was thinking again about our conversation, Kurt entered our apartment and bowed deeply to my father. Kurt's show of great respect toward my father through his manner and speech transformed my father into a proud patriarch before our eyes. His eyes lit up as he sat up in his chair and began asking Kurt a string of personal questions: How long had he lived in the United States? Where did he go to school and what was his relationship to my brother? Finally deeming Kurt a worthy enough translator, my father addressed me.

"Please understand that it was hard for me to get these papers about your mother," he began. "It took me a long time to find them. In Korea, a woman is listed under her father's registration paper until she marries. After she marries, she moves to her husband's family records. But you see, your mother was moved to her older brother's records."

"But does my father know for sure that she is alive?" I asked Kurt.

"Your father says the records show that your mother is alive and not married. In Korea, when a person dies, she is crossed off her family papers with a black *X*."

My father spoke again for a long time as Kurt smiled and nodded in agreement with him. Finally Kurt turned to me and said, "See? Yesterday was all a big misunderstanding. Maybe you misunderstood what your father said and that is why you were so upset. I think it was the language barrier."

Both men smiled at me as if trying to calm a temperamental child.

"Well," Kurt said, "do you have any other questions for your father?"

I could sense the meeting drawing to a close. Perhaps John was right. The cultural differences were just too great for my Korean father and me to understand each other. I had learned enough about the Korean rules of etiquette to know further questions would be useless now. Kurt would not be comfortable interrogating an elder on my behalf, especially about sensitive topics. No matter how much I craved a frank discussion with my father, it would not happen in a society that honored age, spoke in measured words, and strove for harmony above all else—even above truth.

I slowly shook my head and smiled. "No, I have no more questions."

My father smiled with relief and said, "Let's get some lunch."

15

My mother's family register passed from my father to brother, and still I had no copy of my own. My brother took over the search for my mother, promising to run her name through the police records and also to track down the addresses for my aunt and uncle. "You must be patient," he told me each time I asked about his progress. Feeling the search spin out of my hands, I waited each day for news about my mother while my emotions shifted between hope and mistrust.

While I waited, John and my daily lives in Seoul and exposure to Korean culture progressed at a rapid pace while I attended school and John taught English. During our free time, we explored the city as much as possible, from hiking the high, jagged mountains to exploring the vast markets. Wherever we went, John continued to stand out as the foreigner while I attempted to blend in—a strange role reversal for us. With his thick wavy brown hair and deep-set eyes that alternated from blue to green with the color of his shirt, John had quintessential American good looks, and Koreans reacted to him with a mixture of awe and good-natured curiosity. He prompted stares from older people, while children often reacted with giggles and exclamations of "*Mee-gook saram!* American!" Although thousands of American soldiers were stationed at a military base in Seoul, they seldom wandered far from Itaewon, the shopping and eating district that catered to English-speaking tourists, located near the base. Elsewhere, especially on the crowded public buses, an American was a rare sight. Students of all ages took advantage of this opportunity to practice their English skills with a native speaker.

One day while we were touring an ancient palace in downtown Seoul, a flock of elementary-school boys descended on John. Their teacher explained that his English class was on a field trip hoping to find American tourists to interview. The boys, sporting cropped hair and light blue dress shirts, gathered around John while giggling and shoving each other.

"What—is—your—name?" they asked in robotic pronunciation in between wide grins. "How—old—you—are? What—is—your—hobby?"

I tried answering one of the boys, but he was more interested in speaking English with a "real American" than with me. When we got up to leave, some of the boys asked John for his autograph. "Sign! Sign!" they shouted, shoving slips of paper at him. They ran away squealing and I overheard one boy say, "He looks just like Tom Cruise!"

This sort of fascination was not limited to young boys.

John encountered a crowd of curious Korean grandfathers while hiking in the hills behind our apartment. These *harabojis* met regularly at the top of the hill, where they exercised, drank, and gossiped together. When they saw John approaching, they pointed and chattered among themselves in a chorus of voices that became faster and louder. Finally, one of the old men walked toward John while staring at the mass of blond hair that blanketed John's arms. He looked down at his own smooth, brown arm. When he reached John, the grandfather touched the coarse hair, timidly at first, then like a mischievous child pulling at grass.

"Come see the forest," he yelled, and waved his friends over. Soon John was surrounded by an excited group of Korean grandfathers.

I also generated plenty of curiosity among Koreans as soon as they discovered my inability to speak the language.

"Were you adopted?" Some people guessed immediately and reacted with sympathy and kindness. Korean women, especially, were curious about my adoptive parents and fawned over me like surrogate mothers.

A few people, however, became upset.

"Why don't you know your own language?" a taxi driver asked me.

"Because I grew up in America."

"But you are still a Korean!" he chided.

For days afterward I found myself thinking about the taxi driver's comment. So many times I have wondered what it would have been like to have grown up in Korea. But I would always be destined, it seemed, to *look* like an outsider in one country and *feel* like an outsider in another.

I thought about Sandy, one of the first Koreans I met after going away to college in California. She was a Korean immigrant in her fifties who worked at the campus library with me. She was petite and had a pretty oval face painted with bright makeup. She spoke English with an accent and students sometimes had difficulty understanding her. The first day I arrived for work, she studied me carefully and finally asked, "You Korean?"

"Yes."

"But you don't look too Korean."

"Well, I am," I answered, surprised by her comment and wondering how I could change my degree of Korean-ness.

"You are too tall. Korean women are tiny. You know"— she lowered her voice to a whisper—"Koreans are the most beautiful of all Asian women. What? It's true! Much prettier than Japanese women. Everybody knows that."

From that day on, Sandy acted like a pesky aunt, as if our shared Korean heritage gave her license to pry. Her favorite topic was my adoption.

"So your adoptive mom, is she white?"

"Yes."

"Does she have blond hair?"

"No, Sandy." I sighed. "She has red hair. See the resemblance?" I showed her a piece of my hair.

She slapped my arm away. "Your American parents, are they nice to you? They like you, treat you okay?"

"Of course! They love me just like their other children."

"Oh they have other children. They white?"

And so it went, until her questions became even more annoying.

"You like white men or Asian men?" she asked one day as casually as if asking me whether I liked coffee or tea.

"I don't know."

"I only see you with white boys. Why?"

"Well, there weren't any Asian boys where I grew up, so I guess I'm not used to dating them."

"You'll grow out of it. You only like American boys because you're young. You know better as you get older. My daughter also liked American men, but now she's dating a Korean man," she said with a big smile.

Remembering her words all of these years later made me smile. I would never fit her model of a proper Korean woman.

But she would be proud to know that I had returned to Korea to learn about my culture, even if I had married a white man.

Word of my search for my birth mother spread among the large group of Korean adoptees at school. Like me, they had returned to study the language and search for their birth families. Perhaps because we were swinging from the same pendulum of fascination and repulsion with Korean culture, I found a sympathetic ear among them. Without stating it out loud, we shared an innate sense of being "inside-outsiders" in Korea.

It took only a couple of days before all of us Korean adoptees in school formed a loose network. We had an uncanny ability to spot another adoptee in a crowd. Of course, that was easy to do in Korea, where chances were good that anyone who looked like a Korean in his or her twenties, but couldn't speak the language was an adoptee on a pilgrimage to the homeland. What surprised me was the sheer number of adoptees who had returned and the varied places we came from—the United States, Canada, Norway, and Sweden. We pulled together like members of a secret club, interrogating each other and comparing childhood experiences. There was an unspeakable joy in discovering someone who understood the paradoxes even before you explained them.

The first Korean adoptee I met was Dong-soo. When he heard me speak English with a group of students after class one day, he made a beeline across the cafeteria.

"Hey, were you adopted?" he asked casually. "I was wondering, because, well, I was adopted."

"Yes, I was. I was adopted when I was seven."

He smiled as if reacquainting himself with an old friend. "Seven? Wow, that's old! Do you have many memories of Korea, then? I was a baby, so of course I can't remember anything."

"Yes, I lived with my mother and grandmother until I left, so I remember them. Where are you from?" I didn't recognize his accent.

"Sweden."

"Sweden?" Before I met Dong-soo, I had been under the misconception that only Americans adopted children from overseas.

"Yeah, there are quite a few of us in Sweden, you know. Where are you from?"

"Salt Lake City, Utah."

He gave me a mocking grin. "How many Koreans live in— where is it?—Salt Lake City?"

"Hardly any." I laughed. "Only me, I think."

"Well, there are more than ten thousand Korean adoptees in Sweden and many in my hometown. I helped form a Korea club there that meets every month to eat Korean food and just get together for some fun."

"Really?" After growing up in Salt Lake City, I couldn't imagine openly celebrating adoption and Korean heritage like that.

As we became closer, I learned that Dong-soo and I had traveled similar paths. Neither one of us had shown much interest in Korea as a child or teenager. He grew curious about his Korean heritage as an adult, after he was hospitalized with a serious illness. While in the hospital he met a Korean couple who encouraged him to visit his homeland just once, when he got well. The first time he visited Korea, Dong-soo said he felt like he had come home. He fell in love with everything about Korea, and this was now his fifth extended visit. Unlike me, he had easily slipped into the culture and felt as comfortable as a native. He was completing a master's degree in Korean studies.

"Every chance I get, I come to Korea. Back home, everyone calls my apartment Little Korea because I have the Korean flag hanging on the wall and I'm constantly talking on the phone to my Korean friends. This time when I am here, I want to meet a nice girl."

"Yeah, you only like Korea for the women," I quipped.

"I know. It is good to be a man in Korea. I need to find myself a good traditional Korean wife to take home with me."

I gathered from his tone that he was only halfway joking. As much as I hated to, I had to admit that Korean men had it good and were pampered like kings. Who wouldn't want a traditional Korean wife?

Dong-soo introduced me to other adoptees. There was Pia, who had located her Korean mother only to be rejected by her. She was told that her mother didn't want to see her and to never contact her again. All of us quietly shared Pia's pain, which heightened our own fears of rejection. There was Yvonne, who was able to find her mother and six older siblings. Unlike Pia, Yvonne's was a remarkable and joyous reunion. She learned that her father was killed in a car accident while her mother was pregnant with her. Already struggling to support six children, her mother decided to give Yvonne up for adoption in the hope that she could find a better life in Norway. Yvonne was majoring in Korean and spending time with her new extended family in Pusan, a seaport city about four hours south of Seoul. She had a younger sister in Norway who was also adopted from Korea. But interestingly, her sister had little interest in finding her birth parents.

And there was Kim, Dong-soo's friend from Sweden. One look at Kim and you could tell he had not grown up in Korea. Besides his ponytail, he had a confident, slightly cocky air about him that said "visiting foreigner."

"So, I'm curious because I have a Korean sister who also was adopted. What was it like for you growing up?" he asked during our first meeting.

"Well, you know . . ." I searched for a way to condense my experience into a few phrases. "I was the only Asian at my school, so I think it was difficult for me that way. I remember wanting to be white and look like everyone else."

"Really? But why? You seem like a nice person with an outgoing personality, so I wonder why you felt like that. I guess I had a totally different experience. I always thought that the fact that I looked different worked to my advantage. In school, all of the girls liked me because I was so unique looking." He bent his fingers into a set of quotation marks. "They thought that was way cool. But maybe it's a guy thing, because I know my sister has some issues about her appearance and all that."

I felt a slow blush spread across my face. How pathetic I sounded in the shadow of his self-confidence. All this time I had attributed my adolescent self-doubt and identity crisis to the mere fact that I was a Korean in a white society, when maybe it was an inherent defect in my personality.

Eager to change the topic, I asked Kim the inevitable question. "So why did you return to Korea? Do you plan to search for your birth parents?"

His earlier confidence faded and a slight look of discomfort appeared in his handsome eyes. "Yeah, I tried, but got nowhere. It's okay, though. I don't really care if I find them or not. It's not a huge issue for me. I'm just here to learn Korean, have some fun, and party for a while."

Dong-soo and I exchanged knowing looks across the table. I knew from earlier conversations that Dong-soo had chased every possible lead in search of his birth parents, without luck. He was trying not to let the futile search become an obsession. "What can I do?" he asked with a resigned look in his eyes. "I want to find my Korean family more than anything. But I can't spend the rest of my life thinking about that. Otherwise, I'll drive myself crazy."

• • •

Several weeks later, our landlord's daughter called me in an excited voice. "Quick, turn on the TV! There is a show on that's just like your story. Oh, it's so sad." She sniffled.

When I flipped on the television, I was surprised to see a somber-looking Kim appear on the screen. "My name is Kim and I am twenty-eight years old. I was abandoned at a train station in Taejon when I was two."

Kim's nonchalance had been fake after all. He had joined other adoptees on a call-in television program trying to reunite adopted children with their birth families. This was the show Miss Yoo had told me about the first time we met. Some adoptees flashed their baby pictures; others gave their Korean names and birth dates while a dramatic Korean voice-over contemplated the tragedy of adoption on children's lives.

The show was sentimental, but I stayed glued to the screen. My empathy for other adoptees turned into an inner shame that I was just another statistic, one of thousands of children who had been given away. The melodrama of an on-camera reunion between mother and child had a soap-opera-ish quality to it. Cameras closed in on a white-haired, stooped woman wailing in the arms of her newly found middle-aged son.

I tried hard not to be moved by the spectacle. But as I gazed at the old woman's tears, my thoughts turned to my own Korean mother and grandmother. I wondered if they were watching.

Later, the program turned into a tabloid-style exposé of racism in America. The camera followed a teenage girl, a Korean adoptee who had grown up in a white family in a Chicago suburb. She snapped her gum and spoke about her harsh life in America. "I, like, never got along with my adoptive parents," she said. "I suffered a lot of racism. One time I went into a store and the clerk just like followed me around, just because I was, like, Asian, you know? When I asked my parents about it, they, like, said I must have deserved it."

I couldn't believe this babbling teenager was the chosen representative of Korean adoptees living in the United States. The Korean host nodded at the girl sympathetically and was apparently almost moved to tears as he explained to the television audience the racism Asians in America encountered on a daily basis. The program then turned to stock footage of Korean shopkeepers whose stores had been looted and destroyed during the riots in Los Angeles after the Rodney King verdict. Watching the films of the riots themselves, especially from the perspective of a Korean, was horrifying. No wonder some Koreans looked at me with pity when they discovered where I lived.

I was the first to admit there was racism in America, but I felt suddenly defensive about my adoptive country. I didn't need anyone's pity, and besides, Korea seemed to have its own racist views of neighboring Asian countries, African-Americans, and darker-skinned people in general. The fact that its population was nearly completely homogenous, combined with the country's long history of invasions by foreign powers, made Korea's racist views and fear of foreigners all the more prevalent. I hoped television viewers realized this girl was not representative of all, or even a majority, of Korean adoptees. Most adoptees I met felt that they had entered loving families, complete with ups and downs and all of the quirks that come with any family—adoptive or biological.

The program demonstrated the pain Koreans felt about foreign adoption. On the one hand, Koreans admired foreigners who adopted their nation's children and were sincerely grateful to them for taking care of the children when their own countrymen would not. It was not unknown for a foreign couple traveling to Korea to pick up an adopted child to be stopped on the street and given heartfelt thanks by complete strangers. But underneath the gratitude lay great shame and embarrassment at the legacy of being a "baby-exporting" nation. Korea tried to reduce the numbers by setting a limit on foreign adoptions each year. But with the latest economic crisis, the number of children being given up for adoption had swelled and the government temporarily lifted the cap on overseas adoptions.

Korea's attitude toward adoption was best expressed by the country's own president. A speech given by President Kim Dae-jung to a group of visiting Korean adoptees was circulating over the Internet among adoption circles.

"I am pained to think that we could not raise you ourselves, and had to give you away for foreign adoption," he said. "The reason for the adoption was primarily economic difficulty. But there were other reasons. Koreans traditionally have a habit-of-the-heart that places too much importance on blood ties. And when you don't have that, people rarely adopt children. So we sent you away. Imagining all the pain and psychological conflicts that you must have gone through, we are shamed. We are grateful to your adopted parents, who have loved you and raised you, but we are also filled with shame . . ."

Although his words were heartfelt, I found little comfort in them. I did not want to bear the shame of a nation.

My friend Yvonne and I took off our shoes and stepped into the hallway of the Holt Orphanage, where we were greeted by the combined scent of baby formula and messy diapers. It was afternoon feeding time and we joined a group of volunteers who alternated between giving bottles and changing diapers, under the direction of the busy Korean women who worked there.

Holt was the Eugene, Oregon–based agency through which both Yvonne and her sister had been adopted. Adoptees who returned to Korea almost always visited the orphanages where they had stayed. And even though this was not my orphanage, it was difficult not to feel an immediate bond with the babies there. The facility was a three-story Korean-style building that housed twelve to fifteen children, divided by age, on each floor. The top floor held the younger babies—the youngest of which had been born just one day before. Her tiny pink body lay in an incubator with a strip of gauze taped over her eyes to protect them from the light. Another baby girl, in the incubator next to her, was born the week before. Her faint cry sounded like a meow from a newborn kitten. Rows of cribs held the other babies, ranging in age from the newborns to six months old.

It's easy to fall in love with babies even when they're not your own—especially ones in need of homes. But what I felt was more than adoration. When I looked into their faces, I was moved by a sense of camaraderie. Twenty years from now, some of them would return to this very orphanage in search of answers. As I gazed down at the tiny bodies lying in cribs and on blankets on the floor, I was overcome with emotion. Not any sort of pity, but a sudden realization of the decision each of their mothers had made. At first there was anger and a temptation to pass judgment—how could any mother give up her baby like this?

But the anger gave way to something more complicated.

I understood my own mother and forgave her. I prayed that each of these children would one day do the same.

A white marker board on the wall held a long list of babies' names and birth dates. Some also had adoption dates along with their destinations: Oregon, Norway, Canada, Minnesota. The opposite wall was covered with a collage of photographs of infants in their new homes surrounded by parents and extended family members. Grinning moms and dads held their new babies dressed in Halloween costumes and Christmas dresses. Although these babies could not comprehend the photographs, the wall was a reminder to the adults at the orphanage of the bright future awaiting these children overseas. Each child who had been matched to adoptive parents had a disposable camera with his or her name written on it. Employees of the orphanage were encouraged to take pictures of the children at play to send back to anxiously waiting parents.

We were directed downstairs to continue the never-ending ritual of feeding and changing. Each room was staffed by a Korean caretaker who worked a twelve-hour shift. Each time we came, however, we found several other volunteers there to help care for and play with the children. These infants did not fuss or cry as much as children who have the luxury of a doting parent by their side. Here, they had to wait their turns in a room full of infants. Many lay quietly on the floor, learning to roll over onto their stomachs or flop onto a playmate next to them. When they did get held, many smiled, slobbered, and cooed to show their appreciation. Some babies performed a series of cute new antics in order to hold my attention before I moved on to someone else. As I picked up one baby boy, other tiny heads looked to see who was getting the attention. I ran clumsily from one child to another, wanting to hold them all at the same time. There were never enough volunteers to give each child the affection he or she deserved. After each visit, we left happily exhausted and covered with that day's slobber and spit-up stains to show for our work.

At night, my thoughts and dreams were filled with babies— their sweet powdery scent, fuzzy black heads, drool dripping off chubby cheeks, and pink fingers wrapped tightly around my finger. I grew to miss their physical presence in my arms. One particular little boy, whom I nicknamed Happy Baby, won my heart. He was always eager to see me and greeted me with a smile that revealed two front teeth. He kicked his tiny legs up and down in a dance of excitement. Even if I caught him in the middle of a rare cry, he changed to a grin when I smiled and talked to him. Happy Baby had light brown almond-shaped eyes that explored everything around him with fascination. I thought about how his world would open up once he found a home filled with books and toys and loving parents who would play with him all day long.

I saw that he did not have the name of a country written on the board after his name.

16

Dear Mom,

  *I can't believe how fast the time in Korea is going
and that it is already Thanksgiving. Korea, of course,
doesn't celebrate Thanksgiving, but there is a similar
holiday called* Chusok, *the fall harvest celebration.
This is a national holiday and many Koreans travel to their home-
towns to be with relatives. The stores are filled with holiday foods—
ginseng cookies and colorful rice cakes shaped like half-moons. (The
moon is supposed to be full and the most beautiful of the year during
Chusok.) For Chusok, children and women dress up in colorful
hanboks—bright greens and pinks, although not as pretty as mine!
Although we expected to, we didn't hear from my brother or sister, or
dad. Our upstairs neighbors must have felt sorry for us, because last
night, the mom knocked on our door holding a tray of homemade
dumpling soup, braised beef, and rice cakes.*

  Remember my first Thanksgiving and the drumstick?

  *I have been thinking a lot about my adoption. I think that giving
me up for adoption was the kindest thing my family could have done*

for me. I have been thinking a lot about what makes a family. In Korea, the bloodline is so important, but I don't know.

Anyway, I am grateful that I didn't have to grow up a dutiful girl in Korea. I am reading a collection of folktales and the moral of every story is for the wife to sacrifice herself for her husband and in-laws.

—Katy

Hello All,

We have continued to meet with Katy's brother about once a week. Koreans, especially men, like to drink alcohol a lot, so we usually end up going out for dinner then drinks. Every once in a while, Katy's brother opens up and tells us about himself and his family, but most of the conversation is the usual low-key kind since we must speak through a translator.

We have seen Katy's father only once in the last month. There was an awkward moment when he told Katy that he has a third family (and that Katy has another brother and sister). Last week, though, he dropped off a present for each of us (a peace offering?) and we hope that we will see him more regularly. Once again, one of the difficulties is the language barrier and we usually don't have a translator when we talk with him. We also realize that he is alone raising two teenagers and is possibly unemployed. Not exactly an easy life for a seventy-two-year-old man.

For a while it felt like each time we met with Katy's family, they surprised us with another information "bomb" about their family. Hopefully, we have now learned about most of the family secrets and can continue to get to know them. Some things are still difficult, though. Katy implied to her brother that she would like to meet his family, but then he told her that his mother does not know Katy is in Seoul. We also do not think he has told his son about her yet. We think his wife knows, but she never comes out with us. We also haven't seen Katy's sister since our initial meeting and are unsure why. Katy questions herself about whether she did something wrong.

Katy has spent time this past week trying to locate information about her mother. Katy's father has tried to become actively involved in the search, but we think that is a mistake. Since we don't know anything about her parents' past, and the reasons why they separated, I think that any possible reunion should be for Katy and her mother alone. Although it is difficult for Katy to communicate what she wants to her father, I think he knows how she feels, but does what he wants anyway. However, until we actually find out if Katy's mother is alive, and if she wants to meet with Katy, we won't have to make any decisions about the details.

—John

Dear Mom,

My brother called yesterday to give me an update about my Korean mom. He said he ran her name and birth date through a police computer database going back for twenty years. But they were unable to find any type of records for her. That is strange since Koreans keep notoriously good records. If she had gotten married, had children, or died, there would surely be records of those events. When I questioned my brother further, he said the government building that may have housed her records burned down and maybe the papers were destroyed. That explanation also sounded strange. He asked me to be patient and not take action on my own.

He did find an address for my mother's younger sister and an older brother. He wants me to wait until he confirms that this is their current address. He didn't say what will come after that, but I would like to write or contact them and ask for their help in locating information about my mother.

In a rare moment of candidness, he asked me what I expected from a meeting with my mother. I told him that I didn't know exactly, *just that I want to find her and let her know that I am okay. I assured him that if she couldn't meet with me, I would understand. He said, of course I had a right to meet my own mother. But he didn't sound very convinced.*

                                                        —Katy

17

Each time my father and brother told me to be patient,
I suspected they were really asking me to give up
the search for my mother. Out loud, they promised to help me find her. But the look behind their
eyes begged me not to ask any more questions,
not to stir the waters for fear of creating lasting ripples. I didn't
know whether they acted out of fear and concern on my behalf
or for themselves. But the more they stalled, the more determined I became to find my mother and give her voice—even
if that meant defying the wishes of my father and brother by
going behind their backs. I had a right to hear my mother's story
and she had a right to tell it.

In the end, it was John who convinced me to take up the
search on my own.

"If you really want the truth, you're going to have to look
on your own," he said. "I don't think you can depend on your
Korean family. It's just too hard for them."

I knew what he said was right. And so I found myself back
at the doorsteps of Korea Social Services, my orphanage. The

first time I returned there, I had felt like a lost child searching for the way home. This time, however, I came as a determined adult ready to demand the information that was being kept from me. Every person has a right to know whether her mother is alive or dead. If my mother didn't want to see me, I was prepared to accept this and honor her wishes. But I could no longer hang in midair, suspended between hope and despair.

John and Mr. Sim came with me, John for support and Mr. Sim in case I needed a translator. The three of us walked in and asked to speak with Miss Kim, the social worker who had helped me find my father. Our visit was not unexpected, since Mr. Sim had called ahead and explained my situation. A woman named Miss Kim, but not the same person who had helped me the year before, led us into a conference room and told us to wait. She returned ten minutes later with my case file. On the way over, I had prepared a speech in my head to plead my case and beg to know the truth about my mother and explain my good intentions. But before I had a chance to speak, the woman glanced at me, then at John and Mr. Sim, and began our meeting in a curt tone. Unlike the first Miss Kim, her English was flawless and there was no need for translation.

"Our records show that you visited us a year ago. And at that time we helped you find your father. So what can we do for you now?"

I felt like a child being chided without understanding why. She glared at me from across the table and folded her hands on top of the brown folder. This reception, so different from my first visit, when Miss Kim had held my hand as she talked soothingly, came as a shock.

"I'm here hoping to get some information about my mother."

"Well, why don't you ask your father to help you?" She continued her glare, then looked down at her watch.

Her words were like tiny pricks to the skin. I tried to keep my voice steady as I explained, "I did ask my father to help me. But first my Korean family told me my mother was dead, then changed their minds and said she was alive. Now I don't know what to believe and came here searching for the truth. I just want to know the truth."

When I saw that she was unmoved, I continued, "My father and mother were separated. They were never married, so I don't really think my father has any information about my mother or can help me find her. That is why I came back here."

"Oh, I see."

I waited for her to say more, but there was only suffocating silence under the fluorescent white light of the room. I had come to demand answers and yet I felt like the one being interrogated. I thought about the advice I'd received from my friends at school. They said Korean law had changed recently to give adoptees access to their adoption records. Many of them had obtained copies of their files from their orphanages. "All you have to do is insist they make you a copy," they said. "If they give you any trouble, tell them that you have a legal right to this information."

Trying for a strong and steady tone, I asked, "Could I please have a copy of everything in my records?"

She was prepared for my question and opened the file. "I can make copies of some papers in here, but I can't show you any personal information about your mother. We have an obligation to protect your mother's rights and privacy. You understand that, don't you?" Her condescending tone was not lost on me as she paused for emphasis. "Any contact you make with her would have to be through us."

Her last comment was a reference to our attempt, the week before, to locate my mother by running her name through a police computer. One of John's students had a relative who worked as a police investigator, and when he heard about my search, he had offered to help. But he called us from the police station, saying he needed to confirm my adoption and could we give him the name of the orphanage, which we did. But I now understood how my decision to involve a third party had upset this woman and caused her to view me as a threat. No one— not my father, brother, or this social worker—wanted me to search for my mother on my own.

As I glanced at the open file, I noticed that some of the papers that had been there on my previous visit had already been re- moved, including the page with my mother's signature. All that remained were the caseworker's typed reports.

"Here, you may look at this," Miss Kim said, handing me a typed letter written in English. "If you want, I can make you a copy to take with you."

It was the agency's response to my American mother's letter years before, when she asked them about the photographs of my Korean family and confronted them about the lies they had told her.

About the picture: After Ji-yun left the country, her maternal grand- mother moved and we are still in the process of locating her. When we locate her I plan to have a discussion with her about the pictures. In the caseworker's opinion, the pictures seem to have been taken at the maternal grandmother's house.

Family background: Ji-yun's mother is a single girl and had an affair with a married man. From the beginning, Ji-yun's father was indifferent to Ji-yun and Ji-yun's mother. Since Ji-yun was born, she was reared by her maternal grandmother at her maternal grand- mother's house and she understands that her father is a bad man.

Since her mother had been working, she does not have any close relationship with her mother either. Her maternal grandmother kept telling her that she was being sent to the United States as an adoptive

child and that was a great opportunity for her. She is a gentle child
and I think that she will adjust very fast if somebody pays enough
attention to her and treats her warmly. Since she was born out of wed-
lock, her name is not on the family register.

Her mother is to be married very soon, and for the future of both
the child and her mother, they have decided to relinquish her for a
foreign adoption.

Nothing in the report came as a surprise to me, yet my eyes
stung as I finished reading it. These words were forthright,
whereas the people I had been dealing with were not. They
confirmed my growing suspicions and proved that I was born
out of the most common of mistakes—an affair with an older
married man who had turned indifferent. I was an illegitimate
child and a permanent scar on my mother's reputation. She had
to be rid of me in order to marry. Even as I repeated that
thought, I could not be angry or even blame my mother. What
other choice did she have? Instead, my anger turned toward my
father for putting my mother in such a situation and for being
indifferent, for causing endless shame while bearing none himself.

After Miss Kim handed me a copy of the report to take home,
I tried one last appeal for more information.

"I understand that my mother may be in circumstances where
she can't meet me. I know that she may be married and have
other children. I don't want to ruin any life she has built for
herself. I just want to know whether she is alive or not, and for
her to know that I am here if she wants to meet me."

She remained silent, so I continued.

"The last time I was here and met with the other Miss Kim,
she promised to look for some information about my mother.
She told me that she was able to locate an aunt, but I never
heard anything more."

"Oh really? I don't know anything about that."

"Do you have information about this aunt—maybe in my records somewhere?"

"No, there is nothing here about an aunt."

She closed the file. There was nothing I could say to convince her that I did not mean to be a threat to my mother's new life.

On the way out, I saw Miss Kim of the year before in the hallway. She recognized me right away and we embraced.

"I received your card and photograph from Idaho," she said. "I am so happy that you came back to Korea." She gave me a sympathetic smile, as if she already knew the outcome of my meeting but there was nothing more she could do.

On our way back to the bus stop, Mr. Sim asked us to follow him around the corner and into a police station. "I'm going to see if they can give me an address for your aunt and uncle," he told me as he pulled out the sheet of paper I had given him earlier. Inside the station, Mr. Sim spoke with an officer behind the counter, who glanced over at me and smiled before walking over to a computer. He returned a few minutes later and handed Mr. Sim a slip of paper.

"He gave me the addresses of your aunt and uncle," Mr. Sim said. "If you want, I can write to them on your behalf and tell them that you are searching for your mother."

I nodded eagerly, surprised at how easily he had obtained this information.

"Okay. I will try my best to contact them for you. I will write them a letter today when I return to the office," he promised.

The three of us boarded a bus and headed back to town. Narrow streets and one-story shacks turned into skyscrapers and traffic jams as we approached downtown. Returning to the orphanage the first time had evoked a joyful sense of familiarity and memories from childhood. But I did not know what to make of this most recent trip and the cold reception I received.

No one, it seemed, wanted me to ask questions about my mother.

I thought about the social worker's defensive attitude and what that could mean. Perhaps my mother really was dead and she wanted to protect me from the bad news, which seemed to be a natural Korean instinct. Or my mother was alive, they had contacted her, and she had said she didn't want to see me. Perhaps in some people's eyes, believing my mother was dead was better than rejection. Or the woman at the orphanage had just been doing her job, which was to protect the mothers who had given up their children. My mind reeled with confusion and endless guesses.

"I hope you find your mommy," Mr. Sim said quietly. "I know she would want to meet you. Of course every parent wants to meet their child."

He said it with such certainty, as if this was a universal and known fact. But if my mother wanted to find me, all she had to do was return to the orphanage as my father had done. But then, she was a woman with much more at stake than a man.

In a sudden burst of clarity, I knew without a doubt that my mother was alive. Why else would the social worker feel such a strong need to protect her? I imagined a new life for my mother, married to a kind husband, with several children in their teens. I understood why she couldn't meet me. Korean society did not easily forgive women. Her family's discovery of a former child could lead to disdain from her in-laws, divorce, and eventual ostracism for her current children. The discovery of a secret past would be the ultimate source of shame in a society that honored a woman's chastity above all else. This sounded melodramatic to my Western mind, but I also knew it was reality in Korean culture.

The more I thought about the social worker's refusal to help me, the more I began to see her unwavering position as something to admire. She was simply protecting my mother and all other unwed mothers who came to the orphanage in desperation. She was keeping an old promise to my mother, all the while trying to protect my feelings as best she could. No matter how much I begged for the truth, she would never tell me that my mother did not want to see me. In her view, it was better to answer with silence or lies. Even better, if she could somehow convince me to stop looking.

Maybe it was time to give up the search. Who was to say my quest for the truth and the past was more important than my mother's honor? My mother was alive, but I would never meet her.

I attempted to come to peace with that stark reality.

"Your brother has news about your mother..."

My brother asked us to meet him at a restaurant, and when we got there we found that along with his usual friends he had brought a new translator—a Korean-American from Los Angeles named Gilbert. As Gilbert spoke his first sentence, everyone at the table stiffened in anticipation of his next words.

It had been weeks since my visit to the orphanage, which I had never mentioned to my father or brother. But after that visit, I stopped asking them for updates.

I hadn't expected any news about my mother and I wasn't sure if I wanted to hear what my brother had to say. I searched his face for a hint of the impending news, but his face was masked with a forced smile. I saw a weary look cross John's face as he reached for my hand under the table. I took a deep breath and braced for the translator's next sentence. I had the feeling that whatever it was, this news would bring me to the end of my search.

The words fell out of his mouth in one graceless tumble.

"Well, your brother is sorry, but he found out that your mother died ten years ago."

My brother continued to smile as the translator spoke.

"She was killed in a car accident. Your grandmother is dead also."

I gaped in the direction of the man's face as if I could see the actual shape of his words floating in the air and drifting toward me. My first thought was not about the meaning of the words themselves but about the scene around me—the smile on my brother's face, the slump of John's shoulders, the tone of the translator's voice as he spoke. Then something in me snapped, and the words burst like tiny explosions in my head. *Sorry but . . . mother died . . . killed . . . dead.* Gilbert had uttered those words so quickly and casually, as if discussing the fate of some unknown stranger on the street.

"This is my mother you're talking about," I wanted to scream. "How would you feel if I just told you *your* mother was dead?"

Just as quickly my anger turned into shock. Every emotion in my body came crashing together and I was suspended between belief and disbelief. Just as I had convinced myself of my mother's life, my brother reaffirmed her death. As much as I questioned my brother's motives, a part of me believed what he was saying, just as I had believed him the first time he told me my mother was dead. And the news of her death stung just as much, perhaps even more, because it was now clouded by a web of lies. I tried to hold back my tears and sort through the tangle of emotions enveloping me.

What finally surfaced was a suspicion that I was not being told the complete or even a partial truth—without which, I would forever be lost in a game of guesses.

I was suddenly sober. "How did my brother get this information?" I asked Gilbert. "I mean how does he know for sure this time?"

There was a silence as people shifted in their seats. I got the sense that I was being "un-Korean" once again. But I could not let this meeting drop into obscurity.

"Is there a death certificate?"

"No, there is no death certificate." Our translator answered calmly without consulting my brother.

"But I thought Koreans kept detailed records of every death."

Another long silence followed before Gilbert broke into what sounded like a carefully scripted speech. My brother remained silently by his side as he spoke.

"Your mother died alone, so there was no one to report her death on the family register. That is why your father thought she was still alive when he looked at her family papers. She never married, and her mother—your *halmoni*—had already died. So I think your mother died all alone."

He was the only one at the table who looked me in the eyes as he spoke one last sentence. "I think her situation was very sad."

Even through my suspicions, I could no longer hold back my tears. As much as I tried to convince myself that all of what I was hearing was a fabrication, dictated by a pretense of "protecting me," I dwelled on my mother's death. I pictured her sprawled in the middle of a road, her body flopped over like a rag doll next to a mangled car. Her hair matted and covering her face, her red lips turning a deep purple. She had died alone, without anyone even to report her death. Thoughts of my mother all alone—without her mother or daughter, without anyone to grieve the loss of her life—replaced my earlier thoughts of her happily married life. The loss of her young life was worse than the thought of never meeting her.

Of all the possible scenarios my brother could have told me, I never imagined one so tragic. I sat paralyzed by the image of my mother's death.

"Wait, what about her relatives—her brother and sister?" I asked, still trying to push my brother into a corner. "Did my brother talk to them? He said he was going to contact them. Their names were on the family register."

Gilbert had been prepped, even on this.

"Right," he answered. "Your mother does have a sister and brother listed on the family documents. Your brother had a detective—I think a friend of your sister's—call them. But they acted like they didn't care about your mom. You see, they didn't know her very well."

These were the people Mr. Sim had promised to write to on my behalf. I hadn't heard a response from them.

"Your brother thinks it would be best if you didn't contact them, since they have no memories of you. He doesn't think they really care about you or your mother."

With each statement, I felt the sides of the box close in on my mother. I tried desperately to think of another angle to adopt or a way to trap my brother into confessing the truth with a carefully crafted question.

As my mind raced, our translator answered a question that it had not even occurred to me to ask.

"I'm sorry, but there is no burial site for your mother, so you cannot visit her gravesite either."

With that, my mother's fate was tightly sealed so that I could never reach her. I ran out of the restaurant so that no one else had to witness my tears.

When I came back inside, I was surprised to see that the topic of my mother had been erased from the conversation and replaced by the business of eating and drinking. Koreans seemed to me overly sentimental on the one hand and heartless on the other. I suffered my grief in silence while my brother and his friends did their best to act like nothing had happened.

I had no choice but to play along and swallow one bitter bite after another.

Afterward my brother took us to a bar located below my sister's office. While everyone else was removing their shoes and arranging themselves around a low table, my brother whispered to me, "*Unnee* is working upstairs. Let's go say hello." I followed him up a narrow staircase to a small corner office that housed my sister's two-person graphic-design company. I caught my older siblings exchange looks, as if they were passing a secret code. My brother quickly left the room while my sister took my hand and led me to a seat. This was the first time I had seen her in months.

"Katy," she said, studying my face while her eyes wrinkled into concern. She smoothed my hair like I was a child. "Did *Oppa* give you the news about your mommy?"

I nodded, too exhausted by the evening's events to speak about it.

"Oh." She searched for the proper words then said, "You look tired. Get lots of rest this weekend and stay healthy. Don't drink too much tonight." She patted my back and opened her mouth to say something else, but let the subject drop unspoken.

Back at the bar, I found my brother slamming back shots of *soju*. I chased him with shots of my own, wanting desperately to get drunk. After several drinks, I remained stubbornly sober even as my brother's eyes glazed over and he began to slur his words.

"Ka-ty." He grabbed my hand. "Ka-ty," he repeated several times. "I'm sorry."

As his words spilled out, he leaned his head on my shoulder and began to cry silently, releasing tears down his hollowed cheeks in a rare show of emotion. I patted his back and stroked his head, filled with equal doses of love and suspicion. As he continued to cry, I covered my brother's hand with mine until our long fingers meshed into one continuous line.

"When I found out the news about your mother, my heart was broken," he said. "This is hard for both of us, but you have to be strong. We, Sister and I, sat down with our mother last night and told her about you, that you were in Seoul and we had seen you. At first she was upset. But then her heart became so heavy after hearing about how your mom died. Our mother said she wants to meet you and adopt you as her own daughter, since you no longer have a mother. So now my mom is your mom too. She says to think of her as your true mother now."

"You know, you're very lucky, because your brother's mommy is now your mommy too," Gilbert added.

My head spun with alcohol, the cloud of cigarette smoke around the table, and this latest news. I didn't know whether to feel grateful for my brother's mother's pity and generosity, or insulted. Couldn't they understand that I didn't *need* another mother? I already had a mother in America. It wasn't a mother figure I sought as much as an understanding of my past, and this could only come from my Korean mother, not a surrogate. I thought again about my mother dying alone in a car accident, with no death certificate, burial site, or relatives who cared. The story my brother had told me did not make any sense. If my mother was dead, there had to be some evidence or record of her passing; otherwise how could my brother know the details? The only thing I could conclude was that he had fabricated this elaborate story for the purpose of *kibun*—the complex Korean code of saving face and preserving honor and harmony at the expense of all else. He wanted to erase all traces of my mother so that we could carry on our lives unfettered by the past.

18

> *Katy, I am so sorry about last weekend.*
> *I think, I made a lot of mistakes that time.*
> *I wish you understand me.*
> *Tomorrow afternoon, I'm going to call at your*
> *house.*
> *I want to buy a tasty food for you.*
> *I think we will be there about 1 P.M.*
>
> —*Oppa*

My brother was eager to lay the topic of my mother to rest, even as I struggled with the mystery of her fate. Even though I didn't believe the story of her death, the emotional damage was done. For days afterward, the vision of my mother's car accident flashed in my mind like a lingering doubt. As much as I tried, I couldn't comprehend why my brother had chosen to make up this horrific story. My brother had once told me that he believed in telling the truth. Why couldn't he trust me with it?

He would forever protect me from the truth whether I wanted it or not. With time, I came to understand that he was also protecting his own mother by wiping my father's old mistress from the picture. Only through my mother's removal could I be fully accepted into his family. I realized this as soon as he introduced me to his wife and son.

His wife, Gyung-hee, was studying English and became our new translator and go-between. John and I began receiving frequent E-mails from her, written on my brother's behalf. After our male translators, she was a welcome feminine presence that softened some of my brother's qualities and gave us an air of a family unit.

Gyung-hee, who I was directed to call *Sae-unnee* or "new sister," stood a full head shorter than I am and looked more like a college student than a mother. She wore her short brown hair pulled back into a ponytail and sported rectangular tortoise-shell glasses, blue jeans, and a bright orange turtleneck sweater with the Gap logo printed across the chest in oversized letters. Before greeting me, she handed me an enormous glass jar of her mother-in-law's homemade *kimchee* with both hands and giggled at her gift. Her smile was warm and sincere and I immediately liked her. Her son hid behind her legs, peeking out with shy curiosity at his new aunt and uncle who couldn't speak Korean. He stared at John with big open eyes, smiled, then whispered something to his mother with a boyish grin.

"Kang-san says John looks like an American movie star, but has hairy arms," she translated with a laugh.

My nephew was eight years old and a younger replica of my brother and father. His straight wispy bangs hung above his narrow eyes and his long oversized ears stuck out from his head. His wide, slightly crooked front teeth seemed out of place in his delicate mouth. He had a thin lanky body and skin the color of light caramel. When I looked at my nephew, I had an image of my father as a child, close to the age I was when I left Korea. As if reading my thoughts, my brother laughed and told me the name of a popular Korean snack, which was made by pouring dough into rows of fish-shaped molds.

"In Korea, that is what we call people who look alike, like they came from the same mold one after another. Our father, Kang-san, and I are the same," he said proudly. He shoved his son forward and instructed him to bow to his new *komoe,* or aunt.

My nephew shot me a look of curiosity before shifting his eyes to the ground and muttering a quick *"Anyong-ha-sayo."*

I stroked the top of his fuzzy head and smiled at his striped blue T-shirt that had a familiar little red tag on the side of the pocket that said VELIS—a Korean variation of the Levi's brand.

We left for our Sunday outing looking like the picture of a Korean family, indistinguishable from any other family with the exception of John—the *Meegook saram.* I welcomed the opportunity to meet my brother's family, but was preoccupied with thoughts of my mother. I wanted the copy of my mother's family register that my brother had promised me. I plotted the best way to ask for it later that day. He might give it to me now that he believed the search for my mother was over.

Given the unease I felt toward my brother, my nephew Kang-san was a welcome distraction. He sat next to me in the backseat of the car squirming and playing with the headset he brought with him. I tried a few words of Korean on him, hoping he would understand me.

"Do you go to school?"

He nodded.

"Do you like it?"

My short, grammatically incorrect Korean sentences seemed to amuse him and he began to relax. "Yes, school is okay except for this one time my teacher hit me. Pow." He feigned being punched in the face.

"Hit you?" I asked, duly horrified.

"Yes!" he replied. "In Korea, if you are bad, teachers can hit you. But I didn't do anything wrong."

From my own memories of going to school in Korea, I knew he was exaggerating only slightly. I had finished first grade and a part of second grade. I had visions of sparsely furnished classrooms with shared wooden desks arranged in long neat rows, paperback books protected with plastic covers, and backpacks decorated with Western-looking cartoon characters. I remembered standing in front of the class to receive my punishment—a slap on the palms with a wooden ruler. In Korea, school brought an end to the carefree days and brief leniency afforded to children. From the moment they entered a classroom, students were pressured to study hard, with the goal of entering a prestigious university to study traditional fields such as math, science, or business. Korean education drilled three words into the minds of its youth: *discipline*, *obedience*, and *diligence*. My two years of Korean elementary school had more than prepared me for my academic career in America.

Kang-san was the first Korean with whom I could carry on entire conversations with ease. It didn't matter to him that my Korean was at an infantile level. When my vocabulary ran short, he eagerly filled in the blanks with gestures or simpler words. And I quickly discovered how much he loved to talk. "I'm studying English at school," he told me. "I have these flash cards at home too. I know 'ant'—it's *gae-mee* like the American movie *Antz*. But my mom says you are my aunt."

While Kang-san tried to teach me Korean in the backseat, we crossed a long bridge over the Han River and headed into a trendy and expensive district of Seoul. The south side of the river was home to newer, more modern buildings and Koreans considered it a more prestigious area than the north. We drove into a hip new district marked by nightclubs, bars, and Western restaurant chains. My brother wove through thick crowds of congregating college students and parked in a plaza that reminded me more of Old Town in San Diego than Seoul. We stood on the cobblestone walkway surrounded by quaint stucco Mexican and Italian restaurants. My brother thoughtfully selected an American rock café meant to resemble the Hard Rock Café. After Korean-style family meals, it felt strange for each person to be handed separate menus, silverware, and individual plates of food. Like a good sport, my brother ordered the "American platter"—a hamburger patty, frozen yellow corn, and cold canned pork and beans. John and I grimaced at his plate of food. My *oppa* wanted to give us a taste of home, but we had grown to prefer the food and style of eating of Korea. We would take *bulgogi* and *kimchee* over a hamburger any day.

Throughout the meal, I studied my brother in his new role as father and husband, warmed by this new aspect of our relationship. Regardless of his lies, I knew that his intentions were good—even if I didn't agree with his tactics.

Gyung-hee, who was embarrassed to speak English in front of us, apologized many times before building up enough courage to say what was on her mind.

"Katy and John, I am so happy to finally meet you. *Oppa* has told me so much about you. Since you have come to Korea, Katy, *Oppa*'s heart has been filled with happiness."

Before we parted, my brother handed me a copy of my mother's family register as if he had been reading my mind.

"Here," he said casually, without mentioning the documents by name.

I took it as a gesture of closure, ending one chapter of our relationship before moving on to the next.

"Katy, I wish for you to meet my mom," he then said. "She is anxious to meet you and wants to have you and John to our house for Lunar New Year. She wants you to spend the night at our house—if you feel comfortable."

John and I happily (and nervously) accepted the invitation.

"Erasing" my mother had opened the way for me to finally meet his mother.

Lunar New Year was by far the most important holiday in Korea— like Christmas and New Year combined into one day, along with everyone's birthday. In the true spirit of "the group" over the individual, Koreans celebrated a universal birthday. Regardless of their actual date of birth, everyone grew a year older on Lunar New Year. No expenditure of money or energy was considered too great in preparing for this occasion, and the entire city bustled with activity in the days before the national three-day holiday. Everywhere we went we saw elaborate flower arrangements, special wine and liquor sets, and gift baskets of fruit, rice cakes, and cookies displayed in shop windows.

We knew that my brother's family would take extra care preparing for our first visit to their home. We were also aware of the Korean tendency to spend too much, relative to their means, so as not to offend guests or appear less successful than they wished to appear. John and I would be treated like royal guests in accordance with unsurpassable Korean hospitality. We were honored to be inducted into *Oppa*'s family and excited to get a true taste of Korean culture, but we grew nervous as the big day approached. The culmination of all of the twists and discoveries about my Korean family hinged around this woman who was my father's first wife, the mother of my half brother and sister, Kang-san's beloved *halmoni,* and now, my surrogate Korean mother. I worried about her reaction. Would I remind her of my mother, the young mistress responsible for breaking up her marriage? Her discomfort would be understandable, as was mine.

We prepared for the momentous visit by walking all over the

city to select gifts for each member of the family. We bought a box of cream-filled chocolates for Gyung-hee, English picture cards for Kang-san, English conversation books and tapes for my sister, a Dave Matthews CD for my brother, and a bouquet of yellow flowers for his mother. Lastly, we bought a chocolate cake for dessert. We found the most expensive bakery and chose the largest round cake in the display case, one decorated with long slivers of dark chocolate sitting atop sugary white frosting. We had heard how in Korea, the wrapping and presentation of gifts were almost more important than the contents, so we searched stores around our neighborhood for wrapping paper and bows.

That morning, I took an extra-long time getting ready, feeling almost as nervous as I had been the day I met my father. I had a sneaking suspicion that I would be examined under a microscope and wanted to make a good impression for my brother's mother, whom I referred to simply as "the grandmother," since I could not bring myself to call her my mother. I went to the unusual bother of curling my long hair, putting on extra makeup, and choosing an outfit that would make me look slim, as was befitting a Korean woman. My nervousness soon rubbed off on John, who had the added pressure of not understanding or speaking Korean. Also, as an American and my husband, he would be elevated to a higher status and be put on display—something I knew he dreaded. With frayed nerves, we set off on the bus and subway loaded with our gifts, cake, and overnight bag.

The grandmother greeted us at the doorway rubbing her hands on her flowered apron. *"Ii-ee-go!"* she screeched. "Is this our Ji-yun-ah? *Yea-puh-yo!* Very pretty, so thin, so tall. *Ii-ee-go!"* She grabbed both sides of my waist and pinched the skin, stroked my hair, and lifted my chin to examine my face more closely. As she continued uttering a string of loud compliments, I caught a flash of pain cross her face and her eyes glistened momentarily. But she quickly smiled and laughed as she led me by the hand into her house.

It was easy to tell that she had been a beauty when, as a young woman barely out of her teens, she married my father. Now sixty-one, she still had a lovely young face that was a perfect oval covered in shiny, smooth, white skin and thick black curly hair pulled back at each side in barrettes. Her full red lips gathered in a natural pucker that highlighted her high cheekbones. Her large round eyes held a flirtatious spark when she spoke and the scooped neckline of her dress showed off her girlish figure. She was hardly the vision of the old Korean grandmother that I had in mind!

She took our bags and coats and stared at the chocolate cake with a funny expression on her face before carrying it out to the back porch like a sack of laundry. We sat on a couch in the main room of the house, where she continued to size me up by patting my thighs and squeezing my wrists. "Oh, you are too skinny! Oh, you are too cold. *Ii-ee-go!*" She jumped up and cranked up the heat in the already toasty room. Her zealousness made us laugh with affection and a little bewilderment. After she had squeezed all the appropriate limbs of my body, the grandmother moved on to John—the first American, we were certain, to grace her home. "John is so handsome," she said, examining his sharp profile, stopping at his large pointed nose. She stared at him curiously, then let out a teasing laugh.

After our inspections were over, she hopped up from the couch and began serving us. She unfolded a low lacquered table in the middle of the room and instructed us to sit on the floor. A cousin, who had lived in the States and spoke English, had been invited to join us and help translate for my brother. While we sat around and visited with the cousin, the two women— Gyung-hee and the grandmother—shuffled back and forth from the tiny kitchen to the family room like two servants in a palace. Soon a procession of Korean dishes decorated our table. Green onion pancakes, braised *bulgogi* beef, *chop-chae* clear noodles with vegetables, batter-fried zucchini slices, meat-filled steamed dumplings, spicy tofu soup, homemade cabbage-and-radish *kim-chees,* and a tray of expensive sashimi (sliced raw fish), which the cousin had brought as his gift. Our cousin, my brother, and Kang-san eagerly delved into the sashimi like my family at home ate chocolate-chip cookies. It was then that I realized with embarrassment that our gifts had been a total flop. We had selected all the wrong things—especially the box of chocolates and cake. How could I have forgotten my own aversion to the overly rich sweets that I had first encountered in America? For years, my American mother had substituted fresh fruit pies for my birthday cake, which I was unaccustomed to eating. But over the years, my family converted me into a certified chocoholic. I realized too late that a better gift would have been expensive liquor, fresh fruit, rice cakes, or this sashimi.

We chased down bites of delicious food with a potent Korean wine as new dishes continued to arrive at the already colorful table. While the women ran back and forth, my brother barked orders to the kitchen to bring more dipping sauce, glasses of beer, more of this and that, until I grew embarrassed and made my way into the kitchen. I found my two female in-laws squatting on the floor of the cramped kitchen chopping vegetables and frying Korean pancakes on a portable gas burner. The grandmother's rhythmic chopping and the sizzle and crackle of oil filled the room. Every inch of available space was occupied by some essential ingredient of a Korean kitchen—strings of dried fish and red chili peppers, jars of ginseng roots and other medicinal herbs, pots of barley tea, marinating soup bones, sheets of dried seaweed, and most importantly, two enormous rice cookers busy at work in opposite corners of the room. Baskets and trays of food covered the floor and table and spilled out on to a small balcony.

Gyung-hee explained that they were preparing enough food for the next day as well. It looked like enough food to feed us for a month.

"Can I help you cook?" I asked shyly.

The grandma sized up my soft hands and looked up at me with amusement before directing me to kneel by the cutting board on the floor. She was slicing long tubes of rice cake, which would be put into the soup traditionally eaten on New Year's Day. She demonstrated how to slice the rubbery tubes at a forty-five-degree angle, then handed me the large butcher knife. I was thrilled to be put to work, but the grandmother quickly grew impatient at my slow pace. Either that or she was worried I would slice off a finger with her sharp knife and mess up her kitchen. She laughed and snatched the knife away, giving me a light shove out of the kitchen and telling me to *mogo, mogo*— eat, eat! For a brief moment, I felt like a failure but was relieved to escape back to the living room, where all I had to do was eat until my stomach bulged out happily.

During the weekend, we never saw my brother step foot into the kitchen, even to retrieve his own glass of water. And the two women never left the kitchen, except for a brief minute when my brother ordered his mother to sit down and have a drink of beer with us.

She took a gulp and released a deep burp before addressing me. "Ji-yun-ah, think of me as your mother now."

She waited for my response with what I guessed was a look of pity in her eyes. I was sure my brother had told her the same story about my mother dying alone, without even a burial site for me to visit. I swallowed the urge to tell her that I didn't need her to be my mother—I was still searching.

When I remained silent, she continued with a laugh, "Please

visit us often. Maybe you and John can stay an extra night? Yes, you must stay another night and come again—maybe next weekend. Please eat, eat some more, *mogo, mogo.*"

I wanted to give her a compliment and express our gratitude in her own language, but my Korean, which had been steadily improving until then, suddenly became a jumble. I couldn't remember the most basic phrases. "Thank you. You are very beautiful," I tried to tell her.

She laughed and slapped her thigh as she corrected my Korean. "*Moshisoyo,* not *mashisoyo!*" (I had just told her she was delicious.) "You must study hard so we can talk to each other one day. I am too old to learn English, so you must learn Korean quickly."

I nodded, deciding not to attempt any more Korean and vowing to study harder. I let our cousin take over as translator. "Out of all of my aunts, she is my favorite," he said, smiling at the blushing grandmother. "Don't you think she is beautiful? Your sister looks exactly like her mother and your brother looks exactly like your father. That is why our side of the family hates your brother." He laughed.

Even though my sister lived in the house with my brother, his family, and their mother, she remained strangely absent during the time John and I were there (which was particularly odd, given the family holiday). I guessed that she had been against telling their mother about me.

My sister was the only one in the house who had a Western-style bed and we were directed to sleep in her room. The apartment was located on the second floor of a run-down complex decorated with hanging laundry and pots of garlic and green onions set out on porches and balconies. It consisted of two small bedrooms occupied by my sister and the grandmother, a kitchen, a bathroom that doubled as a laundry room, and a central family room that served multiple functions as the eating, gathering, and sleeping area. After an afternoon and evening of continuous eating, the lacquered table was folded up and set against a wall. The women raced to wipe the floor on their hands and knees and brought out a pile of thick quilts that would serve as a bed for my brother and his wife.

Before going to bed, Kang-san practiced his newly acquired English skills loudly enough for the neighbors to hear. He arranged new vocabulary words that he'd learned from flash cards into phrases that garnered a great deal of laughter. "I'm a handsome boy!" he screeched. "My ugly father. My fat aunt Katy! Monkey Uncle John."

Each night, Kang-san slept on the floor with his grandmother in an adjoining room. "If I wasn't there next to her, *Halmoni* wouldn't be able to go to sleep," he whispered.

I glanced at the room with a feeling of envy as I remembered sleeping on the floor with my own *halmoni*. Although she was different from Kang-san's grandmother, we had been just as close.

A stranger viewing my *halmoni* for the first time might see a harsh, almost cynical look engraved into her face. She was not the type of Korean *halmoni* to pat her grandchildren with exaggerated worry or overaffection, starting each sentence with a high-pitched *Ii-ee-go! Ii-ee-go!* while clucking her tongue and shaking her head. She displayed little emotion—never raised her voice, yelled, or cried, at least never in front of me. She was not wrinkled and frail like many grandmothers, who were permanently hunched over from years of squatting on their heels and stooping over to cook, clean, and scrub laundry on wooden washboards propped against the floor. Neither was she delicate or beautiful like my mother. But there was something enormously comforting about her rough hands.

Images of my *halmoni* drifted back and forth in my mind like a lazy wave: snuggling next to her on a warm floor under a heavy quilt. Riding on her back when I was too sick to play outside. Clasping her hand when we ventured into the streets of Seoul. In our own neighborhood, she often sent me around the corner to buy a bag of yellow-headed soybean sprouts shaped like music notes—*kongnamul*. We both squealed in delight the day she found a sparkling silver coin nestled in among the sprouts. "*Aiee yah!* This is a sign of good luck," she said, patting my head. From that day on, we always checked our sacks of sprouts for lucky coins.

I still find myself checking sacks of vegetables.

The next morning, I awoke at 5 A.M. to the sound of the grandmother washing in the bathroom. I pictured her squatting on the floor, scrubbing her face, hands, and feet from a series of plastic buckets containing cold water. The sound of her clearing out each nostril, then hawking on the floor like a man echoed throughout the house and made me giggle under the sheets. Soon the clatter of pots and pans and the sizzle of her cooking wafted in from the kitchen and filled the house. As I lay in bed listening to the sounds of my brother's house come alive, I was filled with a range of emotions tugging at me in all directions. There was a feeling of distant familiarity and the amazement of waking up in a Korean household. I was overwhelmed with gratitude for the way my brother and his family had adopted us as their family. But there was also a sense of discomfort, like we were putting on a show. Our conversations swerved around the topics of my adoption and American family, and of course, the fate of my Korean mother. Throughout the weekend, I had the urge to pull Gyung-hee aside and ask, "So tell me, what *really* happened to my mother?" I came close to asking several times, but didn't want to put her in an impossible position.

An hour later, when John and I stepped out of the bedroom, the grandmother was already setting up the meal table in the middle of the room.

"Oh, you must be so hungry!"

She must have thought we had tapeworms. The thought of more food this early in the morning turned my stomach, since I was still full from the night before. "No," I insisted with a smile. "John and I don't usually eat breakfast."

"What? *Ii-ee-go!* How can you not eat breakfast?" she asked in horror. "Don't you know it's unhealthy to skip a meal? How can you give birth to a healthy baby if you skip breakfast? *Mogo! Mogo!*"

After affectionately scolding his mother, my brother encouraged us to eat a small portion of *ddok guk,* the rice-cake soup eaten on New Year's Day. For Koreans, breakfast consisted of the same foods eaten at lunch and dinner—a bowl of rice, *kimchee,* and soup. John and I took deep breaths and tried to make room in our ballooning stomachs. We took our seats on the floor and were served two huge steaming bowls of soup. I recognized the slices of rice cake the grandma had chopped the day before sitting in a light broth flavored with strips of seasoned beef, scallions, minced garlic, toasted sesame seeds, and strips of toasted seaweed. The rich aroma tempted, and eventually won over, our reluctant appetites. But she didn't stop there. Bowls of *kimchee,* rice, and other dishes soon filled our table as we held our stomachs and groaned at the feast being thrust upon us. It was a wonder so many Koreans remained so skinny with such doting and food-obsessed mothers.

While we ate, Gyung-hee helped her mother-in-law prepare a picnic for the graveside ceremony. We were driving to the countryside to visit our ancestors' graves, we were told, and to meet other relatives for a picnic. My brother explained how on New Year's Day, Koreans performed a ceremony at the graves of male descendants' parents and grandparents, which were usually located next to each other. Because of our family's unique situation, we would visit the graves of my brother's *maternal* grandparents. The absence of a father created endless complications and opportunities for shame in the patriarchal Korean customs and ceremonies. Our father's betrayal was continually thrust in the faces of his children and former wife, reminding them of their demoted status in society.

After breakfast, we loaded boxes of food into a rented van and drove for about an hour outside the city until we reached open pastures and hills. We saw dozens of Korean families—the women and children dressed in colorful *hanboks*—walking up the mountain and dotting the golden hillside. Families gathered at the foot of their ancestors' graves, which formed rows of oblong mounds covered in dry grass and colorful wildflowers. We joined the crowds hiking up the mountain and met distant relatives from the grandmother's side of the family. My brother introduced me as his sister and I felt a pang of guilt for any embarrassment I may have unintentionally caused the grandma. Everyone in her family would recognize me as the mistress's daughter.

While the men chatted, the women prepared a makeshift altar at the foot of the two graves. They spread out a blanket and arranged the specially prepared foods according to complex ancient customs. Red food was placed toward the east; white toward the west. The women carefully peeled the tops off pears and apples and stacked them into pyramids on both sides of the blanket. They set out plates of whole fried fish, colored rice cakes, marinated and fried beef strips, tempura vegetables, round ginseng cookies, peeled raw chestnuts, and the other foods I had seen the grandmother prepare the day before. A glass of *makkoli,* a milky-white rice liquor, was poured for each of the ancestors. Long sticks of incense were lit and placed in the middle of the altar. When the ceremonial table was prepared, we waited for the oldest male relative to arrive, since only he could lead the official ceremony. Finally, several men dressed in black robes arrived and began the ritual. First, the leader bowed twice before the altar, lowering his forehead flat to the ground. He then poured the liquor over the grave and bowed twice more, joined by the rest of the males. Finally, the entire group bowed together two more times.

After the solemn ceremony, the mood quickly changed to that of a festive picnic and family reunion. Relatives caught up on one another's lives and gossiped as the eating and drinking began in full fervor. Everyone took off their shoes and arranged themselves on blankets around plates of food. Just then the afternoon sun broke through the hazy sky and released warm rays of sunshine on our cool faces. Amazingly, I found myself grazing on the tasty food once again—and enjoying it with renewed appetite. Home-brewed jugs of *makkoli* passed freely among both the men and women. All over the grassy hillside, groups of families shared food and drink while children chased one another between rows of burial mounds.

As I took in the vibrant scene, I could not remember the last time I had visited a cemetery back home. In America, graveyards were haunted and creepy places—definitely not sites for a picnic! We also did not honor or remember the dead with such comfort and vitality. But maybe it was time to change my own perception of death and graveyards. I made a silent vow to visit my grandpa Art's grave when I returned home and perhaps even pour him a shot of Irish whisky.

As we prepared to leave, the sight of a traditional-looking *haraboji,* or grandfather, with a long, shaggy white beard and thinning gray hair made his way down the mountain. He was dressed in a white male *hanbok* vest and rounded baggy pants that hung from his hips. The dignified elderly Korean man fit the grandfather mold perfectly as he walked down the steep mountain with the aid of a long wooden stick. But just before I turned my head away, I saw him drop the stick, slip on a bright yellow helmet, rev the engine, and zoom away on a motorcycle.

On the way home, the grandmother held her head and moaned, "I drank too much." But the liquor eased the way for other pains as well. She began sobbing and speaking in a sharp voice that differed from the light demeanor she had shown before. As she spoke in rapid Korean, I made out my Korean name, a reference to my father, and a few other angry words scattered here and there. When Kang-san saw his *halmoni*'s tears, his own eyes clouded over and he became silent. Right then, I wished I could disappear and ease her pain.

My brother stared at his mother silently through his rearview mirror, his eyes begging her to stop. When we got home, she went straight to her bedroom and slammed the door.

"Is she okay?" I asked *Oppa*.

"She was remembering the past with our father. When I think about what our father did to women not once, but twice or more times, I really hate him." My brother spoke with disgust in his voice in a rare moment of honesty. "I made a vow in life never to be like our father."

"Our mother doesn't like your father," Gyung-hee said with a nervous laugh. "Maybe she hates him."

"Our father was very popular with women when he was younger," my brother explained as Gyung-hee translated his words. "Our father was much sought after. He was a good catch—the youngest of four children from a wealthy family. He graduated from Korea University, the most prestigious university at that time. He owned his own business and was successful and handsome."

I felt the bond with my brother grow stronger with each word he spoke about our father—the man responsible for connecting us by the same paternal blood coursing through our veins. And with each description and newly discovered fact, my father began to take on new dimensions. I had encapsulated him into a regretful old man estranged from his children. But where I saw an old man with a *kimchee* stain on his tie had once been a brilliant, handsome man with the world at his fingertips. I tried to imagine my father as the baby of the family, college student, eligible bachelor, husband, and lover.

As a sullen mood settled over us, Gyung-hee pulled out an old family album and opened to wedding photographs of her mother-in-law and my father. The first photograph was a storybook image of a Korean bride and groom on their wedding day. My father was a strikingly handsome thirty-year-old with thick, jet-black hair slicked back from his wide forehead in a loose wave. His face was finely chiseled, with a sharp chin and long stately nose, his sparkling dark eyes brimming with quiet self-confidence. His full lips froze somewhere between a smile and a snicker. His picture-perfect wife was more than ten years his junior. A cascade of long black hair, piled high on her head and loosely curled at the ends, framed the young bride's face. I recognized the grandmother's same beautiful oval face and full lips. She looked so frightened, and a little sad, standing there next to my tall father in his dark pinstripe suit and white gloves.

The couple had not fallen in love on their own. As was the custom in those days, their marriage was arranged by a matchmaker hired by the families. Once the two families agreed to the terms of the arrangement, the bride had no choice but to follow the orders and, in effect, relinquish relationships with her side of the family. From that day on, she would devote her life to her husband's family until she had a son of her own. But my father's first wife had no reason to be dissatisfied at first. After the wedding, the couple moved into their own apartment, located on the top floor of one of the tallest buildings in downtown Seoul, where my father operated his clothing export business. And since my father was the youngest son, the bride was not burdened with the responsibility of caring for her in-laws and suffering the notorious cruelty of mother-in-laws that every young Korean woman feared. That job fell to the wife of the eldest son.

But hints of a gloomy future appeared soon enough, Gyung-hee said. "During the first week of their marriage, a young woman came to our mother's door, crying and demanding to see your father. Our mom always says that was the first sign of bad luck."

The image of my father's old lover coming to the door turned to thoughts of my own mother and how she must have felt when she learned she was pregnant. And later, when she realized that my father was not going to marry her.

"Our father—a playboy." My brother interrupted my thoughts, shaking his head. "Many women liked him, so he became—what is the word? An egotist! He is still an egotist."

We turned the page of the album and came to a photograph that captured a lifetime of emotion frozen into a single, still moment. It was a family portrait that at first glance appeared to be the vision of a perfect, wealthy family. But upon closer examination, I noticed that sitting next to her confident husband, the now older bride wore the same frightened, sad expression she had worn on her wedding day. But instead of youthful, she now looked matronly next to her three young children. Her face had filled out and she wore her hair cut short around her face. Tiny lines were etched around her mouth. My brother and his twin looked into the camera with their hair combed back into the same wave as their father's and their ears sticking out from their heads. Their older sister, my *unnee*, wore a scowl on her face, which was framed on both sides by long, neat braids with ribbons tied at the ends. Her eyebrows furrowed in a way that made her appear older than she was.

My brother laughed and shook his head when he saw the photograph. I picked up the album to take a closer look and wanted to weep for this family that was going to be destroyed. I wanted to wipe that confident smirk from my father's face and comfort the young woman in the photo, the woman who now welcomed the child of her husband's mistress into her home. I had helped reopen old wounds that had never fully healed. How could they, in a society that revolved around husbands and fathers?

We heard the grandmother cough from the next room.

"Please don't mention your father around her," Gyung-hee pleaded. "Or around your sister."

Later that evening, we completed the New Year's celebration with our *sae-bae,* or ceremonial bows, to honor living parents and grandparents. We had heard young people refer to the yearly custom fondly as collecting their "bow rebates," since children received envelopes of money—their *sae bae tone*—after performing their bows. In our case, an exception was made and we received our bow rebates even though we were beyond the acceptable age. The grandmother positioned herself at one end of the family room, sitting cross-legged on the floor. Kang-san went first, bowing respectfully to the ground as we had done before the graves earlier that day, followed by his parents, then us. After each bow, the proud grandma handed each of us a long white envelope filled with wide green Korean bills.

After the *sae-bae,* we played *yoot*—one of the most popular

Korean games for all ages, traditionally played on New Year's Day. The game was played with four wooden sticks, carved so that one side was flat, the other rounded. Players took turns throwing the sticks into the air, then adding up the points depending on how the sticks landed. While we played the game with Kang-san and *Oppa,* the women continued to serve us refreshments of rice punch and sliced fruit.

To everyone's secret relief, John and I politely refused the invitation to stay an extra night even as the grandma insisted with renewed vigor. She would not let us leave until we sat down for yet another meal. That was not negotiable. Just before we left, the grandma grabbed my arm.

"Ji-yun-ah, why don't you and John have a baby yet?"

I'd already learned my lesson, so instead of answering her question, I laughed uncomfortably, hoping that would suffice for an answer.

But she was undaunted. "The next time you come to Korea, I want you to come with an *agi,* a baby!" she demanded while pinching my arm for emphasis.

19

Dear Katy,
    My mom-in-law was very happy to meet you.
    She thanks you for growing-up as good lady.
    And she thanks John for loving you.
    She wanted talk to you a lot of things.
I think that she sympathizes with you.
I think, because she had a hard time in past.
So, she considers you as a daughter.
She is not your blood mother, but I wish you think her as your another mother.
But, I don't want to force you. Just remember she very very loves you.

                         —Gyung-hee

Katy, I need more time to think about our father.
I think that all of us (you, sister, and me) had not a good thought about our father.
But let us try to understand him.

I think, maybe all parents' mind is the same.

—Oppa

My brother asked us to keep our visit to his house a secret from our father. I had little choice but to agree, but that secret was the beginning of more to come. And those deliberate deletions, along with many more unspoken thoughts, widened the gulf between my father and me until we were like strangers again. For every timid step we took closer, we drifted two steps apart, as if pulled back by a wave of regrets and silent accusations.

I guessed that my brother had told him the same story about my mother's death as he told me. But my father did not mention it or offer condolences, as he had done the first time. If he brought up the subject of my mother, how could he explain his earlier insistence that she was alive and not married?

As each meeting became more strained, my father began relying on a "cup of courage" from under a sidewalk *soju* tent to get him through. It was easy to recognize the evidence of these outings on my father's face. The puffy red flush of his cheeks, along with his potent breath and frequent trips to the toilet, became a regular greeting when he arrived at our door. Even so, he never failed to bring a gift—a bouquet of white lilies, a stack of plastic bowls, or a sack of grapes. The value of the gifts increased with our level of tension, as if the gifts could express what my father could not.

On this day, my father knocked at our door with a portable radio-and-cassette player. He rushed to our bed and gestured for John to come examine his gift.

"John, English station here," he said, turning the dial until "Oh Susie Q, baby, I love you" blasted from the old radio. He laughed and his smile became wider as John bowed and thanked him. He then pulled out a wall calendar from a plastic bag and handed it to me with disappointment on his face when he noticed we already had one hanging on the wall. As I accepted his gifts, I wanted to hug him and bring a smile to his lips, as I knew I could. I wanted to tell him about the wedding pictures I had seen and ask him about his life. What had his childhood been like, his parents, his time in the army and the Korean War, his marriage, his first wife and his three children? I longed to uncover the handsome, confident man I had seen in those photographs and understand what had made my mother fall in love with him.

But we sat quietly, studying each other until I broke the silence.

"John, why don't you take a picture of me and my father?"

My father's eyes lit up and he jumped from the bed to straighten his plaid scarf around his wool coat. He licked his three middle fingers and patted his already smooth hair while standing in front of our full-length mirror. He then repeated the process, primping and preening like an actor about to take center stage. As I watched his reflection in the mirror, I tried to picture the handsome gentleman who had broken so many hearts. He was the same cocky man, yet now old and alone. The formerly thick wave of his greased hair was still the same jet-black color, but now slightly thinner and limp across his lined forehead. For the first time, I noticed how the thinning circle on the back of his head had become discolored to a coppery brown (as if he were suffering from a bad dye job). Properly groomed, he turned around for the photograph with a stately look on his face, his mouth pulled into his characteristic long line across his face. He reached out for me to stand next to him until our shoulders touched and our fingertips brushed.

"One more." He gestured to John to take another picture, then another.

After the pictures, we resumed our previous quiet until he got up and said, "I go now."

At the doorway, he turned around with a strained smile on his face. *"Bo-po."* He pointed to his cheek and said, "Give Daddy a kiss." I brushed my lips against his cheek like a reluctant child following orders. As I turned away, he grabbed both my shoulders, pulled me toward him, and planted his lips on mine with a loud, exaggerated smack of dry lips.

"Ah, like this," he said with a laugh. As he noticed the startled expression on my face, the smile dropped from his face and he quickly shut the door behind him.

That night I had a dream about my father. It was his birthday—perhaps *hwangap*, his important sixtieth birthday, when Koreans believe a person has completed his full life cycle. At first, I worried about who would plan his celebration, because not observing the symbolic event would be a shame too great for anyone to bear. But I discovered that someone else had already planned the party. I went to the ceremony in his honor and saw him from across the room, sitting cross-legged on the floor with his long back curved over like the neck of a goose. His back was toward me and I couldn't see his face, but I knew that it was my father from the tightening knot in my chest. Then I saw a wooden table where an aged book sat open. When I walked over to the book, I discovered long columns of names and realized that my father had written down his family history for all to see. Nothing detailed, just a long list of secret wives and children, and more children we had never known about. As I read the names, I was ashamed of my father's life and our blemished family history laid open for all to read.

I glared frantically at my brother, who in reply shrugged his shoulders, as if to ask, "What can I do about it?"

I studied the book once again, but this time I was filled with relief at finally discovering the remaining secrets of my father's life. I felt an intense burden lift.

Suddenly I was in the middle of the celebration, being introduced to a line of children. A little girl with long hair and familiar dark eyes looked up at me curiously. As I took her slender hand, I thought to myself, "Oh, you are one of my father's daughters."

But the girl and I never spoke before I awoke.

That same night, when I went back to sleep, I had another dream, this time about my Korean mother. In the dream, I was sitting on a bed beside my uncle—my mother's older brother whose name was listed on the family register. I begged him to help me find my mother.

"Please, you have to help me," I cried. "What child does not have a right to meet her own mother? Please."

At first, he pretended not to know where she lived, but finally gave in to my pleading. He resolutely picked up the phone and dialed a number while I waited by his side. I could hear a muffled voice on the other end and knew that it belonged to my mother. As I heard the echo of her angry words, I realized my worst fear was coming true.

"Why are you bothering me?" I heard her tell my uncle. "You know I don't want to see her. I can't . . . ruin my life . . . Don't call again."

The line went dead.

The scene shifted from Korea to John's and my home in Boise. I was walking down the street with John, sobbing uncontrollably into his chest. He led me by the arm as I hid my face from people we knew for fear they would ask me about Korea and whether or not I had found my mother. I was too ashamed to tell them the truth, that my mother did not want to meet me.

I awoke the next morning with wet tears still rolling down

my face. When I realized it was just a dream, I made the decision to write to my uncle myself. Perhaps I could persuade him to help me, like in the dream.

Dear Mr. Lee,

My name is Katy Robinson, but you may know me as Kim Ji-yun, your niece who was adopted to the United States twenty-two years ago. I am now twenty-eight years old and have returned to Korea to learn about the place where I was born and lived for the first seven years of my life. You may already know that a part of my journey home is concerned with searching for information about my mother and grandmother. I feel, at this point, that you are the only person left who may be able to tell me about their well-being. I understand that my mother, your sister Kyung-woo, is probably married and built a new life for herself after I left. It is not my intention to disrupt her life and current family situation. I would simply like her to know that I grew up well and give her the opportunity to meet me someday if she wishes. I also would like to thank my mother for the sacrifice she made to give me a better life, and I hope with all my heart that she too was able to create a new beginning for herself, as I did.

I have many memories of my childhood in Korea, especially the loving care of my grandmother. I remember the kung namul *soup she made when I was sick, her carrying me outside on her back, and the pink* hanbok *she brought to the orphanage for my trip to America. One of my last memories is saying good-bye to my mother and grandmother at the airport.*

I long to meet my mother and grandmother if it is possible. I do not know what kind of memories or feelings you may have for me. I only reach out to you with the hope that you may find it in your heart to help me.

—Your niece,
Kim Ji-yun

Just as I finished writing the letter, the phone rang.

"I have not yet heard back from your uncle, but I have been in touch with your aunt," Mr. Sim announced. "I have her phone number and you can call her yourself if you would like. Her name is Sunny and she speaks English very well. She is expecting your call."

20

My heart pounded as Mr. Sim read the phone number. My aunt and my mother's sister—finally, I had a tangible physical link to my Korean mother within my grasp. Her flesh and blood. Surely her own sister would know what happened to her, regardless of what my brother said. Besides, my aunt couldn't be indifferent to my mother and her fate if she had responded to Mr. Sim's letter and wanted to talk to me. Just when I was ready to give up hope, this was the sign I needed to continue.

I gazed at the phone number and tried to summon the courage to call her. I wondered what kind of reception I would get and what she would tell me about my mother. What if my aunt commanded me to stay out of my mother's life? What if she confirmed her death? I remembered my brother's warning and knew that contacting my mother's relatives directly was a bold move. Each step I took closer to my mother increased the risk of rejection or of some unexpected discovery that might shatter my fantasy of her.

For six days, I studied the phone number.

Finally, I dialed the number, halfway hoping that no one would answer.

"*Yobo-sayo?*" a female Korean voice answered.

"Hello." I cleared my throat and felt my face turn hot. "Is Sunny there?"

Silence.

"This is Katy. I think Mr. Sim called you about me?"

More silence. I wondered if my aunt really was expecting my call or if Mr. Sim had made that up. I was getting ready to hang up the phone when a sleepy voice finally replied.

"Oh yes." She spoke more excitedly now. "I was so shocked to hear that I am an auntie!"

It was funny how much younger she sounded when she spoke English instead of Korean. Her English was perfect and laced with an Australian accent. I wondered if Mr. Sim had found the right person.

"You know I don't really know your mother," she said.

"Oh." My heart fell with her words.

"I mean, I guess she *is* my sister—but only a half sister. We have the same father but different mothers."

"Oh."

"Your grandfather married your grandmother and had your mom and a son. I think their son died, so your grandfather left your grandmother. At least that's what my mom told me when I told her about you and that I was an auntie."

My head was spinning with excitement; each word she spoke was another piece of the puzzle. "So my grandfather is your father, right?"

"Right."

"But you never knew my mother?"

Click. The line went dead. I tried calling again, but got busy signals. I waited in agony while I sorted through the new revelations about my mother and her family. Thirty minutes later, the phone rang.

"Hi, it's me. Sorry, we were talking on my cell phone and the battery died. I had to call Mr. Sim to get your phone number. Anyway, what was I saying?"

"My mother—"

"No, I never met her. I think your mother is quite a bit older than I am because I'm only twenty-eight."

"That's the same age as me," I said, stunned. How could I have an aunt who was my age? Before, I had pictured a typical Korean aunt, an *ajuma* with curly hair and a loud-patterned blouse and slippers.

"I know, it's a bit confusing, isn't it? But I'm still your auntie, so you have to show me proper respect." She laughed. "Anyway, doll," she continued in an Aussie drawl, "after your grandfather left your grandmother, he met my mom and they had me. But he left us when I was three and I haven't seen him in— let's see—more than ten years? He moved on to God only knows how many other women. He's a no-good Korean bastard, you could say."

Her bluntness startled me.

"Sorry, but it's true!" she said.

Her manner of speaking was so un-Korean and such a refreshing change. I felt my earlier nervousness fade away as I said the first thing that came to mind. "That sounds just like *my* father! I came to Korea and discovered that he has children by three different women. Can you believe my father is seventy-two years old and has two *teenage* children? He was married before and had children who are my half brother and sister. Then he had an affair with my mom and had me. He left us and got married and had more children. Both sides of my Korean family sound so crazy, but everyone keeps telling me that it is very rare for Korean men to have more than one wife."

"Rare—yeah, right. I'm afraid not, doll. Listen, what are you doing today? I live in Taejon, which is about four hours away. But I was planning to come into Seoul today anyway, so why don't we meet? If you want. I'll make my boyfriend, Eric, come with me."

"Yes! I would love to meet you."

"Okay, then, can you meet me at the train station? I think there is a train that gets in around four-thirty. I'll be with Eric. He's American. Let's meet by the McDonald's inside the station, okay?"

A glamorous woman dressed in leopardskin boots waved to me from across the train station.

"Katy? I'm your auntie!" she said, and gave me a hug.

My aunt's physical appearance took me as much by surprise as her Australian accent had on the phone. Her long hair was streaked with brown-and-gold highlights and hung down her back in a fashionable shag style cut into the shape of a *V*. The most striking feature was her eyes, lightened by colored contact lenses so that they glowed with a golden catlike hue. I guessed that she had undergone the popular cosmetic surgery to create a "doublelid" above her eyes, which otherwise closely resembled mine. When I first arrived in Korea, I was shocked to discover how many Koreans resorted to cosmetic surgery to give their eyes a rounder, more Western appearance. There also was surgery to make noses appear pointed and faces more narrow (by shaving down the cheekbones). This obsession to look more Western was the last thing I had expected to see in Korea, which was so proud of its unique culture. But the surgery was practically de rigueur for models, actors, and anyone else who wanted to be considered beautiful by modern standards. My aunt fit the mold of modern beauty in every way. Above her modified eyes, her eyebrows were plucked almost bare, and in their place, dark sloping lines were drawn in. Her outlined lips were filled in with frosty lipstick. Befitting the rest of her style, she wore a form-fitting white cotton blouse, tight black stretch pants, and leo-pardskin half-boots topped with white fur around the ankles.

In my jeans and denim shirt, I towered above her.

"I knew it was you as soon as I saw your nose!" she said. "My mother told me, just look for the family nose—it will be exactly like yours!"

I was astonished to discover that her mother had been right. At first glance, we looked nothing alike. But under all of her makeup, we shared the same small flat nose and oval-shaped face. In fact, our resemblance was so uncanny that we could have passed as sisters. We laughed at each other's nose—our family trait—and hugged again. We walked arm in arm to the train-station McDonald's, where we met John and Sunny's boyfriend Eric. Sunny and her American boyfriend made quite a pair, es-pecially in a conformist society like Korea. Eric, a New York native, sported a biker-style black leather jacket, an earring in his right ear, and a bandanna around his balding head. His long blond ponytail hung down his back. Eric and Sunny had met at a university where they both taught English.

"I was so relieved that you spoke English," I told her.

"Well, Eric always corrects my grammar, but I think I speak pretty well. I lived in Australia for eight years and first learned to speak English there."

After a while, Sunny and I pulled out our respective copies of our family register so we could compare information. We unfolded the papers that traced the family lineage of my grand-father—Sunny and my mother's father. She had an older and thicker version of the document, which contained Chinese characters written in long vertical rows. She translated their meaning and pointed to various boxes.

"So this is your grandfather here, and his first wife—your grandmother. This is your mother. My papers are so old and faded that I can't read all of it. Let me see yours." She took my copy and quickly flipped through the pages. I watched as her face froze and her hand began to tremble at first, then visibly shake.

"What is it?"

She swallowed several times and I saw tears form in her eyes. Finally: "This says that my father died two years ago. I didn't know."

Neither my father nor brother had said anything about my maternal grandfather. I felt bad that I hadn't known and that Sunny had to discover the news like this. I knew how it felt to receive such news and shared her grief, sharpened by the shock. I wished I could comfort her, but could think of nothing to say.

"I haven't spoken to my father for ten years," she said, wiping her eyes, "and the last time we talked, we got in a big fight. I yelled at him and told him I hated him and never wanted to see him again. He wrote to me one time after that and asked me to forgive him. But I never replied. Nobody even contacted me when he died. I don't know how I'm going to tell my mother."

Even though she was struggling to keep a grip on her emotions, I could detect the clash of anger, shock, grief, and most of all, regret. Sunny's strained relationship with her father so closely resembled mine, with both of my fathers, that it was easy to see myself in her place. I would grieve not so much for the physical presence of a father in my life, but for the missed opportunities, for not accepting my father's apology when I'd had the chance. Not making peace with him before it was too late.

I gazed at Sunny and wished I could reverse time for her.

"Did you know that your grandfather was a famous politician in Korea?" Sunny said after a long pause.

"Really?"

"Yes, during the 1970s. He had a lot of fame and money, but then lost an important election. Your mother's situation—having a baby out of wedlock with a married man—is bad today, but would have caused an even bigger scandal in those days, especially for someone like your grandfather. That's what my mother remembers hearing about your mother—the scandal. She never knew your mother, but heard about her from her husband and from other relatives."

"Has your mother heard anything else, like where my mother might be living now?"

Sunny paused for a second to study my face. "I asked her that today before I left to meet you. My mom said she thinks your mom moved to Chicago."

"Chicago—as in the United States?" A tingle of excitement shot up my spine and gathered at the back of my neck. At first, I was certain that I had not heard correctly. But then my mind filled with images of my mother riding the el in Chicago and walking along downtown streets dressed in stylish American fashion and dark sunglasses.

"Yeah, that's what my mom heard. But that was years ago, so we're not sure where she is now." Sunny's voice dropped a notch. "Your mom probably had a lot of pressure put on her, you know, to give you up for adoption. She may have been forced to move out of the country. I'm just guessing, though."

"Chicago," I repeated numbly, then raised my voice. "Wow! Here I am looking all over Korea and she could be in Chicago. Did you hear that, John—Chicago!"

John's silence communicated his doubt about this latest information.

But I wanted to believe. Even as I latched on to this latest twist, I found it annoying that Koreans never had a reliable source for their information. It was always an intuition, an implied, but not certain, truth. A belief based on folklore or something someone "heard" from an unnamed someone else. If my mother moved to Chicago, I wanted proof.

"Do you think there is any way to find out for sure if my mother moved to the States? What about her brother? Mr. Sim says he lives in Seoul and I wrote him a letter. Wouldn't he know what happened to her?"

Sunny turned the pages of the family register and found the name of the uncle to whom I referred.

"Oh, this person is not really my brother or your mother's brother. After your grandfather left my mother, he remarried and had this son by another woman. So he would be, I guess, my half brother and your mother's half brother. But chances are, he may not even know anything about your mother. I'm guessing he doesn't. That wouldn't be something the family would talk about."

"Have you ever met him?"

"No, never."

I understood now why my uncle had not responded to Mr. Sim's letter or phone call. My little branch of the family had nothing to do with him and he probably had no information about my mother. He may not even have known that she existed. My mother was like a diseased limb snipped off the family tree. I pictured what my Korean family tree might look like on a diagram—spindly branches spinning off and twisting this way and that, fostering half siblings and half relatives until the whole thing looked like a giant knot of tangled twigs and broken branches.

"Would you ever want to meet him?" I asked Sunny while thinking about my own Korean brother.

"No, I don't think so. He didn't even contact me when our father died. And now I doubt he would have anything to do with me. Oh well, I don't need him anyway. To hell with him."

"Hey, before you got Mr. Sim's letter, did anyone else try to contact you about me? My brother said he tried to call you."

"No, I never heard from anyone else."

The tragedy of a young woman falling in love with an older married man and bearing his child was becoming a familiar Korean tale, at least in my family. I learned from Sunny that her mother had been in her twenties—probably close to the same age as my mother, who would have been her stepdaughter—when she met my grandfather.

It was strange to think about my grandfather. I couldn't remember ever meeting him or even seeing him from a distance. But looking back, I did feel the financial impact of his invisible presence and eventual departure during my childhood. When I was younger, my mother, grandmother, and I had lived comfortably in a large house that had a gated backyard lined with rosebushes. One particular photograph from that time shows my grandmother dressed in a floor-length fur coat and looking robust as she held my hand. I too was dressed in a fashionable new winter coat trimmed with a black fur collar. It must have been after my grandfather left us that our resources started dwindling. We moved out of the big house. I went to live with my father's relatives in the village, and my mother and grandmother moved to an apartment in the city. There were other moves, too hazy to remember. There was a period when my grandmother and I took random jobs, one of which was to assemble tiny plastic toys, seal them in cellophane paper, and deliver them to neighborhood stores.

Now, when I passed by one of those toy shacks located across the street from elementary schools and filled with comic books, school supplies, and toys, I would remember squatting on the floor with my grandmother in front of rows of plastic parts and rubber bands. (Was it then that she commented on my fingers? "Ji-yun-ah, you have such long pretty fingers," she said. "I just know that someday you will grow up to play the piano.")

It had never occurred to me as a child that my grandmother had once been a beautiful bride, wife, and a mother. In her later years, most would describe her as handsome rather than pretty. The softest—and oldest-looking—parts of her body were her drooping breasts, which gathered in round cradles just above the waistline of her dress. I had been shocked the first time I saw the lumps of flesh dangling from her bare chest like two wrinkled eggplants.

Even as an adult, I never paused to consider the complexity of my grandmother's life. But with the information Sunny now provided, pieces of my grandmother's life began to take shape. She lost her only son, was blamed for his death, and abandoned by her husband, who left her for a younger woman almost the same age as their daughter. She then watched her own daughter continue the cycle by becoming the mistress of an older man, nearly the same age as her father.

Your father is a bad man! I heard the echo of my grandmother's voice tell me once again. No wonder she hated my father with such ferocity. She had known, even before my father did, what would become of her daughter.

How is it that mothers always know?

"Oh, Sue." I now heard Grandma Ruth's voice, as she began her familiar litany. "How I prayed to God you wouldn't marry that man. I knew as soon as I met him that he was no good for you."

I think she disliked him as much as my *halmoni* disliked my Korean father. And like *Halmoni,* Grandma Ruth was my best defense against my father's temper. No matter what he did, I could always count on her to take my side and demonstrate her disdain for my father in ingenious new ways. One Christmas, for instance, she gave my father a tin of Poppycock with a red bow on top and a cream-colored woman's sweater in a size small. She kept a straight face as she watched my father open her gift. There was a mischievous twinkle in her eyes.

My father was predictably furious. "Why does your mother even bother giving me a gift at all?" he hissed to my mom.

On several occasions, Grandma told me in secret how my mom had passed up a chance to marry an older wealthy man who had taken her to Hawaii and begged her to marry him. She shook her head at my mother's missed opportunity.

How many opportunities had my Korean mother missed because of me?

Perhaps it had been my grandmother's idea to give me up for adoption, her way of breaking the cycle and ensuring that I would not repeat the same mistakes or suffer the same punishment as the two generations of women before me. Certainly, she did not want me to grow up with the mark of shame as an illegitimate, fatherless child. My *halmoni* had wanted for me the things she could never give me in Korea. She never told me that getting married and having children (particularly a son) were the ultimate goals in life, even though that was what many Korean girls grew up believing. Instead, she preached to me about the importance of education and encouraged me to become a doctor. To get an education, she said, was the reason she was sending me to America. Perhaps because of this, I have never taken my education at any level for granted.

I saw her face once again—the determination in her eyes. Lips stretched tight across her face, enclosing everything she could not explain to me before I left. As I thought about her in this new light, I longed to run into her open arms and tell her that all of her hopes for me had come true. No, I did not learn to play the piano in America, I would tell her. But I had infinite freedom to shape the course of my life in ways unavailable to her or my mother.

I wanted to thank her for the photographs of my childhood and tell her that I never forgot.

Most of all, I wanted to take away her pain, shame, and guilt until the sloping lines of her face lifted into a carefree laugh. I wanted to take her rough hands in mine and waltz barefoot with her across a room.

John's and my day with Sunny and Eric turned into a weekend as we attempted to catch up on a lifetime. At some point during our time together, it occurred to me that Sunny was to my *halmoni* what I was to my brother's mother. How complex the concept of "blood ties" could be in a society that honored the family bond above all else. Would my grandmother welcome Sunny into her home in the same warm manner that I had been received in my brother's home?

I couldn't get enough of Sunny or what she had to tell me about our family. In Sunny, I saw myself, or what I might have been had I stayed in Korea. And in learning about her mother's life, I felt somehow closer to my own mother. Her mother's life, after all, paralleled my mother's, with the one exception: my mother gave me up for adoption, whereas Sunny's mother decided to keep her and raise her as a single mother.

"I owe my mother everything," Sunny mentioned several times during the weekend, as if seeing me—a Korean adoptee— were a reminder of her good fortune. No Korean would ever look upon her with the mixture of pity and shame that the word "adoptee" evoked. "Even though her life was difficult, I owe her for not giving me up for adoption or something else," she said, unaware of the impact her words had on me.

Sunny spoke openly about her life. After my grandfather left her, Sunny's mother struggled to raise her daughter alone. She did not have the support of any family members since she had shamed them by getting pregnant out of wedlock. And with a child, she had no hope of ever getting married or finding a good job.

"The two of us scrounged to get enough to eat and moved from one tiny apartment to another," Sunny said. "My mom couldn't find a job or make a living in Korea, so she moved to Japan and left me with my aunt."

In Japan, she was able to conceal the stigma of being a single mother and get a decent job, earning enough money to send to her sister in Korea for Sunny's care.

"But I never saw any of that money spent on me," Sunny said with a trace of bitterness. "My aunt just spent it all on herself, even though my mom was working for me." After a few minutes of silence, she repeated her earlier sentiment. "I am so thankful that my mother never abandoned me even though I made her life more difficult. She never gave me up."

I was shocked to hear that Sunny and her mother had lived apart for fifteen years in that arrangement. It was true that her mother hadn't given her up for adoption, yet they did not live together. How difficult and lonely life must have been for them both. I couldn't help but wonder how close I had come to that same life. Besides the poor economic circumstances, there was the lifelong stigma of being an illegitimate child.

Sunny read my thoughts. "You know, in Korea, if you grow up without a father, it's a big black mark against you. I couldn't help the fact that my father left us, but it affects my life even now. If I apply to a university, they want to know my father's name and my family history. If I apply for a government job, the same thing. Everything revolves around the father and his family name."

Each time I studied Sunny, I knew that my life just as easily could have been hers. She looked at me too, with that same knowledge in reverse. The funny thing was, we both were secretly a little envious of each other and yet eternally grateful for the decisions our mothers had made and the way our lives turned out. It was difficult to say which of our mothers had made the greater sacrifice. Perhaps they were both equally painful and honorable.

Despite our differing circumstances, Sunny and I both were independent, feisty, and driven. She succeeded in school, won scholarships, and was on track to become an elementary-school teacher when she suddenly quit and announced that she was moving to Australia. Despite pleas and threats from her mother, Sunny moved overseas alone and without a job.

We gazed into each other's eyes with love and admiration. Mulling over our family history, we finally shook our heads in disbelief and toasted the crazy men in our family.

The encounter with Sunny left me in a whirl of new discoveries and questions. The first thing I wanted to confirm was whether or not my mother had moved to the United States. The same tingling sensation trickled down my spine each time I thought about her living in Chicago, speaking English, and living as a Korean-American, just like me! Through all of the unexpected twists in my search for my mother, I seized each new possibility as if it were the one true thing. With each new revelation, my hopes and fears bubbled to the surface all over again, so that I rode a constant roller coaster of emotions.

I struggled to keep the latest news a secret from my father and brother. As far as they were concerned, I had finally accepted my mother's death and ended my pursuit. How could I tell them that I had contacted my aunt against their wishes and discovered so much more than they were willing to tell me?

This would prove my distrust, and shame them so deeply that we might not be able to continue a relationship. And so I continued the game of well-intended lies by keeping half of my life a secret from the male side of my Korean family.

Subconsciously, I pitted my father against my mother and perhaps even resented that it was him I found instead of her. While my father stood before me, anxious to reenter my life, I obsessed over my mother, who was now like a saint dead and risen again several times. Her stature grew so much in my mind that nearly every thought revolved around her. I wished that I could tell people what her favorite color was, a unique saying that belonged to her, or a particular song she sang to me as a child. But there was little evidence left in my mind of our seven years together. There was just a wound waiting to be healed.

As my mind became murky with all the choices, possibilities, and unanswered questions, I felt my body buckle under the stress. I felt pulled in every direction and yet powerless to control my own movement. Everything—the Korean culture, my brother, my father, and even my mother—weighed on me with their silent expectations, and my body began to mimic my mental state. The first thing I noticed was that I couldn't see clearly anymore. My vision became increasingly blurred each day, as if a thin cloud were passing through my eyes. No matter what I tried, I could not wipe away the fog.

21

On the morning we were scheduled to visit my aunt Sunny and her mother in Taejon, I awoke with worsening vision. Things appeared spotted and hazy, as if blocked by floating mist. I guessed it was from fatigue or stress and went to my morning class. But when the words of my Korean textbook began floating above the page like an ethereal gas, I knew something was wrong. I slammed my book shut and ran home to tell John that I had to see a doctor immediately. But we had no idea where to go, whom to call, or how to communicate my problems in Korean. Finally, we called the U.S. army base and asked if we could see a military doctor.

"Are you or your husband enlisted?" a man asked.

"Well, no. But I'm an American citizen." When the man sensed the panic in my voice, he referred me to an English-speaking ophthalmologist at the nearby Korea University Hospital. At the hospital, a nurse waved us into a cramped office. The first thing I noticed was a briefcase filled with glass lenses of varying size and thickness. They looked like antiques. Then

I saw the doctor place one of those lenses on the machine he was using for my examination. He tilted my head in various directions and studied my retina. Beads of sweat formed on the young man's forehead as he spoke in strained English. "Miss, have you been in a car accident?"

I shook my head.

"Did you hit your head on something?"

"No."

"Did someone hit you?"

"No. What is it? What's wrong with my eye?"

"Well, I think you have a hole in your right retina."

A detached retina is common among boxers and head-injury victims, but in my case, no physical event had contributed to the condition. My eye had self-destructed with no apparent medical explanation other than a hereditary weakness. The next morning, I was rushed into emergency surgery at a Seoul hospital and underwent a three-hour operation. There was no time to prepare me for the relative bliss of general anesthesia, as my case was so severe the doctor feared I might lose my sight if I waited one more day.

The operation brought back memories of being in a hospital in Korea as a child. I was strapped to a steel table and my hair was pulled back and covered by a knitted white cap. When the doctor approached the side of my neck with a sharp object, I screamed and told him I was going to pee on the table if he did not let me go—the best threat a five-year-old could conjure up. He called in reinforcements to pin my legs down.

This time, they called John into the operating room to calm my cries. An eternity later, I found myself spinning in a small hospital room filled with strangers. A Korean family occupied the bed on the opposite side of the room about an arm's length away. Apparently, the woman was having surgery the next morning, and her husband, son, and mother had come along to keep her company for the night. They were making themselves at home, watching loud television and pulling out snacks they'd packed in their bags. Soon I heard voices talk about me like I was an invisible.

"Poor thing! Do you think she's Korean?"

"Of course she is, can't you tell?"

"But she can't understand us. Her husband looks American. Ask him if he's hungry."

I heard a little boy's giggle.

"Go ahead! Practice your English. Ask him if he likes pizza!" I heard the grandma urge.

A shy voice turned toward John. "Pizza, you like?"

As evening approached, the grandma showed John how to pull out the cot from underneath my bed and make it into his bed for the night. She gave him a pillow and a blanket and then pulled out her own cot from under her daughter's bed, and the four of us slept together in the tiny room.

I was released from the hospital two days later, but not before John had paid the bill in its entirety. He asked if he could take me home in a taxi, then return with the money after he went to the bank, since no one carried around that kind of cash.

"No," the nurse replied with a nervous smile. "Give money, then can take wife."

A few days later, my brother and his wife accompanied us to the hospital.

"Oh Katy, I'm sorry." I sensed the horror in Gyung-hee's voice as she greeted me. I had not seen myself in the mirror since the surgery, but John told me that my face looked like I had been in a prizefight. The outer area around my eye was black-and-blue and puffed out to the size of a golf ball, the inside raw and swollen. Gyung-hee rubbed my back and held a garbage sack to my mouth while I vomited.

"What caused Katy's condition?" I heard my brother ask the doctor.

"In Katy's case, I think the weakness in her eye is hereditary. In addition to her severe myopia, she had some lattice degeneration that has been there for quite some time. Do you or anyone else in your family have weak eyesight or any other eye problems?"

"No, no one in our family has bad eyes. Nobody, not even our father, wears glasses." My brother turned toward me and said, "It must come from your mother's side of the family."

The Korean doctor looked at me, slightly puzzled. "Does your mother have weak eyes?"

"I don't know," I said, unsure how to answer his question in front of my brother. "I was adopted and I don't have any medical information about my mother."

My medical history was not something that I had ever wondered about—until now. What else, other than weak eyes, had my mother passed on to me? What other surprises or illnesses lurked in my future, and what would I unknowingly pass on to my own children? I wondered how I could learn about my medical history without finding my mother and asking her directly. Since the adoption agency had told my American parents that I was abandoned at birth, my case file held no medical information other than that I'd had chicken pox. That my eye suddenly fell apart in Korea, giving me my first glimpse—no pun intended—into a hereditary weakness, seemed like a sick joke. This was one more thing I shared with my Korean mother—long legs, flat noses . . . and bad eyes.

A second surgery to repair my retina was followed by two months of recovery. During this time, I had to remain facedown in bed while the gas bubble the doctor injected into my eye to help hold the retina in place dissolved. Suddenly the only thing that mattered was saving my eyesight. I dropped out of school and could no longer continue to search for my mother. I had reached the end, both emotionally and physically. During the many silent hours, marked only by the throbbing in my head, I wondered if my illness was fate's way of telling me to leave my mother alone. Just when I had discovered Sunny, the closest link so far, I was no longer able to search for clues to my mother's life. As an understanding of my mother's past was just beginning to develop, my vision narrowed to the darkened blur under my nose.

I was helpless in all ways.

After the surgery, John was at my side as a full-time nurse and companion, and my brother and his family visited us every other day. John and I awaited the now familiar rustle of plastic sacks in the hallway and the timid knock on the door. My brother alternately came with his mother, wife, or his son. When his mother came, a burst of activity immediately filled our apartment.

"*Ii-ee-go!* We are so worried about you. You are getting so skinny. How can you have a baby if you don't get better? How is John getting along by himself?"

"He's managing fine and taking good care of me," I assured her.

"But who buys groceries or cooks?"

"John can do it."

"*Ii-ee-go!*" She clucked her tongue in disbelief.

Every time she visited she brought a half-dozen metal containers of food—rice, a special chicken-and-ginseng soup, beef, dumplings, and toasted seaweed. Like most Koreans, she believed illness could be cured through a regimen of carefully prepared foods and medicinal herbs. She took special care in preparing the meals she brought for me, alternating between various comfort foods—seaweed soup, pine-nut porridge, and my favorite, *samgae-tang*: a chicken, garlic, ginseng, and rice soup that was as comforting as chicken noodle soup back home. As soon as she covered our kitchen table with bowls of food, she instructed us to *"mogo, mogo"* as she cut up some fruit for dessert, washed the dishes, and scrubbed the floor on her hands and knees.

"She doesn't need to do that," John told my brother. "I cleaned the floor yesterday."

"What?" The grandmother looked up with surprise. *"John* scrubbed the floor? Oh, what a good husband you have! Not like a Korean man." She slapped her thighs and laughed. We weren't sure whether it was out of admiration or amusement. But when she found dust on our back porch, she moved her scrubbing outside, still shaking her head and laughing.

"It's okay," my brother said. "She is just acting like a Korean mother. It makes her happy."

John's cleaning abilities didn't help convince the grandmother of his cooking abilities, however. She fretted over our every meal and left enough food to last us until her next visit. Before she left, she measured everything into pans that could be easily reheated on the stove.

"John, just heat this meat and eat it with this rice tomorrow, okay?"

John smiled and nodded obediently.

My brother also seemed amused by John and his role as my attentive caregiver. "I don't know how he can stay cooped up in this apartment all day," he told me. "Isn't he bored? If my wife got sick, I would still have to get out of the house. My mom would take care of her."

As my brother massaged my back like a professional masseur, he named off certain muscles, bones, and stress points in the body. Koreans are deeply in tune with the human body. Instead of turning to synthetic drugs to relieve their ailments, each person practices his own brand of medicine, which tends to be an eclectic blend of ancient practices, folklore, and a knowledge of and faith in natural herbs and roots.

He squeezed a spot under the small toe of my right foot. "This is the pressure point for your eye," he said. "Can you feel it?"

"Uh-huh," I said, although I wasn't really sure what I was supposed to be feeling.

"Do you still have that scar from your surgery as a child?" he said while rubbing my neck. He went to the exact spot behind my ear and found the scar with his finger.

"You know about that?" I asked with amazement.

"Yes, of course! I was there with you. I held your hand during the whole thing. You had a growth removed from your neck." He ran his fingers over the small rise of the scar. "It wasn't a big deal, but you kicked and screamed like a wildcat."

My brother's memory of my childhood surgery was yet another piece of our shared past. At that moment, I felt closer to him than I'd ever felt before. My illness had wiped away any sense of pretense or ceremony between us. Since my American mother could not be here, my brother immediately took over and lent us his own family. He arranged his work schedule around visits to our house, and in addition to the foods his mother prepared for us, he stocked our refrigerator with ice cream, juice, and treats for John. During these visits, he seemed at ease. For the first time, I felt truly a part of his family—a relative by much more than blood.

But as John and I grew closer to my brother and his family, my father seemed to vanish from the scene. He didn't even know about my surgery. His visits had slowly ceased as our relationship became more and more strained by the question of my mother and the pressure to meet his other children. I had not spoken to him in more than a month when he called one day.

"How are you?" he asked from a street pay phone.

"*Appa,* I'm sick."

"What is it? *Comghi*—a cold?" His voice was thick with concern.

"No, it's my eye—it hurts." I spoke in simple phrases because I did not know the Korean words to explain a detached retina or the surgery I underwent. "I was at the hospital."

"Which hospital?" he yelled into the phone.

"Yonsei Severance."

"What?"

"Yon-sei Severance Hospital."

"I want to see you." He switched to English.

"No! I think it's better if we don't meet—because of my eye."

Through his silence I pictured my father's face at that moment, twisting with a mixture of anger and hurt—mostly the latter, I guessed. I wasn't sure why the thought of his visit filled me with such dread, but it seemed like just one more thing I could not handle. He would see me and ask what happened with alarm and I wouldn't be able to explain to his satisfaction. He would feel responsible and want to help me, when there was really nothing he could do.

"I have to be in bed and rest," I finally said in a pleading voice.

"Okay. Take care of yourself and rest."

Tears filled my eyes as I hung up the phone. I was frustrated that I could not explain my condition to him and that I had inadvertently pushed him away. I had come to Korea to be with him. Yet I dreaded his visits, his voice on the phone, his questions that sounded like barks, and his looks, which filled me with guilt and regret. If only he had told me everything at the beginning, my disappointment might have been less now. Each of us evoked such a tangle of emotion in the other that neither of us could express how we truly felt. But the one thing I knew for certain was that as long as I was in Korea, my father felt responsible for my well-being. He would be sick with worry, wondering what was wrong with me.

I asked John to write my brother an E-mail on my behalf.

Dear Oppa,

I am writing to ask you for a favor. Please call our father and tell him about my eye surgery. He called today and I told him that I was sick, but my Korean was not good enough to explain everything. Please explain what happened and tell him that I need to stay in bed, facedown, for the next two months. Tell him not to worry.

Katy and John,

We received your E-mail.

Oppa called your father like you asked. But he feels that our father is old and his condition is not so good, so we decided not to tell him about your surgery.

We hope that you understand us.

—Gyung-hee

I didn't understand. Instead of communicating what I wanted, he had done the exact opposite, essentially lying to our father. And now there was an unspoken expectation that I would back up that lie. I felt trapped once again by a cultural protocol I did not understand. Instead of calming my father's worries, we were deceiving him "for his own good." I thought about how terrible my father would feel when he saw me and discovered the truth. I was stuck between respecting my brother's authority and deceiving my father. The only solution I could think of was to avoid my father for as long as possible.

Since I avoided my father's phone calls, he had no way of knowing how much I had wanted to do just the opposite—include him in my recovery.

In the meantime, my brother and his family continued to take care of John and me. One day, my brother's mom was performing her usual cleaning ritual when she turned to me suddenly and asked, "Ji-yun-ah, do you like your father?"

"Omma . . ." My brother tried to cut her off.

"Well, do you?" she asked again.

I was fully aware of being thrust onto forbidden ground, territory that was filled with emotional land mines. I grappled for the right words to answer her in Korean. "Yes. I don't know; it's confusing."

My hesitation cracked open the door just enough for her own opinions to come crashing through.

"Your father—he is *ja-il napoon saram!*" Her usually playful voice turned high and shrill and her face scrunched into a scowl as she spat the words. "Your father—he is Number One Bad Person in all of Korea!" She glared at my brother with hatred in her eyes and spit on the ground for emphasis.

My brother and I exchanged looks of surprise and burst out laughing.

"Omma," my brother pleaded. I could tell from the tone of his voice that my brother had heard this tirade before. The grandmother's comment no longer struck me as humorous as I thought about my brother's dilemma, being caught between his mother and father. Korean society demanded filial duty, yet his mother would see any kind gesture toward our father as a personal betrayal.

"Well, he is," she continued sputtering. Her anger at my father soon overflowed onto my brother. "Do you know what a bad person your father is, do you? Don't laugh. It's not funny how bad he is. You go ahead and laugh then. You go right ahead and call him up. Go ahead! What do you care how much he hurt me or how bad he is?"

At first, my brother brushed off his mother's words with a wry smile. But when she continued, his pleading turned threatening. *"Omma!"* She gave her son one last glare and stepped outside, still muttering. As I took in the scene that was unfolding before me, it slowly dawned on me—the reason he had not told our father about my surgery. It wasn't to protect our father—it was to protect his mother! I suddenly understood the complexity of my brother's situation. He was forced to choose between his father and mother at all times. He had to decide which one should take care of me during my illness, and he had selected his mother over our father. If the two distant "planets" ever collided or even passed by each other, a firestorm would erupt. His mother's brief tirade was just a preview.

22

At the end of May, as I was recovering from a second surgery, my American mother made the journey to Korea. I had always envisioned the last step toward wholeness as having my two mothers—the Korean one and the American one—in the same room with me. That way, I would not have to talk to one mother about the other. Perhaps that dream would never come true. For now, I would have to settle for my mother meeting other members of my Korean family.

I waited for her visit with building excitement. My mother often vacationed and traveled with John and me, but this journey covered more of an emotional distance than a physical one. I needed her to see where I had come from and to acknowledge my culture and identity separate from hers. The journey back to Korea had been my choice, but I knew that it involved my mother as well, in ways I could not fully understand. During my time in Seoul, and perhaps even before then, an unease had settled between us. Initially, I had needed the emotional distance to begin the search for my Korean mother, yet I hoped that my mother understood that no one could ever replace her. One woman was an elusive ghost while the other had been faithfully by my side. For the past year, my mother had been a helpless spectator, watching me take one emotional tumble after another. As I instinctively turned to her for comfort, I knew, before she even tried to offer it, that she could not understand. It was difficult for me to explain the differences between and the necessity of each family—the one who gave me birth and the one who raised me. Each represented a part of me, although I could not say with much clarity where one influence ended and the other began.

Now my mother would finally come to Korea. My two families were so different, with me as the only bridge between them.

This was not lost on my American mother or my Korean father and brother, each of whom looked forward to the meeting with a sense of nervous anticipation. I knew that my American and Korean families wanted to impress each other and express their gratitude. I hoped the meeting would not be too uncomfortable for any of us.

My mom burst through the door in a jumble of luggage, gifts for my Korean family, and packets of instant American foods. Although it had been less than a year, it seemed like an eternity since we had seen each other. In my sickness, it was my American mother's face that I longed to see. When she finally arrived, it was the best feeling in the world to be folded into her arms and hear her voice.

"Oh, my baby girl," she exclaimed, "you are so skinny. I see that it will be my job to fatten you up!" She showed me the instant packets she brought to make some of my favorite foods from home—tacos, spaghetti, and scalloped potatoes.

Seeing her here, in Korea, reminded me just how far I was from home and how different the context of our lives had become.

"Our apartment is too small." I wanted to apologize to her as my father had apologized to John and me on our first day in Korea. I also wanted to ask "What in the world did you bring?" as I stared down at her enormous pieces of luggage occupying our floor.

Normally, when we got together, our time and energy were spent going from one activity to another. We had arranged my mother's trip to Korea months in advance and had planned to tour the country with her for three weeks. But with my illness, we were forced into a subdued state of togetherness in our cramped apartment—my mother and I sharing the bed while John slept perpendicular to us on the floor, his head pressed against the refrigerator and his feet touching the bedpost.

After a few days, my mother became restless. For as long as I could remember, she had been involved full throttle in a thousand different activities—raising four children while working full-time and attending school until she earned a doctoral degree in education. In her latest job, she lobbied Utah legislators for more education funding and ran the largest youth-in-custody program in the state. Everywhere she went, my mother made friends quickly and was always up for an adventure—the more exotic the better. Her boundless energy had never been more apparent than it was in the setting of the Zen-like state of calmness John and I had reached during my illness. For us, simply listening to music or a book on tape was enough to entertain us for hours. By contrast, my mom listened while sewing, solving a crossword puzzle, playing cards against the computer, or entreating us to play another game of Scrabble. Even though John took her out shopping and hiking in the mornings, I knew other markets, sights, and restaurants constantly beckoned to her as the minutes ticked by inside the four pastel walls of our apartment.

Our opportunity to escape came the next week when the

doctor finally said the magic words: "The second surgery was successful, and the gas bubble is small enough so that you can lift your head now."

"Really?" I could hardly believe the ban had been lifted— after three long months!

"Yes, you can resume all normal activities, except for flying, until the gas is completely gone."

I straightened my neck, feeling like a turtle poking its head from its shell for the first time. I felt a foot taller, and was amused to see the faces of the doctor's assistants, who had previously been mere blurs and buzzing voices. When we walked outside, I was surprised by the vibrant colors of summer after a wet spring (and months of looking at the ground). I had missed the early bloom of spring and Seoul's most beautiful season. But plenty of white, pink, and purple blossoms remained, like splashes of glowing color on an already bright cityscape. I soaked up the scene, which hit me afresh, like my very first time in Korea.

To celebrate my upright position, we took my mom downtown to T'apkol (pagoda) Park, named after the ten-tier marble pagoda inside. The park was a great place to walk and people-watch, as it was the favorite hangout for elderly men who gathered in clusters to play chess or seek respite from the summer heat in the shade of pine groves. Next, we took her to Namdaemun Market, which was overwhelming in its size and the kaleidoscopic array of goods it offered for sale. This market, one of the largest in Seoul, was the city's epicenter of chaotic commerce. We passed by rows of pig heads, buckets of live turtles and eels, traditional ceramics and masks, mountains of clothes, and enough leather goods to fill a dozen malls back home.

That night we met my brother, who had been waiting to entertain my mother ever since her arrival. He wanted to give her a taste of Korean culture, so we met him in Insadong at our favorite restaurant, Arirang, named after a famous Korean song.

"I'm so nervous to meet your brother," my mom had confessed while curling her hair and putting on her makeup. "I wonder what he will think of me."

I knew he was probably wondering the same thing. "Oh, don't worry," I told her. "He is very excited to meet you."

But I recalled what he had said after I showed him a picture of my mother.

"*Oppa,* this is my mom," I said, pointing to her photo.

"John, your mother is very beautiful," he responded, much to John's and my surprise. It was simply impossible for him to imagine or acknowledge my adoptive American mother.

Remembering that response, I wanted to hold my mother in front of my brother as proof of my family back home and of my American identity. At the same time, I wanted my mother to recognize my Korean family and heritage. I kept these thoughts to myself as we arrived at Arirang and met my brother and Gilbert, who came along to translate. Seeing Gilbert again reminded me of his words the last time we had met: *Your brother is sorry, but he found out your mother is dead.* But I found that my animosity toward him had dissipated with time and I was relieved to have a translator on hand. My brother, dressed in his finest shirt, tie, and jacket, bowed to my mother and shook her hand enthusiastically.

Introductions and greetings were exchanged and I was grateful for Gilbert's ability to put my mother and brother at ease. He seemed anxious to explain to my mother that, although he lived in Seoul with his family, he was an American citizen, having grown up in Los Angeles. This fact seemed to elevate his status with my brother, who looked to Gilbert for explanations of how things were done in America. We sat on floor cushions at a table directly in front of the stage where dancers would later perform. My brother ordered a six-course royal banquet and an expensive bottle of "one-hundred-year wine." When the delicately shaped bottle of sweet wine arrived, he poured my mother's glass in the ceremonious manner normally directed toward him. He then gazed at my mother, fully taking in her face for the first time.

"Your mother is so beautiful, like Miss America," he said, with a hint of awe in his voice. "Please tell her she looks so young and her eyes are so beautiful."

I repeated my brother's compliments to my mom, whose eyes sparkled as she blushed and countered, "Miss America? Hardly! But thank you. Tell your brother that he is very handsome."

"*Oppa,* my mother says you are very handsome," I said, enjoying this exchange.

"Thank you," he said in English. Then in Korean: "Katy and I look alike."

"Do you think my brother and I look alike?" I asked my mom.

"Yes." She paused. "I see the resemblance."

"We are sorry that Katy has had such a difficult time in Korea and been ill. We're sorry that we could not do more for her during this time."

"But you have done so much. I really thank you and your family for taking such good care of her since I could not be here. You have been so kind and generous."

This time, my brother's eyes sparkled with pride. "What was Katy like as a child? She must have been very difficult."

"Oh no. She was an angel. She has brought me nothing but happiness. We are more than just mother and daughter; we are good friends. I feel so lucky that she came into my life."

My brother laughed and shifted uneasily. "I know there must have been difficulties. Children are always difficult. Thank you for raising her so well."

"No, she really was an angel. Thank you for being so kind to Katy and John this year."

"Katy and I both shared difficult times in our childhood. But our family is good, honest people."

"Yes." My mom was at a loss for words, but recovered. "This year has meant so much to Katy."

The conversation volleyed back and forth in carefully formulated compliments. While Gilbert took over the translations between my mother and brother, I willingly faded into the background, enjoying the position of a casual bystander to this cultural exchange between two strangers getting to know each other. It was an odd sensation to see my mother set against this Korean backdrop. For most of my life, I had been the person who stood out in a crowd as someone who didn't quite belong. But now here was my mother, with every one of her Western features illuminated in my brother's eyes—her white skin, deep round eyes, red hair. I could guess the thoughts that were scrolling though my brother's mind: "This is who raised Katy, how she grew up." What, then, was my mother thinking as she looked across at me sitting next to my Korean brother?

As I watched the two of them, I began to notice small cultural nuances—the subtleties that were lost on my mother and would have been lost on me too if not for my year of viewing life through Korean lenses. I noticed, for instance, the diligent watch my brother kept on my mother's shot glass to make sure it never approached emptiness during the long evening. The "honorific" manner in which he poured the liquor each time, using his right hand supported by his left. His unusually reserved drinking, straight posture, and frequent bows of the head. He wore the mask of a host and I could see the invisible wheels turning in my brother's mind as he carefully formulated his thoughts and words before speaking them. There were endless small gestures of respect. Waiting for my mother to take the first bite. Ordering the most expensive dishes and setting the best ones closest to her. Handing her the largest piece of beef. Smiling often and complimenting her on her deft use of chopsticks (even as she held them too low and frequently crisscrossed them clumsily, so that I didn't know whether to laugh or wince). I saw my brother watch nervously as my mother shifted her long legs under the table.

"Sitting on the floor was a bad idea," he whispered to me. "Does she need a chair?"

"No," I whispered back. "She's fine."

"Does she want a fork? Ask her."

"Mom, do you want a fork? They can bring you one."

"Oh no," she answered, checking my face first to see whether she should be embarrassed.

From my brother's side of the table, I now observed my mother's gestures, and for the first time saw her as distinctly American, the way my Korean family must have seen John (and me?). Her lovely round eyes, sparkling jewelry, and most of all, a confident manner that immediately set her apart from most Korean women. Instead of feeding herself last and clucking with concern over everyone else (something that came as naturally to Korean mothers as breathing), she assumed the position of honored guest with an easy grace. I watched the way she took the best morsels of fish and meat without noticing that my brother and Gilbert ate hardly anything during the meal. The way she downed her wine before refilling my brother's glass, asked for some water, passed with her left hand, and looked around the table for a saltshaker. The way she held her chopsticks casually pointed up in the air, stretched her long legs out in front of her to shake them awake, and talked to Gilbert about California's education system as my brother sat uncharacteristically ignored and shut out from their private conversation. Didn't she notice the break that caused in the harmonious flow of the group?

But it was not with mounting criticism that I observed these subtle gestures. What I felt was more like a dawning revelation that I had, perhaps, become more Korean during the past year. One culture was not necessarily better than the other, and for the first time I could see that I contained qualities of both. But the differences were fascinating. With my mother, for instance, what you saw was what you got. Every emotion and thought lay open and exposed on her face, ready to slip from her tongue and make instant contact. She embodied the American declaration of individuality: if she had a craving, she satisfied it. If a thought came to mind, she shared it. If she found herself in the seat of honor, she happily claimed it. My brother, on the other hand, was concerned, foremost, with the harmony of the group at the expense of self-comfort and moments of frivolity. His was a life of self-restraint, as I had come to understand. Gracious and selfless host that he was, one had to guess and pull at the thoughts behind his masked face, subtle gestures, and unspoken words.

I studied the faces of my American mother and Korean brother, both of whom, at that moment, I found more endearing than ever before. And when I finally snapped out of my trance-like state, I discovered that I needn't have worried. Sometime during the evening, at which exact moment I could not say, my mother and brother had connected without much effort from me.

"Let's go to a teahouse," I heard my brother say. "I want to continue talking to your mother."

My mom eagerly obliged, and at the teahouse, I found her and my brother smiling at each other with genuine warmth.

"Katy has always been a little bit stubborn," my mom said, to my moaning objection. "Her brothers used to tease her a lot. When she would get angry at them, she would jump into a karate stance and practice her moves on them like this." My mother was encouraged by my brother's laughter. "And when her father spanked her for being naughty, she would stand up, put her hands on her hips, and say, 'Daddy no spanky Katy!' "

"Even though we grew up apart, I think Katy and I are the same," my brother said.

Then, to my surprise, he reached across the table and took my mother's hand in his playfully. "I can read your palm," he told her. "Oh, I see that you are very intelligent! And see this line here? It shows that you will have a very long and happy life."

They laughed and held hands for a moment longer.

"I think your brother liked me, don't you?" my mom asked on the way home.

"Yes. Did you like him?"

"Oh yes!" she said, her eyes still sparkling.

If my two mothers ever were to meet, I wondered how they would hit it off. Which of their qualities would I find in myself and how would I come to terms with those two sides?

The next night as John and I were getting ready for bed, we heard a knock at the door that was so loud and unexpected that it startled all of us. Before anyone could move toward the door, we heard a key enter the lock, turn, and click. My father suddenly stood before us, staring down at my mother. He was dressed in his navy-blue suit and tie, as if prepared to look his best for this unannounced introduction to the woman who had raised his daughter. His face was red with the bloom of alcohol, the smell of which emanated from his every pore. What followed his sudden entry was one of those uncomfortably slow moments where everyone gazed wide-eyed at the other. When we snapped to, a painful embarrassment seeped into the room.

My father laughed nervously and extended his hand to my mother, who jumped to her feet, rearranged her shirt, and gave a high-pitched hello.

"I was at a party in your neighborhood, at Korea University, so I thought I would stop by," he said to no one in particular.

"Oh, well, it's nice to meet you finally, Mr. Kim," my mother said, unable to hide her discomfort.

He then turned to me and saw, for the first time, my eye. His earlier pleading smile disappeared and was replaced by a look that was as close to dejection as I'd ever seen on an adult face. He gaped at me, taking in my swollen eye and weakened body, which was twenty pounds lighter than the last time he saw me. I lowered my head, but could still feel his eyes burning into me.

"Hel-lo," I stammered, my face flushed with shame and anger, and not knowing what else to say. "I guess you already met my mother."

For months since my surgery, I had been successful in keeping my father at bay while my brother's family took care of me. But now I felt like a criminal caught in the act. Still, what gave my father the right to burst in on us like this? If only he had waited for a few days, for the meeting my brother had arranged at a restaurant. My mother had wanted to prepare for the meeting, to look her best and figure out what to say to my father.

"I didn't know you were this sick," he said, in a way that made me want to cry. It was as if we were back on that bus and he was asking me, "Why didn't you tell me? Don't you love me?"

I was unable to think of a way to explain how I had meant to tell him, tried to tell him.

He turned to my mother with a look of shame. "I am so sorry you came to Korea and had to see Katy like this." He paused to compose himself. "I didn't know what had happened to her. She never told me."

He addressed me once more: "You kept telling me that you were okay, not that you were like this! I wanted to come and see you on your birthday, but you told me not to come." For a second, he looked as though he might cry. But then he took a seat, cleared his throat, and spit. As I heard the spit land on the floor, I didn't know whether my father had momentarily forgotten where he was or if his spitting was an act of defiance, the last vestige of his male pride.

My mom watched in amazement.

After a few more minutes of brewing silence, my father left as abruptly as he had come.

It was another sign of my brother's comfort that he invited my mom over to his house for dinner. We welcomed the opportunity for my mom to meet my sister, my brother's family, and his mother. And more than any fancy restaurant, this would truly give my mom a sense of Korean culture. The thought of the grandmother and my mother meeting brought a smile to my lips. The grandmother had adopted the role of surrogate mother to me during my illness and I wondered how these two women would get along. I could only imagine how long the grandmother must have spent in her tiny kitchen preparing the banquet for my mother's arrival. My brother explained beforehand that I would have to assume the role of translator because he did not want to invite an outsider to join us on this family occasion in his home.

The grandma greeted us at the door with her usual zest. "Ji-yun-ah—why, you look so much better! *Ii-ee-go!* It must be your mother's good care that has made you so well. You must have been waiting for *her* cooking."

I translated the grandma's words to my mom, who quickly replied, "Yes, I think so. When I first saw her, I couldn't believe how skinny she had become. She looked like she had been in a concentration camp!"

I winced inside as the grandma looked to me for a translation.

"Oh, my mother says that I am much better thanks to your kind care. My mother asks me to thank you for taking care of me all of these months when she could not be here and for feeding us so well," I said with added enthusiasm.

The grandmother beamed at my mother and protested, "Oh no, no! It is your mother who has made you better. *Ii-ee-go!* We were so worried about you all these months. Oh, how much we worried. Thank goodness that your mother is finally here and you are well. Tell your mother she is so beautiful and so young looking."

I turned to my mother. "She says that you are very beautiful and young looking."

This time my mother beamed and protested, "Oh no. Tell her she is the one who is very beautiful."

To the grandma: "My mom says you are very beautiful!"

After this initial greeting, both women smiled at each other contentedly, not able to understand a word of each other's language and therefore unable to gauge my budding abilities as their translator.

We entered the family room to find two low lacquered tables pushed together in order to hold a mind-boggling assortment of dishes. The grandma had prepared the best delicacies, including a whole steamed fish decorated with colorful strips of white radish, carrots, and spinach. My mom gasped in amazement as the grandmother smiled proudly. My mom soon learned the grandma's favorite words: *"Mogo! Mogo!"*

"This looks beautiful! Thank her for preparing such a wonderful feast."

"Oh no! I wish I could have done more, but I had such short notice," the grandma answered as she motioned for us to take a seat on the floor. "We are sorry we couldn't meet your mother earlier, when she first arrived. But your *oppa* has been busy preparing for a concert."

When everyone had gathered around the table, my mom presented colorfully wrapped gifts to each member of the family: A glass platter that my brother Dave had made in his home kiln for my Korean brother. Watercolors of Utah landscapes for each of the women. Expensive perfume and fragrant soaps for the grandmother and my sister and a *Star Wars* T-shirt for my nephew.

"*Ii-ee-go!* Look at that," the grandma exclaimed to Kang-san when he eagerly held the shirt to his chest.

"Is *Star Wars* popular here too?" my mom asked.

"Yes, of course," my brother answered. "Kang-san wants to see the new movie when it comes out."

Before the grandmother opened her package, she instructed my brother to get my mother's beautifully wrapped gift and watched as my mother opened it. It was a custom-made "name chop," an official stamp of one's Chinese name that Koreans used in place of a signature on important documents. My mother's, however, was engraved with her American name, Sue. A Korean mountain scene had been carved into the marble handle.

"I bought this at a shop in Insadong," my brother said, "where a friend of ours works. He had to work very hard to finish it in time for your mother's visit."

I thanked him on behalf of my mother and myself and noticed that he took more joy in giving this gift than in receiving his. After the exchange of gifts, my mom quickly became the center of attention and focus of all eyes as we waited to see what she would pick up first with her chopsticks. John and I were surprised, but happy, to see that my sister was present for this occasion after seeing her only once in the past five months. In fact, it was my sister who seemed to take the greatest interest in my mother.

"Katy, how old is your mother?" she asked.

"Sixty-one."

"Oh, that's the same age as my mom! Katy, I heard that your mother works. What does she do?"

"She runs an education program for the state of Utah." I attempted to explain in a mixture of Korean and English, looking to Gyung-hee for help. "She has her doctorate in education administration," I bragged.

"Oh! She is a career woman," the women said in chorus, duly impressed. "Your mother must be very intelligent." But afterward, I wondered if my bragging had offended the grandmother or if being a single "career woman" at my mother's age struck my Korean family as odd. I wondered if they would point to my mother later, after we left, as another example of the unraveling fabric of American society, with its high divorce rate and disrespect for elders (since my mom lived alone, and not with one of her three sons).

"So does your mom live alone?" my sister asked.

"Yes, ever since she and my father divorced."

"Oh." My sister laughed uncomfortably and exchanged a quick look with her mother before lowering her head into her rice bowl. But a few minutes later, her curiosity was once again piqued. "But, Katy, in America, how far away from your mother do you live?"

"What did she say?" my mother asked, reminding me of my duties as translator, which I had forgotten.

"She asked how far we live from each other in the States." Then in Korean: "I live in Boise. My mom lives in Salt Lake City. It's about five hours away by car."

"How often do you see each other?"

"Every other month or so. Sometimes John and I drive down. Sometimes she flies up." I turned to my mother: "They are asking how often we see each other."

"Boise is very beautiful," my mom said, bypassing my slow translation to talk to them directly in loud English.

My sister understood my mother and responded, "Oh yes. It must be very beautiful and clean—not like Seoul. Here we have so many people and it is so crowded. What does your mother think about Korea?"

"They want to know what you think about Korea," I said to my mother.

"It's very beautiful! John took me hiking and around the city while Katy was sick. And this week, we had a chance to go to the markets and palaces. There are so many beautiful temples and palaces, and so much to do and see here. And the people are so friendly and beautiful too."

When I translated my mother's response, my Korean family laughed with delight. Then, as if embarrassed by their momentary show of pride, my sister-in-law Gyung-hee added, "But don't you think Seoul is very polluted? These days, we are very concerned about the number of cars and the bad air. I think Idaho must be very pristine and clean, compared to Korea."

The Korean way would have been to reaffirm the earlier compliments of Korea and smooth over sensitivities about Seoul's worsening air quality. But my mother, understandably, was not used to this familiar Korean pattern of self-deprecation in search of reaffirmation of what was good about their country.

"Yes, Idaho is very clean because there are not many people there," she answered. "In Boise, there is a big river that runs through the middle of town." My mom demonstrated the river with a snaking gesture of her hand.

"A river," I translated to the group.

"Idaho is famous for white-water rafting," my mother continued. "When I went rafting with Katy and John, the river was very high and we went through some huge rapids. Maybe when you visit us in Boise, we can take you rafting."

Everyone paused to hear my translation. "Rafting," I said in English as if leading a game of charades. My mom motioned a series of waves with her hand.

"Oh, *rafting*." Gyung-hee laughed and translated to the rest of the group, who was enjoying my mother's gift for gab much more than I was.

"I don't think *Oppa* would like rafting," Gyung-hee said with a laugh. "He is afraid of water."

"Rafting—me, no!" My brother motioned with his hands.

"Oh no, you would love it," my mom persisted.

My mother's enthusiastic talk about Boise seemed to confuse my sister. "Does your mother live in Boise?" she asked me.

"No, she lives in Salt Lake City, but she often visits us in Boise."

My mom was off again: "There are also lots of city parks in Boise all named after the wives of rich men, like Kathryn Albertson Park—what's the other one, John? Oh, Julia Davis Park and Ann Morrison Park. Tell them John will name a park after you one day."

"Oh mom!" I moaned, "I am not going to tell them all of that. Why would they care about some park in Boise?"

"They do too care," she said in that familiar mother-knows-best tone. "They want to know where you live."

By this time, Gyung-hee had the Korean-English dictionary out and clapped as she deciphered one of my mother's words.

I could see that the conversation was drifting away. I decided to take some liberties as translator and redirect the focus.

"My mom thanks you for your kindness and wants to invite all of you to America someday. You are welcome to stay at her house."

"Thank you!" My brother's family nodded and smiled at my mother. "Maybe Kang-san will go to America one day, and your sister will go to find a husband, but it is too late for me," the grandma said, half joking, half serious. "My brain is too old to learn English."

"But you don't have to know English to visit," I replied.

"*Ii-ee-go!* How would I get along? Your Korean is not good enough to talk to me." She laughed. "No, your sister, brother, and Kang-san can go and just leave me here to die."

"*Omma!*" my sister said in expected protest.

Toward the end of the evening, I noticed the two older women sitting next to each other on the floor, holding hands like two girlfriends and looking into each other's eyes with smiles on their faces. I was surprised by how comfortable each of them looked. The grandma patted my mother's freckled hand as she spoke, the sound of her words rising from deep within her chest and striking the air with intensity.

"Ji-yun-ah, tell your mother that I've had a very difficult life," she said. "I think raising children is the most difficult thing in life—especially when a woman has to do it alone."

"Yes, tell her I agree," my mother responded. "Tell her that I admire her strength. I was also divorced, but at least I had an education and a career to fall back on. I went back to school and got my degree and was able to continue working. I think I had an easier situation because of that. She must be a very courageous woman. She can be very proud of her children and everything she has accomplished, despite her circumstances."

"My mom says that you are a strong and good person," I translated, purposefully leaving out the rest. "You are a good mother to good children. My mother also had difficult times in her life, with my father and the divorce."

There was a visible shift in the grandmother's eyes, which glistened after those last words. She gazed at my mother with affection, as if a secret had just passed between them. "Even though we cannot talk to each other directly, I feel that our hearts are the same and that we understand each other. I have done the best I could. I feel very badly about Ji-yun's father and the situation that she was in."

"You don't need to be sorry, because otherwise I would not have had Katy in my life. And having her in my life has been the greatest gift." My mother's eyes also shone as she smiled and squeezed my hand.

"Still, I think she is confused about her father, and so is her brother and sister. They feel the same way about him, I think."

"Yes, Katy has not had an easy relationship with her father—in Korea or America."

"It is the exact same for Ji-yun's brother and sister."

The women sat together a few more minutes in silence, holding and patting each other's hands.

For the official meeting with my father, we arrived at a classy restaurant with high tables and chairs, similar to the first place my brother and sister had taken John and me nine months before. Gilbert was there to translate once again, and we waited for my father's arrival. A cloud of unease hung over our table as we recalled my father's surprise appearance a few days before. Thinking about that night, I was angry all over again. Why did he have to ruin the meeting and embarrass himself like that? I pictured his red face and the spit landing in the middle of our floor.

My father approached the table and I reluctantly rose to my feet and bowed, following my brother's lead. My father looked at me tentatively, as if sensing the reluctance in my polite gestures. I tried to smile, but knew that my look was sullen at best. Gilbert began to introduce my father and mother with an air of ceremony, but my father cut him short.

"We've already met," he said, and nodded to my mother with a short smile. He cleared his throat and took a seat next to my brother as a heavy silence weighed down upon the table. Seeing the two of them—my father and brother—together for the first time took me aback. The resemblance between them was even more uncanny in person, as they sat side by side. My older brother suddenly seemed so small sitting next to our father. He also seemed uncharacteristically shy in my father's presence.

"*Aboji,* how is your health these days?" my brother asked him.

"Fine, fine. I am a strong person, but how about you?" He took a long look at my brother before declaring, "You are so skinny! Aren't you eating well?"

A sheepish smile spread across my brother's face and I could tell he was moved by my father's attention. "Yes, I am eating well," he replied. "I'm just skinny, like everyone else in our family."

My father smiled.

"Here, try this," my brother said, picking up a piece of beef with his chopsticks and setting it into my father's bowl. This time, it was my father who was moved by my brother's show of concern. I watched this exchange between my father and brother with curiosity and the slightest bit of envy. But soon my feelings turned into an inexplicable sadness. Perhaps it was the hidden discomfort in the scene. My father's overstated air of pride thinly masked his embarrassment in my mother's company. He ignored my mother and avoided my eyes as well, focusing instead on my brother. For his part, my brother tried his best to put a happy spin on the occasion, smiling and doting on my father like a love-starved child. My brother, I realized, was acting partially out of instinct, and partially to make up for my lack of initiative. As much as we wanted to be a normal family, we never would be. Perhaps each of us had failed in our filial duties, and it was too late now to salvage the harmony of pretense.

My mother responded to the situation by striking up a conversation with Gilbert, who sat directly across from her. I sat at the middle of the table, feeling trapped by the clashing forces sectioning off our table into discordant fragments. My father felt this too, as he cleared his throat in that familiar manner and waited for his opportunity to speak. Taking my cue, I whispered to my mother: "Sorry to interrupt, but I think my dad wants to say something to you. And you know, this is the last time you'll see each other, so now is a good time if you have anything to say to him before you leave."

"Oh, okay." She shifted in her seat nervously and looked up at my father, who was watching her. "Tell him that I am so happy for this opportunity to meet him and thank him in person. I feel very fortunate to have Katy in my life, and for that, I am grateful to him."

Gilbert translated her words.

My father nodded gravely. "I think that I have already thanked Katy's mother in a previous letter for raising Katy so well and providing for her when I could not."

I was surprised at how curt my father's words sounded in Korean. I had expected him to break into a long-winded speech of gratitude to my mother. But his words sounded better in Gilbert's translation, so that the curtness was lost on my mother.

"You don't need to thank me," my mother responded. "I think much of the work was already done when she came to us. It is you who I thank."

A hint of a smile touched my father's lips before he became somber again. "I'm just sorry that Katy's mother had to come to Korea and see her daughter in such bad health. I wish I could have done more to prevent this. I hope that she was not too worried."

Before my mother could answer, I jumped in, suddenly feeling protective of my father. "*Appa,* don't worry," I said, moved by his sad expression. "My eye is healing well and I am better now. So there is nothing to worry about."

"We didn't want to concern you because there was nothing anyone could do," John added. "This would have happened to Katy, regardless of where we were—in Korea or back home. We are just glad that Katy is better now, so please don't worry anymore."

After John's words, my father's face relaxed for the first time.

"Of course I was worried about Katy, but I knew she was being well cared for," my mother said. "Thank you for everything you have done for Katy this year, for finding such a nice apartment and helping her to learn about her heritage."

My father smiled, but didn't reply. He suddenly seemed tired and uncomfortable once again. When it appeared that no one had anything more to say, the meeting came to an end. My brother asked Gilbert to drive John, my mother, and me to a subway stop.

"I need to speak to our father a while, in private," my brother said to me, protectively guiding our father out of the restaurant.

I bade my father good-bye with a quick bow and watched as he and my brother walked down the street to find a coffee shop. As I saw the two figures turn the corner, the same sadness I experienced earlier came rushing back. I knew that my brother had felt it as well. Perhaps he was trying to make up for that now, with our father.

23

In June, my mom returned to Salt Lake City and we were down to our last few weeks in Seoul. With the strain of the surgery and the failure to find my mother still hanging over me, I was ready to leave Korea behind. We packed our belongings and reluctantly agreed to spend our remaining days at my brother's house. With our original four bags loaded into the trunk of my brother's car, we pulled up to his house. As I opened the door, I heard the patter of the grandma's slippered feet running down the stairs.

"Is that our Ji-yun-ah?" she yelled. "Has she arrived?" She stared, a little panicked, I thought, at our luggage and led us up the stairs. "Here, you and John can have Sister's room. Put your luggage over there." She pointed to the back patio. Within a few minutes, she was bringing us a tray of food. "Here, sit down. You must be hungry. *Mogo, mogo.*" The rest of the day was divided between snacks and meals, which seemed to appear before us in one continuous procession.

My nephew, Kang-san, arrived home from school at three

o'clock, red-faced and sweaty and happy to see us. Within seconds, the grandma was stripping off his pants and doting on him. "Oh, you are so hot! Here, drink some juice. Say hello to your aunt Katy and uncle John. Go in and wash your face and feet."

When his mother came home, Kang-san asked her if he could order a pizza.

Gyung-hee nodded reluctantly when the grandma burst into the room. "Pizza? *Ii-ee-go!* You don't want that, do you? I'll make you a snack—" But then she glanced at John and me and quickly changed her mind. "Of course, order a pizza if you want. Kang-san likes American food."

But a few minutes after we finished eating our pizza (Kang-san slathering hot pepper paste all over his), the grandma brought out a full-course Korean meal.

"Almoni," Gyung-hee said, "we already ate."

"But that was just pizza, not a meal!" she declared.

Early the next morning, we awoke to the sound of splashing and scrubbing coming from the bathroom. Since the door was open, I peeked in and was horrified to discover the grandma squatting on the floor in front of a washboard—with a pair of John's socks in her hands! She rubbed soap over the brown-stained heels and scrubbed it against the washboard as if in a battle. She rinsed and started the process again.

"Ji-yun-ah," she called out, slightly out of breath, "where are John's underpants?"

When I didn't answer right away, she reached under her sweats and pulled the waistband of her panties. "Go and bring them to me. Bring me yours too!"

I went to our bedroom and announced to John, "She's in there scrubbing your dirty socks. And she wants me to bring her your underwear."

"You're kidding. Hey, you can't take those to her," he said, reaching for his boxers.

"I know, but if I don't, I'm afraid she will come in here and search for our dirty clothes on her own. Here, hide those at the bottom of our bag and I'll go wash these myself."

I returned to the bathroom and practically wrestled the washboard away from her. Assuming the squat position, I tried to imitate the grandma's quick movements with a large square bar of her homemade soap. She left the room, laughing, but returned a few minutes later to check on my progress. "Rinse one more time!" she scolded. "Otherwise, John will get a rash." Then she grabbed the boxers from my hands, held them to her face, and sniffed. "Good! Now they are ready to be hung outside."

While she hung the laundry from a line stretched across the back porch, I was surprised to discover a brand-new electric washing machine sitting there, unused. "Why didn't we use this?" I asked her.

"Not as good as my hands," she answered. "I don't trust that to get the clothes clean."

Later that morning, a man's voice yelled from the stairwell. I opened the door to discover an enormous bur sack filled to the brim with long heads of Chinese cabbage, used to make *kimchee*. "It's time to make a batch of summer *kimchee*," the grandma announced behind me. "I'll teach you how so you can make it for John at home."

For the next three days, I observed the ancient art of making *kimchee*. Traditionally, housewives made enough *kimchee* in the autumn and summer to last the rest of the year. They stored the cabbage—which is pickled with sea salt, along with green onions, red peppers, garlic, and other ingredients—outside, in thick ceramic pots, which were buried during the winter. Nowadays, fresh vegetables are available year-round, so that *kimchee* can be made more frequently, and in smaller portions. The popular side dish can also be bought in any supermarket, although every Korean is partial to his mother's homemade variety.

Although Gyung-hee and I tried to help, the grandma was the *kimchee* master. She began by spreading the fifty or so heads of cabbage into large plastic buckets on the bathroom floor. After sprinkling a generous amount of salt over them, she filled the buckets with water and let them soak overnight. The next day she returned from the market with sacks of various greens, fresh garlic, large round Asian pears, and other secret ingredients. Hunched over a large steel bowl on the kitchen floor, she began creating a bright red pepper paste, which would be slathered between the leaves of cabbage.

Watching her work reminded me of Grandma Ruth's attempt to make me a batch of *kimchee* when I first arrived in America. Soon after she heard how every Korean child grew up eating *kimchee*, she decided to make me some, just as she imagined my Korean grandmother had done. It didn't matter that Grandma had never tasted the dish herself, she was sure she could teach herself how to make it.

"The recipe called for more red pepper," she informed us, "but no one on earth could possibly eat that much hot pepper!"

Mom and I exchanged the uh-oh look.

Instead of following the recipe exactly, Grandma improvised a little here, a little there, she said. Everyone knew what that meant—trouble. She never followed a recipe, or any other directions for that matter, *exactly*. Even something as simple as Rice Krispies Treats would come out lodged with foreign objects such as raisins, walnuts, or M&Ms. She proudly set a big glass jar of *kimchee* on the kitchen table, along with a tin of her homemade shortbread cookies. She waited for me to take a bite. It was bland and tasted a little strange, compared with what I had eaten in Korea. But I didn't have the heart to tell her this.

"Um, it tastes good! Thank you, Grandma," I said with all the enthusiasm I could muster.

"You eat that up and I'll make you some more," she answered proudly.

But my family practically barred me from the refrigerator. Each time I pulled out the jar of *kimchee* and opened the lid, someone commented on the strong smell.

"Gad! That stuff really reeks, Kate." My youngest brother complained the loudest.

"Well, I think your milk reeks!" I said, suddenly feeling defensive about my *kimchee*. But inside, I felt self-conscious. In Korea, the familiar peppery smell always made my mouth water for the ensuing meal. But in America, the distinct smell seemed out of place. Soon I became too embarrassed to eat it anymore.

My brother's household included three generations under one roof, and if that wasn't enough, we added another layer of relations to complicate matters. It was easy to understand, now, why young people in Korea seldom stayed home in the evenings or invited friends over to their homes. The cramped quarters allowed for zero privacy or even room to relax and let down your guard. Thus, children took to the neighborhood streets to play; young people flocked to coffeehouses; and the men went to bars. The women, of course, were left at home to do the chores.

Each morning (including Saturdays, which were a part of the Korean workweek), my brother went into the office around 9 A.M. and didn't come home until way past dinnertime. In fact, it was common for him to stay out half the night drinking with his coworkers (as we knew from experience) and roll home reeking of *soju*. *"Yobo!"* we heard him yell to his wife late one night as he climbed the stairs. "Darling! I'm home." I heard

Gyung-hee stir herself awake and greet my drunken brother at the door. This kind of behavior, it seemed, was almost expected from Korean males.

But the family was untraditional in other ways. My older sister, for instance, had decided never to get married. "Because of what your father did," Gyung-hee once whispered to me. Instead, she focused on her career and earned an income that she gave to her mother to run the household. Perhaps because of this, my sister enjoyed a status unheard of for a single Korean woman. She came and went as she pleased, was spared household chores, and could stay out all night with impunity. Her mother and sister-in-law treated her as the princess of the house, washing her clothes, serving her food, and bringing her vitamins in the morning.

Gyung-hee, by contrast, was like a servant whom everyone bossed around, including her son. But unlike most married woman, she still attended university to work on her master's degree in psychological counseling. She wanted to be a marriage counselor—quite a revolutionary idea in Korea.

"I think there is a great need," she said shyly. "Every woman I talk to is very unhappy in their marriage and they want to talk to someone. Korean husbands stay out late every night and drink a lot. Some hit their wives. But it is very difficult to convince Korean people to go to a counselor. Koreans hate telling their problems to a stranger. I hope this will change and counselors will become more accepted. Are there many marriage counselors in America?" she asked.

"Yes. Marriage counselors and therapists, in general, are very popular. It seems like everyone I know has been in counseling at some point. My parents went to a marriage counselor, and all of us went to family therapy before they got divorced."

"But if so many people go to counselors, why are there so

many divorces in America?" She looked genuinely shocked. Although it was now legal in Korea for women to ask their husbands for a formal divorce, and divorce rates had increased recently, the number was still only a fraction of the rate in the United States.

"I don't know," I answered, wondering how many marriages counseling actually saved.

"Maybe American marriage counselors are not so good," she said, laughing.

While I admired Gyung-hee's ambition, I could not picture her with a career outside of the home, like my sister had. She seemed in constant demand at home, jumping to her mother-in-law's aid, my brother's wishes, and her son's demands. She did have it easier than most married women, I supposed, since the grandma took over the household cooking and most of the chores. She was far from the tyrannical Korean mothers-in-law John and I so often heard about. "My mom-in-law has lots of energy," Gyung-hee said. "She is always running around doing something."

It was clear that when it came to household matters, the grandma was in charge.

Kang-san—the only child, and a son to boot—was the focus of constant attention from the three women of the house, each claiming an equal stake in how he was raised. The grandma's zealous worry toward me was quadrupled on Kang-san until every other word out of her mouth was *"Ii-ee-go!"* followed by a pinch, squeeze, or affectionate pat. After walking home from school, Kang-san would shed his school clothes in the middle of the room. After eating the ice-cream bar his grandma bought for him, he was out the door to play with neighborhood boys.

John and I became like second grandchildren in the house, the grandma still trying to fatten us up.

"*Mogo, mogo!* You are too skinny," she said every day. "Oh, John does not like the food! It is too spicy, too salty. Why doesn't he eat more?"

We had never eaten so much in our lives. Three meals a day, plus several snacks scattered in between. The best part of our meals was when Gyung-hee had a chance to sit down and talk with us. We learned that all of Gyung-hee's psychology textbooks were written in English, so her skills were better than she had let on. During these casual chats, we were able to learn more about my brother and about things that he would never tell us himself. We learned, for instance, that my brother had once owned a video store. He bought a building and lived upstairs with his wife and son. At the same time, he started a magazine about the movie industry with his wife's help.

"What happened to his video store and the magazine?" I asked.

"It went bankrupt," Gyung-hee said matter-of-factly. "And since he didn't have money to repay his loans, he fled. He went to live with my brother in another city for a year until he could work and earn enough money to repay his debts."

I wondered how my brother would feel about his wife telling me all of this. I also wondered how his current business was doing.

"Your *oppa* is a strong person, willing to take many risks in order to succeed," Gyung-hee said. "In the old days, I worked beside *Oppa,* supporting whatever he was doing. But during those days, I often felt bad about myself and had a low self-image. That is why I decided to go back to school to become a counselor and earn an income."

While I was becoming closer to and more comfortable with Gyung-hee, the distance between my sister and me remained the same.

She seemed to steer around me, alternately reaching out and pulling back. During my favorite times with her, she teased me, just as I had imagined an older sister would. "You speak Korean like a two-year-old *agi*—baby!" She laughed. "But I speak English like a baby not even born." At other times, I watched her follow my movements with detached curiosity. Under her cool exterior, I sensed a constant anxiety for her mother, whom she had protected since our father left them. Sometimes I saw the familiar scowl creep up on her face—the same one I had seen in the photograph of her as a young girl.

As we checked off our remaining days in Korea, my sister made it her duty to guide us around the most beautiful and interesting areas of Seoul. We drove for hours outside the city, until we saw open hills and vast fields of lush green rice paddies dotted with the long necks of white cranes. We took a ferry to a remote island and hiked up the mountain until we found ourselves beneath an amazing carving of Buddha's head, his long and wise ears drooping to the edge of his round face. She took us to Independence Hall, a Smithsonian-like museum commemorating Korea's long and bloody struggle against colonialist Japan. Groups of young schoolchildren snaked around graphic exhibits of Japanese torture chambers. Teachers told them to never forget the horrors inflicted on the Korean people by the Japanese.

She drove us to the edge of the demilitarized zone with North Korea, where from an observatory, South Koreans could look through coin-operated telescopes at their impoverished neighbors to the north. The barren landscape evoked both sympathy and fear: sympathy for the people of the same Korean blood, and fear of the North's unpredictable military dictatorship, which, seemingly at any moment, could declare war on the South. The basement gift shop exhibited worn clothing from North Korea and touted smuggled goods for sale, including a certain type of buckwheat noodles made only in the North, special liquors, and even bottles of northern soil.

It was outside this gift shop that a bumblebee flew up John's pants and stung him several times on the thigh. Nearby, two old Korean women pointed and stared in fascination at the foreigner screeching and jumping up and down. The sight of an American was rare at this observatory, since U.S. citizens could take a special "DMZ Tour" that brought them closer to the border than South Koreans were allowed to venture.

"That must have been a North Korean bee," one of the old woman said. "They hate Americans!"

Later that day, my sister asked me, "Katy, are you happy to be going home?"

I pondered her question in silence and wondered if I should answer truthfully. Of course I was happy to finally go home after all these months of illness and a whole year away. I missed my family and friends. I craved a sense of familiarity and the comforts of my own home.

When I remained silent, Gyung-hee answered for me. "*Un-nee,* of course Katy wants to go home. America *is* her home. She has her family, friends, and job there."

My sister studied me suspiciously for a while longer, as if waiting for me to give a different answer. When I remained silent, she got a funny look on her face and walked away.

The next day, we bade good-bye to the grandma and promised to return to Korea soon with, yes, a baby.

"Ji-yun-ah, what are you going to eat in America? Are you sure you can't take some of my *kimchee* with you? I could put a container in your bag."

"*Omma,*" my sister pleaded. "Mo-ther, put that away! The

customs agents will just take it from her. They won't allow her to take food."

"All right. How about some seaweed, then?"

"No, she can buy that at home."

The grandma was still fretting when I hugged her to my chest. "Please come visit us."

"Oh no! I'm too old! But maybe if you find a nice American man for your sister to marry, she will visit you in America. Or maybe our Kang-san will want to attend school in America one day." The grandma smiled while my sister grimaced behind her.

Next, I quickly squeezed my sister.

"Katy, take good care of your health and build up your strength again. Rest and then work hard," she said.

I hugged Kang-san and waved good-bye as my brother and Gyung-hee drove us to the airport. My brother had arranged for us to meet our father there so he could see us off. We drove through town one last time, the skyscrapers, mountains, and people becoming a blur through our window. As we drove, I thought about the incident with my sister the day before with a tinge of guilt. I wondered if I should have obliged her by pretending to be sadder about leaving. In many ways, I was sad to leave Korea, with so many things still unsettled and undiscovered. The year seemed both like an eternity and a blip in time. How much more time would I need to better understand my father or to gather more information about my mother, or perhaps even to find her? It was funny how long and short a year could be. Long enough to change my life and crumble all of my childhood fantasies, and yet short enough to leave me incomplete and wishing for more.

Epilogue

I have played and replayed the scene when I last saw my mother and grandmother at Kimpo Airport and wondered how we could have parted so quietly.

And now I find myself back at the airport, only this time I know that I am heading home. Not to the place where I was born, but to a place that my birth mother wanted to create for me all those years ago. I look into my father's face and see a lifetime of regrets mixed with sorrow and an old man's pride. We both search for words, which refuse to slip off our tongues.

Finally, my father forces a smile. "You are lucky to have such a good husband to take care of you. He will be happy to return home to his family, I think."

I translate my father's words for John and he answers, "I'm going to miss Korea a lot. I'm sure we will be back."

My father searches my face with hope to see if what John says is true. "Yes," I assure him. "We will be back." The minutes tick by and I search for the right words to leave with him.

"Appa," I say, and grab his hand, "I know how much trouble you went to preparing for our arrival in Korea. Thank you for everything."

"The apartment was so small. I'm sorry."

"You don't have to be sorry—for anything." As these words fall from my mouth, my father suddenly appears older and more vulnerable. When had this aging taken place and why hadn't I noticed earlier? I circle my arms around his slumped shoulders and hug him before I turn away.

With each step I take away from my waving father, I wait for the voices to return.

"Okay, I returned to Korea like you told me," I want to lift my head and shout up to the sky, "and where were you? Now what?"

There is only silence.

This time I continue forward, not because I am obeying orders, but because I truly want to go. But with each step, I feel those same two ghosts at my back and my heart twists inside me for my failure to bring my mother and grandmother back to life. What is it about a childhood fantasy that makes it so hard to let go of? I wonder if my mother is destined to remain a figment, an image of the past—the one who sent me on my way, but will not return to see her finished product. Having no face to replace the one in our last photograph together, I picture my mother once more and realize that I am now older than she was at the time I last saw her. Even as I age, her face will always remain the unsmiling one in the Polaroid.

In the absence of the person, I am left clinging to insignificant reminders. The way she combed my hair and cut my bangs, pasting down wisps of hair with a lick of her finger. In the packet of photographs from my grandmother, one particular picture flashes before my mind's eye. I am sitting on the floor in my favorite position: the insides of my bent knees pressed flat against the warm floor and my feet fanned out to the sides so that my legs form a W. My hair is braided and twisted into coils above my ears with large red bows wrapped around them—definitely my mother's doing, I think. I am dressed in typical layers with wool socks pulled over my white tights and the straps of my overalls crisscrossed over my chest to keep them from slipping off my shoulders (definitely my grandmother's doing). My head is cocked to the side and I look as though I am about a second away from sticking my tongue out at the person holding the camera, who could only be my mother.

As I think about that moment, I can almost feel the warmth of her love. But as a child, I had sensed other emotions as well, too complex to name. There was the time my mother returned late one night and began arguing with my grandmother. Eavesdropping from the other room where they thought I was asleep, I didn't understand exactly what they were talking about, but knew my mother had done something bad. The hiss of angry words, mutual accusations, my name (that threw me into a panic—what had I done?), and finally, the burst of my mother's uncontrolled sobs. When I could no longer feign sleep, I peered into the room just in time to see my mother run into the bathroom and vomit on the floor with one violent heave. Seeing my mother slumped over like that, still sobbing as she choked and spat, suddenly flipped my own stomach upside down. I sensed her desperation and knew that it somehow involved me. I ran to the bathroom and found myself squatting next to my mother, getting sick just as she had a moment earlier.

Recalling that scene now, I can only guess what the argument was about. She had been with my father, met another man, or said yes to a marriage proposal. Or perhaps that was the day she decided to give me up for adoption.

That night, I think, was the only time I ever saw my mother cry.

And now what? Should I try to follow her elusive steps back across the Pacific to my adoptive country—to Chicago? I thought about my father's words to me during our first meeting, about how he had been planning to search for me in New York, but I had come to him first. I listed the steps I could take to search for my mother in Chicago: look up immigration records, try to track down a Social Security number, hire a private investigator, put an ad in the newspaper.

Or should I wait for her to come to me, however long that might take?

Just before I step onto the plane, I hear the echo of people's voices back home in my head. *How was Korea? Were you able to find your mother?*

How will I answer them? I wonder.

I could tell them that I once thought the past was like a puzzle that would lock neatly together once I found all of the missing pieces. But even then, the picture constantly shifts, one piece connecting while another is discarded. I thought that if I could look into my birth mother's eyes, all of my questions would be answered, all of my aches soothed.

As the plane takes off, I close my eyes and imagine a new scene to replace the childhood fantasy.

We no longer meet in a hotel room.

With a dull ache that has traveled from my chest to my head, I try to picture how my mother might have aged in twenty years. Perhaps tiny lines are now etched around her eyes and mouth and wisps of gray streak her hair. Her body is a bit plumper through the chest and hips.

I imagine that my mother is married to a kind man who does not know of her past, but would forgive her if he did. She has other children now—at least one son and perhaps two daughters. She is a kind and patient mother who understands the ache of first love and the fickle hearts of handsome men much more than her children will ever know. Her children will doubt her, just as she doubted her own mother and my child will someday doubt me.

There is a comfort in the cycle that will connect generations of women, Korean and American.

In the quiet of my heart, I look out the window of the plane and whisper to my mother's ghost down below, "*Omma,* I forgive your imagined sins. No, please do not apologize to me for failing in your duties as a mother. Thank you for loving me enough to raise me for the first seven years of my life and for letting me go when it was time."

As the ghost fades away into the distance that becomes Korea, I envision a twisting family tree and mark my place twice.

DEVELOPMENT FROM WITHIN

SURVIVAL IN RURAL AFRICA

Edited by
D.R.F. Taylor and Fiona Mackenzie

London and New York

First published 1992
by Routledge
11 New Fetter Lane, London EC4P 4EE

Simultaneously published in the USA and Canada
by Routledge
a division of Routledge, Chapman and Hall Inc.
29 West 35th Street, New York, NY 10001

Typeset in Baskerville by
Pat and Anne Murphy, Highcliffe-on-Sea, Dorset
Printed in Great Britain by
Biddles Ltd, Guildford and King's Lynn

British Library Cataloguing in Publication Data
Development from within: survival in rural Africa.
1. Africa. Rural Regions. Economic conditions
I. Taylor, D.R. Fraser (David Ruxton Fraser) 1937–
II. Mackenzie, Fiona
330.96
ISBN 0–415–03567–8
ISBN 0–415–03991–2 pbk

Library of Congress Cataloging in Publication Data

Development from within: survival in rural Africa / edited by
D.R.F. Taylor and Fiona Mackenzie.
p.   cm.
Includes bibliographical references and index.
ISBN 0–415–03567–8 – ISBN 0–415–06991–2
1. Rural development – Africa, Sub-Saharan – Case studies.
2. Community organization – Africa, Sub-Saharan –
Case studies.
3. Cooperative societies – Africa, Sub-Saharan – Case studies.
I. Taylor, D.R.F. (David Ruxton Fraser), 1937–
II. Mackenzie, Fiona.
HN780.Z9C643   1992   307.1'412'0967–dc20
91-10050 CIP

722758

CONTENTS

List of tables	vii
List of figures	ix
Notes on contributors	xi
Preface	xiii
List of abbreviations	xvii

1 DEVELOPMENT FROM WITHIN? THE
STRUGGLE TO SURVIVE   1
Fiona Mackenzie

2 LOCAL FARMER ORGANIZATIONS AND RURAL
DEVELOPMENT IN ZIMBABWE   33
Lovemore M. Zinyama

3 THE INDIGENOUS RESPONSES OF A GHANAIAN
RURAL COMMUNITY TO SEASONAL FOOD
SUPPLY CYCLES AND THE SOCIO-
ENVIRONMENTAL STRESSES OF THE 1980s   58
George J.S. Dei

4 THE CO-OPERATIVE CREDIT UNION
MOVEMENT IN NORTH-WESTERN GHANA:
DEVELOPMENT AGENT OR AGENT OF
INCORPORATION?   82
Jacob Songsore

5 SURVIVAL IN RURAL AFRICA: THE SALT
CO-OPERATIVES IN ADA DISTRICT, GHANA   102
Takyiwaa Manuh

6 LOCAL COPING STRATEGIES IN MACHAKOS
DISTRICT, KENYA   125
Peter O. Ondiege

CONTENTS

7 HOUSEHOLD BASED TREE PLANTING
  ACTIVITIES FOR FUELWOOD SUPPLY IN
  RURAL KENYA   148
  Noel A. Chavangi

8 LOCAL COPING STRATEGIES IN DODOMA
  DISTRICT, TANZANIA   170
  Japheth M.M. Ndaro

9 THE INFORMAL SECTOR: A STRATEGY FOR
  SURVIVAL IN TANZANIA   197
  Alice Nkhoma-Wamunza

10 DEVELOPMENT FROM WITHIN AND SURVIVAL
   IN RURAL AFRICA: A SYNTHESIS OF THEORY
   AND PRACTICE   214
   D.R.F. Taylor

   Bibliography   259
   Index   276

TABLES

1.1 Ghana and Zimbabwe: summary of UNICEF's process
and outcome indicators   12

1.2 Sub-Saharan Africa: annual percentage cuts in per
capita GDP and health and education expenditure   13

3.1 Seasonal economic cycle of Ayirebi, Ghana   64

3.2 Food strategy responses of twenty Ayirebi households to
seasonal nutritional stress by income status   67

3.3 Monthly breakdown of the yearly record of money order
transactions conducted at the Ayirebi Post Office
(1981–3)   70

3.4 Summary results of a seasonal weekly survey of the
portion of a 12-hour day spent on various activities by
both sexes in twenty representative Ayirebi households   72

4.1 Regional distribution of credit unions affiliated to
CUA 1984/5   88

4.2 Distribution pattern of major credit unions Upper-West
Chapter 1985   89

4.3 Per capita savings and loans by district, Upper-West
Chapter   90

4.4a Upper-West Chapter: trends in savings and loans   91

4.4b Deflated values   91

4.4c US dollar equivalent   91

5.1 Ada agro-economic subzones, population, arable,
grazing and total areas   105

vii

5.2   Age and sex composition, Ada Songor Zone 1984   106

5.3   Economic activity, Ada Songor Zone 1984   106

5.4   Regular school attendance, Ada Songor Zone 1984   107

5.5   Amenities in six sample villages in Ada Songor Zone
      1988   112

6.1   Growth rates of real gross domestic product (GDP)
      1964–87   127

6.2   Proportion of households/holders by size of holding   129

6.3   Population projections by Division 1979–90   132

6.4   Population densities per Division   132

6.5   Medical services ratio 1983 and 1987   134

6.6   Major disease incidence 1987   134

6.7   Crop production trends 1983–6   141

6.8   Crop area yield trends 1983–6   142

6.9   Price trends for food crops 1983–8   142

6.10 Price trends for cash crops   143

6.11 Livestock population trend   144

6.12 Milk production and revenues 1980–7   144

7.1   Summary of monitoring results of the 25 groups in
      Kakamega District   163

8.1   Cross-section of coping strategies in Dodoma District 174

FIGURES

1.1 Growth of gross domestic product in Africa 4

2.1 Principal agro-ecological regions of Zimbabwe 35

2.2 Zimbabwe: major land use divisions 40

2.3 Mhondoro and Save North communal areas: the survey areas and major land use divisions south of Harare 45

5.1 Map of Ghana showing the study area 104

5.2 Map of Songor Lagoon and surrounding villages 108

ix

CONTRIBUTORS

Noel A. Chavangi, Researcher, formerly with the Kenya Woodfuel Development Programme, Nairobi, Kenya.

George J.S. Dei, Assistant Professor, Department of Sociology and Anthropology, University of Windsor, Ontario, Canada.

Fiona Mackenzie, Associate Professor, Department of Geography, Carleton University, Ottawa, Ontario, Canada.

Takyiwaa Manuh, Research Fellow, Institute of African Studies, University of Ghana, Legon, Ghana.

Japheth M.M. Ndaro, Director, Institute of Rural Development Planning, Dodoma, Tanzania.

Alice Nkhoma-Wamunza, Acting Director, University Library Services, University of Dar es Salaam, Tanzania.

Peter O. Ondiege, Lecturer, Department of Urban and Regional Planning, University of Nairobi, Kenya.

Jacob Songsore, Senior Lecturer, Department of Geography and Resource Development, University of Ghana, Legon, Ghana.

D.R.F. Taylor, Associate Dean (International), Faculty of Graduate Studies and Research; Director, Carleton International; Professor, Department of Geography and School of International Affairs, Carleton University, Ottawa, Ontario, Canada.

Lovemore M. Zinyama, Senior Lecturer, Department of Geography, University of Zimbabwe, Harare, Zimbabwe.

PREFACE

In 1981 one of the editors (Taylor) was involved in the publication of *Development from above or below?: the dialectics of regional planning in developing countries* (Stöhr and Taylor 1981). The arguments for development 'from below' are now fairly well known. Succinctly, development 'from below' considers

> development to be based principally on maximum mobilization of each area's natural, human, and institutional resources with the primary objective being the satisfaction of the basic needs of the inhabitants of that area. In order to serve the bulk of the population broadly categorized as 'poor', or those regions described as disadvantaged, development policies must be oriented directly towards the problems of poverty, and must be motivated and initially controlled from the bottom. There is an inherent distrust of the 'trickle down' or 'spread effect' expectations of past development policies. Development from below strategies are basic-needs oriented, labour-intensive, small-scale, regional-resource-based, often rural-centred, and argue for the use of 'appropriate' rather than 'highest' technology.
>
> (Stöhr 1981: 1–2)

As originally expressed, 'development from below' had several weaknesses. Regional political economy critics drew attention to the neo-populist or Utopian origins of the paradigm and its lack of adequate theoretical underpinning. In essence, the problems emanated from the lack of theorizing of social relations with respect to the composition of the State, the existence of class and gender differentiation, and, in turn, State–local relations. Writers such as Charles Gore (1984), for example, showed how problematical is the assumption that regional planning ('from above' or 'from below') takes place in a

political vacuum. Regional planning, he proposes, is one of the instruments at the disposal of those who wield power within the State and can be understood only as an integral component of State policy. It may be used to legitimate government authority; chameleon-like, it may also be used to promote the material interest of those in power (Gore 1984: 242–58).

A lack of theorizing of the State in turn fed into a conception of society as undifferentiated or homogeneous. It was assumed, for example, by Stöhr (1981) that, by definition, local communities had commonly held interests and would act together in these interests. But the conflation of 'place' with 'people' in terms of identifying interest groups is problematical for the refinement of theory which seeks to be relevant to the diverse realities within Africa. Finally, the degree of conflict or confrontation that is likely to emerge in the event of significant mobilization locally, whether with local authority or that of the State, was ignored.

In all three of the above areas, substantial rethinking is necessary to ensure the development of theory that has greater historical and social specificity within Africa, as Hyden (1983) calls for. This can emerge only through an iterative process whereby small-scale event (at the intrahousehold level and through local community action) is examined in the context of large-scale process. It was in order to explore this relationship, specifically to focus on local-scale organization ('from within') in the context of economic crisis in Africa, that this book has been produced.

Through an analysis of case studies at the local level (all too frequently ignored as theorists measure success through the applicability of universals), which are set within the political and economic context of the State, the underlying objective of the book is to focus on the relationship between local action and macro event. The intent is to move beyond the rhetoric that has come to surround the concept of 'development from below', which is adopted now in the discourse of institutions such as the World Bank, to examine issues raised by earlier work. Drawing from the case studies, the aim is to suggest avenues for future theoretical exploration. Fundamentally, the book illustrates the diverse means by which women and men in rural Africa struggle to survive.

In the first chapter, Mackenzie examines alternative analyses of and prescriptions for the deepening crisis in Africa. Her concern is to expose questions which arise from such analysis with respect to the potential for local organization to effect positive change in rural Africa.

This sets the context for the following eight chapters, presenting eight case studies which are written from very different theoretical perspectives. The first of these is Zinyama's study of 'Local farmer organizations and rural development in Zimbabwe'. This chapter is particularly interesting because it argues that there is a very positive relationship between the State and local organizations.

Next are three case studies from Ghana, each of which gives a very different perspective on local initiatives. In Chapter 3 Dei describes the response of a community in southern Ghana to the growing stresses facing the people in the 1980s. Here the community appears to have acted as an entity and there is no evidence in the study of differentiation. This is quite different from Chapter 4 by Songsore, who discusses the co-operative credit movement in northern Ghana and shows that differentiation and conflict clearly exist. This is true also in the third case study from Ghana by Manuh. In Chapter 5 she documents the continuing political struggles and tensions of the salt co-operatives in Ada District. These demonstrate the complexities of intra-community relationships and the ambivalent relations among the State, local government, traditional authorities and the local people.

Two case studies are drawn from Kenya where local organization is largely seen as an extension of State planning. In Chapter 6 Ondiege looks at the situation in Machakos District and in Chapter 7 Chavangi considers some of the experiences of the Kenya Woodfuel Development Programme, drawing much of her material from experiences in Kakamega District. In both of these case studies the relationships between government and the local people appear to be quite different from the situation in Zimbabwe and Ghana and non-government organizations (NGOs) and international aid agencies are major actors. The case studies conclude with two studies from Tanzania. In Chapter 8 Ndaro looks at the experience of Dodoma District and argues that local initiatives will remain marginal to the development process unless they are integrated with the planning efforts of government. In Chapter 9 Nkhoma-Wamunza provides a fascinating description of the struggle which faced the women of the village of Utengule Usangu in Mbeya District who were attempting to organize beer-brewing co-operatives. Here, gender oppression was a major factor in undermining their efforts.

The book concludes with a chapter by Taylor which attempts to synthesize theory and practice relating to 'development from within' in Africa.

In *Development from above or below?*, it was argued that:

The validity of development approaches will not be determined as a result of theoretical and ideological debate, but in the realm of practice. The peasant families of Africa . . . are more likely to judge the validity of a strategy from its results rather than its ideological or methodological soundness.

(Stöhr and Taylor 1981: 458)

It is clear from empirical evidence that existing strategies, whether socialist or capitalist, have not brought the results expected of them. Sandbrook has posed the question:

Is it wholly unrealistic to hope that, out of systemic crisis and popular disillusionment and withdrawal can emerge the self-reliant and communitarian basis for the construction of more organic and satisfactory economic and political structures? Or are statist top-down forms of capitalism and socialism the only practicable frameworks for economic development today?

(Sandbrook 1986: 331)

Development 'from within', like development 'from below',

argues for flexibility and is as much an ideology as a strategy. It is a way of looking at development rather than a rigid set of policies and ideas. In practice there will be many responses to it over both time and space.

(Stöhr and Taylor 1981: 458)

Robert Chambers (1989b: 24) has argued for an 'ideology of reversals' which starts with the priorities and conditions of rural people. Development from within is an example of such an approach. Both editors hope that this book will make a contribution to a greater understanding of the realities facing the people of rural Africa and that out of such an understanding will come both new theory and practice which are based on 'development from within'.

D.R.F. Taylor and
Fiona Mackenzie

ABBREVIATIONS

AAF–SAP	African Alternative Framework to Structural Adjustment Programmes
ACCOSCA	African Confederation of Co-operative Savings and Credit Association
AFC	Agricultural Finance Corporation
APPER	African Priority Programme for Economic Recovery
ASAL	Arid and Semi-Arid Lands
ATAF	Ada Traditional Area Fund
BSACo	British South Africa Company
CBS	Central Bureau of Statistics
CCA	Canadian Co-operative Association
CDR	Committee for the Defence of the Revolution
CDTF	Community Development Trust Fund
CEG	Commonwealth Expert Group
CIRDAFRICA	Centre on Integrated Rural Development for Africa
CMB	Cotton Marketing Board
CUA	Credit Union Association
DDC	District Development Committee
DFRD	District Focus for Rural Development
ECA	Economic Commission for Africa
ECOWAS	Economic Community of West African States
EEC	European Economic Community
EIU	Economist Intelligence Unit
ERP/SAP	Economic Recovery Programme/Structural Adjustment Programme
FAO	Food and Agriculture Organization
FCS	Farmers' Co-operative Societies

GATT	General Agreement on Trade and Tariffs
GDP	Gross Domestic Product
GMB	Grain Marketing Board
GNP	Gross National Product
IDS	Institute of Development Studies
ILO	International Labour Organization
IMF	International Monetary Fund
KVIP	Kumasi Ventilated Improved Pit
KWDP	Kenya Woodfuel Development Programme
LPA	Lagos Plan of Action
MIDP	Machakos Integrated Development Programme
NBC	National Bank of Commerce
NFAZ	National Farmers' Association of Zimbabwe
NGOs	Non Government Organizations
OAU	Organization for African Unity
ODA	Official Development Assistance
OECD	Organization for Economic and Cultural Development
PAMSCAD	Programme of Action to Mitigate the Social Costs of Adjustment
PDC	Provincial Development Committee
PDCs	People's Defence Committees
PHC	Primary Health Care
PNDC	Provisional National Defence Council
S&C	Savings and Credit Societies
SAPs	Structural Adjustment Programmes
SHG	Self-help Group
SPUs	Seed Production Units
TDC	Town Development Committee
UNCRD	United Nations Centre for Regional Development
UNECA	United Nations Economic Commission for Africa
UNICEF	United Nations Children's Fund
UNPAAERD	United Nations Programme of Action for African Economic Recovery and Development
UWT	Umoja wa Wanawake wa Tanzania
VIDCO	Village Development Committee
VSL	Vacuum Salts Limited
W/G	Women's Group
WADCO	Ward Development Committee

WB	World Bank
WCED	World Commission on Environment and Development
YSWGED	Yalta South Women's Group Enterprise Development

1

DEVELOPMENT FROM WITHIN?

The struggle to survive

Fiona Mackenzie

INTRODUCTION

Social struggle within rural Africa, whether it takes a visible form of
co-ordinated action *vis à vis* local power structures or less overt but
perhaps more sustained forms of 'everyday' resistance (Scott 1986) at
intra or extra household levels, dispels any myth of an undifferentiated, immobile peasantry through whom a strategy either of 'grass-
roots initiatives and community self-management', as proposed by
the ECA (Economic Commission for Africa) (UNECA 1989a: 47), or
of greater community responsibility for 'development', in the words
of the World Bank (WB 1989: 54), may be glibly promoted. Such
strategies may indeed be a cheap 'development platform' (to paraphrase Watts, 1989: 6) at a political moment when the more difficult
options of challenging the protectionism of industrial economies and
renegotiating terms of trade are ignored and when state intervention
is made the scapegoat for policy failure. But the proponents of these
strategies, albeit they are analysing African crises from different
ideological perspectives, fail to examine critically the outcome of their
proposals. To call for the 'empowerment' of local people is to
challenge social structure. Profoundly, one is dealing with 'politics'
not 'policies', with 'struggle' and not 'strategy', as Weaver (1984:
138) points out.

In order to explore the interface between these antonyms, to
investigate the nature of local action in the context of a deepening
crisis in Africa, authors were invited to examine how members of
communities in specific rural localities drew on their own resources,
or attempted to gain access to resources controlled by others, as they
sought to survive. A critical question which is raised by the authors'
research is whether the action that they identify may be seen as being

1

a coping mechanism, as a result of the extent to which it meets the practical needs of everyday life, or as being of strategic significance (Molyneux 1985), in that it challenges social structure through a reconstruction of gender or of 'class'[1] and thus concerns empowerment.

The objective of this introductory chapter is to provide a conceptual context within which the case studies may be situated. As an entry point, the crisis in Africa is examined from the perspective of two multilateral institutions, the UNECA (United Nations Economic Commission for Africa) and the World Bank. Through an analysis of the contradictions posed, in particular by the Bank's agenda of continued structural adjustment, the opportunities for and constraints against local mobilization are exposed. Issues of sustainability and of popular participation are explored in the context of the debate between these two institutions.

Through the *African Alternative Framework to Structural Adjustment Programmes for Socio-economic Recovery and Transformation* (AAF–SAP) (UNECA 1989a), the ECA has brought to centre stage an alternative discourse for Africa to that of the World Bank, premised on human centredness. Reaffirming a commitment to an 'internally-generated self-reliant process of development' (Adedeji 1989: 5), which was first articulated in international fora through the Lagos Plan of Action and the Final Act of Lagos (1980), the Framework's rationale lies in 'immersing short term stabilization and adjustment with long term social and economic transformation' (UNECA 1989a: 33). Endorsed at the OAU summit in July 1989 by member states, AAF–SAP challenges blind adherence to the externally motivated prescriptions of stabilization and structural adjustment of the IMF and World Bank. Its progenitors argue, indeed, that these two institutions, in so far as their prescriptions divert attention from the root causes of crisis in Africa and focus instead on the 'symptoms and consequences of Africa's underdevelopment' (Adedeji 1989: 7), mask the nature of Africa's crisis and hence its sustainable resolution, thus contributing to its aggravation.

MEASURING THE ECONOMIC CRISIS

Methodologically, it is impossible to define either the crisis in Africa in general, or the impact of structural adjustment programmes in individual states specifically, on the basis of quantitative data (Berry 1984b: 61; Bienefeld 1989: 4–5; Loutfi 1989: 138–40; Watts 1989: 9).

Official statistics, or 'facts', as Michael Watts points out, are elastic. Frequently, the problem is less one of 'theory shaping fact' than of 'fiction masquerading as fact' (Watts 1989: 9).

Seldom are the contradictions that can be generated by reliance on macro economic data more flagrantly displayed than in the recent interchange of documents between the World Bank (WB/UNDP 1989) and the UNECA (1989b). While the WB/UNDP insist that SAPs have assisted economic performance and that strongly'[2] adjusting countries perform better than countries with 'weak' or no programmes (WB/UNDP 1989: 30, Table 20), the ECA accuses the Bank of faulty methodology. Selectivity in compilation, presentation and analysis of data, the ECA contends, has been exercised with respect to time periods under review, the establishment of base years, the inclusion or exclusion of data sets and the country groupings of African states. Groups of states have 'strong', 'weak' or no reform programmes, yet no definitions of terms are given and clusters are inconsistent with previous Bank practice (UNECA 1989b: 1–7). The data, the ECA proposes, 'seem to have been chosen, at least in some cases, to fit pre-conceived conclusions' (ibid: 6). The result is tautological; those countries that are 'winning' are those that are strongly reforming.

Where data are not available, optimism prevails, leading the Bank to conclude that 'the crisis seems less precipitous and the road to recovery more obvious and more manageable' (WB/UNDP 1989: 1):

> The growth that appears to be resulting, at least in part, from this reform and adjustment helps raise living standards overall and especially for the poor. The agricultural reforms that many countries have adopted, for example, increase the earning of small farmers – who make up about 80 per cent of the population of Sub-Saharan Africa and include most of the poorest people.
>
> (WB/UNDP 1989: iii)

Using the same data set, the ECA turns the table on the Bank, arguing that the latter's compilations for the period 1980–87 showed that countries with strong SAPs had the worst economic performance of any group.[3] The negative annual average growth rate of – 0.53 per cent of this group contrasts with + 2.00 per cent for countries with weak SAPs and a strong + 3.5 per cent for countries with no SAPs.[4] The negative growth rate of the strongly adjusting countries, the ECA points out, leads to an average growth rate for all SSA for

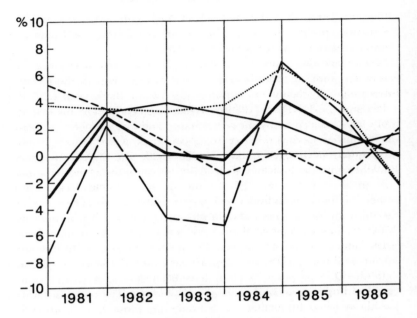

Strong-adjusting: *Burundi, Central African Republic, Congo, Cote d' Ivoire, Gambia, Ghana, Guinea, Guinea-Bissau, Kenya, Madagascar, Malawi, Mauritania, Mauritius, Niger, Nigeria, Senegal, United Republic of Tanzania, Togo, Zaire.*

Weak-adjusting: *Benin, Burkina Faso, Comoros, Equatorial Guinea, Ethiopia, Liberia, Mali, Sierra Leone, Somalia, Sudan, Zambia, Zimbabwe. (Rates exclude Comoros and Equatorial Guinea; 1986 and 1987 excluding Somalia).*

North Africa: *Algeria, Egypt, Libyan Arab Jamahiriya, Morocco, Tunisia.*

Other Countries: *Angola, Botswana, Cameroon, Cape Verde, Chad, Djibouti, Gabon, Lesotho, Mozambique, Rwanda, Sao Tome and Principe, Seychelles, Swaziland and Uganda. (Rates exclude Djibouti; 1986 and 1987 excluding Angola).*

All Africa

After UNECA 1989a: 22

Figure 1.1   Growth of gross domestic product in Africa[1]

the same period of + 0.24 per cent (UNECA 1989b: 10). Figure 1.1 illustrates the annual fluctuation for each of the groups, but it is important to recognize intra-group variation in economic performance, which is dependent on a complex number of factors, including *inter alia* 'weather, conditions of commodity markets, inflow of external resources, the debt situation and structural determinants' (UNECA 1989b: 11). Thus, the ECA argues, 'any attempt to establish a one-to-one relationship between growth trends and the adoption or non-adoption of SAPs is prone to oversimplification and fallacy' (ibid.).

Equally alarming in the construction of an argument is the Bank's ability to use an indicator such as current account deficit (by its own reckoning illustrative of 'deterioration' of economic circumstance, WB 1988b: 2) as indicative of success (WB/UNDP 1989: 29). The Bank argues that only those countries with strong SAPs have been able to 'sustain a progressively widening current account deficit in 1986 and 1987' (ibid.: 28). For Africa as a whole, the deficit increased from $3.9 billion (US) in 1980 to $20.3 billion (US) in 1988 (Adedeji 1989: 10).

The implications of this situation for foreign-borrowing are clear. Although it is frequently pointed out that Africa's debt (which has risen over the decade 1978–88 from $48.3 billion [US] to $230 billion [US], Adedeji 1989: 10) is low, high debt service ratios cast into doubt the ability to sustain even current economic performance. In Ghana in November 1989, 70–75 per cent of export earnings were directed towards debt servicing (*West Africa*, November 1989). For Kenya, the equivalent figure during 1989 was close to 40 per cent (EIU 1989: 4). Even the Côte d'Ivoire, so long exhibited as a 'miracle' of economic performance, now recognizes the costs to political and economic stability of a soaring debt burden.[5]

The problems associated with the continued reliance on external sources for the direction of economies will be examined shortly but it is important to note here, in terms of methodology, that accurate data are more difficult to obtain now than a decade ago (Loutfi 1989: 142). This problem relates, in part, to cutbacks in government expenditure (ibid.) and, in part, to what is actually being counted. This concerns not only 'counted' crops such as cocoa in Ghana, which at various times has escaped official marketing channels by finding more lucrative markets in neighbouring Côte d'Ivoire or Togo (Bequele 1983; Green 1988) and so evading Ghanaian statistical records, but also the lack of visibility of a large sector of the economy, which Jamal (1988) refers to as the 'unconventional economy').

In the everyday struggle of survival in Africa, the majority of rural and urban households survive through juggling a myriad of activities. Even where there is access to a formal sector wage or salary, the reality for only a minuscule percentage of the households, this income provides but a small proportion of daily needs. At the height of the 1983 crisis in Ghana, brought to a head by the drought and rapid inflation of food prices, UNICEF estimated that the minimum wage would cover 2.6 per cent of a minimum 'socially acceptable household budget' for a family of five; the salary of a middle level civil servant would cover 5.9 per cent (Loxley 1988: 9). Households of five members in the low income areas of Accra, Nima and Maamibi spent over eight times the minimum wage in order to survive (ibid.).

Green's (1988: 15) reconstruction of the budget of a Ghanaian household with a male clerk as wage earner in late 1985 illustrates where, in an urban area, the extra income is generated. Wages here provided 25 per cent of household expenditure. A further 25 per cent came from housing and other allowances, tips and sales memos. The wife's income from the sale of vegetables and other 'informal' sector activities and income from other household members accounted for the remaining 50 per cent. With a freezing of wages in 1988, the relative proportion of household income from this source will have decreased, with a return closer to the figures of 1983.

Phenomenal growth in the 'unconventional' or 'informal', but largely uncounted, sector is widely reported as a response to economic crisis in Africa (for example, Colclough 1988; Evans 1989; Green 1988; Loxley 1988; Maya 1988; Onimode 1989a; Tibaijuka 1988). Individuals with or without wage or salaried employment frequently have three or more 'jobs'. The growth in petty trading among women and children has been particularly rapid, yet concomitant with a squeezing of retail margins. Loxley (1988: 39) suggests that, in contrast to wholesale traders whose monopolistic organization allows them to compensate for measures of structural adjustment, such as devaluation of the currency and import liberalization in Ghana, retailers are faced with increasingly intense competition, leading frequently to depressed earnings from this source.

For measuring the economic crisis, there is a woeful lack of adequate data on the distributional consequences of current structural adjustment policies. The political consequences of this omission became most obvious in the riots of December 1986 and June–July 1990 in copperbelt towns in Zambia. Extensive rioting followed the

removal of the maize–meal subsidy by the government (Colclough 1988: 60; Young 1988: 25; *Globe and Mail*, 6 July 1990) in a context where miners, particularly those in the middle and top grades, were disproportionately affected by the economic reform programme. Loxley (n.d: 25) illustrates how, for these two groups of miners, real wages fell 77 and 84 per cent respectively between 1981 and 1986. In contrast, the wages for lower paid miners fell 56 per cent in real terms. Both real per capita GDP and real value-added in the mining industry dropped by 19 per cent over the same period.

Available data from critical sources draw attention elsewhere to the widening disparities among social classes as a result of current policy implementation (Bienefeld 1989; Colclough 1988; Longhurst *et al*. 1988; Loxley 1988). Bienefeld (1989: 70–2), for example, illustrates how, in Tanzania, social polarization is growing rapidly as a consequence of an Economic Recovery Programme which is squeezing the majority of the peasantry who were previously 'protected' by policies which accorded priority to food security. The abandonment of pan territorial pricing exemplifies one instrument operating here. However, recent studies commissioned to support the work of the Commonwealth Expert Group on Women and Structural Adjustment, published by the Commonwealth Secretariat (1989), indicate that analysis of the distributional impact of economic reform programmes must proceed beyond an investigation of urban/rural and rich/poor to an examination of the differential impact on individual household members.

The conceptual point that analysis, or measurement, of the economic crisis must focus on the intersection of class and gender may be underlined through an examination of the repercussions of removing subsidies of food staples, such as maize, in urban areas and raising producer prices of the same crops in rural areas. Evidence from Munachonga's (1986) survey, Sanyal's (1984) doctoral thesis on urban agriculture, and the study by Evans and Young (1987) of household labour allocation in maize producing households in Northern Province, Zambia, which is drawn on by Evans (1989), provides some insights into this issue.

The maize subsidy, Evans (1989: 28) notes, was the 'cornerstone of Zambia's pricing policy', since maize consumption provided 50 per cent of calorie intake for the population. Removal of the subsidy resulted immediately in a substantial increase in the cost of living. In urban areas, where the lowest income groups spent 77 per cent of their monthly income on food, the impact was dramatic (Evans 1989:

33). Munachonga (1986) argues that the strain created particular hardships for women on account of intrahousehold practices of income allocation and control. Her data indicate that men's differential access to income meant that women seldom controlled sufficient resources to provide meals for the family. Women's responses, in addition to borrowing money, were to change consumption patterns through buying less food, buying cheaper and especially less protein-rich food, and reducing the number of meals per day. More positively, some women in Munachonga's survey began to grow their own food. Among poorer households, this frequently entailed travelling to vacant land in the urban periphery; for less poor households, plots close by were common. Production in both cases was primarily for household consumption. From Sanyal's (1984) study, it is evident that vegetable growing could provide for half of household expenditure on food. For 'better off' low income households, 13 per cent of expenditure on food originated from home cultivation (Evans 1989: 31). Female-headed households were particularly vulnerable to food price increases, since not only was their labour insufficient to engage in urban agriculture but also there were fewer economically active members on whom to draw for resources (Evans 1989: 34).

The differential impact on women, contingent on socioeconomic and marital status, of the elimination of the maize subsidy is further evident in rural Zambia: the study by Evans and Young (1987) in Northern Province distinguishes among households on the basis of whether or not maize is produced for the market. Evans (1989: 37–8) points out that only a small percentage of small-scale producers benefited immediately from an increase in the producer price of maize, as the majority of farmers grew cassava, millets and sorghum, the prices of which were not increased. Drawing on an ILO report of 1987, Evans points out that average per capita cash income for the economically active population in this sector actually dropped by 13 per cent between 1976 and 1985. 'Rural producers reliant on selling "traditional" food crops (predominately women)', she writes, 'found their incomes being squeezed by stagnating producer prices and rising transport costs on the one hand, and rising consumer prices on the other' (1989: 39). Frequently, in households headed by women, whether widowed, separated or in a polygamous marriage, insufficient labour and lack of capital with which to purchase seed and fertilizer meant that maize was not grown (Evans 1989: 41).

Among those households which produced maize, the study by

Evans and Young (1987) found evidence that an increased focus on production for the market intensified gender struggle within the household. The labour allocation survey revealed 'that a major interest amongst men in cultivating hybrid maize was to gain direct control over cash income' (Evans 1989: 42). Despite the fact that women provided more labour time in maize production than men, men managed to gain access to the proceeds of the crop through payments from the marketing union and through controlling expenditure. Evans notes that while some women were given money for clothing for the household this did not cover other expenses. Although the survey indicated that women retained 'more or less direct control' of income from other crops, the increased hectarage under maize meant that less land was allocated to millets, beans and groundnuts, and that women had less time to spend on these crops. Also, prices for these crops were much lower than for maize. Further, as Evans notes, 'the purchasing power of such income was declining as crop prices failed to keep pace with the prices of processed and manufactured goods' (ibid.). Evidence from Ghana and the Côte d'Ivoire similarly illustrates the lack of benefit accruing to women from incentives for the production of cash or export crops (Commonwealth Expert Group, 1989). Women's withdrawal of labour from export crop production as a consequence of lack of control over the proceeds is well documented (Carney 1988; Mackenzie 1986; Mbilinyi 1988).

The only exception to this trend of declining income for female farmers, as explored in the Zambian case study, is that of women brewers of beer which is made from millets and maize. This most lucrative form of non-farm income had two negative side-effects, however. First, it led to a decline in food stocks available for household consumption. Second, an increase in the incidence of domestic violence is attributed to growing alcoholism and to women's increased income which threatened the intrahousehold balance of power (Evans 1989: 43).

A negative change in women's bargaining power *vis-à-vis* men is seen to result from other policies carried out under economic reform programmes. Evidence from Tanzania (Tibaijuka 1988), Nigeria (Onimode 1989a) and Zambia (Evans 1989) illustrates the impact on women of cutbacks in formal sector employment. Although Evans (1989: 21) points out that, in Zambia, cutbacks in the formal/public sector had a proportionately greater impact on men because more men are employed in this sector, retrenchment has affected chiefly

9

low-skilled, low wage labour, and so women have been heavily affected. This fact, and the inadequacy of the wage or salary to ensure household reproduction, has led to an explosion of activity in the 'informal' sector, as has already been identified. Much of the increased activity comes from a multiplication of women's labour in this sector. Tibaijuka's (1988) survey of 134 women in low income areas in Dar es Salaam is instructive here. All of the women were involved in income-generating activities, such as petty trade, beer brewing, poultry raising, tuition and tailoring. Seven only of the 134 women had 'professional' jobs. Despite this active and increased participation in economic activity, 58 per cent of the women interviewed said that they had been forced to reduce the number of meals from three to two in their households; 61 per cent indicated a reduction in protein-rich foods (1988: 37–40).

Clearly, as has been pointed out previously, intense competition in the 'informal' sector, as more and more people strive to survive, squeezes profit margins in a context where declining real incomes decrease the purchasing power of urban consumers for goods and services from this sector (Evans 1989: 19). Women are particularly affected. They are likely to be 'downwardly mobile' because of involvement in less profitable enterprises compared to men, and a lack of access to capital and to material resources, for example, premises for storage (Evans 1989: 21).

Untangling the distributional effects of SAPs is complex and requires much further research which links micro analysis with an understanding of macroeconomics at the national and international levels. However, as has been demonstrated through discussion of research which was conducted under the auspices of the Commonwealth Secretariat, data are sufficient to counter arguments such as Loutfi's (1989: 139) that, as the 'informal' sector is a source of economic refuge, the policy impact of SAPs is of little relevance to the functioning of the economy. An intensification of social struggle, as polarization of wealth becomes more deeply embedded, is played out at the intrahousehold level as individuals strive to ensure household survival. The 'African social fabric', as AAF–SAP contends, is in danger of collapse (UNECA 1989a). It is in this light that Adedeji (1989: 12–13) questions whether the SAPs are even a 'temporary palliative' for the problems that Africa faces. They have led, he argues, to an 'erosion of national sovereignty', in terms not only of a hijacking of economic policy to external design but also of a neglect of the human dimension of the crisis.

10

THE 'AFRICAN SOCIAL FABRIC'

In part, the neglect to which Adedeji refers is reflected in a reversal in the 1980s of gains which were made in the previous two decades in levels of nutrition, health, the provision of safe water and education. Green (1988: 7) cautions that there is a danger, when analysing the human condition today, of ascribing the prevalent decay solely and universally to SAPs. In Ghana, he notes, only belatedly did the Provisional National Defence Council (PNDC) begin to address the deteriorating social conditions that preceded the crisis of 1983 and agreements with the World Bank and IMF, by means of the Programme of Action to Mitigate the Social Costs of Adjustment (PAMSCAD) (Ghana 1987). The central issue in analysing this crisis, fundamentally of social reproduction, concerns the extent to which present policies not only undermine previous gains, the focus of Green's (1988) analysis, but also shape, through an intensification of class and gender contradiction, the ability of people to actualize their own survival. In this section, the distributional effects of declining public sector support for health and education are discussed. Again, as would be expected, and as argued so vehemently in UNICEF studies, the cost is disproportionately borne by the poor, by women and by children.

Table 1.1 illustrates the contrasting situation for Ghana and Zimbabwe, countries for which comprehensive data are available from UNICEF's case studies. The dramatic decline in wellbeing which is illustrated in Ghana is related to economic crisis and cutbacks in government social expenditure, both before and after agreements with the IMF/World Bank (Table 1.2). Cuts in Ghana in public expenditure for health are reflected in decreased access to and decreased quality of these resources, in contrast with Zimbabwe. Maya (1988: 27) notes that in Zimbabwe government spending since 1983/4 through Labour and Social Welfare, the main channel for public sector social spending, has decreased by 50 per cent, but that this figure is probably misleading, reflecting temporary payment increases in the face of drought and demobilization. Maya argues that health in particular has remained a government priority even in the face of policies of structural adjustment.

In Ghana, cutbacks have been massive. With respect to health personnel, Ghana lost over half of its doctors between 1981 and April 1984 (Commonwealth Expert Group [CEG] 1989: 57). In 1983, only one of the graduates of the University of Ghana Medical School,

11

Table 1.1 Ghana and Zimbabwe: summary of UNICEF's process and outcome indicators

| | *Ghana* *(1979–85)* | | *Zimbabwe* *(1980–84)* |
	late 1970s	*1980s*	*1980s*
Process indicators			
Average calorie availability as % of requirements	88%	68%	N/A
Access to/use of health services	Decrease of 11% p.a.		Increased coverage of health care and preventive service
Access to/use of education services	Positive change (Primary enrolment rate [6–14 years] constant)		Postive change (Primary enrolment rate [6–14 years] up to 20% per annum)
Outcome indicators			
Infant mortality rate[1]	86%	107%	Positive (qualitative assessment)
Child death rate[2]	15%	25–30%	N/A
Pre-school malnutrition	35% (1980)	54% (1984)	Constant (1982) 18–22% (1984) 16–25%
Primary school quality	Negative		N/A
Disease prevalence	High morbidity, increased yaws and yellow fever		Positive decline in incidence of disease
Population below poverty line:			
rural	60–65% (1974)	70–75% (1984)	
urban	30–35% (1974)	45–50% (1984)	

Source: Cornia 1987: 24–6

1 IMR, per 1,000 live births
2 CDR, per 1,000 of the population aged 0–15 years.

Table 1.2 Sub-Saharan Africa: annual percentage cuts in per capita GDP
and health and education expenditure
(cumulative totals given in parentheses)

	Health 1979–83	Education 1978–83	GDP 1980–5
Ghana	− 15.8[1] (− 40.3)	− 9.5[1] (− 25.9)	− 4.4 (− 20.1)
Malawi	− 9.8[1] (− 26.6)	+ 7.0[1] (+ 31.1)	− 1.1 (− 4.9)
Sudan	− 9.5 (− 32.9)	− 16.8[1] (− 42.4)	− 2.6 (− 12.3)
Togo	− 7.5 (− 26.8)	+ 3.3 (+ 13.9)	− 3.7 (− 17.2)
Liberia	− 6.9 (− 24.9)	− 0.6 (− 2.4)	− 7.1 (− 30.8)

Source: Compiled from Table 3.3, Pinstrup-Andersen *et al.* 1987: 76

1 1979–82.

Korle Bu, remained in the country (personal interview with Dr
Ampofo, Professor of Medicine, 1986). One-twelfth of Ghana's
nurses left in 1982 (CEG 1989: 57). Pinstrup-Andersen *et al.* (1988:
72) note that cutbacks in financing health in Ghana at the height of
the economic crisis in 1982–3 resulted in inadequate infrastructure
for the basic health programme. For example, in the Accra region, 20
of the 57 refrigerators essential for maintaining a cold chain for
vaccines were unusable. The outcome indicators (Table 1.1) of child
survival and welfare reflect this situation.

Evidence from Zambia parallels Ghana's experience, and has been
directly attributed by the Bank to the reform programme carried out
under its auspices (Evans 1989: 22). Again, a decline in the provision
of health care is evidenced by a fall in real per capita expenditure; a
loss of medical personnel (between 1983 and 1986, the ratio of doctors
per 100,000 people fell from 13 to 5); and a drop in the real value of
the drugs budget (in 1986 under 25 per cent of its 1983 value) (ibid.).
The provision of health care in rural areas has particularly been
jeopardized. In a 1986 survey, 73 per cent of rural health centres had
unfilled staff positions, 51 per cent of the vehicles were in disuse, and
there was a lack of essential drugs and equipment. (Drugs were available on the parallel market but at a highly inflated price; Evans 1989:
44.) As Evans points out, those services most used by women and
children required increased costs, both directly for increased distances, and indirectly as more time away from productive work
ensued (ibid.). Where user fees are required, as in urban centres in
Zambia (Evans 1989) or more widely spread in Nigeria (Onimode
1989a), data indicate decreased use of health facilities by the poor.

The long term effects of these policies may not be assessed at present but an increase in maternal and child mortality, particularly in the perinatal period, and an increase in low birth weights are seen by researchers in Tanzania (Tibaijuka 1988: 12) and Zambia (Evans 1989: 24) as evidence of an ominous trend. The escalating decline in adequate nutrition supports this view. Data in Table 1.1 illustrate the situation for Ghana. As in Zambia, malnutrition is associated with the dietary changes documented in the previous section, which are associated with declines in real income for the majority of the population in Ghana and Nigeria (Onimode 1989a: 15). It is also associated with a change in balance of power within the household. Evans (1989: 45) draws on a 1986 survey in Zambia to argue that 'child welfare in households with a variety of individual farming and food processing enterprises is significantly better off than in households whose resources and labour are concentrated in the hybrid-maize farming of one member'. Evidence from Western Kenya (Kennedy and Cogill 1987) and Longhurst's (1988) analysis of the relationship between export/cash cropping and intrahousehold malnutrition suggests that the degree to which a woman controls the income from such crops is a critical determinant of nutritional adequacy among children. In Zambia, Evans (1989: 24) draws attention to the increase in hospital deaths of children which are 'attributed' to malnutrition; they are a minute percentage of those suffering from inadequate nutrition.

Cutbacks in government budgets for health inevitably shift the burden of health care to the household, causing acute problems for low income households, and particularly women, as the prime individuals responsible for such care. The opportunity costs in terms of income generation or agricultural production, and thus potential ability to increase the level of consumption, are high. As the CEG summarizes, the strain on women's labour time increases:

> More time as producers, working outside the home, to contain the falls in household income; more time as home managers and mothers to protect family health and nutrition in the face of rising food prices, reduced incomes and reduced social services; and more time as community organisers to help counter some of the adverse effects through community action.
>
> (CEG 1989: 62)

With respect to education, cutbacks in expenditure and the implementation of user fees again affect the poor and women differentially. In Zambia, where user fees were not as yet introduced for primary or

14

secondary education in 1985, it was estimated that parental expenditure for items (uniforms, books, paper, transport) required for one child to attend primary school averaged one-fifth of per capita income (CEG 1989: 56). For secondary schooling, the cost was nearly half of the average per capita income (Evans 1989: 27). Given the existing bias against female education, which is evidenced in literacy rates for 1985 for the country as a whole (48 per cent of the female adult population, compared to 29.5 per cent of the male, was illiterate), higher female dropout rates and lower participation rates in secondary and tertiary educational institutions, as Evans (1989: 26–7) argues, discrimination against women is likely to be 'aggravated' during a period of structural adjustment.

Direct evidence of the impact of user fees on school attendance comes from Bendel State, Nigeria, but unfortunately this is not disaggregated by sex. Subsequent to the introduction of school fees in 1982, primary school enrolment fell from 90 to 60 per cent within eighteen months (Cornia 1987: 34). An escalation of these trends may be anticipated, with a disproportionate effect on women/girls from low income households, as it is their unpaid labour time which is bearing the hidden cost of cutbacks in public social sector spending and their participation in education which is curtailed first under conditions of economic stress. An intensification of female labour as a result of economic reform programmes is widely documented (CEG 1989; Evans 1989; Tibaijuka 1988).

ENVIRONMENTAL COSTS

The relationship between the economy and the environment has until recently been invisible in analyses of the economic crisis in Africa. However, inspired no doubt by the popular attention given to the Brundtland Report (WCED 1987), both AAF–SAP (UNECA 1989a) and the Bank's publication *Sub-Saharan Africa: from crisis to sustainable growth* (WB 1989) include the environment as a cost connected to economic insecurity.

Although given only brief attention, AAF–SAP (UNECA 1989a: 11) links the aggravation of an environmental crisis to poverty and the increasing severity of the economic crisis: '[I]ncreased poverty induces the poor to degrade further the physical environment as they struggle to eke out a precarious living'. While AAF–SAP may be criticized for not integrating the relationship between poverty and environmental degradation more centrally in its analysis and

recommendations, its statements are less schizophrenic than those of the Bank.

Early in its report (WB 1989: 44), the Bank characteristically holds up population pressure as the primary cause of environmental degradation. Subsequently, the link between poverty and environmental cost is made, albeit within the context of a neoclassical growth paradigm:

> low prices for produce coupled with uncertain land tenure make conservation financially unattractive. . . . A more prosperous rural environment – resulting from the removal of price, exchange rate, and fiscal and other distortions together with greater security of tenure and improvements in productivity – is necessary for farmers, forest dwellers, and pastoralists to have an interest in conservation. Conservation will fail unless it appeals to the farmer's self-interest.
>
> (WB 1989: 101)

The argument that policies pushed by the Bank, specifically those geared to an expansion of export production and hence further integration into the world market system, increase the contradiction between the economy and the environment is ignored.

But it is precisely through what Redclift (1987) has termed the 'internationalisation of the environment' that the contradictions for 'sustainable development' are exaggerated. The central contradiction with advanced capitalism, in terms of its relations with the third world, concerns the way in which 'the labour process, the means by which the social mediation of nature is achieved, succeeds in transforming the environment in ways that ultimately make it less productive' (Redclift 1987: 51).

Redclift's argument is succinctly summarized at the conclusion of his earlier book:

> poor people impose excessive strains on the carrying capacity of the natural environment because of the structural demands imposed on them. The need to increase cash income, repay debts and meet the necessities of the household impinge upon poor people while they are held in a vice by the terms of trade which govern intersectoral and international relations. As 'development' removes them from control over their own environment, this control is assumed by transnational companies and capital-intensive technologies. As some activities,

especially those of women, are transferred from the household to the market place, the environment is relocated not as part of a *local* system of production, but as a link in the international division of labour.

(Redclift 1984: 130)

The solutions, to follow Redclift's (1987) reasoning, lie not with technological tinkering ('environmental management' carries with it a 'facade of technical objectivity'; 1987: 138) but with a profound redistribution of the means and resources of production. In this light, Redclift (1984: 23) argues, it is 'intellectually dishonest' to suggest population increase as a cause of environmental deterioration.

Redclift does not pursue his analysis of the political economy of the environment 'downwards', as Blaikie (1989: 26) suggests, to examine the 'dialectic between environmental and social change' (ibid: 22) in terms of differential gender access to and control over land, livestock, labour, and decision-making at the level of the household. Yet it is at this level, it may be argued, that the 'simple reproduction squeeze' (Bernstein 1979: 427) is most keenly felt. In Africa south of the Sahara, where women are the prime agriculturalists, maximization of short term economic gain through mining of the resource base may outweigh the long term consequences of this action. The option value (Blaikie 1989: 22) of investing in the maintenance of soil fertility, for example, may decrease as a consequence of the stress to meet immediate needs. It may become a less viable strategy for women where security of tenure is threatened through the increasing polarization in rural society and where they need to strengthen social relations which ensure access to land, to follow Berry's (1989: 44–8) argument, demands the diversion of surplus from direct investment in production. As Berry (1989: 49) argues, where there is substantial insecurity, common survival strategies include 'maintaining as liquid a position as possible in one's asset holdings. People are reluctant to tie up capital or fixed assets or long-term projects and prefer to hold commodities . . . or to specialise in activities with rapid turnover (such as trade) rather than in those with long gestation periods.'

As relations of production change within the household under economic stress and as commoditization of production increases, the household becomes a more 'deeply contested terrain' (Watts 1989: 12; Guyer and Peters 1987; Carney 1988; also Vaughan 1985). One outcome, as women strive to meet their responsibilities for household maintenance, is indeed to increase pressure on the land (Mackenzie

17

1991). As undermining of the resource base continues, a cycle of environmental decay increases rapidly the reproduction costs of the household (Blaikie 1989: 28). Thus the contradiction between land use management for agricultural production and the long term sustainability of the resource base is intensified.

As a corollary to this argument, the integrity of local environmental knowledge systems (Belshaw 1979; Kjekshus 1977; Igbozurike 1971; Richards 1979, 1983, 1985) is not in question. Use or misuse of the environment by individuals from specific socioeconomic strata is, as Watts (1989: 15) explains, 'a function of the intersection of resource managers with extrahousehold, non-local circuits of accumulation and surplus extraction'. Nevertheless, it may be argued that, as the option value of maintaining a sustainable resource base declines and as cropping strategies based on exportable commodities prevail, a further subjugation of the 'ecological specificity' (Richards 1983: 56) of local knowledge is likely. Women's relationship to the land alters through a reproduction squeeze, commodity production is maximized at the expense of long term land sustainability, and thus a particular knowledge base is threatened. The ecological costs of the devaluation of such knowledge are intimately linked, as Stamp (1989: 129) illustrates, with the pervasive imposition of Western 'knowledge' on Africa and the construction of knowledge about Africa through a process whereby dominant power structures are reinforced. It is with this process, yet a further implication of Africa's loss of sovereignty, that the recent ECA documents take issue on a large scale.

COUNTERING THE EROSION OF SOVEREIGNTY

Diagnosing the crisis in Africa in terms of external dependence, which created social and political structures leading to a polarized society, the Lagos Plan of Action (LPA) and the Final Act of Lagos (1980) sought resolution of the crisis through a long term strategy of self-sustaining development based on the maximum internal use of Africa's resources (UNECA 1980). Faced with a balkanized continent, the LPA placed emphasis on national and collective self-reliance, the alleviation of poverty and a raising of living standards, and an egalitarian society (Adedeji 1985; Asante 1985; Lardner 1985). In this analysis the environmental costs of the prevalent approach were ignored, although the ecological implications of policies towards agriculture were considered in commentaries (Daddieh 1985).

18

However, by 1985, with a deepening economic crisis, the analysis in the African Priority Programme for Economic Recovery 1986–90 (APPER) had been modified, despite an affirmation of the principles of the LPA, to include a frank acknowledgement of 'internal factors' which contributed to the crisis. The lack of implementation of the LPA was considered to be due to 'insufficient structural transformation and economic diversification' from an inherited colonial structure (UNECA 1986: 7). As the crisis intensified, policy makers shifted their attention to short term crisis management through stabilization and adjustment programmes (UNECA 1989a: 10).

Identification of endogenous factors in APPER indicated considerable responsibility within Africa for the crisis. Among the factors were: structural imbalance (e.g. urban–rural; disparities in income distribution); population increase; the inadequacy and misdirection of human and financial resources; inappropriate economic strategies and policies; poor economic management; inadequate institutional and physical infrastructure; the 'persistence of social values, attitudes and practices not always conducive to development'; and political instability (UNECA 1986: 9). Among the exogenous factors identified were: international recession; commodity price collapse; adverse terms of trade; decline in real terms of ODA; increasing protectionism on the part of northern markets; high interest rates; currency fluctuations; and high debt and debt servicing obligations (ibid.: 10).

As a result of this analysis, solutions to the crisis were sought through a balance between external and internal measures. APPER refers to 'shared responsibilities' and 'a genuine partnership' between Africa and the international community (UNECA 1986), a co-responsibility which was accepted in the UN Programme of Action for African Economic Recovery and Development 1986–90 (UN-PAAERD) (UN 1986a). The approach was expected to lay the basis for self-sustained development but subsequent years have proved this not to be the case, as illustrated in earlier sections of this chapter. An ECA survey of mid-1987 documented not only the extent to which African countries were adopting policy reforms under SAPs, but also the lack of support from the international community. Ironically, the year 1986 saw a dramatic drop in the terms of trade of some of Africa's principal exports (Adedeji 1987).

An intensification of the crisis by the end of the 1980s led to a re-examination of previous analysis and policy recommendations on the part of the ECA. Remarkable in the vehemence of the language used, AAF–SAP (UNECA 1989a) considers that the growing reliance on

the direction of African economies by multilateral institutions (the IMF and World Bank), chiefly through the implementation of SAPs, contributes to the crisis rather than resolves it. SAPs, it is argued, deal with symptoms of the crisis, such as budgetary and external disequilibria, rather than root causes; the human costs of SAPs are unsustainable and undermine long term, sustainable development. AAF–SAP notes:

> Unless there is an immediate amelioration in the conditions of the vast majority of the African population, there is a real danger of a systemic breakdown in the socio-economic fabric and the supporting natural environment.
>
> (UNECA 1989a: 10)

Regaining control over the direction of African economies and human resource development is identified as a key to the future:

> The gradual erosion of sovereignty implied in the growing role of officials of international financial and development institutions and donor agencies in policy design, implementation and monitoring without any accountability to the people of Africa will be reversed. . . .
>
> (UNECA 1989a: 49)

AAF–SAP is a 'blueprint' providing the 'broad guidelines and strategies' for long-term, 'human-centred' and 'holistic' development to be achieved through the 'immersion' of short term adjustment with long term social and economic transformation (UNECA 1989a: 33). AAF–SAP argues that

> Africa has to adjust. But, in adjusting, it is the transformation of the structures that fundamentally serve to aggravate the African socio-economic situation that constitutes the focus of attention. As such, adjustment and transformation must be conceived and implemented as inextricably linked and intertwined processes such that progress will be made simultaneously on the two fronts.
>
> (UNECA 1989a: 33)

The dichotomy between long and short term is resolved, in the document, through the 'endogenisation of development' (UNECA 1989a: 13).

Analysis of Africa's predicament proceeds, according to AAF–SAP, from a political economy perspective. In fact, this includes neither a debate over the role of the state nor a serious attempt to break

out of the duality (external/internal) of the conceptualization of previous documents. There is, however, a significant broadening of the field of discussion.

Consistent with previous theorizing, AAF–SAP again challenges 'the outward orientation' of consumption and production, arguing for the transformation of economic and social structure at the level of production (UNECA 1989a: 12). Principally, this will entail breaking the 'apron-strings of structural and relational dependence' which is most visible in the production of a few primary commodities for export. Africa will not make 'a development break-through' by following this route, it is argued: trade 'dependence' must be changed to trade 'viability' (UNECA 1989a: 13) and this is to be achieved primarily through an increase in intra-African trade. Only through this route, it is suggested, can there be a curtailment of structural dependency, the outward manifestations of which include a 'narrow, disarticulate production base with ill-adapted technology' (UNECA 1989a: 2), a neglected informal sector, a rising debt burden, capital flight, the loss of skilled personnel, declining institutional capability and deteriorating terms of trade. The environment and its degradation are included as an integral component in economic analysis (e.g. UNECA 1989a: 4, 11).

In contrast to earlier analysis, socio-political structure achieves greater visibility in AAF–SAP. The document points to the increasing social differentiation in African society – between classes, gender and ethnic groups – on the basis of economic and political cleavage, and the danger of imminent breakdown. But it also draws attention to the lack of 'democratic political structure' (UNECA 1989a: 7) within African society and calls for democratization of society and accountability of those in power to their electorate.

On a broad scale, AAF–SAP tackles the relevance of present institutional capability in resolving the crisis. Public administration is charged with a 'siege-mentality' which is responsive to '*ad hoc* crisis management' (UNECA 1989a: 33) at the expense of long term economic planning. Blame is placed on the increasing role of 'foreign experts and managers' and on the continuous rounds of negotiations with aid agencies and with creditors for debt rescheduling. The result is that 'the scope for independent policy-making and rational economic management in Africa has gradually diminished and narrowed' (UNECA 1989a: 8). Reinforcing national economic management capability is a key to restructuring.

Policy instruments which are designed to address these questions

are organized in the Framework broadly around four themes: the strengthening and diversification of production capacity, including a focus on agricultural investment for food production; improving the level of income and the pattern of distribution; redirecting public expenditure towards measures to promote the satisfaction of basic needs (limiting debt service ratios is one instrument through which this may be achieved); and fostering appropriate institutional support to ensure adjustment with transformation (UNECA 1989a: 38–43). It is in this last context that community institutions, specifically indigenous NGOs and self-help programmes, are identified. The authors of AAF–SAP write as follows:

> At the institutional level, there is need for excessively central-ised bureaucracies to yield to local decentralisation, grass-roots initiatives and community self-management. . . . [T]he increas-ing role of the people in adjustment with transformation should facilitate the functioning of a system of checks and balances and safe-guard against bureaucratic excesses.
>
> (UNECA 1989a: 47)

Further, AAF–SAP's implementation

> must be based on a genuine and active partnership between the government and people through their various political, social and economic organisations at national, local and grass-roots levels.
>
> (UNECA 1989a: 49)

'Vigorous' government support for grass-roots' initiatives is called for (ibid.).

The extent to which such grass-roots initiatives may facilitate development 'from within', i.e. may be strategic in intent rather than merely coping with crisis, is the central question of this book. It is dis-cussed in this chapter after the Bank's proposals are analysed. It is important to note at this point, however, that AAF–SAP fails to consider the socioeconomic climate, the degree of differentiation, within which community initiatives are to flourish. 'Differentiation' may appear in the Framework's analysis, yet a fault line between theory and prescription emerges, owing to the failure to investigate social relations which have led to present practice. In AAF–SAP, as in previous UNECA documents, an underlying contradiction is buried in the supposed neutrality of bureaucratic discourse; namely, that those accepting the report were themselves assisted in reaching

their position by market forces, particularly through integration into the international economy and present 'development' approaches, and yet are to be the instruments to foster 'another' development.

Community initiative is one of several recurring themes which are identified as having significance in terms of ways forward in AAF–SAP but which are inserted by the World Bank, through its recent response to the ECA, *Sub-Saharan Africa: from crisis to sustainable growth* (WB 1989), into an ostensibly alternative analysis. Acknowledging here the depth of the crisis in Africa, that social progress is in danger of erosion as hunger increases and as ecological degradation accelerates, the document similarly argues that the approach to development must be broadened from purely monetary considerations to become human centred:

> Improving health, expanding education, ensuring food security, creating jobs: these are the priorities shared by all the partners in Africa's development.
>
> (WB 1989: 186)

Continuing, the Bank argues that 'deep transformation of the production structure is required' through a long term strategy (ibid.: 186). Successful SAPs, the fulcrum of sustainable change, must go beyond stabilization in order to 'achieve a genuine transformation of production structures' (ibid.: 189), taking account of the social impact of adjustment measures. There is to be more investment in education, health, science and technology, infrastructure and environmental protection.

In the search for common 'high ground' in the discourse on African crises, the Bank also talks of equitable growth, not in terms of a 'distribution of wealth' but concerning 'access to assets and poverty alleviation' (WB 1989: 38). Self-reliance is acknowledged as a legitimate notion, albeit framed within arguments of comparative advantage. An increase in intra-African trade is seen as one route to this end. A continued insistence on a retraction of state intervention is tempered by an acknowledgement that short term intervention, for example in the area of food subsidies or in the provision of some public goods, may be necessary (ibid.: 55)

However, such calls, as well as those for greater democratization, consonant at the level of rhetoric of those of AAF–SAP, lie uneasily with the renewed commitment to the free play of market forces. As Hutchful (1990) argues, schizophrenia is evident in philosophical and practical posturing; in the tendency to mask old policies with new

slogans; and in discussions which deal simplistically with some very difficult issues, such as those of local empowerment.

Consistent with previous analysis, namely the 'Agenda for Action', or the Berg Report as it is frequently named (WB 1981), and *Toward sustained development in Sub-Saharan Africa* (WB 1984a), the present report dwells on internal explanatory factors. A brief consideration of terms of trade, for instance, admits that for poorer sub-Saharan countries the situation is particularly difficult but that southern Asian countries in similar circumstances have 'coped better'. Africa's deteriorating economies, the Bank reasons, 'must be attributed in large part to a combination of high population growth and low GDP growth (WB 1989: 25). Population, as in previous reports, in relation to 'development' and, incidentally, environmental degradation (ibid.: 22), becomes part of a simple Malthusian equation, dissociated from historical context. Declining returns on investment are blamed for Africa's increasing uncompetitiveness internationally in agriculture and industry; in turn, poor public sector resource management and 'bad policies' are viewed as culprits. In the words of the Bank: 'Together these have undermined the efficiency of the private sector and have added greatly to the high cost of doing business in Africa' (WB 1989: 27).

Despite a partial apologia for co-responsibility for 'inappropriate' investment (WB 1989: 27), the Bank once again casts public sector management as the scapegoat for economic failure, and so continues to rely on policy instruments drawn from classical economic theory. In the words of AAF-SAP (UNECA 1989a: 18): 'output, employment, and prices (including wages, interest rates and the exchange rates) are best determined by the free play of market forces, and . . . prices are the most effective instruments for the efficient allocation of resources'. The main components of this 'monetarist jigsaw' (Adedeji 1989: 16), whose composite picture varies little from country to country, include: demand restraint, primarily through cuts in government expenditure, public sector employment and real wages; a pricing policy which aims at decontrol of price structures, including the elimination of subsidies and the imposition of user fees for public services; trade liberalization involving currency devaluation and foreign exchange auctions; credit reform principally through the setting of higher interest rates and the provision of increased agricultural credit; privatization of, for example, parastatals; and institutional 'strengthening' (Commonwealth Expert Group 1989: 45; Loxley 1988: 12–17).

24

It is against this continuation of previous economic direction, of orthodox structural adjustment, that the Bank's emphasis on community initiative may be assessed. Is local level empowerment part of the 'arsenal of new conservatism' emanating from the US (Hutchful 1990), the cheap 'development platform' of Watts (1989: 6)? Or is it, indeed, a sustainable critical component in directing the future? The Bank does suggest:

> Like trees, countries cannot be made to grow by being pulled upward from the outside; they must grow from within, from their own roots.
>
> (WB 1989: 194)

The Bank's arguments for local empowerment rest on two pillars: the first is an appeal to 'indigenous African values and institutions', particularly 'primary group loyalties', or a communal tradition (WB 1989: 60); the second concerns a debate which is couched in terms of not merely the public (state) sector *vis-à-vis* the private sector but also decentralization of institutional structure among central authority, local government and local communities (ibid.: 55) in order to ensure efficacy in development initiative.

It is worth quoting at length to illustrate the flavour of the Bank's proposals with respect to African 'tradition' and community initiative:

> History suggests that political legitimacy and consensus are a precondition for sustainable development. A sound strategy for development must take into account Africa's historical traditions and current realities. This implies above all a highly participatory approach – less top-down, more bottom-up than in the past – which effectively involves ordinary people, especially at the village level, in the decisions that directly affect their lives.
>
> (WB: 1989: 60)

'Africa has rich traditions of community and group welfare', the Bank writes:

> This is reflected in the widespread practice of sharing among people, with its emphasis on grassroots initiatives and community-based projects. Such cooperation tends to be spontaneous and informal.
>
> (WB 1989: 168)

25

African intellectuals, the Bank continues, have frequently noted the failure of post-independence development strategies to draw on 'the strengths of traditional societies' (WB 1989: 168). But, the Bank proposes: 'Communal culture, the participation of women in the economy, respect for nature – all these can be used in constructive ways' (ibid.).

The 'informal' credit system or indigenous methods of crop husbandry *inter alia* have a role to play. Without romanticizing 'the traditional sector', the Bank's purported aim is to support it through the 'modern' sector, rather than undermine it. Pragmatism is to prevail:

> Community-based development projects provide an avenue for mobilizing community savings in cash or labour for a range of local activities. Much community development in Africa has been carried out by local self-help – for example, the construction, repair, and maintenance of community facilities. Because those involved are direct beneficiaries, motivation tends to be high. Such projects are an effective means of using free resources to meet the community's most urgent needs.
>
> (WB 1989: 169)

Earlier in the report it is noted that:

> [m]any basic services, including water supply, health care, and primary education, are best managed at the local level – even at the village level – with the central agencies providing only technical advice and specialized inputs.
>
> (WB 1989: 54)

In order to facilitate local initiative, the aim should be, in the Bank's words: 'to empower ordinary people to take charge of their lives, to make communities more responsible for their development, and to make governments listen to their people' (ibid.). Later in the report, the following words are used: 'The challenge is to build on this solid indigenous base, with a bottom-up approach that places a premium on listening to people and on genuinely empowering the intended beneficiaries of any development program' (WB 1989: 191).

Empowerment is to be achieved, essentially, through 'a more pluralistic institutional structure' (WB 1989: 54), specifically through a devolution of authority from central to local government and through closer linkage with non-governmental organizations. The Bank argues as follows:

Involving central bureaucracies may stifle local initiatives. Thus NGO support structures should be encouraged to serve as a link between the state and thousands of small self-help and community development efforts. Such NGOs are closer than government to the rural communities, . . . highly motivated, cost conscious, and sympathetic to labor-intensive approaches, and flexible – a quality that stems from their small size and decentralized decision-making. Both local and foreign-based NGOs should be encouraged.

(WB 1989: 169)

The pervasive paternalism of the document aside, the assumptions in the above argument may be questioned on four fronts. First, the Bank draws on a notion of 'tradition' and communal solidarity, devoid of historical context, as an unchanging and unchallenged sphere of practice without ideological imputation in order to suggest prescriptions for future actions. But 'tradition' or 'custom', Glazier (1985: 231) suggests, is a 'continuously evolving code', used by individuals or groups of individuals to create strategies which 'serve economic or political ends' (ibid: 28). It is a malleable and manipulable instrument to which individuals from different genders, generations and classes have access (Mackenzie 1990; Stamp 1987) and which may be used to foster social differentiation (also Chanock 1985; Moore 1986; Parkin 1972).

This point is a critical one: societies may contain values and expertise far more consonant with a sustainable development ethic – including that of community responsibility – than that of a development model imported by outside agencies, but to assume that such societies are undifferentiated, that all interests are served through subscription to 'community development efforts' (WB 1989: 169), is to mythologize. Hyden (1980) notwithstanding, differentiation within the peasantry has created its own series of emergent and frequently conflictive interests (for example, Bernstein 1979; Kitching 1980), played out further in the reconstruction of gender (for example, Mackenzie 1990; Mikell 1989; Robertson and Berger 1986; Stamp 1987). The objectives of different interest groups may be served through community initiative, as Wade (1988) has illustrated with respect to collective decision-making *vis-à-vis* scarce resources in the very different socio-political context of 'village republics' in southern India, but this may not be universally assumed. Thomas (1988: 22) has argued, with reference to Harambee and the politics of

self-help in Kenya, that 'strong communal identities' frequently coexist with 'nascent class awareness'. Subscription to community solidarity may also coexist with contradictory gender awareness (Mackenzie 1990; Stamp 1987). The outcome may be the complex interplay of allegiances which in certain situations takes the form of collective community action while at other times the structure of such communities may be challenged from within.

Second, the Bank's prescriptions can be challenged for the assumption of 'free resources' (WB 1989: 169) that may be put to use to meet community needs. Labour no more than capital is a 'free resource' in the provision of basic needs: opportunity costs are implied in both. Again in Kenya, activities carried out under the aegis of Harambee do enable rural communities to command resources, through patrimonial linkage, from an urban élite with a need for a secure power base in the rural area, and thus at one level represent a form of progressive taxation. But they also serve to legitimize inequalities in the post Independence state (Thomas 1988), an argument which is pursued at the more general level by Brett (1988: 10). Thomas writes:

> The rhetoric of Harambee stresses cooperative effort for the benefit of all. The reality of Harambee underscores a system in which some communities, some groups, and some national-level elites benefit far more than others.
>
> (Thomas 1988: 23)

As Harambee activities frequently rely on women's labour (Thomas 1985), the stress on their contribution to community welfare may frequently be disproportionate to their gain. Continued reliance on their labour input in such activites becomes more problematical under structural adjustment programmes where increased responsibility for productive and reproductive tasks in rural areas falls to women, as discussed in the previous section.

This is not to argue that strategies created at the local level are not, and have not been, vital to survival in rural Africa, as several of the case studies illustrate. But it is to expose to scrutiny further curtailment of state responsibility.

A third area of concern for the Bank's new found panacea for Africa's ills lies in the assumption that 'local' empowerment is politically of no consequence to those in power at the level of the state. Here the Bank falls into the populism of early proposals for development 'from below' (see Forbes 1984: 130–5; Gore 1984: 222–32). Arguing for the ascendancy of territory rather than function as a key

principle for social organization (for example, Friedmann and Weaver 1979; Friedmann 1981), such proposals focus on internal territorial integration through the

> maximum mobilisation of each area's natural, human, and institutional resources with the primary objective being the satisfaction of the basic needs of the inhabitants of that area.
>
> (Stöhr and Taylor 1981: 1)

In order to achieve equitable development, Stöhr and Taylor argue, 'development policies must be oriented directly towards the problems of poverty, and must be motivated and initially controlled from the bottom' (ibid.). Further,

> Development 'from below' strategies are basic-needs oriented, labour-intensive, small-scale, regional resource-based, often rural-centred, and argue for the use of 'appropriate' rather than 'highest' technology.
>
> (Stöhr and Taylor 1981: 1–2)

Selective regional, or spatial, closure (Stöhr and Tödtling 1979) is viewed as a critical instrument in achieving these ends.

But development 'from below' is labelled neo-populist by Gore (1984: 165) and utopian by Forbes (1984: 134) precisely because, although it may draw from political economy in considering, for example, the spatial transfer of surplus (Forbes 1984: 134) or the empowerment through participation of the poorest members of society, it fails to construct a coherent analysis which connects the different actors, or interest groups (class, gender, ethnic group), within society. As Forbes (1984: 134) points out, it is a theory of policy rather than of explanation. The contradictions that may evolve in terms of state–local relations, of classes, or of genders, are ignored. Indeed, the interests of individuals or of groups are frequently equated with territorial interest, 'an ecological fallacy' in Gore's (1984: 225) conception: it does not follow that development measured at a certain level of aggregation denotes benefits to all members of that group.

The empowerment of individuals or groups within a community concerns, by its nature, political action. The realization of strategic needs (Molyneux 1985), which go beyond those of 'coping mechanisms' or 'practical needs', reorders social relations. And these may be perceived as a threat, not only to local interests but also to state power. Nowhere is this clearer than in the response of the Kenyan state to the

activities of the Kamiriithu Community Educational and Cultural Centre in Limuru. On two occasions, the first in 1977 after ten performances of the play *Ngaahika Ndeenda* (I will marry when I want), the second in 1982 after rehearsals for another play at the University of Nairobi, state authorities forcibly halted the performances, detaining writer Ngugi wa Thiong'o who had been involved in the production on the first occasion, and destroying the open air theatre in Limuru on the second.

Kidd (1982: 48) has asked why popular theatre, produced by workers and peasants, provoked the hostility of government: 'Why has a program which has significantly reduced illiteracy and alcoholism, increased employment opportunities, fostered a people's culture and raised the awareness and participation of villagers been suppressed?' The answer, in his subsequent analysis and in Ngugi's (n.d.) writings on the subject, identifies the theatre as a site of resistance, of struggle, and the dramas created as expressions of a growing conscientization of the people involved. 'Understandably', Ngugi (n.d: 126) writes, 'the wealthy who control the government did not like the stark realities of their own social origins enacted on the stage by simple villagers.'

Similar presumptions to those of the Bank are found in AAF–SAP, as has already been suggested. Where the state is a 'continual site of struggle' (Kitching 1985: 132), the primary concern of the contending interests which comprise the state is the reproduction of their own 'class' position (Dutkiewics and Shenton 1986). Thus, the political and economic restructuring necessary to facilitate empowerment may be unlikely to proceed far. With specific reference to the Berg Report and demands for a reduction in state intervention, Dutkiewics and Shenton (1986: 114) argue that the 'ruling groups' are in effect invited 'to commit political suicide'. Any strategy of decentralization in this context may be no more than a guise for the exertion of further central control (ibid: 111; Olowu 1989: 202. Gore 1984: 249–58). The 'metonymical' nature (Gore 1984: 258) of such policies allows the state both to resolve conflicting interests within it and to legitimate its continuation in authority.

To what extent, then, can local, non-governmental organization thrive? Can it provide, except under the most repressive regimes, resolution of problems of poverty, as Sandbrook (1986) claims? Is a threat to the rules of the game, which are operative in 'macro arenas' (Goulet 1989: 168), more or less likely to be tolerated as states retrench, in terms of the provision of social welfare, but increase

repression in an attempt to enforce unpopular policies which are demanded through SAPs (namely the urban riots in Zambia in June 1990)? This fourth area of concern is neglected by both AAF–SAP and the World Bank.

The case for local empowerment may be strong – based on an ecological and environmental rationale (Richards 1979, 1983, 1985; Bell 1979; Chambers 1988; Thomas-Slayter and Ford 1989), on the reality of social and economic diversity (Chambers 1988; Taylor 1989; McCall 1988; Oakley and Marsden 1984), or on the ideology of a 'moral incentive' for equitable development and political democracy (Goulet 1989: 172). However, local organization, even if it originates in response to crisis, as 'the spontaneous mobilisation of a powerless group to defend itself against destruction', may yet contain, Goulet (1989: 167) argues, the 'latent seeds of organisation for multiple new developmental actions'. In this sense, the line drawn between that which may initially appear as a coping mechanism or action to meet a practical need and that which is of strategic significance may be blurred. And in the transfer of consciousness from one to the other, the transition to the 'macro arena' (the 'ever widening arena of decision making', which implies the maturation of a 'social force wielding a critical mass of participating communities' [Goulet 1989: 168]) will indeed challenge the interests of those in power both within the local community and at wider levels of social organization, the state.

NOTES

1 Gender is taken here to refer to the *social* construction of differences between women and men. Following Robertson and Berger (1986), the concept of access to and control of critical resources is used to analyse the relationships of men and women to the means of production. Such a definition of class, Robertson and Berger suggest (1986: 21), is 'more sensitive to local conditions and social structure' in Africa, and allows for an analysis of both class and gender struggle within and outside the household.

2 With respect to the Bank's classification of countries with 'strong' or 'weak' reform programmes (WB/UNDP 1989: 33, Note b), the UNECA (1989b) points to the lack of clearly developed criteria to distinguish among African countries. The Bank defines as 'strong' those countries with SAPs with the WB/IMF during 1985–7. But, the UNECA (1989b: 4) points out, 'neither the count of 19 countries resulting from this classification nor the reference period stated are adhered to in other parts of the Report'.

3 ECA calculations were based on World Bank GDP data (in constant 1980

US dollars, market prices) and countries were grouped according to those in the Bank's list. But the annual average growth rates for the groupings calculated by the ECA were based on weighted averages rather than the unweighted ones of the Bank (UNECA 1989b: 10).

4 These data differ from those given in AAF–SAP. Countries with strong SAPs are estimated in AAF–SAP to have had an overall average annual growth rate of 1.5 per cent in the period 1980–87. 'Weak-adjusting countries' recorded an overall average annual GDP growth rate of 1.2 per cent and 'non-adjusting countries' a rate of 3.1 per cent (UNECA 1989a: 22–3). These are the data used in Figure 1.1, and represent subsequent calculations to those in UNECA 1989b.

5 Abdoulaye Kone, Economy and Finance Minister, quoted in *Globe and Mail*, 2 July 1987 and referred to by Bienefeld 1989: 73.

2

LOCAL FARMER ORGANIZATIONS AND RURAL DEVELOPMENT IN ZIMBABWE

Lovemore M. Zinyama

INTRODUCTION

The political history of Zimbabwe from colonization in 1890 to the present has had a controlling influence on state policies for the development of those parts of the country that were set aside for settlement by the indigenous blacks *vis-à-vis* areas that were alienated for the incoming white settlers. Colonial state policies favoured the latter areas, thereby creating and perpetuating a dual socioeconomic structure which was characterized by wide spatial inequalities. The post-independence government that came to power in 1980 has sought to reduce these racial and spatial inequalities by giving priority to the development of the previously neglected areas that are home for the country's black peasant farmers who make up some 60 per cent of the national population. However, some commentators contend that recent gains in agricultural production and rural development, with their focus on the existing peasant areas but without substantial agrarian reform, are likely to be unsustainable. It is argued that the government's current policies and strategies have failed to address directly the problems facing the rural peasantry in Zimbabwe. These problems, which are a legacy of ninety years of colonial rule, include rural overpopulation and a deteriorating human–land ratio, environmental degradation, low rural incomes, and a lack of both rural and non-rural off-farm employment opportunities.

In the meantime, the small-scale subsistence agricultural population is compelled by harsh economic and environmental conditions to evolve a variety of strategies for mitigating the persistent rural poverty and hardships. This chapter examines some of the local-level initiatives that small-scale peasant farmers in Zimbabwe adopt in

33

order to improve their levels of agricultural production and hence their household incomes, with particular emphasis on the role of grass-roots voluntary farmer organizations. In many ways, these organizations complement the government's efforts to develop the previously neglected peasant farming areas. Given the unique circumstances of the decolonization process in Zimbabwe, where independence was won after a bitter war whose brunt was borne by the rural population, the development of these areas is seen as a two-way partnership in which the government contributes from the top while the farmers contribute from below. The focus of this chapter is on the latter, using the case of local peasant farmer groups as an example of 'development from within' or the 'self-reliant and communitarian' approach to rural development that has recently been suggested as one possible way of solving the African economic crisis (Mackenzie and Taylor 1989; Sandbrook 1986). Such community-based developmental organizations may

> also permit villagers, by defining their own needs, designing and implementing their own projects, to educate themselves in organizational dynamics and self-government. In time, this local capacity for organization and confidence may increase popular pressure for change at the territorial level.
>
> (Sandbrook 1986: 331)

The Zimbabwe experience in recent years provides an additional dimension to the theme of this book. In most African countries today, governments are retreating from the rural areas, leaving the rural population to evolve its own coping strategies and organizational structures in order to mitigate the deteriorating economic conditions. In Zimbabwe, on the other hand, the opposite prevails at present, with the government actively seeking to improve rural living standards through the development of social and economic infrastructure, the improvement of health and sanitation, and the provision of agricultural extension, marketing and credit services. Local farmer initiatives for the development of their areas and their agricultural capacities have generally received support from the government and, in some cases, from the private sector and from non-governmental organizations. Thus, in the Zimbabwean context, local-level initiatives or 'development from within' need to be regarded as complementary to the government's efforts of 'development from above'. It is therefore inappropriate to regard these local initiatives primarily as a reaction to the withdrawal of the state from the rural areas.

The chapter is divided into four parts. The first section briefly describes the principal agro-ecological regions into which Zimbabwe is divided for commercial farming purposes. The second section provides an overview and comparison of colonial and post-colonial government policies for the development of the black peasant farming areas. The third section discusses the four agricultural subsectors in the country and the changing role of black farmers in the national economy. The fourth section discusses how peasant farmers in two of the communal farming areas are using grass-roots voluntary organizations as a means of self-reliant resource mobilization in order to overcome felt agricultural resource constraints.

AGRO-ECOLOGICAL REGIONS OF ZIMBABWE

Zimbabwe has been divided for agricultural purposes into five agro-ecological regions (commonly known as Natural Farming Regions), mainly on the basis of the amount, reliability and variability of their rainfall (Vincent and Thomas 1961). Conditions become increasingly

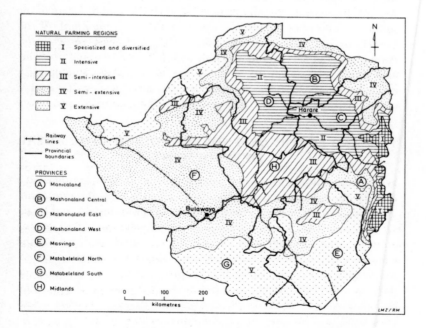

Figure 2.1 Principal agro-ecological regions of Zimbabwe

35

marginal for crop production from Natural Region I to Natural Region V as rainfall decreases in both amount and reliability. For commercial farming purposes, Regions I and II, with high and reliable annual rainfall in excess of 750 mm, are suitable for specialized farming (i.e. plantation crops such as tea and coffee) and intensive crop and livestock farming respectively (Figure 2.1). Agro-ecological Regions I and II respectively cover 1.8 per cent and 15 per cent of the country along the eastern border highlands and on the central plateau in the north and east. Region II is the breadbasket of the country, contributing up to 90 per cent of the national annual crop production.

Agro-ecological Region III receives moderate rainfall, between 650 and 800 mm per year, but much of it falls as infrequent heavy downpours which, combined with the high summer temperatures, reduce its effectiveness for crop production. The region is also subject to mid-season dry spells, thereby making it suitable for semi-intensive farming and marginal for enterprises based on dryland crop cultivation alone. Region III covers 18.7 per cent of the country, surrounding Natural Region II but with the largest expanse to the south and west of the central plateau. Natural Regions IV and V occur to the south and west of the country as well as in the low-lying Zambezi and Save-Limpopo valleys in the north and south east respectively. Annual rainfall is less than 650 mm with frequent seasonal droughts and severe mid-season dry spells. These areas are suitable only for extensive livestock and game ranching. Natural Regions IV and V occupy 37.8 per cent and 26.7 per cent of the country respectively.

PRE- AND POST-INDEPENDENCE POLICIES FOR RURAL DEVELOPMENT

When Zimbabwe attained independence in April 1980, it inherited a racially divided, dual socioeconomical structure. On the one hand, there was a modern sector comprising the urban-industrial and large-scale commercial farming subsectors which were controlled by the minority white settlers who made up less than 5 per cent of the national population. On the other hand, there was a predominantly subsistence agricultural subsector that provided a livelihood for some three-quarters of the black population. Throughout the colonial period, a variety of legislative and socioeconomic impediments had been used to minimize the permanent migration of blacks into the white-controlled areas, confining the men instead to oscillating labour

migration and forcing them to sojourn in town while their families remained in the rural areas (Patel 1988; Zinyama and Whitlow 1986). At the 1982 census, only one-quarter of the black population was urban, a figure far below that of several other African countries at a comparable level of development. Even today, a decade after the colonial influx control measures were removed and after the country has experienced rapid urban growth arising from rural out-migration, the rural areas continue to support the majority of the population. It is to these rural people that the post-independence government is giving priority in the allocation of national development resources.

Following colonization of the country in 1890 by the British South Africa Company (BSACo), land was divided along racial lines in such a way that blacks were mostly confined to agriculturally marginal areas in Natural Regions IV and V. In 1969, with the enactment of the Land Tenure Act, the last major piece of colonial legislation for dividing the land, the country was divided equally between blacks and whites, with each group getting 46.6 per cent of the total land area, and the remainder was designated as national parks and forest areas (Christopher 1971; Floyd 1962). The areas that were set aside for blacks (previously called Native or African Reserves and now Communal Lands) not only experience low and unreliable rainfall but also have poor sandy soils derived from granitic rock formations as well as large tracts occupied by exposed granite domes which reduce the amount of land available for cultivation (Whitlow 1980a, 1980b). Three-quarters of the communal farming areas are situated within Natural Regions IV and V, compared with 49 per cent of the former white large-scale commercial farming areas. Almost two-thirds of the land in Natural Region I and three-quarters of that in Region II falls within the previously white-owned large-scale commercial farming sector.

In the early years after colonization, blacks were able, by increasing their agricultural output, to meet not only their new tax liabilities, imposed by the colonial administration, and other emerging requirements for cash but also the growing demand for food in the newly established towns and mining settlements. However, as the settler agricultural sector became more firmly established with active government support during the first two decades of this century, it became necessary, first, to ensure a source of cheap labour for white farms and mines and, second, to protect the agricultural produce markets, for the benefit of white farmers, by eliminating competition from black farmers. The government instituted a series

of measures which restricted access by black farmers to agricultural input and output markets and support services (i.e. research, extension and credit facilities). This combined with diminishing productivity from impoverished soils in increasingly overcrowded reserves, reduced black farmers' net returns from agriculture and compelled them instead to sell their labour on the white-owned farms, in the mines and in the towns. The communal areas henceforth served as cheap labour reserves for the modern white-controlled sector of the national economy. Meanwhile, increasing overpopulation within the communal areas over the years has exacerbated problems of land shortage, of the cultivation of marginal lands on steep hill slopes and long stream banks, and of general land degradation through soil erosion and deforestation (Whitlow 1980a, 1988). Not surprisingly, therefore, black farmers during the 1970s contributed less than 25 per cent of the national annual agricultural output while over 90 per cent by value of all of the agricultural produce marketed through official marketing boards came from some 5,000 white large-scale commercial farmers (Republic of Zimbabwe 1982).

At independence in 1980, the new government came to power committed to transforming the national economy and society to socialism and, as a more immediate task, to redress the inherited social and spatial inequalities. It immediately embarked on a dual rural development strategy involving, on the one hand, the redistribution of land and resettlement of land-hungry peasants on former white-owned large-scale farms and, on the other, increased state support for farmers within the existing communal areas.

The government had originally planned to resettle some 162,000 families by 1985. However, by the middle of 1989, only some 52,000 families had been resettled on nearly 3 million hectares of land under different settlement and land use models (*The Herald*, 4 August 1989; Kinsey 1983; Zinyama 1986a). The resettlement programme has progressed much slower than originally envisaged for a number of reasons, including: constitutional constraints on land acquisition, which were imposed on the government at the Lancaster House conference in London prior to independence; lack of money for land purchase and development; recurrent droughts during the mid-1980s; the continuing dominance of settler economic planning ideology; and the co-optation of newly affluent and influential blacks into the landowning classes (Munslow 1985; Stoneman and Cliffe 1989; Weiner 1988; Zinyama *et al.* 1990). Although the resettlement programme was aimed at redressing inequalities in the distribution of land, it has

effected little change in terms of both the total amount and the agricultural potential of the land that has been transferred to date. Much of the land that has so far been transferred for resettlement is situated in agro-ecological Regions III, IV and V. Furthermore, the programme has been scaled down considerably. The 1986–90 National Development Plan proposed the resettlement of only 15,000 families per year (Republic of Zimbabwe 1986). Even this reduced target of 75,000 settler families over five years is unlikely to be achieved. (The constitutional restrictions on land acquisition fell away in 1990 and it still remains to be seen whether the pace of the resettlement programme will accelerate.)

The government has been more successful in the measures that have been taken to improve agriculture and general living conditions within the communal areas. These measures include: the provision of schools, health services, and improved water and sanitation facilities; the decentralization of government services; and improved accessibility of such services through the development of rural service centres at district level (Gasper 1988; Wekwete 1988; Zinyama 1987a). Measures taken to improve the farmers' levels of agricultural production, and hence on-farm incomes from sales of crop surpluses, include: the establishment of a network of official marketing depots covering most of the rural areas; the provision of agricultural credit and extension services; and the improvement of the rural road network (Zinyama 1986a). Local-level participation in the identification, articulation and implementation of development projects within the communal areas has been facilitated by the democratization of local government and the establishment of a hierarchy of development planning fora at which the local inhabitants are represented in Village, Ward and District Development Committees (VIDCO, WADCO and DDC), up to the Provincial Development Committees (PDC) (Mutizwa-Mangiza 1986)

THE CHANGING ROLE OF BLACK PEASANT FARMERS

Today, four distinct agricultural subsectors exist in Zimbabwe. These are: (a) the large-scale commercial farming sector; (b) the small-scale commercial farming sector; (c) the communal farming sector; (d) the resettlement areas (Figure 2.2).

The large-scale commercial farming sector occupies some 12.8 million hectares of land, covering approximately 33 per cent of the total land area. The sector comprises some 4,500 farming units which

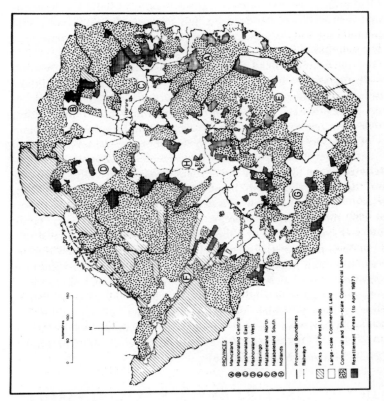

Figure 2.2 Zimbabwe: major land use divisions

range in size from less than 200 to over 8,000 hectares, mostly under freehold tenure. These farms were previously exclusively owned by whites, but today some wealthy blacks have acquired properties within this sector.

The small-scale commercial farming sector comprises some 8,500 units on land that was set aside during the colonial period for the few blacks who wished and could afford to purchase land under freehold and leasehold tenure. The farms are generally less than 150 hectares in size. The sector occupies some 1.4 million hectares, or 3.6 per cent of the total land area.

The communal farming sector occupies some 16.4 million hectares of land, or 42 per cent of the total land area. The sector supports, directly from agriculture, about 60 per cent of the national population. The average size of arable holdings in the communal areas is about two hectares, held under usufructuary rights. In addition, farmers have access to communal grazing land.

The fourth subsector, the resettlement areas, is a post-independence development. The resettlement areas occupy about 8 per cent of the national land area at present. As mentioned earlier, much of the resettlement land has been at the expense of the large-scale commercial farming sector, although some vacant state land has also been utilized for the resettlement programme.

Since 1980, black small-scale farmers in the communal, small-scale commercial, and resettlement areas have greatly increased their crop production levels as well as their share of total marketed agricultural produce as a result of the support and incentives given by the government. This is particularly true for maize and cotton, their principal cash crops. Maize is also the staple crop in the country. Until 1980, black farmers accounted for less than 10 per cent of the maize and less than 25 per cent of the seed cotton that was sold annually to the respective official marketing organizations, the Grain Marketing Board (GMB) and the Cotton Marketing Board (CMB). Today the black small-scale farmers account for a little over 50 per cent of both the maize and cotton that is sold annually to the respective marketing boards. Sales of maize to the GMB from black farmers have increased sixfold from a pre-independence peak of 84,300 tonnes, which were sold after the 1977–8 season, to over half a million tonnes per season today. These figures exclude retentions for the farmers' subsistence requirements. Similarly, the amount of seed cotton that is sold to the CMB has more than doubled from less than 45,000 tonnes annually before independence to over 100,000 tonnes per year today

(Agricultural Marketing Authority 1988; Cotton Marketing Board 1988; Grain Marketing Board 1988).

Such progress can only be described as remarkable, especially when viewed against a backdrop of the recurrent severe droughts of the mid-1980s. Many observers have commented on this apparent Zimbabwean success story in transforming the peasant agricultural sector within such a short period of time. However, these figures, while certainly impressive at the national scale, hide substantial spatial and social disparities in the transformation of the country's peasant agricultural sector. The continuing maldistribution of land across the agro-ecological regions, which was described earlier, exerts a considerable differentiating influence on the current spatial development pattern of the peasant sector (Stanning 1987; Zinyama 1988a). For instance, the three provinces of Mashonaland Central, East and West, which are located in agriculturally favourable areas on the central plateau, support about 28 per cent of the total black farming population. The communal, small-scale commercial, and resettlement areas within these three provinces have experienced the highest and most consistent increases in crop sales to the marketing boards since 1980 (Zinyama 1988a). In seasons of normal rainfall, the three provinces contribute between 55 and 65 per cent of the total maize that is sold by black small-scale farmers countrywide. This rises to over 95 per cent following severe droughts when lower rainfall areas are hardest hit. Some two-thirds of all of the maize that was sold to the GMB by black small-scale farmers during the period 1980–86 came from a little over one-quarter of the farming population who are fortunate to live in these three provinces. An even greater pattern of inequality emerges with respect to sales of seed cotton to the CMB. Some two-thirds of the annual cotton output of the small-scale farming sector (i.e. equivalent to 20–25 per cent of the total national output) comes from two major producing areas in the north west, in the Midlands province, and in the north, in the Mashonaland Central and West provinces. The comparative study by Rohrbach (1987) of two communal areas, Mangwende, which is 80 km east of Harare in Natural Region II, and Chivi, some 370 km to the south in Natural Region IV, also demonstrated that the relative impact of any policy or institutional intervention depends very much on the agro-ecological conditions of the areas concerned.

Intra-community differences by age, gender and status have also been reported in other studies of the peasant agricultural sector. For instance, in Wedza communal area south of Harare, Callear (1984)

42

found three categories of households which were particularly disadvantaged: (a) young families with little land, mainly because of growing population pressures, with few or no cattle and with few or no implements because they had not yet had time to accumulate the necessary farming assets; (b) widows, especially if they had school-going children whose daily labour time was eroded by schooling; (c) families of some labour migrants. The three categories of families failed to earn adequate incomes from both on-farm and off-farm activities. Similar intra-community disparities were reported by Gobbins and Prankard (1983) from four communal areas north-west of Harare, in the Mashonaland West province. In their study, Gobbins and Prankard (1983) classified farming households on the basis of whether or not a family member had undergone formal on-farm training in agriculture under a government extension worker, thereafter qualifying to be known as a 'master' farmer. In all four areas, master farmers had access to more land and family labour, owned more draught cattle, used more purchased crop inputs, particularly fertilizers, and generally had a more balanced mix of resources than non-master farmers. The former also obtained higher yields and incomes from crop sales. The authors suggested that it was members of families who were already wealthy who trained to become master farmers, thereby adding formal technical knowledge to their existing favourable resource base. The result would be an accentuation of intra-community socioeconomic inequalities.

Overall, the regional and social disparities emerging from the commercialization of peasant agriculture suggest that on-farm incomes for a large proportion of communal farmers, especially in the low rainfall areas, have changed little from what they were before 1980. The benefits from the new rural development thrust are largely accruing to the small number of peasant farmers who are fortunate enough to be located within the better agro-ecological regions. Elsewhere, farmers continue to be handicapped by the constant threat of drought and food shortages, by increasing land shortages, by infertile soils and by low agricultural production. Given the social and regional disparities in food production and distribution, it is not surprising that malnutrition continues to be a major public health problem in many parts of rural Zimbabwe (Republic of Zimbabwe 1986), in particular in low rainfall areas where a considerable proportion of children are undernourished even during supposedly good crop years. Overall, post-independence agrarian restructuring has been limited. The success to date in raising agricultural productivity

within the communal areas appears to be merely short term; it does not provide a long term solution to the problems of rural development in Zimbabwe (Munslow 1985; Weiner 1988; Zinyama *et al.* 1990).

Government efforts to develop the rural areas of Zimbabwe, as discussed above, represent the 'development from above' approach. The success in implementing these programmes has been made possible partly by the unique circumstances surrounding the decolonization of the country, whereby the liberation war in the 1970s was fiercest in the rural areas, so enabling the nationalist forces to mobilize and identify with the rural population. Thus, the priority given to rural development after independence was the new government's way of thanking the rural populace for its support during the war. The remainder of this chapter will focus on some of the ways in which farmers themselves are contributing towards the improvement of both agricultural production and on-farm incomes through sales of surplus crops in two of the three communal areas: a process of 'development from within' which, as mentioned earlier, is complementary rather than being an alternative to the macro-level strategies and programmes of government.

LOCAL ORGANIZATIONS AND RURAL DEVELOPMENT: A CASE STUDY

The study areas

During 1983–4, a survey was undertaken by the author to examine the factors influencing agricultural change and development in two communal areas, namely Mhondoro and Save North (Zinyama 1988c). The former is situated about 40 km south-west of Harare while the latter is 150 km south-west of the capital (Figure 2.3). Mhondoro is therefore more accessible than Save North to national markets, infrastructure and other agricultural support services which are available within the capital city and other urban centres. At the 1982 census, Mhondoro had a population of 59,800 people in some 10,900 households while Save North had 62,900 people in 12,600 households. In Mhondoro, population densities ranged between 23 and 107 persons per km^2 for individual enumeration areas, with an average density of 46 per km^2. Average density in Save North in 1982 was 48 per km^2, varying from less than 20 to a little over 100 per km^2 for individual enumeration areas. In Mhondoro, 430 randomly selected households (4 per cent sample) were interviewed. In Save North, 371 households (3 per cent sample) were interviewed.

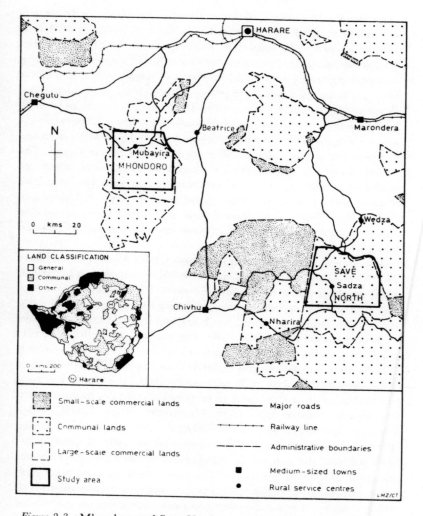

Figure 2.3 Mhondoro and Save North communal areas: the survey areas and major land use divisions south of Harare

The two communal areas are situated in Natural Farming Region III, with moderate rainfall of 650–800 mm per year. Soils in both areas are largely sandy, derived mainly from granitic rock formations. Although the soils are light and relatively easy to cultivate, they are inherently infertile, they drain freely and dry out quickly. This

45

gives them a low water holding capacity. Therefore, moderate and infrequent rainfall and poor soils combine to make rainfed crop cultivation not only risky but also expensive where the farmers attempt to apply the recommended quantities of inorganic fertilizers for optimum crop yields. In both areas, the average amount of arable land per household was 2.1 hectares, although 60 per cent had less than two hectares each. Another one-third had what could be termed, by communal area standards, medium-sized holdings of between 2.1 and 4 hectares. Only 5.4 per cent of the households in Mhondoro and 1.9 per cent in Save North had more than four hectares each. The principal crops in both areas are maize and groundnuts, which are grown by virtually every household, with maize being grown as both a staple and a cash crop. Minor crops include cotton in Mhondoro, and in Save North small grains such as bulrush millet (*Pennisetum typhoides*), sorghum (*Sorghum vulgare*) and finger millet (*Eleusine coracana*).

In common with other communal areas, both Mhondoro and Save North have, since independence, witnessed major changes in agricultural practices and crop production levels. The survey showed that the proportions of households using improved agricultural techniques, particularly chemical fertilizers and hybrid maize seed, have increased considerably since 1980. For instance, only 33 per cent of the households in Mhondoro (and an even lower percentage in Save North) were using chemical fertilizers for maize production before 1980, compared with over 90 per cent by 1983. The changes in agricultural practices are reflected in crop yields and sales to the marketing boards. Maize sales from Mhondoro to the GMB, which averaged 1,014 tonnes annually during the pre-independence period 1974–9, quickly rose to 14,038 tonnes for the 1981–2 intake year. This followed the nationwide bumper harvest of 1980–1 which was the result of a fortuitous coincidence of several factors, namely: good rains; the return to relative peace and improved security over much of the country; a massive government pre-planting price increase of 41 per cent to Z$ 120 per tonne for top grade maize; and the distribution of free seed and fertilizer packs as part of an internationally supported programme of post-war rural reconstruction and rehabilitation. There was a drop in sales to pre-1980 levels during the next two intake years, 1982–4, because of severe droughts during the 1981–3 seasons. However, maize deliveries from the area reached a new peak of 15,112 tonnes in 1984–5, before dropping to 12,174 tonnes for the 1986–7 intake because of poor and erratic rainfall

during the previous 1985–6 growing season. Similar trends, though with lower figures, have occurred in Save North where maize sales to the GMB have increased from a pre-independence annual average of 95 tonnes during the period 1974–9 to 7,868 tonnes in 1984–5 and 5,601 tonnes for the 1986–7 intake year.

However, these aggregate figures hide substantial age, status and gender differences in crop production and sales. Generally, households with permanently resident middle-aged male heads performed better than households with either female heads or those with younger, absent, male heads. Households in the former category had more land, more farm equipment and more draught cattle than the other two categories. A large proportion of the crops that were sold in each area came from a small percentage of the sample farming population. For instance, in Mhondoro, 25 per cent of the households were not selling any maize while another 22 per cent sold less than ten bags (one bag equals 91 kg). Only a little over 10 per cent of the households sold over 50 bags of maize annually. In Save North, the proportion of households who sold little or no maize was even greater, as much as 75 per cent in a fairly good season, while less than 3 per cent sold more than 50 bags.

The respondents were asked what they considered to be the major obstacles that were hindering them from increasing their crop production. In both areas, the five most frequently cited constraints related to the lack of adequate farming resources. These were, in descending order of magnitude: (a) lack of money to purchase farm inputs, particularly fertilizers; (b) lack of farming implements, especially the ox-drawn single furrow plough; (c) lack of draught cattle; (d) inadequate family labour (Zinyama 1988b). An understanding of these constraints, as perceived by the farmers themselves, is essential if one is to understand the nature of local group activities in which farmers participate voluntarily, thus giving such organizations greater prospects for success.

Local farmer organizations in rural development

One of the strategies that is being used by the farmers to raise their level of crop production and on-farm incomes is participation in local voluntary organizations for collective action, as the farmers seek to overcome their felt resource constraints. Given the relative weaknesses of peasant households when they act individually for purposes of resource mobilization and acquisition or when they deal with the

state or other external agencies, collective local action becomes a vital strategy for rural development. Moreover, the process of rural development entails increasing the participation of the people concerned in the decision-making process, and this can be enhanced through local groups. Local farmer groups can also be used to facilitate the collective purchasing and transport of agricultural inputs, marketing of produce, and the timely mobilization of labour for a variety of tasks such as ploughing, planting or weeding.

The distinguishing feature of these collective local action groups is self-management. Where the group is formally structured, management will be done through a committee which is elected by the farmers from among themselves. Self-management sets these groups apart from externally sponsored organizations which rely on governmental or non-governmental professionals and technocrats not only for advice but also for leadership. The principles governing such farmer groups are therefore voluntary membership, government by agreement, and social control through peer pressure (Bratton 1986, 1987). The problems that can beset group projects which are initiated from above without prior involvement of the target population have been clearly documented by Sibanda (1986) in a study of a goat breeding project that was intended to benefit the women of Muzarabani Communal Land in the Zambezi Valley in northern Zimbabwe.

Bratton further argued, as a result of his work elsewhere in Zimbabwe, that farmer groups are most likely to form and to succeed in those parts of the country where services from the various economic sectors, both state and private, are well represented and that they are least likely where the latter are weakly represented. He observed that:

> Autonomous farmer organizations are most likely to arise where effective state and market institutions provide stimulation and support. It is also vital that the policy regime allows sufficient 'space' for unaffiliated and autonomous organizations to exist.
>
> (Bratton 1987: 226)

The importance of state support for local voluntary organizations, particularly during their formative stages, was also highlighted by Brett (1988). He noted that the development of autonomous local organizations was not a substitute for effective public service provision, 'but only possible where it can grow effectively in association

with it' (Brett 1988: 10). It can therefore be hypothesized that, given the current favourable national policy environment for local-level co-operative action, such organizations will be better developed and more effective in Mhondoro than in Save North because of the former's greater accessibility to the national economic heartland and larger marketable crop surpluses.

Mutual-help groups

A number of local voluntary farmer groups, traditional and modern, informal and formal, are found in both Mhondoro and Save North. First, there are the mutual-help groups which provide a means for overcoming labour and other resource constraints that households may face. The informal type of mutual-help group (called a *nhimbe* in the vernacular) is where a farmer provides beer and food in return for the collective labour of friends and neighbours on a particular day and for a specific task. The more formal type (*jangano*) is where a small number of friends or relatives agree to help each other by com-bining their labour on a regular rotational basis for such tasks as ploughing, planting, weeding or harvesting. In the former, both males and females pool their labour and other resources for the day. In the latter case, men usually work together mainly at ploughing only; the more prolonged activities such as weeding or harvesting usually involve women and children working co-operatively.

Analysis of the demographic structure of households in the two areas showed that those with female heads (i.e. widows and divorcees) accounted for 21 per cent and 14 per cent of all households in Mhondoro and Save North respectively. Although the remainder were headed by males, two-fifths of the male heads of households lived away from home as migrant workers. Thus, the agricultural labour input, day-to-day management and routine decision-making on the family farm were the responsibility of women in a large majority of households. Household labour was further reduced by the fact that two-fifths of the *de facto* or resident population were children attending local schools. Therefore, although the average household size for the resident population alone was 5.3 in Mhondoro and 5.5 in Save North, the actual amount of full-time labour which was usually available for agriculture was only two persons per household in both areas (Zinyama 1986b). Again, households with female heads and those where the male head was absent (i.e. female-managed house-holds) generally had less family labour than those with resident male

heads. Given the high incidence of male absenteeism and the post-independence expansion of educational opportunities for rural children, it is therefore not surprising that farmers identified the shortage of family labour as one of the principal constraints against increasing their crop production. One way in which they were trying to overcome this problem was through the formation of mutual-help groups.

Mutual-help groups involving the pooling of scarce production resources also help to improve access to essential production assets and implements among rural households, particularly where inequalities exist in the ownership of resources. For instance, some 30 per cent of the households in both Mhondoro and Save North did not own an ox-drawn single furrow plough, the standard implement for land preparation in communal area agriculture. A little over one-third had no draught cattle, and a further one-fifth had between one and two animals only to provide draught power. The latter group of households were in almost as precarious a position at the end of the long dry season, which coincides with the peak demand period for draught power for land preparation (November–December). Over-all, a little over half of the households in both areas could be said to suffer, to varying degrees, from a shortage of draught power. Only 56.7 per cent of households in Mhondoro and 59.6 per cent in Save North had both ploughs and draught cattle of their own. One-quarter of the households in each area shared either a plough or oxen, usually with other members of the extended family, for which no payment was made. Another 18.2 per cent in Mhondoro and 10.8 per cent in Save North hired ploughs and/or draught cattle from other families, with payment being made in cash or in kind. Although the practice of sharing helps to improve access to resources, it also means that land preparation cannot be completed on time for all households, with a consequent loss of yield because of failure to take advantage of the early season rains. The most disadvantaged households with respect to ownership of farming implements and livestock were, first, female-headed households and, second, newly established households with younger male heads who have not yet accumulated an adequate range of assets (Zinyama 1987b).

Farmer training groups

It is now the general policy of government agricultural extension staff to work with groups of farmers rather than visit them individually on

their landholdings. Given the current poor ratio of farmers to extension staff, the group approach enables extension workers to reach more farmers than would otherwise be the case through individual farm visits. Interested farmers within an area organize themselves into groups that meet regularly with the local extension worker for training and information dissemination. These groups are called Master Farmers' Clubs. A 'master farmer' is one who has successfully completed a prescribed programme of on-farm training under the supervision of the agricultural extension staff. In mid-1983, there were 96 master farmers' clubs with 4,671 members in Mhondoro, an average of 49 members per group, both males and females. The primary function of these groups is to train farmers and to improve the farmers' standards of agriculture. It is important to emphasize that, although the farmers receive technical support from government extension staff, the formation of the groups is largely initiated by the farmers themselves who are also responsible for their management through committees which are elected from among themselves.

Membership of master farmers' clubs is open to all interested farmers, including prospective trainees, regardless of gender, age or status. In both Mhondoro and Save North, membership was divided more or less equally between males and females. Male members are usually drawn from those who are permanently resident at home. Many of the female members are wives of absent migrant workers (female farm managers). Equality of membership in such skills training groups is being actively encouraged by the government as part of its efforts to raise the social and economic status of women in both rural and urban areas. Thus, a similar pattern was reported by Smith (1987) in her study of the participation of women in producer co-operatives in Zimbabwe. Although the research in Mhondoro and Save North did not examine the participation of women in decision-making within these groups, the observations by Smith for the producer co-operatives seem to be applicable to the communal areas as well. She noted that women, although enjoying equality in terms of membership, participated less than men in decision-making either as members of management committees or through contributions at general meetings. Reasons why women are under-represented in decision-making include: heavy domestic workloads and other socio-cultural demands which prevent them from serving in elected positions and which reduce their ability to travel and to represent their organizations externally, lack of administrative experience;

attitudes and prejudices against the election of women to positions of leadership.

Membership of farmer training groups is also differentiated in terms of social status and age. First, members tend to be drawn from the middle and upper social strata of the rural population, that is from households who already possess adequate land, farming implements and cattle. They are also more likely to have greater access to sources of cash (e.g. from crop sales, from loans from the Agricultural Finance Corporation, or from migrant labour remittances) with which to purchase farm inputs such as hybrid seed and chemical fertilizers. These groups therefore exclude the poorest of the farming population. Second, the majority of members are drawn from middle-aged and older households rather than from younger, more recently established families. The latter have fewer agricultural resources and, where the husband is employed elsewhere, the wives tend to have a more negative attitude towards farming (Zinyama 1988b). These wives frequently spend most of the dry season away from the family farm with their husbands, returning only at the onset of the rains. They are therefore unable to participate in much of the dry season training activities, in land preparation or in collective input procurement with other farmers.

Agricultural marketing groups

The third category of local farmer groups are those which are engaged in the purchasing of agricultural inputs and in the marketing of commodities to the statutory marketing boards. Membership of these marketing groups frequently overlaps with that of master farmers' clubs. This category includes voluntary savings or thrift clubs which are initiated and run by the farmers themselves with the assistance of their agricultural extension workers and, in some cases, with that of the country's two fertilizer companies. In Mhondoro, other savings groups are supported by the charitable organization, the Catholic Association, under its Silveira House Agricultural Project, as part of its programme of 'mushandira pamwe' (working together) groups, and by the multinational agricultural chemical company, Ciba-Geigy, under its 'kohwa pakuru' (expand your harvest) programme. The Catholic Association and Ciba-Geigy have been operating in Mhondoro since the early 1970s and 1981 respectively. Both distribute input packages either on loan (now using funds obtained from the Agricultural Finance Corporation) or for cash and

they require that farmers work in groups on each task such as planting, weeding, harvesting and marketing. This obviously reduces the unit costs of loan administration, particularly where it involves the processing of large numbers of small loan requirements from the farmers.

Members of savings clubs hold regular meetings at which they deposit money into a club fund. The money is then used for purchasing inputs collectively for the next agricultural season. The quantities of inputs that are ordered by each member will depend on his/her requirements and on the amount of money that has been deposited with the club. At least two major cost advantages accrue to farmers who are members of these clubs. First, by obtaining their fertilizers directly from manufacturers in bulk at wholesale prices, which also carry cash discounts, the farmers benefit from lower purchasing costs. Second, the companies will then deliver the fertilizer to an agreed collection point (e.g. the home of the club chairperson) at much lower cost than if the farmers transported their inputs privately by hired lorry or on buses. During the 1982–3 and 1983–4 seasons, farmers who were members of savings clubs in Mhondoro paid between 15 and 20 per cent less for each 50 kg bag of chemical fertilizers, inclusive of transport, than non-members who purchased their requirements individually either at their local business centres or from the towns. (The fertilizer companies can also arrange to obtain and deliver hybrid maize seed and other chemicals for the farmers at the same time as they deliver the fertilizers.)

Farmers' groups for purchasing inputs are more numerous and have operated for longer in Mhondoro than in Save North. Some of the extension workers in Save North made initial attempts during 1982 to organize and convert some of the master farmers' clubs into savings clubs for input purchasing. A few of the farmers purchased their inputs through the clubs for the 1982–3 season. However, output that year was so severely cut because of the drought that most farmers were unable to obtain money to continue their club subscriptions in preparation for the next season (1983–4). Thus, in 1984, only 7 per cent of the households interviewed in Save North were members of savings clubs (most of which were largely inactive), another 4 per cent had ceased to be members, and the remainder were not members at all. In more recent years, the number of savings clubs has increased, mainly through the addition of functions to existing master farmers' clubs. In Mhondoro, a few of the savings clubs were started in the early 1970s but most of those operating

today were formed after 1980. By mid-1983, at the time of the survey, there were 88 clubs with 4,313 members throughout Mhondoro, an average of 49 members per club.

A brief outline of two of the most successful savings clubs in Mhondoro is indicative. Savings club 'A' was formed in May 1982 with 35 members. By October of that year, membership had risen to 63. The members had purchased chemical fertilizers valued at $Z 3,843, an average of Z$ 61 per member, in preparation for the 1982–3 season. Savings club 'B', the oldest in Mhondoro, was formed in 1972 with 37 members. In September 1983 it had 107 members. By September 1983, the members had already bought Z$ 7,970 worth of fertilizers for the 1983–4 season. The club had also just completed, out of its own resources, the construction of a large brick-under-asbestos building which was to be used as a club office and a farmer training centre, as well as providing storage space for agricultural materials.

The varying history of collective groups in Mhondoro and Save North, as outlined above, accounts for variations in the impact of these groups as agents of change in the two areas. In Mhondoro, 47.2 per cent of the households were members of savings clubs, through which they purchased their inputs, compared with only 6.7 per cent in Save North. These savings clubs provide a vital vehicle by means of which farmers in the communal areas, given their limited individual input requirements and lack of money, can reduce costs of purchased inputs by buying collectively in bulk. Membership of such clubs also suggests that the farmers are looking beyond the traditional inputs of unimproved maize seed and cattle manure and that they are searching for alternative modern inputs which will give them greater yields, more marketable surpluses and higher incomes from farming.

It was therefore not surprising to find that farmers who were members of clubs not only applied more appropriate quantities of chemical fertilizers to their crops but also produced and sold more than non-members. The importance of appropriate fertilizer applications was highlighted by Tattersfield (1982). Using data from the large-scale farming sector, he estimated that proper application of the full package of modern technology, derived from research, would have resulted in an increase in maize output per hectare of 325 per cent over the output for 1950, with almost two-thirds of that increase coming from the application of nitrogenous fertilizers and a little under one-fifth from the use of hybrid maize seed varieties. The survey in Mhondoro showed that three-quarters of the households

who used little (under 50 kg) or no chemical fertilizers on their maize crop during the 1981–2 season harvested less than ten bags of maize each (one bag equals 91 kg), and only 4.5 per cent of them gathered more than 30 bags. On the other hand, of the 121 households who used more than 300 kg of chemical fertilizers, 82 per cent obtained more than 30 bags each, with 13 households harvesting over 100 bags each. (The recommended minimum levels for maize are 250–300 kg per hectare, i.e. 5–6 bags of 50 kg each, comprising three bags of basal and two bags of top dressing nitrogenous compound. The average area that was planted with maize was 1.1 hectares.) About 50 per cent of the households that were members of savings clubs used more than 300 kg of fertilizers for their maize production, compared with only 14 per cent of the households that were not members. Out of the 76 households that harvested more than 50 bags of maize in Mhondoro, 77 per cent were members of savings clubs.

Similar results were reported by Bratton (1986) from four other communal areas of Chipuriro and Dande in the north of the country, Wedza in the centre and Gutu in the south. He found that farmers working in groups consistently produced more, both per unit of land and per household, and sold more than farmers working alone. More significantly, he found that farmers who were organized into groups for purposes of input acquisition performed better than those who merely pooled their resources of labour or draught power at the village level. The former performed better because they were more likely than the latter to receive the full package of agricultural support services, namely extension advice, fertilizers, hybrid seed, and market access.

Overall, during the past decade, farmers in Mhondoro have been more successful in transforming their agricultural practices and in raising average productivity levels than farmers in Save North. While these emerging regional differences are attributable to a number of factors, the existence of viable savings or thrift clubs, which farmers can use to mobilize effectively local capital resources, has certainly been a major contributing factor towards the greater agricultual success in Mhondoro.

CONCLUSION: SOME POLICY CONSIDERATIONS

This chapter started by examining the current macroeconomic environment for rural development in Zimbabwe. Unlike other African countries where national policies are generally unfavourable

towards the rural sector, thereby adding to its stagnation, the rural areas in Zimbabwe are fortunate in that the government is currently giving them high priority. There is therefore considerable complementarity between the efforts of the state and those of the rural population itself to develop the rural sector. To illustrate the latter's contribution, the second part of the chapter focused on the role of local voluntary farmer organizations and on how they can provide an effective grass-roots vehicle for overcoming constraints that are identified by the farmers themselves as hindering their agricultural activities. In Mhondoro and, to a lesser extent, Save North, these farmer groups are helping to overcome problems arising from household labour shortages and from inequalities in access or ownership of agricultural resources. Such group activities should be actively encouraged; at the same time, they should not be strangled by restrictive rules and regulations nor have their principal advantages of voluntary membership, self-government and peer control removed from them.

Lack of money with which to purchase agricultural inputs, particularly fertilizers, was the most frequently cited constraint faced by farmers in both Mhondoro and Save North (Zinyama 1988b). While the provision of institutional credit for small-scale farmers by the Agricultural Finance Corporation (AFC) since 1978 has gone some way to help them, a number of problems remain. For example, 90 per cent of the loans are short term or seasonal for crop production purposes; the AFC tends to favour farmers in the wetter regions who are able to present viable cropping programmes when they submit their applications for loans (Zinyama 1988a). The frequent droughts that are experienced in low rainfall regions, where the majority of communal area farmers live, reduce the ability of farmers to benefit from the loans because they are then unable to repay them. Some farmers who have accumulated substantial debts are now evading repayment by selling their crops indirectly through GMB-approved grain buyers or through other farmers. As a result, in 1988 the AFC announced a change in policy: to move gradually from individual to group lending in order to reduce the problem of non-payment by small-scale farmers. However, the proposed debt collection system involving mandatory joint liability can also give rise to other problems. For instance, the whole group may opt not to repay its loans to the AFC: or, because the lending agency will automatically deduct the debts of defaulting members from the accounts of paying members, a situation of 'internal indebtedness' may arise within

groups. Whether credit is given under individual liability or mandatory group liability, the risk of increasing rural indebtedness is very real. The recurrent droughts in low rainfall regions and the likelihood of rising rural indebtedness raise an important policy issue concerning the role of voluntary savings or thrift clubs in alleviating the problem of capital shortage among communal area farmers. The establishment of a network of viable savings clubs would help to reduce such indebtedness, particularly in the event of crop failure, as the farmers would purchase their inputs out of their own savings rather than through loans. The clubs could thus provide an effective vehicle for the mobilization of local capital resources for agricultural and rural 'development from within' at much lower unit costs both to the state and to the farmers. In the long run, and by broadening their range of activities, the clubs could even form the basis for the development of co-operative agricultural production units, in line with government policy for the socialist transformation of the economy and society.

3

A GHANAIAN RURAL COMMUNITY

indigenous responses to seasonal food supply cycles and the socio-environmental stresses of the 1980s

George J. S. Dei

INTRODUCTION

This case study examines the nature of the adaptive resources of the people of Ayirebi in south-eastern Ghana to local food supply cycles and to a national economic crisis of the 1980s which was triggered by world recession and aggravated by drought, bush fires and the influx of Ghanaian deportees from Nigeria. Ayirebi is a forest, food farming community with a population of about 4,300 made up of 2,021 males and 2,279 females.[1] It is located in the Eastern region of Ghana about 45 km from Akyem Oda and 180 km north of the Ghanaian capital, Accra. The town covers an area of approximately 1.75 km² The inhabitants are Twi-speaking, belonging to the matrilineal Akan sub-group known as the Akyem.

Ayirebi is without electricity or a piped water supply. Firewood is used for household cooking purposes. Kerosene lamps and lanterns supply household lighting. The water supply comes from streams, wells and rainfall. A non-bituminized feeder road from the nearest urban centre of Akyem Oda leads to Ayirebi and its surrounding villages. Government-built infrastructure in the town includes a police station, post office, health centre, two cocoa buying agencies and three public elementary schools. Community initiated facilities and services include a market square, public conveniences, a chief's palace and a rural bank. Other services which are prominent in the community are a private health clinic, three private vocational schools, and stores (for the sale of provisions, health drugs, toiletries,

stationery, alcohol and drinks). There are also shops for artisans in blacksmithing, woodcarving, tailoring, hairdressing, as well as radio, watch, footwear and bicycle repair shops.

METHODOLOGY

This study was conducted primarily through active participant and non-participant observations of the everyday life in the community, the gardens and the bush, i.e. forest). The total study sample was 412 households, representing a quarter of all Ayirebi town households.[2] With the assistance of two local schoolteachers, these households were the focus of demographic, ecological and socioeconomic surveys which were conducted through interviews and the administration of questionnaires. The research sample had a total population of 1,543 people. Their age and sex distribution show 731 (47.4%) males; 812 (52.6%) females. The youth population, defined as 0–20 years, was 647 (41.9%) and the adults and elderly, 896 (58.1%). The active adult population (i.e. 21–64 years) is made up of 408 (45.5%) males and 488 (54.5%) females.

Four major climatological and ecological periods can be identified in the community. These are a main dry season that falls between January and March; a main rainy season from April to June; a pre-harvest season, July/August to September; and a main harvest season lasting from October to December. In gathering seasonal data on food supply cycles, the rainy season and the pre-harvest season were appropriately combined into the lean season. The seasonality of data dealing with household consumption and other economic activities which are presented in this study thus refers to a harvest season (October 1982 to December 1982); main dry season (January 1983 to March 1983); and lean season (April 1983 to September 1983). Each of these periods was sampled for data collection (between seven and fourteen days) to reflect seasonal differences and/or fluctuations in subsistence and other economic activities. From the initial 412 households, 20 representative households were further selected on a non-random, statistical basis for the more detailed study of the seasonal variation in household food procurement, distribution and consumption patterns, as well as to keep periodic activity diaries.[3]

THE LOCAL ECONOMY

Nearly 90 per cent of the adult population of this town depend directly on farming for their livelihood.[4] They produce both

subsistence and cash crops. The local staples are plantains, manioc, maize, cocoyams, yams, rice and green leaf vegetables such as tomatoes, pepper, okras, onions, and garden eggs or egg plant. Other economic activities include hunting and gathering of wild forest resources, raising of livestock, and arts and crafts. Colonial and post-colonial changes introduced into the economy include the production of such cash crops as cocoa, kola nuts and palm oil, and a subsequent articulation with the national market economy and/or wage labour.

Since cocoa was introduced in 1879 as a commercial crop, it assumed an important role in the Ghanaian economy (Senyah 1984). The production of this crop was embraced by most farmers as it could easily co-exist with food farming for local consumption needs. Cocoa continues to be the chief crop of most major farming communities in the forest zones of southern Ghana. Its cultivation has dominated all other agricultural activities in the country (Wilks 1977: 490). The largest concentration of cocoa farms in Ghana today is found in the forest areas of the Brong Ahafo, Ashanti, and parts of the Central, Western, and Eastern regions of the country.

The leading position of cocoa in the farming economies of some Ghanaian communities has in the recent past suffered a gradual setback. Beginning in the late-1920s, a multiplicity of factors has diverted attention from the overwhelming production of cocoa to that of staple foods in certain forest farming communities.[5] One such community is Ayirebi, where the farmers have for a long time concentrated upon subsistence crop production.[6] Food farming there (and in the wider context of the Ghanaian forest zone) at the beginning of this century was mainly for subsistence, as there was no incentive to produce food crops on a large commercial scale. Owing to the bulky and perishable nature of most of the foodstuffs, and to the lack of communications and of proper organization among the producers, food farming in the past was usually not as profitable as cocoa. Therefore, most farmers preferred to grow cocoa wherever possible. But, as Boateng (1959: 68) points out, the scarcity of food which began during times of war and the need to feed large numbers of troops gave considerable stimulus to food production between 1939 and 1946. Government bulk-purchase organizations were set up at various centres; and the increasing demands of the urban centres over time have provided an incentive for food farming. It is therefore not surprising that, in all areas where the growing of cocoa has been unsuccessful, a food production industry has emerged. Contemporary events show that Ayirebi has become a town known for its

food production. Food crops which have been grown there for local consumption are now sent regularly to the urban centres of Akyem Oda, Akyem Swedru, Koforidua and Accra.

Lineage control of land used to be a marked feature of the Ayirebi economy. Family land was vested in the matrilineage and every member of the lineage had the right to farm freely and to build on such land. The individual controlled only the usufruct of the land and could not alienate it nor transfer the rights to use family land or farms following matrilineal inheritance. Since colonial times, however, the emergence of such cash crops as cocoa and coffee, together with the demand for timber and gold mining concessions, have encouraged the wholesale alienation of land by some chiefs and lineage elders, at the expense of their subjects' rights, and a trend towards individual ownership of land has emerged (Dickson 1969; Manoukian 1964). In the contemporary period, the concept of family land is still upheld and a great proportion of food and non-food cash crops are produced on such land. However, land has come to be regarded more and more as a commodity, with the state and other wealthy individuals in the community striving endlessly to annex substantial portions of all land available. Thus the concepts of family land, stool land (land under custodianship of a chief), individually owned land and state land co-exist in the daily lives of the Ayirebi people (Dei 1987).

The 1982–3 survey of food farm plots which were owned by the sampled Ayirebi population showed an average farming household having between two and three separate farms. The study also showed household differentiation in the size of farm plots. Of the total of 412 research sample households, 124 (30%) households each had between 0–3 hectares of food farm plots; 140 households (34%), 3–6 hectares; 86 households (20.9%), 6–9 hectares; 41 households (10%), 9–12 hectares; and 21 households (5.1%), over 12 hectares (Dei 1987: 117ff.).

Generally, the basic production unit comprised a husband, wife, children and one or two matrilateral kin. This group could either be the sole production unit occupying a house or compound, or it could form part of a larger group occupying a compound. In this latter instance, the compound would be sub-divided into a number of separate (and independent) production units. It was also possible for a large group organized around a segment of the matrilineage (an elder woman and her sister or her daughters; or a man and his sister or his sister's children) to be the sole production unit within the compound or dwelling house (Dei 1986; Hill 1975).

Members of a household share farming activities, working together on the farm land that was acquired through the matrilineage and/or the custodian of the stool (i.e. village chief or sub-chief) or through the individual's personal effort (i.e. outright purchase) (Dei 1987). During periods of major economic activity (e.g. preparation of the land for farming, or harvesting of farm produce), when agricultural work intensifies, households may request the assistance of available extended family labour. Other 'external' sources of labour which are available to the household production unit include seasonal migrants from the northern parts of the country and casual wage labour provided by the town youth. There is also the formation of such partnerships as *nnoboa*, collective self-help groups of age mates helping each other in farming activities (Arhin 1983: 472). The adult males perform the task of clearing the forest and preparing the land for farming. Women, the young and the elderly in the household do the planting and harvesting of the crops, occasionally receiving some assistance from the adult males. Both sexes make joint efforts to keep weeds out of the food farms by using such farming tools as the hoe, digging stick, cutlass and axe. The principal methods of farming are shifting cultivation on bush farms, and intensive cultivation in the gardens and farm plots that are closer to the homesteads.

Ayirebi has fast become a market centre for the surrounding smaller communities. Traders and other visitors from both distant and nearby communities converge on the town to sell and buy foodstuffs as well as other goods at the local retail shops. There are established foodstuff dealers in the community, most of whom act as middlemen and women who make weekly bulk purchases of food items for traders in the Ghanaian urban centres. These foodstuffs are transported to the cities in hired articulated (trailer) trucks, which converge on the town on the Tuesday and Thursday market days. Established political structures, such as the Town Development Committee (TDC) and, more recently, the Committee for the Defence of the Revolution (CDR),[7] help to supervise the sale of farm produce in the local market, as well as to regulate the activities of the food dealers and urban traders.

Another sphere of Ayirebi's town involvement in the national market economy can be found in the government's employment of a handful of local residents as agricultural workers in the cocoa and oil palm plantations near Akyem Oda.[8] There is also rural migration of some town youth to the cities and urban centres, in search of non-existent white-collar jobs and a perceived 'better' standard of living.

The Ayirebi seasonal economic cycle (see Table 3.1) shows an alternation between periods of abundance and relative scarcity in household food supplies. Notwithstanding the effectiveness of local farming strategies in meeting the basic food requirements of households, periodic food shortages of brief duration do occur among households, particularly in the lean season of late May to August. Ordinarily, the situation may be attributed to unpredictable ecological and logistical factors, such as erratic and inadequate rainfall, crop destruction by pests and diseases or a temporary inefficiency in household productive strategies (e.g. poor management and/or sudden cutbacks in household labour supply resulting from illness during a farming season).

In 1982 and 1983 certain socioeconomic and environmental changes had implications for the successful adaptation of the Ayirebi community. The world recession adversely affected the Ghanaian economy, with the result that the national government could not afford to pay for imports of food, fuel, medical supplies, and other services and facilities which are associated with housing, clothing, education, transportation and communication, employment and industry. Consequently, local shops and stores were empty of such imported food items as milk and milk products, vegetable oil, flour, oats, sugar, tinned meat and fish. There were nation-wide shortages of basic amenities such as toiletries, textiles, health drugs and stationery. This period also coincided with the worst national drought in forty-eight years. Poor rainfall led to a general water scarcity, forcing people in towns and villages to walk long distances in search of water for household use and consumption.

Ayirebi town experienced these hardships, recording its poorest ever rainfall as reflected in both the total amounts and number of days of rainfall. In the past, Ayirebi annual rainfall had averaged 1,680 mm. Between October 1982 and September 1983, however, the total annual rainfall dropped to 933 mm.[9] The situation was more acute in the months from November to March when food planting activities reached a peak. Rainfed cultivation was affected. The drought also encouraged a series of bush fires that destroyed food crops, such as plantain, yams, cocoyams and cassava, as well as cocoa farms (Dei 1986). In the national food economy, the drought and bush fires worked in particular to depress production and to raise demand, which invariably worsened the problem of food availability. Even rural communities, which were spared the full impact of the world recession (on account of their minimal connection with the

Table 3.1 Seasonal economic cycle of Ayirebi, Ghana

Period	Ecological conditions	Productive cycle farming activity	Food cycle (food supply)
January–March	Main dry season: characterized by a dry parching land wind	Beginning of the agricultural season: preparation of fields, cutting, burning and tilling of farm land.	Farm food supplies partially available from previous harvest season. Cassava and cocoyams left in the fields may be harvested at this time. A second maize crop planted in early September is harvested February–March.
April–June	Main rainy season: with peak of rains in June	Farm activities continue with the sowing of seeds and crops at the onset of the first rains.	Food supplies in some households may be near exhaustion, causing episodic food shortages beginning in late May. The relatively lean season for cultivated
July/August/September	Pre-harvest season: low rainfall in July–August and a second rainy season in September–October	Farming labour increases, including weeding of fields and tending to crops, thus increasing the expenditures of labour on the farms.	foodstuffs continues to August, resulting in a marked dependence on forest plants and game. Early maize may be ready for harvest towards the end of August, helping to alleviate food shortage. Individuals may also make craft items to obtain additional income for food purchases at the local market.
October–December	Main harvest season: rains that began in September continue into October; November sees the beginning of the main dry season, continuing through December–March.	October–November is a period of intense harvesting of foodstuffs; the second half of the season is a period of leisure from farm work. Crafts and other community festivities peak. Social gatherings and collection of some forest products are undertaken but their contribution to household income and food supply is not particularly significant.	A season of relative plenty and abundance of food supplies for the community at large. The harvest permits the lavish consumption of food that accompanies the celebration of socio-religious activities. Brisk market activity as articulated trucks converge on the town to cart away foodstuffs to urban centres.

See also Fortes and Fortes (1936) and Hunter (1967).

global economy), were struck by the drought. For the Ayirebi community, an additional stress was the return of 298 town residents (about 7% of the town's population) who had been deported from Nigeria in the early months of 1983.[10]

HOUSEHOLD-LEVEL COPING STRATEGIES

The farming economy

The successful adaptation of the Ayirebi people to such stresses, particularly seasonal food supply cycles, can in part be attributed to the strength and viability of the household subsistence farming economy. There is great diversity of cropping patterns among local farmers. As part of indigenous safeguards against food scarcity and prolonged periods of hunger, local farmers have devised two growing seasons for maize. The main season maize, which is planted in April, may be ready for harvest towards the end of August (i.e. during the lean season), while the second crop, which is planted in early September, helps to extend the household food supply with the harvest in February and March. Cassava (*Manihot esculenta, Crantz*), the most versatile of the local staples, also assumed greater importance in the local diet during the stress period. Its capacity to grow and yield well on low fertility soils, its ability to withstand locust attack and drought, and its low cost of production provided the economic incentive for local farmers to use it as a replacement for staples such as yams. Cassava is a reliable year-round source of calories and a famine reserve crop. Many farmers leave unharvested actual surpluses of the crop on their farms, in order to constitute a valuable reserve in the event of a relative failure of other staples in a farming season. Its roots survive well when stored in the ground, to be harvested only when required. With its ability to increase the caloric yields and to extend the harvest season, cassava, in effect like cocoyam, serves to lessen the full impact of the lean season on most farming households (see also Annegers 1973: 256).

Like cassava, cocoyam (*Xanthosoma saggittifolium* or *Xanthosoma maffaffa*; and *Colocassia antiquorum schott* or *Colocassia esculenta*) is another important root crop that keeps well either in the field or in storage, and is therefore available throughout the year. The matured crop can be stored underground, as it were, and harvested only a little at a time when cocoyams are needed. In this manner it is common for harvesting to extend over four to five years (Karikari 1971: 9). An

early and late crop of cocoyams may be taken, depending on the type of planting material. When land on which cocoyam has been planted is cleared again after a long fallow, small seedlings of the crop, with no traces of the tubers, may appear. These mature quickly and may be harvested after six months. Cocoyam is usually the first crop to be taken on land after clearing a secondary forest. Not only does the root crop spring up underneath burnt cocoa farms but its tubers can also lie dormant for several years. The local farmers have also developed a habit of digging out and removing mature cocoyams from the parent plant before the smaller ones are fully mature and the entire plant is lifted. By harvesting individual cocoyams when they mature, losses from rotting and premature germination are held to a minimum. This practice constitutes an important safeguard against future food scarcity or hunger.

As part of the indigenous strategies to cope with the stress on household food supplies, Ayirebi women devised additional processing methods for cassava and cocoyam to make them edible irrespective of their natural state. The skin of cocoyams under normal favourable circumstances would be discarded. However, during this period of hardship, the women spent some time drying the cocoyam skins before milling them into a flour and preparing them at extremely hot temperatures for consumption.

Another coping strategy was the pragmatic dependence on the local market on the part of households. Particularly during the lean season, households facing deficits in their food supply would obtain their food requirements from the relatively well-off farmers who had been able to produce surplus for the market. Payments for such market foods varied from monetary payments to exchanges of forest collected food items.[11] It is during this lean season that some degree of difference emerges between households and their diets in terms of both content and source of food supplies. Distinguishing Ayirebi households by income, the picture that emerges suggests that differences in source and content of household diets can in part be attributed to differences in economic status. Table 3.2 shows the responses by income status of twenty representative households which were selected non-randomly for the study of the sources of the household food supply during the lean season (see also Dei 1986).[12] The income brackets were chosen arbitrarily.[13] In meeting the cash demands of augmenting household food supply from the local market, households rely on accumulated earnings from previous sales of farm produce, wild forest resources, sales of arts and crafts, wage labour, services and rental income, remittances and welfare, and livestock rearing.

Exploitation of wild resources

Hunting and gathering has been an economic strategy which was utilized in the past by some Ayirebi households in response to the seasonal fluctuations in food supplies. In 1982 and 1983, households were observed to be reverting to dietary patterns that relied heavily upon the surrounding natural environment. A wide variety of edible and non-edible (medicinal) wild products, such as roots, fibres, leaves, bark, fruits, seeds, nuts, insects, molluscs, sap and syrup was exploited largely by Ayirebi women and children to satisfy basic household needs. The women experimented with four new varieties of plants for cultivation purposes. These were: *Dioscorea praehensilis* (bush or forest yam), a root crop locally referred to as '*ahabayere*' and normally classified as a semi-wild yam; *Afzelia bella*, a wild plant locally referred to as '*papaonua*', the leaves of which are used as vegetables in soup; *Napoleona vogelii*, known as '*obua*', whose fruits are eaten as a delicacy; and *Blighia welwitschii*, known locally as '*akyekobiri*', the leaves of which are also used to flavour soup.

Table 3.2   Food strategy responses of twenty Ayirebi households to seasonal nutritional stress by income status

Status*	Contribution to household food supply from four sources in the lean (pre-harvest) season (%)			
	Farm	Bush	Market/Store	Other (kin and close friends)
Wealthy n = 3	75	2	16	7
Middle n = 10	65	8	19	8
Poor n = 7	55	20	10	15

*Wealthy = annual cash income (i.e. market proceeds of all economic production) of C 8,000 + ;
  Middle = annual cash income between C 4,000 and C 8,000;
  Poor   = annual cash income of less than C 4,000;
         where one cedi (C) = US$ 0.36 (1982–3).

Households found local substitutes for imported sugar and cooking fat in honey and palm oil respectively. After extracting the oil from the palm kernels, the women utilized some of the palm oil products,

together with wood ash, to make local substitutes for the scarce imported soap. The hunting and trapping activities of Ayirebi farmers and male professional hunters also provided the community with a steady supply of bush animal protein. These included: mammals (grasscutter, *Thyromomys swinderianus*; giant rat, *Critetomyx gambianus*; antelope, *Neotragus pygamaeus*; brush-tailed porcupine, *Atherurus africanus*); reptiles and aquatic species (such as molluscs, crabs, clams, tortoise, giant forest snails); and a wide variety of birds, invertebrates and insects (Dei 1986).

Non-agricultural production

The research period also witnessed a marked resurgence in local skills in non-agricultural production, particularly among the male population. The Ayirebi environment provided enough raw materials to produce a wide variety of products for both household use and sale on the market. Activities included blacksmithing, tinsmithing, basket-weaving, straw-work, barkcloth-making, woodcarving, mud-brick and tile-making. These are viable economic activities that enable the practitioners to supplement their household income and food supply.[14] Households which were unable to afford the services of skilled artisans or the high prices of imported building materials (e.g. cement, iron roofing sheets) made some cash savings by constructing and repairing their houses themselves out of local raw materials. During the research period, when imported cement and iron roofing sheets were scarce, most houses were constructed or repaired in the community with mud-bricks and thatch roofs. Both basketry and thatch roofing manufacture are also crucial for food storage purposes. The resurgence in the importance of blacksmiths in the community can be attributed to the absence from the local market of such farm implements as cutlasses, knives, and axes. Local blacksmiths are increasingly relied upon to produce these implements. They accept old farm implements from the local farmers and reforge them for recycling (see also Posnansky 1980: 2419). This revival in the work of blacksmiths is confirmed by the interest shown by some local male youths in becoming apprentices of the trade.

Remittances and welfare

A feature of wage labour of some significance to the household economy and to rural adaptation in general is the remittances of

urban wage earners to their kin and friends in the village. Within the Ayirebi community the wage earners are predominantly males and their remittances usually take several forms. These include clothing, footwear (both old and new), money (to help kinsfolk in their farming, or as kin contribution towards a family project, funeral celebration or household maintenance), and imported consumer goods such as food items and medicine. Cash remittances, in particular, are significant in the household farming economy. The money received can be used to hire seasonal or casual wage labourers on the family farms.[15] Studies of money order transactions at the Ayirebi Post Office during the three-year period 1981–3 show a relatively steep rise in cash remittances in the difficult months of May and June 1983 (i.e. lean season period) over previous years (see Table 3.3).[16] A possible explanation for this is that, during the crisis period, when urban wages were inadequate to meet rising food prices, urban wage earners found it necessary to devise alternative strategies. They remitted cash to their rural kinsfolk very frequently, in order to obtain some food items directly and also to assist kinsfolk in hiring seasonal or casual wage labour for family farms. In some cases, the cash remitted was clearly earmarked for the establishment of new farms on the family plot on the wage earner's behalf.

COMMUNITY-LEVEL COPING STRATEGIES

Self-help and mutual aid have been cornerstones of the Ayirebi community-wide responses to the hardships of the early 1980s. The remarkable extent of social responsibility that was exhibited by the people is a testimony to the effective organization of the Ayirebi social and economic structures as well as its political leadership patterns. For example, to cope with the problem of scarcity of good drinking water during the 1982 drought, the eight-member Town Development Committee (TDC) in conjunction with the local Committee for the Defence of the Revolution (CDR) effectively mobilized the Ayirebi male community to construct both compound and community wells.[17] With regard to bush fires, a number of small fire-fighting groups of farmers who shared boundaries was formed. Town residents of both sexes, through a labour pool, assisted in the replanting of individual burnt farms. Victims of bush fires were financially assisted through voluntary contributions from the community.

The reintegration of the 298 returnees from Nigeria into Ayirebi society was viewed as the responsibility not only of the individual

Table 3.3 Monthly breakdown of the yearly record of money order transactions conducted at the Ayirebi Post Office (1981–3)

Year	JAN		FEB		MAR		APRIL		MAY		JUNE		JULY		AUG		SEPT		OCT		NOV		DEC		TOTAL	
	N[1]	A[2]	N	A	N	A	N	A	N	A	N	A	N	A	N	A	N	A	N	A	N	A	N	A	N	A
1981	12	850	4	205	—	—	1	22	—	—	2	34	1	26	4	123	7	202	8	350	3	125	9	518	51	2,455
1982	18	1,307	9	620	2	32	1	29	5	75	2	326	2	62	5	240	8	407	9	353	8	238	10	620	85	4,309
1983	23	1,876	10	877	2	150	2	53	11	850	15	1,504	6	408	7	210	–	–	–	–	*Not available*		–	–	76	5,928

1 N = Number of individuals reporting to the Post Office to conduct money order transactions.

2 A = Total amount involved in all transactions for the particular month. Amount in cedis (C), where one cedi = US$ 0.36 (1982–3).

household and families concerned but also of the wider community. The local chief, after consultations with his elders, took the first initiative and released a total of 2.5 hectares of stool land to the returnees for farming on a co-operative basis. Town residents with uncultivated lands were also encouraged to lease them out to interested individual returnees for farming. To reciprocate such community gestures, some returnees shared part of their acquired wealth from Nigeria with other town residents.[18] They also formed a voluntary body, the 'Ayirebi Agege Boys and Girls Association', which occasionally conducted two-hour clean-up exercises to improve sanitary conditions in the town. They assisted the various town committees to mobilize the local population to conduct other self-help projects effectively (e.g. the construction of four new public conveniences, using primarily local materials, within a period of two months between April and May 1983).

As part of the community coping strategies for the stress in the domestic food economy, town residents communally brought additional land into production. A series of community level co-operative farms were established (e.g. Town Co-operative farms, farms of the returnees from Nigeria, and the Ayirebi community farms). The local CDR in 1983 also secured an additional two hectares of stool land for community farming. During the same period, a group of women in the community obtained four hectares of stool land in order to establish a communal rice farm. In May 1983 the local chief, attempting to lessen the effects of the lean season's food supply on all Ayirebi households, appealed to the successful farmers to help their unfortunate counterparts who were experiencing hardships from poor harvests. Farmers with surplus food for sale were to make sure that local needs were satisfied first before supplying external markets. The appeal demanded that foodstuffs for sale were to be displayed at the Ayirebi market, in order for needy households to have the first right of purchase, before being sent to the established food dealers in the community. The local CDR saw to the execution of this measure which, despite a few grumblings, was largely adhered to by the farmers.

The extent to which the varied coping strategies were gender specific has already been pointed out: men hunted, engaged in non-agricultural production, constructed household and community wells and performed wage labour, while women gathered wild products, experimented with the cultivation of varieties of wild plants, made local substitutes for imported soap and vegetable oil, and developed

Table 3.4 Summary results of a seasonal weekly survey of the portion of a 12-hour day spent on various activities by both sexes in twenty representative Ayirebi households (no. of hours)

Seasonal cycle	Farm work[1]		Food processing[2]		Transport and maintenance[3]		Building repairs[4]		Child care[5]		Non-agri. production[6]		Total work	
	M	F	M	F	M	F	M	F	M	F	M	F	M	F
Post harvest season (Jan–Mar)	5.1	3.0	0.3	3.5	0.5	0.8	0.5	—	0.1	1.0	0.3	0.4	6.8	8.7
Lean season (April–Aug)	4.0	3.7	0.4	3.0	0.4	0.9	0.9	0.1	0.2	1.0	1.1	0.5	7.0	9.2
Harvest season (Oct–Dec)	1.9	2.2	0.6	3.7	0.7	1.3	0.6	0.1	0.1	0.8	1.4	0.7	5.3	8.8

1 Refers to actual work relating to field preparation, cutting, planting, weeding, harvesting and transporting produce to the household.
2 Activities associated with food processing and preparation, e.g. sun-drying, cleaning, peeling, winnowing, milling, cooking and serving of meals.
3 Includes collection of firewood and other fuel, fetching of water, laundry, sewing and household cleaning, washing of dishes, transportation of foodstuffs to market, and marketing.
4 Construction of new homes, repairs on existing structures.
5 Tending of children to bed and school; child learning; health needs of children.
6 Time devoted to wood and other fibre work.

additional processing methods for some crops. A seasonal weekly survey, which was based on observations and on interviews regarding household daily activities and the time spent on each, was conducted among adults of both sexes in the twenty representative households mentioned earlier. Data are summarized in Table 3.4. A basic finding is that men's work, although at times more strenuous, is generally limited to specific seasons unlike that of women (see also Brandtzaeg 1982; White 1976). The men may spend a great deal of their time performing farm work, but the contribution of women is equally significant. The role of women in agricultural production receives added significance when work relating to travel and household maintenance, food processing and preparation for consumption is taken into account. Men do not take part in some of the activities relating to household maintenance but, when all groups of activities performed in a day are totalled, the labour input by women, measured by time spent on the various activities, is far greater than that of the men. However, it should be stressed that, on the whole, the research period witnessed a remarkable degree of co-operation between the genders to find solutions to common problems both within the household and community and on the farms.

Normally, one would expect that the effects of severe economic hardships would be manifested in the conduct of social relations. That is, social conventions such as 'sharing, hospitality and generosity will go by the board in times of scarcity', while individual household needs and welfare become the prime concern (see Turton 1977: 188, on Ethiopia). This was not the case in the Ayirebi community. Largely through self-help, mutual aid, sharing and generosity, the local population was able to cope with ensuing hardships. There was a cultural awareness and acceptance that the main causes of the environmental crisis were human induced. The crisis was widely attributed to the breakdown of respect for customs, including one's obligations to kin and neighbours. There had been frequent condemnation from the aged in the community of the contemporary rising trend towards greed and the craze for self-aggrandizement at the expense of others. There was also a feeling that certain customary restrictions that were being increasingly ignored (e.g. restrictions on bush burning during certain periods and under certain conditions) were based on practical knowledge which had been acquired by the town ancestors. Such knowledge derived from long-term experience of subsistence strategies in an environment which was subject to the vagaries of climate (Posnansky 1984: 2163). In large measure, then,

the drought was seen as a punishment from the gods and ancestors in order to make the living aware of their neglect of adaptive customary behaviour and of the need to live harmoniously in the community (see also Turnbull 1972: 284). It is in this light that one has to understand the success of the local authorities in mobilizing the people to combat the hardships that they were facing and to fight for group rather than individual survival.

The study of criminal records at the local police station does not provide any significant evidence of strain in social relations during this period. The 1982–3 police records on crime, and other household or community disputes, show no marked increases over previous years. Sixty-one cases, including bodily assault (fighting), drinking abuse and insulting behaviour, breaking of national curfew hours, theft of household property and food crops (including bush animal protein from farm traps), were reported to and investigated by the local police officers.[19] In living memory, there has been no charge of murder, manslaughter or sexual abuse in the community. Those cases of bodily assault that have been reported are usually in the form of fist-fighting; implements such as knives and cutlasses are rarely used to inflict wounds. Of 15 bodily assault cases which were reported during the research period, knives were used in only four to inflict injury. The foregoing, however, is not intended to mean that Ayirebi social life was without an incident which could be attributed to the hardships of the stress periods. During the lean months of May to June 1983, there were occasional complaints of theft from farmlands involving food-crops such as cassava, plantains and cocoyams. These incidents were rarely reported to the police. The local chief, through the town crier, communicated to his people the need to be vigilant and he warned that offenders, when caught, would be severely dealt with. Other indicators of the effects of economic stress include a few observations of people calling in outstanding debts and pressing claims which, in less difficult or normal times, they might not have done (Turton 1977: 190). On the whole, community life was peaceful and in stark contrast to the stories of increased crime rate and commotion in the cities and urban centres, as reported in the national daily newspapers.

DISCUSSION

This study has focused on how one Ghanaian community has responded to the processes of change. The vitality of the rural survival strategies of the people of Ayirebi in combating the effects of seasonal

food supply cycles and of other contemporary socioeconomic and environmental stresses has been explored. It was shown how local self-sufficiency in food and other basic requirements was achieved in the community through four related factors: the strength and viability of the subsistence farming economy, which showed great diversity in cropping pattern; the adoption of hitherto underutilized subsistence practices (e.g. hunting and gathering of wild resources, and a resurgence of non-agricultural production); a pragmatic dependence on the local markets and/or cash economy; and the extent of social responsibility which was exhibited by community members.

While the coping strategies which are discussed here may not be altogether new, they have re-emerged in the contemporary scene in ways that clearly demonstrate the creativity and resourcefulness of the local people. In the Ayirebi community the local people are using all of the resources that are available to them from past experience to combat the stresses and strains that are brought to bear on existing means of satisfying basic necessities of life. Such micro-level studies of the nature of the contemporary adaptation of rural communities provide useful lessons not only in crisis containment but also, more importantly, in development planning; specifically, on the necessity of building thriving, self-reliant, self-sustainable local and regional communities in contemporary Africa.

This study raises issues regarding the nature of local–State relationships, particularly in the context of some of the structural adjustment programmes that are recommended by the World Bank for tropical African economies (WB 1981, 1984a). The active role of the State in promoting export-led development through cash crop production and the free play of market forces is seen as essential for the long term development of the African economies. Primary importance is attached to external assistance in the developmental process (Hinderink and Sterkenburg 1987: 271–3). A basic problem with export-led development relates to the continued subordinate position of African economies in international terms of trade and division of labour. The effects of the world recession of the 1980s on African economies reaffirm the fact that the State cannot guarantee the availability and growth of fair markets for national export products. This means that the State has to reassess its role in the developmental process. It must promote reforms that not only make for the efficient allocation of available resources, but also utilize indigenous creativity and resourcefulness in order to improve upon the living conditions of the rural majority.

The Ayirebi case study offers some useful insights in this direction. A socially responsible local leadership is leading the way to addressing pressing issues of communal interests during stressful situations. There is grass-root level participation in village decision-making, and the crucial issue of access to productive resources, particularly land, is being addressed. Local checks on the activities of 'external' forces in the domestic economy (e.g. marketing intermediaries; food dealers) ensure that external demands do not adversely affect local needs and requirements. Other areas of spontaneous action on the part of Ayirebi farming households to combat the socio-environmental stresses on the local economy have been spelt out. The noted inter- and intra-village integration involving households' pooling of resources and labour power constitute effective strategies for self-sustained and self-reliant development.

Participation in the cash economy can, to some extent, make a contribution to a farming household's ability to cope with national economic crisis, by making other sources of revenue available for other household purchases. However, a deeper involvement at the expense of subsistence production can also have detrimental effects in terms of local food self-sufficiency. The consequences of cash tree cropping on the local food requirements of developing African countries have been far reaching. In most of these countries, the redirection of agricultural efforts away from food crop production to cash tree crops has worked to the detriment of household, community, and national levels of food adequacy. The question which readily comes to mind is whether the observed local food self-sufficiency in the Ayirebi community is attributed to the primary importance of food production, for both household consumption and the external market, over non-food cash cropping (e.g. cocoa). There is limited and inconclusive evidence to answer this question, and further research in other Ghanaian communities is needed. At the national level, however, certain facts are clear and relevant. Since the turn of this century, a significant factor influencing food production in Ghana has been the introduction of cocoa as a cash crop. In areas where cocoa is dominant, the best land is allocated to this crop, while food crops are relegated to the poorer land. The continuing government emphasis on export cropping to the neglect of small-scale rural food production has necessitated the importation of food items to supplement local production. In fact, some of the more recent national policies to combat the effects of the 1982–3 drought and bush fires (such as those relating to cocoa rehabilitation and replanting) involve large tracts

of potential foodcrop land, which may seriously influence total food output in the country in some years to come.

Further research is also needed to assess the degree to which the coping strategies of the Ayirebi community have been continued long after the 1982–3 drought. But it is important to point out that, after the rains came in June 1983 and in 1984, Ayirebi households could still be observed as being engaged in the major survival strategies discussed. These included: a continuation of food collecting and hunting activities; experimenting with additional varieties of plants for cultivation purposes; non-agricultural production; use of local substitutes for imported soap, vegetable oil and sugar; and expanded processing methods for staples such as cocoyam and cassava. Future research is needed to identify whether or not there is a continuance of the changes that were observed in land use and allocation, in food crop diversification, in farm labour adjustments, in household remittances and welfare, and in the wider community responses to ecological and other stressors.

Further studies are necessary before generalizations can be made from the results of research in Ayirebi. Nevertheless, this study questions conclusions about the state of African economies which are based solely on macroeconomic data, themselves measuring for the most part production for the external market and omitting from consideration local survival strategies.

ACKNOWLEDGEMENTS

This study was conducted in 1982 and 1983 for my doctoral dissertation in Anthropology at the University of Toronto. I am grateful for the comments received on this study from Professors Richard Lee and Maxine Kleindienst of the University of Toronto, Professor Merrick Posnansky of the University of California, Los Angeles, and Professor Alejandro Rojas of the Faculty of Environmental Studies, York University, Toronto. I am deeply indebted to the chief and people of Ayirebi, near Akyem Oda in southeastern Ghana, for their warm hospitality. Funding for this project was provided by the University of Toronto through the award of a Connaught Scholarship.

NOTES

1 This figure is based on projections of Ghana's population growth for the 1980s from the 1970 census of 3,450 for the Ayirebi town (Central Bureau of Statistics 1982). The official report of a late-1984 population census which was carried out in the country had not been published at the time of writing.

2 The household refers to a group of people usually (but not necessarily) living in a house or compound who have a common food supply, pool their incomes for common support and regularly use and share the contents of a cooking pot.

3 Food records were kept in both the local language, Twi, and in English. In some of the households, the help of those with some formal education was sought for this detailed study.

4 A study of the occupational characteristics of the 412 sampled household heads (of whom 96 [23.3%] were female and 316 [76.7%] were male) shows that 396 (96%) consider farming their primary occupation while two mentioned hunting and trapping. The remaining 14 primary occupations were: herbalist (1); fetish priest (1); tailor and seamstress (2); trader (4); police officer (2); school teacher (2); shoe repairman (1) and transport driver (1). Fifty-six (13.6%) of the household heads indicated hunting and trapping as a secondary occupation.

5 Among the factors accounting for this development are ecological problems (drought, bush fires, soil erosion), diseases (such as swollen shoot), the problem of agricultural labour, and the failure of successive Ghanaian governments to provide adequate incentives to cocoa farmers (see Senyah 1984). Because of the declining revenues of some cocoa farmers, individual attempts are being made now to devote land to the cultivation of foodstuffs for both domestic and commercial purposes (Atsu 1984).

6 Hill (1963) has detailed the crucial role played by a group of migrants from Akuapem, Ga, and Shai in the hills above Accra in creating the Ghanaian cocoa industry. Starting in 1892, they migrated eastward to the present state of Akyem Abuakwa, where they bought large tracts of uncultivated land from absentee landlords. These migrants occupied an area further to the south east of Ghana than where Ayirebi town is located, and their settlements post-date the known early history and evolution of the Ayirebi community. The early settlers of Ayirebi were food producers. In later years, when the successful cocoa enterprises of the Akuapem migrants became generally known, cocoa growing became a feature in the Ayirebi economy. However, the cocoa farmers of Ayirebi (unlike those migrants of Akuapem) primarily relied on lineage and stool land (land under custodianship of a chief), as well as family labour, while combining their cocoa farming activities with food production (Wilks 1977: 526).

7 The members of the Town Development Committee (TDC) are selected by the local chief in consultation with his elders. Membership of the Committee for the Defence of the Revolution (CDR) is open to all town residents. This latter body was formerly called the People's Defence

Committee (PDC). It is a more recent political action group, the idea for which was introduced by the ruling Provisional National Defence Council (PNDC) government since 1982.

8 This wage sector is, however, not a well developed feature in the local economy. Fewer than a hundred individuals in the town are employed by the government as agricultural workers. Interestingly enough, although these are supposedly full-time employees collecting monthly salaries, they normally report for duty only twice a week and spend most of the remaining time working on their farms. In my conversations with agricultural workers, they unanimously pointed out that the government rarely pays their wages regularly, and that at times they are not paid at all for three or four successive months. The workers are thus forced to embark upon their own farming as a means of obtaining a sustained livelihood.

9 See Ghana Meteorological Services, Annual Rainfall Reports, Headquarters, Accra, Ghana.

10 The 298 returnees were made up of 210 males and 88 females with ages ranging from a three-month-old baby to a 49-year-old adult. Two hundred and seventeen of the returnees resettled in Ayirebi between January and April 1983, with the other 81 arriving between May and October 1983.

11 The importance of the local market increased during the season of relative scarcity in so far as household food consumption needs are concerned. The market prices of the basic staples (cocoyams, plantain, cassava and yams), as well as other protein-source foods (such as meat and fish), also tend to fluctuate with seasonal variations in supply. In the lean season, because of relative scarcity of some basic staples on the market, higher prices are demanded for the products on sale. But, just as market purchases of basic staples for local household consumption may rise during this lean period, those of meat and fish, as well as other protein-source foods, show a steady decline. The lean season witnesses an increase in the relative contributions of game from hunting and trapping activities, which supply most of the protein required in household diets. With the emergence of the harvest season, the importance of the market for household food supply reverses, with a period of increasing dependence on self-produced foodstuffs and a decrease in the contribution of purchased basic staples to the calorie content of the average household diet. However, as this period also coincides with the festive and ceremonial season which entails increased consumption of protein-source foods, market purchases of meat and fish (particularly of smoked herring and catfish) show a steady rise over those of the previous season.

12 In providing such information it is borne in mind that monetary income alone may not always give a complete and accurate picture of the economic status of the individuals involved. The income data should be supported by additional consideration of other important assets in the form of such immovable property as house and land. Before drawing conclusions on economic status, this researcher compared the income data and his observations of household property (e.g. land, houses) with the views of other community members. The income data are considered to be a relatively good index of, or a close approximation to, economic status.

13 The minimum daily wage was C 12 at the beginning of the research period. Although incomes expressed here may appear rather high for the predominantly small-scale rural farming households, they are if anything on the low side. Owing to prevailing high inflation levels in the country (in 1982–3 over 350%), these incomes do not reflect actual purchasing power.

14 There were a few instances, observed during the research period, of local artisans (blacksmiths, woodcarvers, bamboo and basket weavers) accepting food items for their manufactured products, as was usually the case in the past.

15 Most of the wage earners living outside the community, in order to make sure that their future food requests to rural kinsfolk will be heeded, try to remit some money to the farmers at the onset of the farming season and also during the harvest season. Other wage earners also provide some of their income to their rural kin so that the latter can employ farm labourers to set up local farms on behalf of the urban workers.

16 A certain amount of caution should be exercised in reading and interpreting the figures because of the problem of inaccurate record keeping at the Post Office. It is also possible that some monetary transactions of this nature might have been conducted by a few local residents at the major Post Office of Akyem Oda rather than at Ayirebi, or that people do not cash their money orders immediately. Also, most of such monetary remittances do not necessarily come to Ayirebi residents through the local Post Office. Substantial sums of money are received through the personal visits of the donors themselves, or via their friends and other visiting relatives. Some allowance must also be made for inflation and the increase in money supply in the country over the past two years. None the less, the comparative figures for three years lend credence to an argument for the increasing importance of cash remittances during the stress period of 1982–3.

17 The digging of wells was initially a voluntary exercise. As the water supply situation worsened and additional community wells had to be established, the local CDR instituted a penalty of C 20 (i.e. US$ 7.20 in 1982–3) for households whose male adults failed to provide communal labour.

18 The arrival of the returnees temporarily brought some goods into the community, such as soap and toiletries, clothing and textiles, tinned foods, health drugs, building materials (iron nails and tin roofing sheets), as well as household effects, such as tape recorders, stereo equipment, mattresses, trunks and suitcases. In addition, there were ten chain-saws, two mini-Toyota buses, and five electric generators, the presence of which helped in the farming, transportation, and energy requirements of the local population respectively.

19 During the fieldwork, countryside curfew hours were in force from 10:00 p.m. to 5:00 a.m. daily. Also, the figures for cases reported to the local police include crime and assault cases from other small communities within the immediate vicinity of Ayirebi. Civil cases involving land disputes and marital conflicts usually end up in the local chief's arbitration courts rather than with the police. Cases involving witchcraft

accusations are normally dealt with by the local fetish priests. Finally, it is stressed that not all criminal or assault cases necessarily end up in the hands of the police. Therefore, caution must be exercised in placing too much reliance on the figures provided.

4

THE CO-OPERATIVE CREDIT UNION MOVEMENT IN NORTH-WESTERN GHANA

Development agent or agent of incorporation?

Jacob Songsore

INTRODUCTION

Although it is generally accepted that credit plays a crucial role in the expansion and development of productive forces, social scientists, in addition to the World Bank and other donor agencies, are only now assessing the part that bank credit has played in the centralization and concentration of capital in the process of accumulation. This process had long been observed by Lenin in his analysis of finance capital (Lenin 1978: 30–59; see also H.T. Thomas 1988: 8).

At the micro level, the role of the financial system is to provide adequate savings and credit facilities to individual households whilst, in a macroeconomic context, financial institutions have the basic functions of channelling capital from savers to investors. An efficient financial system is consequently assumed to have a considerable positive effect on increasing welfare and stimulating economic activity and development. As a result 'credit is now the largest component in the World Bank's agricultural lending . . . and many governments of developing countries have assigned to credit the lead role in rural and industrial development programmes' (H.T. Thomas 1988: 10).

In the normal workings of a capitalist economy, financial institutions collect all kinds of financial revenue which they place at the disposal of the capitalist class. A study of the workings of formal financial institutions in the underdeveloped economy of rural Ghana has come up with similar conclusions. As the researchers put it:

> By providing liquidity in quite a selective way, primarily to the powerful and alert members of rural society, the banks

contribute greatly to a redistribution of wealth in favour of these 'elites'. Although the rural people would not use this terminology, it is the view held by the majority of the rural people and one which they do not hesitate to express; 'They only help the big shots to become richer'.

(Bentil *et al.* 1988: 126)

The *laissez-faire* operation of banking institutions in Third World countries and more especially in Ghana has had two consequences: first, the denuding of impoverished rural regions which are of little interest for the accumulation of much of their locally generated capital and, second, the creation of isolated pockets of rural poverty, i.e. the classical labour reserves. The latter have few modern financial institutions. Indeed, where these exist, they hardly serve the interest of the numerous illiterate rural peasant men and women in the lower ranks of the social ladder.

For example, in Ghana it is widely recognized that commercial banks have served to mop up and transfer rural savings to the capital markets of the Accra-Tema metropolitan area, the national capital, and to a lesser extent to other large metropolitan areas such as Kumasi and Sekondi-Takoradi. Such capital drained from cocoa and food producers has then been reallocated for foreign monopolies and other business interests which are located in the non-indigenous economy, i.e. those economic sectors with very few spin-off effects on the petty commodity sector of the national economy.

Of late, in order to stimulate a stagnating rural economy which has grave consequences for the national economy, rural banks have been established as a way of reducing these flows. This does not imply that there have been no initiatives on the part of the rural poor to adopt mitigating or survival strategies as a way of coping with the haemorrhage of capital and the limitations that are imposed on their productive activities and welfare services by their incorporation into the capitalist world economy.

These initiatives have taken the form of rotating credit associations known as '*susu*' and the development of the co-operative credit union movement. These indigenous rotating credit associations provided the basis for the development of the new organizational form of co-operation through the credit unions, since, without this spirit, the credit union movement might never have gained ground in the region. Where such organizational forms to defend the interest of the poor are lacking, both the rural and urban poor fall into the hands of

'usury' money lenders who step in to fill the gaps that are left by finance capital.

North-Western Ghana, as the name implies, lies in the north-western corner of Ghana. For the purpose of credit union administration, North-Western Ghana includes the present Upper-West Region, and the Bole and Damongo Districts within the Northern Region which currently operate under the Wa Chapter Head Office of the credit union movement. The region represents the worst pocket of extreme poverty in Ghana, with no modern industry except a cotton ginnery, few parastatals and a predominance of peasant agriculture using the most rudimentary technology. Out-migration to the southern mines and cocoa farms has been the lot of young men, leaving behind a population comprised largely of women, children and the elderly (Songsore 1983; Songsore and Denkabe 1988).

The underdevelopment of productive forces in the region can best be understood in the context of internal contradictions arising out of its colonial incorporation into the world capitalist sphere as a regional periphery of a peripheral state. All available studies indicate that the poverty of its people has further deepened as a result of, on the one hand, the ripple effect of the contemporary crisis of underdeveloped capitalism and, on the other, the marginality of the 'distant' poor in the area from the focus of the ongoing Economic Recovery/Structural Adjustment Programme (ERP/SAP) of the state. The politically powerless peasant producers in the region, whilst sharing few of the benefits of the ERP/SAP, have had many of the burdens of economic recovery pushed on to them.

Since this IMF/World Bank fashioned programme is based on an export-led strategy of economic recovery, resource flows in terms of loans have been directed to cocoa producers, and to the mining and timber industries in southern Ghana, to the neglect of food producers in the region. By contrast, as a result of the effects of devaluation of the local currency, liberalization and price de-regulation on the prices of inputs and consumer goods, the interregional barter terms of trade have shifted against rural food producers in the region. Utilization of health, potable water and educational services have all declined because of the imposition of high user charges. The imposition of higher user fees and the withdrawal of supplementary feeding programmes have caused a sharp drop in attendance at child and maternal welfare clinics. This is occurring at a time of drastic cutback in so-called nonproductive expenditure in the social sector. The worst hit have been women and children from very poor households.

Among these, children under five and pregnant and lactating mothers have been most affected. The overall quality of life among these people is the worst in Ghana (Songsore 1989).

Credit, by enabling peasants to expand and develop income-generating activities and by supporting payments of water tariffs, health charges and school fees, could be a vital tool for empowering the rural poor to cope with the consequences of the current crisis. By so doing, credit from these local co-operative credit unions could serve as vital instruments for achieving development from within and below (Mackenzie and Taylor 1989: 133).

In response partly to the area's neglect since the colonial period and partly to the pressures for cash mediated subsistence consumption and the intensification of commodity production, the Co-operative Credit Union movement in Ghana was born in the north-west of Ghana in 1955 (Songsore 1982: 3). The movement was to serve as a focal point for the endogenous, grass-roots mobilization of local resources for local development within the limits set by the national and international system. It is very often the belief that, through the organized collective action of communities at the local level, the poor can fashion a suitable response to their progressive marginalization by the normal workings of finance capital.

This paper reviews state policies and the development of institutional credit in this largely neglected rural region and attempts to situate credit unions in the context of this general development. A major proposition which is advanced is that the co-operative credit union movement has served more as a vehicle for the penetration of capitalist production relations in this regional periphery rather than as a development agent addressing the needs of the majority of the members.

Pertaining to the above proposition, the paper discusses urban—rural contrasts in access to credit; differential class and gender access to credit; and peasant protest and crisis in the credit movement. In conclusion, suggestions are made which are aimed at recapitalizing and redirecting the credit unions towards the genuine developmental aspirations of the rank and file membership, especially women who are among the least heard. It is only through such reforms that the movement can serve the interest of the poor and thus become an effective coping mechanism for the poor.

THE POST-COLONIAL STATE AND THE DEVELOPMENT OF INSTITUTIONAL CREDIT IN NORTH-WESTERN GHANA

As a result of the low level of development of productive forces, a situation which was bequeathed by colonialism (Bentil *et al.* 1988: 11; Songsore 1983), both foreign and national banking institutions have been slow to develop in North-Western Ghana in contrast to their early development in the more monetized export-oriented areas of Southern Ghana. In the colonial period, for example, only one branch of the Standard Bank was located at Wa to serve the whole region. It was later replaced by a branch of the Ghana Commercial Bank in the same town. This was the only source of bank credit in this area of over half a million people until the 1970s.

Two new branches of the Ghana Commercial Bank have now been opened in Lawra and Tumu. This is partly in response to the expansion of government administrative institutions and schools in these district centres but also because the rural credit unions, which have long existed in these districts operated deposit accounts with this Bank thereby ensuring their viability. In order to stimulate agricultural development in the area, the Agricultural Development Bank now operates branch offices at Wa, Lawra and Tumu. Besides these, there is a branch each of the Social Security Bank and Co-operative Bank at Wa which, since 1983, has served as regional capital of the new Upper-West Region comprising the districts of Wa, Lawra and Tumu. The Co-operative Bank also has branches at Tumu, Jirapa and Hamile, all in the Upper-West Region. Two rural banks now exist in Jirapa and Nandom through the energies of their Youth Associations.[1]

Similar developments in commercial banking have taken place in Bole and Damongo Districts which, although they lie within the sphere of the Upper-West Chapter of the Co-operative Credit Union Movement which is headquartered at Wa, are administratively within the Northern Region. Damongo and Bolé Towns each have a branch of the Ghana Commercial Bank. In northern Ghana as a whole (consisting of the Upper-West, Upper-East and Northern Regions), where about 20 per cent of the total population lives, there were in 1988 only 45 bank offices, which amounted to a mere 8.6 per cent of the country's bank offices. The ratio of inhabitants to banking outlets reaches a high of over 1:58,000 with average catchment areas of 5,300 km^2.

This very low bank density seems to be one reason why the entire North accounts for only 3.9 per cent of all formal sector credit and 2.8 per cent of all formal sector deposits. . . . The insufficient supply becomes all the more obvious if one takes into account the internal concentration of banks in the three regional capitals Tamale, Wa and Bolgatanga: almost half of the bank offices in the North are located in these cities while only one-sixth of the northern population live there. This implies that the ratio of inhabitants to bank offices in 'rural northern Ghana', outside of the regional capitals, is close to 1:100,000.

(Bentil *et al.* 1988: 66)

By contrast to the recency in the evolution of banking services in the region, a phenomenon largely of the mid-seventies and eighties, co-operative credit unions have been in existence in this area since 1955.

LOCAL INITIATIVES AND THE EMERGENCE OF THE CREDIT MOVEMENT IN THE AREA

The pioneering work which led to the establishment of credit union associations in the area was undertaken by Rev. Father John McNulty among Dagaaba peasants in Jirapa parish within the Upper-West Region. This Canadian-born priest was inspired by his experience with credit unions in Canada, where they emerged in poor rural areas among the working class and craftsmen with the object of providing a collective response to their poverty through mutual self-help (Chitsike 1988: 34; Credit Unions Association [CUA] 1971: 1). He pursued the idea among the very poor parishioners in Jirapa. After several months of intensive discussions in a basic membership education programme, the first parish (associational) type of common bond credit union in Ghana was founded in September 1955 in Jirapa (CUA 1971: 1; Van Den Dries 1970: 34).

Thereafter, the credit union movement was actively promoted by the entire Catholic Church hierarchy in the Wa diocese, leading to the establishment of a credit union in every parish town. From Wa diocese the idea spread to Navrongo and Tamale diocese in Northern Ghana. The preliminary work in the parish towns was delegated to the parish priests. All but five of the twenty-two major credit unions within the Upper-West Chapter, as of 1985, were based at parish stations. For the five which lay outside mission stations, the missionaries still played an important animating role in their establishment.

As many as seven credit unions were already in operation within the North-West before the Ghana Co-operative Credit Unions Association Ltd (CUA) was formally registered in March 1968. CUA serves as an umbrella organization for all primary societies affiliated to it. CUA relates to the primary societies through the regional offices of these societies, which are known as chapters.

The role of the National Association is mainly supervisory. It aids existing societies in training officers and members; helps in the establishment of new societies; provides financial aid to member societies; represents the member societies in dealings with the government; and represents the member societies at the international level. The various chapters have the authority to act on behalf of the National Association at the regional level although this is exercised in consultation with the National Association (CUA 1978: 15).

Table 4.1 Regional distribution of credit unions affiliated to CUA 1984/5

Chapter	Credit union	Membership	Savings (C)	Loans (C)
Ashanti	29	4,913	13,984,465.00	12,531,594.00
Brong Ahafo	19	4,587	28,762,433.96	26,205,041.63
Central	15	1,748	2,776,064.03	2,527,265.63
Eastern	9	1,155	1,074,005.00	992,625.00
Greater Accra	47	9,491	21,305,677.00	17,566,489.00
Northern	7	2,010	1,809,355.00	1,624,479.00
Western	13	5,710	11,958,352.00	8,994,535.00
Volta	NA	NA	NA	NA
Upper-East	7	3,256	2,823,071.38	1,714,836.27
Upper-West	22	17,382	62,231,741.54	43,019,718.00
Totals	168	50,252	146,725,164.91	115,176,583.53

Source: CUA Office, Accra

As of the 1984/5 fiscal year, CUA embraced a total of 168 primary societies with a total membership of 50,252 persons. The regional breakdown is shown in Table 4.1. The total savings of all credit unions stood at 146,725,164.91 cedis while total loans were 115,176,583.53 cedis.

The Upper-West Chapter accounted for 13.1 per cent of the number of primary societies, 34.6 per cent of total membership, 42.4 per cent of total savings and 37.3 per cent of the total loans. The position of the Upper-West Chapter in the Co-operative Credit Union

Movement is a noteworthy achievement given the level of poverty in the region. These savings and loans have been mobilized entirely from the efforts of the rural poor.

The district by district distribution pattern of the major credit unions in the Upper-West Chapter is shown in Table 4.2. There is a concentration of societies, membership, savings and loans within the Upper-West Region from where the credit union idea diffused to the Northern Region. The two most populous districts of Wa and Lawra with the highest number of parish stations also have the highest number of societies.

Table 4.2 Distribution pattern of major credit unions Upper-West Chapter 1985[1]

	No. of societies	Membership	Savings (C)	Loans (C)
Districts Upper-West Region				
Wa	8	4,302	16,189,997.81	8,950,490.00
Lawra	8	6,597	15,199,401.16	11,019,016.80
Tumu	3	2,696	14,474,738.32	9,243,553.70
Districts Northern Region				
Damongo	1	2,029	5,379,635.99	4,290,472.10
Bole[1]	2	2,418	11,454,481.64	9,917,863.70
Totals	22	18,042	62,698,254.92	43,421,396.30

Source: Upper-West Chapter head office, Wa

1 Data for 1984 were used for Fielmun and Babile (Upper West Region) while data for 1986 were used for Bole (Northern Region) owing to deficiencies in data.

In terms of per capita savings, Tumu District tops the list followed by Bole and Wa Districts, as shown in Table 4.3. The per capita savings levels for the credit unions in Damongo and Lawra Districts fall below the mean per capita savings level for the Chapter which stands at 3,477.05 cedis. In terms of loans, the average loans per head are highest in Bole followed by Tumu. All other districts had below average performance, taking the mean value for the Chapter as a whole. The reason for lower savings rates and per capita loans in Lawra, Damongo and Wa Districts may be that the levels of loan delinquencies are higher for the oldest credit unions in these districts. This fact might have served to dampen the enthusiasm of most rank and file members in credit union activities.

Table 4.3 Per capita savings and loans by district, Upper-West Chapter

	Savings per head (C)	Loans per head (C)
Upper-West Region Districts		
Wa	3,763.36	2,080.54
Lawra	2,303.98	1,670.30
Tumu	5,368.96	3,428.61
Northern Region Districts		
Damongo	2,664.50	2,125.00
Bole	4,737.17	4,101.68
Mean for Chapter	3,477.05	2,408.02

Source: Upper-West Chapter head office, Wa

In nominal cedi terms, the capital base of the credit unions in North-Western Ghana has shown a positive trend. For example, savings grew from 16.4 million cedis in 1979/80 to just over 66 million cedis in 1986. Loan portfolios also grew from 7.5 million cedis to almost 46 million cedis in the same period (Table 4.4a). In real terms the capital base of the Upper-West Chapter showed a rather drastic shrinkage from 16.4 million cedis as savings in 1979/80 to a mere 5.8 million cedis in 1986.

This had a corresponding effect on loan disbursements (Table 4.4b). The 1981/2 financial year showed a slightly better picture because of the rigid enforcements of price controls in the first year of the December 31 Revolution when the popular classes had a strong influence on policy. This situation stands in sharp contrast to the sharp decline from 1982/3 to 1986 as a result of the very drastic devaluation of the cedi from under three cedis to one dollar (US) to over ninety cedis to one dollar (US) by 1986.

The progressive decline in the value of the cedi to the US dollar is reflected in the dollar equivalents presented in Table 4.4c. There are a number of reasons for the shrinkage in capital base of credit unions in the study area. First, the high import content of manufactured items and the limited price support for food crops which were produced in the area worsened the terms of trade of rural producers and thereby made it more difficult for peasants to sustain and increase their savings. The second major reason was the decline in

Table 4.4a   Upper-West Chapter: trends in savings and loans

Year	Savings (C)	Loans (C)
1979/80	16,441,235.37	7,575,367.26
1980/1	25,892,709.46	14,553,861.82
1981/2	36,144,337.00	19,035,228.00
1982/3	49,734,545.00	23,693,918.00
1983/4	63,617,224.06	46,766,326.49
1985	62,698,254.92	43,421,396.80
1986	66,156,635.00	45,897,307.00

Table 4.4b   Deflated values (using 1979/80 = 100)

1979/80	16,441,235.37	7,575,367.26
1980/1	11,952,315.00	6,721,547.80
1981/2	13,649,384.00	7,188,377.80
1982/3	8,428,443.70	4,013,680.40
1983/4	7,724,479.60	5,678,423.40
1985	6,896,939.60	4,776,444.70
1986	5,842,272.50	4,053,177.40

Table 4.4c   US dollar equivalent (US$)

1979/80	5,978,033.00	2,754,403.40
1980/1	9,414,588.90	5,291,783.80
1981/2	13,142,080.00	6,921,208.90
1982/3	2,446,939.60	1,165,248.70
1983/4	1,768,558.80	1,300,103.80
1985	1,153,647.80	798,953.68
1986	740,954.31	514,049.83

Source: Calculated from data collected from Upper-West Chapter head office, Wa, using Quarterly Digest of Statistics, March 1988, Accra, Ghana

confidence that peasants had in the credit unions as seen in the declining number of active members for some of these credit unions. For example, the total active membership dropped from 25,830 in 1983/4 to 16,290 in 1986.

Perhaps the most important issue relating to the development of credit unions is their role in the stimulation of endogenous rural development initiatives by these neglected rural poor, to which we now turn.

THE ROLE OF THE CREDIT UNIONS IN RURAL DEVELOPMENT

In order to address this important question, an analysis is presented below of the sectoral and spatial structure of credit distribution and issues related to class, gender and access to credit. For this purpose five credit unions, namely Wa, Hamile Town, Jirapa, Kaleo and Ko Credit Unions, were selected for closer study.[2]

In terms of effective utilization of savings as credit, most credit unions were found wanting. Out of the five selected credit unions, only the Wa and Hamile Town Credit Unions were effectively utilizing their deposits as loans to their members. Well over 75 per cent of the savings of the Wa Credit Union and all of the savings of the Hamile Town Credit Union were out in loans. By contrast, under 50 per cent of savings of the remaining three Credit Unions were given out as loans. The main reason for the difference lies in the contrasting world outlooks between the commercially minded Islamic Wala ethnic group, which dominated the Wa and Hamile Town Credit Unions, and the agrarian peasant-oriented focus of the other three unions that were located in the Dagaba area. Generally, poor peasants were found to be more averse to risk relative to the more opulent merchant class. Because of the low returns on investment in agriculture, given the vagaries of the weather, peasants living close to the margin of survival are more cautious of getting into debt. By contrast, given the highly inflationary situation which Ghana has gone through, speculative and rentier activities in the commercial sector have tended to confer windfall gains on rural merchants. More recently, the pattern has changed for the other credit unions. They now have higher percentages of their resources being utilized as loans because of the demonstrated effect over time of the advantages to be derived from access to credit and the penetration of the rural unions by urban-based elements.

The sectoral distribution of loans for all of the credit unions surveyed showed a high concentration of loan portfolios in the productive spheres, namely trade and small-scale industries, agriculture, housing, health and education. For example, over 90 per cent of the loans in Wa, Hamile Town and Jirapa were investment loans. For Kaleo and Ko Credit Unions the proportion of investment loans were 75 and 60 per cent respectively.

Within the productive sector, trade and small-scale industries together accounted for between 50 to 80 per cent of the total loans,

with agriculture and housing each having a range of 3–16 per cent of the total loans from year to year. Health and education-related borrowing had the lowest percentages, generally ranging from below 1 to 5 per cent.

Only a small fraction of the loans were for consumptive purposes and these were distributed among the following categories: family use, purchase of private transport, repayment of loans elsewhere, purchase of foodstuffs and the settlement of bride price or dowry. The purchase of cars, motor bicycles and bicycles was the most outstanding single expenditure item in this category because of the high capital outlay required per unit item.

The per capita concentration of loans was much higher when borrowing was for investment rather than for consumption. The very poor members of the unions made the heaviest demands on loans for the purpose of consumption but, while they accounted for between 50 to 98 per cent of the number of beneficiaries, their relative share of total loans was generally under 30 per cent from year to year. One could conclude with some justification that the credit unions, by supporting investments in the productive base of the regional economy, have been vital instruments in rural development.

Going beyond mere sectoral aggregates, one notices: (a) a skewed distribution of credit in favour of the urban and rural centres where the credit unions are located as against their wider catchment areas; (b) a further polarization of capital in the hands of the local dominant classes; (c) a distribution of credit in favour of male members of the respective credit unions.

Taking the issue of rural/urban contrast, the privileged position of credit union centres, as opposed to the settlements in their respective catchment areas, is very stark. For example, in the case of Wa Co-operative Credit Union, all but 2 per cent of the loans went to Wa based members alone. The picture was slightly better for the Jirapa Credit Union where almost 21 per cent of total loans went to about 32 per cent of the total beneficiaries in the outlying villages. A further improvement in the position of satellite villages as opposed to the credit union station town was observed in the case of Kaleo Credit Union. About 45 per cent of the loans went to 43 per cent of the total beneficiaries in the surrounding villages. Ko Co-operative Credit Union was the only exception to the rule. Over 60 per cent of the loans was utilized by 82 per cent of beneficiaries in outlying villages.

The overall bias in favour of urban or 'rurban' centres can be explained largely by the sectoral concentration of loan portfolios in

such urban activities as commerce and industry, and the distance decay effect in the spatial pattern in the relative use of an innovation by people living within the spheres of contact of the origin of an innovation. The special case of Ko Credit Union can be explained in terms of the overall rural character of the centre, apart from the existence of a Catholic mission station and the credit union. In addition, within its catchment area lay such large centres of very profitable commercial maize farming as Lambussie, where an emerging stratum of capitalist farmers has been making heavy demands for credit to finance fertilizer purchase and tractor hire services. The Lambussie area is well known in the region for 'large-scale' maize production and recently the Lambussie *Kuoro* (chief) won the 'best maize farmer of the year' award in Ghana.

In terms of the relationship between class and access to credit, loans were heavily concentrated in the hands of a few beneficiaries in the upper stratum of regional society in the cases of Wa, Hamile and Jirapa Credit Unions. In the case of Jirapa, about 60 per cent of the total loans was utilized by a mere 2 per cent of the total number of beneficiaries. For Wa, between 68 to 80 per cent of total loans was absorbed by between 6 to 10 per cent of loan beneficiaries. The situation was almost the same for Hamile where about 41 per cent of the loans was concentrated in this stratum, involving only 6 per cent of the total number of loan beneficiaries. The opposite, however, was true for Kaleo and Ko Credit Unions where nearly all of the loans went to the lower and a few middle strata of rural society. In the case of these two credit unions, per capita loans were also much smaller.

Even for these rural-based credit unions, such as Kaleo, Ko and many of the others, the current pattern is one in which the few better-placed urban and rural bourgeois elements, consisting of merchants, contractors, civil servants, chiefs and *kulaks*, i.e. farmer-traders, have seized control of the management of the unions and as a result have begun to appropriate a larger share of total loans to themselves. This tendency became ascendant in the seventies when the Catholic Church, partly in response to pressures from the local dominant classes, decided to withdraw priests from the position of treasurer in the various co-operative credit unions. The newly appointed treasurers were very often barely literate in accounting knowledge. These clerks soon became pawns in the hands of local notables and were found approving and granting loans to members of the various committees, which was against the rules.[3]

Available evidence suggests that most of the credit unions have lost

huge sums of money through misappropriations. In one case alone, a treasurer misappropriated five million cedis from union funds at Damongo; at both Wa and Bole, over four million cedis each of union funds could not be accounted for.

In almost all of the credit unions, those who owed huge sums of money and who have defaulted with repayments are the chiefs, local contractors, merchants, middle-level servants and members of the various boards of management. Most of these loans were granted as 'trust' loans, without any collateral, by the loan committees. In the case of Lawra Credit Union, the repayment of loans due from two such individuals alone would be enough to put the credit union back on a very sound financial footing.

Poor peasants, rural women and workers are rarely mentioned, if at all, among the list of loan defaulters. Poor people very often seek only genuine loans, which they do pay back as they generally do not want to be disgraced. By contrast, the well-connected in society know that they can escape exposure by members of the loan committee. Rank and file members often do not understand the financial mess that their unions may be facing until such time as they cannot withdraw money from their savings because of an acute liquidity crisis.

The members of the various management boards have also undertaken poor investment projects, using union funds, with the result that such investments have served as drains for credit union resources. One good example is a hotel complex under construction at Wa, using resources from the local credit union. Others include a co-operative store and a petrol dump owned by the Jirapa Credit Union, a tractor hire service run by the Kaleo Credit Union and a fuel dump operated by the Busie Credit Union. The Tumu Credit Union has used union funds for the construction of bore-holes. All of the investments which were aimed at expanding the capital base of the respective unions are operating at a loss.

Owing to the out-migration of adult males, women outnumber men: in 1970 the ratio of males to females was 89.2:100 and this increased only slightly during the 1984 population census to 90.3:100. The discrepancy was greatest among those aged 15 to 40, the years of greatest migration. This situation is not reflected in membership lists of the various credit unions, as women often account for under 30–40 per cent of total membership. While a number of women may 'put away' their small savings in the credit unions to avoid the predatory attitudes of their husbands, most women have not benefited from the credit facilities in their respective unions. Most men in the region do

not like their spouses to have financial autonomy as, in their view, it erodes their position of control. Women's chances are better when they place group savings in the credit union. The *pito* brewers' association in Ko is among a few women's groups which have utilized the loan facility of the Ko Credit Union. There are hardly any women representatives on the committees of the various credit unions operating in the area.

Although the parent association (CUA) was established in 1968, specific provision of credit for women began only in 1984 when CUA helped market women in the port area of Tema to establish the first market women's credit union in Ghana. The success of this union has led to the establishment of four more market women's credit unions, two in neighbourhoods within Tema and two more recently at Kaneshie and Nima, both in Accra. The latter two were established with the encouragement of the Canadian Co-operative Association (CCA). There are prospects for the establishment of two more women's credit unions in Accra, in Makola Market and 31st December Market (Ghana 1988: 1–2).

Similar credit initiatives are being introduced in North-West Ghana under a 'Credit for Women Project' which is being initiated by CCA in partnership with CUA. This pilot project is targeted towards three zones, namely the Upper-West Chapter in the North, the Greater Accra/Coast Area in the South and Brong-Ahafo Region in Central Ghana. The Upper-West area has been included because 'it is the birthplace of the African credit union movement, and it is currently the source of 50 per cent of the savings which have been deposited in CUA's Central Fund' (Ghana 1988: 2). This move is designed to facilitate access to credit for women credit union members for productive activities such as trading, agricultural production, food processing and marketing. It is also intended to provide the selected credit unions with the capacity for continuing management of savings and credit programmes for women and to increase women's credit union membership.

CRISIS AND PEASANT PROTESTS WITHIN THE CREDIT UNIONS

Under the emerging chaotic and undemocratic political system, many chiefs, traders, retired civil servants and public servants, who secured 'trust' loans without the usual collateral or guarantors, have refused to pay back the money, with the result that a number of these primary

societies now face serious problems with loan repayment. Individuals among these groups have taken huge loans of between 300,000 to one million cedis for well over five to ten years without having repaid a pesewa. In the case of three credit unions, Hamile Town, Nandom and Wa, the liquidity problems are so severe that individual members cannot even withdraw money from their savings accounts. This has led to the collapse of the Hamile Town Credit Union.

In Nandom the situation was so grave that peasants in a fit of anger and protest literally drove off the treasurer and some other committee members. As a result, the parent credit union is facing *de facto* liquidation; peasant confidence has been completely destroyed. From the mess has emerged a farmers' co-operative credit union, the Kuob-Lantaa Credit Union. The peasants have refused to admit any literates into the new union, since the literate 'élite' were blamed for the frauds in the Nandom Credit Union.

A recent audit task force has revealed that the current liquidity crisis within most of the credit unions has been aggravated by plain theft of resources by treasurers and some members of the various committees in the chapter. About 20 million cedis have been lost in IOUs and other such fictitious loans to members of the various committees. Since the inception of these unions, no dividends have been paid to members because of staff incompetence.

Other problems relate to bad management and the overall lack of democracy within the unions. For example, in theory the supreme authority of each society is vested in the members, who exercise their power through voting at annual and special general meetings, but in practice the involvement of the general membership in the operations of these credit unions has been virtually absent. Meetings are either not held at all or are held but no elections take place, the rank and file membership merely endorsing the nominations of candidates that are made by influential members of the unions.

The checks and balances that were carefully negotiated between the various committees, namely, the committee of management, the loan committee and the supervisory committee, never worked either because of collusion among the various bodies or because of ignorance, particularly on the part of members of the supervisory committee which should oversee the operations of the management and loan committees (CUA 1988: 12–17). Most of the treasurers were selected on trust and lacked any accounting background. This was one of the main reasons why dividends could not be calculated and paid to members even though some profits accrued, largely in the

form of interest on savings with the commercial banks. Auditing of accounts, if undertaken, was carried out by incompetent personnel who could not detect frauds.[4]

Summarizing, one could argue that, quite apart from managerial problems, it has been the progressive alliance between the local dominant classes and elements of the credit union bureaucracies, who themselves are aspiring petty bourgeois, that has served to exclude the poorer groups from access to credit union funds. Through the agency of the credit unions, capital is in the process of penetrating and partially dissolving the pre-capitalist economic forms in the region in its quest for a general commodification of the regional economy. By assisting the 'large-scale' commercial farmers to purchase improved seeds, fertilizers and tractors, the credit unions are encouraging the development of capitalist production relations in agriculture. Part of the loans to traders is used for the speculative purchase and hoarding of local foodstuffs at harvest time. This is often sold back to poor, distressed peasants who might have sold cheaply at harvest time only to find themselves having to buy back grain at double the harvest time price during the 'hunger season'. This tends to have a magnified negative redistributive effect on incomes. At the same time, by offering credit to traders, there is an expansion of trade in imported manufactured goods thereby helping to draw peasants more and more into the market economy and away from the production of use value in the crafts industry. A skewed income distribution also tends to expand the market for imports of luxury goods into the region, such as cars, motorcycles and imported foods. In the end, both the relative and absolute poverty levels of the poor peasantry, a large proportion of whom are women, have been deepened, giving rise to a heightened awareness of class conflict among the poor peasants.

CONCLUSION: STRATEGIES OF REVIVAL AND PEASANT CONTROL

In order to reorient the credit unions towards their initial goal of supporting the developmental initiatives of the poor majority, a number of considerations are being implemented by the management of CUA for all credit unions in Ghana. These include: (a) measures to re-capitalize the credit unions; (b) intensification of the educational training programmes for members and their mass involvement;

(c) the recovery of loans from defaulters together with improved staffing with competent personnel.

As has been indicated in the analysis, the high rate of inflation in Ghana, the devaluation by over 8,000 per cent of the cedi between 1983 and 1988, and the high levels of fraud and default in loan repayment for some primary societies, have all served to erode the capital base of the credit unions in the area. The women's credit initiative, which is being funded largely by CCA, is in the process of establishing a revolving fund of Can.$ 268,110 which is targeted on women in the three pilot zones of Greater Accra/Coast Area, Brong Ahafo Region and the Upper-West Chapter. About 30 credit unions from the three pilot areas will benefit; in addition, at least ten new, women-centred credit unions will be established in the pilot areas. All of the individual loans in the beneficiary credit unions will be for purposes of production only, and will have a maximum maturity of three years. A minimum of 10 per cent counterpart contribution will be required of all participating credit unions. The total funding involved, which includes provision for training, personnel, transport and management support, is Can.$ 429,300 with Can.$ 68,360 of this amount being CUA's contribution to the project (CCA and CUA 1988: 6–8).

As a component of the project, there is to be a greater involvement of women in the management of the various credit unions. For example, CUA will have to add at least two women to its Central Fund Committee, which will select the 40 credit unions to receive the group loans. The 40 selected credit unions will add at least two women each to their credit committees to decide which of their members will be given individual or collective loans (CCA and CUA 1988: 4).

At the end of the three-year project period the following results are expected:

(a) A total of 1,100 credit union members from the three sample areas will have received 1,400 new loans for productive purposes;

(b) A total of 960 women trainees from participating credit unions will have received general leadership and/or general business training;

(c) A minimum of ten new, women-centred credit unions will have been established as part of the 40 credit unions participating in the project;

(d) The membership of women in the 40 participating credit unions will have doubled from the beginning to the end of the project period;

(e) A minimum of 10 per cent growth in the assets of the CUA's Women's Revolving Credit Fund will have been achieved each year (CCA and CUA 1988: 7).

About 33 per cent of the total beneficiaries will come from the credit unions in the Upper-West Chapter, which will help to strengthen access to credit by women who are among the poorest members of regional society. At the same time it will improve democratic participation in the activities of the various unions, an important animation programme for women in the area.

Another initiative by the CUA is also under way with the Food and Agriculture Organization (FAO). If it is approved for support, the FAO is to assist in educating farmers in the various credit unions on marketing and credit management. Links will also be established with the Farmers' Services Centres, Ministry of Agriculture and Barclays Bank in order to pre-finance input delivery to farmers who belong to specific credit unions.[5]

The World Bank, which has been impressed by the better performance of the credit unions concerning savings mobilization in remote rural areas and by the lower loan delinquency averages compared to the banks, has expressed interest in financing small-scale industries in particular and the rural sector in general through the credit unions.[6] Repayment rates of between 92 and 100 per cent can be found in well functioning unions (Bentil et al. 1988: 115).

While the average loan delinquency level is below 30 per cent in the credit unions, it is estimated that the national average for banks in Ghana is above 60 per cent (Hubbert 1988: 15). Although four separate World Bank teams have recommended the channelling of financial credits to the credit unions, the disbursement of funds continue to be targeted only to rural banks.

An audit task force has been reviewing the operations of the credit unions while auditing and updating their records. A recovery of delinquent loans is part of the programme of reorganizing and recapitalizing the credit unions. In the Upper-West Chapter specifically, the Catholic Diocese of Wa has commissioned a study of the Upper-West Chapter credit unions as a basis for reorganizing and reactivating the poorly run ones (Wa Diocese 1987). If all of these schemes by CUA and the Church get off the ground, the credit unions will be sufficiently recapitalized to play a more useful role in the development of their catchment areas.

In the sphere of mobilization, the education committees of the

respective credit unions in the region, which are either non-existent or dormant, need to be activated to educate the rank and file members in their general responsibilities and rights. In this regard it is necessary to enlarge the membership of the various committees to reflect the social base of the credit unions. While other financial institutions are not interested in why people save, why they want to build up capital or where the money comes from, the credit unions must be interested in people's objectives for saving, including a study of their investment plans as a way of contributing to each individual or group realizing its objectives (de Stemper 1988: 10). More credit should be directed towards group farmers, women's groups and the poorer strata of the primary societies.

Last, there is the need to strengthen the managerial capacity of the various credit unions in the Upper-West by hiring competent treasurers and officers. These are some programmes of action which will help to mitigate the harsh reality of the Structural Adjustment Programme in Ghana among the neglected rural poor in the Upper-West (Songsore 1989). Through these reforms the credit unions will be better placed to become focal points in the struggle for fundamental changes in the relations of production by poor peasants and their class allies, the urban working class, at some future date.

NOTES

1 Data from a recent survey of financial institutions in the Upper-West Region.
2 Except where otherwise stated, much of this section derives from Jacob Songsore (1982: 6–26) and further discussions with Catholic priests in the Upper-West and with the general manager of CUA, Accra.
3 Wa Diocese 1987: 1–2. Discussions with CUA general manager, priests and other people concerned with credit union work in Upper-West Region.
4 Discussions with general manager, CUA, Accra, 1988; see also CUA 1987b: 8–9.
5 Discussion with CUA general manager, 1988; see also CUA 1987a: 5.
6 Discussion with CUA general manager, 1988.

5

SURVIVAL IN RURAL AFRICA
The salt co-operatives in Ada District, Ghana

Takyiwaa Manuh

INTRODUCTION

The poverty of theories on African development has been laid bare as the crises engulfing African economies have deepened. From east to west, north and south, hopes for African 'breakthroughs' have shattered as the ravages of the world capitalist market destroyed hopes of controlling national economies, of formulating rational planning, either by state or market forces, Sender and Smith (1986) notwithstanding. Even the Côte d'Ivoire, the sometime success story of Africa, is now struggling to stay on its feet.

Documentation on the nature and extent of the crises has come from many sources, and diligent perusal of annual World Bank reports from the early 1980s, for instance, provides eloquent testimony of the manifestations of the crises, even as there are disagreements about their origins (WB 1984b, 1985, 1986). Similarly, UNICEF's reports on the state of children in Africa present the crises from the viewpoint of the most vulnerable groups – women and children in urban poor and rural communities (UNICEF 1984, 1985). More recently, Onimode (1989b) and others have presented overviews and case studies of the crises and the programmes of adjustment which have been put in place in several countries as an answer to the crises. Overall, the crises and the accompanying structural adjustment programmes (SAPs) have led to a massive deterioration in the quality of life for poor urban and rural dwellers, further deepening the rural/urban divides which exist in almost all African countries. However, the various strategies for rural development have, like national development programmes, largely failed to alleviate the deprivation that rural communities experience and most rural people have been left to their own devices. Brown (1986) and others have

described the framework, strategies and policies for rural development which have been formulated in Ghana, with little success, by successive regimes. What is remarkable about the contributions in the volume edited by Brown is that, with the exception of one paper (Boateng 1986) which describes governmental and voluntary participation in rural development, most contributions focus almost solely on theoretical issues, institutions and resources, and planning for rural development but say little about what rural people do themselves about their situation. Yet, it is clear that, for most rural dwellers, survival and the little development that has come their way have largely resulted from their own efforts.

In this chapter, we present the organization of co-operatives in the Ada Songor lagoon area (see Figure 5.1) as an instrument of struggle and a coping strategy by rural people, in the face of dispossession by powerful capitalist interests and state neglect.

THE ADA DISTRICT

Introduction

Ada is located in the Dangme East District of the Greater Accra region of Ghana and covers an area of 546 km². Ada Foah is the administrative capital where government offices and functionaries are located, and Big Ada is the seat of the paramount stool and the traditional capital of the Ada state. The population of Ada was 68,923 in 1984, of whom 36,564 were female and 32,359 male. Population densities are generally high, with about 126 persons per km², which is higher than the national average of 50 persons per km², and decrease from the coast inland.

Climatic conditions

The climatic condition of the District is dry equatorial; Ada is located between Accra and the Volta which is the driest part of the entire West African coast. The vegetation is short grassland with small clumps of bush or a few trees and the soils are coastal sandy, tropical black clays and lateritic sandy soils. There are two rainfall maxima, but the dry season is very marked and evaporation exceeds rainfall in eleven months of the year. Mean temperatures are around 27°C and mean annual rainfall is between 737 mm to 889 mm. Given these features, the scope for agriculture is limited to short term crops or

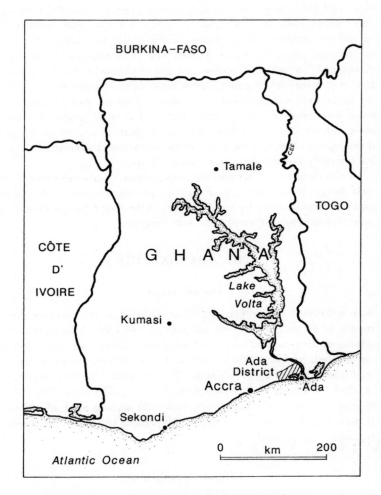

Figure 5.1 Map of Ghana showing the study area

crops which can survive on intermittent rainfall, and only about 47 per cent of the arable land is under cultivation at any one time. The main crops grown are cassava, maize, tomatoes, okras, peppers, bambara beans and groundnuts, with the latter four crops interplanted on cassava, maize or tomato farms. Table 5.1, which shows agro-economic subzones, population, arable and grazing land in the Ada zone, adequately portrays the characteristics of the zone and

104

Table 5.1 Ada agro-economic subzones, population, arable, grazing and total areas

Zone description	Total area (ha)	No. of people	Arable areas (ha)	Grazing areas (ha)	Arable area per person (ha)	No. of cattle	Grazing area per cattle unit	Remarks
1 Coastal fishing villages	6,160	8,734	460	1,150	0.05	336	3.42	West Songaw probably includes grazing used by saltings subzones
2 Islands and estuary	1,130	3,111	765	—	0.25	—	—	
3 Market and urban	650	9,156	negligible		negligible	—	—	Some farming in adjacent areas
4 Fishing and farming coast, East Songaw[1]	3,860	4,604	405	3,080	0.09	1,556	1.97	Includes Midier grazing
5 (a) Angaw[1] Valley, Gorm								
(b) lower	4,840	5,259	2,295	1,880	0.44	1,111	1.65	
(c) upper								
6 Marsh grazing	6,110	3,831	495	5,220	0.13	2,299	2.27	Both Obanes included
7 Kasseh, Toje Red Sands	7,640	6,172	5,490	1,190	0.89	441	2.70	Probably some grazing on arable
8 Hwakpo-Koluedor Sege	7,100	4,989	3,110	3,350	0.62	1,152	2.91	
9 NW inland grazing	15,750	1,946	770	15,140	0.40	4,757	3.18	Probably grazing outside area
10 Saltings	1,100	2,168	negligible	510	—	1,514	0.34	Must be grazing outside area
11 Lagoons, rivers	11,170							
Totals all zones	65,510	49,970	13,790	31,520	0.29	13,178	2.31	

Source: Ada farming households survey, 1983

Note: [1]'Songaw' is also spelled 'Songor' in some texts; similarly 'Angaw' and 'Angor' are interchangeable spellings.

consequent settlement and occupational patterns. At least 45 per cent of the total area is covered with marshes, saltings, lagoons and rivers, which effectively sets the limits of economic activity. A significant feature of the Ada District is the high ratio of livestock, arising from the fact that the zone is relatively free from the tse-tse fly. Thus, in spite of constraints of water and marginal grazing land, cattle-rearing is an important economic activity. In addition to livestock, there are large flocks of sheep, goats and many pigs.

The Ada Songor zone: demographic and socioeconomic characteristics

Of the 68,923 persons in Ada District, about 24,152 persons or 35 per cent live around the Songor lagoon in some twenty villages. Of these, 12,924 are female and 11,228 are male. Tables 5.2, 5.3 and 5.4 show the age and sex composition of the population, economic activity and regular school attendance for the zone.

Table 5.2   Age and sex composition, Ada Songor zone 1984

Sex	All ages	Below 1 year	1-4	5-9	10-14	15-24	25-44	45-64	65 and over
M	11,228	312	1,858	2,066	1,288	1,981	1,992	1,048	683
F	12,924	376	1,980	2,235	1,351	2,225	2,522	1,440	795
Total	24,152	688	3,838	4,301	2,639	4,206	4,514	2,488	1,478

Source: Ghana 1984

Table 5.3   Economic activity, Ada Songor zone 1984

Sex	Total age 15 and over	Employed		Unemployed	Homemaker	Other
		Total	Agriculture, hunting, forestry and fishing			
M	5,704	4,987	4,339	36	37	644
F	6,982	6,317	1,678	29	130	506
Total	12,686	11,304	6,017	65	167	1,150

Source: Ghana 1984

Table 5.4 Regular school attendance, Ada Songor zone 1984

Sex	Total age 6 and over	6–14 years			15–24 years			25 years and over		
		Never	*Past*	*Present*	*Never*	*Past*	*Present*	*Never*	*Past*	*Present*
M	8,577	1,584	150	1,146	757	758	466	2,546	1,170	—
F	10,114	2,158	124	850	1,473	563	189	4,194	563	—
Total	18,691	3,742	274	1,996	2,230	1,321	655	6,740	1,733	—

Source: Ghana 1984

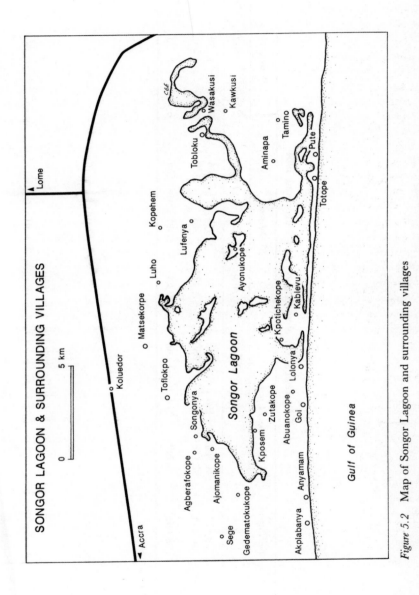

Figure 5.2 Map of Songor Lagoon and surrounding villages

Settlement in these villages dates back almost to the time when the Adas found themselves in their present homeland. The Songor lagoon area is inhabited by Tekperbiawe, the clan which traditionally 'owns' the lagoon, and other Ada clans. The lagoon provided fish in the rainy season and salt in the dry season and has centrality of place in the cultural and religious lives of the villagers. These villages have been linked to many places inland through the production of salt in the lagoon which has attracted traders from far and wide. In addition, trade in smoked fish was carried on with towns as far away as Mangoase, Akuse, Agormanya and other places on the Volta (see Figure 5.2). In return, the traders, mostly women, carried back cocoyams, palmnuts, bananas, oranges and other food items which were unobtainable in the Ada environment. In addition to trading, other Ada migrated with their families in the 1920s to the cocoa growing areas in Akim and around Koforidua in order to establish cocoa farms or to work as caretakers on the farms of wealthier farmers. A few also went to forest sites to log timber in order to make canoes and boats.

The main occupations of people in the Ada district are farming, fishing, livestock rearing, and trading, with the majority of employed people working in agriculture and related activities including fishing (Table 5.3). Surprisingly, salt mining is not listed under economic activities although it formed and remains an important occupation for villages around the lagoon. In part this may be attributable to the time of year when the census was conducted, when the inhabitants may have been engaged in other activities; it could also reflect the ecological changes which occurred with the construction of the Volta Lake and which blocked the entry of sea water into the lagoon and made salt winning a precarious occupation; lately, it might also have reflected the conflicts over access to the lagoon after private salt winning companies came in, depriving local people of access.

At present there is only one industrial establishment in the Songor zone, Vacuum Salts Limited, which employs about two hundred people on a casual basis. In addition, the salt co-operatives also employ a number of young people as waybill clerks and secretaries. The remaining salaried employment is by the central government and district council which employ teachers. The overwhelming majority of the inhabitants are self-employed farmers, fishermen and saltwinners, individuals often combining two or three occupations at the same time. In addition to these usual occupations, a few men are tailors, carpenters, shoemakers, fitters, distillers of *akpeteshie* (the local

gin), cassava mill operators, weavers of mats for fencing compounds and ceilings, makers of straw mattresses, kraal owners, and carvers. Some women trade in both local produce and industrial products, sell cooked food on an itinerant basis or in the small local markets, are chopbar keepers in villages along the main road, are processors of cassava into dough or *garri* for sale in Kasseh and Accra markets, are sellers of drink, or are weavers of baskets for transporting crabs, a speciality in the Ada district. Most of these occupations are usually combined with farming, fishing or salt winning. Since these occupations yield variable returns, migration is widely adopted as an alternative.

Infrastructural facilities and community amenities

Water supply

In all of the villages, the existence and level of basic amenities is very low.[1] Water is a major problem for most villages around the lagoon as the level of salinity in the soils is very high. To compound the problem, there are few streams flowing into the lagoon, thus making most villages dependent on dug-out ponds which dry out quickly or which are easily contaminated by cattle and other animals. All communities report that they buy water during at least three months of the year for domestic and other uses. Water thus constitutes an important item of household expenditure.

Health facilities

In addition to problems with water, which also pose a threat to health, the lack of adequate health facilities is a major constraint facing the inhabitants of the Songor zone. The nearest health facility is more than 30 km from most villages. There is dependence on traditional birth attendants (*tbas*), herbalists and rudimentary community clinics.

Energy sources

There is no electricity in any of the villages surveyed, nor indeed in any of the villages around the lagoon. Vacuum Salts Limited has a generator but electricity does not extend to the village near where it operates. The major sources of energy are fuelwood and charcoal for cooking and domestic uses, and kerosene for lighting.

Educational facilities and enrolments

Since the early 1950s, primary schools have existed in nearly all of the villages and middle schools have been added to some of these.

Table 5.5. presents a summary of the basic services and facilities that are in place in six selected villages.

THE ADA SALT TRADE

Extensive documentation of salt production and marketing indicates that Ada salt has been produced and traded for over two centuries. Isert, a French traveller in the 1780s, gave a detailed account of the salt industry at Ada in 1784. He wrote: 'To each house at Ada were attached huts each of which could store at least fifty tons of pure salt' (Isert 1793, quoted in Dickson 1969). According to Isert, the Adas looked down on agricultural activities, preferring instead to engage in salt mining and fishing. They sold the products to the people inland and bought food from their neighbours. Dickson (1969) also states that 'the salt works at Ada [were] probably rather large and important, since there were few profitable alternative occupations other than fishing in the Volta and neighbouring creeks'. Clearly, then, the reasons why Ada people engaged in fishing and salt mining lay more in their natural environment than in preferences. As the above description of climatic conditions showed, this is an area of lagoons and marshes, backed by inland grassland plains and supporting little agriculture.

Ada salt was traded throughout the country, and Bosman (1705, quoted in Dickson 1969) claimed that the salt trade rivalled that of gold in profitability, with a handful of salt worth one or two slaves. Together with fish, the salt was transported to Kete Krachi where it was sold to trading caravans from northern Ghana (Dickson 1969: 180). Ashanti was also an important market for salt from Ada, carried there along the great east–west routeway that linked Kumasi with the oracle Odente at Krachi.

The Ada salt trade continued and survived throughout the colonial period in spite of the competition from imported salt and the imposition of taxes. Ada salt was preferred to other varieties of salt on the market and competed favourably, despite higher transportation costs. Sutton (1981) gives an informative account of the trade, its marketing network around the country, and the virtual monopoly of the Ada traders. While salt collection was regarded as a task mainly for

Table 5.5 Amenities in six sample villages in Ada Songor Zone 1988

Main activity by village	Population 1984	Access by road (main, feeder)	Vehicle based in village	School (primary, middle, junior secondary))	Health facility[1]	Water supply[2]	Tractor in village	Mill	50% of buildings with metal roofs	50% of buildings with block walls	Artisan (carpenter, fitter, tailor)	Production co-operative
Marine fishing												
Lolonya	2,284	F	yes	P,M	CC,HB,TBA	R,P,T	no	yes	yes	yes	C,T	yes
Anyamam	2,739	F	yes	P,M,JS$	CC,HB,TBA	PB,W,T	no	yes	no	yes	C	yes
Agriculture/ livestock/saltwinning												
Koluedor	2,572	M	yes	P,M,JS$	CC	P,R,T	yes	yes	no	no	C,F,T	yes
Matsekorpe	825	F	yes	P,M	HB,TBA	P,W,T	no	yes	–	–	–	–
Adjomanikorpe	700	F	no	–	HB,TBA	P,R	yes	yes	no	no	no	no
Lufenya	430	F	no	P	HB,TBA	W	no	yes	no	no	no	yes

Source: Survey data, field observations

1 CC = Community clinic; HB = Herbalist; H = Hospital; TBA = Traditional British attendant.
2 R = River; P = Pond; T = Tanker; PB = Pipe borne water; W = Well.

women and children, control of the trade was in few hands, as investment was required in the form of canoes and hired paddlers. Later,
more successful traders such as the Ocansey and Dumas families
bought steam launches for navigation up the Volta. The salt trade
formed an important, albeit not the sole, source of accumulation for
such traders (Moxon 1984).

In the past, the process of collecting salt from the lagoon demonstrated community management of a natural resource. The Volta
enters the sea at Ada Foah and, as Sutton (1981: 50) recounts, before
the construction of the dam, the Volta and channels leading to the
lagoon flooded their banks around September–October. As flooding
retreated, brackish water was left in the lagoon and, as the sand bar
was narrow and fragile, sea water could also enter at high tide. In any
case, the water would be saline, as the Volta was tidal for some
kilometres upriver. If the lagoon dried out before the rains came,
about 2.5 cm of salt was left. When this occurred, the Libi Wono and
Woyo, priest and priestess of the Tekperbiawe clan, would be
informed. At the direction of the Ada *mantse*, the paramount chief,
they would place sticks and watchmen on the paths leading to the
lagoon and would cause an announcement to be made, placing a ban
on salt winning in the lagoon. This measure ensured that no one
collected the salt before it was all exuded, and gave equal access to all.
It further maintained the process of collection firmly in the hands of
the priests and the chiefs, who levied tolls on salt won. By January,
the process would have occurred and the lagoon would be left to dry
out for about three months. When the priests and elders determined
that the salt had sufficiently matured, the ban would be lifted and
people could then go out to win salt. Tolls were collected on the salt
and were shared between the paramountcy in Big Ada and the
priests.[2]

From all accounts, salt did not form in the lagoon every year.
However, given the size of the lagoon, which was 13 km long and
8 km at its widest, even occasional production from the entire lagoon
would result in storage of large amounts from year to year.[3]

From about 1960 the lagoon began to fail. This was in part caused
by the creation of the Volta Lake and the construction of Akosombo
dam which had deleterious effects on the lagoon, leading it to dry out
more frequently. At the same time, the entry of sea water into the
lagoon was impeded both by silting at the mouth of the Volta and by
the control of flooding that was required for the dam to generate
hydro power (Anim 1959; Sutton 1981: 50).

In the 1970s, two private companies, Vacuum Salts Limited (VSL) (owned and managed in principal by the Appenteng family) and Star Chemicals Limited, were given leases by local chiefs which were subsequently confirmed by the government, to win salt from virtually the whole expanse of the lagoon. A part of the lagoon was reserved for the Ada Traditional Council. This area was considered sacred by the inhabitants as the abode of the goddess of the lagoon. However, from the point of view of the inhabitants, the area was unsuitable for salt winning. It received hardly any sea water for the necessary concentration to be achieved for forming salt. In addition, the area was far from most of the villages.

In the early 1980s, conflicts erupted between the lagoon dwellers and the two companies over access to the lagoon. In particular Vacuum Salts Limited, had constructed dykes and embankments across the lagoon and had stationed armed guards there to prevent the villagers from exercising any rights to the lagoon. Although the actual operations of the companies were outside the lagoon (for example, Vacuum Salts possessed several pits which were used as crystallizing pans, these being fed by sea water which was pumped in through a pipe), the companies claimed monopoly rights over about two-thirds of the lagoon. Ada people were arrested on charges of stealing salt, were locked up in cells and were constantly routed by the police who acted on behalf of the companies. It was during this period that a salt co-operative, the Ada Songor Salt Miners' Co-operative Society, emerged to organize the saltwinners and to act as a focus in the struggle to regain rights over the lagoon.

In 1985, the government finally intervened in the conflict when a pregnant woman was shot and killed in a raid. A committee of enquiry was set up to investigate the grievances of the inhabitants arising from the operations of the companies, to ascertain whether these operations had resulted in any hardships to the people, and to make necessary recommendations.[4]

THE SALT CO-OPERATIVES

In Ada, as in other districts in Ghana, there are four main types of co-operative societies which reflect the predominant occupations and the needs of members for inputs for production: co-operative farming societies, fishermen's co-operatives, bakers' co-operatives, and *akpeteshie* distillers' societies. These societies usually flourish in periods of scarcity and reflect the constraints that farmers, fishermen,

bakers and distillers, for example, face in their productive activities. Their main aims are to secure inputs, in the form of fertilizer, cutlasses, outboard motors, nets, flour, sugar and loans, for members. They are registered with the Department of Co-operatives, operated under the latter's regulations, and depend on it for access to inputs.

However, in the Songor zone, the salt co-operatives are new and different. Although they have utilized the co-operative form and regulations, they are different in conception and function. These co-operatives arose from the struggle of Ada people, predominantly the inhabitants of the lagoon area, to regain sovereignty over the lagoon. Originally, one co-operative society, the Ada Songor Salt Miners' Co-operative Society, emerged in 1984. Currently there are some ten societies, most of whom operate provisionally under licence from the Department of Co-operatives, but by far the best organized is the original society. Its attempt to emerge as an engine of development in the zone will now be considered in detail.

The Ada Songor Salt Miners' Co-operative Society

In 1983, the People's Defence Committees (PDCs), which had been formed in communities and workplaces following the events of 31 December 1981 in Ghana, took over the operation of Vacuum Salts Limited (VSL) while Star Chemicals Limited was confiscated by the state. By 1984, the situation had reversed; the former management of VSL under the Appenteng family resumed their position and subsequently barred access to the lagoon by the inhabitants. The potential for improving the livelihood of the inhabitants that had been demonstrated during the administration by the PDCs led to the mooting of the co-operative idea by some local activists and their allies as a means of combating VSL. In January 1984, contacts were made with leading personalities in the villages around the lagoon. The co-operative concept was explained to them, resulting in member groups being formed in some six villages to win salt. By October–November 1985, when the government announcement was made which allowed anybody to win salt in the lagoon, membership of the Co-operative comprised 3,200 people or about one-sixth of the total population of the Songor zone.

At first, the general need of the population for money led to very low prices for salt in Ada. A 75 kg bag of salt cost only C 40 in Ada

but sold for C 600 in Accra, only 80 km away. Attempts were therefore made to increase the price through levying a toll on each bag. This money was to go into a development fund to benefit the area. A customs duty was also exacted, which was paid directly to the government, and the Co-operative issued waybills and customs receipts to buyers. In time, personnel from the Customs, Excise and Preventive Services were stationed at buying points around the lagoon to collect duties. By 1986, which the Co-operative reckons as its best year of operations, its assets totalled some C 15 million (US$ 100,000 at 1986 rates). Most of this revenue was put into treasury bills for a year. This choice of investment was due to a large extent to the role played by a director and leading figure in the co-operative movement who was an accountant. Such involvement by a professional raises possibilities about the roles that African professionals can play in sustaining and facilitating the development of rural communities.

Ironically, the financial success of the Co-operative was to evoke demands from sections which had played little or no part in its struggles. The first of these was the District Administration in Ada Foah which was faced with a financial crisis following the government's cuts in subventions to district councils as part of the Structural Adjustment Programme on which it had embarked. District councils had to meet 50 per cent of the salaries of their staff from the beginning of 1987, and so the Ada District Council passed a by-law in 1986 which authorized it to collect a toll of C 60 on every bag of salt sold. As has been shown above, the villages around the Songor benefited little from the operations of most governmental departments in the District capital. Thus, initially, the Co-operative refused to pay. Later, the Co-operative unwillingly paid one million cedis on account because of the harassment of its customers by militiamen acting at the instigation of the District Council. In spite of the payment, the District Council itself issued waybills to certain villages around the lagoon to collect tolls on its behalf, on the understanding that they would share the money in the proportion of two to one. The formation of other co-operative societies around this time further undermined the Ada Songor Co-operative's stand against the Council, since these other societies acceded to the Council's demand to pay tolls. The Ada Songor Co-operative finally agreed that the District Administration could station personnel on their premises to collect the tolls.

The Ada Traditional Council was the other body which began to make demands on the Co-operative after the District Council

succeeded in collecting its tolls. The Council insisted that the Co-operative should pay a toll of C 50 per bag for the development of Ada and the upkeep of the chiefs, as royalties for the use of the lagoon. Although the Co-operative refused to accede to their request, it decided as a gesture of goodwill to make contributions to the annual Asafutufiam festival in 1986. As part of this contribution, two Kumasi Ventilated Improved Pit (KVIP) latrines were started in 1986 at Big Ada and completed in 1987, at a cost of C 1.1 million paid for by the Co-operative, with the help of National Service personnel and communal labour by the townspeople. However, these contributions did not appease the Traditional Council and since 1988 it has used the Ada Traditional Area Fund (ATAF) to market salt and to collect tolls on its behalf.

The Ada Songor Co-operative Society has a management commit-tee made up of 24 members, seven of whom are elected, while the rest are observers. This committee meets monthly to discuss develop-mental and other objectives of the society, as well as to deal with any problems which may arise. There is also an 18-member secretaries' committee, which is made up of the secretaries and their assistants from constituent villages, which meets on an *ad hoc* basis. Finally, there is the general meeting which is supposed to meet fortnightly, but which in reality rarely meets. This creates the paradox of a body which, although well organized at the top, is almost non-existent at the grass-roots level. The explanation given, that most women who are the majority of members are interested only in winning salt and have no time to participate in meetings, can only be partial. More fundamentally, it reflects not only the failure, so far, to translate the co-operative idea into reality for individual co-operators in the peculiar circumstances of the Songor area but also the internal contradictions which have emerged from within the ranks of the co-operative society itself. Thus, while co-operatives of the old type were concerned primarily with enhancing the benefits to their co-operators, the Ada Songor Society has set itself broader development aims and objectives which can only be realized over the medium to long term, and not necessarily at the individual level. The realization of these objectives, however, demands the strong participation of members, and the inability to involve rank and file members in its activities further delays progress. Part of the inability to integrate members stems from the male-dominated structures. So far, only one woman stands out alongside the men even though salt winning itself is an occupation dominated by women. In addition, the scheduled

meeting times do not coincide with women's time-use patterns and do not, as a result, enhance their participation.

Problems with conceptualizing and realizing the potentials of this new type of co-operative have been compounded by allegations of financial irregularities, embezzlement and non-accountability within the Ada Songor Co-operative Society. This has occasioned internecine strife and thrown rank and file members into confusion and suspicion, leading to the mushrooming of societies in virtually every village. At the same time the Co-operative's funds have been blocked. The Department of Co-operatives, through its District officer, appears not to have been of much help and to have no faith in the capabilities of the salt co-operatives. Beyond recommending that the co-operatives be grouped in zones and that a curb be put on the number of co-operatives which can be formed in the area, the Department has not been in a position to enforce its own regulations concerning the formation of societies. Regular audits have not been performed as required by law, nor have annual general meetings been held, which are to be attended by officers of the Department. More recently, the Dangme East District Secretary has called for a reorganization of the co-operative system around the lagoon, and for the Department to perform its statutory duties.[5]

Despite these difficult problems, the Ada Songor Co-operative Society can claim successes in the initiation of development projects in some of its constituent villages, albeit at a slower rate than projected. In general, development projects are determined by felt needs of the people, and the provision of water has been identified as the major problem. However, given the high salinity and the sandy soils, it has not been possible to dig many wells, as the well casings easily settle. World Vision International, an international voluntary development organization, has been approached to help with the construction of bore holes in villages around the lagoon, and it is expected that this will begin shortly.

The construction of classroom blocks for existing schools is seen as another priority to enable the schools to function well, and the Society has provided roofing sheets, timber, cement and other materials for constructions in Matsekorpe, Koluedor and Anyamam, while townspeople have provided communal labour. There are also plans to put up KVIP latrines around the banks of the lagoon for salt winners. Some pits have been dug but are not completed. Finally, in order to secure vehicular access to sites along the lagoon, the Society has engaged in road maintenance and in the construction of culverts.

Erosion is heavy around the lagoon owing to the high salinity, and the articulated trucks which ply around the lagoon, also put a heavy strain on the existing roads. However, following the formation of the other co-operatives, the Society is unwilling to bear all of the costs of road maintenance, and so it has proposed a co-operative union to discuss services and cost-sharing for the use of the lagoon as well as general management of the lagoon.

The Society has also constructed offices for its own use and is now building warehouses to store salt for an export drive to Nigeria and neighbouring ECOWAS countries. It has formed a marketing company, African Salt Limited, to be in charge of this, and the company has already started operations.

THE STRUGGLE OVER THE SONGOR LAGOON AND POWER RELATIONS IN ADA

In the 21 July 1989 issue of the *Daily Graphic*, it was reported that the president of the Ada Songor Salt Miners' Co-operative Society, who is also an Assemblyman, had been dismissed from the Assembly following a letter he had written headed 'Attitude of PNDC District Secretary for Dangme East and Officials of the Department of Co-operatives towards the Ada Songor Salt Miners' Co-operative Society Limited'. While the legality of the purported dismissal of the people's nominees by an assembly remains to be tested, the above incident illustrates the mounting contradictions between, on the one hand, the co-operative societies as new engines for development around the Songor zone and, on the other hand, the interests of the District Administration and chiefs who have long considered the lagoon as a source of revenue for development in the District and traditional capitals of Ada. This section discusses the interplay of forces, both local and external, who are dominant actors in the continuing struggle to define the rights of access to, and the use of, proceeds from the Songor lagoon.

The State and the Songor lagoon conflict

The role of the State in the conflict over access to and control of the lagoon has depended on which forces have been able to mobilize the apparatus of the State to their side. Initially, in 1982, when the PNDC came to power professing to speak for the masses, the then People's Defence Committees (PDCs) were sufficiently emboldened

to take control of the salt companies' premises and operations and to administer them. However, this control was ended in 1984, when a government announcement was made which restored the management to Vacuum Salts Limited and Star Chemicals to their owners. Effectively, however, only VSL resumed production while Star Chemicals shut down. The leadership of the PDCs was castigated and accused of maladministration and embezzlement. Following the ascendancy of the attacks by government on external and internal exploiters, and the adoption of an economic recovery-cum-structural adjustment package, the scope for private capital expanded somewhat in order to secure the confidence of much needed investors. In this climate of *laissez-faire*, it was important for Appenteng, VSL and other investors to be assured of governmental non-interference with their entrepreneurship. Indeed, the State intervened on their behalf, as is shown in accounts of workers' struggles in the PNDC period, from the turnover of the Ghana Textile Printing Company to the case of the Assene metal workers (see, in particular, Graham 1989).

During the period 1984–5, the full power of VSL and the Appentengs was unleashed on the people of Ada, who had their salt seized in markets at Kasseh and Dawa and in raids on their homes (Memorandum presented to the Amissah Committee of Enquiry by Ada Songor Salt Miners' Co-operative Society, 1985). Salt was seized at barriers erected by the police, acting on the instigation of VSL, on the pretext that it was stolen. The fledgling Ada Songor Salt Miners' Co-operative Society had its offices raided several times by customs officials and had its books taken away. Watchmen and other employees of VSL brutalized Songor residents who were found near the lagoon and confiscated implements used in winning salt. Some members of the Appenteng family were accused by residents of personally administering cruel and inhuman punishment such as forcing men and women to drink concentrated salt water from the lagoon.

Finally, police detachments were used to intimidate, assault and batter Songor residents, resulting in the notorious raid on 17 May 1985, at the lagoon site near Bonikorpe village, in which a pregnant woman was shot dead. In addition, other residents sustained injuries. At this point, the State intervened, this time on the side of the Songor residents. An inquiry was ordered into the grievances of the residents, and access to the lagoon was granted to all, saving actual trespass on the premises of VSL.

But the State's intervention was only partial, and not definitive, as

since the submission of the Amissah Committee of Enquiry Report of Ghana (Ghana 1986), the findings have not been published. Further, the State has revalidated the leases to VSL, without any publicity, and has thus undermined the findings of the Amissah Committee on the operations of the two salt companies. In addition, technical teams have been appointed which have sought to denigrate the operations of local saltwinners, thereby setting the stage for banning local people from winning salt. For example, the report of the Technical Team appointed by the Ministry of Lands and Minerals Resources in July 1988 proposes that the lagoon should be exploited by companies using more 'scientific' methods to win salt.[6] However, as evidence before the Amissah Committee of Enquiry clearly showed, there was little, if any, difference between the technologies used by local winners of salt and by the two private companies: for instance, Vacuum Salt Limited, contrary to its name, was not using methods of vacuum extraction in its operations but, like the local winners, private companies depended on the over-abundant sunshine to collect salt from its evaporation pans.

In these circumstances, it is apparent that factions within the State apparatus are mobilized in support of VSL and its claims, and are sometimes able to further VSL's aims. However, while the contest may be unequal, residents of Ada Songor are not without their champions. From time to time, seemingly unexpected announcements are made to their benefit. Thus, in October 1989, the management contract was terminated between the government, as leading shareholder, and VSL, as represented by Appentang & Co., and the Appenteng family were banned from the area as a result of continuing acts of harassment (*Daily Graphic*, 30 October 1989). But, given the equivocal position of the State *vis-à-vis* Songor, the State cannot be relied upon to protect the interests of the residents. This was apparent recently in Ada when a demonstration was organized to protest against the extortionist acts and bias of the District Secretary against the salt co-operatives. It resulted in the arrest of a militant priest who was released only after intervention from Accra. However, populist measures do have their value and, from time to time, the State can be relied upon to come to the defence of Songor residents, under strong pressure from lobbyists.

The salt co-operatives and local authority holders

The salt co-operatives have suffered not only from the power of the State, which often mobilized support of VSL, but also from the power of local authority holders. As adverted to above, control over salt production in Ada has been a matter for dispute among priests, local notables and the Ada *mantse*, and, according to Sutton, conflict raged during the colonial period over claims to particular shares.

The role that the chiefs and local notables played in the acquisition of the Songor lagoon by the two companies appears not to have been salubrious; a charitable view could be that they were impressed with the prospects for developing the zone that were held out by the companies. Even then, they were soon disenchanted and refused to accept the royalties proffered, on the grounds that they were too paltry. With the emergence of the salt co-operatives and their generation of funds, the chiefs, through the Ada Traditional Council, have insisted on what they see as their due and have demanded allowances for their upkeep and contributions to other causes. While the co-operatives have sometimes been obliged to keep the peace, there has also been conflict. The chiefs used the Ada Traditional Area Fund (ATAF) to market salt on their own behalf, as distinct from the interests of the Songor residents.

The chiefs have allied themselves with the District Administration to challenge the hegemony of the Ada Songor Salt Miners' Co-operative Society, and have not been averse to acts of intimidation. The role of the presiding member of the District Assembly, who is also chair of ATAF, is being investigated. He is currently suspended from duty.

For the chiefs and notables in Ada, it would appear that the lagoon exists as a source of accumulation for development in Big Ada and in Ada Foah and its environs, but not around the lagoon itself. Thus, it would appear that in part the present conflict centres on whether this historical function will be maintained or whether the lagoon will serve more directly the interests of the Songor zone as a whole. The existence of other co-operative societies with less well-defined aims and objectives has been used to force the Ada Songor Salt Miners' Co-operative Society into line. Its own organizational weaknesses militate against action to confront the chiefs and other local interests successfully.

The needs of the District Administration for a local source of revenue to meet the costs of decentralization, in the absence of strong

central government support, have placed it on a collision course with the salt co-operatives. The failure to engage in dialogue and a consensual approach to resolving matters results in the issuing of edicts and commandist postures which serve only to polarize positions and to create antagonism. So far, few benefits of development, as pursued by current or past district administrations, have accrued to the residents of the zone and notice has been served that, instead of waiting, the people are mobilizing themselves to deliver what they need.

CONCLUSION

Will the co-operative societies survive all of these onslaughts? It is clear that they face serious internal organizational problems which have to be resolved effectively if this new co-operative concept is to have any salience for the membership. Effective participation by the rank and file, especially women, accountability and probity of officers, and a more cohesive organization need to be built up in order for the co-operative to carry out its developmental tasks with greater success. In a situation of plurality of co-operatives, co-ordination needs to be enhanced among the several co-operatives and common tasks shared to avoid unnecessary and unhealthy duplication and rivalry. Such understanding may well pave the way for the merging of nonviable co-operative societies to ensure viability. The unity that derives from this co-operation could then be used to confront the interests and forces which are marshalled against the co-operatives and could lead to the development of the potential of the area to provide a better life for the inhabitants.

NOTES

1 The lack of social amenities and infrastructure in Ghana, particularly in rural areas, has been noted in the Ghana Living Standards Survey, which was funded by the World Bank, and some measures are proposed to deal with this issue. See WB 1988a.
2 Sutton (1981: 50) alludes to conflict between the priests and the Ada *mantse* over the division of tolls, and to contradictory accounts about the actual division of tolls.
3 Sutton quotes Hutter, who had been the agent of a company at Ada since 1896, on the volume of salt production from the lagoon (Sutton 1981: 51). Nowadays, customs and excise proceeds show the volume of salt that is traded in a season, although it is still difficult to tie these figures to production in any particular year.

4 This was the Amissah Committee of Enquiry set up by Executive Instrument No. 12 of 1985.
5 This is with reference to the address by the District Secretary at the first ordinary sitting of the Dangme East District Assembly where he called for the reorganization of the co-operative system being operated by salt-winners in the Songor lagoon, the financial backbone of the district. This was to correct the situation whereby a society comprised only the executive, and he asked for the submission of full membership lists. See *Daily Graphic*, 27 April 1989.
6 This is a reference to the 'Report (interim) of the Technical Team for Songor lagoon, presented to the PNDC Secretary for Lands and Mineral Resources, Accra, Ghana, July 1988'.

6

LOCAL COPING STRATEGIES IN MACHAKOS DISTRICT, KENYA

Peter O. Ondiege

INTRODUCTION

Africa's economic structure defines the essential features of her central problem of underdevelopment. The basic bottle-necks that arise from structures of production, consumption, technology, employment and socio-political organization include problems of mass poverty, food shortage, low productivity, weak productive base and backward technology. The fundamental problem of Africa is that of

> a vicious interaction between excruciating poverty and abysmally low levels of productivity in an environment characterised by serious deficiencies in basic and social infrastructure, especially the physical capital, research capabilities, technological know-how and human resources development that are indispensable to an integrated and dynamic economy.
>
> (OAU 1986: 4)

The crisis is exacerbated by factors that affect economic performance. These include inflation, export earnings instability, balance of payments deficits and rising debt burdens which are the direct result of the lack of structural transformation, the rather unfavourable physical and socio-political environment of African economies and their excessive outward orientation and dependence.

Africa's economic structure is characterized by a predominantly exchange economy, narrow production base, neglected informal sector, environmental degradation, urban bias of public policies and openness, and excessive dependence on external factor inputs.

Most African countries depend on agriculture for employment, income, foreign exchange earnings and government revenue, and yet

125

agriculture is still characterized by traditional production techniques and a generally low level of productivity. Most efforts to transform this sector have been concentrated on the export subsector, ignoring the food and raw materials subsectors. While women play an important role in agricultural production, especially the food subsector, their role as producers and agents of change in the much-needed rural transformation has been severely constrained by their meagre share in the means of production (land, capital, credit, technology, etc.) and by their marginalization in production relations. Thus, owing to the weak agricultural base, the industrial sector has also remained structurally weak and narrow and with insufficient internal linkages.

African economies have also tended to ignore the informal sector which is currently estimated to account for 20 per cent of total output and over 20 per cent of the total labour force. This sector plays an important role in production, distribution, finance and employment creation in the African economies and needs, therefore, to be given serious consideration to help to reform Africa's economic structure.

Natural and human factors have continued to erode the natural resource base which is needed to sustain Africa's development. These factors include over-use and misuse of the soil, poor conservation policies, overgrazing, deforestation, drought, salination, river system pollution and water-logging. The cumulative effect of these factors has led to reduced carrying capacity of the land at present levels of technology, reduced productivity, social dislocation and accentuation of absolute poverty in the rural area.

The past development strategies that stressed industrialization and urbanization have failed to sustain growth of these economies. Objectives of providing dynamic forces for the structural transformation of their economies and promotion of equitable growth have not been successful.

In sub-Saharan Africa, the rural population seems to be the most affected as even minimum basic needs have not been adequately provided. Thus, in these economies, national development should be essentially concerned with rural development. This entails promotion of agricultural and non-rural farm activities, and increasing economic and social welfare levels of the population through employment creation, rising income and poverty reduction. The ultimate aim of rural development should be to improve the earning capacities of farmers and off-farm workers and also to provide services and living conditions which are better adapted to their needs. To achieve

this, it is imperative to provide an enabling environment that will allow the participation of local rural people in conceptualizing, implementing and managing their development programmes.

In 1948 Kenya's population was 5.25 million which increased to 8.6 million by 1962. By 1979 the population had reached 15 million and it is expected to rise to 24 million in 1989. The majority of these people are living in rural areas with only 15 per cent living in urban areas. The population is estimated to be 35 million persons by the turn of the century, with an estimated urban population accounting for only 25 per cent of the total (Kenya 1989b). Essentially, then, the rural areas will still have a majority of the population.

Table 6.1   Growth rates of real gross domestic product (GDP) 1964–87[1]

Year	Agriculture	Manufacture	Government services	Other	Total GDP
1964–71[2]	4.2	8.2	9.8	6.9	6.5
1972	7.6	7.3	12.8	3.6	6.8
1973	4.4	14.4	6.3	1.0	4.1
1974	– 0.2	5.9	6.8	4.0	3.1
1975	4.6	4.0	8.5	– 0.01	3.1
1976	3.7	14.0	5.1	2.0	4.2
1977	9.5	16.0	5.1	6.1	8.2
1978	8.9	12.5	6.4	8.4	7.9
1979	– 0.3	7.6	7.1	7.7	5.0
1980	0.9	5.2	5.6	5.2	3.9
1981	6.1	3.6	5.3	6.9	6.0
1982	11.2	2.2	3.8	1.4	4.8
1983	1.6	4.5	4.2	1.5	2.3
1984	– 3.9	4.3	2.9	2.7	0.8
1985	3.7	4.5	4.2	1.5	4.8
1986	4.9	5.8	6.3	5.4	5.5
1987	3.8	5.7	5.7	4.9	4.8

Source: Kenya 1989b: 5

1 1964 prices for 1964–71 and 1982 prices for 1972 onward.
2 There were extensive revisions in major series affecting GDP calculations in 1972. Any linkages between 1964 and 1982 based series should therefore be interpreted with these revisions in mind.

The rapid population increases have resulted in high pressures on land such that land subdivisions and inequities are growing. In addition, there are rising employment problems and pressures on other resources. Growth rates of agricultural production in Kenya, which averaged 4.2 per cent per annum between 1964 and 1971,

increased to 7.6 per cent in 1972 and then started to decrease until 1976 (see Table 6.1). Farm production is also affected by weather changes; for instance, in the 1983/4 drought, agriculture fell by 3.9 per cent.

Kenya has also been faced by unemployment programmes since independence. The historical urban unemployment has been 16.2 per cent (Kenya 1989b) and is not expected to change in the coming few years. In rural areas, the employment problem mainly has been underemployment and not open unemployment. There is therefore a need to encourage those activities that enhance employment in rural farm and non-farm activities as well as those of urban informal activities where underemployment problems exist. These, if enhanced, may increase rural incomes, reduce poverty levels and thereby increase gainful employment.

In Kenya's rural sector, increasing population pressure on limited arable land has resulted in a large number of small landholdings which are insufficient to support household production (Table 6.2). These co-exist with large, underutilized holdings. This has led to poor agricultural growth rates. There has been continued pressure on other resources and unemployment and underemployment problems have been increasing since independence. These have resulted in low income earnings and poverty of the rural households, which seem to have increased with population growth rates.

There is need to emphasize the urgency for implementing human-centred development programmes which imply that mass poverty must be alleviated in order to increase people's welfare. Development has to be engineered and sustained by the people themselves through their full and active participation, and should not be undertaken on their behalf. It may be argued that the major cause of failure of development models of a macro nature in Africa is the inadequate attention and recognition given to local micro initiatives in rural areas. In rural economies local people have developed different strategies to cope with development problems. These include ecological, socioeconomic and political strategies.

A number of African countries have of late realized the significance of local initiatives in coping with development problems in rural areas and are now trying to incorporate them in their planning strategies. Kenya, like many other countries in the Third World, has been pursuing policies with mixed results which are aimed at promoting rural development. Past policies have not been very successful and so, in 1983, the Kenya government shifted the responsibility of planning

Table 6.2 Proportion of households/holders by size of holding

| District | No holding | Holding size in acres | | | | | | | | Total |
		Up to 2.0	2.1 – 4.0	4.1 – 6.0	6.1 – 8.0	8.1 – 10.0	10.1 – 15.0	15.1 – 20.0	Over 20.0	
Kilifi	—	36	22	12	10	4	14	1	1	100
Kwale	—	30	26	15	12	4	5	3	5	100
Taita-Taveta	—	52	16	10	5	3	6	4	4	100
Machakos	—	30	15	15	6	10	8	5	11	100
Kitui	6	17	20	13	7	7	15	3	12	100
Meru	2	47	32	9	4	3	2	1	0	100
Embu	1	42	25	12	6	9	4	0	1	100
Nyeri	1	62	18	11	5	0	1	0	2	100
Murang'a	—	65	21	5	3	2	3	0	1	100
Kirinyaga	—	51	24	15	8	2	0	0	0	100
Kiambu	8	68	16	4	2	2	0	0	0	100
Nyandarua	2	27	21	10	9	3	7	5	16	100
Nakuru	22*	25	23	10	4	7	3	4	2	100
Nandi	6	25	16	10	9	8	12	6	8	100
Kericho	—	25	22	10	6	7	14	7	9	100
Uasin-Gishu	3	28	11	10	5	10	11	10	12	100
Trans-Nzoia	7	45	19	12	5	5	2	1	4	100
S. Nyanza	2	47	14	8	4	5	4	6	10	100
Kisii	1	58	25	9	1	2	1	3	—	100
Kisumu	—	59	22	9	5	4	1	—	—	100
Siaya	—	42	28	14	6	3	3	—	4	100
Kakamega	—	59	23	5	5	3	2	2	1	100
Bungoma	2	27	32	14	6	5	9	2	3	100
Busia	—	23	29	20	9	5	6	6	2	100
Mean	5	40	21	10	5	5	5	4	5	100

Source: Kenya 1989a: 28

*Mainly workers on large-scale farms and estates but including farming members of land-buying companies whose farms had not been sub-divided at the time of the survey.

and implementing rural development from the headquarters of relevant ministries to the districts. This strategy of 'District Focus for Rural Development' (DFRD) reflects recognition of the importance of involving the local people in the development. Its purpose is to broaden the base of rural development and to encourage local initiatives in order to improve problem identification, resource mobilization, and project design and implementation. A further objective is to encourage and increase communications between the local community and government officers working in the district.

The success of this DFRD strategy is debatable. One issue concerns how much economic, administrative and financial powers should be given to the districts in order to enhance the successful implementation of the strategy. On paper, the DFRD strategy provides a policy environment that can accommodate local initiatives and strategies for rural development. It is too early to assess the full implications of the strategy.

This chapter examines local coping strategies of Kenya's Machakos District. The main objective is to identify and analyse the coping strategies that people have adopted in view of development problems in this district.

BACKGROUND OF THE DISTRICT

Machakos covers an area of 14,250 km^2 and is situated in a transition area between the rather dry, south-eastern parts of Kenya and the wetter, high central part that borders Nairobi City. It is predominantly a semi-arid area with a bimodal rainfall pattern. Rainfall in the area is inadequate and unpredictable, a factor which, when combined with shallow soils, steep slopes and unstable surface soil structures, makes water and soil conservation for farming a delicate issue. On the basis of agro-ecological potential, Machakos is divided into low, middle and high potential zones which constitute respectively 56.2, 38.4 and 5.4 per cent of the agricultual land.

The District has been known as a 'Problem District' in Kenya since the colonial period. The earliest problem was overstocking, later it was soil erosion, and then overpopulation. The population is now estimated to be 1.5 million and is concentrated on the more fertile parts of the central hill masses.

The consequence of the variable rainfall pattern is that, in four years out of ten, there is a major drought (Were and Akong'a 1981). For instance, in 1930–1 there was major flooding and between 1940 and 1944 there was famine. In the period 1951–2 heavy rains destroyed crops, resulting in famine and in 1965–6 there was another drought. In 1980, the food crop failed, although people claim that they had money to purchase food. In 1983–4 a major drought in the country led to food shortages which affected Machakos District severely. Generally poor soils and the arid climate contribute to low agricultural potential, which makes smallholding rainfed farming difficult in more than 75 per cent of the District. Soil and water conservation are necessary in order to have adequate farm production.

During the colonial period, there was a breakdown of the farming system cycle of land use and regeneration. This took the form of squatter settlement in unpopulated areas of Ukambani and common grazing land of the Yatta plateau. A shorter fallow system resulted (Meyers 1981). There was increased bush clearing, felling of timber and the subsequent demarcation of new holdings. At the same time, the population was expanding resulting in a growing fragmentation of landholdings. By the 1930s, land tenure was increasingly under individual control. The combination of these factors led to intensified soil erosion by the mid-1930s.

After the Second World War, poor agricultural production and famine relief became the order of the day and the government had to send in relief assistance to the District. The Akamba who occupy the District faced resettlement as well as soil and water conservation pro-grammes which were instituted by the government. Within five years, soil erosion control was so successful that farm production increased, enabling the District to be a net maize exporter. However, this situation was unsustainable in the long term as the programmes had failed to integrate cropping and livestock components of the farming system.

In the late 1970s, Arid and Semi-arid Lands (ASAL) became a major concern of the independent government. The Machakos Integrated Development Programme (MIDP) was started in 1978 by the government, in co-operation with the European Economic Community (EEC). The focus of the MIDP is on resettling people in the former scheduled areas (of large-scale holdings), on crop and animal husbandry promotion, on the expansion of community services, and on income and employment promotion. MIDP is also concerned with soil and water conservation as well as providing essential infrastructure and water supplies.

Population, employment and incomes

The Akamba ethnic group occupies the District. The group is concentrated mostly on the more fertile parts of the central hill masses. Population densities decrease in a south-easterly direction where rainfall is less in both quantity and reliability (Tables 6.3 and 6.4). Machakos District had a higher population growth rate of 4.2 per cent than the national average of 3.9 per cent according to the 1979 population census. The current population is estimated to be 1.5 million people with the high potential zones still having high population growth rates and hence increased densities.

Table 6.3 Population projections by Division 1979–90

Division	Residential area (ha)	Population (000's)			
		1979	1988	1989	1990
Central[1]	727	82.2	121.1	125.7	130.5
Kathiani	1,069	74.4	109.5	113.7	118.1
Kilome	1,323	152.4	224.4	232.9	241.9
Mbooni	535	92.6	136.4	141.5	147.0
Makueni	2,005	125.9	185.4	192.4	199.9
Kibwezi	3,400	98.9	145.7	151.2	157.1
Yatta	2,459	137.2	202.1	209.7	217.8
Kangondo	598	133.0	195.8	203.2	211.1
Mwala[2]	1,332	125.5	184.8	191.7	199.2
Total	13,448	1,022.1	1,505.2	1,562.0	1,622.6

Source: Kenya, Machakos (1989a)

1 These divisions did not exist at the time of the 1979 census.
2 Residential area: where people can settle, excluding water bodies.

Table 6.4 Population densities per Division (persons/km^2)

Division	1979	1988	1989	1990
Central	113	166	173	180
Kathiani	69	102	106	110
Kilome	115	170	176	182
Mbooni	180	255	265	275
Makwueni	63	93	96	100
Kibwezi	29	43	44	46
Yatta	56	82	85	89
Kangundo	222	328	339	353
Mwala	94	139	144	149
District density	76	112	116	121

Source: Kenya, Machakos (1989a)

Most of the labour force in the District is self-employed. Total wage employment, according to the Central Bureau of Statistics (CBS), was 41,293 (1986) with the two towns of Machakos and Athi River in the District accounting for 33 per cent of all wage employment. Labour in wage employment was 7 per cent in 1980, only rising to 8.7 per cent in 1988, and is expected to fall to 8.4 per cent by 1993 (Ondiege 1989).

This implies that over 90 per cent of the District's labour force is employed in farm and non-farm activities in the rural areas, predominantly in smallholding farming and pastoralism.

The main source of income in the District, as in many others in the country, is agriculture, which accounted for 50 per cent of the total according to the 1982/3 CBS Rural Household Budget Survey (Kenya 1988). Off-farm enterprises, salaries and wages, and other sources respectively accounted for 17, 24, and 9 per cent. The average monthly income, including cash and in-kind, was Kshs 864 in 1981/2. The nominal rural per capita income had decreased to Kshs 628 per month, according to estimates from the rural incomes in the District for the year 1986, although income in the urban centres in the District averaged Kshs 1,860 per capita (Ondiege 1989). The situation is likely to foster more migration into urban centres in the District thereby leading to increased urban unemployment.

The decreased nominal rural per capita income between 1981/2 and 1986 is an indication of a growing population that outstrips the growth of agricultural and livestock production. In response, farmers in Machakos are diversifying their sources of income through improved agricultural practices, the adoption of new crops, and non-farm activities. Often such activities have been carried out by self-help and women's groups, the objective being both to increase food production and to generate income to improve living standards.

Access to social facilities such as health have been affected by the increasing population. For instance, the ratio of medical staff to population increased between 1983 and 1987. This implies that a medical officer working in 1983 had to attend to more patients in 1987 than he/she did in 1983 (Table 6.5), a situation that is likely to affect the health standards in the District. One solution to this problem is to train more medical staff and to intensify primary health care (PHC) programmes in the District, since most of the major diseases in the District (Table 6.6) could be prevented if nutrition and water facilities were improved. The ratio of hospital beds to population between 1983 and 1989 has improved, however, though few new health facilities were constructed between 1979 and 1987. Infant mortality rates have decreased from 109 deaths per 1,000 live births in 1979 to 65 in 1987 (Ondiege 1989).

Some of the health facilities and those for education have been built on a self-help basis by the local people, to supplement government efforts, in the realization of the deteriorating situation in the District.

Table 6.5   Medical services ratio 1983 and 1987

	1983	*1987*
Projected population	1,239,822	1,500,000
Bed population ratio	1:1,196	1:1,149
Medical personnel/population ratio		
Medical officers	1:29,520	1:34,091
Kenya registered nurses	1:10,891	1:18,519
Enrolled community/enrolled nurses	1:2,109	1:4,389
Clinical officers	1:23,393	1:20,270
Public health officers	1:72,931	1:136,364
Public health technician	1:14,417	1:16,304
Pharmacists	1:59,039	1:71,429

Source: Kenya, Machakos (1989a)

Table 6.6   Major disease incidence 1987

Disease	*Number of patients*	*Percentages of total*
Malaria	397,989	26.53 (28.62)[1]
Disease of respiratory system	310,008	20.66 (22.0)
Disease of skin (including ulcers)	115,577	7.70 (9.63)
Diarrhoeal diseases	74,973	4.99 (5.00)
Internal worms	57,848	3.85 (3.96)
Ear infections	39,707	2.64 (—)
Eye infections	31,836	2.12 (2.20)
Rheumatism, joint pains, etc.	25,624	2.00 (1.9)
Pneumonia	26,966	1.79 (—)
Accidents (including fractures, burns, etc.)	26,811	1.78 (2.05)

Source: Kenya, Machakos (1989a)

1 Numbers in ( ) are 1983 percentages.

COPING STRATEGIES

The District is faced with land shortage, population pressure, physical resource base deterioration and the vagaries of an erratic climate. The Akamba have adopted a number of ecological, social and economic strategies to cope with this problem. Some strategies were started before the MIDP was launched and represent initiatives which were undertaken by the local people themselves.

These strategies are undertaken by individuals and, more importantly, by organized groups in the locality. In Ondiege's survey (1989), the main ecological strategies included bench terracing and tree planting, dam construction, afforestation and water conservation. The economic strategies included farming, goat, poultry and bee keeping, ranching, dairy farming and fishing. People were also involved in employment and income-generating activities such as construction of rental housing, constructing and operating shops and storehouses as well as operating book shops and restaurants. There were also savings and credit, consumers', and farmers' co-operative societies. Social strategies were geared towards home improvement and welfare in general, whereby members contributed money to help one another. Groups were also involved in the construction of education and health facilities.

There was a total of over 115 Self-help Groups (SHG) and Women's Groups (W/G) which were engaged in ecological activities. In economic activities there were 96 SHGs, 249 W/Gs, 73 Farmers' Co-operative Societies (FCS), and 19 Savings and Credit Societies (S & C) in the District. Some of the SHGs and W/Gs combined these activities with social ones. Most of the groups were formed in the last decade, although these activities were carried on previously in order to cope with the deteriorating rural situation in the District. Many of these organized groups are registered with the District authorities. Although co-operative organizations existed in the 1960s, a number of them were registered after independence.

Structure, organization and strategies of the groups

Most of the women's and self-help groups are basically organized at the village and sublocational levels. Membership is mainly female for SHGs and W/Gs have only women as their members. The analysis of several groups will serve to identify some of their main characteristics.

The Kundi ya Kuela Mbesa W/G, based in Kisuini village of Machakos municipality, started in 1983 and has a membership of 28 women. One of the members says that 'the local people thought of the idea because of their needs, so they wanted to get together to solve their problems and meet their needs. There was no support from outside.' This is a W/G whose members contribute money to a common pool from which members can borrow at a reasonable interest rate. The group is facing problems of late payments of contribution and poor records of repayment. As a result, the group has

no plans for expansion, which may be construed as implying poor management.

Another group, Ngenda SHG, whose chairperson is a woman, says that the initiative originated from the local people. The group was formed in 1981 and has 16 members. The main activity is the running of a shop but members also engage in organizing weddings and in making group presents to members' families. The members are planning to purchase their own plot where they will construct shop premises. This implies that they are not currently experiencing problems. In contrast, Kanzokea W/G in Kangundo Division started in 1978 and has 50 members who carry out bench terracing, horticulture and also contribute money to the group. All of these activities were started by the local people with some advice from people outside the locality. The group is said to have declined in the 1970s, owing to poor leadership, but was revived in 1981. It is currently facing financial problems.

In Yatta Division, 31 women's groups, who share a tradition of farming and weaving sisal baskets, amalgamated to form Yatta South Women's Group Enterprise Development (YSWGED) in 1986. However, the individual groups have been in existence since 1978, each being headed by a woman. Membership of each group ranges from 18 to 74 individuals, aged between 16 and 100 years old. The majority are illiterate.

The basic aim of amalgamating in Yatta was to mobilize women for socioeconomic activities, to create awareness of their potential and to raise living standards. The main focus of YSWGED is to transport members' handicrafts and grains to Yatta Women's Centre and to collect water, thereby lessening the demands on women's labour; to advertise in order to promote handicraft sales; and to use scales to ensure accuracy when buying and selling grains. YSWGED is run by an elected committee with representatives from each of the 31 groups. Their staff is composed of a general manager, storehouse manager, handicraft workers, grain store workers and labourers and strappers (employed on casual terms), and two watchpersons, all of whom are women.

YSWGED is one of the most organized women's groups in the sample. Since unification, the group has completed construction of their multi-purpose centre. Member groups have also started small projects such as group farming, building lodgings, shops and meeting places, rabbit rearing and purchasing plots. They participate in community projects such as building nursery and primary schools,

soil conservation and road construction projects. YSWGED has been appointed as an agent of the National Cereals and Produce Board which purchases and markets cereals that are produced in the entire country. The group has had technical support from the Danish Volunteer Service and financial support from the Kenya Rural Enterprise Programme. In both cases the YSWGED approached the two donors.

In Mwala Division, Ndubi W/G started in 1969 with basket making and later bought a *posho* (maize) mill. In 1970 they embarked on buying plots on which they constructed rental housing to generate income for members. The group's activities were initiated by the local women themselves without outside help. They sell their baskets locally and lack organized marketing channels.

In Central Division, Ndulu W/G, which started operation in 1978, focused mainly on rental housing construction and basket making, with the objective of income generation. In Mbembani W/G, the activities are mainly poultry keeping and rental housing construction, so that members are able to diversify the sources of their incomes. These activities are meant to capture the growing market in Machakos Municipal Council where these groups are located. Wittu wa Mwene W/G, which started in 1952, has as its main activities home improvement, money contributions to improve members' welfare, and coffee growing.

It can be seen from the comments above that leadership of these groups is by women. The groups have initiated activities that may lead to improved rural development, as activities address local needs, i.e. food production, employment and income generation. The groups are found practically in all locations of the District and membership numbers are between 10 to 100 SHG and 15 to 100 per W/G. The majority of W/Gs which were surveyed had between 20 and 60 members per group.

The SHGs have a mixed membership of women and men with the former dominating. Ondiege (1989) found that most of the activities of these SHGs were socio-ecological, although there was a tendency for each group to engage in all types of activities. For instance, the main activities of Manzaa SHGs in Kilome division were the construction of dams and water tanks to conserve water and the growing of horticultural crops, i.e. vegetable and fruit, while Kyanguli SHG was involved in tree planting to conserve soil, citrus fruit growing, and money contributions by members for welfare activities.

The women's groups are said to have contributed the lion's share

137

in the mobilization of communities at the grass-roots level, especially in the implementation of self-help projects and income-generating projects (Kenya, Machakos 1987). Women's groups were mainly involved in soil conservation, shop keeping, trade, storehouse keeping, goats, pigs and bee keeping, basketry, maize milling, tree planting and construction of dams. There were over 249 W/Gs involved in economic activities in the District (Ondiege 1989).

Women are viewed as increasingly significant participants in socio-economic and ecological conservation activities in the District in response to the deteriorating rural situation. In addition, the formation of large numbers of these groups, which are controlled and managed by women, also indicates an attempt to gain access to and control over resources that have historically been dominated by men. Women have actively taken the leadership of these groups so as to 'create awareness of their potential, raise living standards so that they may continue to develop and help their families and the community' (Kenya, Machakos 1987). They may have found it more expedient to form groups rather than to try to do it individually, as it is easier for them to compete effectively against men as a group rather than as individuals in order to obtain access to and control of resources.

Initially, about 1945, co-operative societies were restricted to coffee co-operatives which were started by white settlers. More recently, co-operatives have been formed by handicraft makers and sand harvesters in the District. The latter, mostly men, collect sand from riverbeds and load it on trucks for sale not only in the District but also, more importantly, in Nairobi where the construction industry is growing very fast. In Mwala Division, Wamunyu Handicraft Co-operative Society was formed in 1965 with the objective of promoting wood carving and basket making and marketing. This group has had mixed results but has also helped to reactivate the old crafts industry in the District.

The significance and potential of these 'coping strategies' for enhancing rural development is discussed below.

SIGNIFICANCE AND POTENTIALS OF COPING STRATEGIES

The strategies that are adopted by these local people have been on the increase and have contributed highly to the local economy (Kenya, Machakos 1987). To turn first to ecological issues, soil and water conservation and afforestation are vital in an environment that is

fragile and prone to ecological disasters; local strategies supplement government efforts in this sphere. For instance, in Kaiti area, 13,850 seedlings were planted and 991 ha of bench terracing were constructed. In Tawa, Mbooni division, 13,309 ha of land were terraced, 5,180 ha cultivated and 9,791 ha of bush cleared. In Kilome Division 46,850 ha were terraced, while in Kathiani Division 6,443 ha of land were terraced and 43 ha cultivated. All of these were done on a self-help basis.

Bench terracing helps to check soil erosion when sudden and short rains fall after long spells of dry season. This is reinforced by afforestation activities which are undertaken by women and men of the area. These activities help to improve agricultural productivity which in turn helps to maintain minimum subsistence and to improve the communities' nutrition levels and living standards.

The annual report for the District by the Ministry of Culture and Social Services (Kenya, Machakos 1987) estimates that the self-help projects which were undertaken by the local people contributed about 54 million hours of labour worth Kshs 8.5 million, cash worth Kshs 2.9 million and materials worth Kshs 2.2 million, totalling Kshs 13.6 million for the year. These organized SHGs and W/Gs have helped in mobilizing local physical and human resources when implementing their socioeconomic coping strategies. They have also led to the revival of local crafts and industries and to the emergence of new institutions and economic activities in the area.

The new economic activities in the area include the construction of rental housing, shops and *posho* mills. New institutions that have emerged are the co-operative societies and women's groups, some of which have formed development enterprises such as the YSWGED. Basket making and wood carving ventures by W/Gs, SHGs and co-operative societies have led to the revival of old crafts and industry in the District.

Akamba are famous for wood carving, which is said to have been introduced in Wamunyu area around 1920 by one of the Akamba. This activity has mobilized human resources and export sales for the region and the country thereby earning foreign exchange for the economy. The Wamunyu Handicraft Co-operative Society has contributed to increasing employment opportunities for the local people, to income earnings and export sales. The Society estimates that the handicraft industry in the area employs about 2,000 persons in the location, out of which 700 are members. In 1987 the share capital was Kshs 11,250 and the turnover, Kshs 939,963. The Society has

opened a showroom at Wamunyu trading centre and, in a way, has boosted the growth of the centre's trade and other trading centres in the area.

Kenya's *cyodos* (sisal baskets) and wood carvings are famous in European and American markets; the biggest share in terms of production of *cyodos*, as well as wood carvings, comes from Machakos District. During 1987, Machakos District Handicraft Centre in Machakos town assisted the women's groups by buying products locally and selling them overseas for a total of Kshs 374,185. Most Akamba use the proceeds from handicraft sales to augment family incomes, which helps to maintain the minimum subsistence needs of the local people. They combine handicraft making and farming, concentrating on handicrafts during the off-farming seasons and thus providing employment throughout the year. With proper marketing, handicrafts could increase local people's incomes far more than is currently the case, as at present great portions of the profit are received by middlemen (Mukoko 1987).

Farming activities have improved food production in the District, raising incomes of those growing cash crops and helping to improve people's living standards (Tables 6.7–6.10). For instance, in 1987, the Co-operative Societies which are mainly found in Central and Kangundo Divisions had a total of 150,087 members with a share capital of Kshs 74.97 million. The year's turnover was Kshs 287.85 million with Coffee Co-operative Societies contributing Kshs 164.81 million. In 1988, coffee earning in the District was Kshs 290 million, showing the great contribution that the local farmers were making to the economy.

Available statistics for 1983 and 1986 show that crop production and hectarage for most crops have been increasing (as may be seen in Tables 6.7 and 6.8) in the years between 1983 and 1986. There has been a great increase in the growing of traditional food crops such as sorghum, millet and cassava, which are suitable crops for semi-arid areas. Yields per hectare have also increased as a consequence of the adoption of new farming techniques by individual and group farmers, as discussed earlier.

In Table 6.9 we note that prices increased in 1984, decreased in 1985 and from then on increased in nominal values. The price increase was a consequence of the drought of 1983/4 which affected the whole country, resulting in food shortages. However, good weather conditions in 1985/6 contributed to food price reductions as a result of bumper harvests.

Table 6.7 Crop production trends 1983–6

Major crops	Metric tonnes		% change
	1983	*1986*	
Food crops			
Maize	121,940	178,780	47
Pigeon peas	5,840	15,840	139
Beans	69,850	56,100	– 20
Cowpeas	10,790	20,410	89
Green grams	1,060	3,320	213
Sorghum/millet	2,210	5,440	146
Cassava	6,050	19,180	217
Horticultural crops			
Bananas	18,600	16,280	– 12
Cabbages/kales	32,290	96,150	198
Onions	430	15,560	3,519
Tomatoes	12,690	126,470	897
Citrus	8,200	55,250	574
Passion fruit	720	860	19
Pawpaw	23,800	26,400	10
Irish potatoes	—	29,760	—
Industrial crops			
Coffee	22,688	28,421	25
Cotton	4,890	2,400	51
Sunflower	130	450	246

Source: Kenya, Machakos (1989a)

Similar trends are noted in Table 6.10, owing to the same 1983/4 drought. The effect of the drought may have influenced farmers to double their efforts when weather conditions changed. They also illustrate the vulnerability of a farming system which is based on rainfed agriculture and the need to improve on irrigation schemes in such regions of the country if productivity is not to be adversely affected. If farmers manage crop production efficiently, it is estimated that the average gross margin per day for coffee growers is Kshs 50 in the central hill mass areas, while for those in lower areas, who are growing cotton with sunflower as main cash crops and maize, beans and pigeon peas as food crops, the equivalent figure is Kshs 18. Thus, coffee farmers would be wealthier than other farmers if they were to manage their farming efficiently, other things being equal.

Table 6.8 Crop area yield trends 1983–6

Major crops	% change in ha 1983–6	Yield/ha (Kshs)	
		1983	1986
Maize	32	900	1,000
Pigeon peas	70	450	630
Beans	13	900	830
Cowpeas	35	450	630
Green grams	162	450	540
Sorghum/millet	120	570	640
Cassava	98	5,000	8,000
Bananas	45	6,300	9,000
Cabbages/kales	32	6,640	1,500
Onions	1,386	6,143	14,962
Tomatoes	534	18,940	29,758
Citrus	192	6,508	15,014
Passion fruits	20	14,400	14,962
Pawpaw	11	2,164	2,131
Irish potatoes	—	—	8,000
Coffee*	9.7	1.3 kg/tree	1.5 kg/tree
Cotton	60	162	200
Sisal	1	1,211	1,372

Source: Kenya, Machakos (1989a)

Note: Coffee is given in kg/tree, not a cash equivalent as coffee is determined based on an average kilogram yield per tree.

Table 6.9 Price trends for food crops 1983–8

Food crop	Unit of sale (kg)	Kshs					
		1983	1984	1985	1986	1987	1988
Maize	90	220	320	270	280	270	290
Pigeon peas	80	360	520	400	450	540	700
Beans	80	480	600	480	520	540	540
Cowpeas	80	380	480	400	430	450	560
Green grams	80	640	720	620	700	790	720
Millet	80	600	720	620	630	640	720
Sorghum	80	340	420	380	320	480	315

Source: Kenya, Machakos (1989a)

Table 6.10 Price trends for cash crops

Period	Coffee (millions)			Cotton (millions)	
	Production cherry (kg)	Turnover (Kshs)	Net payments to farmers (Kshs)	Production (kg)	Value (Kshs)
1983–4	22.6	148.6	78.6	4.4	20.2
1984–5	16.9	174.5	130.7	2.1	9.9
1985–6	28.4	270.9	226.2	7.5	34.1
1986–7	25.6	92.5	78.1	1.3	6.2

Source: Kenya, Machakos (1989a)

The growth of citrus fruit and vegetables increases the fruit and vegetable supply and consumption in the area and also generates income for members of these groups. This helps to diversify food production and intake in the area and to improve the health conditions of the local people. According to the District Commissioner, Machakos District Co-operative Union has been licensed to export horticultural produce. This will boost production, increase income for farmers in the District and also earn the country foreign exchange.

The production and hectarage of horticultural crops have increased in the period between 1983 and 1986 (Tables 6.7 and 6.8) and yields per hectare have risen greatly. For example, the yield per hectare of onions and citrus fruit has more than doubled (Table 6.8). This expansion is likely to increase further as the co-operative society concerned has been authorized to export the produce, reflecting their importance in the District. This will increase farmers' income and improve their living conditions. Fruit and vegetable production is also important when enhanced with irrigation schemes, especially smaller scale schemes that farmers can handle easily.

Livestock farming contributes to beef and milk production, both of which have a ready and wide market in nearby Nairobi City. New production techniques, such as cross-breeding, and access to veterinary training improve the production of cattle. Livestock production has generally been increasing in the District as seen in Tables 6.11 and 6.12. However, in 1984, owing to the effects of the 1983/4 drought, production decreased except for those animals that do not rely heavily on rainfed farming, such as dairy cattle, which can be zero-grazed, and improved poultry. Milk production, however,

decreased in 1984. The most drastic decrease occurred among goats and sheep which are reared for the most part in the drier, southern parts of the District.

Table 6.11   Livestock population trend ('000s)

Type	1980	1982	1984	1986	1987
Beef cattle	395.1	435.6	314.0	322.4	338.5
Dairy cattle	10.1	16.7	23.3	30.6	31.9
Goats	437.3	551.5	235.0	217.0	227.0
Sheep	187.5	298.5	82.9	18.3	91.7
Pigs	0.1	0.2	0.4	0.2	0.2
Improved birds	25.0	28.0	34.5	47.9	53.0
Local birds	1,000.4	975.0	235.0	468.0	590.1
Rabbits	2.6	5.1	4.0	7.9	9.0

Source: Kenya, Machakos (1989a)

Table 6.12   Milk production and revenues 1980–7

Year	1980	1981	1982	1983	1984	1985	1986	1987
Total milk production (million kg)	1.1	1.1	2.1	2.2	1.7	3.9	5.4	5.7
Revenue from sales (million Kshs)	3.2	3.2	6.2	7.8	6.6	13.0	15.2	15.4

Source: Kenya, Machakos (1989a)

This trend of production shows how reliance on rainfed livestock in semi-arid areas can have disastrous effects. It shows the importance of water availability, hence the need to conserve the ecology and diversification of farming techniques and sources of income if living conditions of the local people are to be maintained and improved.

Rental housing construction by these groups helps to alleviate housing shortages in the area and also assists in increasing the quantity and skills of artisans working in the construction industry. This activity, together with the construction and running of shops, storehouses and restaurants, will create jobs and diversify the sources of income for local people.

It has been noted above that W/Gs helped in mobilizing communities at the grass-roots levels in the implementation of self-help projects, especially those for generating income. About 48 per cent of the activities of W/Gs were economic in nature and 23 per cent were ecological. Women's and self-help groups augment the economic activities that are carried out by individual men and by co-operative societies which are dominated by men in terms of leadership. These societies contribute greatly to the local economy in terms of food production, trade and other activities which generate income and employment. Those that experience managerial and organizational problems need to be supported by the authorities concerned so that achievement of their potential, like that of women's and self-help groups, can be facilitated to the maximum.

A number of groups have plans to expand and some have already expanded and diversified, such as Mbembani W/G, which has started construction of rental housing over and above poultry keeping, and Katelewa FCS, which has bought a farm with cattle on it at Namanga. The Yatta South Women's Group Enterprise Development has also expanded its socioeconomic activities, as discussed previously. The potential of these micro-level groups, in terms of contributing to the economy and rural development in Kenya, is great; an enabling environment which recognizes the micro-level activities that are initiated by the local people is essential to ensure that such initiatives are sustained.

CONCLUSION:
THE SUSTAINABILITY OF COPING STRATEGIES

To sustain coping strategies, these groups may benefit from some outside assistance in the form of material inputs and equipment for production, technical advice, credit or grants where necessary, and organizational and management training.

Although most of the activities that were identified above were initiated by the local people, there has been some support from both inside and outside the District from the government, churches, NGOs and foreign government agencies. Most of the soil and water conservation activities have received help from the MIDP. Other agencies which have assisted include: UNICEF, SIDA of Sweden, the Danish Volunteer Service and the Nordic Co-operative Project. In 1986–7, the MIDP assisted 25 SHGs in the District with materials worth Kshs 6,875 per group and twelve W/Gs with materials worth Kshs 4,000 per group.

During 1986–7, people's contributions and efforts attracted government and NGOs assistance amounting to Kshs 3.8 million. The NGOs contribution was Kshs 3.6 million, while the central and local governments respectively contributed Kshs 155,387 and Kshs 64,370. This shows great financial reliance on NGOs which are generally funded from overseas. This trend is likely to continue for some time, as many foreign-funded NGOs as well as donor agencies are increasingly interested in funding local groups in the country. This should be encouraged, provided that it does not destroy local initiatives. Such contributions and assistance add substantially to the sustainability of these micro-level activities.

Most of these activities are locally initiated and implemented although some external support has been received. The groups should be encouraged to be self-reliant by making financial and material contributions for themselves; only after this should they be considered for outside financial help. Some groups which seem to be successful in our sample, such as the Kamoli Ka Irongom W/G in Kibwezi and YSWGED in Yatta, are those that have made self-contributions and have then approached NGOs and governments for help. The groups that are mainly involved in socio-ecological activities should be encouraged to diversify and to include economic activities which will enhance the group's survival and self-reliance.

The groups that were studied did face varied obstacles and problems in attaining their objectives. Problems included: financial mismanagement by their leaders; inadequate financial support and insufficient inputs of new materials and equipment; lack of elementary skills by a majority of members, including high illiteracy rates; poor marketing channels; and inadequate infrastructure. These difficulties require active and flexible responses in a timely manner by the government and by NGOs and other agencies working in the area. This support should be given in a way that does not discourage these micro-level initiatives but instead enhances their development.

The NGOs and other donor agencies should continue to support these activities, especially through provision of technical and financial information and infrastructural support as well as management and organization training, since they are better placed to do so. The government should provide the overall stimulative policy framework. Regional or rural planners need to take into account the activities of local people and to integrate their initiatives and activities when planning for these areas. They must also allow local people to participate fully in the planning stages.

ACKNOWLEDGEMENT

I should like to acknowledge the support of the United Nations Centre for Regional Development under whose auspices some of the data used in this chapter were collected.

HOUSEHOLD BASED TREE PLANTING ACTIVITIES FOR FUELWOOD SUPPLY IN RURAL KENYA

The role of the Kenya Woodfuel Development Programme

Noel A. Chavangi

BACKGROUND TO THE KENYA WOODFUEL DEVELOPMENT PROGRAMME

Both the Kenya National Energy Symposium, held in November 1978, and the International Workshop on future energy policy issues for Kenya, held in May 1979, highlighted the need for Kenya to address the issue of woodfuel scarcity in the country and the problems of ensuring its future sustainable supply. At present, fuelwood accounts for 53 per cent of the total energy consumption in Kenya and is dominant in the rural areas (which use up 72 per cent of the total fuelwood consumption in Kenya). Charcoal accounts for 6 per cent of the total energy consumption in Kenya and is dominant in the urban centres (which use up 50 per cent of total charcoal consumption in Kenya). Fuelwood is mainly produced and consumed in the agricultural areas of high and medium potential, while charcoal is produced in the semi-arid areas and consumed in the urban centres (O'Keefe *et al.* 1984).

In view of the crisis in the woodfuel energy sector, the Beijer Institute of the Royal Swedish Academy of Sciences was invited in 1980 to assist in carrying out a system-wide analysis of the woodfuel supply situation in Kenya, which would form the basis for future programmes of energy provision. As a result of the analysis, a woodfuel supply strategy was outlined in the 1984–9 development plan of Kenya (Kenya 1986). It stresses the need for agroforestry

programmes, peri-urban plantations, industrial plantations, and active participation of the Ministry of Energy (MOE) in continuing rural afforestation and soil conservation programmes.

The Kenya Woodfuel Development Programme (KWDP) is one of the projects operating under the auspices of the Ministry of Energy. The overall objective of the KWDP arises from one of the main findings of the study, to the effect that woodfuel (fuelwood and charcoal), as both a non-commercial and commercial source of energy, accounts for about three-quarters of the total energy base of Kenya and that the scope for employing other locally based energy sources is limited. In addition, the economic trend is unlikely to encourage a move from woodfuel to other fuels (oil or coal). As a consequence, woodfuel will continue to play a dominant role within the energy economy of Kenya (O'Keefe *et al.* 1984).

The greatest proportion (80 per cent) of Kenyans live in the agricultural lands of high and medium potential, which have a high degree of land demarcation and privatization and therefore offer almost no possibilities for the promotion of communal fuelwood plantations (Bradley 1984). Efforts towards the supply of energy for the millions of Kenyans living in these areas thus have to concentrate on the promotion of increased tree planting activities on individual household land (Van Gelder and Kerkhof 1984). The KWDP has worked with farmers in Kakamega and Kisii Districts of Kenya and in the process has gained useful experience in efforts towards developing viable agroforestry practices which are aimed at increasing the fuelwood supply to rural households. The objective in this chapter is to indicate the role that the KWDP has played in establishing, with farmers, self-sustaining innovations that would result in increased tree planting activities for fuelwood supply in rural areas. A particular concern is to focus on the way in which the KWDP has confronted male control of tree resources, in a context where women are responsible for gathering fuelwood for their energy needs. In the first section of the chapter, the philosophy and objectives of the KWDP are outlined. The case study of KWDP activities in Kakamega District which follows indicates the response of communities to the Programme.

The KWDP

The KWDP is basically a research and development programme whose objectives centre on the concept of sustainability. To achieve

this end, its concerns are: to develop replicable and participatory methodologies through which locally feasible agroforestry recommendation and locally tailored extension approaches and methods can be designed to ensure the effectiveness of woodfuel development at the district level; to verify both the feasibility of agroforestry recommendations and the effectiveness of extension approaches/methods, through which rural households can be encouraged to increase their woodfuel production for self-consumption and for the market and to economize on fuel consumption and end-uses; to assist in the development of Kenyan capacity to prepare, execute and monitor district fuelwood projects; and to develop a monitoring methodology at both district and national levels.

To achieve these objectives, a sequential implementation strategy covering several phases is adopted. First, a district resource analysis is carried out. In the initial phase the natural and human resources are thoroughly studied and analysed. District-level information which is derived from aerial photographs is combined with documentary information on population, soils, rainfall and land tenure. Analysis of these data indicates the extent of ecological zones, community differences and, hence, the selection of representative communities. From this base, particular households are selected for the field-based investigations in an effort to define more specifically the woodfuel problem and to lead to the design of interventions in subsequent phases (Bradley 1984). The strength of this approach emanates from the development research concept of involving the local communities in project identification and design.

In the second phase, the agroforestry and cultural backgrounds of the people are determined and defined. The information obtained contributes towards the design of the interventions that accommodate indigenous expertise and practices. The KWDP strives from the outset to determine who the target group is, what it needs and how the people themselves perceive the potentials for and constraints to achieving a desirable solution that is acceptable and appropriate to each cultural setting (Chavangi et al. 1986). After field trials of technical options, the KWDP launches a series of training programmes for extension staff of agencies which are already operating in the districts. This ensures that the tree planting messages are fully integrated within already existing extension services and that information is relayed to a larger community after the KWDP activities have been phased out of a district.

150

KAKAMEGA: A CASE STUDY IN KWDP ACTIVITIES

Kakamega District

Kakamega District, which has been the focus of KWDP activities since 1984, is representative of the densely populated, high-potential agricultural areas of Kenya. It has population densities, which rise to 1,000 inhabitants per km^2, and small farms averaging under one hectare in size, resulting in very heavy pressure on the land for food and fuelwood. Most of the land has been consolidated and registered in individual title. Little communal land remains. The degree of involvement of farmers in tree-raising activities is high, resulting in significant woody biomass coverage on the farms, with a large proportion of the trees having been planted by the farmers themselves. The extent of the farmers' existing knowledge on tree-raising techniques is great, giving a valuable reserve of indigenous experience which had hitherto been much underestimated and thus remained unexplored.

The KWDP survey, the main source of data for the following discussion, showed that, in Kakamega District as a whole, the area that is covered by trees and shrubs on farms in rural areas increases as the population density increases and as average farm size decreases. The proportion of on-farm woody biomass which is deliberately planted and managed increases similarly. Approximately 20–25 per cent of the area of farms is covered by trees and shrubs of which about 75 per cent have been deliberately planted. As many as 79 per cent of farmers plant seedlings or sow seed directly; about 38 per cent of farmers raise seedlings in small (on-farm) nurseries, with the number of seedlings raised varying from a few hundred to over a thousand.

Owing to the high degree of land demarcation and privatization tree-raising activities are very much confined within each household. Opportunities for establishing communal fuelwood tree plantations are almost non-existent, so there is no doubt that any efforts to introduce a programme with the ultimate aim of providing a self-sustaining supply of fuelwood has to concentrate on the promotion of tree planting for fuelwood on individual farms. The survey results gave firm grounds for believing that the observed fuelwood shortage is the result not of a shortage of woody biomass on individual farms but of social and cultural forces within the households which determine control over and access to the wood produced.

It was found that trees are planted and managed by farmers in

151

Kakamega District for many purposes: poles or timber for construction: split wood for sale; wood for making charcoal; and trees for use in rituals and religious ceremonies. There is a District preference for exotic tree species, such as eucalyptus, cypress and pine, which are regarded as cash crops or as a form of investment to pay for school fees. Indigenous tree species are rarely planted because they are thought to be able to grow on their own. In only a few areas are indigenous tree species, such as *Sesbania sesban*, deliberately grown on agricultural land. Sesbania is generally regarded not as a tree but as a plant which enhances soil fertility (by nitrogen fixation) and so is tolerated by farmers. This species has been effectively adopted as a source of fuelwood by the women in these areas. The KWDP is adopting this line of approach by introducing similar tree species (to Sesbania) which can serve the same purpose but which bypass the cultural blockage.

Considerable variations over small areas were found to exist both in the tree configurations (woodlots, hedges, trees within agricultural land) that are found on the farms and in the tree species (mainly exotic) that are grown within them. Tree production activities and preferences are to a very large extent locally determined. Farmers exchange seeds and/or seedlings with relatives and neighbours within their immediate surroundings in preference to relying on centralized nurseries which may be too far away to have any direct influence. The diffusion of innovative practices or new species throughout a community of farmers (as occurred with the spread of *Eucalyptus saligna* and other exotic species in Kenya) takes place gradually and cautiously at first, based on personal interactions.

A cultural survey revealed that only men have permanent rights to ownership of land. Trees are often planted to demarcate farm boundaries and thus serve to demonstrate ownership. Since trees are regarded as permanent features of the landscape, only men are able to plant them and to have sole rights to the use of them. A woman does have certain rights of access to her husband's land but not to trees deliberately planted on it. As a consequence, women do not enjoy the freedom to participate effectively in tree-raising activities. However, it is the woman's responsibility to provide for the household fuelwood needs. Fuelwood has until recently been regarded as a common and free good that may be collected from areas of 'natural vegetation' near or on the farms in the District. However, these sources have dwindled, primarily as a result of increasing population pressure, and

women now have to walk longer distances in search of fuelwood or have to raise funds to purchase fuelwood.

Thus, fuelwood procurement was identified specifically as a woman's task. The KWDP considered that it would therefore seem logical to work through women in efforts to increase the supply of fuelwood to the rural households. However, the existence of myths (taboos) that influence the behaviour of women became a major obstacle to introducing a project aimed at increasing the participation of women in tree planting. To overcome this, an awareness programme has been developed which exposes the issue within the community so that it can be discussed and pragmatic solutions sought. The mass awareness activities, which are based on popular theatre (drama), are aimed at the community and the focus is on providing not only a mirror (to stimulate reflection) but also desirable images to catch the people's imagination and thus stimulate action-oriented discussions. The drama has now been developed into films for ease of handling. The awareness programme focuses on encouraging tree planting for fuelwood as a new concept or innovation since, hitherto, trees were rarely planted for fuelwood although fuelwood occasionally has been obtained as a by-product.

Farmers' tree planting activities

In each subregion or zone, there are a locally preferred mix of elements (woodlots, hedges, wind-rows, trees on agricultural land) and tree-raising activities, depending on local perception and practices regarding the agricultural production system. Some types of tree planting configurations are found on virtually all farms, i.e. trees in cropland, and trees in home compounds and hedges.

On-farm agroforestry practices

Investigations which were carried out to assess the actual practices by which the on-farm woody biomass is established revealed the importance of planting new species in the District. It was estimated that in the District over 42 per cent of the farmers had planted trees on their farms during the previous year. It is also recognized that the bulk of these newly planted trees come not from official nurseries, such as those of the government, forestry department or chiefs, but from the farmers' own nurseries or neighbours' on-farm nurseries. There exists a free sharing of seedlings between neighbours. Direct sowing

of tree seed and the collection of wildlings are also widespread
practices in tree regeneration efforts on the farms.

Species preferences

The seedlings that are most commonly planted are exotic. In
Kakamega, 85 per cent of the seedlings raised, bought or obtained for
free were exotic tree species (mainly *Eucalyptus saligna* and to a lesser
extent *Cupressus lusitanica*), whereas, of the wildings collected, 52 per
cent were indigenous species and 39 per cent were fruit trees. About
half of the trees sown directly were exotic species, mainly *Acacia
mearnsii* (Black Wattle), *Eucalyptus saligna, Cassia siamea* and some
indigenous species, mainly *Sesbania sesban* and *Croton microstachys*, in
some parts of the District (Van Gelder and Kerkhof 1984).

Tree ownership uses

Trees are planted for various reasons across the District but mainly
for construction poles and timber and as a form of investment, to be
sold for cash. Such activities are under the control of men. Trees are
also planted as a legal requirement for land demarcation purposes,
hence the presence of hedges (as boundary features) on virtually all
farms in the District. In Kakamega District, the planting of trees is
mostly done by the men. As trees are generally viewed as men's
property, men decide what to plant, where to plant and when to
harvest. This is seen to be in line with the fact that, in most societies,
men are the legal owners of the land and therefore have control over
most of the farm resources.

Access to and control of household resources

In general, men and women have differential access to resources at
the household level. Men, in their capacity as traditional heads of
households, are usually in control of major household resources of
economic importance. This control, as has been shown above,
encompasses trees and hence men are found, in general, to control
the planting and managing of trees on the farm, especially in the
communities where traditions are observed to be relatively strong.
The current trend in farm forestry activities focuses mainly on trees
as a form of family investment (cash crop concept) and tends to over-
look the requirement for a rational approach to total household tree

and tree product needs. Thus, it is found that the heavy involvement of men, to the exclusion of women, also means low priority for women's needs for tree-related resources (firewood, fodder, raw materials for crafts, medicinal herbs) in relation to seemingly more pressing needs of the household. The service role of trees in agroforestry systems, including enhancing the production of organic matter, maintaining soil fertility, improving soil structure and thus reducing soil erosion, are all factors which are of major importance in subsistence agriculture (mainly done by women) and which are usually overlooked. To achieve a balance in providing for the total household woody biomass requirements, most of the issues raised above have to be considered and tackled at the household level. The focal point is the need to foster increased involvement of women in tree planting activities at the household level, in efforts towards providing for women's specific needs, enhancing their status, and thus increasing their self-confidence and pride. There are certain tasks that have been associated with women since time immemorial. Women still feel a sense of fulfilment in being able to meet the demands of these tasks. For rural Kenya, the provision of fuelwood is one such task.

KWDP INTERVENTION STRATEGY

Equipped with the knowledge that farmers in Kakamega have built up a large body of knowledge of agroforestry practices that are applicable to their particular farms, the KWDP mapped out intervention strategies that involved: creating an awareness of the fuelwood issue as a family problem to be tackled by both men and women; increasing dialogue within the households on fuelwood-related issues and initiating discussions towards common solutions; increasing the scope of tree planting by women through the introduction of the concept of multipurpose tree species, which can be managed by women; promoting woody species which are relatively fast growing and which do not yet have a cash value attached to them. These species are planted specifically for fuelwood but they also improve soil structure and soil fertility because of their nitrogen-fixing ability. In view of small farm sizes, multipurpose species are essential. A series of interrelated agroforestry and extension activities for the implementation of the overall programme was developed. These activities included: on-farm trials with individual farmers; the group extension approach; and a mass media approach, involving use of drama, films, printed pamphlets and brochures and radio messages.

On-farm trials

Initially the programme carried out reconnaissance research covering just over 520 farmers in Kakamega. In Kakamega, 28 farms were selected for on-farm trials, on the basis of farm size and gender of the farm manager. Farm sizes varied from 0.5 ha to 7 ha. Of the 28 farms, three belong to widows, five belong to women whose husbands work away from the farm (female-headed households because of migration), and 20 belong to married couples, both of whom reside on the farm. Farmers were provided with a few seedlings of quick-growing fuelwood species and small amounts of seed. Each farmer received 15–20 seedlings of three species and 50 seeds of one of the species. Four species were used: *Calliandra calothysrus, Leucaena leucocephala, Mimosa scabrella* and *Gliricidia sepium.* The KWDP was particularly interested in what farmers would do with the new materials on the bases of their existing knowledge of tree growing.

The choice of these four species was greatly influenced by the observed practice of women planting Sesbania in Ebusikhale in Kakamega. Sesbania has been accepted as a fuelwood species that women are allowed to plant and harvest. This species is locally considered to be a shrub, rather than a proper tree. Consequently, planting of this species does not establish any right to land. Furthermore, the species is not considered to be commercially valuable.

The farmers were given no technical information but the KWDP made arrangements for close observation of what the farmers did and discussed the activities with them constantly. The on-farm trials aimed: to create an environment for interacting with several farmers and building a relationship of mutual trust; to learn as much as possible of their knowledge on tree-growing and management (this approach was intended to expose the KWDP extension workers to the concept of learning from and with the farmers); to provide for individual farm visits to elicit information from farmers to identify problems; and to facilitate, from the outset, the participation of the farmers in finding solutions to the identified problems.

The KWDP staff members, therefore, decided to experiment with other designs with the farmer in order to take into account the farmer's knowledge and experience. The approach relied on mutual agreement as to where to plant the trees and, later on, to establish appropriate harvesting regimes. Together, extensionists and farmers have formulated ideas as to the most appropriate intervention strategies.

Although it is acknowledged that the small size of the trials dictates that the information be treated cautiously, there are a few worthwhile conclusions that emerge from a critical assessment of the trial on 28 farms in Kakamega.

The on-farm trials were used to initiate dialogue with the farming community. All efforts were geared towards understanding the community, analysing the fuelwood situation as perceived by the community, and stimulating the people into identifying possible solutions to the problem. Many of the options and questions that were raised through these farm trials have continuously been used in developing technical and extension options for the KWDP and in setting up the trials. The specific issues that were identified for further experimentation on a wide basis, in efforts towards assessing possible viable options, included: planting sites; spacing within the different configurations; performance of the various species; tree management practices for various end-use purposes such as fuelwood, fodder, soil conservation; compatibility with crops; resistance to insect and disease attacks; and seed handling and storage. The farmers in turn have become aware that they can solve part, if not all, of their fuelwood problems by raising trees which are fast maturing and which provide an opening to the cultural barriers that inhibit women's participation in agroforestry activities (Chavangi and Ngugi 1987).

One of the KWDP's objectives was to discover how local knowledge systems about trees would influence farmers' use of seed and seedlings. Survival of the planted seedlings was very impressive. On the whole their performance was observed to be encouraging, although not all did well (namely *Gliricidia sepium*), as many different planting strategies were used. An interesting range of tree planting configurations and sites was observed: the trees were planted in hedges, on agricultural land, near homesteads, on terraces, in tiny woodlots and as scattered trees all over the farms. Sometimes the trees were planted in pastures, and this led to destruction by animals if the trees were not protected. This problem is an off-shoot of the fact that three of the species that were used in the trial are palatable to animals. From comments by farmers, it would appear that they have intentions of planting the fuelwood trees on favoured land, which is a promising possibility (Chavangi and Ngugi 1987).

Harvesting of the trees had been sporadic. In most cases, farmers appeared to be waiting to see how big the trees would grow. On six farms where trees had been harvested by the end of two years, they were mainly used for fuelwood; indeed, the need for fuel was often

identified as the reason for harvesting. Other uses were as rails for the construction of granaries and as supports for banana trees. The use of the foliage from the trial species for fodder was also observed. Those who had used the species for fuel indicated their satisfaction with the fuel qualities of the species, to the extent that those who wanted to continue growing the fast maturing species would do so for fuel in most cases; fodder and building materials were also mentioned as end-uses. On most of the farms, seed had been harvested from the trial species by the end of two years of growth.

No clear harvest pattern emerged from the 28 trials but obviously the number of farms in the trials was too small for such a pattern to emerge. It does appear, however, that the KWDP needs to support on-station experimental data with a wider body of data from farmers, a process which is already being undertaken.

Although most of the farmers had harvested seed within the first two years, only two farmers had established a nursery after harvesting the seed. There was some concern about the reasons why the farmers did not establish nurseries, direct sow and coppice regularly at a higher level. Why do the farmers keep seed and where and how do they store it? Why do they prefer giving seed away? While it is possible that they do intend to establish nurseries in the future, only about three said that they would do so. Perhaps the KWDP has expected too much in too short a period of time. There is a need to communicate with the farmers regarding the coppicing qualities of Calliandra in particular, and direct sowing for other species. It would appear that a majority of farmers are not aware of the coppicing characteristics; they also have not tried planting cuttings.

Although direct sowing was tried, it has been too limited. Only two farmers directly sowed the seed. Direct sowing is a convenient and easy method of regenerating some of the species, and it is assumed that the farmers thought of trying this out because they had previously done so for species such as *Markhamia platycalyx*. Collection of wildlings should also be encouraged so that it becomes widespread and intensified. Collection of wildlings has also been undertaken by the farmers, and some farmers are experimenting with coppicing of the species at a regular interval.

There seems to be no pattern in how the trial farmers perceive the species. Some species have drawn considerable comment while others have been mentioned only once or twice in passing. Leucaena, for example, has been noticeable for its horizontal growth and slowness in increasing in diameter and for its prolific seeding. Calliandra, on

158

the other hand, has often been identified for its ornamental characteristics, while Sesbania appears to have been easily acceptable but
not particularly noticeable. Not many comments have been for-
warded about Mimosa but, amongst all of the trials, there has been a
general impression that the farmers, especially the men, have been
watching Mimosa with keen interest. This is suspected to have something to do with *Mimosa scabrella* showing signs of growing into a big
rounded tree, in comparison to the other species, which are shrubby.

From the discussions with the farmers, it appears that the species
have raised great interest among the neighbouring farmers. In fact,
in a majority of cases, the seed that was harvested by the farmers had
been given away to neighbours, friends and relatives. Judging by the
high incidence of this, it would appear that the species are diffusing
rapidly amongst the farmers. Some farmers also indicated that their
neighbours had been asking questions about the trees.

Measurement of attitudes or perceptions is normally difficult since
these are hard to gauge from brief interviews with a respondent. Also,
attitudes and perceptions may change from time to time, or even from
place to place, depending on the surroundings and context of a discussion. Nevertheless, long term interaction with an individual or
individuals can lead to an understanding of their attitudes, whether or
not these alter. In the case of the KWDP's trials with 28 farmers, it has
been possible to gain a general view of what the farmers really think of
the trial species, and how they perceive them in terms of their possible
contribution to the household energy budget and other farm needs.

The issue of how ownership affected management and harvesting
was broached in the structured discussions which took place on a
number of farms. Some women claimed ownership of the trees but on
most of the farms the trees were reported to be owned by 'the family';
a few women considered the trees as belonging to their husbands,
even though the husbands do not live on the farms and did not participate in raising the trees. There was no distinct difference among
farms in terms of who cared for the trees: on most farms, the husband
and the wife or son cared for the trees jointly. In other cases, it was
reported that the whole family looked after the trees. In a few cases, a
woman cared for the trees on her own.

In some cases, women indicated an intention to regenerate more
trees in the future for fuel and other needs, such as the building of
granaries. Where the men expressed an intention to regenerate more
of the species, the intended end-uses were more ambivalent; a list of
uses, such as construction poles, railing and fencing materials, was

given, sometimes with reference to particular species such as Calliandra, Mimosa and Sesbania. Fuel was also mentioned by men but it was difficult to ascertain the priority that they assign to different uses. A few men indicated that they wanted to grow trees for fuel for their wives, which in itself is a promising development.

It was apparent that, barely two years after the trials began, some farmers had already given up on the species. In one particular case, a woman who was interviewed indicated her husband's dissatisfaction with the species and stated that they had no intention of regenerating any more trees. She was not willing to express her own opinion on the species but claimed that her husband, who had expected to be given Eucalyptus and Cypress, had received only fuelwood species which he did not believe were worth growing.

Male ownership of the trees appears to be a prominent feature. In those cases where the trees had not been harvested at all, the most common owner was a man. Nevertheless, there are indications that some men have already left the job of caring for and harvesting trees to their wives, while others do it for them. It would appear that some men are keen on leaving the species to grow for a longer period of time in order to observe them. So far, male ownership does not appear to have affected adversely the orginal intention of promoting cultivation of trees for fuelwood, since the majority of harvested trees have been utilized for this purpose.

Generally, interplanting of the trees with crops was observed to be an acceptable practice. Some women have been impressed by the fact that, having been unable to grow *Eucalyptus saligna* (a common species in Kakamega), they have now found some species which they can plant in cropland. Judging from the indications on planting site preferences, it is also possible that the farmers will in future experiment with the trees in a variety of planting sites. However, it is recognized that a farmer, in order to make meaningful decisions on the most productive planting site, needs to grow many more trees than the small number given to the 28 farmers.

The KWDP has realized the importance of explaining to farmers the growth characteristics of the trial species and their 'shrub-like' features, since unrealized expectations could cause adverse reaction to the fuelwood species. Such explanations help to avoid disappointment on the part of the farmers at the poor performance of the trees. Those who had been expecting the trial species to grow into big, thick trees were disappointed when they realized that this would not be the case for some of the species.

The group extension approach

During November 1984, the KWDP decided that the trials on the 28 farms were sufficiently promising that larger scale, on-farm trials of the same species could be implemented, based on the group extension approach. Interested neighbours of the initial 28 farmers were brought together in groups. Where it was not possible to form a group on this basis, existing organizations were used, including a women's group, a church group and an adult literacy class. Also, one youth and one men-only group were formed.

In total, 25 groups were formed in Kakamega with 520 members. The majority of group members (75 per cent) were women. The average size of each group was 25, with members basically from the immediate neighbourhood and drawn from the same social class. Most participants were from the middle economic level of the community, rather than the very poor or the well-off.

The extension staff held, on average, three separate discussions per group, generally at two-week intervals. Through problem-solving tactics, the group members were assisted in analysing the fuelwood situation, defining the problem and coming up with possible solutions to the identified fuelwood problem. The group members were then encouraged to work out a course of action which was aimed at meeting their needs. Any external assistance which was needed was also determined.

The overall strategy, apart from learning about the possible motivation components around which an effective awareness programme could be designed, was to learn about various technical practices of farmers and the adaptability of the selected fuelwood species. Areas of specific emphasis were: species performance; spacing trials; tree management practices for various end-use purposes; planting sites; regeneration methods; compatibility with crops; resistance to insect attacks; and alternative uses, such as fodder, soil conservation and soil fertility improvement. Seed handling and storage were also monitored.

The few seedlings trials that were conducted all over the District, using the 28 farmers, had raised a lot of interest. Believing that such interest could be indicative of a positive demand for seed, group members, assisted by project staff, decided to establish Seed Production Units (SPUs) which could also be used as demonstration plots. The functions were specified as follows: to monitor seed potentials of the new species; to function ultimately as seed orchards

for the community; to demonstrate the growth performance and characteristics of the new species and to promote community interest and stimulate discussions; to facilitate choice of species once an individual had decided to try planting of introduced species; and to involve school children, both girls and boys, in raising trees for fuel-wood, as a possible means of overcoming cultural constraints. Each group aimed at establishing one SPU but only 16 groups succeeded. Of these, 10 SPUs are located on farmers' lands, 5 are in church compounds, and 1 is on public land. Additionally, 14 SPUs were created on school compounds and 4 on public land.

A group activity such as this was greatly encouraged so as to promote and maintain group identity. Thus, the project promoted the establishment of an SPU in which all group members could actively participate during group meetings. In addition to the group activity, each member decided to plant trees on his or her land. Married women had to negotiate individually with their husbands while youths had to negotiate with their parents for land. The KWDP supplied members with seedlings. Each member decided on the number of seedlings, subject to a maximum of 250 seedlings, and chose the type of seedling to be supplied from a selection of four species. Slightly over 100,000 seedlings were distributed, with an average of 150 seedlings per farmer.

Group extension activities were monitored in May 1987, two years after seedling distribution. Out of the 520 farmers who participated in Kakamega, 109 respondents were interviewed. These 109 were randomly selected and therefore did not take into account the propor-tion of female-headed households. Of the 109 respondents, 83 per cent (96 respondents) had trees still surviving; 52 per cent (57 respondents) had harvested the trees. Of these 57 respondents, 65 per cent had harvested for fuelwood, 14 per cent for fodder and 14 per cent for other reasons, such as for construction rails.

Only some farmers planted these agroforestry species in their agri-cultural fields. No negative effects of the trees on the maize and beans crops were reported, and trees were considered to be compatible with crops. A few farmers reported increased maize yields during the second year (Chavangi 1988).

As indicated in Table 7.1, generally 30 per cent of those involved in tree-raising activities are women. However, women were responsible for 50 per cent of wildling collection and 80 per cent of direct seeding (Chavangi and Ngugi 1987).

The impact of the group extension approach comes out quite

Table 7.1 Summary of monitoring results of the 25 groups
in Kakamega District

Activity (%)	Husband	Wife	Son	Others[1]	Total (N)[2]
Tree ownership	65	30	<5	0	109
Tree management	44	32	13	11	109
Tree harvesting	60	30	8	2	57
Seed harvesting	44	15	15	26	26
Nursery establishment	37	0	37	24	18
Wildling collection	25	50	25	0	12
Direct seeding	—	80	20	0	5

1 Others include: daughters, in-laws, labourers, neighbours, friends, and other
relatives.
2 N = 109.

clearly in discussions with participants, both women and men. The
group extension efforts have been effective in improving the fuelwood
situation for individuals, as illustrated by the experience of Rispa
Akhoya from Eshianda sublocation of Marama Location, Kakamega.
Her church group, the Mother's Union, has participated in the
KWDP group approach extension efforts since 1984. She received
250 seedlings in early 1985 (March–April) and first harvested in
December of the same year. As she relates, involvement in the
KWDP activities has been a positive experience for her:

> I am glad that I participated in the activities of the programme
> right from the start and that I did not ignore them as I had done
> with earlier programmes, such as the Sugarcane and Poultry
> ones. My main fear was in regard to the credit element, in case
> my land could be auctioned if not successful.
>
> I am a Christian and so the cultural beliefs did not bother me
> very much. I attended the initial meetings, requested 250 seed-
> lings, and planted them in a woodlot and a few in the home
> compound. I am grateful for the encouragement I received
> from KWDP staff. My trees did well; I only lost a few from
> insect attacks.
>
> Before participating in the fuelwood production activities, I
> had a major fuelwood problem. But since I started harvesting
> the trees, I have enough fuelwood and I have even sold some. In
> 1986, I increased my woodlot with another 400 trees. I raised the
> seedlings in a small on-farm nursery using seed from my older
> trees. In 1987, I planted another 200 trees along the terraces.

I have been very happy with the programme activities. I have very good firewood, I have shared the seeds and wildlings with my neighbours, and I am encouraging more women to take up the fuelwood raising activity.

(Chavangi 1988)

From the experience and information gained from both the on-farm trials and the group extension activities in Kakamega, a number of conclusions were reached. First, the idea of tree planting for the specific supply of fuelwood has to be introduced in the communities as an innovation. Second, men have to plant these trees to assist their wives in producing fuelwood or they have to allow the women to plant and use the trees for fuel. Third, tree-raising for fuelwood touches on the culturally determined relationship between husband and wife and upon traditional tree and land ownership issues. Finally, an 'awareness raising' programme is needed, and forms the basis of the mass media extension approach.

The mass media approach

Both intensive work with individual farmers and the group extension approach have been conducted in only 11 out of 202 sublocations in Kakamega. To disseminate information more broadly and to encourage participation in tree-raising activities, the KWDP has launched a mass media programme. This programme first sought to raise awareness about fuelwood issues and to provoke discussions of problems and possible solutions. Later, the mass media messages presented more technical information on tree-raising. The KWDP has employed drama, films, public rallies (community and school based) and school field days to sensitize communities to fuelwood issues. These public events have been supplemented by printed extension materials, such as a picture-story (comic book), whose written messages focus on tree-raising techniques. Radio messages have been utilized also. Messages have been transmitted in serial form (drama, film, radio or pamphlets) to provide 'boosters' to maintain farmers' interest. To ensure that issues which are raised by the mass media efforts take root and are sustained in the community, the KWDP relies on the farmer-to-farmer extension approach that is supported by follow-up activities with groups and individual farmers.

One drama production was pre-tested in November 1985 and shown in January/February 1986 at 14 different sites. A total of

16,500 people (7,700 adults and 8,800 children) attended the drama. One week later follow-up meetings were held with interested farmers to discuss the issues raised and to give demonstrations on nursery establishment, root pruning and other techniques. On these occasions, seed was distributed to 3,630 farmers. Three months later, in May 1986, 777 of the 3,630 farmers were interviewed to monitor the results. It was found that 73 per cent of those interviewed had established nurseries with the seed taken.

Although the play was well received, the KWDP decided to replace it with a series of films. Problems had arisen in performing the drama as a result of illness or lateness on the part of the actors. Also, the logistical problems that were involved in transporting a cast of over twenty individuals were considerable. Films were shown in 18 different sites during July and August 1987. Out of 24,747 attending the shows, 70 per cent were children, 15 per cent youths, 8 per cent adult females, and 6 per cent adult males. The opportunity was taken to distribute 10,966 seed packages.

The KWDP extension staff noted a generally favourable audience reaction to the films. As illustrated by comments expressed in Murhanda sublocation, the films generated much discussion:

'It's good to have brought the film during the day so that we can also see it.' (Female adult)
'My home is the same as that one, only I cannot break a chair or the house. In fact, I am afraid I don't know what to use when the rains come. Ask whether they have those trees to give us.' (Female adult)
'Can women really plant trees?' (Female adult)
'I saw a woman in the film buying firewood. How many things shall I be buying in my life? Food, clothes, fees, and also firewood? No! I will plant my own trees for firewood!' (Male adult)
'This depicts our daily lives. It comes from nowhere but our homes.' (Female adult)

(Chavangi 1988)

In November 1987 a monitoring exercise was undertaken to assess what farmers did with the seed that they obtained after the film shows. On average, 84 per cent of those who took seed had established on-farm nurseries.

The guiding principle for future work is based on the understanding that the Ministry of Energy has no intention of establishing a parallel extension system to those already existing within the collaborating

ministries. Therefore, the energy message to the farmer has to be integrated within already established extension agencies. In line with this, activities which are planned for the next three years focus on the integration of fuelwood energy plans with other rural development activities. For the planned activities to begin smoothly, a workshop is viewed as important for coming up with recommendations as to how to proceed in efforts towards establishing mutual linkages among activities.

OVERALL CONCLUSIONS

Work with farmers in the on-field trials, the group extension approach and some initial monitoring of results from the dramas and films have led the KWDP to a number of conclusions. The initial problem that was identified in Kakamega, namely that domestic woodfuel shortages are caused, not by technical problems, such as lack of knowledge of the benefits of planting trees, but by socio-cultural constraints, was correct. Individual farm visits have proved invaluable for learning from and with the farmer. These visits have been especially useful for eliciting information regarding the identification of problems and for stimulating experimentation.

The group extension approach has proven effective in verifying the KWDP's understanding of the community's perspective, in formulating a description of the system, in helping to establish priorities, in setting up workshops and seminars, and in evaluating and pre-screening ideas. The initial focus on introducing as an innovation the idea of tree planting for the specific supply of fuelwood has been effective in sensitizing farmers to the need for increased tree planting activities. The end-use, however, is determined by the most pressing need at the time of harvest. Thus, the multipurpose species that were introduced offer the greatest long term flexibility.

Since the programme has undertaken several activities to promote women's participation in tree-raising, it is difficult to assess the impact of each activity separately. Overall, it seems that efforts to promote community and household discussions of fuelwood issues have been most significant. All of these efforts – working with individual farmers, groups, and the larger community through mass media approaches – have encouraged the planting of trees for fuelwood by both women and men. Where cultural beliefs concerning the division of labour by sex are still strong, extension approaches focusing on working with the household as a unit are proving effective.

The focus on planting quick-growing, multipurpose agroforestry tree species has encouraged the participation of women. These species are slowly being accepted as fuelwood species. By offering alternatives that do not clash with existing patterns of tree use, such as the use of timber as cash crops and as a means of establishing claims to land ownership, the eventual result should be a greater control of fuelwood trees by women.

Since the KWDP activities took place in only a small proportion of District sublocations, it is considered too early to assess whether or not the overall fuelwood situation has improved. Of course those farmers who have participated in growing fuelwood species for at least two years, a majority (20 out of the 28 in the on-farm trials and 65 per cent of group members interviewed) of those harvesting trees have used the wood for fuel. This information suggests that the fuelwood situation for participating households has begun to improve. It should be noted, however, that the number of seedlings involved was small (up to a maximum of 250 seedlings per household). Preliminary estimates indicate that an average household of six persons would require approximately 1,000 trees to attain self-sufficiency.

REMAINING QUESTIONS

First, for any innovation to take root, people must be able to observe benefits from their efforts. Further assessment is needed of self-sufficiency in fuelwood on the small farms using on-field trials. Further experimentation is needed on the technical performance of the species and on the fuelwood quality in order to formulate technical recommendations, including issues such as planting sites, spacing, regeneration methods and management practices for various end-use purposes.

Second, little research has been carried out on indigenous tree species that can contribute to the fuelwood supply. The effect of establishing an economic value for tree products, especially seed, must be examined in order to determine whether this can promote interest in fuelwood species. Third, promoting tree-raising which is less labour-demanding must be further assessed as to whether such practices can effectively encourage women's participation.

Finally, it has not been determined whether direct promotion of tree planting for fuelwood encourages increased planting of indigenous tree species for fuelwood supplies. If this should prove to be the case, then planting trees for fuelwood will have become established practice.

SUMMARY

For the KWDP activities carried out in Kakamega, the Initial District Resource Analysis has proved invaluable (Bradley 1984). This analysis helped in identifying the main fuelwood shortage indicators, in understanding the fuelwood problems as perceived by the communities, and in designing a realistic woodfuel implementation strategy.

The KWDP has utilized two broad approaches in order to improve the fuelwood situation in Kakamega. First, there has been a focus on initiating dialogue among women and men at the community level in the hope that such dialogue filters through to the household level. This approach was necessary in Kakamega because women, recognizing that fuelwood procurement was their task, believed themselves to have failed if they sought their husbands' assistance. On the other hand, men did not want to be associated with the fuelwood issue because it fell outside their mandate. Thus, the provision of fuelwood had to be recognized as a task which, owing to changing circumstances, needed the co-operation of husband and wife. It was necessary to bring the two parties together to discuss the issue, so that there would be a recognition that fuelwood could no longer be handled by women alone and that men's involvement was necessary.

Second, once solutions were agreed upon and action taken, the availability of seed of the quick-growing, multipurpose agroforestry species provided possibilities for the direct participation of women. The species were considered to be shrubs and not trees, and so the cultural taboos limiting women's participation in tree-raising activities could be overcome. The two approaches, therefore, were complementary. Given the situation in Kakamega, one could not have succeeded in the absence of the other.

However, planting of multipurpose tree species for increasing fuelwood supplies to rural households must be seen as an introductory effort. Communities are starting to think of fuelwood as a resource which can no longer be obtained for free but which has to be either produced or purchased. The fuelwood development efforts, therefore, have to be viewed as supplementary to other efforts which are designed to increase the availability of forest resources, such as the supply of fuelwood as a by-product on the farm and the collection of fuelwood by women.

To increase fuelwood supplies where strong cultural divisions of labour are found, the strategy of working with households and

encouraging the participation of men, women and children seems to work better than focusing on the women only. The guiding principle here is for trees to be planted for fuelwood regardless of who actually does the planting. If this is achieved, then the provision of fuelwood is no longer an issue specific to women.

The mass media approach has proved effective for the purpose of sensitizing communities to the fuelwood problems, of stimulating discussions, of raising interest and of initiating action. To sustain interest and maintain action, support through the other extension methods, such as approaches involving both, is necessary. This ensures the achievement of visible results that can initiate the diffusion process.

8

LOCAL COPING STRATEGIES IN DODOMA DISTRICT, TANZANIA

Japheth M.M. Ndaro

INTRODUCTION

This is a case study of the local or community level strategies that people have devised and adopted in response to, and as a means of coping with, the recent economic crisis on the one hand and the hostile ecological conditions on the other. The economic crisis has arisen as a consequence of the interplay of two types of factors: internal and external factors. The internal factors that have consistently affected economic performance in Tanzania include:

1 Insufficient resources for agricultural development compared with the high priority given to industry. Between 1976 and 1986, the agricultural sector received only 13.54 per cent of capital investment compared to 24.20 per cent allocated to industry (United Republic of Tanzania 1986).

2 Inadequate producer incentives and marketing/distribution systems. Since the mid-1970s, the real producer price index of all export crops has fallen consistently. Between 1982–3 and 1984–5, real producer prices were increased by 5 per cent per year but producer prices in real terms are still only half of what they were in the early 1970s (Odunga *et al.* 1988). On the distribution front, the main problem to be faced is that the country's physical infrastructure has been deteriorating for want of essential repairs and maintenance. Such deterioration has inhibited the timely movement of agricultural products and inputs to the rural areas.

3 Expansionary fiscal and monetary policies which added to inflationary pressures and thus to exchange rate over-valuation. Economic growth in Tanzania has been characterized by high inflation in recent years. The rate of inflation in 1984 accelerated to

over 36 per cent from an annual average of 11 per cent during most of the 1970s, as measured by the National Price Index.

4 Unfavourable weather conditions. Until the early 1970s, Tanzania was largely self-sufficient in the major food staples: maize, paddy, sorghum and cassava. This situation abruptly changed in 1973 when drought struck many parts of the country. Following this situation, over the last two decades, Tanzania's performance in agricultural production has varied considerably from severe food crises, such as in 1974–5 and again in 1982–3 to 1984–5, to comfortable surpluses, as in 1986–7 and 1987–8.

5 Domestic economic dislocation, in particular foreign exchange shortages affecting the supply of fertilizers, agro-chemicals, farm equipment, incentive goods, and constraining crop processing and transportation. The scarcity of foreign exchange considerably reduced the country's ability to import machinery and other inputs for most sectors in the economy, and caused a sharp decline in the quality of essential services, particularly health and education.

External factors have also contributed to the general economic decline. The budgetary situation deteriorated sharply after Tanzania's unaided effort in Amin's war of aggression in 1978–9 and the effects of the break-up of the East African Community. The 1979 increase in petroleum prices added US$ 150 million to the annual oil import bill. This increased to US$ 180 million in 1986 (United Republic of Tanzania 1986). Fuel shortages in recent years have had a crippling effect on economic activity and on the quality of life throughout the country. Meanwhile, a world recession and declining commodity export prices caused a major deterioration in the terms of trade. The trade deficit worsened as a result of the 1980–1 drought which necessitated large imports of food grains (Odunga *et al.* 1988).

The combined effect of these factors has, over time, greatly reduced the ability of the government to meet most local needs satisfactorily. The shortage of foreign exchange has led to underutilization of capacity in industrial establishments as a result of the inability of the government to import spare parts, raw materials and new machinery. As a consequence, a prolonged shortage of industrial incentive goods, such as clothes, sugar, cigarettes, soap, and torch batteries, has prevailed in the country. Community services such as health and education have also been handicapped. Import requirements of medicines, medical equipment, training materials, laboratory equipment and chemicals cannot be sustained. Joseph

Warioba, the Prime Minister and First Vice-President, has put the argument more succinctly:

> although the Economic Recovery Programme shows positive signs, the country's economy is still bad. The economy still suffers from constraints such as undercapacity utilisation, unfulfilled agro-needs, crop haulage and storage. People in the villages experienced problems of unsold crops or lack of transport and high prices for inputs. In towns, workers also were facing problems as their income failed to meet basic needs due to continuous decline of the shilling. People should therefore join hands with the Government in undertaking different projects as the only sure way to better their lives.
>
> (*Daily News*, 3 April 1989)

The study area is Dodoma District, located on the Central plateau of Tanzania, some 500 km west of Dar es Salaam. Dodoma District has a dry, savanna-type of climate which is characterized by a long, dry season lasting between late April and early December and a short, wet season occurring in the remaining months. The District is one of the least developed areas in the country and is the poorest in terms of income per capita. The District economy is almost entirely dependent on arable farming and animal husbandry. Agriculture is characterized by low productivity, resulting from low erratic rainfall, high evapo-transpiration and low moisture-holding capacity of the soils. These conditions, together with widespread overstocking and overgrazing, make the District susceptible to extensive soil erosion and creeping desertification.

The unpredictable nature of the prevailing rainfall pattern has made the District prone to food deficits. Although the population has responded to this challenge by planting drought-resistant crops such as sorghum and millet, this strategy has not turned Dodoma into a food surplus district. Moreover, the prevailing rainfall pattern contributes significantly to the acuteness of the water supply problem in the District both for household and livestock use.

On the socioeconomic front, the existing economic crisis nationwide, as argued above, coupled with unreliable weather conditions in Dodoma District, has created unbearable living conditions. The hardest hit by the crisis are the peasants, the youth, women and low-income earners. These groups have been forced to seek additional or alternative employment to augment their incomes. Moreover, community services, such as health and education, have also been

handicapped by shortage of foreign exchange and the inability of the government to allocate adequate resources to these sectors. The movement of goods and services in rural areas has also been constrained by transportation bottle-necks in the economy.

The purpose of this study is to show how local populations have responded to the various problems discussed above in the light of examples taken from Dodoma District. The coping strategies which are outlined in the study have the objectives of meeting subsistence needs and of preventing a drastic fall in living standards of the local population in the face of the prevailing economic crisis. The strategies are implemented locally by means of small-scale activities which are geared to the capabilities of the individuals, groups and villages concerned.

PHASES OF COPING STRATEGIES IN DODOMA DISTRICT

In Table 8.1 a cross-section of local coping strategies in Dodoma District is presented. As the coping strategies were started in different time periods, a distinction is made between new and revived activities.

In Dodoma District, three phases of locally initiated coping strategies are clearly distinguishable. The first phase was the ten-year period after independence, 1961–70. During this period, the inhabitants of Dodoma devised and adopted strategies that did not conform with the political slogan of nation building which was dominant in the early 1960s. The strategies were concerned with trade and exchange, local crafts and industries, the construction of small dams and the opening up of new lands to facilitate shifting cultivation. They did not, for example, consider building schools or dispensaries or constructing roads. To a large extent, coping strategies in phase one were essentially survival strategies.

The second phase covered the period from 1971 to 1978 during which villagization campaigns were taking place across the country. This phase marked the abolition of locally based institutions, such as local authorities and co-operative societies, coupled with promises by the central government to meet expenses for local basic needs, in particular health, education and water. In concrete terms, the phase involved moving people in rural areas to specific locations in order to establish nucleated or *Ujamaa* villages where the government was to provide schools, health and water facilities. This arrangement quickly gained considerable goodwill among the people. In reality, however, it stifled local self-initiative in some parts of the District.

Table 8.1 Cross-section of coping strategies in Dodoma District

Major strategy or response	Activity undertaken	Main focus and objective of activity	Initiators	Contribution of activity	Degree of spread	Activity: new or revived
Economic	1 Local crafts and industries	Income generation	Individual artists	Production of household items, farm implements	Widespread among poorer people. Blacksmithing and metal trades involve mainly unemployed poorer youth groups.	Revived
	2 Exchange and barter trade	Increase food stocks for households	Individual households	Aversion of hunger and possible famine	Widespread among poorer people	Revived
	3 Charcoal making	Income generation	Individual peasants	To increase household incomes and provide energy to urban dwellers	Widespread among poorer people	New
	4 Selling animals	Income generation to pastoralists	Individual pastoralists	To provide income to pastoralists and manure/fertilizer to farmers to increase production	Widespread sale of manure largely by wealthy livestock owners	New
	5 Vegetable gardening	New employment and income generation	Individual youth and women's groups	Human resources mobilization	Moderate activity largely of middle-level income peasants	New
	6 Local beer making	Employment and income generation	Individuals and women's groups	To augment household incomes and employment	Widespread among poorer women	Revived

Category	Activity	Objective	Participants	Benefit	Extent	Status
Economic (continued)	7 Opening up of kiosks			Employment	Moderate mainly among middle-level income peasants	New
	8 Door-to-door salespeople	Employment and income generation	Individual young men and women	Employment	Moderate	New
Social	1 Building dispensaries and clinics	To provide health care	Local village leaders	Ensuring a healthy population	Moderate	New
	2 Building primary schools and vocational centres	To provide primary and post-primary education for their children	Local village leaders	Raising the literacy level of the population and improving skills in various trades	Widespread	New
	3 Building of small dams	To provide water for household and livestock use	Local village leaders	Improving water supply system in villages during the dry season	Moderate	Revived
	4 Transportation	To provide rural transportation of inputs and outputs, and to facilitate human movement	Local village leaders	Crop haulage, human transport and incomes to village governments	Moderate	New
	5 Savings and credit societies	To provide cheap loans to members	Groups of people	Financial resource mobilization	Moderate largely among middle-level households	New

Table 8.1 Cross-section of coping strategies in Dodoma District (*continued*)

Major strategy or response	Activity undertaken	Main focus and objective of activity	Initiators	Contribution of activity	Degree of spread	Activity: new or revived
Social (*continued*)	6 Burial societies	To provide a social service to bereaved families	Groups of people in Dodoma urban	Social cohesion	Moderate largely among middle-level income groups	New
	7 Milling machinery	To provide milling services to villagers	Women's groups in villages	Lessening of the burden on women	Moderate	New
Ecological	1 Afforestation	Control of soil erosion and desertification	Local leaders	To prevent soil erosion and desertification and to provide soil cover	Widespread	New
	2 Destocking	Control of soil erosion	Local leaders	To prevent soil erosion, to improve the livestock herd	Low	New
	3 Opening up new farmlands	To increase agricultural output	Individual peasants	As a cushion against low productivity	Moderate	Revived

Source: From surveys conducted by the author between July and December 1988

In the third phase, after 1979, local self-initiative in development activities had virtually disappeared as people depended more and more on government handouts. At the same time, this phase coincided with general economic decline in the District. The occurrence of drought conditions in 1981–2 and again in 1983–4, accompanied by general price increases, shortage of industrial incentive goods and a rise in the cost of living, pushed many people in the District almost to the point of destitution. This situation left the population with no alternative other than to revive and intensify previous local initiatives and to contrive new ones. The range of coping strategies in force after 1979 is indicative of a dramatic increase in the number and types of self-help initiatives that have emerged or re-emerged in the wake of a deepening crisis in the district.

Clearly, coping strategies in Dodoma District have emerged in response to various historical developments. It is therefore important for our analysis to distinguish the circumstances in which each strategy emerged or re-emerged.

Phase I: 1961–70

An important characteristic of Dodoma District before and after independence has been the recurrence of drought and famine (Brooke 1967; Ndorobo 1973). Brooke has documented several drought years, beginning as early as 1919–20 up to and including 1961–3. This documentation highlights the fact that drought gave birth to famine and that people devised and adopted several strategies to deal with such situations. Among the coping strategies that were adopted, barter and exchange, and migration to other parts of the country were the most prominent. In other situations, people learned to store food in a common pool (normally near the residences of their chiefs) during good years and would use the grain stock in years of shortage. In the case of barter and exchange, people traded livestock for grain or exchanged their labour for grain. Discussions with knowledgeable people in the District corroborate Brooke's documentation of this phenomenon.

With the increasingly unreliable rainfall conditions in the District, grain shortage has remained a major bottle-neck facing the people. Moreover, lower returns from agriculture resulting from low erratic rainfall, high evapo-transpiration and low moisture-holding capacity of the soils prevented households from satisfying their subsistence

needs even in years of adequate rainfall. The inhabitants of Dodoma responded by expanding the practice of shifting cultivation in their farming systems. Knowledgeable people in the village suggest that shifting cultivation became more widespread in the District in the 1950s and that, since then, peasants have opened up new farmland whenever the existing land became exhausted.

A related ecological problem that afflicted the rural population in Dodoma in this period was the lack of water for domestic and live-stock use during dry seasons. Although the post-independence government embarked on a rather ambitious programme to provide water to villagers by sinking boreholes and shallow wells and by con-structing dams at Hombolo, Ikowa, Buigiri and Matumbulu, these efforts benefited just a few villages. In the majority of the villages, water supply remained an acute problem. Consequently, as early as 1962, people in a number of villages initiated the construction of their own dams to alleviate the problem. Attempts by the villagers of Chololo and Nala are worth mentioning in this respect.

Local initiatives were also prominent in the crafts and industrial fields in the period under review. The remoteness of most villages in the District prevented peasants from acquiring modern industrial goods such as household utensils and farm implements. Local crafts and industries emerged in Dodoma not only as a reaction to the non-availability of industrial goods but also evolved as part of the *Wagogo* culture. Traditionally, crafts and industries were limited to specific clans and such specialization remained in force even in this period. Crafts industries were scattered throughout the District, but the scale of production of the implements was not large. Moreover, this activity facilitated barter trade among the people. It was only in the late 1960s that the produce from this activity found its way into modern exchange channels and this development motivated artisans to improve both the quality and quantity of their products. All in all, the Arusha Declaration (Nyerere 1967) and the *Ujamaa* policy (Nyerere 1968), which marked an important milestone in the development of the country as a whole, did not inspire the people of Dodoma to engage in development initiatives that were alien to their sociocultural environment.

Phase II: 1971–8

One of the outstanding developments in this period was the villagiza-tion of the District which involved moving people either to the location of existing social services, such as schools, dispensaries,

water points, and trading settlements, or to new areas. The size and layout of the new villages were based on the economics of providing social services and not on production. Consequently, Dodoma villagers did not alter their pattern of cultivation, crops grown or life pattern. Thus, they remained vulnerable to the exigencies of weather, low productivity and possible stagnation. Instead of developing an attitude of self-reliance, villagization temporarily caused some villages to become more dependent on government than was formerly the case (Kauzeni 1988). Given this situation, the survival strategies that were started in the previous phase were continued, and sometimes intensified. Attempts to construct earthen dams were made in several villages: Gawaye (1975), Mbabala B (1978) and Ntyuka (1981). Villagers opened up new farmlands to augment food production and hence continued to practise shifting cultivation. Barter and exchange increased because of the social and economic dislocation arising from villagization.

A development that contributed to the emergence of new coping strategies in Dodoma District was the decision of the central government to transfer the capital from Dar es Salaam to Dodoma in 1972. This action brought about a very rapid increase in the population of Dodoma Town from an estimated 38,000 people in 1972 to an estimated 158,000 people in 1978 (United Republic of Tanzania 1982). This sudden increase in population created new and additional demands for various items that could be obtained locally. The most critical of these were charcoal, firewood, vegetables and animal manure. Most of the new migrants needed charcoal and firewood as energy while the few who opened up vineyards created a ready market for animal manure. This development motivated villagers living around Dodoma Town to engage in charcoal production and the sale of animal manure to town dwellers. The former activity was carried out mainly by poorer members of the community, the latter by wealthier livestock owners. In addition, the middle-level peasantry found a ready market for vegetables and responded by growing this crop more intensively, particularly during the dry season.

A further development during this period was the establishment of village co-operative shops. Village shops were established in Dodoma in 1976 following the Bihawana Declaration which made it compulsory for each village in the District to establish a shop. Villagers were motivated to found shops not only to obtain the needed shop services but also as an investment outlet for their savings. From this explanation, it is clear that the idea of starting village shops was

initiated by government rather than by the people themselves. In fact, it was in the form of an 'operation'. People's initiatives were limited to the way in which such shops had to function: for example, the number and size of shares to be contributed, the type of commodities to be sold in the shop and the management of the shop.

A particularly vivid example of a locally motivated strategy in this period concerned the poor rural transportation system. Rural transportation in Dodoma District had been neglected by the central government for a long time. This neglect affected not only the movement of people but also the transportation of crops from production sites to marketing centres. The late delivery of agricultural inputs to rural areas also worried local leaders. As a consequence, between 1973 and 1978, villagers and their leaders took the initiative by purchasing vehicles on a self-help basis: some villages (Chamwino, Msanga, Kigwe, Mwitikira) bought lorries, other (Mlowa Bwawani, Mlowa Barabarani, Mpunguzi, Mvumi) bought tractors and a few (Mpunguzi, Hombolo Bwawani, Chamwino) purchased buses (Mulazi 1984).

Phase III: 1979

Underlying the social and economic performance of Dodoma District after 1978 was the nationwide economic decline arising from the interplay of factors, as outlined in the introductory section, and the peculiar ecological conditions of the District. The long drought that affected the District between 1980–1 and 1982–3 created unprecedented hardships for the people, particularly in rural areas. Thousands of tons of food were brought into the District by the government to avert possible famine. Because of the magnitude of the problem, the government directed wholesale institutions, such as the Regional Trading Company and the National Milling Corporation, to sell food and other essential goods to co-operative shops only. This action gave rise to the mushrooming of such shops at workplaces in Dodoma Town and to the opening up of women's shops in rural areas.

The food crisis added another burden to an already endemic problem of scarcity of industrial goods such as soap, salt, sugar, matches, torch batteries, clothes and cooking. Long queues of people waiting to purchase food and other essential commodities at designated co-operative shops were common in most parts of the District. From villages surrounding Dodoma Town, between 1982 and 1985, people commuted on a daily basis to the town to buy food and other

items. As a result of the severity of the crisis, well placed town dwellers even managed to trade maize flour to villagers for cattle or goats.

On the social front, community services such as health and education faced fundamental problems. The government had invested heavily in social services, especially health, education and water supply, yet at the end of the 1970s none of these services could obtain the necessary operational support (Coulson 1982). Hospitals and dispensaries in the District found it difficult to secure the required medicinal supplies. In fact, until recently, more and more people have been paying for medical services in private hospitals or dispensaries. The illusion of free medical care is disappearing fast in Dodoma District. In some of the villages, the people no longer depend on modern medical services, relying instead on the services of herbalists.

Education has also suffered severely. In the majority of primary schools within the District, pupils have to sit on the floor as there are no desks. Even with the re-introduction of local authorities, schools are starved of funds to purchase stationery for the children. The buildings of most schools are in appalling condition because of inadequate maintenance. Moreover, the District economy is unable to absorb primary school leavers, many of whom migrate to urban areas to look for paid jobs only to increase the number of unemployed youths in towns. With regard to water supply, the situation has been very similar to other community services. Many villages, such as Nala and Zepisa, which had water supply systems, no longer enjoy the service because of the lack of spare parts to rehabilitate them.

In general, the increase in the cost of living arising from high rates of inflation, the scarcity of foreign exchange, the shortage of essential industrial incentive goods and the deterioration of community services have had the combined effect of reducing the standard of living and quality of life of the District's population. The picture that emerges after 1979 is one of a deepening economic crisis that significantly altered the lifestyle of the population in both rural and urban Dodoma. Trade liberalization and good weather conditions have eased some of the socioeconomic difficulties which were experienced after 1979, particularly after 1986 (Odunga et al. 1988). But this encouraging performance has become meaningful in Dodoma only after the people themselves had devised alternative means of survival.

Several such strategies were continued from previous phases. Examples are barter and exchange, shifting cultivation, local crafts

and industries, and income-earning strategies such as beer making. Others included charcoal making, vegetable gardening, selling animal manure, and transportation. New activities that emerged in the wake of the deepening economic crisis in the District included: the formation of savings and credit societies, the emergence of burial societies and building co-operatives, the initiation of income-earning activities such as the opening up of kiosks, the mushrooming of door-to-door salespeople among the middle-level peasantry, and the formation of youth and women's groups as a means of pooling labour and other resources among poorer members of the community in order to obtain economies of scale in production.

To summarize, the people of Dodoma District have engaged in self-help activities of different types for a very long time. The range and diversity of these activities has increased and intensified over the years because of the social and economic upheavals that have confronted the District. For example, in the past, crafts and industries were confined to certain clans only. However, over time, this trade has spread to other people, particularly youths who have formed small-scale industrial groups and have improved the quality and quantity of their products. Even the marketing of the product is much more commercialized than previously. In addition, women's groups are playing an increasingly visible role in crisis response, whether the crisis arises from natural disasters such as drought or from development policies. For example, women's groups in the District are now involved in income-generating activities, such as vegetable shops and maize milling, to supplement family incomes. Individually, women brew beer to generate income.

In Phase I, it was found that the strategies that emerged were mainly directed to the subsistence needs of the population. However, in the most recent past, this concern has broadened to include self-help activities which are service-oriented. Communities have found it necessary to supplement government efforts in fields which were previously provided by the government, such as health, education, transportation, and the control of soil erosion and desertification. The initiatives by local communities are indicative of development 'from within' which requires government recognition and support. The intervention by rural communities has come at a time when government ability to marshal resources for development has deteriorated drastically. In the next section, a detailed description is provided of the interventions that were made by the rural communities in Dodoma District in the wake of the economic crisis.

COPING STRATEGIES AND RESPONSES

Among the coping strategies studied here, a distinction can be drawn between those which are intended to deal with the economic crisis (local crafts and industries, metal trading, exchange and barter system, charcoal making, selling animal manure, vegetable gardening, local beer making); those which arise from the failure of the government to deliver essential services to the population (housing and credit co-operatives to provide social services such as health, education, water, housing, transport, credit, and burial services, formation of clubs and groups such as youth and women's groups); and those which are intended to deal with the hostile environment (drought, low productivity, desertification, soil erosion).

Economic strategies

The widespread development of economic coping strategies and responses in Dodoma District has come about in the wake of the economic crisis confronting the local population. This development is expected to produce multiple benefits for the local population:

(a) The generation of additional income to households;
(b) The creation of employment for the population throughout the year;
(c) Increasing food stocks in food-deficit households.

Local crafts

Handicrafts are a long-established local occupation in Dodoma District. The craft persons are private artists who are located all over the District and who are engaged in trades such as pottery, and in the manufacturing of wooden trays, carvings, mortars and stools. They have few tools and usually use a tree or a simple hut for a workshop.

Pottery is almost completely carried out by women. The product is a popular cooking utensil which is used in most rural households and in some urban households. With the existing high prices of industrially produced cooking utensils, locally produced pots are cheap substitutes for rural households and low-income earners in urban areas.

The manufacture of wooden trays, carvings, mortars and stools is undertaken exclusively by men. The items produced are household necessities in rural communities. There are no specialized groups of

183

people involved in these crafts. The items are simple implements which do not require sophisticated technology in their production. Moreover, because of the numbers of artisans involved and the simplicity of the tools used, the scale of production for each artisan is small. Some of the items find their way into the Dodoma urban market and therefore earn income for the artists.

Blacksmiths and metal tradesmen

Blacksmiths provide an important service to farmers by manufacturing farming tools such as cutlasses, hoes and harvesting tools. This trade was neglected in the District development strategy for a long time. In the past, blacksmiths and metal tradesmen have operated in Dodoma on either an individual or family basis, their scale of production remaining small. Recently, youths have organized themselves into co-operative groups with the purpose of increasing the scale of operation by taking advantage of organized marketing.

Three co-operative groups were studied during the initial survey. The first is the Nzuguni Youth Group which has 20 members. This group manufactures traditional knives, spears and hand hoes. The group is based at Nzuguni Village, some 10 km east of Dodoma Town. The second group is the Muungano Talawanda Group which has 50 members and is based in Dodoma Town. The group makes traditional metal items such as cutlasses, knives, hoes, and charcoal stoves. A third group, which is also based in Dodoma Town, is the Awamu Vijana Group. This group has 20 members and makes buckets, charcoal stoves and cooking utensils.

Exchange and barter trade

Unreliable rainfall has made Dodoma District an area prone to food deficits. Although the population has responded to this challenge by growing drought-resistant food crops, particularly sorghum and millet, this step has not made the District a food surplus area. Exchange and barter trade are the main strategies that continue to provide relief for a large section of the rural population. Barter trade in Dodoma District is a common feature in the exchange relations between November and March each year. In the main, the exchange is between food grains and livestock. The survey revealed that, in the 1987/8 farming season, two tins of maize flour were being exchanged for one goat. The survey also revealed that in certain cases grain is

exchanged for labour. This happens when a member of a household which is facing food shortage works on another family's farm for several days/weeks and is paid in kind. This practice is quite common among the *Wagogo* in Dodoma District and is known as *kuhemea*. Considering that Dodoma District is a very dry area and that for most years the majority of the rural population do not satisfy their subsistence needs for five months in any one year, barter trade is an important strategy for alleviating hunger and human suffering which is caused by intermittent unfavourable weather conditions.

Charcoal making

This activity is more widespread in villages surrounding Dodoma Town. A study by Graham Thiele has shown that charcoal making is most popular in those villages which are less than 24.3 km from the town centre (Thiele 1984). Participants, who are from poor households, are mainly young men, although in certain instances middle-aged men are also involved. Most of the participating population undertake this activity on a part-time basis in the farming season but are fully engaged in the dry season, that is, from May to November of each year.

Charcoal is normally sold to Dodoma Town residents. The survey showed that the price of charcoal varies from season to season. In the farming season, prices are normally higher than average, indicating that fewer people are involved in charcoal making and that household food stocks in the villages are lower than the required level. It is common in Dodoma Town to see charcoal traders buying grain or maize flour after selling their charcoal. Moreover, since about 90 per cent of Dodoma Town residents use charcoal as fuel, charcoal making is a response to the energy needs of the urban population.

Selling animal manure

The application of animal manure in farming is not a new development in Dodoma District. What is new is the realization by pastoralists that farmyard manure is a resource that can be used to augment their incomes. Before 1982, animal manure was given free to grape farmers and orchardists. However, with the increasing number of grape farmers in the District, wealthier livestock owning families started on their own initiative to sell animal manure to vineyard owners in 1982. With the escalation of prices for industrial fertilizer,

farmyard manure is becoming not only an important substitute but also a popular fertilizer among grape farmers, vegetable gardeners and orchardists. With a large livestock population, the potential for expanding the use of animal manure in Dodoma District is substantial.

Vegetable gardening

Vegetable gardening is an off-farm seasonal activity that has been initiated by enterprising young men largely from the middle peasantry. The activity has gained momentum in the last five years in both scale and extent. It is an important activity in the dry season where small-scale irrigation is used and is more common in those villages where small dams have been constructed. In the case of seasonal rivers which dry up in the dry season, young men dig holes in the sand from the riverbed using shovels to obtain water for their small plots. Men from more than thirty villages in Dodoma District are actively engaged in this activity. A large part of the crop, predominantly tomatoes and onions, is sold to Dodoma Town residents and a small portion is exported to Dar es Salaam. Vegetable gardening enables an important section of the rural community to be actively involved in productive work throughout the year.

Beer making

Local beer making is not a new activity in Dodoma District but has become more popular as an income-earning activity among women from low-income groups and petty traders. More than 98 per cent of those who were interviewed indicated that their involvement in beer making was in response to the current economic difficulties facing them. In rural areas, this activity is found in almost every village. It is an important income-earning strategy after the harvest season; in the farming season, grains are normally in short supply and beer production is reduced. Moreover, village governments and local authorities normally forbid people from engaging in the activity at this time to ensure that villagers do not exhaust available grain. In urban Dodoma, this activity is undertaken throughout the year. The very high price of industrially produced beer has contributed significantly to the high demand for locally made beer in Dodoma Town. For example, by the end of 1988, the former was selling at $2.00 per litre compared to $0.33 per litre for the latter.

Social and political strategies

Social coping strategies in Dodoma District emerged as responses to unfulfilled government and political promises to deliver essential services such as health, education or water after the villagization campaign in 1976. In another development, the emergence of such local initiatives was pre-empted by government policies which advocated the doctrine of self-reliance as a follow-up to the Arusha Declaration (Nyerere 1967) and the post-villagization policy. This development is aimed at:

(a) Complementing government efforts towards their own development;
(b) Providing important services to local communities such as health care, education and transportation;
(c) Widening opportunities for individuals or organized groups and mobilizing capabilities and resources for common beliefs;
(d) Preventing a drastic fall in living standards for local communities and improving their quality of life.

Provision of health care

Health care is an essential service in any community. With the nucleation of the population after villagization in 1976, demand has increased but, over the years, has not been met because of the economic difficulties confronting the country since 1977. The government no longer commits enough resources to this sector. The enthusiasm that accompanied the provision of this service motivated village communities in Dodoma to initiate the construction of health facilities in their areas on a self-help basis. Village leaders first discuss the matter among themselves and then table the issue before the village community. When the idea is accepted, village leaders hold discussions with authorities to establish whether or not it falls within the government policy of service provision.

After the District authorities have accepted the village request, village leaders mobilize the community to construct the facility. The villagers' contribution is normally in the form of labour and money. Technical assistance in the building of a dispensary is normally provided by the Department of Community Development through its building brigade. In certain cases, building materials are obtained through assistance given by non-government organizations such as the Community Development Trust Fund of Tanzania. For example,

the dispensary-cum-clinic at Mahoma Makulu Village was built by way of self-help and received material assistance from the Dodoma Municipal Council and the Community Development Trust Fund of Tanzania. Several other villages in Dodoma District have constructed health facilities in their areas in this way.

Education

Subsequent to villagization in 1976 and the adoption of the policy of universal primary education in November 1977, each village was motivated to build its own primary school where such service was non-existent. The initiative normally came from village leaders and government officials at the district level.

Rural communities, in their attempt to provide this service for their children, have built classrooms and teachers' houses on a self-help basis. In some cases, entire primary schools have been built in this way while, in others, building materials have been provided by government and by some religious institutions which are based in the District. About 60 per cent of the primary schools existing in Dodoma District have been built through self-help.

Universal primary education has also created a problem in the form of youths completing primary education in large numbers. In Dodoma District in the last five years, only about 2 per cent annually of primary school leavers receive post-primary education. This means that 98 per cent of youths completing primary education join the pool of unemployed youths. Rural communities, with the help of local institutions and non-government organizations, such as Oxfam, World Vision and the Community Development Trust Fund (CDTF), have responded to this problem by building multipurpose community centres. In such centres at Mbabala B, Mpunguzi and Kigwe villages, youths train in skills such as carpentry, tailoring, blacksmithing and pottery (Hiari 1982).

Water supply

The problem of water for various uses in Dodoma District is critical because of the unreliable nature of rain or surface water. In the dry season, water availability is problematic not only for household use but also for livestock use. During this season, large herds of cattle are frequently moved long distances in search of water. The survey showed that pastoralists move their cattle over distances averaging up to 25 km in search of water and pasture.

For household use, villagers who are far away from reliable water sources, such as shallow wells or boreholes, frequently obtain their water by digging small wells in the dried river beds. The difficulties which are associated with this popular method of water harvesting indicate that the magnitude of the problem is not being adequately tackled. Several villages in Dodoma District on their own initiative now construct small dams to deal with the problem. Examples of such villages include Chololo (1962), Nàlà (1962), Gawaye (1975), Mbabala B (1978), Ntyuka (1981), and Ihumwa (1981). The main handicaps to the provision of water in this way are the lack of expertise, the limited technological base, and the lack of equipment and implements on the part of the villagers (Ndaro 1987). With assistance from government or NGOs, this method of water conservation would provide a more certain means of water harvesting in water-starved villages in the District.

Transportation

Over the last two decades, various initiatives have been taken by villagers to provide transportation in their areas on a self-help basis. The main initiative has come from local village leaders who have been inspired by political and government officials within the region. Villagers make their financial or equity contribution through village governments. The main support has come from the National Bank of Commerce (NBC) through its subsidiary, the Karadha Company Ltd, and the Co-operative and Rural Development Bank. Advisory and technical support has come mainly from the Co-operative Division at the District Headquarters.

The initiative has resulted in the acquisition of vehicles by villages. Since 1973 the distribution of ownership has been of the following order; 24 villages have acquired lorries, 5 villages have purchased tractors, while 3 own buses. The objective of the villages in acquiring vehicles is threefold: to provide rural transportation for agriculture inputs and farm produce; to facilitate human movement within the district; and to increase/expand village government coffers. The collective initiative by village communities to provide transport services for themselves is directed to finding a solution to the problem of rural transportation (Mulazi 1984).

Co-operative savings and credit societies

These are registered societies which are started through the initiative of the members themselves. Members are mainly employees in

189

different institutions in urban and rural areas. The main purposes of such societies are twofold: one is to provide cheap loans to members in case of problems such as bereavement, sickness, or school fees for their children; the other is to provide cheap loans to members for personal development, such as farm expansion, or for the purchase of important but rather expensive household items such as bicycles, radios or radio cassettes.

There are a total of sixteen such societies in Dodoma District. Three-quarters of the societies are located in Dodoma Town, while the remainder are found in rural areas of Dodoma District. The collective effort which is shown by such groups of people is designed to mobilize what little financial resources are available for their own development. Existing co-operative savings and credit societies in Dodoma have so far made it possible for members to engage in farm expansion, poultry projects, purchase of building materials, and other self-development activities.

Burial societies

Burial societies have been initiated by individuals from middle income households in urban areas for the purpose of assisting one another in cases of bereavement. Ten such societies are known to exist in Dodoma Town. Each burial society has a fund which is established through members' own contributions. The specific objectives of burial societies are:

(a) To provide financial and other material support to bereaved family members of the society;
(b) To assist in the transportation of the body of the deceased to the original place of domicile for burial;
(c) To provide assistance to members or travellers belonging to their region who happen to be in financial difficulties or need of material support.

Youth groups

In the last decade, several youth groups have emerged and formed co-operative ventures. These groups are of a social and economic nature. Two types of youth groups have emerged in Dodoma District, those which are spearheaded by religious institutions and those which are organized by the Department of Youth and Culture.

Among the former, two were visited during the survey: the Evangelical Youth Group is involved in pig and goat rearing projects in Hombolo village, while the Anglican Cathedral Group is engaged in vegetable gardening and fruit farming projects. In addition, this group cultivates drought-resistant crops such as sorghum and cassava. A total of 80 youths aged between 12 and 35 years are involved in these projects.

In the case of the youth groups that are organized by the Department of Youth and Culture, only one such group was visited. The Mpunguzi Youth Group, which is based at Mpunguzi Village some 21 km south of Dodoma Town, is involved in grape farming, an important cash crop in the district. The group consists of youths who have organized themselves into a farming brigade, after realizing their own common purpose of raising their incomes by pooling whatever resources they had, especially their labour.

Women's groups

Several types of women's groups can be identified: tailoring groups, co-operative shops, milling machine projects, and informal women's groups which are spearheaded by religious institutions. Although these groups may be perceived as responding to the prevailing socio-economic crisis in Dodoma District, they also represent an opportunity for women to acquire access to and control over resources in a society where these are frequently denied to them. In Wagogo society, control over land and livestock is overwhelmingly in male hands. Women's groups therefore provide women with a means to improve their access to resources without interfering with such rigid relations of production.

Tailoring groups

In the survey, six women's co-operative groups were visited. The women form their associations voluntarily, members contributing to a common fund in the initial stages of the association. After registration, assistance in the form of material support is sought from the Department of Community Development or some other donor agency. The women's group at Bihawana Village was assisted by a religious organization called World Vision.

Co-operative shops

These shops are spearheaded by the local branch of Umoja wa Wanawake wa Tanzania. Thus, the membership is confined to UWT members. There were more than fifteen women's co-operative shops run by the UWT in Dodoma District in 1984. However, by 1988 this number had declined to six. Factors which contributed to this decline included: very low initial capital; management problems arising from members' inexperience; and high operational costs.

Milling machine projects

Over the last decade, many women's groups in the villages, under the auspices of local UWT branches, have endeavoured to acquire milling machines in their villages. In certain villages, women's groups started other economic ventures, such as restaurants or co-operative farms, in order to raise funds for the purpose of acquiring milling machines. However, available evidence suggests that this method of raising funds has not been successful for many groups. Consequently, more effective methods have been sought. The most popular method has been to approach local non-government organizations, particularly the CDTF. In such situations, milling machines are delivered only after the relevant group has constructed a permanent structure to house the machine. Examples of women's groups which have acquired milling machines in this way are those in the villages of Mzakwe, Mlowa Barabarani, Nzuguni and Zepisa.

Informal women's groups

These are essentially voluntary groups which are initiated by religious institutions. The most active religious women's groups, which are found in Dodoma, belong to the Lutheran Church, the Anglican Church, the Roman Catholic Church and the Seventh Day Adventist Church. The groups are involved in tailoring, weaving and gardening. Initially, members contribute money to a common fund which is used to purchase the needed inputs. Material support is obtained from the relevant religious institutions. Proceeds from these activities are used by members to supplement their household incomes.

Ecological strategies

The strategies which are investigated in this category are devised in response to, and as a means of coping with, the hostile natural environment prevailing in Dodoma District. The strategies are directed towards the prevention of further degradation of the environment which is caused by soil erosion, deforestation and creeping desertification. The principal objective of these strategies is to improve environmental protection and living conditions through measures such as soil erosion control, afforestation, and desertification control.

Soil erosion control

In Dodoma District, soil erosion is caused by two main factors: overstocking, and deforestation as a result of charcoal making, house building and shifting cultivation. It follows that both pastoralists and agriculturalists contribute in one way or the other to soil erosion.

Responses or local initiatives from pastoralists and agriculturalists to soil erosion control are still neglible in Dodoma District. One possible approach to soil erosion control is destocking. In Dodoma, however, it is estimated that, since the introduction of such efforts in the mid-1970s, destocking has been insignificant (under 5 per cent) largely because pastoralists consider their livestock as capital investment. Pastoralists are not prepared to reduce the size of their livestock herds by selling or slaughtering them (Mascarenhas 1977). Village leaders, with the assistance of local district authorities, are attempting to circumvent this problem by designating specific areas as grazing land. It is thought that the restriction imposed on pastoralists by village government leaders will motivate them to reduce the size of their herds.

Deforestation and desertification control

Another approach to soil erosion control is afforestation or the planting of trees and the exercising of strict and conscious control in tree felling. In Dodoma District, there is considerable evidence to suggest that tree felling is undertaken indiscriminately, i.e. without any planned tree harvesting. Tree-cutting is undertaken either to enable peasants to acquire new farmland or to facilitate the production of charcoal and firewood for sale in Dodoma Town. Both practices are discouraged by the government as they constitute the main cause for the creeping desertification in Dodoma region.

Afforestation campaigns have taken place in villages and primary schools for several years now. In the process, village governments have designated specific areas for tree planting. During the survey it became clear that each village which was visited had established an average of three hectares of trees, which had been planted following the intervention of the village government. Primary schools had also planted an average of half a hectare at the time of the visit. In addition to these efforts, individual villagers are encouraged to plant trees near their households. Seedlings are normally supplied by local government authorities based at the District Headquarters. The survey also indicated that, so far, four villages have established their own nurseries to meet the ever increasing demand for seedlings in their areas.

IMPLICATIONS FOR RURAL/REGIONAL DEVELOPMENT

Local coping strategies are attempts by communities to provide essential goods and services in their own areas with little or no assistance from the state. The nature and scope of the activities that have been described in this study are manifestations of an approach to socioeconomic development which is grass-roots based. Specific strategies vary according to both socioeconomic stratum and gender.

The local provision of goods and services on a self-help basis, rather than a reliance on government assistance, is an important feature of a locally based rural/regional development paradigm. However, in the context of rural/regional development, there is a problem in that many local initiatives tend to be ignored in the mainstream planning process. In practice, such initiatives tend to have certain characteristics in common: they are often badly designed; they expect a great deal to be achieved in a short time from the use of meagre resources; they contribute little to raising the consciousness of local communities; they include activities which are marginal (in terms of both sustainability and expansion); and they are part and parcel of rural/regional development plans which are formulated and implemented by government. One result is the perpetuation of marginal social and economic roles for local-level coping strategies, which acts as a constraint on the potential for local populations to promote their own development.

There is, of course, no blueprint for achieving rural/regional development but the integration and co-ordination of local coping strategies with government initiatives may help to start such a process.

This approach can be adopted by a committed government and by organizations with decision-making power and access to knowledge and resources that can be used by local populations in their struggle for improvement and self-sustenance.

CONCLUSION

Grass-roots involvement in self-help activities has a long history in Tanzania, which can be traced back to 1967 when the policy of socialism and self-reliance was elaborated in the Arusha Declaration (Nyerere 1967). However, this policy did not provide for sufficient prominence being given to local strategies in national, regional or even district development plans. Instead, government initiatives continued to be given more prominence in development plans. Even with decentralization (Nyerere 1972), it has not been possible for local initiatives to filter upwards. Self-help initiatives are widespread in Dodoma District and other parts of Tanzania, as indicated in the study. In spite of this, local populations have been handicapped by their restricted access to finance, technology, organizational and management skills, advisory and technical services *inter alia*. To produce sound results, local coping strategies must solve the problem of access to these essential inputs.

In some instances, outside promotion of local coping strategies has been effected in Dodoma District. For youth groups, this intervention has taken the form of the Youth Development Task Force (Akator 1988); in the case of women, Umoja wa Wanawake wa Tanzania has had some influence. While the degree of contact with locally based groups has varied, such bodies have exerted little effect on mainstream decision-making. Of course, they have served to channel funds for short term, small scale projects for youth and women's groups, but their impact on grass-roots development has tended to be slight. Although there appears to be a serious need to re-assess their role, this does not mean they should be dismantled. The challenge is to make them more effective. Members and staff need adequate training in organizational, leadership, planning and management skills. Such institutions can play a catalytic role, working with local government not only to review and improve people's programmes, in line with acceptable targets and commitment for grass-roots development, but also to participate in the monitoring and evaluation of overall programmes. Their influence on district or regional decisions is likely to depend on their links with the grass-roots, since

organizations with a substantial power base among the people are less easily ignored.

ACKNOWLEDGEMENT

I should like to acknowledge the support of the United Nations Centre for Regional Development under whose auspices some of the data used in this chapter were collected.

9

THE INFORMAL SECTOR
A strategy for survival in Tanzania
Alice Nkhoma-Wamunza

INTRODUCTION

In Tanzania, the participation of women in the informal sector must be seen in relation to the deterioration of the subsistence economy. In the rural areas, women constitute the majority of the population and form 80 per cent of the agricultural producers but they are also the most marginalized section of the population. Women's access to land, credit, agricultural inputs and technical know-how is limited compared to that of men. Further, although women work so hard, they are not the main beneficiaries of the products of their labour (Muro 1987). Women are rarely represented in public decision-making bodies nor do they effectively participate in the decision-making process as in other fora; in fact, they have limited control over factors that are vital for their economic survival.

The continuing economic crisis in Tanzania has affected women and children more than men since it has led to cuts in public spending in areas which most concern women, such as social and health services. For example, government expenditure on health declined from 9 per cent of total expenditure in 1973–4 to 4.9 per cent in 1982–3 to 1985–6. Similarly, government expenditure on education declined from 14 per cent during 1975–6 and 1977–8 to 9 per cent for the 1982–3 and 1985–6 period. Primary education has been the most seriously affected. Here government expenditure declined from a high of 19.9 per cent of total capital expenditure in 1982 to 11.9 per cent by 1986 (Havnevik *et al.* 1988). For a country that is trying to eradicate illiteracy and to strengthen its human capacity in the management of various sectors, these cuts have had a negative impact on the effort to improve the capacity of national human resources.

Such cutbacks reflect the post-independence economic performance

of Tanzania. Tanzania's economic growth rate in the 1960s and early 1970s ranged between 5 and 7 per cent annually. But from 1973 to 1978 the economy began to decline rapidly; GDP averaged only 1.5 per cent per annum. Between 1978 and 1985, real income stood at 2 per cent while GDP stood at 10 per cent below the 1978 levels. There was, however, a slight increase in the growth rate of 0.3 per cent between 1985 and 1986 to 0.6 per cent from 1986 to 1987 (Havnevik *et al.* 1988). The deteriorating economy has meant a dramatic reduction in real earnings. The value of the T Shs to US$ 1 has continued to decline from T Shs 17 in March 1985 to T Shs 145 to US$ 1 in November 1989. One result has been an increase in the number of women and children living below the poverty line. Between 1972 and 1984, the average real wage in industry declined by 70 per cent. The high rate of inflation and devaluation has meant an increase in the cost of living while low wages and poor employment opportunities face the majority of women who are unskilled. By 1980 women constituted only 15 per cent of all wage and salaried employment. As a result, more women have been forced to engage in income-generating activities in the informal sector in order to sustain their families and to increase their purchasing power.

As elsewhere in sub-Saharan Africa, the current economic crisis in Tanzania is characterized by low per capita incomes, low production, slow export growth, weak balance of payments, shortages of foreign exchange and essential goods as well as inadequate recurrent funds for the operation and maintenance of services. African countries have responded to the crisis by introducing various adjustment programmes in order to contain the situation. In the case of Tanzania, various structural adjustment programmes have been introduced, none of which has seriously taken into consideration the specific needs of women. Instead, the programmes have worsened the condition of women. The National Economic Survival Programme of 1981–2 focused mainly on the management of the external sector imbalance, increasing exports, marketing of food surplus, controlling government expenditure and producing essential goods for industry. Despite the good intentions of the programme, it did not address the specific needs of women. There was no mechanism in the programme through which women could have had access to the resources to improve production.

As the crisis deepened in the 1980s, it was felt that the National Economic Survival Programme was not adequate. Thus, the 1982–5 Structural Adjustment Programme was introduced. Like its predecessor, it did not attempt to address the specific needs and problems

of women agricultural producers, such as issues of access to land or farm inputs, credit or division of labour. Instead, the removal of food subsidies and reduced support to social services negatively affected women and children. Trade liberalization made matters worse because few could afford to buy the goods that were imported.

Since the first two structural adjustment programmes failed to meet their objectives, the government introduced the 1986–9 Economic Recovery Programme (United Republic of Tanzania 1986) which aimed to increase both food and cash crops, to improve marketing structures and resources in the agricultural sector and to rehabilitate supportive production infrastructure. None of the three programmes gave due consideration to the vital role played by women in production, marketing or distribution.

The participation of women in the informal sector, in order to generate additional income, is not a new phenomenon for women in the urban and rural areas of Tanzania. However, the current economic crisis and the monetization of subsistence has created a high demand for cash to meet the rising costs of food items, clothing and other basic needs. This situation has negatively affected the nutritional welfare of children who are left in the care of either other children or ageing grandmothers. In many cases, children are forced to work late hours to help their mothers to generate income through petty trading; sometimes this results in their being absent from school.

Another factor which has led to women's increased involvement in the informal sector is male migration, especially from rural to urban areas. Migration has contributed significantly to the increase in female-headed households, which in turn has meant women taking initiatives to generate income through the informal sector to enable them to provide and manage family needs in the absence of their husbands. The informal sector, therefore, has provided an opportunity for women to earn independent incomes but it also has meant a shifting of family responsibilities on to women and additional workloads for the already over-burdened women. Since women's involvement in the informal sector is undertaken concurrently with other household chores and agricultural cash food crop production, this situation in turn has serious implications for the health and nutritional status of both the women and their children.

Cultural factors have also contributed to more women engaging in cash-earning activities, since women in many African societies are brought up to take responsibility for providing food for their families.

From early childhood a girl is taught the virtues of hard work. Parents will influence their sons in the choice of a spouse by emphasizing the qualities of hard work in a young woman. Girls grow up believing that food provision and household care are their sole responsibilities, thus furthering the unequal sexual division of labour.

It is not surprising that so many women are turning to income-generating activities in the informal sector in order to earn extra income and to supplement other sources of income for the continued sustainment of their families. It is no longer possible for low income and peasant households to subsist on the low wages and income from agricultural produce, the prices of which are determined in international markets. By taking on income-generating activities, women are increasing their workload and stress but they are also becoming innovative and are developing informal support systems as they struggle for the betterment of their families' livelihoods. For example, they draw on *Update*, a rotating savings and loans system, to which each makes a monthly contribution. In turn, a lump sum of money is allocated to each member for investment in a business or to purchase household items which would otherwise be beyond reach.

Women are also creating employment opportunities for other women. The major areas of concentration for women's activities are in food processing, bun and bread making, petty trade, poultry, pigs, pottery, dairy cattle, transport, handicrafts, tailoring and embroidery, food vending and brewing. According to women, the monthly earnings from these activities are much higher than the official minimum wage of T Shs 2,500 per month. The high incomes in this sector have attracted many women in formal wage employment, thus tripling the workload of most women. For example, a woman in formal wage employment may keep up to 400 poultry while women keeping poultry on a full time basis may keep between 500 and 5,000 poultry and realize more than T Shs 300,000 per year.

This chapter presents a case study of women brewers in Utengule Usangu, a *Ujamaa* village in the Mbeya Region. It is a study and history of women's struggles. It illustrates their strengths, weaknesses, aspirations and determination for survival despite the many obstacles and constraints. The struggles also show us lessons which can be learned and which perhaps can contribute towards developing alternative mechanisms to deal with similar problems. The material in this chapter is based on earlier fieldwork and research, sponsored by ILO Geneva, on employment opportunities for rural women in

Tanzania. The methodology that was used involved case history studies, participatory observation, meetings, discussions and interviews.

BREWING

For the majority of women in rural areas and for rural–urban women, brewing is not only a major contribution and source of income but also a lucrative business. Indulgence in brewing is an activity which women take on in addition to their other daily household and agricultural chores.

In Tanzania, women from different parts of the country brew different types of alcohol; for example, *komoni* and *kangara* which are made from grains such as maize, millet or sorghum, *mbege* which is made from unripe bananas, *bonasi* from ripe pineapples, *ulaka* from the cashewnut, *dengerua* from sugar cane and *wanzuki* from honey. While the above types of alcohol are controlled and prepared mainly by women, there are other types of brews of which men are the main producers. For example, men prepare *ulanzi* (bamboo) or *mnazi* (palm) wine. The actual preparation of these is not a demanding task; it does not involve cooking or the fetching of fuelwood or water as is the case in the brews that are prepared by women. The wines that men produce are tapped straight from palm trees or bamboo shoots. They are not labour-demanding, although they do require skills such as climbing the tall palm trees and tapping. In addition, whereas ordinary brewing is the domain of women, distilling spirits such as *gongo* is dominated by men. Distillation involves technological innovation with which men tend to be more conversant. However, more women are now learning the skills of brewing *gongo*.

Brewing is a demanding, labour-intensive activity requiring large quantities of water and fuel. For many women, the search for water means walking long distances to rivers, streams or wells. Even for those women with access to piped water, the presence of a water supply system is no guarantee that a regular supply of water will be maintained. Often many of these supply systems cease to function owing to a lack of spare parts, poor operation and maintenance and a lack of trained personnel to operate and maintain them. Where training has been given in operation or maintenance, those trained have always been men despite the fact that women are the drawers of water. Until recently, development aid programmes have not adequately addressed this issue when sponsoring village water projects.

For many households in Tanzania, fuelwood is the main source of energy for cooking and especially for the brewing process. The demand for fuelwood is so great that women now have to walk longer distances in search of fuelwood for both household consumption and petty trade activities, such as baking bread, making bricks and drying tobacco, since it is no longer possible to find fuelwood nearby. The government and various non-governmental and international organizations in Tanzania are just beginning to emphasize the importance of increasing local awareness of the hazards of environmental degradation and of the need to preserve and plant trees for the future supply and source of fuelwood.

The Utengule Usangu Brewers

Utengule Usangu is a small *Ujamaa* village in the Usangu plains in Mbeya Region. The village is about 60 km from Mbeya Town. By 1982 the village had a population of about 1,860 with a total of 340 households. The major economic activities are farming and animal husbandry. Rice, maize and sorghum are the major food and cash crops. Some cotton is also grown as a cash crop.

Beer brewing among the Wasangu (the people of Usangu) is as old as their history. It plays an important social, religious and economic role. In pre-colonial days, the presence of beer played a significant role in the organization and mobilization of labour for agricultural production or for any task that required significant labour power. However, during the colonial period, beer brewing became a new source of income to pay poll tax.

Today, income from brewing continues to be the major reliable source of income for many rural women and has made it possible for women to pay their share of the development levy that was introduced by the government in 1982. Every able-bodied individual over 18 years of age, employed or unemployed, man or woman, is expected to pay this levy to finance the local government authorities. For many rural women this has meant an additional financial burden. Often, women with a reliable source of income from brewing and petty trade have no choice but to pay the levy for their husbands who may not have the money at the necessary time. Men frequently rely on income from seasonal crop sales, payment for which is often deferred by crop buying authorities. Whether women in the rural areas should pay the development levy has been the subject of much debate in the country. In 1982–3, the village government collected T Shs 26,589 from

villagers compared to T Shs 12,413 from market traders. This may be an indicator of the role of beer brewing in the economy of the village.

Brewing is predominantly a female occupation because the tasks involved fall within the gender division of labour for women, e.g. drawing water, collecting fuelwood, grinding or pounding, and cooking. Some of the drudgery in brewing has eased through access to technological innovations such as grinding machines. Today, women rarely use the mortar and pestle except when small amounts of grain need to be ground. At the time that this research was undertaken, the village had three grinding mills which liberated women from the tedious process of pounding the grain with a mortar and pestle. However, when there is no diesel or when the mills break down, especially when no spare parts are available, women must either resort to the traditional way of grinding or travel to another village with a milling machine. Most women prefer to walk the long distances to the next milling machine rather than use up their energy through tedious pounding.

The process of brewing is very demanding. Women wake up very early to light the fire, draw water and mix the ingredients. They must collect sufficient fuelwood. In some cases, women with means or younger women prefer to buy fuelwood from fellow women or men rather than fetch it themselves because of the long distances involved and to avoid having to carry a heavy load on their heads. In all of these activities women make use of their support systems to ease the drudgery and work burden, so that the drawing of water, the collection of fuelwood and the preparation process of brewing is often done with the help of friends. In some cases, child labour is utilized. This is noticed especially in the rural–urban periphery of Dar es Salaam where young girls help their mothers to sell drinks to customers.

These support systems/networks and the co-operation are necessary to ease the work burden since, apart from brewing, women must also perform all other daily chores. The support networks are not confined to the preparation of beer but extend to co-operative child care. Often a friend or relative will offer to look after another woman's children while the latter is busy brewing or selling.

Brewing is a technique and those without the specific knowledge or skill or those who would like to earn money but cannot brew for religious or other reasons will often ask a friend to brew for them as long as they provide the ingredients, water and fuelwood. Here support systems are used by women to enhance the economic capacity of fellow women.

The whole brewing process, including the boiling, mixing, cooling and serving stages, may take between eight and ten hours, spread over a period of one week. Meanwhile, preparations for the next brew are made so that immediately after one brewing is sold out, production of the next brew begins. How much and how often a woman brews depends on her need for cash and the time available. Some women may brew between 90 and 180 litres of beer per week. The price of a litre of beer varies between T Shs 20 and T Shs 30. In urban areas, the price ranges between T Shs 30 and T Shs 40 per litre. Earnings from brewing vary from individual to individual depending on the amount brewed. By 1982, T Shs 600 per person per brew was considered to be the highest, whereas recently women in villages in Mbamba Bay in Ruvuma Region indicated that they earned between T Shs 2,000 and T Shs 3,000 per person per brew. In Dar es Salaam, a woman may earn up to T Shs 6,000 per brew in a day, assuming that she does not sell on credit to some customers and that the quality is good. This difference in earnings can be explained by the rise in prices of food items and the devaluation of the Tanzanian shilling against the US dollar.

On face value, the earnings appear high. However, the money is spent quickly because of the prohibitively high costs of food and other essentials. In 1989 in Dar es Salaam, a kilo of meat cost up to T Shs 300 whereas in the rural areas a kilo of meat sold for about T Shs 150. A loaf of bread sold at T Shs 70. The official price of a kilo of sugar was T Shs 100 but often the price was inflated to T Shs 200 on the black market because unscrupulous entrepreneurs created deliberate shortages so that they could earn more on high demand goods. Sugar is currently one of those essential foods that is subject to government control. Only those shops designated by the government, such as the National Milling Mobile Shops, sell at the official price. Despite control, the *walanguzi* (unscrupulous entrepreneurs) sell it at an inflated price. Given the fluctuating prices, most women are unable to save; earnings go to purchase the highly priced raw materials. Even if they could save, the absence of accessible banking facilities is a problem. Those women who are not engaged in brewing earn a living by selling cooked food at public places or practise in other types of petty trade.

The social and economic backgrounds of the brewers differ, including teachers and nurses in addition to peasant women. Those in wage employment who participated in the study confirmed that they earned more from brewing than from their salaries. Brewers in

Utengule Usangu are of all ages; women from the age of 16 onwards engage in this activity. Young girls learn the art of brewing from their mothers at an early age. When older, they brew independently to earn cash. For the younger women, cash earned is spent mainly on material goods such as fashionable clothes. With older women, money goes into sustaining their families and extended families. Cash is needed for clothes, school uniforms, fees, basic essentials such as salt, sugar, soap, kerosene and medicine, in addition to amounts for hiring farm labour, tractors or ox-ploughs and carts for the transportation of agricultural products. It is also needed to pay their poll tax or development levy. In most urban areas, only older women who are married, divorced or widows brew beer.

Women have worked out their own mechanism of production control by brewing in turns so as not to saturate the market. Controlling the supply on the market ensures equitable distribution of income from brewing among themselves. Brewing is a risky business; if the brew turns out to be bad, it is thrown away and the woman loses the costs and the potential income of the inputs. Quality of brew is important if it is to sell.

The amount of brewing activity varies from season to season. Soon after harvest there is more brewing activity than during cultivation and harvesting time. Grain, such as maize or millet, is in abundance during harvest time and there is also plenty of money in circulation after the sale of the crops. By November, brewing activity slows down as women are busy tilling the land in preparation for planting and weeding. For some women the brewing business continues but on a smaller scale, while others brew in order to harness labour for agricultural production.

Both men and women indulge in drinking beer, either in small groups or as individuals. Opening hours for *vilabu* (s. *kilabu*) (beer halls) are 3.00 p.m. to 10.00 p.m., Monday–Saturday, and from 10.00 a.m. to 10.00 p.m. on Sunday. The hours of *vilabu* are deliberately controlled by the village government so that the more productive morning hours are spent in agricultural production. Women must brew sufficient quantities of beer to keep circulation of money within the village; if they do not, then their husbands will spend money on beer in the next village.

Since brewing is a lucrative business, more men are engaging in this trade than ever before. Because men have the time and the resources, they buy beer wholesale from women and resell it at slightly higher prices. Normally two or three men team up and buy a

large quantity of beer from women at lower prices before it is taken to the beer clubs (*vikao*) (s. *kikao*). Then the men take the beer to small private rooms alongside the women's main beer club and sell it from there. Their pattern of selling is different, as all the men who wish to drink make a down payment as calculated by the businessmen. For example, a group of ten men may contribute T Shs 30 each for a 20 litre bucket of beer. The businessmen make a profit of T Shs 200, having bought the beer wholesale from the women at T Shs 100. In the end, the businessmen earn twice or three times more than the women. On the other hand, the idea of selling wholesale appeals to women, who are happy to be released from having to stay at the *vilabu* until the beer is sold out and so can spend the time on other chores. It is possible that women may be pushed out of actually selling beer and instead will remain at the periphery, enduring the drudgery of fetching wood and water and of coping with the practical aspects of brewing, while men assume the role of middlemen and control the beer trade.

Some women, however, have caught on to the new tactics that men are employing. They do not brew, but buy wholesale from fellow women and resell it to patrons in large quantities. In this way, they earn twice as much as they paid for the brew and have more time to carry out other household chores.

THE UTENGULE USANGU BEER PROJECT

This section will describe a case study of a women's co-operative venture in beer brewing, how they organized, what they achieved and the problems that they encountered in the process.

In 1969 a group of ten women came together and discussed the setting up of a beer club (Kilabu cha Akina Mama). The idea originated from some of the women who had accompanied their migrant husbands who worked on sisal estates in Tanga and Morogoro Regions. By setting up this co-operative venture the women were responding jointly to common problems which faced them within the community and the household. Their immediate goal was to generate enough money to buy a milling machine to ease the burden on themselves and other women of pounding grain. They also wanted to start a co-operative shop. The group thus began to organize and they elected a chairperson, secretary and treasurer. Any woman could join as long as she was willing to contribute labour for setting up a building, e.g. by collecting thatching grass and plastering walls. Each

member was also expected to contribute T Shs 2. Initially the women set up business under a tree. Business was good, especially between June and October when there was plenty of grain available and more money in circulation. There were many potential customers as well, such as the cattle owners and other traders who came monthly to sell their products. The money that was collected by the women from sales went into improving their premises. By 1970 the women had constructed a complete new building and business was thriving. They were even able to hire the services of a watchman and a sweeper whom they paid from the proceeds of beer sales. They built two latrines on the premises. The women held regular meetings to review progress on their activities and to receive and discuss the treasurer's financial report. At these meetings they also formulated guiding rules on how to run the club. The women were happy with the progress made. They had organizing capabilities and were a highly motivated group. Business began to pay off.

However, this state of affairs did not last for long. With success came problems. The women began experiencing interference from male parties who had vested interests in the activities of the group. One businessman in particular tried to bring about confusion in order to break up the group. For example, he spread false allegations against the treasurer by stating that she was misusing the group's funds for her own gain. Members began to distrust each other. The group was also subjected to a lot of pressure from the village group leaders. The women were asked from time to time to make financial contributions for village activities which needed financing. The group was politically vulnerable and any attempts to protest were quashed with threats to close down the club. On other occasions, a health officer would be called in to condemn the premises as unhygienic, with threats that the club would be closed down unless the women paid a fine; the women always paid the fine. Such tactics employed by men were eroding the group's enthusiasm. Their confidence was also being shattered. The women were made to feel as if they had no right to organize and that they ought to be grateful as the village government was doing them a favour. Ultimately the group began to disintegrate.

Finally, in 1972, the women were dispossessed of their club on the pretext of mismanagement. The village leaders used their power to appropriate property which legally belonged to the women. But the motivating force came from the businessman who colluded with the village leaders. The club was transferred to the businessman. He took

over from the women, without compensation, what they had collectively built up.

The women did not accept this takeover silently. They protested to the village government but received neither sympathy nor support, not surprising since the village government at that time comprised men only. Towards 1974, the businessman who had taken over the *kilabu* failed, in part because the women brewers organized collectively and resisted the takeover by deliberately refusing to supply him with beer. They still controlled the brewing because they made the beer in their homes. Instead of supplying beer to the man's business, they 'illegally' sold it in their homes or in other secluded places. The women thus reunited and gave each other moral support. The male drinkers too were supportive, as their allegiance lay with those who could supply them with the beer that they wanted. This silent and effective protest put the women back into business. In 1975 the *kilabu* was returned to them. Business began to flourish and by the end of 1976 they had managed to save enough money to buy a house from a farmer for T Shs 5,000. This was converted into a second *kilabu*. The women also paid for the renovations, building materials and two lamps.

The group was expanding; by 1976, there were about 40 members. Some women, especially those who brewed beer as a full time activity, became more successful than others. There were, however, organizational problems within the group. The treasurer and chairperson were frequently under attack for taking undemocratic decisions. They were accused of collaborating with the village leaders, since they made fiscal contributions to village activities without first consulting the group. Another of the organizational problems was the low level of training in book-keeping. Solidarity within the group began to deteriorate. In 1977, the village government called a meeting in the spirit of trying to assist the women to resolve their differences. The leaders advised the women to split into two groups and to share their assets. The group split into two and each group began to run its own *kilabu*. Later, each group elected its own office bearers.

The year 1978 was one of uncertainty for the women. The village leaders continued to harass them and to interfere with the groups' activities. One day, the two groups, who were summoned on short notice to a meeting organized by the village government, found themselves the centre of discussion. They were informed that the village government had decided to take over and run the two clubs

as a village project. The women were also informed that both the watchman and the sweeper would now be paid by the village government. Although the women protested, they were told that the decision was final and that there would be no compensation for the appropriated property. Not all of the men supported the takeover but those who sided with the women could not effect a change. After the meeting, the two treasurers were summoned individually to the village office and each was asked to surrender whatever cash was in her possession. One handed over T Shs 600 while the other surrendered T Shs 1,400 in cash and each relinquished the inventory of her group's assets. The assets were also appropriated. Although the main reason that was advanced for the takeover of the clubs was the need for the village to have an income-generating project, other reasons were cited by both men and women in the village. One such was that the economic independence that the women had achieved threatened the men. This did appear to be the major reason for the takeover, since, during informal discussions with the village leaders, this author was told: 'walikuwa wanaringa sana hao wanawake na hela zao (the women had become big-headed)!' The village government could have initiated a project of its own but it was more interested in this project because it was lucrative and well established.

Since 1978 the project has become the major source of income for the village. With this income the government is able to employ a full time clerk of accounts, watchmen, herdsmen and a shop assistant. The control of beer brewing was such a decisive issue because it was not only lucrative but also a source of regular income. There is very little chance that the women will ever regain their clubs. The women did attempt to raise the issue of the hijacking by the village government with an official of the Tanzanian Women's Organization (Umoja wa Wanawake wa Tanzania), who paid a one day official visit to different villages in the area. At a public meeting she confronted the village government on the issue, charging them with taking advantage of their privileged positions. She appealed to the village government to return the clubs to the women. However, there was no follow-up to her visit and the issue has remained unresolved.

Organized as a co-operative, the women achieved unity, acknowledged their ability to run an independent economic venture and were able to make collective democratic decisions. They also benefited by owning property. Most importantly, they achieved economic independence and stability and the ability to decide how to spend their money, which in many cases went to sustaining their families.

Economic independence also gave them confidence, although this confidence was ultimately regarded as a threat by the men, who thought that they were losing control over their wives. This was a problem particularly for those men who had no regular source of income of their own. Economic independence also meant that the women had taken up an extra burden to support their families. The consequence of takeover of the project by the village government was that the women were not able to realize their original goals of buying a milling machine and of opening a co-operative shop with a view to expanding their business.

Women continue to brew individually but now more and more men are entering the trade as middlemen. They buy the beer wholesale from the women at the low price of T Shs 300 for 90 litres of beer and set up their own businesses of *vikao*. Here they reap high profits, since whoever joins a *kikao* pays a fixed rate in order to be a member. These middlemen earn up to four times as much from one *debe* (20 litres) of beer. Some women are now going into wholesale buying and setting up of their own *vikao*.

CONCLUSIONS

Economic ventures which are undertaken by women have many things in common. The activities are normally marginalized and they lack recognition from policy makers and sometimes from community leaders in the allocation of resources, such as access to credit, loans and land, even though the success of these ventures contributes to the sustainment of the family. Lack of training in project management and basic book-keeping skills affects the continuity of a project. Similarly, the absence of banking facilities within walking distance affects women's ability to reinvest and so strengthen their economic capacity. At times, when women have entrusted money for safekeeping among themselves, to husbands or to the village government, they have found that the money has disappeared when they need it.

Poor leadership and lack of training in leadership skills and group management sometimes lead to mismanagement of resources, destruction of group dynamics, and vulnerability to manipulation by unscrupulous village leaders or other interested parties who may end up controlling the project or taking over from the women. Often, women's projects lack markets because women have no access to vital marketing information and marketing strategies or even to information on viable and profitable project ventures. This can also be linked

with the high rate of illiteracy and the low levels of education and technical know-how. It is also true that, in rural areas, projects are often imposed upon women's groups by donors without the donors first consulting the women to find out what the women's priorities are.

Inadequate legislation has also had adverse effects on women, in that no protection for women's economic groups is ensured. An example is the Tanzanian Co-operative Societies Act of 1982 which was enacted to provide for the formation, constitution, legislation and functioning of co-operative societies as instruments for implementing the policy of socialism and self-reliance. Sections 22 and 23 of the Act provide for the formation and recognition of only one co-operative society in a village. Women's economic groups, which are often not part of the village co-operative society, are therefore not covered under this Act, leading them to be placed at a disadvantage. Even when women's economic groups can form a branch of the main co-operative society in a village, they cannot function entirely under the control of women since the society falls within the jurisdiction of the village government which is dominated by men. The Co-operative Societies Act does not affect women's groups in urban areas where the independent formation of women's groups is not controlled by legislation. A review of this Act would be in order so as to allow for the formation of independent co-operative societies in the rural areas.

In order to understand more fully women's economic and political situation, it is necessary to analyse customary law and property rights and the implications that these have for the rights and full participation of women. It is common knowledge in Tanzania that the majority of women in both urban and rural communities are governed by customary law which is overwhelmingly used to male advantage. However, with increasing conscientization some women are becoming aware of their legal rights. For example, there have been cases where women have sought court decisions on child custody and maintenance, on marriage and divorce and the division of matrimonial property. One of the landmark cases in matrimonial property in the Tanzania Court of Appeal concerns Civil Appeal Case No. 9 of 1983, involving Hawa Mohamed and Ally Sefu (Dar es Salaam Registry, unreported). The High Court held that child care and housework which is done by a wife should be regarded as contribution and joint effort towards the acquisition of property.

In this ruling the High Court set a precedent by recognizing the contributions that a wife makes in the home for the well-being of the family. This decision could not have happened if Hawa had not

contested the division of property in court when the marriage broke down. What is also significant about this case is the recognition by some of the legal authorities that customary law has to change with time but that this can come about only if people, and especially women, initiate the changes that are required in collaboration with women's organizations, parliamentarians and the legal profession. Rutashobya (1988) has argued that:

> The customs and laws of our society can be changed to accord women the rights, respect and dignity which they rightly deserve if each one of us realizes that he or she has a duty to take part in building new social attitudes in which all people are regarded as of equal social worth so that the criteria for the allocation of private and public responsibilities is not sex but the individual's potential contribution.
>
> (Rutashobya 1988)

Various developments are taking place in Tanzania through the Law Review Commission. Among the laws being reviewed is the Law of Marriage Act No. 5 of 1971. Women have also expressed concern about the need to review the Customary Law Declaration Order No. 4 of 1963, the Employment (Amendment) Act No. 20 of 1975, the Income Tax Act No. 3 of 1973 and the Affiliation Ordinance Cap. 278 because 'provisions in these legislations deny women certain rights or adversely affect their interests' (Sinare 1988).

In addition to legal barriers, women's economic activities are often hampered by lack of adequate financial resources. There being no alternative, women tend to be satisfied with the little cash that they earn from an economic activity because of their pressing needs for cash to purchase the basic necessities. There is little scope for investment. Nevertheless, independent incomes give women a more self-sufficient stance in the family and it makes them more secure and less vulnerable to mistreatment by husbands.

The independence, security, confidence and self-respect that women achieve through economic activities sometimes have negative implications, since most men feel threatened because they do not like to lose their position of power in the family. Some men go to the extent of forbidding their wives from participating in economic ventures. Further, when women do achieve economic independence, men often retire from providing for the family and so the women are left with yet another burden of making ends meet to sustain the family while the men spend their income unilaterally on durable goods.

Within the context of the structural adjustment and economic recovery policies which have been introduced in Tanzania over the past decade, women's abilities to meet these responsibilities have been further strained. In these programmes, low priority has been given towards the allocation of resources which would otherwise raise the productive capacity of women. In addition, the low levels of education and of technical and managerial expertise of women and their lack of access to credit have meant that most women cannot own property or take up top management positions or similar jobs to enable them to exercise their capabilities in influencing decisions that affect their lives.

In the informal sector, women have found a venue through which they can interact and be exposed to political issues and economic practices. Participation in the informal sector has in turn contributed towards raising women's consciousness, as the case study on beer brewing in Utengule Usangu illustrates.

10

DEVELOPMENT FROM WITHIN AND SURVIVAL IN RURAL AFRICA

A synthesis of theory and practice

D.R.F. Taylor

INTRODUCTION

The purpose of this chapter is to draw on the empirical evidence that is presented in the case studies, together with other sources, and to attempt to point to new directions for both development theory and development practice in Africa. This linkage between theory and practice is important, although it was pointed out in the Preface that

> The validity of development approaches will not be determined as a result of theoretical and ideological debate, but in the realm of practice. The peasant families of Africa . . . are more likely to judge the validity of a strategy from its results rather than its ideological or methodological soundness.
>
> (Stöhr and Taylor 1981: 458)

Good practice must be based on an understanding of the theoretical underpinnings of the approach being used. Although difficult to define, 'development' is generally agreed to include a series of components such as increased economic growth, equity and distribution of the fruits of that growth, control of the population of its own destiny and the achievement of qualitative transcendental values. Development cannot be defined in purely quantitative terms and differs over both time and space. It is best defined in terms of the aspirations and values of people in their own social context and, in this sense, is probably only really meaningful at the sub-national scale.

214

THE CRISIS OF DEVELOPMENT IN AFRICA

Mackenzie analysed aspects of the major elements of crisis in Chapter 1. Although quantification at the macro level is fraught with difficulties, there is no doubt that at this level the quality of life for the majority of Africa's inhabitants has been declining in both absolute and relative terms. For many parts of Africa there is no compelling evidence that 'development', however defined, is taking place. Increasing degradation would be a better description than 'development' for the current trends. Adebayo Adedeji (1989: 33), the Secretary-General of the Economic Commission for Africa, has outlined the major features of this debilitating crisis which he sees as having three major manifestations:

(a) A deterioration in the main macroeconomic indicators;
(b) A disintegration of productive mechanisms and infrastructural facilities;
(c) An accelerating decline in social welfare.

To this list could be added an increasing deterioration of the physical environment. The figures that he quotes are disturbing, to say the least. Between 1980 and 1988, per capita income for Africa as a whole fell steadily by 2.6 per cent per annum and wage employment fell by 16 per cent. GDP per capita in 1978 was US$ 854; by 1988 it was US$ 565. In 1978 the per capita growth rate was 3.03 per cent; in 1988, it was – 0.88 per cent. Growth rates in all sectors are dropping and Africa's inflation rates are rising. The debt burden has risen from US$ 48.3 billion in 1978 to over US$ 230 billion in 1988 and debt servicing obligations now exceed 100 per cent of export earnings in several African countries. The scale of the debt servicing problem has reached such a level that, despite Official Development Assistance (ODA) flows, there is a net flow of capital from developing to developed countries in many instances. The terms of trade have continued to deteriorate, resulting in an annual loss of approximately 10 per cent of export earnings. Adedeji's comment is that:

> The cumulative toll of this unremitting decline for a whole decade on our society is clear and unmistakable. The number of countries classified as least developed among the developing world – the wretched of the earth as they have been categorized – increased from 17 in 1978 to 28 in 1988. And more, I regret to say, are knocking at the door to join. Whereas in 1960 Africa had 124 million illiterates, in 1985 the illiterate population had

increased to 162 million, almost one-fifth of all the illiterate females in the world are in Africa.

(Adedeji 1989: 11)

Equally disturbing was the situation that was revealed by the UNICEF report, *The state of the world's children*, which was released in December 1988. It showed that the impressive gains that had been made in education and health in many African countries, which appear in the ECA socioeconomic indicators (UNECA 1987), have in recent years been seriously eroded.

> For almost 900 million people, approximately one-sixth of mankind, the march of human progress has now become a retreat. In many nations, development is being thrown into reverse. And after decades of steady economic advance large areas of the world are sliding back into poverty. Throughout most of Africa and much of Latin America average incomes have fallen by 10 to 25 per cent in the 1980s . . . In the 37 poorest nations, spending per head on health has been reduced by 50 per cent and on education by 25 per cent over the last few years. In almost half of the 103 developing countries for which recent data are available, the proportion of six- to eleven-year-olds enrolled in primary school is falling . . . The slowing down of progress and the reversal of hard won gains is spreading hardship and human misery on a scale and of a severity unprecedented in the postwar era . . . For most of the countries of Africa, Latin America and the Caribbean almost every economic signal points to the fact that development has been derailed. Per capita GNP has fallen, debt repayments have risen to a quarter or more of all export earnings, share in world trade has dropped and productivity of labour has declined.
>
> (UNICEF 1988: 1)

There is academic debate over the nature and cause of the crisis and some have even questioned the validity of the use of that term. In agriculture it is not clear, for example, if the crisis is one of production, since 'performance failures might easily be attributed to consumption, environmental or distribution crises' (Watts 1986: 377). Colin Leys (1987) argues that per capita food production in Africa may not have declined, despite World Bank (1990) estimates to the contrary, and that what we are seeing is a decline in food exports. This argument can be taken as an indicator that rural people, who are

faced with a variety of problems including inadequate pricing and marketing arrangements, choose to consume agricultural surpluses rather than market them, leading to a situation where production statistics, which are usually of marketed food, go down while the per capita food production remains stable or even goes up, at least in the rural areas.

It is also evident that there are enormous regional variations in the nature and impact of the crisis both among and within African countries, but on balance there seems little doubt that rural poverty is on the increase and that the use of the word 'crisis' is fully justified. There is certainly little evidence from the case studies that, at the local level, Leys' arguments are valid.

The ECA year-end report for 1988 (Economic Commission for Africa 1990) reported a doubling of growth rate for 1988 to 2.5 per cent but this was more than offset by population growth of 3 per cent and the prognosis was that living standards would continue to decline in 1989. Adebayo Adedeji comments that: 'Even this cheerless forecast may turn out to be optimistic if the main underlying assumption with respect to (favourable) weather conditions were to turn out to be misplaced' (Adedeji 1989: 10).

THE CAUSES OF THE DEVELOPMENT CRISIS IN AFRICA

There is no simple explanation for the current state of affairs, since a complex set of external, internal and environmental factors are involved. These are, of course, closely interlinked and no one factor operates in isolation. Recently much attention in the development studies literature has been focused on the role of African states. At the 1987 UNCRD/IDS Nairobi seminar, Ngumbu Mussa-Nda argued:

> The development strategies followed by African countries during the two to three decades of their political independence has gradually led the continent into its present destitution . . . Worse still, all plans designed by those concerned with development, whether social or economic, indicated that without exception, the present policies, plans and strategies are incapable of bringing about any growth recovery in the foreseeable future.
>
> (Mussa-Nda 1988: 3)

The distinguished African geographer Akin Mabogunje later argued in a similar vien. 'It is, however, generally agreed that the false start

in all African countries has been due largely to the high level of governmental and bureaucratic domination of the economy with its consequences of inefficiency, profligacy and inappropriate control' (Mabogunje 1988: 25). These are not exactly moderate statements and, as one author comments, the African state is under attack 'from left, right and centre' (Beckman 1988: 26), which has led to a serious questioning, both within Africa and without, of the role of the state in formulating and implementing policies to alleviate the current crisis. Brett sums up the situation as follows:

> State structures in the Third World are widely regarded as rigid, inefficient, overstaffed and corrupt – systematically exploiting their privileged status to provide minimal services to the public and extract monopoly rents from their clients, while conducting their business in secret to defend their activities from public scrutiny and control. So extreme is the condemnation that fundamental restructuring is usually part of the adjustment programmes introduced by the International Monetary Fund (IMF) or World Bank (WB) where the remedy is often not just the reform of existing structures but privatisation and the enforcement of control by 'market forces'.
>
> (Brett 1988: 4)

Both Brett and Beckman feel that this has gone too far, with Brett insisting 'that the role of the state must remain central in any effective development strategy' (Brett 1988: 4), and Beckman pointing towards the resilience of the post-colonial state:

> The post-colonial state is unlikely to disintegrate through some downward spiral of decay . . . Increasingly sophisticated local ruling classes are busy looking after their own houses as well as their own national development projects. In this, they are prodded, supervised, trained and financed by transnational state organs and foreign aid agencies who have their own stake.
>
> (Beckman 1988: 31)

The role of the state is obviously of critical importance to development from within and consequently will be considered in more detail later in the chapter but, before doing so, some of the external factors influencing the current development situation will be discussed.

Dame Judith Hart, quoted within Oakley 1988, draws attention to some of the more obvious linkages between external factors and the

ability of African states to tackle the challenges of rural poverty. She identified five areas of concern:

1 The collapse of commodity prices, leading to a substantial decrease in funds available to developing countries to finance development. She also pointed out that, given the elasticity of demand for certain commodities, the free market system is weighted against the rural poor. The ECA reported a further decline in commodity prices for 1988 (Economic Commission for Africa 1990) and the value of exports fell 2 per cent from US\$ 51.4 billion in 1987 to US\$ 50.3 billion in 1988. Imports were little changed at US\$ 60.4 billion.

2 The adverse effects of the agricultural policies of industrialized nations which have become increasingly protectionist especially against processed agricultural goods. The EEC policies on self-sufficiency in sugar, for example, have had very negative results for sugar producers. The impasse over agricultural policies at the Montreal meetings of GATT in December 1988 has made matters even worse.

3 The combination of poor commodity prices, the debt-servicing burden, the high price of imports and the impact of the various oil stocks has resulted in a lack of financial resources to tackle poverty and a shortage of foreign exchange.

4 A decrease in real terms of net transfers of ODA. Although there was some improvement in 1988, this was more than offset by the complete drying up of new commercial loans and by the heavy weight of debt re-servicing. Adedeji comments: 'An increasing number of countries are merely deferring the debt-service problem into an uncertain future' (Adedeji 1989: 10).

5 The debt crisis that has forced governments to accept IMF structural adjustment policies which, she argued, have four main elements: a cut in wages, control of the money supply, devaluation, and a cut in public expenditure. As she pointed out:

The implication of this 'adjustment' is *nil or negative growth*. Third World countries are increasingly unable to provide the services for rural development and have also been obliged to cut subsidies for basic foodstuffs; all of which has an immediate effect on the rural poor. In Sri Lanka and Zambia, for example, the IMF *obliged* the Governments to cut subsidies which directly benefited the rural poor. In effect the IMF policies ask the rural

poor to 'enjoy an even greater poverty' and have also been a direct cause of political destabilisation.

(Hart quoted in Oakley 1988: 23)

In the same month as the publication of the UNICEF study, *The state of the world's children*, the OECD released its half-yearly report (OECD 1988). The contrast between them was striking. The OECD report showed an annual growth rate in excess of 4 per cent for member nations. The leading non-Communist industrial economies were reported to be at their 'most buoyant since the early 1970s' and 'The brisk expansion has been widespread. Investment in industry has been growing especially fast' (OECD 1988: 3). The major problems which were identified were growing protectionism and the imbalance among the major industrial trading blocs. Little mention was made of the impact of the policies which have led to this resurgence of growth of the economies of developing nations yet UNICEF observes that the crisis in developing nations 'is happening not because of any one visible cause but because of an unfolding economic drama in which the industrialized nations play a leading role' (UNICEF 1988: 1).

It is important when considering the context for development from below in Africa to examine the relationships which exist at various scales as well as the major actors involved and the relationships among them.

Regardless of which actors are involved in the struggle for development in Africa or at which scale the development problematique is considered, the influence of environmental factors looms large. By far the most significant factor is rainfall. The dynamics of Africa's climatic patterns are complex and by no means completely understood. There is also a tremendous variety and variability of climatic factors which makes the concept of mean annual rainfall almost meaningless in the African context. Three facets of rainfall must be considered: seasonality, reliability and rainfall type. Seasonality is perhaps the best known of these facets. Much of intertropical Africa has a single rainy season although areas closer to the equator have two. In the latter case, the second or 'short rains' period is much more variable and much less reliable than the first or 'long rains' period. Variability and lack of reliability are a feature of Africa's rainfall regimes. Even in areas of high mean annual rainfall, the possibility of drought in at least one year in ten is high. As mean annual rainfall totals decrease, the incidence and impact of droughts become even greater. The droughts of the 1980s, which are mentioned

in several chapters of this book, are by no means unique. Their dramatic economic and social impact puts great strains on the coping mechanisms of African societies and drought has played a major role in causing the crisis that is facing many of Africa's peoples. Variability can range up to 100 per cent of the mean for many regions of Africa, which signifies that a recurring problem is not only drought but also too much rainfall in some years.

Much of the rain tends also to fall in very intense showers, with 100–200 millimetres of rain in a matter of a few hours being not at all unusual. For agricultural purposes this type of rainfall poses problems of rapid run-off and soil erosion.

Most of the soils of intertropical Africa are not very fertile, with a high percentage of lateritic soils which rapidly lose their fertility when cleared of indigenous vegetation.

The African environment is difficult for both agricultural and pastoral peoples and, as it comes under increasing population and production pressure, the difficulties increase.

The impact on agricultural production is direct but what is often forgotten is that the availability of water is critical for all economic activity. Many industries use water more intensively than agriculture. The nature of Africa's physiography and topography makes both access to ground water sources and the use of irrigation difficult and expensive, and so the economic dependence on rainfall becomes even greater.

Both the external and internal factors that have been discussed as causes of the crises facing Africa are probably of less consequence than the impact of Africa's weather and climatic patterns over the last decade.

THE INADEQUACIES OF PAST THEORY AND PRACTICE

Robert Chambers (1989b) argues that 'Historically, the fashions for ideologies, packages and programmes in rural development have changed' and he claims that this is a reflection of changing conditions:

> The lesson is to see ideology and action in context, not as constants, but as arising from and adapting to, as well as moulding, these conditions. In this view they are always likely to be out-of-date, always requiring an imaginative effort to be ahead of current convention.

> (Chambers 1989b: 1–2)

221

He discusses in detail the inadequacies of both the neo-Fabian approaches of the 1970s, which are categorized through redistribution with growth, and the neo-liberal approaches of the 1980s which emphasize structural adjustment and market forces.

A major inadequacy of both approaches has been that they have given inadequate attention to the realities at the local level.

> Both ideologies, and both sets of prescriptions, embody a planner's core, centre-outwards, top-down view of rural development. They start with economics, not people; with the macro not the micro; with the view from the office not the view from the field. And, in consequence their prescriptions tend to be uniform, standard and for universal application.
>
> (Chambers 1989b: 6)

It could also be added that both approaches have so far failed to bring about the results that were expected of them and that African governments which have pursued them have met with little success. It can be argued that any macro-level solution to development in Africa, regardless of its theoretical or ideological perspective, has severe limitations and nowhere are these limitations more obvious than at the micro scale of the African local community, as the case studies in this book amply illustrate. Chambers argues for 'a counter-ideology of reversals' where development theory and practice are driven by 'putting first the priorities of those who are few and peripheral' (Chambers 1989b: 9). Both development 'from below' as originally conceptualized and development 'from within' are such strategies. The general solutions and explanations that are so common in development theory and practice must be complemented by not only an awareness of the need for diversity and specificity but also a recognition that the diversity is critical. 'For some professionals, development is still, consciously or unconsciously, seen as convergent; in the paradigm of reversals, development is decentralized and divergent' (Chambers 1989b: 19).

It is only 'by becoming more complex and diverse that ecosystems and livelihood strategies become more stable and more sustainable. Near the core of this paradigm is decentralised process and choice' (Chambers 1989b: 20). If meaningful development is to occur, it must be defined, motivated and controlled to a much greater degree than at present by the local population itself. The rationale for local initiatives is so compelling that the two major questions are: how can effectiveness be improved and how can they be made more central to

development theory and practice? Following what Chambers (1988) calls a complete reversal of normal bureaucratic procedures, development needs to be turned on its head and to be viewed in a radical way. The word 'radical' is used here in the original meaning of the word, namely, to look at development from its roots. To use a biological analogy which is appropriate to Africa, that part of a maize plant which we do not see, the root system, is much more extensive and complex than that which we do see. Local initiatives and participation have become the imperative of the development decade of the 1990s.

THE CASE FOR LOCAL INITIATIVES

In February 1989 an international seminar was held in Arusha, Tanzania in which four of the authors of this book, Zinyama, Ondiege, Ndaro and Taylor, participated. The theme of the seminar was 'Reviving Local Self-Reliance: Challenges for Rural/Regional Development in Eastern and Southern Africa' and it was jointly sponsored by the United Nations Centre for Regional Development (UNCRD) and the Centre on Integrated Rural Development for Africa (CIRDAFRICA). Many of the ideas in this chapter are built on the opening paper of that seminar, 'Why local initiatives in Africa?: the context and rationale' (Taylor 1989). Seven major arguments were advanced about the necessity for local initiatives and these can be summarized as follows.

1 In the current state of crisis in Africa, local-level initiatives are necessary for survival.
2 African governments, either by choice or by necessity, are unable to provide adequate development services and local people cannot depend on the state to provide them with sufficient means to improve their quality of life.
3 There are unutilized or underutilized resources available at the local scale, including financial resources, which could be mobilized for development purposes.
4 The enormous diversity in rural Africa in economic, ecological, sociological and political terms is such that development can be effectively addressed only at the local level. Chambers captures this well:

Local diversity has many social and ecological dimensions, both within and between areas. Social diversity has many aspects –
ethnic, cultural, economic (concerning wealth, poverty and

access to and control over resources), educational, occupational, gender and age among others . . . Then there are many forms of ecological diversity . . . Differences of soil, slope, vegetation, multiple canopies of plants, multiple tree–crop–livestock interactions, and the number of species exploited, can be mind-blowing. And finally there is diversity which is regularly seasonal and irregular in interannual variation. Nor is this all. Social and ecological diversities interlock and multiply variance. It is easy, once one starts seeing and thinking this way, to regard each place and social group as unique, requiring its own path for development.

(Chambers 1988: 51–2)

5 Economically sound 'sustainable development', as emphasized by the Brundtland Report (World Commission on Environment and Development 1987), has unique meaning at the local level. In terms of the physical environment, it is at the local scale in Africa where environmental degradation or preservation is most likely to occur. Environmental degradation by Africa's rural people is not an act which is bred out of ignorance and greed, as suggested by some authorities, but more often is a result of desperation and the need to survive. Local people have a very special interest in the sustainability of any development initiative. External actors often define policies and impose these by a variety of means on local people. It is the local people who have to live with the results and their caution in adopting new policies is often more than justified.

6 Central planning has inherent weaknesses and the need for decentralization and devolution is paramount not only in Africa but in many other countries, both 'developed' and 'developing' and both capitalist and socialist.

7 Indigenously based knowledge has a major contribution to make to the development process and this local knowledge is effectively found at the local scale.

The importance of local initiatives should not be romanticized. As Mackenzie argues in Chapter 1, the situation is highly complex and a central question is whether grass-roots initiatives are truly strategic in intent and lead to sustainable development action or are merely survival strategies to cope with crisis. Both neo-Fabians and neo-liberals have adopted with enthusiasm the rhetoric of local participation but primarily as an extension and modification of the central premises underlying both paradigms. The answer to some of these

questions lies in the evidence from detailed case studies, such as those in this volume, and it is to them that this chapter now turns.

DEVELOPMENT AND SURVIVAL: THE EMPIRICAL EVIDENCE

Chambers has argued that, in order to understand local realities, it is necessary

> Through local study and individual cases . . . [to] show how varied is that universe of vulnerability and poverty for which we seek simple explanations and single solutions . . . the lesson for the future is to enquire and question, doubting what we think we know and learning from and with those who are vulnerable and poor . . . and to do this, not in one locality, and not for one group only but again and again, in each place and for each sort of person. For that is the surest path to better understanding and to action that will better fit and serve the diversity of conditions and people and their changing priorities and needs.
>
> (Chambers 1989a: 7)

The eight case studies in this book contribute to the empirical base that is required to improve our understanding at the local level.

The case study by Zinyama of local farmer organizations in Zimbabwe is interesting. Zinyama argues that, in Zimbabwe, the government is not retreating but is supportive of local initiatives and that it is therefore not appropriate to consider such initiatives as reactions to the withdrawal of the State from rural areas. Local-level participation has been facilitated by the democratization of local government, a point which is also emphasized by Olowu (1989). Zimbabwe has experienced remarkable production increases in the small-farmer sector since independence in 1980, but these mask both spatial inequalities and intra-community differences of age, gender and status.

> The benefits from the new rural development thrust are largely accruing to the small number of peasant farmers who are fortunate enough to be located within the better agro-ecological regions. Elsewhere, farmers continue to be handicapped by the constant threat of drought and food shortages, by increasing land shortages, by infertile soils and by low agricultural production.
>
> (Zinyama, Ch. 2: 43)

He reminds us that the variability of the African physical environment is a major factor and that the relative impact of any policy or institutional intervention depends very much on the agro-ecological conditions of the area concerned.

Zinyama looks at the history of various forms of local organizations in two communal areas south of the capital city of Harare, including mutual-help groups, farmer training groups, agricultural marketing groups and voluntary savings or thrift clubs. These have achieved considerable success, which Zinyama argues is due to two major factors: the complementarity between the efforts of the State and those of the rural population itself; and the fact that, especially for the Master Farmer clubs, the groups have voluntary membership, self-government and peer control. Voluntary savings clubs have the additional advantage that, in the event of crop failure, farmers purchase inputs out of their own savings rather than through loans.

The evidence from this case study suggests that in Zimbabwe grass-roots initiatives are truly 'strategic in intent' (MacKenzie, Chapter 1) and are much more than simply a means of coping with crisis.

The three case studies from Ghana are quite different from each other and illustrate the diversity at the local level that was outlined earlier in this chapter. George Dei, using participant observation techniques, outlines the adaptive responses of the people of Ayirebi in South-eastern Ghana not only to local food supply cycles but also to a national economic crisis of the 1980s which was triggered by world recession and was aggravated by drought, bush fires and an unexpected influx of Ghanaian deportees from Nigeria which led to a 7 per cent increase of population in the town.

The community managed to cope in a truly remarkable way in the circumstances and Dei's evidence suggests that, despite community differentiation, the community reacted as a group to the crisis facing them. He talks of 'a remarkable degree of co-operation between genders' (Dei, Ch. 3: 73) and of communal cultivation of new land in the form of co-operative farms. Richer farmers who had food surpluses were persuaded by community pressure to offer these at reasonable prices to the poorer members of the Ayirebi community first before attempting to sell elsewhere.

The local explanation for the crisis is also interesting. The people are reported to have seen this as owing 'to the breakdown of respect for customs, including one's obligation to kin and neighbours' and to have explained the drought as 'punishment from the gods and ancestors in order to make the living aware of their neglect of adaptive

customary behaviour and of the need to live harmoniously in the community' (Dei, Ch. 3: 73–4).

Residents of Ayirebi who had migrated to the cities and other regions of Ghana also increased their remittances in both cash and kind to help the community in its time of need.

This case study lends support to the continuance of the 'organic African community' which appears to have been strengthened rather than weakened by crisis. Mackenzie argues in Chapter 1 that it is a mistake to 'mythologize' undifferentiated local communities where the interests of all 'are served through subscription to community development efforts' (Mackenzie, Ch. 1: 27). Although Ayirebi is not an undifferentiated community it appears to have responded to crisis as a community. Whether this is a coping mechanism in the face of crisis which is unlikely to be maintained or a continuing strategy which can lead to sustainable development remains to be seen. The community appears to be meeting its basic needs and has taken steps to increase equity and redistribution. It also appears to have taken cognizance of the qualitative transcendental values which it was argued earlier are an element in defining development. Ayirebi does not appear to be challenging the interests of those in power at the State level but is in fact using the organizational mechanisms of the State, such as the Committee for the Defence of the Revolution and the Town Development Committee, for its own ends. This is a political act but of a different kind from those which are usually thought of as leading to local empowerment. The Ayirebi case does contain the 'latent seeds for multiple new developmental actions' (Goulet 1989: 167) but these would appear to be limited in scope. Dei calls for the State to revise its views on an externally focused, export-led strategy and to build 'thriving, self-reliant, self-sustainable local and regional communities in contemporary Africa' (Dei Ch. 3: 75).

The other two case studies from Ghana lend no support to the existence of an undifferentiated 'organic' community and show evidence of considerable tensions and conflict at the community level.

Songsore analyses the history of the co-operative credit union movement in North-West Ghana, an area which he describes as 'the worst pocket of extreme poverty in Ghana' (Songsore, Ch. 4: 84). Although the co-operative credit movement is an innovation which was introduced by a Canadian Catholic priest, it builds on traditional rotating credit institutions known as 'susu'. The formal banking system has little interest in this poor region which has been hit very hard by the negative impact of the Structural Adjustment Programme

that was introduced at the urging of the World Bank. As the area is ecologically unsuited to the growing of cocoa, it has benefited little from the export-led development strategy which has concentrated resources on the cocoa growing areas of southern Ghana. The inter-regional barter terms of trade have shifted against the rural people of this region and the introduction of user charges has hit social pro-grammes, such as health and education, very hard. Women and children in particular have suffered. To the disadvantaged people of this disadvantaged region, the suggestion that the Structural Adjust-ment Programme is 'succeeding' in Ghana is a travesty of the truth. It is making an already difficult situation much worse.

In these circumstances, credit could be an important tool and the aim of the Co-operative Credit Movement was 'to serve as a focal point for the endogenous, grass-roots mobilization of local resources for local development within the limits set by the national and inter-national system' (Songsore, Ch. 4: 85). Songsore's analysis shows how an institution which was originally established to protect the poor was gradually taken over by members of the local dominant classes. 'Credit unions, by supporting investments in the productive base of the regional economy, have been vital instruments in rural develop-ment' but when, in the 1970s, the Catholic Church withdrew its priests as treasurers the replacement treasurers 'soon became pawns in the hands of local notables' (Songsore, Ch. 4: 94). The result was a crisis in confidence in the co-operative credit movement and an increase in corruption and misuse of funds. Active membership dropped from 25,830 in 1983/4 to 16,290 in 1986 and loan defaults increased in scale. The major defaulters were the 'big men'. 'Poor peasants, rural women and workers are rarely mentioned, if at all, among the list of loan defaulters' (Songsore, Ch. 4: 95) Songsore argues that the Co-operative Credit Union can be of real value but it must be reformed: 'recapitalizing and redirecting the credit unions towards the genuine developmental aspirations of the rank and file membership, especially women' (Songsore, Ch. 4: 85).

This has already begun by a combination of both local and outside action. The Canadian Co-operative Association and the Co-operative Credit Unions Association of Ghana have formed a new alliance to help to revive peasant control of the co-operative credit union in North-West Ghana and to recapitalize the movement. In some areas the peasants have taken action in their own hands.

In Nandom the situation was so grave that peasants in a fit of anger and protest literally drove off the treasurer and some other committee members . . . From the mess has emerged a farmers' co-operative credit union, the Kuob-Lantaa Credit Union. The peasants have refused to admit any literates into the new union, since the literate 'elite' were blamed for the frauds in the Nandom Credit Union.

(Songsore, Ch. 4: 97)

Development from within in North-West Ghana will have to come through strategies of revival and peasant control which are based on women, who are in the majority in the region. Such strategies may not be possible without outside help and support from non-government organizations.

Takyiwaa Manuh's study of the salt co-operatives of Ada District lends support to the argument made by Mackenzie that 'To call for the "empowerment" of local people is to challenge social structure. Profoundly, one is dealing with "politics" not "policies", with "struggle" and not "strategy" ' (Mackenzie, Ch. 1: 1). Manuh argues that 'it is clear that, for most rural dwellers, survival and the little development that has come their way have largely resulted from their own efforts' and that the salt co-operatives are 'an instrument of struggle and a coping strategy of rural people, in the face of dispossession by powerful capitalist interests and state neglect' (Manuh, Ch. 5: 103).

In the 1970s, two private companies were given leases to win salt from the lagoon, thus replacing traditional groups. The area of the lagoon that was left for the Ada Traditional Council was not suitable for both ecological and religious reasons. The locals formed the Ada Songor Salt Miners' Co-operative Society to act as a focus in their struggle to regain their rights. It is interesting that they utilized the form and regulations of other co-operatives in Ghana and that they operate under licence from the Department of Co-operatives like other societies but that they are quite different in both form and function.

The main protagonists are Vacuum Salts Limited, which is owned and managed by a powerful Ghanaian family, the Appentengs, and the local peasant communities living around the lagoon. The Central State has been equivocal in this struggle, orginally allowing a takeover of Vacuum Salts and then restoring it to the Appenteng family. When the Co-operative began to show success, the State

was quick to impose new taxes on their salt production both cent-
rally and through its local agents, the District Council. The Ada
Traditional Council, which is controlled by the Chiefs, appears to
have allied itself with the District Council and is also extracting levies.
The main spokesperson for the local community, the president of the
Ada Songor Salt Miners' Co-operative Society who is also a State
Assemblyman, was dismissed from office by government in July
1989.

It would seem that local people face repression when they become
too vocal in their demands for control of their own destiny and confront the State and its allies. It is likely that local initiatives in such
circumstances will face sustained conflict. It is also clear that traditional structures, such as the Ada Traditional Council, do not always
act in what local communities perceive to be their best interests.
Communities such as Ayirebi appear to be 'invisible' to the State and
do not appear to threaten its interests. The communities around the
Songor Lagoon are a very different matter.

The case study of Machakos District in Kenya by Ondiege is very
much a planner's perspective of local initiatives. He argues for 'an
enabling environment that will allow the participation of local rural
people in conceptualizing, implementing and managing their
development programmes' (Ondiege, Ch. 6: 127). In Kenya the
State is clearly trying to incorporate local initiatives into its planning
strategy and local initiatives are seen as an extension of this strategy.
There is no doubt that mobilization is taking place, with 96 Self-help
and 249 Women's groups in the District together with a number of
Co-operative Societies, but it is not clear if these are a reflection of the
people's perspectives of development priorities or those of the
government.

It is possible that there is a convergence of these two perspectives
especially in the field of income-generating activities. The budget
figures show a high degree of dependence on external funding. In
1986–7, out of a budget of 3.8 million Kenya Shillings for these
activities, a full 3.6 million came from foreign aid agencies and non-
government organizations with only 155,387 shillings from central
government and 64,370 shillings from Machakos District Council.
This lends credence to the view that this form of local development is
the 'cheap "development platform" (to paraphrase Watts, 1989: 6)'
referred to by Mackenzie at the beginning of Chapter 1. On the other
hand, it can be argued that it is in the best interests of the
people of Machakos to participate in these local initiatives, since,

regardless of who initiates them, the benefits accrue to the participants.

The second Kenya case study by Noel Chavangi describes a special programme of the Ministry of Energy to persuade farmers to plant fuelwood, which is a critical input for development in rural Kenya. The Kenya Woodfuel Development Programme is supported by the Swedish International Development Agency. Again, the initiative is clearly an extension of government development policy but an innovative attempt is being made to involve local communities in project identification and design and to incorporate indigenous expertise and practice which is acceptable and appropriate to each cultural setting. The objective is to increase woodfuel production both for self-consumption and for the market and here it appears that the government, in developing its programmes, is making a genuine attempt to listen regarding the realities facing the farmers of Kakamega District. The project is, for example, making a special effort to involve women, who will be major beneficiaries, and is using techniques such as popular theatre to expose issues such as gender relationships which are involved. The main barriers to increased fuelwood production are not lack of knowledge or technical in nature but are sociocultural. Here there has been at least some of the 'bureaucratic reversal' that was called for by Chambers (1988), but the case study is one of mobilization by government rather than local initiatives from the people. The pragmatic view would be that if it increases the supply of much needed fuelwood, which meets local needs, then the form and context of participation are of less concern. If government perceptions of development priorities and those of local people coincide then conflict is unlikely. However, there is an interesting contrast between the government's use of popular theatre in the case of the Kenya Woodfuel Development Programme and its repression of the Kamiriithu Community Education and Cultural Centre, which used the same technique to attack government (referred to by Mackenzie, Ch. 1: 29–30). Once again, if development from within confronts the State in a direct challenge, it is likely to be repressed.

Japheth Ndaro, in discussing local coping strategies in Dodoma District in Tanzania, also takes the view that local initiatives which are not part of the government's plans are likely to remain marginal to the development process. He argues that there have been three phases of local coping strategies since Tanzania attained independence. In the first phase, which he suggests concluded in 1970, the

people in Dodoma District devised local coping strategies which did not fit the government's plans. These involved trade, crafts, industries, the building of small dams and the bringing of new land under cultivation, as opposed to schools, dispensaries and roads which is what the government wanted. Ndaro sees these as 'survival' as opposed to 'development' strategies but it could equally well be argued that the people's preferences did not fit the top-down model of development being promulgated by the government. In the second phase, from 1971 to 1978, villagization was the key factor. During the third phase, which is post-1979, Ndaro argues that the government has stifled rather than encouraged local initiatives. The range of strategies that is described for Dodoma is impressive and people seem to be finding ways to survive in difficult circumstances but at issue is whether these can be sustained over time and how meaningful they are in the current Tanzanian context.

Alice Nkhoma-Wamunza's case study of the women brewers of Utengule Usangu village in the Mbeya Region of Tanzania is an example of how women organized to improve their economic welfare and to retain a greater degree of control of the fruits of their own labours. She illustrates the struggle that women have in a male-dominated society and how, in the long run, their initiatives were taken over by a male-dominated 'community' in the name of the welfare of the wider community and to the detriment of the women of that community. A promising development from within initiative was stifled not because the women threatened state power but because they confronted male hegemony at the village level.

The empirical evidence that is presented in these case studies is both rich and valuable and complements a number of other similar studies by African authors, which will be used to consider the central theme of this chapter which is to point to new directions for development theory and practice. These include studies on Tanzania by Mbilinyi (1989), Kapinga (1989), Ndara and Temu (1989), and Maro (1990); studies on Kenya by Mbugua (1989), Kobiah (1985) and Imoo and Louse (1988); studies on Zambia by Chileshe (1989) and Kalapula (1989); studies on Zimbabwe by Macebo (1988) and Zinyama (1989); a study on Uganda by Ouma (1989); and a study on Ethiopia by Asgele (1989).

DEVELOPMENT FROM WITHIN: KEY COMPONENTS AND PROSPECTS FOR SUCCESS

Development from below revisited

Development 'from within' is based on the concepts of 'development from below', as outlined in *Development from above or below?: the dialectics of regional planning in developing countries* (Stöhr and Taylor 1981). It is perhaps useful to revisit some of the ideas of 'development from below' before considering 'development from within'. Although new in the context of its time, the concept had its roots in the populist ideas of the nineteenth and early twentieth centuries. A number of books advocating broadly similar or related issues appeared about the same time. These included: *Territory and function: the evolution of regional planning* (Friedmann and Weaver 1979), *Self-reliance, a strategy for development* (Galtung *et al.* 1980) and *Alternative Raumpolitik* (Naschold 1978) in German.

Development from below was primarily developed in a 'Third World' context and grew out of a synthesis of a number of different ideas which were broadly related to the emerging number of 'alternative development' strategies. It was influenced by a re-examination of populist and anarchist thought of the nineteenth century, allied to the major contribution of thinkers such as Julius Nyerere and Mahatma Gandhi. Development from below was also strongly influenced by dependency theory and by the concept of an ecologically sound development as advocated by Sacks and his colleagues. Shumacher's concept of 'small is beautiful' and appropriate technology also played a part. The concept of development from below saw development as an essentially indigenous process in which concepts of self-reliance and popular participation loom large. Development from below was based on the maximum mobilization of each area's natural, human and institutional resources, with the primary objective being the satisfaction of the needs of the inhabitants of that area. The dominant building block was the rural, territorially based community at the smallest scale that is efficient and effective. The strategy was basic needs oriented, labour intensive, ecologically sensitive, regional resource based, rural centred and argued for the use of appropriate rather than highest technology.

The concept has now been adopted in rhetorical terms and the slogan 'development from below' has entered the jargon of regional and development planners at all levels. However, there is a lack of specificity of what constitutes 'development from below' and a wide

233

variety of interpretations is given by those involved in dealing with it. Some of these bear little resemblance to the original paradigm and many are in fact antithetical to the original concept.

The original concept was criticized from a number of perspectives. It was argued that there were three major shortcomings: inadequate specification of the theoretical underpinnings of development from below; failure to specify the necessary and sufficient conditions in which development from below could emerge; and failure to add an adequate theory of explanation to what in essence was a theory of policy.

There was also another strand of criticism which did not appear in the literature but was nevertheless very real. Considerable scepticism was expressed by some indigenous planners who said that development from below and concomitant ideas, such as agropolitan development, were just one more example of theories and prescriptions which are developed in the North being applied to the South. It was argued that development from below, before it could possibly be taken seriously, would have to be applied to the industrial nations of the North. There was a suspicion that what was being suggested was a palliative, on acceptance of the inequities of the international system, rather than a device to achieve meaningful change.

Strangely enough, the subsequent development of the concept has taken place almost exclusively in a European context. In the 1980s, several studies on the topic were published, including: *Self-reliant development in Europe* by Bassand *et al.* (1986), *Regional analysis and the new international division of labour*, Moulaert and Salinas (1983), *Economic restructuring and the territorial community*, Muegge *et al*, (1987), and *Endogenous development*, Stuckey (1985).

Self-reliant development in Europe is perhaps the most comprehensive of these and reveals some current thinking in the field. The book itself indicates that interest seems to have shifted from the problems that are inherent in poverty to a means of dealing with the malaise of postindustrial society. A quotation from the Introduction by Brugger and Stuckey will illustrate this:

The demands of economic competitiveness and economic growth conflict more and more frequently with a growing concern for self-development, social morality, and territorial and ecological integrity. We are witnessing a new longing, a longing which reveals a shift in values: from functional goals to territorial life-space, from material gains to emotional and

spiritual needs, from one-sided intellectual training to meet the demands of the computer age to questions about human life and the natural environment. The revolt of youth, the peace movement, concern for health, natural foods and alternative medicine, the continued drive for ecological sanity – despite rising unemployment – are all examples of a new interest in the concept of self-reliance or development from below.

(Brugger and Stuckey 1986: 1)

New terms such as 'endogenous development' have been coined and new meanings given to others. John Friedmann, for example, defines self-reliance as a form of radical social praxis. He argues: 'A self-reliant society is an inclusive, non-hierarchical society that stresses co-operation over competition, harmony with nature over exploitation, and social needs over unlimited personal desire. It represents the one best chance for the survival of the human race' (Friedmann 1986: 211). In yet another apparent shift of thinking, Friedmann, who originally proposed endogenous development as a solution for poverty and dependency in peripheral regions, now argues

that the route to endogenous development within the mainstream of economic policy is virtually closed. It is a viable option only for world city regions that can use their countervailing power to negotiate with global capital and with the state for arrangements favourable to themselves, or to be more precise, to their political and economic elites.

(Friedmann 1986: 211)

He argues further that 'it is virtually impossible to create regional enclaves modelled on social relations that are essentially different from those of the system in dominance' and that hopes to the contrary 'are always dashed [on] the bedrock of reality' (Friedmann 1986: 212). Given this, he therefore talks of 'self-reliant' development as distinct from endogenous development but he sees self-reliance as 'a strategy of social mobilisation for political ends' (Friedmann 1986: 213). He talks of militants organizing people to confront specific questions in the public sphere and to change reality through their own actions. He argues that these militants should use the peripheral regions and the 'internal peripheries' of cities as 'staging areas' for their self-reliant praxis, which he sees as the only viable option that peripheral populations have for their survival and well-being. He sees his self-reliant approach as very much development from below and

235

he claims to have derived it from a combination of utopian, anarchist and marxist thought. Self-reliant development is a way of becoming politically engaged and its ultimate strength 'derives from a deliberate disavowal of formal organisation. The object of the movement is to change reality not administer it' (Friedmann 1986: 213).

The book contains a variety of interesting studies from Switzerland, Austria, France, Belgium, Italy and Scotland, together with three chapters on the historical and theoretical context. All of the authors are purported to share a common conviction in development from below but it is clear that there is little agreement among them on many issues. Even an informed reader who is sympathetic to the paradigm may find the confusion and contradictions difficult to deal with. The relevance of some of the ideas to the developing nations of the world is open to question.

Development from within has similarities with the original concept of development from below but little congruence with current usage of the term in the literature cited above. Development from within is not only possible but also offers the best chance for survival in Africa's current crisis and the key components of development from within will now be discussed.

· Components of development from within

Participation

Participation is a key component of development from within. It is a concept about which much has been written (Oakley and Marsden 1984) and a recent article by Goulet (1989) gives a good overview of some of the main issues. Following Wolfe, participation is defined as 'the organised efforts to increase control over resources and groups and movements hitherto excluded from such control' (Wolfe quoted by Goulet 1989: 165). Goulet argues that there are many kinds of participation and suggests a fourfold typology classifying participation in terms of: (a) participation as a goal or as a means; (b) the scope of the arena in which participation operates; (c) the originating agent of the participation; (d) the moment at which participation is introduced.

This typology provides a useful framework for consideration of the role of participation as envisaged in development from within. Participation is seen as both a goal and a means; it operates primarily at the local community level in the first instance. It is not induced

from above but is generated from below by the populace itself; it can also be generated by the catalytic action of some external third agent. In terms of the timing of the involvement, it begins with the first step of Goulet's sequence: the initial diagnosis of the situation.

Goulet describes the debate between authors such as Freire, who sees participation primarily as a goal and 'some problem solvers [who] defend popular consultation on the grounds that it is the best way of getting the job done or achieving lasting results' (Goulet 1989: 166). Development from within is both a theoretical and a practical concept and as such both ends and means are important.

The scale at which participation operates is at the level of the local community. This is not to suggest, as was the case with the original conception of development from below, that the whole community must always participate as an organic entity. Development from within recognizes the importance of community but also acknowledges that community may sometimes be too large an aggregation and that within communities there is considerable differentiation which is based on issues such as class and gender. This was certainly apparent from the evidence from the case studies. For development from within, participation in all cases will be at a scale much lower than that of the nation state on which much current development thinking is based. It will also be larger than the household. As Goulet has pointed out, 'Depending on the scope of the arena or field in which participation occurs, its impact on development will vary accordingly' (Goulet 1989: 166). In the first instance, this may well lead to the creation of 'islets of social organisation, which obey their own rules of problem solving irrespective of dominant rules governing society at large' (Goulet 1989: 168). An example from the case studies would be the community of Ayirebi, which is described by Dei in Chapter 3. Such an initiative will probably be a necessary first step to ensure that basic needs are met and it has value in its own right at a particular time. In the longer term, however, it must develop further so that local people 'master larger issues transcending the boundaries of their immediate problems' (Goulet 1989: 176). There must be a strategic impact at a larger scale. The best example from the case studies is the National Farmers' Association of Zimbabwe (NFAZ) to which the Master Farmers' Clubs, described by Zinyama (Ch. 2: 51ff.), belong. As Bratton (1990) has pointed out, the Association had in 1988 4,500 clubs nationwide and a membership of 70,000 farmers plus 150,000 other participants and 'can claim without exaggeration to be the only independent, national small-farmers' union in sub-

Saharan Africa' (Bratton 1990: 101). Control of each club remains firmly at the local level but NFAZ plays a significant policy role at the national level and Bratton gives several examples of the importance of this. The aim of NFAZ is to ensure that the problems and views of small farmers are made known to the government and it appears to do this effectively and has considerable political impact.

Participation can come from three quite different sources: 'it can be induced from above by some authority or expert, generated from below by the non-expert populace itself, or catalytically promoted by some external third agent' (Goulet 1989: 166). Development from within does not accept Goulet's use of the term 'non-expert' to describe the local populace. The main agent in inducing participation from above is government and some authorities prefer the term 'mobilization' to describe this process. Governments often view participation as a method of achieving their own goals. Development from within is rarely if ever achieved by a mobilization approach from above except possibly in circumstances where the views and needs of a local community and the goals of the government coincide. But, even in these circumstances, if the local people do not have the decision-making power, true development from within cannot occur. 'Although such "participation" is easy to promote, only with great difficulty can it achieve authenticity. Authenticity means locating true decisional power in non-elite people, and freeing them from manipulation and co-optation' (Goulet 1989: 168).

Bottom-up participation is a key to development from within and the empirical evidence from the case studies and the additional studies cited shows that in Africa today this is largely the result of the 'deliberate initiatives taken by members of a "community of need"' (Goulet 1989: 167).

A third source from which participation can originate is what Goulet calls an 'external third agent'. In the case studies, the role of external agents such as non-government organizations has been shown to be of importance. Although generated from outside the local community,

> intervention by third party change agents differs in important respects from top-down participation induced by the state or other elite groups. Like the form initiated from below, third party participation usually aims at empowering hitherto power-less people to make demands for goods, not to contribute their resources to someone else's purposes.
>
> (Goulet 1989: 167)

There are occasions when development from within can be facilitated by outside assistance, especially in cases such as North-West Ghana, as described by Songsore in Chapter 4, where the community has been progressively weakened over time. This carries with it inherent problems, however, especially if the change agent has an agenda of its own, which is often the case with many religiously motivated institutions. The case study of Turkana by Imoo and Louse (1988) is an apparent example of this.

The Catholic Church initiated a Diocesan Development Education Programme in Turkana District in 1983 which generated a number of promising projects. 'This was the first time that the Turkana people had thought of, discussed and implemented a project on their own, without the direct assistance of a priest, nun or government worker' (Imoo and Louse 1988: 83). As the project progressed, however, problems arose.

> The emergence, therefore, of local indigenous leaders from the Adult Education Programme became a threat to the power and authority of the Catholic Church in Turkana in general and of the parish priest in particular . . . The Church realised that a conscientisation programme like the Adult Education Programme could not be used to divide people into 'Catholics', 'Muslims' or 'Protestants' but to encourage and promote a unity which could eventually become problematic to the institutional Churches. They realised the programme was producing independent thinkers. The Church realised that it had started a programme which was not a vehicle to evangelise people, which was the work all the missionaries had come to do.
>
> (Imoo and Louse 1988: 86–7)

Despite outside evaluations suggesting that the programme should continue 'because it was helping the Turkana people become participants in their own development and decision makers in their historical development' (Imoo and Louse 1988: 87), the Church withdrew its support and closed the programme in February of 1986.

The final point in Goulet's fourfold typology relates to the moment at which participation is introduced. Goulet argues that there is a discernible sequence, beginning with the initial diagnosis of the situation and leading up to discernible final action.

> At any point in the sequence, a non-expert populace may 'enter in' and begin to share in its dynamics . . . Therefore, if one

wishes to judge whether participation is authentic empowerment of the masses or merely a manipulation of them, it matters
greatly when, in the overall sequence of steps, the participation
begins.

(Goulet 1989: 167)

Development from within depends upon authentic participation and
the local populace must enter the participation process at the first
stage and be in control of all subsequent stages of action.

Authentic participation is a necessary condition for development
from within, although it is not sufficient in itself.

Participation, or some active role playing by intended beneficiaries, is an indispensable factor of all forms of development
. . . it is the nature and quality of participation . . . which
largely determine the quality of a nation's development pattern
. . . a policy bias in favour of authentic participation correlates
highly with genuine development.

(Goulet 1989: 175)

Goulet's article concludes with the following paragraph:

Participation began largely as a defense mechanism against the
destruction wrought by elite problem solvers in the name of
progress or development. From there it has evolved into a preferred form of 'do-it-yourself' problem solving in small-scale
operations. Now, however, many parties to participation seek
entry into larger, more macro, arenas of decision making.
Alternative development strategies centring on goals of equity,
job creation, the multiplication of autonomous capacities, and
respect for cultural diversity – all of these require significant
participation in macro arenas. Without it, development
strategies will be simultaneously undemocratic and ineffectual.
Without the developmental participation of non-elites, even
political democracy will be largely a sham.

(Goulet 1989: 176)

From the case studies in this volume and the additional studies cited it
is clear that in most cases African communities are at the 'defence
mechanism' or 'do-it-yourself' stage. There is some evidence of
participation reaching into the macro arena, such as in Zimbabwe,
and of potential for this to occur, such as with the co-operative credit
unions in Ghana, but as yet this evidence is limited. This is not surprising, given both the colonial heritage and the strongly centralized

state planning approaches which superseded them. However, the upsurge of initiatives that is recorded in the empirical evidence is a promising sign of new directions.

Territoriality

A second major component of development from within is that it is a territorial concept. This is seen as being quite different from a spatial concept. Gore, in his stimulating book *Regions in question* (1984), argues that regional development 'theory' has been plagued by what he calls the incomplete relational concept of space. Territory is defined here to include place and the social relations and power interactions which take place within that bounded space. Place has real meaning to most African peoples and it goes well beyond limited economic concepts such as ownership of the means of production. Attachment to place remains, despite physical separation over both time and space. Most Africans, even if they have moved elsewhere, wish to be buried in their community of birth and if possible on their ancestral land. A recent court case in Kenya in 1987 (Wambui Otieno v. Ougo and Sinanga), concerning where a criminal lawyer (S.M. Otieno) was to be buried, is an interesting example of how powerful is the attachment to place of birth. It also helps to explain why the body of David Livingstone was carried by his African followers hundreds of kilometres to the coast after his death.

The attachment to place is of course an extension of the attachment to land, the significance of which is captured well by Wolde-Mariam:

> The very humanity of the person and his status in society is defined mainly by his ownership of land, or more correctly by his membership to a landowning kinship group. Possession of land is therefore sought not only for economic benefits. In fact this is of secondary importance. It is sought more for the status, respectability, dignity and pride that go with ownership of land.
> (Wolde-Mariam quoted in Odingo 1988: 27–8)

The quotation, although indicative of the importance of attachment to both place and land, raises the issue of gender relationships. Women have an attachment to territory, as defined here, but ownership of land and the other social and power relationships which are included in the concept are unequal in almost all cases. This is illustrated by a number of the case studies, perhaps most forcefully by Alice Nkhoma-Wamunza in Chapter 9. Cleavages and conflicts

241

within territorial units, which are based on factors such as gender, will have to be specifically considered. They mark a major difference between development from within and the older concept of development from below. They do not, however, negate the utility of territory as an integral part of development from within.

Territory can obviously be defined at a variety of scales but a precise definition of 'local scale' is a problem. Gore has argued that one scale must be considered as dominant because what is 'endogenous' at one scale can be 'exogenous' at another simply by changing the definition of region.

The definition of local scale will vary from place to place but it will usually be the smallest territory which is effective and efficient and which has meaning for the local people, who will define their own 'life space' in terms of their own values and realities.

Dele Olowu uses the term 'local self-governance' which has some similarities to development from within. He argues that local self-governance has 'three important attributes: locality, primary accountability to the local people, and the presence of important regulatory, economic or social services or a combination of all' (Olowu 1989: 205). He argues that 'smallness/localness' is one of the characteristics which give local self-governance its logic and dynamic and he presents evidence that the arguments of economies of scale in support of the centralization of local government service are overstated. He offers interesting quantitative evidence on the average population for existing local government units in Africa which shows that in only one case, Zimbabwe with an average of 6,000 people per unit, are units of a size which would encourage 'localness'. The figures for other countries in which the case studies in this book are situated are 136,090 (Kenya), 166,386 (Tanzania) and 187,692 (Ghana). In comparison, the figures for France (1,320), West Germany (2,634), USA (2,756), Italy (2,717) and Canada (6,372) are small.

After World War II, the British colonial government instituted a system of local government which marked a departure from the policy and practice of indirect rule. Olowu argues that these systems were remarkably effective because they were efficient, democratic and local. 'In addition the self-governance principle was closer to pre-colonial systems of community governance in most parts of Africa' (Olowu 1989: 206). These flourished for a relatively brief period in the 1950s before independence, after which

the pendulum swung to the other extreme in which African governments, confident about the powers and potentials of central government departments to promote and mobilize development and anxious to integrate their politics and to consolidate the positions of the ruling elites through the elimination of all opposition to their administrations, abolished existing local government structures in favour of structures which were usually adorned with management or development committees whose deliberate powers were severely curtailed.

(Olowu 1989: 208)

Although the brief period of local governance in the last years of colonialism is controversial, and there will be considerable disagreement over Olowu's interpretation, the approach appears to have had advantages. An important point for proponents of development from within is that it was based on a territorial unit at the local scale, often that of the town or village in the Nigerian situation. The case study from Zimbabwe (Zinyama, Chapter 2) may owe some of its success to the local government structures in place there.

None of the case studies in the book explicitly discusses the territorial nature of development from within but territorial organization, a sense of belonging to a distinct community, is implicit in all of them.

Territory refers to both physical and social space. The importance of physical space, the environment in which people live, should not be underestimated. The climate, soils, topography and weather are major factors in determining the pace of development and the success of any development initiative. Zinyama draws explicit attention to this factor which is often underestimated in the social science literature.

Ecology and environment are key factors in the development process and the African environment is incredibly complex and diverse and is far from fully understood. The variations in the micro-environment are considerable and local knowledge of these micro-environments and how best to utilize them resides primarily at the local level. There is a large literature on the importance of indigenous knowledge (Atte 1989; McCall 1988; Richards 1985); and an important element of development from within is the utilization of that knowledge. Such knowledge is often territorially specific.

Although the environmental problems of poverty are quite different from the environmental problems of surplus that are facing post-

243

industrial societies, it is erroneous to think of African societies as being unaware or ill-informed of the need to practise sustainable development. The case study materials show an awareness and concern for the environment and a deep understanding of it. This does not mean that African people have not put their environments under pressure because there is evidence that this does happen. However, this is usually out of necessity rather than choice. Chambers (1989a) edited a very interesting issue of the IDS Bulletin on 'Vulnerability: how the poor cope' which considers some of these issues. In that issue, de Waal discusses the famine situation in Darfur in Sudan and reports that:

> Famine victims in Darfur held that they had no control over their chances of dying during the famine. They did believe that they had power over their chances of preventing destitution, that is, preserving the basis of their livelihood. Consequently, their primary aim during the famine was not to minimise the probability of dying but to keep their animals alive and to cultivate.
>
> (de Waal 1989: 67)

Even under extreme pressure and in the face of death, this particular society was concerned with sustainability.

Territory, as defined for the purposes of development from within, also includes the social relationships of the community inhabiting the physical space. Rural communities are far from homogeneous entities; there are many different actors involved and the tensions and cleavages which exist need to be explicitly considered (McCall 1988). These include what Watts has called 'the rough and tumble of peasant political-economy: namely indebtedness, deleterious terms of trade, gender oppression, local class structure, differential access to and control over resources' (Watts 1986: 382). The case studies reveal ample evidence of this. Songsore's study of North-West Ghana (Chapter 4) is an excellent example of all of the issues listed by Watts, as is Manuh's study from Ada District in southern Ghana (Chapter 5). Alice Nkhoma-Wamunza (Chapter 9) provides evidence of gender oppression, while gender relationships are also a key element in Chavangi's study from Kakamega District (Chapter 7). Gender relationships clearly need particular attention and it has been argued that, in order to improve our understanding, we need to 'pry open the black box of the household'. Sarah Berry argues that:

244

Rather than taking the household as a unit of analysis we need to treat it as a point of departure . . . The questions we need to ask are not how do households decide but rather how does membership in a household affect people's access to resources, obligations to others and understanding of their options.

(Berry 1984a: 23)

Harriet Friedman points out that 'Family enterprise is a battleground over patriarchy where property is immediately at stake' (Friedman 1986: 192), which is especially significant in relation to access to and ownership of land, a critical resource for rural people.

African societies must be understood in their own context. This is by no means static and the argument is perhaps best placed in terms of the co-existence of community cohesion and the tension of different sub-community interest groups which varies over time and space.

The case study by Dei (Chapter 3) and a number of the additional case studies cited show that communities often act in a co-ordinated collective manner. Many African rural societies are organic entities which operate simultaneously at various levels with community cohesion and sub-community tensions existing side by side. Local initiatives at the sub-community level, such as the activities of women's groups, for example, are often organized and implemented in a manner which attempts to avoid confrontation. Contradictions are rarely resolved through confrontations or coercion but rather through negotiation (Watts 1988). Confrontation does take place, as in the cases of the Ada Songor Salt Miners' Co-operative Society (Manuh, Chapter 5) and the Utengule Usangu brewers (Nkhoma-Wamunza, Chapter 9), but this appears to be a last resort when other approaches have failed. Development from within must, however, explicitly recognize and consider the realities of rural society as opposed to the mythology and must also accept that the community is a dynamic and changing entity in many cases.

Development from within argues for the maximum utilization of the resources of a territory primarily for the satisfaction of the inhabitants of that territory. This includes both the physical and human resources of the local community. It is true that many communities are poor in both absolute and relative terms. In cases such as North-West Ghana (Songsore, Chapter 4), for example, both the resource base and the human base have been eroded by induced or forced migration, extraction and exploitation. But it is also true that in many local communities there are resources which remain underutilized or

unutilized. The case studies in this book and those cited in the literature show that, in both human and material terms, much can be achieved by liberating or reviving the enthusiasm and knowledge of local people. In this sense, development from within is a self-reliant concept although, as will be discussed later, it is not an autarchic concept. Relationships with the State, and possibly involvement with third parties such as non-government organizations, are an important consideration for development from within. Selective spatial closure, as described in the original concept of development from below, is still an option for development from within but only in very exceptional circumstances.

PROSPECTS FOR DEVELOPMENT FROM WITHIN

Development from below was described by some authors as utopian. At the time when *Development from above or below?* (Stöhr and Taylor 1981) was written, the political and economic climate in Africa and the mainstream of development ideology was such that the development from below paradigm received little policy acceptance. A decade later, the situation has changed somewhat and the possibilities of a revised and revitalized development from within approach are greater. This does not mean that the paradigm will be easily accepted or that there are still no contradictions but the likelihood of acceptance has increased. It is ironic and unfortunate that the spiral of economic decline which has led to the current crisis in Africa has in itself created the preconditions in which development from within is more likely to be acceptable to local people, African governments, aid agencies, non-government organizations and major international funding agencies such as the World Bank. The crisis has also led to a reappraisal of both ideologies and strategies of development (Chambers 1989b).

From the perspective of the local people has come the realization that they cannot depend on the State either to meet their basic needs or to further their development objectives. As a result, they are taking their destiny into their own hands to a much larger extent than ever before. The realities of the last decade are eroding what is left of the 'colonial mentality' and the dependence on government as the main provider of services and economic opportunities. There are exceptions to this, such as the case of Zimbabwe (Zinyama, Chapter 2), but the emergence of local coping strategies in increasing numbers throughout the continent supports this view.

246

There is general acceptance that African governments, with few exceptions, have been unable to meet their development goals. As a result, either by choice or by necessity, the State is in a sense 'withdrawing' from many of the rural areas (Dearlove and White 1987), at least in terms of the provision of adequate development services, although control functions continue to exist. Several states are involved in Structural Adjustment Programmes, which are based on a resurgence of neo-classical macroeconomic theories, under the guidance of the World Bank. Structural adjustment often involves a severe cut-back in services to rural people. In these circumstances there is some 'space' for development from within to emerge and develop. The control functions of the State continue to exist and it can be argued that in some countries there has been a move away from democratization and a climate of increased repression associated with structural adjustment programmes. But unless the State perceives itself to be directly challenged at the political level it appears to have neither the resources nor the inclination to intervene as it would have a decade ago. Non-government organizations and to a lesser extent aid agencies have policies which favour working at the grass-roots level. Again, this strengthens the opportunities for development from within. Although NGOs cannot fill all of the 'development space' that is left by the State, they can often supply support to development from within initiatives in a much more promising way than the State. The thinking of the World Bank is in favour of 'market forces' performing functions which were previously carried out by the State. There is unlikely to be any objection from the Bank to the emergence of development from within although the reasons for this acceptance may well be quite different from those of the authors writing in this book.

Finally, there is increasing acceptance in academic circles of the need for a 'strategy of reversals' (Chambers 1989b) of which development from within is a good example. Crisis and the changes in attitudes, responses and policies that it appears to have encouraged has created the necessary preconditions for development from within.

DEVELOPMENT OR SURVIVAL

The UNCRD/CIRDAFRICA seminar in Arusha in 1989, which examined a number of case studies on local strategies and initiatives, showed that 'there were numerous individual and group (communal) initiatives, strategies and responses' (UNCRD 1989: 13). The

247

empirical evidence that is presented in this volume and in a number of the other studies cited in the text provides additional proof of that.

A major conclusion of the UNCRD/CIRDAFRICA seminar was that there were two different types of strategies: one which was categorized as 'development oriented' and the second primarily as for 'survival'.

> In some countries . . . communal and social responses had been given major importance and support; hence successful local strategies had emerged through specific local organisations and institutions along with major government and NGO support. [In other countries, however,] the individual responses of rural people had prevailed to a greater extent, especially in cases of stress situations or conditions. The essential distinction between these two types of responses was that, in the former case, local strategies were long lasting and primarily development oriented, while in the latter case they reflected short-term and primarily survival needs.
>
> (UNCRD 1989: 13–14)

This is an interesting and important distinction which requires careful reflection. It is similar in some ways to the distinction between 'strategic' and 'survival' initiations that was mentioned earlier (Mackenzie, Chapter 1). 'Strategic' initiatives are those which lead to impact at scales larger than the local, and which begin to alter power relations at the national scale. This is also a point which is stressed by Goulet in his consideration of participation. He argues that

> the most difficult form of participation to elicit and sustain is also the most indispensable to genuine development. This is the type of participation which starts at the bottom and reaches progressively upward into ever widening areas of decision making . . . It matures into a social force building a critical mass of participating communities now enabled to enter into spheres of decision or action beyond their immediate problem solving.
>
> (Goulet 1989: 168)

Is a distinction between local 'development' initiatives and local 'survival' initiatives valid? Ndaro (Chapter 8), for example, considers many of the initiatives that are taken by the people of Dodoma District to be marginal, as they either are not integrated into government development plans or take different directions from what government would like. He describes as 'survival' those activities such as trade,

crafts, industries, the construction of small dams and the bringing of new land under cultivation but, as was argued earlier, this distinction is dubious because it could equally well be interpreted as an indication that the people did not share the enthusiasm of the government for building roads, schools and hospitals, which Ndaro considers 'development'.

If development is measured by the criteria that were outlined at the beginning of this chapter then the distinction between 'development' and 'survival' becomes more blurred. If 'survival' strategies meet basic needs, as seems to be the case from much of the empirical evidence, is it valid to discuss them as marginal or not worthy of the term 'development'? The people of Ayirebi, for example (Dei, Chapter 3) are increasing economic growth, are concerned with equity and distribution of the fruits of that growth, have some control of their own destiny and appear to be achieving or returning to the traditional transcendental values which are held by the community to be of value. They do not appear to be influencing national policy or power relations in any significant way or 'entering into spheres of decision or action beyond their immediate problem solving' (Goulet 1989: 168). In fact, it might be argued that, by remaining 'invisible' to the State and other powerful actors in Ghana, they are improving their chances of controlling their own development.

Despite these arguments, there is value in considering distinctions between different types of local initiatives but more in order to determine the characteristics which have led to success than to develop typologies.

When the empirical evidence is examined, key elements for success appear to be the development of specific local organizations and institutions, which are controlled by the people themselves, and a degree of external support from an NGO, powerful 'patrons' or even government itself. Another element appears to be a lack of any direct and open challenge to the political power of the State. Bratton argues that what is needed is 'voice', which he sees as quite different from 'empowerment', a concept which he considers 'is used with rhetorical abandon but with little analytical precision in the literature' (Bratton 1990: 95). He argues further that

If 'empowerment' is taken to mean the capacity to get what you want, it is certainly an achievable goal in a local context where community-based organisations can sometimes effectively challenge a traditional power structure . . . But the concept of

249

'empowerment' exaggerates and raises unfulfillable expectations in the context of national politics in Africa. To try openly to rearrange the allocation of resources on which the power structure of the state rests is to run the risk of political repression.
(Bratton 1990: 95)

He uses the example of the National Farmers' Association of Zimbabwe to illustrate the success of a preferred approach. This organization meets most of the conditions under which Bratton argues that 'organisations representing the rural poor are able to attain a modicum of policy influence and to alter the allocation of public resources' (Bratton 1990: 114). These include: the cultivation of formal and informal ties with major political actors; a homogeneous and cohesive membership with membership accountability at the local level; a federated structure to increase its policy voice; specialization in policy issues of limited scope; and a reliance on domestic rather than foreign funding. There may well be considerable disagreement with Bratton over these points but the empirical evidence is clear; open confrontation with government, which is perceived as a threat to the government's political power, leads to repression. Sustainability is a key measure of success and if a local initiative is destroyed then little has been gained.

There is, of course, a very fine line to be trod. There is an increasing danger of local initiatives and organizations being captured or co-opted by government if they come too close. As support of local initiatives and participation becomes increasingly more fashionable in development circles, the autonomous organizations of the rural poor, which were set up by the participants to meet their own needs in ways defined by and acceptable to the community, may be overwhelmed by outside influences and support and, in the process, may be radically changed in character. In many situations local initiatives succeed because they remain 'invisible' to those outside of the society. The 'grey' or parallel economy often fares better in the shadows. Rural people have learned from experience to keep some of their activities hidden, especially from government, which has a tendency to control, regulate or tax such initiatives. Bratton (1989) cites the example of the Savings Development Movement in Zimbabwe, which is described at the local level by Zinyama in Chapter 2.

Unfortunately, the very success of the savings movement in Zimbabwe attracted so much attention that the government found it necessary to intervene . . . By 1987 the government

was able to force changes in the governance of the savings movement by installing their own appointees on the Board of a reconstituted and renamed Self-Help Development Foundation.

(Bratton 1990: 98–9)

The study by Kobiah (1985) of local initiatives in Mathare Valley in Nairobi, although in an urban setting, is another example. The squatter co-operatives which were established by the residents in order to buy the land on which their shanty dwellings stood, in an effort to guard against government raids and evictions, were rapidly taken over by private companies speculating in land. The indigenous local initiatives gradually lost their dynamism as the three major external actors, the government of Kenya, the Nairobi City Council, and the National Christian Council of Kenya, became increasingly significant in decision-making.

Local initiatives are often circumscribed by lack of material resources and by poverty, which are the very conditions that they were formed to overcome. To be sustainable and to grow over time they need access to financial and other resources from outside the community. How to create conditions which allow rural peoples to improve their own lot without losing control of their own initiatives and institutions is an important part of development from within.

RELATIONSHIPS BETWEEN THE STATE AND LOCAL COMMUNITIES

The relationships between the local community and the State have been touched on earlier in this chapter as well as in almost every chapter in the book. These relationships are an extremely popular topic in the current development administration and political science literature on Africa. It is also key to the prospects for development from within.

As the State continues to be unable or unwilling to deal with the current challenges of African development, or implements policies which are seen by rural peoples to be detrimental to their interests, the significance of local organization and initiative increases. However, as both Brett and Beckman point out, the role of the State is still critical and it would be a serious error to underestimate this. Brett believes that there is considerable potential to reform current State practices and argues that 'the role of the state must remain central in any effective development strategy' (1988: 4). He discusses a number

of solutions for increasing flexibility on the part of the State and his observations on what he calls 'co-operative and voluntary alternatives' (Brett 1988: 10) are worthy of careful consideration in relation to the context and rationale for local initiatives. He points out that 'collective organisation requires greater degrees of overall competence than autocratic management' and that 'Voluntary organisation can also transfer the cost of providing services from the wealthy taxpayer to the poorest members of the community and increase inequalities in access to services' (Brett 1988: 10). He goes on to observe that

> these methods [i.e. voluntary organization] can improve service provision and allow local groups to maintain their autonomy against powerful private interests and a distant and perhaps alien state. In most cases success will probably only occur where they are also given substantial degrees of support by state and aid agencies, particularly in the early stages before they have built up their resources and skills. Thus it is almost certainly the case here, as elsewhere, that the full development of autonomous agencies is not a substitute for effective public provision, but only possible where it can grow effectively in association with it.
>
> (Brett 1988: 10)

Beckman cautions that the domestic ruling classes must be taken seriously and not simply dismissed as corrupt, bureaucratically rigid, neopatrimonial compradors. He points out that

> There is also a commitment to the advancement of the nation, as perceived, no doubt, from a particular class perspective. There is a profound resentment of a heritage of foreign domination and racial arrogance, a desire to remove the stigma of inferiority and to seek a rightful place in the community of nations. [This is] a hungry and ambitious class [who] represent a dynamic force geared to expansion rather than decline.
>
> (Beckman 1988: 28)

The current crisis, far from leading to a decline or demise of State power, simply 'hastens historical processes . . . whereby local ruling classes, pampered by state protection, are pushed into deeper water and made to swim' (Beckman 1988: 28). An example might be the steps that were taken by the Nigerian Government, as described by

Mabogunje. These comprise a *domestically* initiated Structural Adjustment Programme which involves 'an agonising reappraisal of the true course of any development effort' (Mabogunje 1988: 17) and the creation of a powerful, new Directorate of Food, Roads and Rural Infrastructure to promote grass-roots social mobilization. If local initiatives are to succeed then it is clear that new power-sharing relationships must be worked out with powerful State actors. External agents, such as international agencies and NGOs, may have a mediating role to play in this process.

Robert Chambers presents the concept of the 'enabling state', which is part of his overall concept of a strategy of reversals, as described earlier. He argues that the paradigm of reversals 'resolves the contradiction between the neo-Fabian thesis that the state should do more, and the neo-liberal antithesis that the state should do less' (Chambers 1989b: 20). The task for Chambers is to dismantle the 'disabling state' and to replace it with 'a state which is not only protector and supporter, but also enabler and liberator' (Chambers 1989b: 20).

Chambers argues that there are three functions of the State which are fundamental for the rural poor: maintaining peace and the democratic rule of law; providing basic infrastructure and services; and managing the economy. He also outlines an agenda for abstention and an agenda for action. Decentralized process and choice are central to his paradigm of reversals and 'In this mode the state is not school but cafeteria, and development is decentralised, becoming not simpler but more complex, and not uniform but more diverse' (Chambers 1989b: 20).

His analysis and suggestions in respect to relations between the State and local community fit well with the concept of development from within. Despite the difficulties, the political climate exists to make development from within possible. There is 'political space' available to allow local communities to establish new relationships between themselves and central government. As Bratton observes, 'the reach of the African state routinely exceeds its grasp' (Bratton 1989: 585) and in the current circumstances the ability of the State to regulate and control has been reduced.

NON-GOVERNMENT ORGANIZATIONS

From the empirical evidence it is clear that the role and significance of non-government organizations has increased. One author has gone

so far as to suggest that 'the 1980s may be known as the development decade of non-government organizations (NGOs)' (Fowler 1988: 1), a view which is echoed by Bratton (1989) who states that

> NGOs have entered the limelight as governments throughout Africa have begun to retreat from ambitious attempts to sponsor socioeconomic development 'from above' . . . Especially in the remotest regions of the African countryside, governments often have had little choice but to cede responsibility for the provision of basic services to a church, an indigenous self-help group, or an international relief agency.
>
> (Bratton 1989: 569)

NGOs have a potential comparative advantage over government in micro-level development but 'you cannot rely on all NGOs in all circumstances to be more effective; being an NGO is not synonymous with being better than government as an agent of micro-development' (Fowler 1988: 23). In some instances, if that potential comparative advantage is not realized, 'The current infatuation of official donors with NGOs will turn into disillusionment, and in the 1990s observers will be writing the obituaries of NGOs in micro-development' (Fowler 1988: 22).

The role of NGOs as perceived by government may be quite different from the perception of their role by local communities. There is congruence in terms of the needs of both people and government for increased resources and the provision of much needed services but the local people appear to view the NGOs as protectors and advocates whereas the government appears to view them as a 'development platform' for activities which they would like to see carried out but either will not or cannot finance from their own resources.

The empirical evidence shows that in many instances where local initiatives have been sustained and expanded there has been some involvement from the outside. The scale and nature of this involvement has varied but it appears to have been important, especially in facilitating the organizational side of local community initiatives and in providing the initial resources to allow these initiatives to be 'jump started'. In some instances the NGOs have been local, in others national, and in yet others international. In both Nigeria and Ghana, men, and to a lesser extent women, who have left their home village or town have been important players in furthering the welfare of their home communities both by remitting resources and by action on

behalf of the community in the wider political and bureaucratic arena (Olowu 1989).

As with government, there is a danger that an NGO, especially one which is based in another country or one which is, say, religion-based and which has a hidden agenda of its own, may subvert or dominate the initiatives of local communities. There is indeed evidence in the case studies cited of this happening. In general, however, the empirical evidence which is available shows that NGOs have been increasingly supportive of local initiatives.

Both Fowler (1988) and Bratton (1989, 1990) explore these matters more fully and the NGOs themselves have issued an interesting Declaration on the African Economic and Social Crisis (UN 1986b). In the emerging new relationship between the local community and the State, the NGOs may have a particularly significant role to play and may act as a catalyst of development from within.

POLICY ACTIONS

Development from within is not a normative concept and, since the major actor in the whole process is the local community itself, it is difficult, if not impossible, to suggest policy actions at the most critical decision-making level. However, it is possible to look at policies which can be adopted by the other major actors, such as government, non-governmental agencies and international funding agencies. The principal conclusions of the UNCRD/CIRDAFRICA seminar provide an excellent synopsis of what is required:

> Given the situation that has been prevalent in the region and the local realities, local initiatives offer great scope for promoting self-sustaining local development and, through it, national development.
>
> It was, therefore, seen as imperative that governments, international agencies, and the NGOs concerned provide a conducive environment and support for the promotion of such initiatives.
>
> (UNCRD 1989: 28)

A number of specific suggestions were made. The role of government was considered 'as crucial in providing a suitable social, economic and political environment in which local initiatives and local self-development could flourish' (UNCRD 1989: 21). The State, therefore, must maintain peace, stability, law and order; provide basic

255

socioeconomic infrastructure and management of the economy; provide a policy framework to encourage local initiatives, including official recognition of local initiatives and institutions as an integral part of the national development effort; provide financial, institutional and technical support for the activities of local institutions and initiatives; decentralize decision-making and adopt a regional or local development strategy in which local resources and institutions would be the major platform of development for the region; and establish a national institution to co-ordinate and link local organizations, initiatives and strategies. The name that was suggested was the National Indigenous Resource Centre or the National Centre for Local Self-Reliance.

> This institution should act as an organiser, facilitator and catalyst, and provide avenues for assistance to local initiatives in terms of funds, technical support, supplies, training and management advice. It could work with communities to modernise local technological capabilities or indigenise appropriate outside technologies. On top of this, it should compile, document and publicise successful local initiatives and strategies (both technical and otherwise) nationwide, to act as incentives to all local communities. Local people across the nation should be appointed members of this national institution.
>
> (UNCRD 1989: 23)

In some ways these suggestions echo those of Chambers (1989b), which were described earlier in this chapter. He argues that the State has done too much in some areas and much too little in others. The role of the NGOs is also considered important in encouraging local initiatives. The UNCRD/CIRDAFRICA seminar suggested: closer co-ordination and less competition among NGOs; that NGOs provide technical, financial, and other information for local initiatives together with management and organizational training; and that the work of NGOs in local communities be guided by a number of basic principles which ensure that the local people are in full control of decision-making and that existing local structures and organizations are respected and built on rather than replaced.

Many of the policy suggestions for NGOs apply to international funding agencies too but it was also suggested that they concentrate on institutional support; finance and design the improvement of local technology rather than the purchase of machinery from abroad; direct efforts to programmes such as public health care and disease

eradication which improve the local environment and make it more conducive to the emergence of local initiatives; and to help to fund research and implementation of local technologies, agricultural systems, manufacturing, etc. which are of direct concern to local people.

Development from within is not primarily a planning strategy but the policy implications of such an approach cannot be ignored if change is to take place.

There are clearly obstacles to be overcome and certain preconditions in which development from within is more likely to emerge. These include: 'the existence of a political will that recognise[s] the role of local initiatives and organisation in local and national development and promote[s] such organisation' (UNCRD 1989: 26); the provision of incentives to local people to meet their own development needs; decentralization and devolution of the structure of government; education and sensitization of local communities to understand the nature of the realities facing them; financial resources and institutions which are geared to the needs of local communities and organizations; training opportunities to increase managerial and administrative skills of local people; and recognition of the potential of local communities, including women, in the solution of their own development problems. In a sense this turns existing development approaches completely on their head.

CONCLUSION

The human potential, basic wisdom and knowledge of Africa's local peoples have been seriously underestimated. To some, they are seen as a major barrier to the development aims both of the African state and of the international agencies which are involved in promoting and guiding what they see as being required for development to take place. They are objects of development who have to be 'modernized', 'mobilized' or 'captured'. A basic objective of development from within is to allow local people to become the subject, not the object, of development strategies. Given the opportunity to do so, they have shown themselves to be perfectly capable of making rational choices regarding their own destinies. Too much attention has been given to the negative developmental aspects of issues such as 'kinship' and not nearly enough to the positive aspects of local community realities on which a more meaningful development can be built. It is hoped that this book has helped to contribute to an increased understanding of a

development from within for, by and with African peoples, as a result of which a new optimism for Africa's future may emerge from the current pessimism.

BIBLIOGRAPHY

Adedeji, A. (1985) 'The Monrovia Strategy and the Lagos Plan of Action: five years after', pp. 9–34 in A. Adedeji and T.M. Shaw (eds) *Economic crisis in Africa: African perspectives on development problems and potentials*, Lynne Rienner, Boulder, Col.

Adedeji, A. (1987) 'A preliminary assessment of the performance of the African economy in 1986 and prospects for 1987', End-of-Year Conference at ECA Headquarters, 2 January 1987, Addis Adaba.

Adedeji, A. (1989) 'The African Alternative Framework to Structural Adjustment', unpublished paper, presented at the University of Ottawa, Canada, 23 October 1989.

Agricultural Marketing Authority (1988) *Cotton situation and outlook report (annual)*, Harare.

Akator, G. (1988) *Youth Development Task Force, weekend seminar report*, Dodoma Municipal Council, Dodoma.

Alila, P.O. (1988) 'Rural development in Kenya: a review of past experience', *Regional Development Dialogue* 9(2): 142–65.

Anim, N.O. (1959) 'A local study of a coastal district', *Ghana Geographical Association Bulletin* 4(2): 16–21.

Annegers, J.F. (1973) 'Seasonal food shortages in West Africa', *Ecology of Food and Nutrition* 2: 251–7.

Arhin, K. (1983) 'Peasants in 19th century Asante', *Current Anthropology* 24(4): 471–9.

Asante, S.K.B. (1985) 'Development and regional integration since 1980', pp. 79–99 in A. Adedeji and T.M. Shaw (eds) *Economic crisis in Africa: African perspectives on development problems and potentials*, Lynne Rienner, Boulder, Col.

Asgele, Tsegay (1989) 'Case study on local people's rural development strategies and responses in the Welo Region of Ethiopia', Paper presented to the UNCRD/CIRDAFRICA Seminar on Reviving Local Self-Reliance: Challenges for Rural/Regional Development in Eastern and Southern Africa, Arusha, Tanzania, 24 February.

Atsu, S.Y. (1984) 'The effect of government policies on the increased production of food and food self-sufficiency in Ghana', Paper read at the International Conference on Food Self-sufficiency in West Africa, University of Ghana, Legon, Accra, 1–3 May.

Atte, David (1989) 'Indigenous local knowledge as a key to local-level development: possibilities, constraints and planning issues in the context of Africa', Paper presented to the UNCRD/CIRDAFRICA Seminar on Reviving Local Self-Reliance: Challenges for Rural/Regional Development in Eastern and Southern Africa, Arusha, Tanzania, 24 February.

Bassand, Michel, Brugger, Ernst A., Bryden, John M., Friedmann, John and Stuckey, B. (eds) (1986) *Self-reliant development in Europe*, Gower, Aldershot.

Beckman, B. (1988) 'The post-colonial state: crisis and reconstruction', *IDS Bulletin* 19(4): 26–34.

Bell, M. (1979) 'The exploitation of indigenous knowledge, or the indigenous exploitation of knowledge: whose use of what for what?', *IDS Bulletin* 10(2): 44–50.

Belshaw, D. (1979) 'Taking indigenous technology seriously: the case of inter-cropping techniques in East Africa', *IDS Bulletin* 10(2): 24–8.

Bentil, B., Gadway, J., Huttenrauch, H., Monikes, V. and Schmidt, R.H. (1988) *Rural finance in Ghana (a research study on behalf of Bank of Ghana)*, September, Accra.

Bequele, A. (1983) 'Stagnation and inequality in Ghana', pp. 219–47 in D. Ghai and S. Radwan (eds) *Agrarian policies and rural poverty in Africa*, ILO, Geneva.

Bernstein, H. (1979) 'African peasantries: a theoretical framework', *Journal of Peasant Studies* 6(4): 421–43.

Berry, S. (1984a) *Households, decision making and rural development*, Development Discussion Paper no. 167, Harvard Institute of International Development, Cambridge, Mass.

Berry, S. (1984b) 'The food crisis and agrarian change in Africa: a review essay', *African Studies Review* 27(2): 59–112.

Berry, S. (1989) 'Social institutions and access to resources', *Africa* 59(1): 41–55.

Bienefeld, M. (1989) 'Structural adjustment and rural employment in Tanzania', Unpublished paper submitted to International Labour Office Employment/Rural project on structural adjustment and rural labour markets in five African countries.

Blaikie, P. (1989) 'Environment and access to resources in Africa', *Africa* 59(1): 18–40.

Boateng, E.A. (1959) *A geography of Ghana*, Cambridge University Press, Cambridge.

Boateng, I.K. (1986) 'Governmental and voluntary participation in Ghana's rural development programme', pp. 27–47 in Brown, C.K. (ed.) *Rural development in Ghana*, Ghana Universities Press, Accra.

Bradley, P.N. (1984) *The District Resource Analysis as applied to Kakamega*, Working Paper 1, Kenya Woodfuel Development Programme, Nairobi.

Brandtzaeg, B. (1982) 'The role and status of women in post-harvest food conservation', *Food and Nutrition Bulletin* 4(11): 33–42.

Bratton, M. (1986) 'Farmer organizations and food production in Zimbabwe', *World Development* 14(3): 367–84.

Bratton, M. (1987) 'Drought, food and the social organisation of small farmers in Zimbabwe', pp. 213–44 in M.H. Glantz (ed.) *Drought and*

hunger in Africa: denying famine a future, Cambridge University Press, Cambridge.

Bratton, M. (1989) 'The politics of government–NGO relations in Africa', *World Development* 17(4): 569–87.

Bratton, M. (1990) 'Non-governmental organizations in Africa: can they influence public policy?' *Development and Change* 21: 87–118.

Brett, E.A. (1987) 'States, markets and private power in the development world: problems and possibilities', *IDS Bulletin* 18(3): 31–7.

Brett, E.A. (1988) 'Adjustment and the state: the problem of administrative reform', *IDS Bulletin* 19(4): 4–11.

Brooke, C. (1967) 'The heritage of famine in Central Tanzania', *Tanzania Notes and Records* 67: 15–22.

Brown, C.K. (ed.) (1986) *Rural development in Ghana*, Ghana Universities Press, Accra.

Brugger, E.A. and Stuckey, B. (1986) 'Introduction: self-reliant development in Europe', pp. 1–8 in Bassand *et al.* (eds) *Self-reliant development in Europe*, Gower, Aldershot.

Bryceson, D.F. and Kirimbai, M. (1980) *Subsistence and beyond: money earning activities of women in rural Tanzania*, BRALUP Research Report 45, University of Dar es Salaam.

Callear, D. (1984) 'Land and food in the Wedza communal area', *Zimbabwe Agricultural Journal* 81(4): 163–8.

Campbell, David J. (1990) 'Community-based strategies for coping with food scarcity: a role in African famine early-warning systems', *Geojournal*, March, 231–41.

Carney, J. (1988) 'Struggles over crop rights and labour within contract farming households on a Gambian irrigation rice project', *Journal of Peasant Studies* 15(3): 334–9.

Central Bureau of Statistics (1982) *Census office report*, Institute of Scientific, Social and Economic Research, Legon, Accra.

Chale, F.U. and Ngonyani, G.H. (1979) *Report on a survey of co-operative income-generating projects for women and its impact on the social welfare of children and the family*, BRALUP Workshop on Women and Development Paper 24, Dar es Salaam.

Chambers, R. (1988) 'Bureaucratic reversals and local diversity', *IDS Bulletin* 19(4): 50–6.

Chambers, R. (1989a) 'Editorial introduction: vulnerability, coping and policy', *IDS Bulletin* 20(2): 1–7.

Chambers, R. (1989b) *The state and rural development: ideologies and an agenda for the 1990s*, IDS Discussion Paper 269, University of Sussex.

Chanock, M. (1985) *Law, custom and social order: the colonial experience in Malawi and Zambia*, Cambridge University Press, Cambridge.

Chavangi, N.A. (1988) Case Study of Women's Participation in Forestry Activities in Kenya, Kenya Woodfuels Development Programme, Nairobi.

Chavangi, N.A. and Ngugi, A.W. (1987) 'Innovatory participation in programme design: tree planting for increased fuelwood supply for rural households in Kenya', Paper presented at the workshop on Farmers and Agricultural Research, University of Sussex, July 1987.

Chavangi, N.A., Engelhard, R.J. and Jones, V. (1986) *Culture as the basis*

for implementing self-sustaining woodfuel development programmes, Kenya Wood-fuel Development Programme, Nairobi.

Chileshe, Jonathan H. (1989) 'Socioeconomic structural change, forms of traditional authority and prospects for local-level development', Paper presented to the UNCRD/CIRDAFRICA Seminar on Reviving Local Self-Reliance: Challenges for Rural/Regional Development in Eastern and Southern Africa, Arusha, Tanzania, 24 February.

Chitsike, L.T. (1988) *Agricultural co-operative development in Zimbabwe*, Zimbabwe Foundation for Education with Production, Harare, August.

Christopher, A.J. (1971) 'Land tenure in Rhodesia', *South African Geographical Journal* 53: 39–52.

Colclough, C. (1988) 'Zambian adjustment strategy – with and without the IMF', *IDS Bulletin* 19(1): 51–60.

Collier, P. (1980) *Poverty and growth in Kenya*, World Bank Staff Working Paper 389, Washington, D.C.

Commonwealth Expert Group on Women and Structural Adjustment (1989) *Engendering adjustment for the 1990s*, Commonwealth Secretariat, London.

Cornia, G.A. (1988) 'Economic decline and human welfare in the first half of the 1980s', pp. 11–47 in G.A. Cornia, R. Jolly and F. Stewart (eds) *Adjustment with a human face: protecting the vulnerable and promoting growth*, Clarendon Press, Oxford.

Cotton Marketing Board (1988) *Annual report*, Harare.

Coulson, A. (1982) *Tanzania: a political economy*, Oxford University Press, Oxford.

CCA and CUA (1988) 'Credit for women', Ghana. Unpublished document.

Credit Unions Association (1971) *CUA Ed-1*, CUA Education/Information Department, Accra, April.

Credit Unions Association (1978) *A history of co-operative credit unions in Ghana, Tenth Milestone 1968–1978*, Accra.

Credit Unions Association (1985) CUA headquarters statistics for 1984/85 fiscal year.

Credit Unions Association (1987a) *Ghana co-operative Credit Unions Association (CUA) limited country progress report for the ACCOSCA biennial meeting and education conference*, Nairobi, 25–29 May.

Credit Unions Association (1987b) *Memorandum on reactivation of Ghana co-operative movement: Ghana co-operative Credit Unions Association (CUA) Limited*, Accra, 15 December.

Credit Unions Association (1988) *Model by-laws and articles of association for Ghana co-operative credit unions*, Accra.

Daddieh, C.K. (1985) 'Recovering Africa's self-sufficiency in food and agriculture', pp. 187–200 in A. Adedeji and T.M. Shaw (eds) *Economic crisis in Africa: African perspectives on development problems and potentials*, Lynne Rienner, Boulder, Col.

Daily Graphic (1989) 27 April, Accra.

Daily Graphic (1989) 21 July, Accra.

Daily Graphic (1989) 30 October, Accra.

Daily News (1989) 3 April, Dar-es-Salaam.

de Stemper, G.A. (1988) 'Progresso social: a mission to help women', *Credit Union World Reporter* 3(2): 8–10.

Dearlove, J. and White, G. (1987) 'The retreat of the State', *IDS Bulletin* 18(3): 1–3.

Dei, G.J.S. (1986) 'Adaptation and environmental stress in a Ghanaian forest community', Ph.D. dissertation, Department of Anthropology, University of Toronto, University Microfilms, Ann Arbor, Mich.

Dei, G.J.S. (1987) 'Land and food production in a Ghanaian forest community', *Africa Development* 12(1): 101–24.

Dickson, K.B. (1969) *A historical geography of Ghana*, Cambridge University Press, Cambridge.

Dutkiewicz, P. and Shenton, R. (1986) 'Debates', *Review of African Political Economy* 37: 108–16.

Dutkiewicz, P. and Williams, G. (1987) 'All the king's horses and all the king's men couldn't put Humpty-Dumpty together again', *IDS Bulletin* 18(3): 39–44.

Economist Intelligence Unit (1989) *Country report: Kenya* 1, London.

Evans, A. (1989) 'The implications of economic reforms for women in Zambia: the case of the Economic Reform Programme 1983–7', Unpublished paper commissioned for the Commonwealth Expert Group on Women and Structural Adjustment.

Evans, A. and Young, K. (1988) 'Gender issues in household labour allocation: the case of Northern Province, Zambia', ODA/ESCOR Research Report; cited in Evans (1989).

Floyd, B.N. (1962) 'Land apportionment in Southern Rhodesia', *Geographical Review* 52(4): 566–82.

Forbes, D.K. (1984) *The geography of underdevelopment*, Croom Helm, London.

Fortes, M. and Fortes, S.L. (1936) 'Food in the domestic economy of the Tallensi', *Africa* 9: 237–76.

Fowler, A. (1988) *Non-governmental organizations in Africa: achieving comparative advantage in relief and micro-development*, IDS Discussion Paper 249, Sussex.

Franke, Richard W. (1987) 'Power, class, and traditional knowledge in Sahel food production', pp. 257–81 in I.L. Markovitz (ed.) *Studies in power and class in Africa*, Oxford University Press, Oxford.

Friedman, H. (1986) 'Patriarchy and poverty', *Sociologie Ruralis* 26(2): 186–95.

Friedmann, J. (1981) 'Regional planning for rural mobilization in Africa', *Rural Africana* 12–13: 3–29.

Friedmann, J. (1986) 'Regional development in industrialised countries: endogenous or self-reliant', pp. 203–16 in Bassand *et al.* (eds) *Self-reliant development in Europe*, Gower, Aldershot.

Friedmann, J. and Weaver, C. (1979) *Territory and function: the evolution of regional planning*, Edward Arnold, London.

Galtung, J., O'Brien, B. and Prieswerk, R. (eds) (1980) *Self-reliance, a strategy for development*, Bogle L'Ouverture, London.

Gasper, D. (1988) 'Rural growth points and rural industries in Zimbabwe: ideologies and policies', *Development and Change* 19(3): 425–66.

Ghana (1984) *Population Census*, Government Press, Accra.

Ghana (1986) 'Amissah Committee of Enquiry Report', Accra, Unpublished document.

Ghana (1987) *Programme of Action to Mitigate the Social Costs of Adjustment*, Government Printer, Accra.

Glazier, J. (1985) *Land and the uses of tradition among the Mbeere of Kenya*, University Press of America, Lanham, Maryland.

Globe and Mail (1990) 6 July, Toronto.

Gobbins, K.E. and Prankard, H.A. (1983) 'Communal agriculture: a study from Mashonaland West', *Zimbabwe Agricultural Journal* 80(4): 151–8.

Gondwe, Z.S. (n.d.) 'Female interstate succession to land in rural Tanzania – whither equality?', Dar es Salaam Women Research and Documentation Project, Dar es Salaam.

Gore, C. (1984) *Regions in question: space, development theory and regional policy*, Methuen, New York.

Goulet, D. (1989) 'Participation in development: new avenues', *World Development* 17(2): 165–78.

Graham, Y. (1989) 'From GTP to Assene: aspects of industrial struggles 1982–7', pp. 43–72 in E. Hansen and K. Ninsen (eds) *The State, development and politics in Ghana*, Codesria Book Series, Codesria, Dakar, Senegal.

Grain Marketing Board (1988) *Annual report*, Harare.

Green, R.H. (1988) 'Ghana: progress, problematics and limitations of the success story', *IDS Bulletin* 19(1): 7–16.

Green, R.H. (1989) *Degradation of rural development: development of rural degradation – change and peasants in Sub-Sahara Africa*, IDS Discussion Paper 265, September.

Guyer, J.I. and Peters, P.E. (1987) 'Introduction: conceptualizing the household: issues of theory and policy in Africa', *Development and Change* 18(2): 197–214.

Havnevik, K.J. *et al.* (1988) *Tanzania country study and Norwegian aid review*, Centre for Development Studies, University of Bergen.

Herald, The (1989) 4 August, Harare.

Hewer, L. (1974) *Rural development: world frontiers*, Iowa State University Press, Des Moines.

HIARI (1982) Newsletter of the Community Development Trust Fund of Tanzania, 10–11.

Hill, P. (1963) *The migrant cocoa farmers of Southern Ghana*, Cambridge University Press, Cambridge.

Hill, P. (1975) 'The West African farming household', pp. 119–36 in J. Goody (ed.) *Changing social structure in Ghana*, International African Institute, London.

Hinderink, J. and Sterkenburg, J.J. (1987) *Agricultural commercialisation and government policy in Africa*, Routledge & Kegan Paul, London.

Hubbert, Lorrie (1988) 'Women's access to credit', *Credit Union World Reporter* 3(2): 15–17.

Hunter, J.M. (1967) 'Seasonal hunger in a part of the West African savannah: a survey of bodyweights in Nangodi, Northeast Ghana', *Transactions of the Institute of British Geographers* 41: 167–85.

Hutchful, E. (1990) 'The emperor in new clothes: new themes in the World Bank's concept of structural adjustment', Paper presented at the Annual Conference of the Canadian Association of African Studies Conference, Dalhousie University, Halifax, May.

Hyden, G. (1980) *Beyond Ujamaa in Tanzania: underdevelopment and an uncaptured peasantry*, Heinemann, London.

Hyden, G. (1983) *No shortcuts to progress: African development management in perspective*, University of California Press, Berkeley.

Igbozurike, M.U. (1971) 'Ecological balance in tropical agriculture', *Geographical Review* 61(4): 519–29.

Imoo, B.V. and Louse, J. (1988) 'Adult education programme Turkana District, Kenya', pp. 79–89 in P. Oakley (ed.) *Proceedings of the international symposium on the challenge of rural poverty: how to meet it*, German Foundation for International Development, Feldafing, FGR.

Jamal, V. (1988) 'Getting the crisis right: missing perspectives on Africa', *International Labour Review* 127(6): 655–78.

James, R.W. and Fimbo, G.M. (1973) *Customary land law of Tanzania: a source book*, East Africa Literature Bureau, Dar es Salaam.

Kalapula, E.S. (1989) 'Responses to drought in Namwala District: local community strategies and initiatives', Paper presented to the UNCRD/CIRDAFRICA Seminar on Reviving Local Self-Reliance: Challenges for Rural/Regional Development in Eastern and Southern Africa, Arusha, Tanzania, 24 February.

Kapinga, N.B. (1989) 'Support to local self-reliant efforts: the approach of Rukwa Integrated Rural Development Project', Paper presented to the UNCRD/CIRDAFRICA Seminar on Reviving Local Self-Reliance: Challenges for Rural/Regional Development in Eastern and Southern Africa, Arusha, Tanzania, 24 February.

Karikari, S.K. (1971) 'Cocoyam cultivation in Ghana', *Legon Extension Bulletin* 13: 1–12, University of Ghana Legon, Accra.

Kauzeni, A.S. (1988) 'Rural development alternatives and the role of local-level development strategy: Tanzania case study', *Regional Development Dialogue* 9(2): 105–38.

Kennedy, E. and Cogill, B. (1987) *Income and nutritional effects of the commercialization of agriculture in southwestern Kenya*, International Food Policy Research Institute Research Report, No. 63, Washington, D.C.

Kenya (1982) *District focus for rural development*, Government Printer, Nairobi.

Kenya (1986a) Sessional Paper No. 1, *Economic management for renewed growth*, Government Printer, Nairobi.

Kenya (1986b) *Development Plan 1984–9*, Government Printer, Nairobi.

Kenya (1987) *Statistical abstract*, Government Printer, Nairobi.

Kenya (1989a) *Economic survey*, Government Printer, Nairobi.

Kenya (1989b) *Development plan 1989–1993*, Government Printer, Nairobi.

Kenya, Machakos District (1987) *Annual report*, Ministry of Culture and Social Services, Nairobi.

Kenya, Machakos District (1988) *Ministry of Co-operatives report*, Nairobi.

Kenya, Machakos District (1989a) *Machakos District development plan 1989–1993*, Ministry of Finance and Planning, Nairobi.

Kenya, Machakos District (1989b) *Machakos District development plan annex*, Nairobi.

Kidd, R. (1982) 'Popular theatre and popular struggle in Kenya: the story of the Kamiriithu Community Educational and Cultural Centre', *Theaterwork* 2(6): 47–61.

Kinsey, B.H. (1983) 'Emerging policy issues in Zimbabwe's land resettlement programmes', *Development Policy Review* 1(2): 163–96.

Kitching, G. (1980) *Class and economic change in Kenya: the making of an African petite bourgeoisie*, Yale University Press, New Haven, Connecticut.

Kitching, G. (1985) 'Politics, method and evidence in the "Kenya Debate" ', pp. 115–51 in H. Bernstein and B.K. Campbell (eds) *Contradictions of accumulation in Africa*, Sage, Beverly Hills.

Kjekshus, H. (1977) *Ecology control and economic development in East African history: the case of Tanganyika, 1850–1950*, University of California Press, Berkeley.

Kobiah, S.M. (1985) 'The origins of squatting and community organization in Nairobi', *African Urban Studies*, special issue 19–20.

Koda, B., Mbliniya, M., Muro, A., Kokubdwa Nkebukwa, A., Nkhoma, A., Tumbo-Masabo, Z., and Vuorela, U. (1987) *Women's initiatives in the United Republic of Tanzania: a technical co-operation report*, World Employment Program, ILO, Geneva.

Kropp-Dakubu (1988) 'Multilingualism in Ada District', *Research Review* 4(1): Institute of African Studies, Legon, Accra.

Lardner, G.E.A. (1985) 'Beyond the neocolonial nexus: inheritance, implementation, and implications of the Lagos Plan of Action', pp. 35–46 in A. Adedeji and T.M. Shaw (eds) *Economic crisis in Africa: African perspectives in development problems and potentials*, Lynne Rienner, Boulder, Col.

Lenin, V.I. (1978) *Imperialism, the highest stage of capitalism*, Progress, Moscow.

Leys, C. (1987) 'The state and the crisis of simple commodity production in Africa', *IDS Bulletin* 18(3): 45–9.

Longhurst, R. (1988) 'Cash crops, household food security and nutrition', *IDS Bulletin* 19(2): 28–36.

Longhurst, R. Kamara, S. and Mensurah, J. (1988) 'Structural adjustment and vulnerable groups in Sierra Leone', *IDS Bulletin* 19(1): 25–30.

Loutfi, M. (1989) 'Development issues and state policies in sub-Saharan Africa', *International Labour Review* 128(2): 137–54.

Loxley, J. (1988) *Ghana: economic crisis and the long road to recovery*, North–South Institute, Ottawa.

Loxley, J. (n.d.) 'Structural adjustment programs in Africa: some issues of theory and policy' (draft).

Mabogunje, A. (1988) 'Africa after the false start', Paper presented to the 26th Congress of the International Geographical Union, Sydney, Australia.

McCall, M. (1987) 'The implications of East-African rural social structure for local-level development: the case for participatory development based on indigenous knowledge systems', Paper presented at seminar in Eastern Africa rural development experience: strategies in local level development, 30 June to 3 July 1987, Nairobi, UNCRD/IDS, pp. 1–36, Nagoya, Japan.

McCall, M. (1988) 'The implications of Eastern African rural social structure for local-level development: the case for participatory development based on indigenous knowledge systems', *Regional Development Dialogue* 9(2): 41–69.

Macebo, L. (1988) 'Vusanami collective farming cooperative society (VCCSL) Zimbabwe', p. 80 in P. Oakley (ed.) *Proceedings of the international*

BIBLIOGRAPHY

symposium on the challenge of rural poverty: how to meet it, German Foundation for International Development, Feldafing, FGR.

Mackenzie, F. (1986) 'Local initiatives and national policy: gender and agricultural change in Murang'a District, Kenya', *Canadian Journal of African Studies* 20(3): 377–401.

Mackenzie, F. (1990) 'Gender and land rights in Murang'a District, Kenya', *Journal of Peasant Studies* 17(4): 609–43.

Mackenzie, F. (1991) 'Political economy of the environment, gender and resistance under colonialism: Murang'a District, Kenya, 1910–1950', *Canadian Journal of African Studies* 25(2).

Mackenzie, F. and D.R.F. Taylor (1989) 'Inequality in Murang'a District, Kenya: local organization for change', pp. 112–39 in K. Swindell, J.M. Baba and M.J. Mortimore (eds) *Inequality and development: case studies from the third world*, Macmillan, London.

Manoukian, M. (1964) *Akan and Ga-Adangme Peoples*, Oxford University Press, Oxford.

Maro, P.S. (1990) 'The impact of decentralization on spatial equity and rural development in Tanzania', *World Development* 18(5): 673–93.

Mascarenhas, A. (1977) 'Resettlement and desertification: the Wagogo of Dodoma Distict, Tanzania', *Economic Geography* 53: 376–80.

Mascarenhas, A. and Mbilinyi, M. (1983) *Women in Tanzania: an annotated bibliography*, Uppsala Institute of African Studies, Uppsala.

Maya, R.S. (1988) 'Structural adjustment in Zimbabwe: its impact on women', Unpublished paper commissioned for the Commonwealth Expert Group on Women and Structural Adjustment.

Mbilinyi, M. (1988) 'Agribusiness and women peasants in Tanzania', *Development and Change* 19: 549–83.

Mbilinyi, M. (1989) 'The role of women in promoting local-level development in East Africa', Paper presented to the UNCRD/CIRDAFRICA Seminar on Reviving Local Self-Reliance: Challenges for Rural/Regional Development in Eastern and Southern Africa, Arusha, Tanzania, 24 February.

Mbugua, Moses G. (1989) 'Kenya Freedom from Hunger Council for National Development: experiences in local-level development', Paper presented to the UNCRD/CIRDAFRICA Seminar on Reviving Local Self-Reliance: Challenges for Rural/Regional Development in Eastern and Southern Africa, Arusha, Tanzania, 24 February.

Meyers, R.L. (1981) *Organisation and administration of integrated rural development in semi-arid areas, the Machakos Integrated Development Plan*, Report prepared for the Office of Rural Development and Development Administration, Development Support Division, Agency for International Development, Ithaca, November.

Mikell, G. (1989) *Cocoa and chaos in Ghana*, Paragon House, New York.

Molyneux, M. (1985) 'Mobilization without emancipation? Women's interests, the state, and revolution in Nicaragua', *Feminist Studies* 11(2): 227–54.

Moore, Henrietta (1986) *Space, text and gender: an anthropological study on the Marakwet of Kenya*, Cambridge University Press, Cambridge.

Moore, S.F. (1986) *Social facts and fabrications: 'customary' law on Kilimanjaro 1880–1980*, Cambridge University Press, Cambridge.

267

Moulaert, F. and Salinas, P.W. (eds) (1983) *Regional analysis and the new international division of labour*, Studies in Applied Regional Science, Boston, The Hague.

Moxon, J. (1984) *Volta – Man's greatest lake*, André Deutsch, London.

Muegge, H. and Stöhr, W. with Hesp, P. and Stuckey, B. (1987) *International economic restructuring and the regional community*, Gower, Aldershot.

Mukoko, R.K. (1987) 'The role of informal sector in rural development: a case of wood carving industry in Wamuyu Location, Machakos District', MA thesis, Department of Urban and Regional Planning, Nairobi University, June.

Mulazi, J.K.N. (1984) '*An evaluation of village vehicle utilization: a case study of selected villages in Dodoma District*', Unpublished post-graduate diploma thesis, Tanzania.

Munachonga, M.L. (1986) 'Impact of economic adjustment on women in Zambia', Unpublished paper commissioned for UNDP Restructuring and Development in Zambia: Roles for Technical Cooperation Group, New York.

Munslow, B. (1985) 'Prospects for the socialist transformation of agriculture in Zimababwe', *World Development* 13(1): 41–58.

Muro, A. (1987) *Education and training of women for employment: the case of Tanzania*, Arusha, 1982, Eastern and Southern African Management Insitute, Ministry of Education, Dar es Salaam.

Mussa-Nda, N. (1988) 'A greater role for local development strategies', *Regional Development Dialogue* 9(2): 1–11.

Mutizwa-Mangiza, N.D. (1986) 'Local government and planning in Zimbabwe', *Third World Planning Review* 8(2): 153–75.

Mwaluko, E.P. (1961/2) 'Famine in the Central Province of Tanganyika', *Tropical Agriculture* 39, Trinidad.

Naschold, F. (1978) *Alternative Raumpolitik*, Athenian Verlag, Kronburg.

Ndaro, J.M.M. (ed.) (1987) *A survey of small village dam construction projects in Dodoma District*, Institute of Rural Development Planning, Dodoma.

Ndaro, J.M.M. and Temu, J.J. (1989) 'Local strategies and regional/rural development in Kenya: a case study of Machakos District', Paper presented to the UNCRD/CIRDAFRICA Seminar on Reviving Local Self-Reliance: Challenges for Rural/Region Development in Eastern and Southern Africa, Arusha, Tanzania, 24 February.

Ndorobo, B. (1973) 'Famine problems in Dodoma District', *Journal of Geographical Association of Tanzania* 3: 26–47.

Ngugi wa Thiong'o (n.d.) 'Women in cultural work: the fate of Kamiriithu people's theatre in Kenya'.

Nyerere, J.K. (1967) 'The Arusha declaration', pp. 231–50 in J.K. Nyerere (1968) *Freedom and Socialism*, Oxford University Press, Oxford.

Nyerere, J.K. (1968) *Freedom and Socialism: a selection from writings and speeches 1965–7*, Oxford University Press, Oxford.

Nyerere, J.K. (1972) *Decentralisation*, Government Printer, Dar es Salaam.

Oakley, P. (ed.) (1988) *Proceedings of the international symposium on the challenge of rural poverty: how to meet it*, German Foundation for International Development, Feldafing, FGR.

Oakley, P. and Marsden, P. (1984) *Approaches to participation in rural development*, ILO, Geneva.

Odingo, R.S. (1988) 'The Eastern African rural settlement pattern and its bearing in local-level development strategy', *Regional Development Dialogue* 9(2): 14–34.

Odingo, R.S. and Okeyo, A.P. (1988) 'The rural development problematique in Eastern Africa', *Regional Development Dialogue* 9(2): i–v.

Odunga, S., Mabele, R.B. *et al.* (1988) 'Tanzania economic trends', *A Quarterly Review of the Economy* 1(1).

OECD (1988) *Activities of the OECD, report by the Secretary General*, OECD Publications, Paris.

O'Keefe, P., Raskin, P. and Bernow, S. (1984) *Energy and development in Kenya: opportunities and constraints*, Beijer Institute, Stockholm, Sweden.

Okeyo, A.P. (1988) 'The role of women in Eastern African rural development', *Regional Development Dialogue* 9(2): 89–101.

Olowu, Dele (1989) 'Local institutes and development: the African experience', *CJAS/RCEA* 23(2): 201–26.

Ondiege, P.O. (1989) 'Local strategies and regional/rural development in Kenya: a case study of Machakos District', Paper presented to the UNCRD/CIRDAFRICA Seminar on Reviving Local Self-Reliance: Challenges for Rural/Regional Development in Eastern and Southern Africa, Arusha, Tanzania, 24 February.

Onimode, B. (1989a) 'Case study on the impact of structural adjustment on women in Nigeria', Unpublished paper commissioned for the Commonwealth Expert Group on Women and Structural Adjustment.

Onimode, B. (ed.) (1989b) *The IMF, the World Bank and the African Debt*, vol. 2, 'The social and political impact', Institute for African Alternatives/Zed Press, London.

Ouma, Stephen O.A. (1989) 'Local strategies and regional/rural development in Eastern and Southern Africa: a report of the Uganda case study', Paper presented to the UNCRD/CIRDAFRICA Seminar on Reviving Local Self-Reliance: Challenges for Rural/Regional Development in Eastern and Southern Africa, Arusha, Tanzania, 24 February.

Parkin, D.J. (1972) *Palms, wine and witnesses: public spirit and private gain in an African farming community*, Chandler, San Francisco.

Patel, D. (1988) 'Some issues of urbanization and development in Zimbabwe', *Journal of Social Development in Africa* 3(2): 17–31.

Pinstrup-Andersen, P., Jaramillo, M. and Stewart, F. (1987) 'The impact of government expenditure', pp. 73–89 in G.A. Cornia, R. Jolly and F. Stewart (eds) *Adjustment with a human face: protecting the vulnerable and promoting growth*, Clarendon Press, Oxford.

Posnansky, M. (1980) 'How Ghana's crisis affects a village', *West Africa* 3306 (December): 2418–20.

Posnansky, M. (1984) 'Hardships of a village', *West Africa* 3506 (October): 2161–3.

Putterman, Louis (1990) 'Village communities, co-operation, and inequality in Tanzania: comments on Collier *et al.*', *World Development* 18(1): 147–53.

Redclift, M. (1984) *Development and the environmental crisis: red or green alternatives?*, Methuen, London.

Redclift, M. (1987) *Sustainable development: exploring the contradictions*, Methuen, London.

Republic of Zimbabwe (1982) *Transitional National Development Plan, 1982/83 – 1984/85*, Harare.

Republic of Zimbabwe (1986) *First Five-Year National Development Plan 1986–1990*, vol. 1, Harare.

Richards, P. (1979) 'Community environmental knowledge in African rural development', *IDS Bulletin* 10(2): 28–36.

Richards, P. (1983) 'Ecological change and the politics of African land use', *African Studies Review* 26(2): 1–72.

Richards, P. (1985) *Indigenous agricultural revolution: ecology and food production in West Africa*, Hutchinson, London.

Robertson, C. and Berger, I. (1986) 'Introduction: analyzing class and gender – African perspectives', pp. 3–24 in C. Robertson and I. Berger (eds) *Women and class in Africa*, Holmes & Meier, New York.

Rohrbach, D.D. (1987) 'A preliminary assessment of factors underlying the growth of communal maize production in Zimbabwe', pp. 145–84 in M. Rukuni and C.K. Eicher (eds) *Food security for southern Africa*, UZ/MSU Food Security Project, University of Zimbabwe, Harare.

Rondinelli, D.A., McCullough, J.S. and Johnson, R.W. (1989) 'Analysing decentralization policies in developing countries: a political economy framework', *Development and Change* 20: 57–87.

Rutashobya, M. (1988) 'Marriage customs and women's legal rights in Tanzania', pp. 29–76 in *Proceedings and papers of the workshop on women and the law: theory and practice*, Dar es Salaam Women Research and Documentation Project, Dar es Salaam.

Sandbrook, R. (1986) 'The state and economic stagnation in tropical Africa', *World Development* 14(3): 319–32.

Sanyal, B. (1984) 'Urban agriculture: a strategy for survival in Zambia', Ph.D. thesis, University of California, Los Angeles; cited in Evans (1989).

Scott, J.C. (1986) *Weapons of the weak: everyday forms of peasant resistance*, Yale University Press, New Haven, Conn.

Sender, J. and Smith, S. (1986) *The development of capitalism in Africa*, Methuen, London.

Senyah, J. (1984) 'Ghana cocoa: more than just a bean', *West Africa* 3483 (May): 1018–19.

Sibanda, B.M.C. (1986) 'Impacts of agricultural microprojects on rural development: lessons from two projects in the Zambezi Valley', *Land Use Policy* 3(4): 311–29.

Sinare, H. (1988) 'Women: do you know your rights? the lack of them?', pp. 17–22 in *Proceedings and papers of the workshop on women and the law: theory and practice*, Dar es Salaam Women Research and Documentation Project, Dar es Salaam.

Smith, S. (1987) 'Zimbabwean women in co-operatives: participation and sexual equality in four producer co-operatives', *Journal of Social Development in Africa* 2(1): 29–46.

Songsore, Jacob (1982) *Co-operative credit unions as instruments of regional development: the example of N.W. Ghana*, Occasional Paper 17, Centre for Development Studies, University College of Swansea, Wales.

Songsore, Jacob (1983) *Intraregional and interregional labour migrations in historical perspective: the case of North-Western Ghana*, Occasional Paper 1, Faculty of Social Sciences, University of Port Harcourt, Nigeria, October.

Songsore, Jacob (1989) 'The ERP/Structural Adjustment Programme and the "distant" rural poor in Northern Ghana', Paper presented at the *International Conference on Planning for Growth and Development in Africa*, ISSER, University of Ghana, Legon, Accra, 13–17 March.

Songsore, Jacob and Aloysius Denkabe (1988) 'Challenging rural poverty in Northern Ghana: the case of the Upper-West region', Unpublished preliminary report for UNICEF, October, UNICEF, Accra.

Stamp, P. (1987) 'Matega: manipulating women's co-operative traditions for material and social gain in Kenya', Paper presented at the Annual Conference of the Canadian Association of African Studies, University of Alberta, Edmonton, May.

Stamp, P. (1989) *Technology, gender and power in Africa*, Technical Study 63e, International Development Research Centre, Ottawa.

Stanning, J. (1987) 'Household grain storage and marketing in surplus and deficit communal farming areas in Zimbabwe: preliminary findings', pp. 245–91 in M. Rukuni and C.K. Eicher (eds) *Food security for southern Africa*, UZ/MSU Food Security Unit, University of Zimbabwe, Harare.

Stöhr, W.B. (1981) 'Development from below: the bottom-up and periphery-inward development paradigm', pp. 39–72 in W.B. Stöhr and D.R.F. Taylor (eds) *Development from above or below?: the dialectics of regional planning in developing countries*, Wiley, Chichester.

Stöhr, W.B. and Taylor, D.R.F. (eds) (1981) *Development from above or below?: the dialectics of regional planning in developing countries*, Wiley, Chichester.

Stöhr, W.B. and Tödtling, F. (1978) 'Spatial equity – some antitheses to current regional development strategy', *Paper of the Regional Science Association* 38: 33–53.

Stoneman, C. and Cliffe, L. (1989) *Zimbabwe: politics, economics and society*, Pinter, London.

Stuckey, B. (1985) *Endogenous development*, NFP 5 Working Papers, Berne.

Sutton, I.B. (1981) 'The Volta River salt trade: the survival of an indigenous industry', *Journal of African History* 22: 43–61.

Swantz, M.L. (1977) *Strain and strength among peasant women in Tanzania*, BRALUP Research Paper 49, University of Dar es Salaam.

Swift, J. (1989) 'Why are rural people vulnerable to famine?'. *IDS Bulletin* 20(2): 8–15.

Taal, H. (1989) 'How farmers cope with risk and stress in rural Gambia', *IDS Bulletin* 20(2): 16–21.

Taasisi ya Watu Wazima Miradi ya Wakina Mama Matetereka (1984) In *Sauti ya Wanawake Tanzania* 1, Idara ya Wanawake, Dar es Salaam.

Taasisi ya Watu Wazima Zijue Haki za Wanawake Tanzania (1987) Dar es Salaam.

Tattersfield, J.R. (1982) 'The role of research in increasing food crop potential in Zimbabwe', *Zimbabwe Agricultural Journal* 16(1): 6–10, 24.

Taylor, D.R.F. (1989) 'Why local initiatives in Africa?: the context and rationale', Paper presented to the UNCRD/CIRDAFRICA Seminar on

271

Reviving Local Self-Reliance: Challenges for Rural/Regional Development in Eastern and Southern Africa, Arusha, Tanzania, 24 February.

Thiele, G. (1984) 'Location and enterprise choice: a Tanzanian case study', *Journal of Agricultural Economics* 35(2): 257–64.

Thomas, B.P. (1985) *Politics, participation and poverty: development through self-help in Kenya*, Westview, Boulder, Col.

Thomas, B.P. (1988) 'State formation, development, and the politics of self-help in Kenya', *Studies in Comparative International Development* 23(3): 3–27.

Thomas, Helen T. (1988) 'Constraints on rural women's access to credit in the Third World: a review of the issues and literature', pp. 6–19 in F. Mackenzie (ed.) *Gender and processes of change in the Third World*, Discussion papers 7, Carleton University, Ottawa.

Thomas-Slayter, B.P. and Ford, R. (1989) 'Water, soils, food and rural development: examining institutional frameworks in Katheka Sub-location', *Canadian Journal of African Studies* 23(2): 250–71.

Tibaijuka, A. (1988) 'The impact of structural adjustment programmes on women: the case of Tanzania's Economic Recovery Programme', Unpublished paper commissioned for the Commonwealth Expert Group on Women and Structural Adjustment.

Turnbull, M. (1972) *The mountain people*, Jonathan Cape, London.

Turton, D. (1977) 'Responses to drought: the Murai of Southwestern Ethiopia', pp. 165–92 in J.P. Garlick and R.W.J. Keay (eds) *Human ecology in the tropics*, Taylor and Francis Ltd, London.

UN (1986a) *Programme of Action for African Economic Recovery and Development 1986–90* (UN-PAAERD), New York.

UN (1986b) 'The declaration of Non-Governmental Organizations on the African Economic and Social Crisis', Proceedings of a meeting of African, Northern and International NGOs at the UN General Assembly Special Session on the Critical Economic and Social Situation in Africa, 26–31 May 1986, New York.

UNECA (1980) *Lagos Plan of Action and Final Act of Lagos*, Addis Ababa.

UNECA, Organization of African Unity (1986) 'Africa's submission to the Special Session of the UN General Assembly on Africa's economic and social crisis', Addis Ababa, 31 March.

UNECA (1986) *African Priority Programme for Economic Recovery* (APPER), Addis Ababa.

UNECA (1987) *African socio-economic indicators 1985*, UN e/f. 87.11.K.8, Addis Ababa.

UNECA (1989a) *African Alternative Framework to Structural Adjustment Programmes for Socio-economic Recovery and Transformation* (AAF–SAP) Addis Ababa.

UNECA (1989b) *Statistics and policies: ECA*, Preliminary observations on the World Bank report: 'Africa's adjustment and growth in the 1980s', Addis Ababa.

UNECA (1990) *Survey of Economic and Social Conditions in Africa 1987/88*, E/ECA/CM15/3/Rev.2, United Nations, New York.

UNICEF (1984) 'Statistics on children in UNICEF assisted countries', Accra, Unpublished document.

UNICEF (1985) 'Situation analysis of women and children', Accra, Ghana, Unpublished document.

UNICEF (1986) 'United Nations Programme of Action for the Economic Recovery 1986–90, Draft basic document, Preparatory Committee of the Whole for the Special Session of the General Assembly on the Critical Economic Situation in Africa, UNICEF, New York.

UNICEF (1988) *The state of the world's children*, UNICEF Publications, New York.

United Nations Centre for Regional Development (1988) 'Eastern African rural development experience: strategies on local-level development', Report of the Proceedings of an International Seminar, Nairobi, 30 June to 3 July 1988, Nagoya, Japan.

United Nations Centre for Regional Development (1989) *Reviving Local Self-Reliance: Challenges for Rural/Regional Development in Eastern and Southern Africa*, Meeting report series no. 31, Nagoya, Japan.

United Republic of Tanzania (1976) *Third five year plan for economic and social development, 1st July 1976–30th June 1981*, Government Printer, Dar es Salaam.

United Republic of Tanzania (1982) *1978 population census vol. 4: a summary of selected statistics*, Government Printer, Dar es Salaam.

United Republic of Tanzania (1984) *National economic survival programme*, Government Printer, Dar es Salaam.

United Republic of Tanzania (1986) *Economic recovery programme*, Government Printer, Dar es Salaam.

UWT (n.d.) *Taarifa ya jumuiya ya Wanawake ya miaka 20 ya Azimio la Arusha na miaka 10 ya CCM*, Dar es Salaam.

Van Den Dries, J. (1970) *Credit union handbook*, Zenith Printing Works, Nairobi, March.

Van Gelder, B. and Kerkhof, P. (1984) *The agroforestry survey in Kakamega District*, Working Paper 3, Kenya Woodfuel Development Programme, Nairobi.

Vaughan, M. (1985) 'Households units and historical process in southern Malawi', *Review of African Political Economy* 34: 35–45.

Vincent, V. and Thomas, R.G. (1961) *An agricultural survey of southern Rhodesia*, Government Printer, Salisbury.

Wa Diocese (1987) 'Reorganization and motivation of credit unions in Wa Diocese', mimeo, Wa, Ghana, December.

Waal, Alex de (1989) 'Is famine relief irrelevant to rural people?', *IDS Bulletin* 20(2): 63–7.

Wade, R. (1988) *Village republics: economic conditions for collective action in South India*, Cambridge University Press, Cambridge.

Wagao, J. (1988) *Analysis of the economic situation of urban and rural women in Tanzania*, UNICEF, Dar es Salaam.

Watts, Michael (1986) 'Geographers among the peasants: power, politics and practice', *Economic Geography* 2: 373–86.

Watts, Michael (1988) 'Idioms of land and labour; producing politics and rice in Senegambia', Paper presented at the Symposium on Land in African Agrarian Systems held at the University of Illinois, Urbana-Champaign, 10–12 April.

Watts, Michael (1989) 'The agrarian crisis in Africa: debating the crisis', *Progress in Human Geography* 13(1): 1–41.

Weaver, C. (1984) *Regional development and the local community: planning, politics and social context*, Wiley, Chichester.

Weiner, D. (1988) 'Agricultural transformation in Zimbabwe: lessons for South Africa after apartheid', *Geoforum* 19(4): 479–96.

Wekwete, K.H. (1988) 'Rural growth points in Zimbabwe: prospects for the future', *Journal of Social Development in Africa* 3(2): 5–16.

Were, S. and Akong'a, J. (eds) (1981) 'Machakos District social–cultural profile', draft report for the Ministry of National Planning and Development, Institute of African Studies, University of Nairobi, Nairobi.

West Africa (1989) November, West Africa Publishing Company Ltd, London.

White, B. (1976) 'Population, involution and employment in rural Java', *Development and Change* 7(3): 267–90.

Whitlow, J.R. (1980a) 'Land use, population pressure and rock outcrops in the tribal areas of Zimbabwe Rhodesia', *Zimbabwe Rhodesia Agricultural Journal* 77(1): 3–11.

Whitlow, J.R. (1980b) 'Environmental constraints and population pressures in the tribal areas of Zimbabwe', *Zimbabwe Agricultural Journal* 77(4): 173–81.

Whitlow, J.R. (1988) *Land degradation in Zimbabwe: a geographical study*, Natural Resources Board, Harare.

Wilks, I. (1977) 'Land, labour, capital and the forest kingdom of Asante: a model for change', pp. 487–534 in J. Friedman and M. Rowlands (eds) *The evolution of social systems*, Duckworth, London.

World Bank (1981) *Accelerated development in Sub-Saharan Africa: an agenda for action*, Washington, D.C.

World Bank (1984a) *Toward sustained development in Sub-Saharan Africa: a joint program of action*, Washington, D.C.

World Bank (1984b) *World development report*, Washington, D.C.

World Bank (1985) *World development report*, Washington, D.C.

World Bank (1986) *World development report*, Washington, D.C.

World Bank (1988a) *Ghana: country economic memorandum*, International Bank for Reconstruction and Development, Washington, D.C., November.

World Bank (1988b) *Report on adjustment lending*, Washington, D.C.

World Bank (1989) *Sub-Saharan Africa: from crisis to sustainable growth*, Washington, D.C.

World Bank/UNDP (1989) *Africa's adjustment and growth in the 1980s*, Washington, D.C.

World Bank (1990) *World development report 1990*, Oxford University Press, Toronto.

World Commission on Environment and Development (1987) *Our common future* (the Brundtland Report), Oxford University Press, Oxford.

Young, R. (1988) *Zambia: adjusting to poverty*, North–South Institute, Ottawa.

Young, Roger (1989) 'Structural adjustment in Africa: roles and challenges for NGOs', Paper presented to Canadian Council for International Co-operation, May, Ottawa.

Zinyama, L.M. (1986a) 'Agricultural development policies in the African farming areas of Zimbabwe', *Geography* 71 (part 2): 105–15.

Zinyama, L.M. (1986b) 'Rural household structure, absenteeism and agricultural labour: a case study of two subsistence farming areas in Zimbabwe', *Singapore Journal of Tropical Geography* 7(2): 163–73.

Zinyama, L.M. (1987a) 'Assessing spatial variations in social conditions in the African rural areas of Zimbabwe', *Tijdschrift voor Economische en Sociale Geografia* 78(1): 30–43.

Zinyama, L.M. (1987b) 'Gender, age and the ownership of agricultural resources in the Mhondoro and Save North communal areas of Zimbabwe', *Geographical Journal of Zimbabwe* 18: 1–14.

Zinyama, L.M. (1988a) 'Commercialization of small-scale agriculture in Zimbabwe: some emerging patterns of spatial differentiation', *Singapore Journal of Tropical Geography* 9(2): 151–62.

Zinyama, L.M. (1988b) 'Farmers' perceptions of the constraints against increased crop production in the subsistence communal farming sector of Zimbabwe', *Agricultural Administration and Extension* 29(2): 97–109.

Zinyama, L.M. (1988c) 'A comparative analysis of social and economic factors influencing agricultural change and development in the Mhondoro and Save North communal areas of Zimbabwe', Unpublished D.Phil. thesis, Department of Geography, University of Zimbabwe, Harare.

Zinyama, L.M. (1989) 'Local strategies and responses and their contribution to rural development in Zimbabwe', Paper presented to the UNCRD/CIRD AFRICA Seminar on Reviving Local Self-Reliance: Challenges for Rural/Regional Development in Eastern and Southern Africa, Arusha, Tanzania, 24 February.

Zinyama, L.M. and Whitlow, R. (1986) 'Changing patterns of population distribution in Zimbabwe', *GeoJournal* 13(4): 365–84.

Zinyama, L.M., Campbell, D.J. and Matiza, T. (1990) 'Land policy and access to land in Zimbabwe: the Dewure resettlement scheme', *Geoforum* 21(3): 359–70.

INDEX

Ada District: 103–23, 229–30;
climatic conditions, 103–6;
infrastructure and amenities,
110–11; salt trade, 111–14;
Songor lagoon area, 106–10
Ada Songor Salt Miners'
Co-operative Society, 114,
115–19, 120, 122, 229–30, 245
Ada Traditional Area Fund
(ATAF), 117, 122
Ada Traditional Council, 114,
116–17, 122, 229, 230
Adedeji, A.: 2, 18, 19, 217;
African debt, 5, 219; African
development crisis, 215, 215–16;
SAPs, 10, 24
Africa: countering erosion of
sovereignty, 18–31; debt, 5, 215,
219; development crisis, 2–10,
215–17, 246; causes, 217–21;
economic structure, 125–6;
environmental costs, 15–18;
growth rates, 3–5, 32, 215, 217;
local diversity, 223; social fabric,
10, 11–15, 216–17
African Alternative Framework to
Structural Adjustment
Programmes for Socio-economic
Recovery and Transformation
(AAF-SAP): 2, 10, 24, 30, 32;
environmental costs, 15–16;
policy recommendations, 19–22
African Priority Programme for
Economic Recovery (APPER),
19

African Salt Limited, 119
Agricultural Finance Corporation
(AFC), 56–7
agriculture: 125–6, 219;
development crisis, 216–17;
Ghana, 59–62, 65–6, 67;
Kenya, 127–8, 140–4; KWDP
and on-farm trials, 156–60;
Tanzania, 170; Zimbabwe,
39–44; see also local farmer
organizations
Akamba people, 131, 134, 139
Akator, G., 195
Akhoya, Rispa, 163–4
Akong'a, J., 130
Akyem Oda, 58
Anglican Cathedral Group, 191
Anim, N.O., 113
animal manure, selling, 174, 179,
185–6
Appenteng family, 114, 115, 120,
121, 229
Arhin, K., 62
Arusha Declaration, 178, 187, 195
assault, 74, 80–1
Awamu Vijana Group, 184
Ayirebi: 58–81, 226–7, 230, 237,
249; Committee for the Defence
of the Revolution (CDR), 62, 69,
71, 78–9, 80, 227; community-
level coping strategies, 69–74;
household-level coping strategies,
65–9; local economy, 59–65;
returnees from Nigeria, 65,
69–71, 79, 80; Town

Development Committee (TDC), 62, 69, 78, 227
Ayirebi Agege Boys and Girls Association, 71

banks, 82–3, 86–7, 100
barter and exchange, 174, 177, 184–5
basketry, 68
Beckman, B., 218, 252
beer brewing by Tanzanian women: Dodoma District, 182, 186; Utengule Usangu, 9, 202–10
beer clubs (*vikao*), 206, 206–10
beer halls (*vilabu*), 205, 206, 208
bench terracing, 139
Bentil, B., 82–3, 87, 100
Bequele, A., 5
Berg Report, 24, 30
Berger, I., 27, 31
Bernstein, H., 17, 27
Berry, S., 2, 17, 244–5
Bienefeld, M., 7, 32
Bihawana Village tailoring group, 191
blacksmithing, 68, 184
Blaikie, P., 17, 18
Boateng, E.A., 60
Boateng, I.K., 103
Bradley, P.N., 149, 150, 168
Bratton, M., 253: local initiatives, 48, 55; NFAZ, 237–8; NGOs, 254; savings development movement, 250–1; 'voice' and empowerment, 249–50
Brett, E.A., 28, 48–9, 218, 251–2
brewing, *see* beer brewing
British South Africa Company (BSACo), 37
Brooke, C., 177
Brown, C.K., 102–3
Brugger, E.A., 234–5
Brundtland Report, 15, 224
burial, 241
burial societies, 176, 190
Busie Credit Union, 95

Callear, D., 42–3

Calliandra trees, 158–9
Canada, 87
Canadian Co-operative Association (CCA), 96, 99, 228
capitalism, 82–3, 98
cassava, 65, 66
Catholic Association, 52
Catholic Church, 87, 94, 228, 239
Chambers, R.: 31, 244, 246; approaches to development, 221–3; enabling state, 253; ideology of reversals, xvi, 222–3, 247, 253; local diversity, 223–4, 225
charcoal, 148, 174, 179, 185
Chavangi, N.A., 150, 157, 162, 163–4, 165
chiefs, local, 113, 122
children, 197, 198, 199, 203
Chitsike, L.T., 87
Ciba-Geigy, 52
class relations: 7, 28; access to credit, 94, 98; farmer training groups, 52; state and local communities, 252
cocoa, 60, 76, 78
cocoyams, 65–6
coffee co-operatives, 138, 140
coffee farming, 141
colonialism, 36–8, 86, 202, 242
commodity prices, 219
Commonwealth Expert Group (CEG), 7, 9, 11, 13, 14, 15, 24
communal lands, Zimbabwe, 37, 38, 39, 41
communities, local: organic entities, 227, 245; participation and, 237; state and, 251–3
community centres, multipurpose, 188
community farming, 71
community initiatives, *see* local initiatives
community-level coping strategies, 69–74
confrontation, 245
Co-operative Credit Unions Association of Ghana, 88, 96, 98, 99–100, 228

co-operatives: beer club, 206–10; Dodoma District, 179–80, 180, 184, 189–90, 192; Machakos District, 138, 230; salt, 114–19, 122–3, 124, 229–30; *see also* credit union movement

coping strategies, *see* Dodoma District; Machakos District

Cornia, G.A., 15

Côte d'Ivoire, 5, 9, 102

cotton, 41, 42

crafts, local: Ayirebi, 68, 80; Dodoma District, 174, 178, 182, 183–4; Machakos District, 139–40

credit: Ghana, 82–3; group lending, 56–7; for transportation, 189

credit union movement: 83–4, 85, 227–9; crisis and protests within, 96–8; emergence, 87–91; revival strategies, 98–101; role in rural development, 92–6

Credit for Women Project, 96, 99

crime, 74, 80–1

culture: tree planting and, 152–3, 156, 168; women in informal sector, 199–200

customary law, 211–12

dams, 175, 178, 179, 189

Dar es Salaam, 10, 179, 203, 204

Darfur, 244

De Stemper, G.A., 101

Dearlove, J., 247

deforestation, 193; *see also* tree planting

Dei, G.J.S., 61, 62, 63, 68, 226–7

desertification control, 193

development: crisis in Africa, *see* Africa; rural, 126–7, 194; strategies, 102–3, 128–30; survival and, 225–32, 247–51; theory and practice, 214; inadequacies of past and present, 221–3

development from above, 34, 36–9, 44

development from below, xiii, 28–9, 222, 233–6, 246

development levy, 202–3

development from within: xvi, 34, 182, 222, 233–58; NGOs, 253–5; participation, 236–41; policy actions, 255–7; prospects for, 246–7; state-local relationships, 251–3; territoriality, 241–6

Dodoma District: 172–3, 195–6, 231–2; 248–9; ecological coping strategies, 176, 193–4; economic coping strategies, 174–5, 183–6; phases of coping strategies, 173–82 (1961–70, 173, 177–8; 1971–8, 173, 178–80; after 1979, 177, 180–2); social coping strategies, 175–6, 187–92

drama, popular, 29–30, 153, 164–5

draught power, 50

drought, 63, 74, 177, 180, 220–1

Dutkiewicz, P., 30

ecological coping strategies: Dodoma District, 176, 183, 193–4; Machakos District, 135, 138–9

Economic Commission for Africa, *see* UNECA

economic coping strategies: Dodoma District, 174–5, 183, 183–6; Machakos District, 135, 139–40

economic crisis: 19–20, 102, 246–7; Ghana, 63–5, 226–7; measuring Africa's, 2–10; Tanzania, 170–2, 180–1; effect on women and children, 197–9

education: Dodoma District, 175, 181, 188; expenditure on, 13, 14–15, 216; Ghana, 12, 111; user fees and, 15; Zimbabwe, 12

employment creation, 200

employment cutbacks, 9–10

empowerment, 249–50; *see also* local empowerment

enabling state, 253

endogenous development, 235
environment: crisis: and economic crisis, 15–18, 220–1; Ghanaian view of causes, 73–4; survival and, 224, 243–4
Europe, 234, 236
European Economic Community (EEC), 131, 219
Evangelical Youth Group, Hombolo village, 191
Evans, A.: 6, 15; health care, 13, 14; maize, 7–8, 8–9; women, 9, 10, 14
exchange and barter, 174, 177, 184–5
export-led development, 75, 228

farmer organizations: co-operatives, 135; credit unions, 100; local and rural development, 47–55, 56–7, 225–6, marketing and purchasing, 52–5, mutual-help, 49–50, state support, 48–9, training, 50–2
farmers' tree planting activities, 153–4
farming, see agriculture
fertilizers, 46, 53–4, 54–5
films, 153, 165
Final Act of Lagos, 2, 18
food: decline in exports, 216–17; prices, 142, 204; production: Ayirebi, 60–1, cash crops and, 76–7, Machakos District, 140, 141, 142, see also agriculture; removal of subsidies, 7–8; shortages, 63, strategy responses, 66, 67, 180–1, 184–5; storage in common pool, 177
Food and Agriculture Organization (FAO), 100
Forbes, D.K., 28, 29
Fowler, A., 254, 255
Friedman, H., 245
Friedmann, J., 29, 233, 235–6
fuelwood: 148; women and procurement, 152–3, 202, 203; see also Kenya Woodfuel Development Programme

gathering, hunting and, 67–8
gender: 7, 28, 31; coping strategies and, 71–3; territoriality and, 241–2, 244–5; see also women
Ghana: xv, 226–30, 242; Association of Co-operative Credit Unions, 88, 96, 98, 99–100, 228; banks and capitalism, 82–3; cocoa industry, 5, 60, 78; Economic Recovery Programme (ERP), 84; economy: 5, 6, 9, effect of world recession on, 63–5; health and education, 11–14; migrants, 254–5; North-West, 84–5, see also credit union movement; People's Defence Committees (PDCs), 115, 119–20; PAMSCAD, 11; SAP, 84, 101, 116, 227–8; see also Ada District, Ayirebi
Glazier, J., 27
Gobbins, K.E., 43
Gore, C., xiii–xiv, 28, 29, 30, 241
Goulet, D.: 30, 31, 227, 249; participation, 236–8 passim, 239–40, 248
Green, R.H., 5, 6, 11
group extension approach, 50–1, 161–4, 166
group lending, 56–7

Hamile Town Credit Union, 92–6, passim, 97
handicrafts, see crafts, local
Harambee, 27–8, 28
Hart, J., 218–20
Havnevik, K.J., 198
health: Dodoma District, 175, 181, 187–8; expenditure, 11–14, 216; Ghana, 11–13, 14, 110; Machakos District, 133–4
Hill, P., 61, 78
Hinderink, J., 75
households: 6, 244–5; Ayirebi, 61–2, 78, coping strategies, 65–9; disadvantaged in Zimbabwe, 43; KWDP, 151, 154–5, 168–9; mutual help and

labour, 49–50, 62; simple reproduction squeeze, 17–18
housing, 68, 144
Hubbert, L., 100
human-centred development, 20, 23, 128
hunting, 67, 68
Hutchful, E., 23–4, 25

Imoo, B.V., 239
incomes: 6, 7, 198; diet and, 66, 67, 79, 80; women, 198, 200, informal sector, 204
India, 27
industries, local, *see* crafts, local
informal sector: 5–6, 10, 126; women in Tanzania, 199–201, 212–13, brewers, 201–10
International Monetary Fund, 2, 219–20
investment loans, 92, 93, 95

Jamal, V., 5
Jirapa Credit Union, 87, 92–6, *passim*

Kakamega District: 151–5, 231; KWDP, 155–67
Kaleo Credit Union, 92–6, *passim*
Kamiriithu Community Educational and Cultural Centre, 29–30, 231
Kamoli Ka Irongom women's group, 146
Kanzokea women's group, 136
Karikari, S.K., 65
Katelewa, F.C.S., 145
Kauzeni, A.S., 179
Kenya: xv, 14, 230–1, 241, 242, 251; agricultural production, 127–8, 140–4; Arid and Semi-Arid Lands (ASAL), 131; debt, 5; District Focus for Rural Development (DFRD), 128–30; GDP growth rates, 127; Harambee, 27–8, 28; households, 128, 129; Kamiriithu Community Centre, 29–30; 231; *see also* Machakos District
Kenya Woodfuel Development

Programme (KWDP), 148–69, 231; group extension approach, 161–4; mass media approach, 164–6; on-farm trials, 156–60
Kerkhof, P., 149, 154
Kidd, R., 30
kilabu (beer halls), 205, 206, 208
Kitching, G., 27, 30
Ko Credit Union, 92–6, *passim*
Kobiah, S.M., 251
Kundi ya Kuela Mbesa women's group, 135–6
Kuob-Lantaa Credit Union, 97, 229
Kyanguli self-help group, 137

labour: mutual help, 49–50, 62, 185; remittance money and hired, 69, 80
Lagos Plan of Action (LPA), 2, 18, 19
Lambussie, 94
land: Ayirebi, 61; distribution in Zimbabwe, 37; gender and access to, 17–18, 152; tree ownership uses, 154
Lawra Credit Union, 95
Lenin, V.I., 82
Leucaena trees, 158
Leys, C., 216
livestock farming, 143–4, 176, 193
loans, *see* credit; credit union movement
local authority holders, 122–3
local empowerment, 25–31, 195–6
local farmer organizations, *see* farmer organizations
local handicrafts, *see* crafts, local
local initiatives: 22–31, 223–5; evidence of, 225–32
local knowledge, 18, 224, 243
local self-governance, 242–3
Longhurst, R., 7, 14
Louse, J., 239
Loutfi, M., 2, 5, 10
Loxley, J., 6, 7

Mabogunje, A., 217–18, 253
Machakos District: 130–46, 230–1;

coping strategies, 134–47,
significance and potentials of,
138–45, sustainability, 145–6,
women's and self-help groups,
135–8; economic background,
131–4
Machakos District Co-operative
Union, 143
Machakos District Handicraft
Centre, 140
Machakos Integrated Development
Programme (MIDP), 131, 145
Mackenzie, F.: 9, 17–18, 27, 28,
231; community, 227; credit, 85;
development from within, 34
Mahoma Makulu Village, 188
maize: Ayirebi, 65; Zambia:
production, 8–9, removal of
subsidy, 7–8; Zimbabwe, 41, 42,
46–7, 54–5
male hegemony, women brewers
and, 207–10, 232
malnutrition, 14, 43
Manuh, T., 229–30
Manoukian, M., 61
manure, selling animal, 174, 179,
185–6
Manzaa self-help group, 137
market, local, 66, 79
market women's credit unions, 96
marketing groups, 52–5
Mascarenhas, A., 193
Mashonaland, 42
mass media, 164–6, 169
master farmers: 43; clubs, 51–2,
237
Mathare Valley, 251
Maya, R.S., 6, 11
Mbamba Bay, 204
Mbembani women's group, 137,
145
McCall, M., 31, 243, 244
McNulty, Rev. Fr J., 87
media, mass, 164–6, 169
metal tradesmen, 184
Mhondoro, 44–55, *passim*, 56
migration: Ghana, 62, 84, 95, 109,
110; Tanzania, 177, 199;
Zimbabwe, 36–7

milling machinery, 176, 192, 203
Mimosa trees, 159
mobilization, 238
Mohamed, Hawa, 211–12
Molyneux, M., 2, 29
Moulaert, F., 234
Moxon, J., 113
Mpunguzi Youth Group, 191
Muegge, H., 234
Mulazi, J.K.N., 189
Munachonga, M.L., 8
Muro, A., 197
Mussa-Nda, N., 217
mutual-help groups, 49–50, 62, 69;
see also self-help groups
Mutizwa-Mangiza, N.D., 39
Muungano Talawanda Group, 184
Muzarabani Communal Land, 48
Meyers, 131

Nandom Credit Union, 97, 229
Naschold, F., 233
National Centre for Local Self-
Reliance, 256
National Farmers' Association of
Zimbabwe (NFAZ), 237–8, 250
National Indigenous Resource
Centre, 256
Ndaro, J.M.M., 231–2, 248–9
Ndubi women's group, 137
Ndulu women's group, 137
Ngenda self-help group, 136
Ngugi, A.W., 157, 162
Ngugi wa Thiong'o, 30
Nigeria, 9, 13, 15, 252–3, 253,
254–5
non-governmental organizations
(NGOs): 22, 26–7, 146;
development from within, 246,
247, 253–5, 256
Nyere, J.K., 178, 187, 195, 233
Nzugumi Youth Group, 184

Oakley, P., 31, 218, 220, 236
Odingo, R.S., 241
Odunga, S., 170, 171
O'Keefe, P., 149
Olowu, D., 30, 225, 242, 242–3,
254–5

Ondiege, P.O., 133, 135, 137, 138, 230
Onimode, B., 6, 9, 13, 102
organic African community, 227, 245
Organization for Economic Co-operation and Development (OECD), 220
Otieno, S.M., 241

participation, 233, 236–41, 248
Pinstrup-Anderson, J., 13
ploughs, 50
popular theatre, 29–30, 153, 164–5
Ponsnansky, M., 68, 73
pottery, 183
poverty, 15–16, 83, 98, 198, 216, 217
Prankard, H.A., 43
priests, 113; see also Catholic Church
property rights, 211–12
purchasing groups, 53–5

rainfall, 220–1
Redclift, M., 16–17
remittances, 68–9, 80
resettlement, Zimbabwe, 38–9
reversals, strategy of, xvi, 222–3, 247, 253
Robertson, C., 27, 31
Rohrbach, D.D., 42
rotating credit associations, 83; see also credit union movement
rural banks, 83, 100
Rutashobya, M., 212

Salinas, P.W., 234
salt co-operatives, 114–19, 122–3, 124, 229–30; see also Ada Songor Salt Miners' Co-op
salt mining, 109
salt trade, 111–14, 123
Sandbrook, R., xvi, 30, 34
Sanyal, B., 8
Save North, 44–55, passim, 56
savings groups: 135; Dodoma District, 175, 189–90; farmers in Zimbabwe, 52–5, 56–7, 250–1;

see also credit union movement
Scott, J.C., 1
seed production units (SPUs), 161–2
Sefu, Ally, 211
self-help groups: 22; Dodoma District, 180, 182, 194, 195; Machakos District, 135, 135–8, 139, 145, 145–6, 230; see also mutual-help groups
self-reliance, 23, 233, 235–6, 246
Senyah, J., 60, 78
Sesbania trees, 152, 156, 159
Shenton, R., 30
shifting cultivation, 178
Sibanda, B.M.C., 48
Sinare, H., 212
social coping strategies: Dodoma District, 175–6, 183, 187–92; Machakos District, 135, 144–5
social relations: Ayirebi, 73–4; territoriality and, 244–5
soil erosion control, 193
Smith, S., 51
Songor lagoon: 106–10, 122; access struggle, 114, 115, 119–21; see also Ada District, Ada Songor Salt Miners' Co-operative Society
Songsore, J., 84, 85, 86, 101, 227–9
sovereignty, countering erosion of, 18–31
Sri Lanka, 219
Stamp, P., 18, 27, 28
Star Chemicals Ltd, 114, 115, 120
state: xiii–xiv, 23; Ayirebi community and, 75–7, 227; development from within, 246, 246–7, policy actions, 255–6; Dodoma district, 232; NGOs, 254; participation and, 238; power, 29–31, and local empowerment, 249–51; relationships with local communities, 251–3; role in African development crisis, 217–18; Songor lagoon conflict, 119–21, 229–30; support for

local organizations, xiii,
Machakos District, 146,
Zimbabwe, xv, 34, 48–9;
Zimbabwean development, 36–9,
44
Sterkenburg, J.J., 75
Stöhr, W.B.: xiv, 233, 246;
development strategies, xiii, xvi,
29, 214
Stuckey, B., 234–5
structural adjustment programmes
(SAPs): 75, 247; impact, 2–5,
10, 19–20, increased rural
poverty, 219–20, social fabric,
11, strong and weak, 31, 32; *see
also under individual countries*
substitute goods/foods, 67–8
Sudan, 244
sugar, 204
survival, development and, 225–32,
247–51
sustainable development, 18, 224,
244
Sutton, I.B., 111, 113, 123

tailoring groups, 191
Tanzania: xv, 231–2, 242;
Co-operative Societies Act, 211;
customary law, 211–12;
development levy, 202–3;
economic crisis, 170–2, 180–1,
effect on women and children,
197–9; Economic Recovery
Programme, 7, 199; health, 14,
181, 197; Law Review
Commission, 212; National
Economic Survival Programme,
198; SAP, 198–9; self-reliance
policy, 187, 195; women:
brewers, 9, 201–3, 232, informal
sector, 199–201, 210–13, *see also*
Utengule Usangu; Women's
Organization, see Umoja wa
Wanawake wa Tanzania; *see also*
Dodoma District
Tattersfield, J.R., 54
Taylor, D.R.F.: 31, 223, 233, 246;
development strategies, xiii, xvi,
29, 34, 85, 214

Tekperbiawe clan, 109, 113
Tema, 96
territoriality, 241–6
theatre, popular, 29–30, 153,
164–5
Thiele, G., 185
Thomas, B.P., 27–8, 28
Thomas, H.T., 82
Thomas, R.G., 35
thrift clubs, *see* savings groups
Tibaijuka, A., 6, 9, 10, 14, 15
tolls, salt, 113, 116–17
trade dependence, 21
tradition, 25–6, 27
training groups, farmer, 50–2
transportation, 175, 180, 189
trapping, 68
tree planting: 176, 194; *see also*
Kenya Woodfuel Development
Programme
Tumu Credit Union, 95
Turkana District, 239
Turton, D., 73, 74

Umoja wa Wanawake wa Tanzania
(UWT), 192, 195, 209
UN (United Nations): Declaration
on the African Economic and
Social Crisis, 255; Programme of
Action for African Economic
Recovery and Development
(UNPAAERD), 19
UNCRD, 247–8, 255–6, 257
UNECA (Economic Commission
for Africa): 1, 31–2, 125, 216;
APPER, 19; economic crisis, 3,
3–5, 217, 219; Lagos Plan of
Action, 18; *see also* African
Alternative Framework
UNICEF, 102, 216, 220
Utengule Usangu: 200, 232, 245;
beer project, 206–10; women
brewers, 202–6

Vacuum Salts Ltd: 109, 110, 114,
120; Songor Lagoon struggle,
114, 115, 120–1, 229
Van Gelder, B., 149, 154
vegetable gardening, 174, 179, 186
vikao (beer clubs), 206, 206–10

vilabu (beer halls), 205, 206, 208
village co-operative shops, 179–80
villagization, 173, 178–9
Vincent, V., 35
'voice', 249–50
Volta River, 113

Wa Credit Union, 92–6 *passim*, 97
Waal, A. de, 244
Wade, R., 27
wages, *see* incomes
Wagogo culture, 178, 185, 191
Wamunyu Handicraft Co-operative
  Society, 138, 139–40
Warioba, J., 171–2
water, 221: Ada District, 110;
  brewing and, 201; Dodoma
  District, 178, 181, 188–9
Watts, M.: 1, 2–3, 17, 18, 25;
  agricultural performance, 216;
  rural communities, 244
Weaver, C., 1, 29, 233
Wedza communal area, 42–3
wells, 69, 80, 118, 189
Were, S., 130
White, G., 247
Whitlow, J.R., 37, 38
wild resources, 67–8
Wilks, I., 60, 78
Wittu wa Mwene women's groups,
  137
women: 126; access to land, 17–18;
  Ada Songor Salt Co-operative,
  117–18; credit unions, 95–6,
  99–100, 229; economic crisis
  and, 8–9, 9–10; health and
  education cutbacks, 14–15; local
  farmer organizations, 51–2;
  Tanzania, *see* Tanzania; tree
  planting, 152–3, 156, 159–60,
  166–7, 168; *see also* gender
women's groups: Dodoma District,
  182, 191–2; Machakos District,

135, 135–8, 139, 145, 145–6,
  230
women's shops, 180
wood crafts, 139–40, 183–4
woodfuel, *see* Kenya Woodfuel
  Development Programme
World Bank: 1, 2, 3, 102, 216;
  Berg Report, 24, 30; credit, 82,
  unions, 100; environment, 15,
  16; local initiatives, 23–7, 28;
  SAPs, 3, 5, 31, 75, 247

Yatta South Women's Group
  Enterprise Development
  (YSWGED), 136–7, 145,
  146
Young, K., 8–9
Youth Development Task Force,
  195
youth groups, 184, 190–1, 195

Zambia: 219; employment
  cutbacks, 9–10; health and
  education, 13, 14, 14–15; maize:
  production, 8–9, removal of
  subsidy, 6–7, 7–8, riots, 6–7
Zimbabwe: xv, 33–57, 225–6, 242;
  agricultural subsectors, 39–41;
  black peasant farmers' role,
  39–44; government development
  policies, 34, colonial, 36–8, post-
  independence, 38–9; health and
  education, 11, 12; Land Tenure
  Act, 37; local farmer
  organizations, *see* farmer
  organizations; National Farmers'
  Association, 237–8, 250; natural
  farming regions, 35–6
Zinyama, L.M.: 37, 38, 39, 42,
  44, 225–6; agricultural
  constraints, 47, 56;
  disadvantaged households, 50;
  wives of migrant workers, 52